About the cover: An artist's conception of the first day of creation, "Let there be light." Was that light the sun, the Big Bang, God's radiance, or something else? Can we even know? See pages 60-62 and 189-190.

THE SIX-DAY WAR IN
CREATIONISM

A New Critique of the Young Earth Reform Movement and Its Excesses

GENE NOUHAN

The Six-Day War in Creationism

© 2022 Gene Nouhan

ISBN 978-1-66786-482-2

eBook ISBN 978-1-66786-483-9

DEDICATION

To: "Elizabeth, Jordan, and Christine,
the cutest little kids I've ever seen."

To my brother Chuck:
We started a journey 50 years ago,
and are now finishing the race.

TABLE OF CONTENTS

PREFACE

When an intelligent person expresses a view that seems absurd...
we should try to understand how it ever came to seem true.
—Bertrand Russell

The Ken Ham/Bill Nye debate was my first encounter with the Young Earth Reform Movement. To my surprise, a friend I hadn't seen in a couple of years helped promote the event. We met because he expressed interest in attending my apologetics class with his wife. So he asked, "Are you going to watch the debate?" I had no interest in it because neither participant was credible on the advertised proposition—Creationism vs. Evolution. Ken Ham is a layman in science and theology, and I always thought of Bill Nye as the "Soupy Sales of Science."

"Are you a *Young Earther* or an *Old Earther*?" my friend asked. I was unfamiliar with those labels, not being plugged into the movement at the time. So I hesitated but then said, "Old Earther." I assumed both labels were simply about the age of the earth. That was a mistake.[1]

A colleague advised me to watch the debate to field questions from the class, should there be any. The course attracted several people with advanced degrees in theology, engineering, and science. My friend has an MBA and his wife a Ph.D. in English, though they could not attend. There were no questions or interest in the Ham-Nye debate the morning after, but it was a sensation elsewhere.

In my wife Susan's office, there was a sharp reaction. One person snapped, "I don't see how you can be a Christian and reject six literal days in Genesis." I think most Young Earthers (YErs) would say that overstates it. Most YErs call other Christians "compromisers," not infidels. Still, we never heard anyone say anything like that, and "compromisers" is not much better.

I did not know Cincinnati and Northern Kentucky were hotbeds for Young Earth Creationism (YEC) due to Ken Ham's Creation Museum and the later addition of the Ark Encounter in Northern Kentucky. I had entered a Young Earth flashpoint in an aggressive movement within Christianity without realizing it. That was February 2014 in West Chester, Ohio.

This book is about the conflict in Christianity over six days in Genesis, thus the title: The Six-Day War in Creationism. Battlelines are drawn primarily

---

1. I knew YEC interprets the six days in Genesis literally but was surprised the label "OEC" usually refers to people who believe the six days are eons or billions of years each. Of course, they do so with no justification except to make the theology of Genesis accord with modern science.

between Protestant fundamentalists and Evangelicals but can also spill onto traditional Vatican 1 Catholics that have become sectarian.[2] The fight is intense, abusive, and often absurd. Unfortunately, the fighting occurs before the public, while neglecting more serious Christian thought, which reflects poorly on Christianity.

YErs call this fight *spiritual warfare*. But when YE reformists claim *as many do* that if the earth is old, God is a liar; that a young earth is a key to all biblical doctrine; or that an older earth threatens to destroy the message of the Cross and Atonement and that YEC is *the key* to reforming the Church and the culture, it is hard to find any clarity in those claims let alone spirituality.

Meanwhile, well-funded Young Earth organizations have persecuted widely respected scholars and Evangelical leaders who think the earth is old and others who accept *Progressive or Evolutionary Creationism*.[3] The surrounding controversy and bad publicity have led some to resign for thinking the "wrong way." Loss of livelihood is the fallout from a campaign of personal destruction in, of all places, Christianity. That is *cancel culture,* which participates in the culture instead of reforming it as YEC promises. The war is on, and it is over six days.

Why me and this book?

Who am I? And why should I write *this* book?

I grew up Catholic with eight years of Catholic school. I accepted evolution at an early age but knew very little of scripture. As a young teenager, the changes with Vatican II led me to look elsewhere. Not knowing the Bible, I was vulnerable to being persuaded by a church that focused on biblical teachings, in this case, The Worldwide Church of God. They accepted the deep age of the universe but not evolution. They produced lavish biblical material free of charge. With little money and little guidance, I converted passionately. There were some beneficial and surprising trade-offs for that decision.

The Six-Day War in Creationism, as I am calling it, reminds me of a rare event in recent Church history that I experienced firsthand. Eventually, I became a pastor in the Worldwide Church of God, which had a Jewish Christian tradition and a fierce orientation to the Hebrew Scriptures. Strangely, almost none of us were Jewish. I am Middle Eastern and Greek by blood. What was I doing in a Jewish Christian Church?

---

2. The attacks come primarily from the Young Earth side as other mainstream Christians are the bear they poke.

3. Some Scholars and Evangelical scientists that have come under fire by YEC are Bruce Waltke, Norman Geisler, Peter Enns, Hugh Ross, Francis Collins, Deborah Haarsma, and William Lane Craig.

Most people thought we were a cult. Why live like Jews if you are Gentile Christians?

The Ten Commandments (particularly the fourth commandment, "Remember the Sabbath.") were central to life in our community—"six days the Lord created the heavens and the earth, and on the seventh day He rested." That created a strong orientation toward the Old Testament. Wasn't the Old Testament the Bible of the early Church? The early Church was also a Jewish Christian Church, not just ethnically but doctrinally. Wasn't that Church full of the Spirit? Maybe there was something to all that, we thought.

Several *presuppositions and claims* informed our distinctive. For example, most Christians believe the earliest Church was the most authentic; it was Jewish Christianity. Keeping the seventh day holy is one of the Ten Commandments. Jesus and Paul customarily attended the synagogue on the Sabbath. We simply followed their example (see Luke 4:16; Acts 17:2), except we attended Church, not the synagogue, and required our members to do the same. Jesus and Paul also made a point to keep the biblical feast days (Matthew 26:17–18; Acts 20:16). So we followed their example.

Furthermore, Christ is our *Passover* (1 Corinthians 5:7), so we kept a "Christian Passover." The Holy Spirit arrived on the day of Pentecost—a *Feast of the Jews*, now Christian. We saw a precedent in all that. Christ typology in the Day of Atonement is obvious, so we celebrated the day and fasted. We believed the Feast of Trumpets typifies Christ's Second Coming at the last trumpet (Corinthians 15:51–54), and the Feast of Tabernacles pictures the millennial reign of Christ. Israel's festivals have striking Christian implications for God's plan (far more than the six literal days in Genesis). So we kept them.

Even Paul said the Old Testament was "God-breathed" and profitable *for doctrine* and instruction in righteousness (1 Timothy 3:16). We used the Old Testament for those purposes, especially doctrine. All this may seem reasonable on the surface, but we adopted this Old Testament orientation as a way of life and made it obligatory for our members and new converts. The New Testament reveals those days—biblical days—as shadows of Christ (Colossians 2:16). Shadows are not a bad thing; they just aren't the real thing. They become irrelevant when what casts them appears.

Shadows (types) lack substance. Jesus supplies it.

The *doctrinal beliefs* of the former Worldwide Church of God are not relevant here, but the similarities in *doctrinal development are*. All the presuppositions of the old Worldwide Church of God seemed to add up to something. We thought the Old Testament was "equal" to the New Testament because they are both God's Word, right? And God's Word is eternal and infallible, period. We unknowingly sublimated the Incarnate Christ's impact and authority over Old Testament interpretation.

We had our explanations, some clever, most not so clever. We did not understand that while the Old Testament was under equal *inspiration*, it was not an equal *revelation* with the New Testament. We thought others were deceived or worse; they compromised the Word of God out of prejudice or enmity against God's word. But we were different from YECs in one significant way— we knew we could be wrong. We were willing to change if convinced. We had some history of doing so.

We boldly proclaimed what amounted to a "Jewish Christian Gospel" (though we were Gentiles) based on the law (or at least some of it) and a literal interpretation of the Old Testament Messianic Kingdom. The "Jewish Christian Gospel" is like the "Creation Gospel" in that there is no such thing. The Gospel is about a new creative act in the Incarnation and its implications for the world. It has nothing to do with genealogies or the mechanisms of physical creation or observing harvest festivals.

YErs often find it necessary to clarify their position on the Gospel. Like YErs, my former Jewish Christian community was unclear on the priority of Christianity's central teachings because our exclusive distinctives overshadowed them.

The earliest Christians considered themselves part of Judaism. Jewish Christians armed with the Old Testament and the teachings of Jesus began to preach after he rose from the dead. But old wineskins cannot hold new wine for very long. It became clear that Christianity was a separate entity from Judaism by the end of the first century, when Christianity officially broke all ties with Judaism. *In reality, the earliest Church was a transitional church—a concept not in our vocabulary at the time.*

The *"soil"* for planting Christianity was indeed the Old Testament. Jesus was Jewish. But by blurring an Old Testament orientation with the Gospel, the Worldwide Church of God (WCG) created a hybrid, mixing our Jewish Christian traditions with the Gospel of Jesus. For us, it was the biblical tradition with "biblical authority." It was the "key to everything." Much like YEC, we attempted to reform Christianity.

Linking our tradition to biblical authority gave our distinctives exaggerated importance they did not have on their own merits. By the mid-90s, the WCG began a path to reforming itself. Within a decade or so and much pain, we managed it. My experience with the WCG has alerted me to red flags in Christian traditions prioritizing Moses, assuming his writings are *covenantal* for the Gospel and Church life. They are not so by definition.

For the first time in Church history, a group like the WCG returned to evangelical orthodoxy in the way it did. We made a systematic appraisal suggested by Bertrand Russell of how our ideas came to seem true. We corrected errors when we discovered them. The more we fixed, the more evangelical orthodoxy appeared on the horizon. A new day was dawning for the WCG.

Many people were frightened, disoriented, and angry. Many also experienced a tangible sense of liberty. For me, the sky felt different. The sky felt larger and lighter, like the breath of God. It was clear that we were badly mistaken all along.

But believing what is badly mistaken does not just happen; it has a process that this book analyzes. We did not realize that a New Testament interpretation of an Old Testament passage was analogous, not literal; it could not establish an obligatory practice or turn an Old Testament tradition into an essential Christian prescription. We took New Testament essentials (about Christ) and infused them into old covenant obligations. That created New Testament requirements by typology or analogy. As a result, we blurred two different covenantal obligations.

We now have a New Creation with Christ—the New Adam. The old is fading away. Jesus said, "You cannot put new wine into old wineskins" (Matthew 9:16). There are many ways to make the "old wineskin" error. The *Old* Testament documents developed under the *old* covenant. Therefore, they are not covenantal for new covenant Christians. The first covenant *is old for a reason*; it cannot bottle the new covenant no matter how carefully one decants it, and the first creation is presently "dissolving" into the New Creation.

John 1:1-14 is the primary creation account for Christians.

This book is *not* about my journey to orthodoxy. It is about bursting a theological bubble that makes one oblivious to basic mistakes, not necessarily the same mistakes, but a similar process and orientation where errors appear camouflaged when they should be obvious. Few people are willing to change their cherished beliefs. Many YErs believe that correcting their primary distinctive is equivalent to calling God a liar and rejecting biblical authority; how open can they be to reassess their views? Throw in conspiracy theories, and a rational discussion is out of the question.

This book is not for crusaders on any side.

The WCG reassessed its theology on God's nature, the Bible's purposes, and the Church's mission. We had to sort out a tangled theological mess. The original denomination's doctrines began with earnest Bible study by gifted lay-people untrained in biblical scholarship and theology. A lack of formal training is considered preferable by some fundamentalists like the former Worldwide Church of God and their current offshoots.

Like YEC, the WCG grew rapidly through persuasive personalities, zeal, and lavish media efforts, and not without making some good points. The WCG soon built colleges and organizations to teach its "discoveries" in the Bible to a new generation. Over the decades, our colleges became more sophisticated in biblical scholarship and other disciplines. Our graduates went on to the best universities and seminaries for PhDs. Some of them returned as professors in our colleges.

I was attending our flagship university when the demands on students in biblical scholarship intensified. A few pastors on Sabbatical who graduated years earlier could not cope with the demands and needed tutoring. A struggle began between a better-educated core and traditionalists.[4]

The conflict was mild at first. Dialogue and debates broke out in my dorm— an education in itself— some of my dorm mates were brilliant. We represented different sides of the issues in the debate. Fourteen years later, there was all-out spiritual warfare worldwide.

In the early days of the YE reform movement of the 1920s, there were untrained teachers, too, with little expertise in biblical scholarship, theology, or field experience in the applied sciences (see chapter 28). They armed themselves only with their homegrown interpretation of scripture and their denomination's distinctives—all that a fundamentalist needs. Today, the language and tone used by YErs are surprisingly like the old WCG and its offshoots. They share a similar orientation toward their exclusive distinctives; *they find their central identity in them.*

But the WCG's errors were broader in scope than those of YEC. Jewish Christianity is more comprehensive than theories on Late Bronze Age cosmology, flood geology, and ancient genealogies. Yet, as we shall see, the impact on the Christianity of YErs is no less apparent.

The way out of any flawed theological foundation begins at its foundation. When scholars outside our Church challenged our unique ideas, particularly on the nature of God, we began to examine the underlying *presuppositions and claims* that grounded our distinctives to meet the challenge. Intellectual honesty requires us to turn a lens on ourselves to discover any hidden assumptions that may be prejudicial. That is what lovers of truth do, no matter how painful.

The bulk of our reassessment focused on three central ideas:

1. The nature of God;
2. The purposes of the Bible; and
3. The Mission of the Church.

Misunderstandings on these can lead to many mistakes in biblical interpretation. What did all of Christianity know we did not or would not accept? A convergence of circumstances "opened the blinds" and gave us *a chance* to see how something so wrong could seem right.

---

4. Some received advanced degrees from other universities for apologetic purposes, i.e., to better defend their tradition against recognized scholarship. They attended top universities with no intention of altering their belief system they thought was inspired by God. The truth is an advanced degree in any discipline does not mean an advanced education if ideology corrupts learning. This is what is meant by "education is the responsibility of the student more than the teacher." A student with an advanced degree without independent critical thinking skills ends up being schooled more than educated, or worse, reeducated ideologically.

An honest and painful reassessment takes courage, education, and discipline. Most of our members came from mainstream orthodox churches. We had reeducated them in a self-styled version of Jewish Christianity. Now they needed to be *re-re-educated* back to orthodoxy. You cannot unscramble an egg. Thankfully, we are not eggs, but you get the point. To revert back was more difficult, emotionally. C. S. Lewis said making progress sometimes means reversing course to discover where you left the track. Similarly, some YErs today were orthodox and mainstream Protestants who converted to YEC.

Many of our people did not have the *will* to do what we asked of them. With a blinding light shining in their eyes, they slipped back into the proverbial cave and settled for the wisdom of shadows. We learned a hard lesson from Mark Twain: *"It is easier to fool people than to convince them they were fooled."*

A new generation of leaders had to convince our people that we were *all fooled.* Not on purpose, of course, but fooled nonetheless. Von Goethe thought, "We are never deceived; we deceive ourselves."[5] Jeremiah wrote, "The heart is fooled more than anything else... Who can know how bad it is?" (Jeremiah 17:9, NLV). It is easier to be fooled than we think. Clever arguments made in isolation can seem persuasive. That's why cross-examination is critical in a just society.

A sizable minority might make the journey back to orthodoxy if they were willing, and in our case, they were. So the WCG was transformed and has since changed its name to the more fitting *Grace Communion International.* Yes, that happened. Only the love of truth and influence from the Holy Spirit can produce that. Personally, my tradition is now closer to the *"Mere Christianity"* of C. S. Lewis, which will be apparent in this book.

I should add that coming from Jewish Christianity into orthodoxy was more enlightening than words can say. I understand why God began His self-disclosure at Sinai, culminating in the events associated with Christ: his life, death, resurrection, and ascension. Our knowledge and understanding of the Old Testament, Jewish thought, and the tensions between early Christianity and Judaism were more advanced than other Christians possessed.

I do not recommend the same journey to get there.

A heads-up

After seeing an interview between Eric Metaxas and Tim Keller, I set out to write a definitive book on age/earth issues in Christianity. Metaxas asked Keller if he knew of such a volume. He did not. Thus this book. You the reader will decide if I succeeded.

The many books I've read on the SDWC are narrow in scope, leaving too many issues unaddressed. So I determined to write a more comprehensive

---

5. Johann Wolfgang Von Goethe, German poet, 1749-1832.

treatment in one volume. This book leaves no reasonable stone unturned and adds many new insights.

There are central terms used in this book that need defining: e.g., "*Young Earth Creationism (YEC)*" usually refers to an elaborate theological system that goes far beyond the belief that the earth is 6,000 years old. YEC is a *movement* characterized by an "*ism*." As with most "*isms*," there are extremes. Here YEC *is not* synonymous with the simple belief the earth is thousands of years old based on a literal Genesis. Instead, YEC is synonymous with the Young Earth Reform Movement, which claims to be a reformation of the Church and culture.

Less used is "*Old Earth Creationism (OEC)*." It accepts the science of the universe's age—about 13.8 billion years, and the earth's age of 4.5 billion. Old Earth Creationists (OErs) generally interpret scripture as *teaching* an old creation, the six days being eons, which I reject. Progressive Creationists, Intelligent Design advocates, generally fall into this grouping, but not necessarily. OErs accept the Big Bang and *microevolution* but far fewer accept *macroevolution* or common descent, aka Neo-Darwinism. *Evolutionary Creationism* accepts common descent of all species by the will of God as He continuously upholds and sustains everything in existence; they generally do not interpret the six days as eons.

By a *nonessential* doctrine, I mean any teaching not essential for salvation nor included in the Gospel message or "evangelism proper." *By evangelism proper, I mean witnessing to unbelievers about the life, death, resurrection, and ascension of God Incarnate, not the practice of persuading Christians of one tradition to join another.* The Great Commission is two-fold: preach the Gospel to unbelievers and make disciples of Jesus. Non-essentials usually refer to distinctives a group is passionate about but belong in discipleship training, not a prerequisite to accepting the Gospel and receiving Christ. Surprisingly, most YErs sound like they agree with this, but significant ambiguity in their messaging creates doubt and confusion on where they stand.

YE leaders are known to persecute Christians and attempt to ruin reputations and careers. I would not lump all YErs in that camp. *I differentiate between those that simply accept a young earth as an opinion from the extremists in the YE Reform Movement. Indeed, this book is for all interested in the issues and who seek a more comprehensive treatment of them; it is for Christians who also have concerns over the damage this conflict is doing to Christianity and are willing to look again fearlessly.*

By "fundamentalist," I usually mean YErs in the Evangelical family. Most Protestant fundamentalists are Evangelicals, but many Evangelicals are not fundamentalists. Moreover, not all YErs are Protestant; as I said, some are traditional Vatican I Catholics, Jews, and Muslims.[6]

I must stress again that the simple belief in a young earth is not my main issue. I have no objection to people with mere opinions about nonessentials *because* they are not essential, even if I strongly disagree with them. Historically, Christians have been free to interpret Genesis literally without damaging their faith because Christianity is about much bigger things. The YE Reform *Movement* is another matter. This book explores whether that movement is a stumbling block to unbelievers. I am under no illusion that this book could move the deeply entrenched YE reform zealot. I've had too many disturbing debates with them. This book is mainly for people who want to know the theological issues better and gain new insights.

There are five parts to this book. The first four address the issues as laid out in chapter 1. Part V changes direction. It compares YE evangelism with historical Christian evangelism. It also puts the SDWC into perspective by contrasting the New Creation over the old creation and John 1 over Genesis 1. Finally, Part V gives us a glimpse at the ultimate end of God's plan—the union of divinity and humanity started by Jesus as the nucleus, putting a new perspective on the six days of creation. The old is fading away.

We have a new beginning, a New Creation, *a New Genesis.*

—Gene Nouhan

---

6. The differences between Evangelicals and fundamentalists are often oversimplified. Evangelicalism is not without an intellectual life. There are moderates and liberals among them. The criticism is that Evangelical intellectual pursuits are in service to apologetics to maintain theological distinctives while avoiding the anti-intellectualism of fundamentalism. But this is true only to a point, and not unique. It is rare that any group: liberal, progressive, or conservative is open to so much change as to cease being that group, in the name of intellectualism. It happens but it is rare. It is my task to separate tradition and disctintives that diverge from core Christian belief or what C.S. Lewis called "Mere Christianity."

I believe AiG is a leading supplier of the most advanced "weaponry" designed to counter the enemy's attacks in this era... I praise God for the advances that many believers are making on various battlefronts as a result of the Lord using AiG to be a part of equipping them for this war.

—Ken Ham

PART I: OPENING REMARKS

1.
THE ISSUES

If the earth is old, God is lying to us.
—Henry Morris

God's salvation plan rests on the foundation laid in the Genesis creation account. An old earth undermines every major doctrine of the Bible.
—Ken Ham

The first chapters of Genesis have been fascinating and frustrating for Christians through the centuries. Several theories on creation find their way into Evangelical theology. The theory that creates the most division between Christians is Young Earth Creationism (YEC), especially in its *reform movement* iteration.

It is a historical fact that all branches of Christianity have allowed for literal and figurative interpretations of the days of creation without judgment on one's character, commitment to scripture, Christ, or the Gospel. The Chicago Statement on Biblical Inerrancy, a highly conservative evangelical group of scholars, omitted YEC for being irrelevant to biblical inerrancy, though some were sympathetic to it. An overzealous YE Reform Movement has become a self-appointed arbiter on faith and acceptance of scripture as the word of God. The mere opinion of six literal days isolated by itself does not create the war.

A *literal* reading of Genesis, for many, suggests the universe could be little more than six thousand years old while scientific evidence for a 13.8 billion-year-old universe (or much older with recent discoveries) claims six-thousand years is absurd. The tension between absolute devotion to literalism and what appears obvious from the evidence helps fuel the conflict.

While this book takes a fresh look at the case for YEC, the simple belief in a young earth, on its own, is not the real issue for me. The quality of one's walk with Christ has nothing to do with that kind of knowledge. Instead, the issues are the *claims and presuppositions of the Young Earth Reform Movement and how their excesses alter historical teachings on God's nature, the Bible's purposes, and the Christian movement.*

Until recently, the age of the earth was not a test of faith. The widespread scholarly opinion considers a literal interpretation of the six days of Genesis implausible on scientific *and theological grounds*. I'll give good reasons for that opinion, primarily on theological grounds, because today's YEC is suspicious of mainstream science, though it is well represented in countless peer-reviewed studies. So a closer look at the theology in Genesis is the direction to take without avoiding science.

Though the age of the earth was not a hot issue in Christianity until modern times, YErs claim the earth's age was never in doubt before modern times, which is not exactly true since the majority opinion in the world, even in parts of Christendom, Judaism and Islam, was a past eternal universe. That idea (and the Steady State Modal) persisted from Aristotle until the mid-sixties with the discovery of the Cosmic Microwave Background. Even in early Christianity, opinions on the earth's age varied from 5000 to 10000 years based on limited historical information and speculation based on hints in scripture. The history of the universe was out of reach.[7]

Perceived threats from science, ANE literature, and biblical scholarship have moved fundamentalists to assert their theological system to the forefront, while Christianity has consistently recognized the freedom of conscience on various interpretive opinions, particularly with nonessentials. People that marshal their freedom at crosscurrents also stir conflict.

Theologians since Augustine have struggled over how much of the creation account to take literally. Think about it. The story[8] tells us about infinite Being acting on a finite universe from an Ancient Near Eastern worldview of the Late Bronze Age. What's to misunderstand! Augustine was disadvantaged, not having scholarship on ANE literature, archeology, and mastery of biblical languages as a background.

Archeologists have unearthed some 500,000 cuneiform tablets from Mesopotamia, Canaan, and countless hieroglyphics from ancient Egyptian ruins. These texts shed enormous light on the Hebrew scriptures, so interpreting Genesis in isolation is out of the question. Scholars have deciphered a small fraction (about ten percent) of these tablets, uncovering surprising new insights. More insights are bound to continue.

ANE literature relates to the Old Testament in unexpected ways. The law Code of Hammurabi, written hundreds of years before the Bible, can be strikingly similar to the Law of Moses. One example is Exodus 21:22: "If men strive together and hurt a woman with child so that her fruit depart, and yet no harm follow; he shall surely be fined."

---

7. Theologians like Augustine and Aquinas stated that creation did not need a chronological beginning since the real miracle is not that anything was made but that any contingent thing can exist on its own. Since God is eternal, He can be the eternal efficient cause of all things in existence eliminating the need for a temporal beginning. Even so, Augustine and Aquinas believed the universe had a beginning as stated in Genesis 1:1.

8. YErs do not like the word *story* in reference to the early chapters of Genesis. That is because stories can be true in the lessons they teach, without being strict history. Attempts to control the *legitimate* use of language (Genesis is clearly a series of stories, i.e., narratives) indicates a weak case. In YEC, Genesis is strict historical narrative and literal word for word. Of course, the word *narrative* means story. Nonetheless, YErs prefer the word *account*. But an account is also a story. Since the word *story* can be history, an account, a narrative, and storytelling, and the lessons are the same regardless, I use them all.

Compare that to the Code of Hammurabi, section 209: "If a man strikes a free woman to cause her fruit to depart, he shall pay ten shekels of silver for her fruit."

Many laws were similar because the culture was similar. Not much changed from Hammurabi to Moses, culturally speaking. *Many laws in both codes were not religious rules but matters of state.* Such similarities at one time were unknown and unthinkable to most fundamentalists and other Christians. However, it is only common sense that a similar view of the world from shared experiences would give rise to similar laws, ideas, and even religious ideas, such as animal sacrifices and harvest festivals also required in scripture.

This Law of Moses about a pregnant woman cannot be *special revelation.* It is hard to see *general revelation*[9] in this law since it puts a price on an unborn child's value, and a meager one at that. This law reflects the mentality of the day. One difference between these two versions of the law might point to a more enlightened feature of biblical law. Notice that Hammurabi defines the type of woman his law protects—a *free* woman—while the same rule in Exodus appears to compensate *any* woman. More significantly, transgressions in Israel were against God, not simply against society or the king as with ANE law codes.

Still, fundamentalists claim *every word* of the Bible was micromanaged from no other source but directly from God. That claim is unrealistic and unnecessary. Divine *inspiration* still stands, but divine *control* over every word claimed by fundamentalists falls.

Furthermore, the discovery of the Sumerian/Babylonian flood account in the Gilgamesh Epic contains surprising similarities to Noah's flood that cannot be coincidental. In both versions, a righteous man built an ark according to divine instructions to save a select group of people and all the animals. Each ark contained a single door with a window.

In Genesis, the rain lasted forty days and forty nights. In the Gilgamesh Epic, the rainfall was much shorter (six days and six nights). The numbers forty and six have *theological* significance to each community and are not likely meant literally in either account. And since the Babylonian story is much older, it is not reasonable to insist that the Genesis account is historically perfect, as if the author intended historical perfection over theological purposes.

A fundamental principle in historiography is that versions of an event written centuries later are unlikely to be more accurate than those scripted close to the event itself, which is common sense. Christianity appeals to that principle

---

9. General revelation refers to what can be learned about God in creation or through natural means. All humans are capable of understanding the Creator this way. Special revelation refers to *God revealing Himself* in scripture and in supernatural ways. General revelation is available to all people and why experience and science can be critical sources of general revelation. The Bible contains both general, special revelation and matters not revelatory.

when Islam claims the Quran, composed many centuries later, is more accurate than the Bible on the same stories.

In both flood accounts, God or gods released the waters above the heavens and under the earth. The heroes let birds loose to seek land; after failed attempts, one succeeds. Both arks came to rest on a mountain. After the crisis, the heroes offered a sacrifice pleasing to their deities (Genesis 8:21). Divine blessings were granted to the heroes in both accounts, and deities promised not to destroy humanity again (Genesis 8:21–22).

There are differences too. The significant difference between the two stories is theological. The reason for divine judgment in the Mesopotamian stories was arbitrary, i.e., the bothersome noise humans made due to overcrowding in a newly developed urbanization. In Genesis, complete moral degradation led to God's judgment. This deep ethical concern of Yahweh might be revealing in the ANE.

Such archeological discoveries shocked people who believed *all* biblical ideas were unique; they still shock. The findings were especially troublesome to those who thought, in some sense, that God wrote the Bible. Why would God use sources for His book? Of course, that is the wrong question. It turned out that there are several Ancient Near Eastern stories written long before the Bible, retold by biblical authors. Were they written mainly for historical or theological purposes?

Many Christians believed that mere cultural practices in ancient Israel were special revelation. Countless archeological discoveries of common cultural ideas throughout the ANE make that assumption untenable. Instead, *archeological discoveries now make it necessary to identify God's self-disclosure (not by the cultural setting but) within the cultural setting as the primary purpose of the Bible.*

God's gradual self-disclosure that culminates in the Incarnation narrows the Bible's purposes and provides perspective on how to read it. In other words, the purposes of the Bible offer a corrective for misusing scripture for other purposes, such as one's exclusive traditions and distinctives or turning the Bible into a scientific textbook. The authors' intentions take precedence over our desires and ambitions.

We must ask, "Did the authors intend to give readers an age for the earth?"

ANE literature related to the Old Testament can be highly expressive, stylistic, rich in figures of speech and strange idioms, with limited vocabulary compared to modern languages. ANE languages emerged from the same area of the world, so reading ANE literature outside the Bible can "sound" much like reading the Hebrew Scriptures. That can be unnerving for Christians when first comparing them side by side. Presuppositions about the Bible contribute to that reaction. Such nervous responses are understandable since we do not know what we do not know until we know it. Even then, most people are still reluctant to continue developing their opinions.

The issues surrounding the SDWC *and the theological system of YEC* are greater in scope than the simple belief that the earth is young from a literal reading of Genesis. Addressing the issues *begins* by justifying the claims that ground literalism. The aim is to determine the literal *and figurative* content of the original writings in *their* setting, not ours. Issues often center on concepts the original readers immediately recognized that are not intuitive to us. Are the areas of dispute theological, scientific, or something else? YEC goes far beyond dating the earth's age. *YEC is a brand of ideas, including numerous presuppositions and claims.*

For example, YErs acknowledge that God made a world that was "very good." However, by that, they do not mean *very good*: they mean *"perfect."* The following quote is sufficient: "There was a *perfect world* to start with described by God as 'very good' (Genesis 1:31)—Sin and its consequence of death entered *the world* that was once a paradise (Romans 5:12ff)."[10] (emphasis mine)

Supposedly, God meant "perfect" but may have misspoken. The Bible does not say the whole world was perfect or a paradise, but that the creation was "very good." Only a garden near the Tigris and Euphrates Rivers was a paradise.

What damage is there to Christianity's overall mission if the YE reform movement is wrong while hundreds of millions of unbelievers think it speaks for Christianity? Is it appropriate to *lead* with and press YEC in evangelistic efforts? Does "Young Earth Evangelism" enrich the Gospel or distract from it? Are people more likely to receive Christ if they believe the earth is young? Is accepting the deep age for the universe synonymous with compromising the Faith or rejecting God, Jesus, and the Bible, as many in the movement believe? If an exclusive, nonessential distinctive is central to a group's identity, is it likely to infringe on the Gospel of Jesus in any way?[11]

※ In "Confessions of a Failed Young Earth Creationist," Daniel Stork Banks writes:

> There are two things I was taught as a new young-earth creationist: "First, that there is a vast conspiracy within the global scientific community against young-earth creation science. [Secondly], *the reason churches are failing* and the culture is secularizing is that Christians have accepted unbiblical "theories" of evolution into their theology.[12]

---

10. From the AiG website (emphasis mine). YErs openly replace the words "very good" with the word *perfect* yet offer no justification for doing so. As we shall see, this kind of move is common in the SDWC.

11. To be fair, YErs are not the only group that evangelizes with privately held or nonessential distinctives. Seventh Day Adventists, Health/Wealth adherents, and Jehovah's Witnesses come to mind. Many groups require their proselytes to accept their distinctives in addition to the Gospel before baptism as in my former fellowship, the Worldwide Church of God.

12. The vast majority of scholars agree that neither Evolutionary Creationism, Intelligent Design, nor YEC are sanctioned or prohibited in scripture since none is explicitly addressed.

Banks describes the personal price he paid for his activism:

It made me very intolerant of contemporary Christians who "compromised" God's word in Genesis through their unbelief. My evangelism no longer started with Jesus but with Genesis, and *my literalistic interpretation of its first two Chapters devastated my ability to evangelize effectively.* I became such an expert in young-earth creationist theology and science that it turned me into a wrecking ball for my faith. Not only did I have to persuade people of God's existence and what Jesus had done for them, but I now had to throw images of triceratops with riding saddles into the mix too.[13] (Emphasis mine)

"My evangelism no longer started with Jesus but with Genesis." - David Stork Banks

Banks' story is not unique; it illustrates a critical point. The *Young Earth Reform Movement* is not merely the belief that the earth is six thousand years old; it is a dogmatic orientation with extreme claims, assertions, and presuppositions. What is clear from Banks' testimony is that excessive devotion to exclusive distinctives that are not essential to Christianity can sidetrack evangelism from the supremacy of Christ and the Gospel's central place in preaching.[14]

In earlier centuries, Christians had speculated about the earth being thousands of years old without an extreme devotion to the concept. The alternative view until modern times was that this universe has an eternal past, now made dubious by Big Bang Theory. There was no knowledge of a much deeper age for the earth, given that the Bible begins with sophisticated agriculture, which came late in the development of modern human culture.

Christians have always been free to accept young or old earth explanations. However, zealots have elevated the modern YE *Reform Movement* and its theological accessories with debatable claims on the purposes of the scriptures and advanced it as a precursor or add-on to the Gospel. YE Reform is the central feature of their evangelism (see Part V, especially Chapters 35-36). The obvious question is, *"If it is not necessary to accept an exclusive distinctive before*

---

13. Daniel Stork Banks, *Confessions of a Former Young Earth Creationist*, Biologos Foundation website.

14. It is a common practice of some groups to connect their unique identifying features to the Gospel. They so permeate their evangelistic efforts with distinctives that the Gospel takes a back seat. I lived that with my Jewish Christian Gospel. Other examples are the "health/wealth gospel" charismatics that require tongue speaking as "proof" of receiving the Holy Spirit, apocalyptic/groups that lead their evangelistic efforts with prophetic scenarios, or others that lead with their unique teachings, like the Jehovah's Witnesses, some Word Faith groups, Seventh-day Adventists, and now the Creation Gospel. I do not mean to say that all these groups are outside the Christian family. It is human nature to make mountains out of molehills. Yet, the content of their evangelism is not explicitly the New Testament message, i.e., sharing in the life, death, resurrection, and ascension of Christ and the ultimate end of his work in the union of heaven and earth, when God will be all in all (Ephesians 1:22–23).

THE SIX DAY WAR IN CREATIONISM

receiving Christ, why place that distinctive at the vanguard of evangelism?" If it is nonessential, its preaching is marketing, not Christian evangelism.

What may otherwise be a simple misunderstanding or difference of opinion on Genesis has developed into the extreme Young Earth Reform Movement. That is not to say that the simple belief in a young earth is radical. Many have assumed the earth was thousands of years old in times past. But an extreme orientation toward an opinion intending to *reform the Church and the broader culture* is new.

Even the framers of the Chicago Statement on Biblical Inerrancy, a highly conservative and sympathetic Evangelical group of scholars, explicitly rejected YEC as essential to biblical inerrancy, something YEC is desperate to claim to legitimize an otherwise nonessential movement. *Norman Geisler, one of the framers, expressed concern when he wrote, "One is surprised at the zeal by which some Young Earthers are making their position a virtual test for evangelical orthodoxy."*[15]

For example, when YErs say, "If the earth is old, God is a liar," how well do they know the nature of the God they worship? If they believe that YEC is the key to every major doctrine of the Bible, and the old earth view undermines the same, how well do they understand the purposes of the Bible? If people accept the Gospel *because* the earth is young— or preach the YE Reform Movement as key to evangelism— how well do they comprehend the Gospel? Those and many other things plague the once innocent notion of an earth thousands of years old. Add to that suspicion and conspiracy theories that replace analysis.

The battle over the nature of creation draws attention away from an unbending reality: *the nature of God.* YErs and most OECs offer little on God's nature and attributes relevant to interpreting Genesis. For example, God is timeless, spaceless, immaterial, and limitless. There is no compromising with any of those. The contents of our universe are time, space, and matter/energy with all their limitations. God's attributes are the mirror opposite. The critical question must be, "Does a literal interpretation of Genesis deny any of God's limitless attributes?" God's nature is always the priority in interpreting. Is there a reasonable interpretation of Genesis consistent with everything we know about God's attributes?

Listen, Christians are free to read their Bibles and draw different conclusions about many things; some will be right, some wrong. It has always been thus. The same freedom should extend to age/earth issues. It is no sin to be honestly mistaken, especially about a nonessential. All Christians make mistakes with the Bible, especially interpreting figurative passages literally and vice versa.

---

15. Norman Geisler. "A Response to Ken Ham and Answers in Genesis," by Norman Geisler, online

Nonetheless, the YE reformer does not believe other Christians are simply mistaken. In an article entitled "Old Earth Creationism: Is it a Sin?" Terry Mortensen writes this:

> If young-earth creationists are right, then my old-earth and theistic evolutionist Christian brethren are wrong and have led much of the Church astray. By accepting millions of years or even evolution, they have contradicted the clear teaching of scripture. They have severely damaged the Bible's teaching about death and unknowingly assaulted the character of God, thereby undermining the authority and reliability of the Word of God and subverting the Gospel, despite sincere intentions to the contrary.[16]

This YE evangelist equates a miscalculation of the earth's age with "severely damaging the Bible's teaching about death." *By death, Mortensen means animal death as if the Gospel is about animal eternal life.* He also claims an old earth "subverts the Gospel," which implies that a young earth (not creation, but a 6000-year-old earth) validates the Gospel. Just how they establish such claims will become clear as we look closer.

Many YErs believe other Christians are complicit in a conspiracy to undermine the Bible and the Christian faith over six days in Genesis. But does YEC make those connections with any perceptible links?

Ironically, YErs assure people that belief in a young earth is unnecessary for salvation or accepting the Gospel, which for them does not go without saying. *Yet, YErs do not explain how a Christian can compromise the Faith, subvert the Gospel, "severely damage" every biblical doctrine, call God a liar, and remain a Christian.* If Christians may do all those things, what exactly does YEC accomplish? If there is no devil in the details, pick any detail you like. For many YErs, YEC is an essential nonessential. This dissonance simply means that far more caution should replace the hyperbolic overreach of radicalized YErs.

It is nearly impossible to have a reasonable conversation with people who entertain conspiracies and attribute sinister motives to those who disagree. Furthermore, these YErs believe that changing their mind would be equivalent to calling God a liar.

Far from reforming the culture, this mentality is the culture.

---

16. Dr. Terry Mortenson, "Old-Earth Creationism—Is It A Sin?" July 1, 2012; last featured July 12, 2020.

Claims and Presuppositions

There is a *one-to-one correspondence* between words and reality [in Genesis].

—Stephen W. Boyd[17]

Some say that before we read the Bible, we have a theology *about* the Bible that is not *in* the Bible. That is, we have *presuppositions*. Not all of them are bad, of course; some are unavoidable. However, regularly checking our presuppositions is a good idea because they direct our inquiries and influence our conclusions, so they must be sound.

There are several presuppositions in YEC that we will assess:

1. Genesis is God's report on the creation, word-for-word, with the so-called "one-to-one correspondence between words and reality" presupposition.

2. The genre of Genesis is "literal historical narrative" and therefore literal in all aspects of history, science, chronology, and theology.

3. Numbered days in the Bible are always literal twenty-four-hours.

4. The phrase "evening and morning" always means a literal twenty-four-hour day.

5. God's appraisal "very good" on day six means "perfect." Since animal death is not perfection, animals must have had eternal life before humans sinned.

6. The motivation behind rejecting YEC is *appeasing* science and the culture.

7. An old universe fosters a conspiracy to undermine the Bible.

8. YEC theology has always been the historical teaching in Christianity.

In addition to these presuppositions, I challenge the following *claims* that keep many YErs on a war footing:

1. If the earth is old, God is a liar.

2. Most biblical doctrines are established by literalizing Genesis.

3. YEC is the key to reforming the Church and culture.[18]

---

17. Terry Mortenson and Thane H. Ury, *Coming to Grips with Genesis,* Kindle edition, page 167. See specifically the essay by Stephen W. Boyd who may be confusing the philosophical definition of a *true statement*, where words are said have a *one-to-one correspondence with reality*, with the genre of Genesis and the intentions of the author.

18. Ironically, there are theistic evolutionists that consider teaching macroevolution around the world is the key to reforming the Church and the culture. This is a progressive idea with a fundamentalist mentality.

4. The Gospel is "rooted" in a literal six-day creation.

5. The concepts in Genesis are not related to ANE concepts.

6. YEC is foundational to God's plan.

7. The six days of Genesis are either literal or billions of years each.

8. The Bible is clear on the age of the earth/universe.

While I disagree with the eighth claim above and intend to give sufficient reasons, that claim alone would not necessitate a book. On its own, belief in a young earth/universe is, at worst, a mistake.[19] However, claims 1–7 are more than simple mistakes. They are symptoms of a mistaken view of Christianity, the Bible, evangelism, and most importantly, God's nature and attributes. I shall make that plain throughout this book.

Though many Christians, in times past, assumed the earth was young compared to today's estimates, they did so for additional reasons other than their understanding of scripture. It will become obvious that the YEC Reform Movement and its theological system are foreign to historical Christianity.

We will discover that *three historical teachings* in Christian thought often surface and provide perspective on the claims and presuppositions on all sides of the SDWC. They are:

1. The historical Christian teaching on God's nature is crucial for putting the language of Genesis into perspective.

2. The misuse of the Bible in Church history led to reforms in biblical interpretation that are useful in the SDWC.

3. The Great Commission in Christianity is first to preach the Gospel to *unbelievers* worldwide in *undiluted form without making demands for what is unnecessary for salvation* and second to make disciples of Jesus Christ with ongoing teaching. Losing sight of that loses perspective on what God is doing in the present.

The battle over age/earth issues is out of proportion to the initial point of disagreement. How does a difference of opinion on interpreting Genesis evolve into the key to everything? Extreme rhetoric has reached the point where Christianity's essentials fade into the fog of an odd form of spiritual warfare. What is the real issue: the age of the earth, hermeneutics, biblical authority, inerrancy, the Gospel, science, conspiracies, lying, all the above...what? The

---

19. Thankfully, there are Christians that believe the earth is young but see the YE Reform Movement for what it is—an non-essential that fights the wrong battle. They simply believe the Bible indicates the earth is thousands of years old. At best, these YErs are right about the earth and charitable about it. At worst, they are mistaken, yet still charitable. Zealots find it hard to be charitable. I did.

rhetoric is excessive, strained, divisive, and often absurd, which is more a sign of our culture than the key to reforming it.[20]

Are all YErs guilty of these excesses? No. Some YErs understand that age/earth issues are secondary and unessential. They don't mix it with the Gospel in evangelism, but they appear to be a minority. This book helps identify the excesses and shows how the YE Reform Movement affects the health of Christianity. The Young Earth Reform Movement is a unique Christian worldview because only the life, death, resurrection, and ascension of Jesus can be:

1. The key to all biblical understanding

2. The foundation of God's plan

3. Foremost of importance to evangelism

4. The key to reforming Church and culture

What kind of Christians would be unclear on these?

---

20. Titus 3:10, "After a first and second warning reject a divisive man [who promotes heresy and causes dissension—ban him from your fellowship and have nothing more to do with him]" (AMP). A person's opinion on the age of the earth based on Genesis does not rise to the level of heresy. However, fanaticism that leads to divisiveness may fall into a similar category.

2.
THEOLOGY OR SCIENCE

If you do not listen to Theology... It will mean that you have a lot of wrong [ideas about God]. Many [ideas today] are ones real Theologians tried centuries ago and rejected.
—C. S. Lewis[21]

Theology is speaking rightly about God.
—Sarah Coakley[22]

Mine anger is kindled against thee, and against thy two friends; for *ye have not spoken rightly about me,* like my servant Job.
—Job 42:7 (KJV)

The case for YEC is simple and compelling as a story: but does that make it good theology? Does YEC agree with historical Christianity about God's attributes? YErs insist that creation took a literal workweek for God—a veritable schedule with six consecutive daily shifts. The seventh day amounts to religious time off for God, i.e., a blessed and holy day of rest (Genesis 2:3). That is how Genesis reads. The literal meaning of words is the primary focus of YEC.[23]

The implications of YE theology on God's limitless nature get little attention from all sides in the SDWC. So, does a literal reading of Genesis impose anything upon God's attributes, or can God's nature provide a corrective for misinterpreting the language?

Nearly 50 percent of Evangelical *pastors* support a young earth, primarily from the branch of Evangelicalism called Fundamentalism. However, far more Protestant, Catholic, and Orthodox clergy—particularly scholars and theologians reject it.[24] YErs insist Genesis 1 is literal history in the modern sense. They

---

21. C. S. Lewis, *Mere Christianity*.

22. YouTube clip from "Closer to Truth" with Robert Lawrence Kuhn, May 7, 2016.

23. YE evangelists would say their focus is really not the literal meaning of words, it is *biblical authority*. But, as we shall see, by biblical authority, YECs have in mind the literal meaning of words.

24. I distinguish between the opinion of scholars and that of pastors because understanding Genesis requires a level of scholarship that most pastors do not possess. This is not a criticism of the pastorate. A pastor's work is a complexity of roles while the scholar's work is highly specialized.

demand that Genesis is God's word-for-word account of His actions and speech at the time of creation that He recounted to Moses.[25]

God was the only one at the creation, so fundamentalists say His "report" on events in Genesis is final. For example, John MacArthur writes, "God Himself was the only eyewitness to the [creation]. We can either believe what he says or reject it."[26] Steven W. Boyd writes, "Since Genesis 1:1–2:3 is narrative, it should be...a concise report of actual events in time-space history."[27]

Therefore, YErs accept Genesis, in their words, *"as written."*

Because YErs believe that Genesis is God's formal statement on a perfect creation, it must be literal and accurate in everything, including scientific and historical details. YErs insist that taking the days of Genesis figuratively undermines every Bible doctrine, compromises the Faith, makes God a liar, etc. Apparently, some YErs believe God does not allow figurative language inside prose narrative because that is equivalent to lying.

But did God *inspire* Genesis or *dictate* it? Did He micromanage or "superintend" every word? Are there no artistic or literary forms in the creation account? Are all the concepts in Genesis unique for the ANE? Were biblical authors oriented toward the scientific or historical precision YEC assumes? How can we tell? Might theological truth be more indicative of the author's purposes?

What kind of "science" was there back then?

"Science" in the Late Bronze Age

Were biblical authors aware of scientific accuracy, even in a moment of inspiration? What kind of science could their readers recognize or even comprehend? The people of the Bible did consider how nature works, which some today might call "science." However, the ancients observed nature primarily for practical living, religious life, and simple survival. The knowledge store and its distribution were minimal in the Late Bronze Age.

The primary tool for observation in the ANE was the naked eye. Their eyes told them that the sun, moon, and stars go around the earth. According to the "science" of the period, which was purely *observational,* they were not necessarily wrong. Today, we look through microscopes and telescopes and accept

---

25. I assume the authorship of Moses throughout because authorship is not an issue for our subject, and it is less awkward than to discuss the theories on authorship. The Pentateuch is historically accredited to the Mosaic Administration who like the President of the USA does not have to physically write all communications attributed to him or his administration. I also refer to "the author" of Genesis as a reminder that I am not insisting on Mosaic authorship of the Pentateuch as we currently have it.

26. Terry Mortenson and Thane H. Ury, eds., "Foreword," *Coming to Grips with Genesis,* 2013.

27. Ibid.

what we see. Galileo said Jupiter has four moons. Was he a fool because we can see seventy-nine moons orbiting Jupiter? His simple telescope pushed the ball forward, which is all we should expect from any generation on the human endeavor we call science. Can there be any doubt that the new ultra-sophisticated James Webb telescope (100 times more powerful than Hubble) will discover stunning new revelations?

We also trust our senses enhanced by our instruments until some new way of observing comes along and corrects what we once assumed. Ancient humans were behind mainly in their tools for observation. Their one "instrument," twenty-twenty vision (or worse), told them the sun, moon, and stars go around the earth, observably and *experientially,* or what theologians call *phenomenologically*, and not what we mean by *scientifically*. They were not stupid but were justified in their belief since the sun did go around the earth from where they sat.

We explain things based on our experiences with them. Our everyday language does not explain phenomena; it describes the experiences we see reflected in the following false but "true" statements:

1. The sun rises in the east and sets in the west.

2. What goes up must come down.

3. Sun at high noon is directly overhead.

4. The moon comes out at night.

5. Days get longer in summer and shorter in winter.

Some reading this list for the first time will realize these ideas are false but "true," and unsettled by mere observation; none is true scientifically. Nonetheless, it is how we perceive each phenomenon. There are countless statements like these in our collective vocabulary; they reflect our shared experiences. Experiences are not lies, nor are they incorrect. They are what they are—experiences. Therefore, it is silly to expect the Bible to be scientifically correct—word for word—to be trusted about their times. Biblical authors could not consider any other language than the language of their experience, and there was no reason for God to point out optical illusions.

Today, we still experience an immovable earth. From our perspective, it is the center of the universe. Those are not scientific descriptions, nor are they objectively true, but they have a kind of accuracy, i.e., they appear irrefutable. It might be surprising that we depend on the precision of our internal navigation systems in our satellites set to an earth-centered universe. That simply works best; it does not make our satellite engineers stupid. Scientists might consider us stupid with a more effective navigational design based on reality many years from now. Until then, we use what works.[28]

The so-called science of the late Bronze Age was imaginative. It had to be. They had no instruments or body of collected knowledge that could inform them analytically. Instead, they had to imagine how the world came to be through association with how things came to be in their experience.

How did the Late Bronze and Early Iron Age Hebrews grow or make things? What was their process? By labor and craftsmanship, artisans learned skills and planned their work. Their schedule was during the daylight from sunup to sundown, six days a week, and they rested on the Sabbath (Psalm 104:23). They constructed buildings by forming materials into various parts and subdividing them into designated sections for assembly. They could only imagine God's craftsmanship similarly. He divided the light from darkness and the waters to open a sky; He also divided the land from the oceans to assemble environments for suitable life forms. How else could they express it? God did not give them His creative secrets or divine timetable.

Thomas Howard captures the ancient's tendency to explain the unknown by association with the known:

This *associative activity* is the opposite of...the scientific method. The imagination handles things not [analytically] but by *correspondences* from other regions of experience. So that, confronted with the furrowed brow of an angry man, the analytic faculty would scrutinize the muscle activity and emotional turbulence...whereas the imagination (the synthetic faculty) might see in miniature something [like a] thundercloud.[29]

In other words, the ancients associated the unknown with what they knew creatively or by analogy. Thunderstorms reminded them of anger. There is a low but reasonable correspondence between storms and rage. Thunderstorms are to "sky behavior" what wrath is to human behavior— loud, uncontrolled,

---

28. Similarly, in Galileo's day, Ptolemy's model of an earth centered universe was surprisingly useful for predicting the movements of celestial bodies and was most convincing by observation. Celestial bodies go around the earth everywhere on the planet, and the earth seems fixed and unmoving. Therefore, Ptolemy's model was the standard model of the universe among scientists in and outside Christianity for a thousand years. It was not mainly a religious idea. Thomas Kuhn writes, "Galileo's law is more useful to science...not because it represents experience more perfectly, but because it goes behind the superficial regularity disclosed by the senses to a more essential, but hidden, aspect of motion. To verify Galileo's law by observation demands special equipment. Galileo himself got the law not by observation...but by a chain of logical arguments." See Thomas Kuhn, *The Copernican Revolution* (Cambridge: Harvard University Press, 1985), page 199. It is universally agreed today that Galileo had not proven his point scientifically. It took another generation for a sun-centered "universe" [solar system] to be established.

29. Thomas Howard, *Chance or the Dance?: A Critique of Modern Secularism*, Second Edition (Ignatius Press, San Francisco CA, 2018); New "Foreword" by Eric Metaxas, Tyler Blanskic, Kindle edition, location 349.

and potentially destructive. Today, we still speak in terms of *nature's wrath* and a *tempest in a teapot.*

The ancients believed that an underlying reality was at work or that everything worked along a train of thought or a cyclical pattern. Today, we call some regular patterns the "laws" of physics, which in reality are not laws, and physics is not a lawgiver. We call it as we see it, too, sometimes with metaphor. The Hebrews saw a reality behind everything. God was the Hebrew equivalent of a Grand Unified Theory. God's nature enabled them to "tiptoe" over science and land on that unified reality that humans have sought since the ancient Greeks.[30]

When the Big Bang was confirmed in the 1960s by the *Cosmic Microwave Background Radiation,* a NASA planetary physicist famously said:

> At this moment, it seems as though science will never be able to raise the curtain on the mystery of creation. For the scientist who has lived by his faith in the power of reason, the story ends like a bad dream. He has scaled the mountains of ignorance; he is about to conquer the highest peak; as he pulls Himself over the final rock, he is greeted by a band of theologians who have been sitting there for centuries. (Robert Jastrow 1925–2008)

To ancient man, everything seemed analogous to something else, even everything else, that is, everything corresponded to or had some connection with the world around it. Neo-Darwinian evolution states that all life is connected and related through a single life form. Why? Because it appears that way. We all depend on observation.

The ancients used the stars they could never reach to guide their travel on land and sea. There is something wondrous about that experience. The starry heavens have governed our daily calendars for millennia. Paganism preoccupied itself with this celestial connection to the point of obsession. It guided their every moment and fated their perceptions of life, especially in the Greco/Roman period. Today's horoscopes are a tongue-in-cheek nod to its darker pagan roots.

Conversely, one of the crudest things of everyday life is dung, the final stage of food *consumption.* It becomes the first stage in food production by returning to the soil as fertilizer. The more cyclical patterns one observes in nature, the more corresponding connections appear. Many are inexplicable. Theoretical physics equates how the universe works up there with mathematical equations formulated here. How can that be? A dumb question to kneejerk atheists. It just can.

---

30. By Unified Theory of Everything, I do not mean in the pantheistic sense as Spinoza meant it, but a conscious reality that upholds and sustains the existence of every contingent thing. Nature is not God but is rather God's operations.

The fine-tuning of the universe displays a surprisingly connected cosmos that makes the modern myth of *unguided* natural selection or *undirected* common descent of all species on earth suspicious. It is not that these processes are suspicious. On the contrary, there is remarkable coherence in them. However, crediting this stunning coherence to "unguided" and wholly "undirected processes" is where the suspicion lies. Is it "possible" that all these connections are wholly undirected? Possible, perhaps, but not reasonable.

Connectedness in the universe is inevitable if the universe came from a singularity. The ancients saw the connectedness without telescopes, microscopes, calculus, or Einstein. The singularity that the Hebrews were familiar with was one God whose name is "I am" or "Existence" (Exodus 3:14).

We see connections in nature between things that appear to have nothing to do with each other. For example, if we say, "That man has no spine," we do not mean that scientifically or analytically. The man is clearly a vertebrate. To us, he moves through life like a "jellyfish," directed by whatever current flows. It turns out this is unfair to jellyfish; nonetheless, this is how the creature appears to us. The travel habits of a jellyfish are not the point. The man is a "milquetoast," a "wimp," "he's yellow," or some other absurd pejorative that, strangely enough, makes sense.

The Hebrews knew that their God transcended nature to their best ability. Yahweh is not a product of the natural world. He is nothing like the gods of the ANE or Zeus and Thor, etc., who were products of this universe and continuous with it. A contingent universe and any others that may exist are dependent on necessary or self-existence for their existence.

In Hebrew theology, the physical creation is not animated by spirits as in paganism. However, it is unreasonable to expect the ancient Hebrews to have the sophistication to make perfect distinctions between the *workings* of a universe they could not explain and the *movements* of the Creator that are beyond all of us.

Nothing in nature is God, according to Genesis. The sun, moon, and stars were not gods or alive but mere functionaries created by Yahweh. All of the creation yields to God. Genesis was more an advancement on God's nature (being One and transcendent) than the universe's shape. The six days in Genesis could fit any ANE creation account apart from the deities involved. Otherwise, the seventh day "Sabbath" rest divorces Genesis 1 from any ANE account. In other words, there was nothing objectionable in the pagan world about the six days except for Yahweh and the theological implications of the seventh-day Sabbath that YEC seems to ignore.

Expecting the ancient Hebrews to have the language to explain accurately how a transcendent source created an immanent universe is not reasonable. Nonetheless, Genesis 1 is a truly remarkable example of God's transcendence expressed with the theological tools of the Late Bronze Age, just as it is.

The ancients had a limited accumulated knowledge transmitted through oral tradition initially. They believed their eyes, and so do we. Discovering how nature worked beyond the unaided eye was not available to them. The ANE lacked thousands of years of accumulated knowledge and advanced instruments that have given us a decisive advantage. These are scientific and secular advantages, not theological ones.

Scientific knowledge developed many centuries after the biblical era. History documents this. Consequently, no biblical evidence exists that God revealed a sun-centered solar system to ancient Israel. There was no purpose in revealing something as basic as a solar system to people who couldn't use it or appreciate it. How would that contribute to an ancient tribal culture in covenant with Yahweh? Why expect God to disclose subtle aspects of physics, chemistry, or biology without the necessary tools to recognize them? That would confuse the Israelites and impose a distracting worldview upon the biblical authors not seen for millennia.

God discloses something far more crucial—I Iimself.

All ancients saw that animals gave birth to their kind—sheep begat sheep that always produced sheep. What else could they think? The Israelites gave God credit for the design. They could reason back that today's sheep came from yesterday's sheep, which came from earlier sheep, all the way back to an original pair of sheep. There is nothing unreasonable about that. Animal pairs were evident and necessary in the ANE. There was nothing in the observations by the ancients to suggest any other "biological" process. Theirs was "naked eye biology."

Even the words *after their kind* do not refer to species or scientific categories, nor is it a revelation. It is a simple observation. In other words, *the revelation is not that animals reproduce after their kind; anyone can see that. The revelation is in who made them that way and why*. Some fundamentalists believe "after their kind" is the revelation of an "immutable biological law of kinds." Yet, YErs also accept the idea that fallen angels copulated with the "daughters of men" to produce a super race of giants (Genesis 6:1–4). These are not only creatures of a different kind; they are from a different universe. Why do they make this exception? Because if Genesis says it, it must be literal despite their "immutable kinds" regarding reproduction. That is, having it both ways.

People all over the ancient world knew that animals reproduced after their kind long before Genesis. They knew from experience in raising animals and watching them in the wild. Who hasn't? The Hebrews brought to the world not just who made them, but who *made them male and female,* i.e., one God who is neither male nor female. Reproducing after kinds refers to a mysterious and wonderous thing in the ANE—sexuality. Pagan gods were sexual. The ANE thought humans were sexual because the gods were that way. Yahweh is not sexual, so He invented males and females. That was different. Hebrew theology was an advance on the transcendent nature of God (the primary purpose of the Bible). Advances on God's nature developed steadily in the Old Testament but have continued at light speed since Christ.

Human origins in ANE creation myths from a first couple (or multiple couples in some accounts) follow a similar train of thought. Some stories speak of multiple couples created in the beginning. Origins also involved gods and a three-tiered universe. The expanse also mentioned in Genesis occurred when a deity, usually with the wind, separated the cosmic ocean into waters above and below the newly opened expanse or blue sky, thought to have a dome-like canopy holding the upper waters in suspension.[31] This action could expose elements locked inside the primordial waters for birthing gods and the various parts of the universe, such as the sun, moon, heavenly bodies, land, and wetlands. The ancients in the Late Bronze Age could relate to this. They did not anticipate a globe, let alone an unbounded universe.[32]

Nowhere in the Bible does God reveal science in advance of human discovery. Instead, He gradually disclosed a theology of Himself that was not discoverable that Christians call *special revelation*. A physics lesson would distract the original readers from essential matters of faith, which were challenging enough. The view of the cosmos in Genesis would have been recognizable in any ANE culture. On the other hand, it was Yahweh and the seventh-day rest that was rejected by those same cultures.

---

31. Attempts have been made to identify this expanse as a hard domed shape shell that physically held back the upper waters above the day and night skies. The expanse everywhere in ANE literature is the result of separating an "endless deep" or abyss of water into two separate bodies, one above the expanse, and one below the expanse. The expanse then consists of the day and night skies as the ancients observed them with moon and stars at night and blue skies with sun, day-moon, clouds, and birds etc., during the day. In other words, the ancients placed the divided waters both beyond the stars and below the earth. *Shamayim*, the Hebrew word for "heavens," translated variously: sky or skies, expanse, and stellar heavens refer to the same thing. Atmosphere is a scientific term without an ancient equivalent. There is no way the ancients knew of various layers of atmospheric gases surrounding the earth, ending at outer space. No evidence shows that the Hebrews of the ANE thought the earth was a sphere before the second temple period. Eratosthenes of Cyrenaica was the first to calculate the circumference of the earth around 240 BC.

32. One Egyptian record speaks of "endless" waters of the primeval world has led some to conclude the waters were unbounded as in an unbounded universe so that there could be no surface of the deep as in Genesis. This hardly seems possible since no such concept of an unbounded physical universe in the modern sense shows itself anywhere in the ANE. "Endless water" is meant vertically, not horizontally, as in a deep abyss of water since most of the created order came out of the watery abyss. Additionally, Egyptian reliefs and paintings in the tombs of the Pharaohs and elsewhere find a three-tiered universe and that the kings would enjoy sailing *on top of the waters* above the heavens alongside Ra, the sun god in the afterlife. One cannot sail on top of infinite waters with no surface. The Egyptian use of the word *infinite* is like the Hebrew use of *forever* and so many other uses in the ANE that likely meant an unknown length too long to measure. Infinite primeval waters likely meant the waters were immeasurable, which, of course, they would have been if they existed.

YE scholars insist that the Bible is "the final authority *in all matters that it addresses,*" including science.[33] But we are talking about the biblical periods of the first or second millennium BC, not astrophysics. The real issues in the SDWC are not about science but theology. For that matter, YEC is the only theory about origins that employs a private science all its own in an attempt to confirm their theology. *Widely recognized biblical scholars do not treat the Bible as a science book, and distinguished scientists the world over do not treat YE science as a science. Strangely, these are YErs who claim to practice a discipline when no one in that discipline recognizes their practice, which is one reason they resort to conspiracy theories.*[34]

The Bible addresses many subjects in the infancy stage of collective human knowledge. That is no criticism of the Bible and would not be an issue unless one thinks that all knowledge "addressed" in the Bible is God's knowledge. That is not possible.

Would we say the Bible is the final authority on matters of engineering? Is it more authoritative on anatomy or medicine? The Bible addresses "matters" that we call science and many others, yet there is no statement on the age of the earth anywhere in scripture. To draw that conclusion, one must string verses together with an outcome in mind called "proof-texting," an illegitimate hermeneutic because the interpreter's purpose replaces the author's purposes. Consider agriculture, food processing, fashion, sanitation, or transportation (boats like the Ark), which are "matters" addressed in the Bible, some extensively. Are they all special revelation? Must we adopt them in our lives? Those are too obvious, one might say. Science is different. But is it?

Why do fundamentalists treat science differently than other disciplines suggested in scripture? Because fundamentalists use the Bible, which is not scientific, to assert their brand of science and exercise their authority. By doing so, it is they who use the Bible (not the Bible itself) to compete with science when they routinely correct the scientific world. That encourages the conflict between them by treading on territory that is not their own.

If we demanded of the world that the Bible be the final authority on the engineering of ships as in the Ark or buildings like Solomon's temple, engineers would push back, too, and rightly so. Remember that the Ark and Temple were God's design *with His specific instructions.* Those are matters God *personally addressed.* So is the Bible the final authority on *everything* or category it addresses? What about economics? Should sheep be currency? No, because we

---

33. Terry Mortenson and Thane H. Ury, eds., *Coming to Grips with Genesis,* Kindle edition, 2013, page 20.

34. The controversy is not in the scientific community but a narrow part of Christianity, showing it has nothing to do with science. This is a six-day war *in Christianity only, primarily among fundamentalists,* primarily among evangelicals.

can see that these are situational customs and technologies based on time-sensitive experiences.

In reality, modern science is incompetent to challenge biblical *theology*, but it is competent to challenge so-called *"Bible science,"* which is like "Bible engineering," "Bible architecture," or "Bible medicine." These are misnomers. There is no Bible engineering; there is only engineering practiced at the time biblical authors wrote. There is no "Bible medicine" or "Bible economics" or building mandates. Engineering, medicine, architecture, and a whole host of other matters like anatomy and reproductive biology that the Bible "addresses" are incidental to the Bible's purposes: the self-revelation of God crowned in Christ and His plan for all times.[35]

To defeat scientific claims, YErs must use scientific methods because the claims of science result from those methods. By their nature and context, the words of a biblical document from the first or second millennium BC do not address science or its methods. Without such distinctions, the parties talk at each other in *different languages* and at cross purposes. YErs should know that speaking in different languages and cross purposes produces *babble*.

The conflict arises when one discipline trespasses upon the other. Science is perceived to defeat theology when believers base their theology on science, opening themselves up to scrutiny. You cannot blame science for that. Science is not so critical of the Bible as it is how the Bible is used to speak for science. Mainstream science helps us understand God's *works* in creation; it does not claim to be God's word. The "Creation science" of YEC is not God's word any more than mainstream science is. For science to defeat theology, it must use the discipline of theology and philosophy. Christians should challenge science when it devolves into theology or philosophy, but we must do that with better theological and philosophical tools.

Since science is *naturalistic*, it cannot speak authoritatively on things that transcend nature, like God, angels, or abstract objects like, numbers, sets, and Plato's forms. Only when Christians usurp the mantel of science does science confront us, justifiably so. If fundamentalists took the same approach to an

---

35. It is hard to explain why people consider some things so important besides that they attach their personal identity to them. That is why ideologies encourage adherents to find their personal identity as a human in their central teachings so they are not likely to abandon them. I had a friend who believed the earth is both the center of the solar system *and the entire universe*, that is, the universe revolves around the earth, daily. However, being a traditional Catholic, his evangelistic efforts were mainly on the earth being the center of *this universe*. He was taught by sectarians that when the Church Fathers all agree on something it must be infallible. He thought if he could convince people on his earth-centered universe, people would become traditional, Vatican I, Latin speaking Catholics. I asked him why his concept of geocentrism was so important. His response was because an earth-centered universe "reveals the love of God." I then asked, "Doesn't the cross satisfy that?" He used the Bible for support much like YErs do though YEC is more reasonable. I was to find out later that a surprising number of people believe in an earth-centered universe—it is a movement too with similar arguments.

earth-centered solar system (and some do) or human reproduction by insisting that only sperm leads to conception—the "biblical view"—we would immediately recognize a misuse of the Bible. We would also find ourselves in a fight with biologists on reproduction.

Biblical authors reflect the development of knowledge in their "public domain." In ancient times (not just biblical), a woman was barren if she could not conceive. After all, if the man planted the seed, females were expected to get pregnant—simple observation.[36]

Christians can sound just as silly on science as scientists like Richard Dawkins when he refers to theological matters. Assuming upon another's expertise without the same specialized knowledge is misguided. Biblical views are irrelevant to scientific discipline because biblical authors do not do science. Science is a naturalistic enterprise, not a theological one. Methods of engineering, medicine, reproductive biology, and many other areas of inquiry were undeveloped in scripture. We understand them as subordinate concepts in the Bible caught in time, not God's revelation breaking through the heavens.

John MacArthur, part pastor/part Reformed scholar, differentiates YEC from science, saying the beginning of creation "*is a theological issue, not a scientific one*" and, therefore, not a matter of empirical evidence.[37] That is true if, by "the beginning," he means *who* began it and how. But what the beginning may have looked like and when it could have occurred may be a matter of empirical evidence. One can have such evidence for the beginning of creation without knowing how it got there. The words "the beginning of creation" muddle the thought. Just when was the "beginning?" The Bible is unclear on that. Why should the beginning be more mysterious than the continuous sustaining of all existence, which Augustine and Aquinas insisted is the more significant operation in creation? Wouldn't the sustainer of creation resist empiricism while age is suited for it?

Theoretical physicists can see physical evidence of continuous causes and effects, tracing them back to the beginning. We are close to "observing" the moment of creation with exceptionally powerful telescopes placed in orbit for a clearer view. In fact, atheistic scientists can see a beginning well enough to look for any measure that pushes it as far back as possible, as in the multiverse.

The physical evidence does not explain the miracle of creation as biological evidence cannot explain *the miracle* of birth. I doubt MacArthur would claim that human conception has no scientific or biological explanation since he must claim the science for his pro-life position on when life begins. Indeed,

---

36. The ancients would have known that seeds could be dormant as in planting crops or when certain men could not impregnate women who could conceive with other men. Even so, ovaries were not understood.

37. Terry Mortenson, Thane H. Ury, *Coming to Grips with Genesis*, Kindle edition, 2013, page 20.

he is happy to use science in service of a miracle since the beginning of life is arguably an equal or greater miracle than material creation.

For YErs like MacArthur, science should be beside the point since science is an empirical discipline while the act of creation is a miracle. Yet, YErs continue to assume a literal Genesis is scientifically accurate and diligently seek to validate their brand of science called *Creation Science*. This inconsistency happens when all roads lead to a predetermined conclusion.

YErs want Creation Science taught in schools. However, if creation is science, it cannot be a miracle. Miracles are not explainable on naturalistic grounds. That is what makes them miracles. The miracle of creation is not just in the mechanisms involved in the things made but also in existence itself, or that anything should exist. How can the universe come into existence that has never existed before? Evolution does not explain the origin of existence. Although physical states can cause other physical states, the reason they exist (their *efficient causes*) must be an independent creative power, e.g., there was no physical state to cause the first physical state! *Material* causes do not ground existence (see the 4 causes online). Even Genesis does not *explain* creation; it declares it: "And God said," "and it was so," etc. *If YErs are right that science cannot explain the miracle of creation, then Creation Science is an oxymoron. If creation is an unexplainable miracle, "Creation Science" would be like saying, "Virgin Birth Science."*

Therefore, YEC contradicts itself. YErs recognize that the creation miracle is not science but theology. Then again, they instinctively know the earth's age, by nature, demands an empirical explanation, so they employ their unique "science." But the earth's aging is a process, i.e., a natural development we can track. Things show their age.

Obscure language on a page from the Late Bronze Age, though inspired of God, does not suffice as a dating device. It is theology, not science. If you claim to know the earth's age, you must explain it scientifically since measuring age is an empirical task, not a theological concept. Therefore, YErs like MacArthur conflate the age of the earth with the miracle of creation. Creation, or existence, is a miracle, regardless of age.

If the earth is young, then show us. Don't just tell us.

Augustine wrote:

Whatever [scientists] assert in their treatises which is contrary to these Scriptures of ours...we must either prove it as well as we can to be entirely false or, *without the smallest hesitation, believe it to be so.*

Augustine might accept deep age "without the smallest hesitation" with today's extensive empirical evidence.[38]

---

38. Since Augustine thought that God created the universe instantly with seeds for life that gradually unfolded, it is conceivable that if he were alive today, he would accept evolution without hesitation.

Science does not claim to understand the pre-Bang singularity, a state where the laws of physics are undifferentiated and time and space break down. The singularity appears unnatural or beyond nature as we have understood it, being without the laws of physics. Currently, the closest science has come to observing the beginning is some 379,000 years after the Big Bang. At that point, the extreme density of light and gases created an insurmountable visual barrier we could not yet penetrate. Because of this, most physicists think it may not be possible to observe the moment of creation. Therefore, they calculate and infer what happened by following the "breadcrumbs" left by the Big Bang, which is not unlike a supernova—call it a "universal nova." We can study supernovas and infer some things about the Big Bang.

One must wonder why the Bible should be accurate in physics but primitive on subjects more relevant to life, such as anatomy, medicine, engineering, or reproductive biology. YErs claim God micromanaged every word of the Bible to avoid any error, so it should be entirely accurate in all disciplines it addresses. Yet, on anatomy, biblical authors indicate that the bowels are the seat of human emotions and that our thought patterns (brain activity) come from our heart muscles. As with many things, those ideas are in the Bible *incidentally*. They have nothing to do with the purposes of the Bible, which have to do with God's self-disclosure, *especially* His plan in the Incarnate Christ.

Reproductive biology in scripture assumes that babies were seeded by sperm alone. Is this God's biology, Bible biology, or ANE biology? If this is Israelite biology, then this was not God's opinion on the matter but culture's idea finding its way into the Bible. Therefore, the Bible does not offer a scientific description of conception. Instead, any "biology" that trips into the Bible's pages is *observational or experiential,* correct on its face but might be technically wrong.

Not *every* word in the Bible is special revelation or even general revelation. If ancient ideas on conception were God's word on human reproduction, God was mistaken, which is absurd since He created us. If ancient authors could not understand what we consider basic science, we assume it was a cultural matter, not instruction from on high. The revelation is not the ancient culture in Israel but God's self-disclosure *within* Israelite society.

Doesn't it make more sense that God's word is in the meaning and lessons of these stories and not so much in the incidentals? The YEC platform depends on incidentals and assumptions, for there is no statement on earth's age anywhere in the Bible. There are no dates anywhere in the Bible. We do not even know when Christ was born! Scientific disciplines were not in development, so science cannot be the intended point. Primitive thoughts occur in the Bible without correction or concern. It is silly to fault God, the Bible, or the Israelites for the realities of the Late Bronze and Early Iron Ages.

Is God responsible for mistaken ideas in the Bible? If so, tell us why.

Why did God let those mistakes go if He could easily correct them, if word-for-word literalism were His priority, or if He was the actual writer? There are many scientific and technological shortcomings with people in Scripture, not because Scripture is unreliable but because it is *genuine*. God is not obsessive-compulsive. The flaws are not *with* the Bible but *in* the Bible; that is, with the times of the authors. There are shortcomings in all periods.

Genesis 1–11 is about prehistory written during the Late Bronze Age; what did we expect to find? Twenty-first-century science? Besides, the authors do not claim to be authoritative in scientific or technological matters secondary to their purposes. The Bible reflects God's presence in authentic times and places. He does not have to prove His *bona fides* to satisfy the anal-retentive, word-for-word scruples of later fundamentalists.

It is an insult to expect God to slip twenty-first-century ideas in the Bible to satisfy curiosity seekers akin to De Vinci Code buffs or Area 51 devotees who treat the Bible like the writings of Nostradamus as if God's self-disclosure is not good enough. *Science did not dominate the ancient world as it does ours, so it could not be relevant, and therefore, science should not dominate the interpretation of the Bible. God's knowledge is not on trial here.*

Hebrew physics or astronomy of the ANE was not God's revelation to the world, nor were the internal workings of organs in the human body. Moreover, procreation is far more relevant to the creation than when it occurred. Reproduction is God's ongoing mechanism for creating living things, yet the Bible is not perfect on the science. It is absurd to expect it to be. Only the notion that God wrote the Bible or dictated every word leads to that.

Another example of ancient anatomy is the brain. There is no word for "brain" in biblical Hebrew. The ancients believed the brain was a useless stuffing in the skull, which is a tempting thought in some cases but is anatomically incorrect! In most ways, Israel was behind the technical advances of the Egyptians, Assyrians, Babylonians, and later Persians, Greeks, and Romans. Honestly, ancient Israel had her hands full with the Philistines. What are we to make of that? Were pagan deities superior to Yahweh? Did pagan gods bless their people more than Yahweh blessed Israel? Or did Yahweh Himself bless those pagan empires?

If God "superintended" every word in the Bible, as YErs claim, must we believe that emotions reside in the bowels and women do not produce eggs?[39] If not, then why is God not a liar on anatomy or biology in YEC, which are as implicit as any age of the earth attributed to scripture? *There are so many ANE assumptions in the Bible that it is more reasonable to suppose science was not high on God's agenda, nor was our idea of science in the authors' consciousness. The*

---

39. For instance, Todd S. Beall writes, "The Bible claims to be the authoritative word of God. This means that God superintended and directed what was to be written." See Terry Mortenson and Thane H. Ury, eds., *Coming to Grips with Genesis* (2013), Kindle Edition, pp. 142–143.

notion that we must get our science from a time when there was no science is not a serious proposal.

Judaism brought enlightenment to the world through theology, wisdom, law, morality, and, most of all, by revealing the source of all things, Yahweh. Contrary to YEC, ancient Israel was not known for enlightening the world with her "science." You would have to go to Babylon or Egypt for greater advancements. Science and technology are neither intrinsically religious nor antireligious areas of study. They are matters of collective human knowledge still in progress. So why do YErs require the Bible to be correct or up on physics but not on other sciences such as engineering, medicine, biology, or anatomy? Why? Because those sciences have nothing to do with the age of the earth.

If we expect the Bible to be relevant to today's science, we will likely force our view on the text. The tendency to read the Bible with a contemporary reader's bias leads to different problems in any generation. As we shall see, many of our interpretive challenges are with primitive languages constantly changing or declining in use.[40]

It is hard to find any place in the Bible where God is concerned about Israel's scientific advancements—just the opposite is true. God warned Israel not to put its faith in technologies, like well-equipped armies and the number of advanced chariots and other weapons in their arsenal. (Isaiah 31:1). They were not to "decipher" the movement and arrangement of the stars (astrology) as in paganism. God seems more concerned about timeless matters regarding His plan and not short-term technical gains.

Besides, it is doubtful that we have much over the ancients from God's perspective. If God explained creation from nothing *precisely*, it is not likely that our best scientists could comprehend it. Our best scientists do not fully understand what they have discovered, including the singularity, the cosmological constant, quantum mechanics, dark energy, dark matter, gravity, light, and many other things we take for granted. Scientists routinely use the word *mysterious* in connection with many aspects of the cosmos. Even Standard Big Bang language is inadequate, which may be a point in its favor.

For example, the Big Bang involved a tiny particle that did not "bang" exactly. A tiny particle called the "singularity" underwent extreme expansion or inflation, like blowing up a balloon at millions of times the speed of light. Our universe would be unfit for life if the expansion rate in the singularity combined with its gravitational pull were any different from the one that occurred.

---

40. Consider 1 Corinthians 13:3 from the KJV: "And though I bestow all my goods to feed the poor...and have not *charity*, it profiteth me nothing." A modern reading might see a flat contradiction in this verse because, today, feeding to the poor *is* charity. Virtually all translations of the Bible are anachronistic to one degree or another because they are modern versions of an ancient text. Therefore, the Bible should be treated with far more discernment on both sides in the SDWC, especially the one to one correspondence to reality, word for word fundamentalist.

Some physicists, popular in media, describe the singularity as a tiny particle of "infinite" or "near infinite" density of light and heat.[41]

As Lawrence Krauss observes, "It is impossible to describe the moment of creation in human language." Undeterred by the word *impossible*, Krauss describes the moment anyway by saying, "From what may have been nothing, we go to a state of almost infinite density and infinite temperature and violence." Krauss is using the word "violence" as a metaphor here.[42]

Metaphor is something scientists depend on more than some are willing to admit. Two other things are striking about Krauss's statement (he describes the beginning of this universe as "the moment of creation"). First, Despite the attempt, Krauss admits that the moment of creation is not explainable with the main thing we use to explain things—words. Is this a veiled way of acknowledging the miraculous? Not hardly; nonetheless, miracles by definition are unexplainable and, according to Krauss, so might be the moment of creation.

YErs claim science cannot explain the miracle of creation, and some scientists seem to agree with the "cannot explain part." Yet YErs believe a document from the Late Bronze or Early Iron ages captures it perfectly, in paleo Hebrew, as if ancient human language shows God's work more than the evidence He left behind.

Secondly, Krauss's statement is an unusual description for a scientist. Any scientist knows that "almost infinite" is infinitely shy of infinite. But some physicists use that language routinely of the singularity, possibly because the singularity was not the universe (i.e., time, space, or matter), nor did it contain the laws of physics. Instead, the singularity "gave birth" to everything in the universe, including the laws of physics. Therefore, the singularity "appears" to have come from the "outside." But there can be no "outside" without space which didn't appear until the Big Bang. Some physicists speculate on the singularity that we may be dealing with something beyond nature, suggesting the "supernatural" or

---

41. We are all familiar with concentrating sunlight through a magnifying glass. The glass intensifies the light enough to start fires easily, and that is from a light that is 93 million miles away. Now imagine all the light in the universe concentrated in a tiny particle. Who is going to measure that?

42. From *How the Universe Works*, Season 1, Episode 1; first aired 4/25/2010. In the same episode, the narrator states that the universe "came from absolutely nothing to everything." Physicists know this, yet they search for how all things can come from nothing by looking for *something* they can call "nothing." Candidates have been quantum fluxes, oscillating universes, multiverses, tunneling universes, De Sitter space, string theory and others, all of which beg the question or kick the can down the road to an earlier beginning. An ultimate explanation must begin with nothing. Science is not equipped to discover that kind of explanation. That is why they search for something they can call nothing. On the TV series *Closer to Truth*, in the episode "How did the Universe Begin?" the renowned physicist Allan Guth states that inflation in the Big Bang effectively destroyed evidence for the beginning of the universe. So scientists theorize about the beginning with *versions of nothing*. Who can blame them?

perhaps "pre-natural." The question should be, how and by what power did the singularity appear? So far, we can only guess.

Many physicists seem intent on finding something they can call "nothing" that could have "birthed" the universe, like quantum tunneling or a fluctuation in a quantum vacuum, none of which is *nothing* or even a vacuum, but an energy field. The struggle for language for the quantum world shows that science has entered a place unlike the standard universe we once knew. How can everything come from actual nothing or even pretend nothing?

According to Roger Penrose, the multiverse is not a theory. He calls it a group of ideas. It is not even a hypothesis because there is absolutely no evidence for it, nor is evidence even possible because we cannot create a bridge from our space into spacelessness in an attempt to "travel" to a neighboring pocket of space. Non-space/time is an absolute barrier. Therefore, the multiverse is not science but a modern myth. I don't use the word "myth" pejoratively. Myths are not lies; they are imaginative explanations about origins that are purely speculative. I hope there is a multiverse; it's not science.

How can a whole universe come from an infinitesimal singularity, unlike the universe it births? By analogy, the human zygote and seeds are like a singularity in that they are tiny and look nothing like the end product they become, yet they contain all that is needed to produce it. Surprisingly, the cosmic singularity was like a universe egg, singularly fertilized with the "DNA" for a developed universe. A woman's fertilized egg lacks any *signs* of human anatomy, but there it is. So how can a *tiny* particle that gives birth to a material universe be infinite?

It is a mystery, a physicist's virgin birth enigma.

When physicists use the word *infinite* in the case of the singularity, they mean an extreme density that allows no measurable quantities of time-space and where the laws of physics break down:

> In scientific terms, a gravitational singularity (or space-time singularity) is a location where the quantities that are used to measure the gravitational field become infinite in a way that does not depend on the coordinate system. In other words, it is a point in which all physical laws are indistinguishable from one another, where space and time are no longer interrelated realities, but merge indistinguishably and cease to have any independent meaning.[43]

Space, time, and matter/energy were one and *simple* as a singularity. They were not separate entities. This "infinite" singularity was analogous to a "trinity" of time, space, and matter—three in one and one in three—inseparable

---

43. See "What is a Singularity" by Matt Williams, in *Universe Today: Space and Astronomy News*, February 16, 2011.

and imperceptible unless a stupendous event revealed its nature. The Big Bang revealed a "trinity" of time, space, and matter that expanded from the singularity, creating the physical universe. Those dimensions are now distinct when they were once indistinguishable. The Incarnation is the event that burst onto the scene and disclosed the ultimate trinity: an infinite Singularity of Father, Son, and Holy Spirit that brought a new creation.

This book contends that our issues in Creationism are more theological than scientific and literary more than literal. Not that science is irrelevant, but science is nearly unrecognizable in Genesis while its theology is profound and often missed. *Therefore, today's notions of science are irrelevant compared to how ANE tribal people expressed their "science."* God seems disinterested in advancing Israel's science which generally lagged behind their contemporaries. In contrast, critical theological ideas were awakening in the Hebrew people.

Science could wait.

Summary

1. God nowhere reveals science in advance of human discovery.

2. God's attributes can provide a corrective for misinterpreting the language of scripture.

3. Ancient Israel's "science" and technology were products of the Bronze and Iron Ages.

4. Judaism brought enlightenment to the world through theology, not science. It is a fact that Israel lagged behind her contemporaries in science and technology.

5. History demonstrates that the science we know developed in increments over very long periods of trial and error.

6. Science is neither intrinsically religious nor antireligious but is a matter of collective human knowledge still in progress.

7. Today's issues in the SDWC are more theological than scientific and literary more than literal.

8. It is inconsistent to require the Bible to be correct on physics while ignoring its primitive ideas in other sciences. Examples are reproductive biology without the female egg, emotions that come from the bowels and thought processes from the heart.

9. God was revealing Himself, not science. God is not a scientist. Scientists discover. God knows all things and creates all things. Artists create. Since God creates, He is more like an "artist."

3.
GOD'S WORD VS. MAN'S WORD

The reality we can put into words is never reality itself.
—Werner Heisenberg

Wherever truth may be found, it belongs to our Master.
—Augustine

Reasonable Christians do not consider a statement false just because an unbeliever says it. Neither is something true simply because a believer says it. Even the devil can tell the truth, and Christians can lie. Since God is truth, all truth proceeds from Him (John 14:6). Hence, Christians believe most truths fall into two general categories: special revelation and general revelation. So any truth in this universe reflects God, as Augustine stated.

Many fundamentalists seem to disagree with this. According to YEC, God says the earth is young, but "man" says the earth is old and there can be no peace. YErs insist that Christians who interpret Genesis figuratively do so to appease the secular culture or join some conspiracy with the scientific community to undermine biblical authority. But Augustine insisted that the creation days were figurative long before modern science. All science has done is help confirm his view as it did with geocentric views of the universe in the Bible that we now take figuratively.

YErs frame the debate within the narrow confines of "God's Word," the Bible, versus "man's word" (science) as if the conflict is over categories and not their content. Science is not "Man's word." Dogma asserted by scientists are not speaking scientifically; Real science discovers and infers. When correct, science discovers general revelation. Science is the most impressive tool humanity has to discover general revelation. Christians should not force what amounts to a categorical debate between science and scripture.

Alvin Plantinga has isolated the alleged conflict between science and religion. Conflict occurs when scientists speak to theology or philosophy without the appropriate education and religious people speak to science without the corresponding preparation. Plantinga distinguishes between *Methodological* Naturalism and *Metaphysical* Naturalism.[44]

Methodological Naturalism is an essential scientific method for understanding nature. But atheistic scientists engage in *Metaphysical* Naturalism, which is not science but philosophy. As Einstein once remarked, scientists

---

44. See Alvin Plantiga, *Where the Conflict Really Lies: Science, Religion, and Naturalism* (Oxford University Press: New York, 2011).

make poor philosophers. The scientific method cannot reach beyond the natural world, so demanding empirical evidence for the supernatural is absurd. The philosophies of scientists outside their discipline are no more authoritative than the layperson.

Forget that by "God's Word," people usually mean their opinion regarding it.

Even Galileo spoke of two books—*the* book of God's Word (the Bible) and the *book of God's works* (meaning information derived from nature or general revelation). He declared that both "books" are harmonious and require interpreters trained for each. The respected evolutionary biologist, Stephen Jay Gould, said that science and religion operate on two different "magisteria," i.e., spheres of teaching authority.[45]

The two books analogy is just that: an analogy. Analogies do not say A is B, but only that A has similarities with B. Nature is only like a book in that it contains information that we can "read" or "translate" in certain ways. Nature suggests types of information we might call languages (mathematics: formula, geometry, and DNA, among others). Anything that we identify as a language has a corresponding class of interpreters. Nature's primary interpreters are scientists. They receive extensive training for analyzing their findings. Humans were made to do science. All evidence suggests they are doing a remarkable job.

Scientists can and do misread nature; that is why dogma and certainty on extremely complex scientific theories are like theology, complete with heresies, censorship, and an inquisitional spirit. Literature, especially ancient literature, is also prone to misinterpretation, if not more so.

The geneticist Francis Collins, who was instrumental in mapping the human genome, calls DNA the *language of God.* Stephen C. Meyer wrote of God's *"Signature in the Cell." Since God created nature, we can learn about Him from the things He made. Beyond that, the nature/book analogy breaks down because nature is not really a book though it contains information, and humans were inspired to write the Scripture but had nothing to do with creating the universe.*

Oddly, many YErs believe the Bible is a better source of information about nature than nature itself. Here is Ken Ham at Answers in Genesis:

---

45. Gregg Caruso, *Was Stephen Jay Gould Right?* April 22, 2014, Real Clear Religion. He writes: "In 1997, the late paleontologist and evolutionary biologist Stephen Jay Gould famously proposed a resolution to the supposed conflict between science and religion. He called it NOMA, or the thesis of *non-overlapping magisteria*. A magisterium refers to a domain of teaching authority. In addition, the NOMA thesis maintains that "the magisterium of science covers the empirical realm: what the universe is made of (fact) and why does it work in this way (theory). The magisterium of religion extends over questions of ultimate meaning, truth, and moral values." According to Gould, since these two magisteria do not overlap there is no real conflict (or at least there should not be) between science and religion. As Galileo put it, "science studies how the heavens go, religion studies how to go to heaven."

Those who promote... [the book of nature] need to understand two crucial fallacies with this idea: first, nature is cursed; second, our observations of nature are not independent from our presuppositions. When we examine these problems, we see that nature should never be put on the same level as the Bible.[46]

Ham identifies two "fallacies" regarding the two-book analogy:

1. "Nature is cursed." Apparently, this means nature is not reliable for information about itself.

2. Our observations of nature are unreliable because they are not "independent of our presuppositions," as if presuppositions are necessarily wrong.

If the first assumption is correct: since nature is cursed, its information is unreliable, we would have to admit that science has been a useless exercise. No one is prepared to do that. If nature's information is unreliable, then even that statement is unreliable. How can we recognize nature's curses without knowing how the natural world is supposed to work? If we isolate the curses, we can see what is left: creation as God intended.

Furthermore, if all nature is cursed, that would include the authors of scripture since they were also part of the natural order. If God can use "cursed" humans to write the Bible so that "cursed" readers can understand it, it follows that cursed humans can comprehend nature (authored by God) by observing it. God created us with the ability to understand and use nature effectively: "fill the earth and *subdue it*" (Genesis 1:28). Other translations say: master it, control it, govern it, which requires extensive knowledge.

Modern science helps restore humanity's dominion over nature.

Catholics and Protestants believe God created an intelligible universe that operates on rational laws. As Einstein said, "The most incomprehensible thing about the universe is that it is comprehensible." If we are solely an ensemble of atoms and molecules, how can we understand anything, let alone ourselves and the universe that produced us?

Paul claims the Godhead is knowable through the creation (Romans 1:20). David said, "The heavens declare God's glory;" in its wonder and beauty, and "we are wonderfully made." Do YErs reject these claims in scripture? Of course they don't. Undeniably, our accumulated knowledge in science has uncovered an enormous amount of reliable information about how nature works. Therefore, what does "nature is cursed" have to do with learning *from* nature?

Nothing whatsoever.

---

46. "Is Nature The 67th Book of the Bible?" April 4, 2016, AiG website.

Ham's second point—we should be "independent of our presupposi-tions"—is itself a presupposition, yet he does not show how his presupposi-tion could be an exception to his arbitrary "rule." If that sounds confusing to you, you are not alone. In Christendom, modern science developed on a major presupposition: God's works are coherent. Therefore, Ham's ideas do not align with historic Christian thought.

For instance, Ham's first presupposition—that nature is cursed—is an assertion without justification. Genesis does not say "nature" is cursed. Instead, it tells us that three suspects in the garden received certain curses: the serpent, the woman, and the man. One of those curses against the man affects the ground to the extent that he uses it for food.

Instead of picking food from an ideal garden, Adam and Eve would have to develop the fields outside, clearing the ground of trees, bushes, and rocks, cul-tivating it, fighting insect infestations, and pulling weeds. Likewise, humans will have to fend for themselves without God's active presence in a tranquil garden. So whatever "curses" mean, it cannot mean nature's findings are misleading or that God damaged all nature's workings because Adam and Eve ate the forbid-den fruit.

Curses likely mean that alienated from God's presence, life is hard and sub-ject to "bad luck."

Genesis lists the curse's effects: difficult crop yield, poor work conditions, painful childbirth, relations between husband and wife, and legless dust-eat-ing snakes. Things will not be so easy now. One must wonder how literal the concept of curses was, particularly the "legless dust-eating snakes." That specific curse certainly meant something. But snakes do not live on a diet of dust, and their slither physiology is remarkably successful. A serious reader might appre-ciate the spirit of storytelling in the language. Nothing kills that spirit more than wooden literalism (see 2 Corinthians 3:6).

It is important to distinguish *science* as the book of nature from *creation* as the "book" of nature. Theologians do not suggest science is the book; instead, nature is the "book" of God's *works* per Galileo. Science is a method or "herme-neutic" used to interpret the "book" of nature. The analogy suggests that nature contains information that reflects its Maker and that we can "read" it. The Bible also suggests this (see Psalms 19:1-4; Romans 1:20).

Today, we can read nature's "languages": mathematics, DNA, the color spectrum of light, and others. Information in the air can be "read" by a blood-hound's sense of smell, which we also use to detect diseases like cancer and epi-lepsy. Marine life uses sonar that gathers information to navigate the worldwide oceans long before humans did.

Nonetheless, the Bible is a book written by humans with ink and assem-bled in pages with a cover. Since creation is cursed and mainstream science doesn't work for YEC, YErs insist, "nature should never be put on the same level as the Bible." There are no "levels" but different sources of information. For example, Christians do not consider the Bible a better source of information for medicine, rocket science, or playing the harp. Yet, YEC says it must be accurate in physics, geology, and biology. Any *special revelation* in either nature or the Bible reflects God's nature.

While the human presence permeates the composition of the Bible, there is no such human presence in the formation of heaven and earth. Therefore, the Bible is less a product of the divine than the universe. That is a fact. God is truly the only "author" of the universe. The book analogy means that God may reveal Himself in both sources, which he does, despite "curses." [47]

Many people believe God has inspired accomplishments by humans throughout history: the Sistine Chapel, the US Constitution and Declaration of Independence, the Emancipation Proclamation, the music of Bach, Mozart, and Beethoven, and achievements like magnificent architecture, brilliant novels, numerous discoveries in science and medicine, and other artistic and intellectual compositions. But, if God inspired (breathed on) them, He did not compose the things these humans created. The human presence is undeniable in works of art and the Bible. Why do YE *reformists* insist that God wrote the Bible? Perhaps to justify literalizing the text and obligating people to their tradition.

Many would say that the Holy Spirit's inspiration for the Bible is unlike his inspiration for art or other giftedness. I have believed that myself, but can we be so sure? YErs believe this difference because it is inconceivable that God painted the Sistine Chapel or "superintend" every brushstroke or chisel in stone by Michelangelo. Yet YErs believe the Holy Spirit composed every word in the Bible but not works of art. Art is more human.

But this, too, is in doubt:

I have filled [the son of Hur] *with the Spirit of God*, with wisdom, with understanding, with knowledge and with all kinds of skills— *to make artistic designs* for work in gold, silver and bronze, to cut and set stones, to work in wood, and to engage in *all kinds* of crafts. (Exodus 31:2–6)

The Holy Spirit inspires gifts for use in service to God to achieve higher results. It does not override the person or their compositions with obsessive control over every stroke of a brush or carving in stone. Christians believe the Spirit gives people abilities and acute awareness but does not do the work for them. God did not paint the Sistine Chapel, nor did He build Solomon's temple. God

---

47. The notion that the Bible must be in accord with nature (or modern science) at the micro or telescopic levels assumes its purpose is to do so. The two "books" do not offer the same kind of information about the same things. The Bible is not an analysis of nature's processes but simple observations, nor is the universe Bible-based. The two books serve different purposes.

does not appear obsessed with controlling every stroke on a canvas, note in a symphony, *or word on a page.*

It should be common knowledge that Christianity furthered the project of modern science not so appreciated among many fundamentalists.[48] YErs call OECs sell-outs and conspirators with science against "biblical authority." That is a rather extraordinary conspiracy over six *ordinary* days. Christianity energized science that developed into modern science. Now YEC is conflicted on the subject.

In reality, surveys of the scientific community over the last hundred years show that the percentage of believers among professional scientists has remained steady at between 30 to 40 percent. About 15 percent are not sure about God or agnostic.[49]

According to "100 Years of Nobel Prizes," the prizes awarded between 1901 and 2000 (one year before 911) reveal that 65.4 percent of all Nobel Prize laureates have identified Christianity as their religious preference. Christians have won 78.3 percent of all the Nobel Prizes in Peace, 72.5 percent in chemistry, 65.3 percent in physics, 62 percent in medicine, 54 percent in economics, and 49.5 percent of awards in literature. Nobel himself was a Lutheran.[50]

If current scientific theories on the universe's age are anywhere near accurate (the evidence is overwhelming), Christianity has a real problem: that YEC should define Christianity for unbelievers.

Augustine recognized the problem 1,600 years ago:

It happens that even a non-Christian knows some things about the earth, heaven, and other elements...in such a way that he holds these by a most certain reason and evidence. But it is a disgraceful and deadly thing that *an unbeliever would hear a Christian speaking about these things as if expounding Christian writings in some delirious manner so that by seeing him wrong about all of [the universe], he could scarcely keep from laughing.* And it is not so annoying that such a Christian errs but that *those outside*

---

48. See Mark A. Noll, *The Scandal of the Evangelical Mind* (Eerdmans Publishing, Co., Grand Rapids Michigan, Intervarsity Press, Lancaster England, 1995).

49. It may come as a surprise that some believers consider themselves "agnostic." Agnostic means not to "know," i.e., that God exists. However, the kind of knowing referred to is empirical or demonstrable knowledge such as fingerprints, DNA, or locating God in space-time. Empirical evidence is for limited creatures in a material universe. Since God transcends empirical data and is not falsifiable, that kind of knowledge is insufficient, nor applicable; therefore, one can only accept or reject the plausibility of God. Believing scientists may consider themselves agnostic in this sense. Immanuel Kant said, "Where reason cannot go, belief is not irrational." The actual percentage of scientists that believe this way may affect the survey's ratios. The percentage of agnostics that believe or lean toward faith, as far as I know, is not tract.

50. Article, "List of Christian Nobel Laureates," *Wikipedia.*

believe [biblical] authors were in fact saying such things."[51] (emphasis mine)

Augustine had no idea how prescient this observation would become. It is undeniable that fundamentalist Christianity has a reputation for lording it over science with its own idea of "biblical authority." The project of science that we understand did not exist in biblical times. Widely recognized biblical scholars reject the idea that the Bible is a science book of any kind. How could it be?

Augustine accepts that "a Christian errs" with science, which he says is "not so annoying," no doubt because he expected some ignorance from such a large population, many of whom were uneducated. However, Augustine abhors it when *unbelievers* associate those mistakes with biblical authority. The bishop had Genesis in mind. He wrote a theological treatise or commentary on *The Literal meaning of Genesis* when he famously said, *"At least we know that the [Genesis creation day] is different from the ordinary day with which we are familiar."* That was some 1600 years ago.

Augustine's counsel is not to confuse opinions on science with biblical authority.

Christians do not use science to undermine the Bible. Science can help us choose one of our own options for interpreting like Augustine's insistence that the days in Genesis are figurative or the earth revolves around the sun instead of the Bible's phenomenological language of an earth-centered universe. YEC is defeated if only one of the six days is figurative like the seventh day. One thousand six hundred years before modern science, Augustine declared that the days in Genesis 1 are undoubtedly figurative. Yet YErs believe Christians use science to undercut the Bible because they believe YE opinions are the Bible. In reality, science undermines YEC.

Moreover, if the YEC movement is mistaken, it exposes the Gospel to unnecessary derision as YErs aggressively pursue potential converts to YEC for the world to see. In New Testament terms, Christians should accept ridicule over the Gospel and Christ crucified, which have always been a "scandal to some and foolishness to others" (Acts 5:40-41; 1 Corinthians 1:18, 23). Nonetheless, it brings unnecessary shame upon the Church when Christians offer needless reasons for those reactions. Outsiders witness many encounters between YErs

---

51. Richard Averback, Todd Beall, C. John Collins, Jud Davis, Victor P. Hamilton, Tremper III Longman, Kenneth J. Turner, John Walton, J. Daryl Charles, Richard Averbeck, Todd S Beall, C John Collins, Victor P Hamilton, *Reading Genesis 1–2: An Evangelical Conversation* (Hendrickson Publishers Marketing, LLC, 2013).

and Christian scholars with a defensive and accusatory tone characteristic of the overzealous YEr.[52]

Are not human words about God's Word still human words? Jesus said, "Father, I ask not only on behalf of these but also on behalf of those who will believe in me *through their word*" (John 17:20). The vast majority of Christians have believed through *their written word, called the New Testament.* Jesus gives them credit for their testimony in speech and scripture. However, the Bible is not enough by itself; it needs competent teachers to expound the word of God.

The New Testament is a series of testimonies, i.e., the genuine testimony of human witnesses. They are not God's testimonies, and God did not reduce biblical authors to quills in His hand; otherwise, they would not be witnessing. So when reading the Bible, how do you distinguish God's "perfect Word" from the author's very human attempt to capture it with human language? Christianity has always rejected the idea that every word of the Bible was hand-selected by God.

How do God's word-for-word "hand-selections" explain the sharp uneven stylistic differences? There are peculiarities, sometimes inelegancies of some biblical authors, and unparalleled brilliancies of others? That is similar to allowing creation to develop its own flaws for a good reason: a certain amount of freedom in creation enables an authenticity in nature's development; it provides a genuine context for rational creatures with free will like humans to emerge. We experience diverse styles and artistry from Moses to Job and David to Paul and John when reading the Bible. Undoubtedly, God allowed freedom in the minds of biblical authors for authentic testimonies. Ethical testimony should be, above all, genuine.

Who is to say that biblical authors are mistaken about their perceptions anyway? Their perceptions may be mistaken, but an accurate portrayal of them is not. We want to know what they thought, even the primitive elements. Not every opinion recorded in the Bible is God's opinion. All biblical sentiments do not originate with God only because they are in the Bible. The Bible is primarily a human product. It just is.

The *personal* witness of each author has survived for a reason. Their authentic perceptions help us understand what *they* meant, not about science (that they didn't know about) but their witness to God's activity in ancient Israel. They witnessed through the lenses through which they saw the world. They were learning about God and His purposes and recorded their experiences.

---

52. See Terry Mortenson and Thane H. Ury, *Coming to Grips with Genesis*, with contributions by several YE evangelists. YE scholars can descend into accusations and judgmental criticisms. The difference in tone between Christian scholars and YE evangelists is evident in the stressed and strained defensiveness of YErs. See also *Reading Genesis 1-2, An Evangelical Conversation* (Hendrickson Publishers Marketing, LLC, 2013) where Todd Beall and Jud Davis represent YEC in discussing differences of opinions on Genesis 1–2.

A serious study of scripture begins with reconstructing the biblical world and not projecting a modern view backward.

The authors of the Bible recorded events and ideas as they perceived them, or else why have authors that do not really author? If God altered the record of their experiences, it questions their credibility as witnesses. Why would God choose such witnesses? If there were no perfect witnesses, and God had to modify their writings, God would be the witness to Himself, defeating the purpose of calling witnesses. The last thing a judge should do is change a witness's testimony. If anything, the biblical authors' genuine experiences and thoughts about them remain important for hermeneutics. It is more important that these works are genuine accounts than technically correct science or rigorous history, which were unfamiliar to the ancient world.

The notion that God corrected everything the authors wrote that was imperfect suggests that biblical authors wrote more for the scruples of later generations than for their immediate audience. But unless the scriptures have a real-world context, they are not genuine. Instead, we would have a Bible written to satisfy future fundamentalists who distort the meaning of inspiration. The Bible being authentic for its day and theologically relevant today makes it impressive.

If there are mistakes in the Bible, we can handle them.

All human language belongs to the human family and is a product of human nature. Our languages reflect our mentality; God does not possess "mentality." The Bible is God's self-revelation primarily in Christ and *translated* into human language for specific purposes that may not always be recognizable to today's readers. Much may be lost in translation, but enough gets through.

Ancient Idiom and the Primordial Past

Notice an extraordinary example of Ancient Near Eastern imagery as Jeremiah describes the coming Babylonian invasion of the land of Judah and Jerusalem in cosmic, even primordial terms: "I looked at *the earth, and it was formless and empty* and at the heavens [sun, moon, and stars], and their light was gone." (see Jeremiah 4:23)

Jeremiah mentions the "earth" as Genesis 1 does, i.e., "formless and empty," but he is referring to the land of Judah and the "heavens" (the local day and night skies): "their lights were gone." This language sounds like the entire planet; indeed, the universe was affected, but this was a local event. Was the whole universe without any light? That sounds more like a blackout in a three-tiered universe. Was the creation reversed to pre-creation conditions? Or is this an ANE idiom? Continuing:

> I looked, and there were *no people; every bird* in the sky had flown away... *Therefore the earth will mourn and the heavens above grow dark,* At the sound of horsemen and archers every town takes to flight... *I hear a cry as of a woman in labor, a groan as of one bearing her first child*—the cry of

Daughter Zion gasping for breath, stretching out her hands and saying, "Alas. I am fainting; my life is given over to murderers." (Jeremiah 4:22-31; emphasis mine)

When the Bible mentions the "earth" and the "heavens," it is often from the perspective of the land of Israel, specifically Jerusalem. That is why God seems to stand at a point on the earth during the creation week. Creation week is one chapter-long Hebraism on the Creator's work and identity: Yahweh Elohim, God of Israel and Creator.

Jeremiah uses language similar to Genesis 1:2 to describe the resulting Babylonian devastation of the kingdom of Judah. His words, "the earth was formless and empty," meaning that no organizing landmarks were recognizable in the ruins. This idiom is what ancient lamentation sounds like when an invader deports an "indigenous world" lost to the chaos of war. It is cosmic in scope because such things cannot happen to the covenant people without God's knowledge or consent. Jeremiah also alludes to the pain of childbirth as with Eve after she disobeyed.[53]

Jeremiah's formless earth was analogous to primordial conditions. In Genesis 1:2, God's attention or favor had yet to address the dark formlessness; in Jeremiah, those chaotic conditions resulted from God's judgment or disfavor. The reader is not required to take the primeval language in Jeremiah at face value because it is idiomatic, which lends some credence that Genesis 1:2 is also idiomatic. What the text says in English is one thing; what it meant to the ancient author is another.

Jeremiah said the "earth was *formless*," but he could not have meant "*the earth* was formless." Instead, *his world* was unrecognizable due to the chaos of war. Perhaps the smoke of battle obscured the local skies (heavens), so the sun, moon, and stars "lost their light" (Jeremiah 4:28). He says there were "no people." The Babylonians killed or deported the nobles, educated classes, and skilled artisans from the earth (land of Judah), so it *felt* unpopulated like New York City during COVID-19 restrictions—also disorienting. Yet, we know that the peasant classes and farmers remained, so a population was left behind. Were there really *no birds* anywhere in the "heavens?" Or were they flying elsewhere or just hiding?

The imagery suggests that the Promised Land (a type of Eden) reverted to the primeval emptiness where the *heavens and earth* had been before day one

---

53. The curse directed toward Eve in childbirth might suggest another ANE idiom. The burden with raising children and losing them to infant mortality, war, famine, and disease fall most heavily on women. The Bible often speaks of the lamentations of women in times of war in terms associated with the pains of childbirth. Women who lose their husbands, sons, and daughters that are slaughtered or taken into slavery, are left alone and powerless in the world or taken into slavery themselves. The point is that the real pain in birthing children is seeing them suffer, which would increase immeasurably in Eve's world after turning away from God.

of creation week. In other words, both descriptions are idiomatic. They express a world with no functioning landmarks. On the one hand, God's favor lifted the formless void in Genesis 1:2; on the other hand, God removed His favor from Jeremiah's Judah.

Without God's grace, there will be disorder in Eden, Judah, or anywhere else.

Disorder and order are natural tensions in our world. They seem to track good and evil or can act as substitute terms. As God proceeds during creation week, the lack of order for life before day one gradually becomes a well-ordered world for human flourishing by day six. The Babylonian armies destroyed only Judah, particularly Jerusalem, despite Jeremiah's cosmic references.

Jeremiah gives us insight into an ANE idiom. Exaggeration better expresses lamentation, whereas literal terms are inadequate. The destruction seemed total: "the whole earth," "the heavens," "every bird," "no people," and the travail of childbirth. Taking these allness statements at face value is reading like a novice. Using these specific statements is an ANE way of saying, "Our whole world is ruined," not unlike a phrase we might use if a catastrophe "ruined everything" for us.

Jeremiah would not use factual reporting in literal terms like "We were defeated in battle" or "The destruction was in the millions of shekels." Judah's only connection to the world detached itself as far as Jeremiah was concerned. Nonetheless, God left a silver lining, a connecting thread between Himself and Judah through the prophet, namely the promise of return after seventy years of captivity. That occurred under Cyrus the Great, king of Persia. God restored Judah to their ancestral home—just barely. Nonetheless, God remembered His people.

Ironically, the Jews still considered themselves in "exile" after returning because of continuous occupations by the Babylonians, Persians, Greeks, and Romans. So they looked for the Messiah to come and restore the land and the *kingdom* to Israel (Acts 1:6).

Today, we use idiomatic expressions to describe a sporting event or an actual catastrophe, but we would not use ANE idiom because we do not relate to it. Our cultural norms are often unrelated to those of the ANE. Our figures of speech are very different and likely unrecognizable in any ANE language like bombed: blasted, wiped out, leveled, cratered, the "nuclear option," or MAD (mutually assured destruction) and MADD (mothers against drunk driving). Cultures with different languages and experiences can form idioms in unique ways that are incomprehensible when translated word for word. Therefore, literal translations can be misleading. We have our idioms and hyperboles, but they can be very different.[54]

Reading the Hebrew Bible outside its ANE context can make grasping the authors' meaning a hit-or-miss effort. We may not take much of Jeremiah's words literally, but we cannot ignore the imagery. That would strip his lament of its pathos, which was the point of the imagery.

The Bible is a witness or a collection of witnesses to God's presence among humans in history—*their* history. It is simply out of context to read modern science into the biblical text or make it adhere to something unrecognizable to the author and his audience.

In the case of YErs, expecting God to correct Bronze Age perceptions of physics or biology creates a disconnect between God's revelation of Himself and the life situations He encounters. We can see that God did not correct all ancient Israel's perceptions of the world. As we shall see, many ideas in scripture were prevalent throughout the ANE. God was not rearranging Israel's life situation but revealing Himself within it.

There is simply no evidence to the contrary.

Summary

1. *Science is not "Man's word." Christians use science to discover general revelation related to God's word.*

2. The Bible is not a science textbook. Its purpose is God's self-disclosure culminating in the Incarnation, not to reveal scientific data.

3. The Bible is God's Word translated into man's words.

4. God did not write the Bible; He inspired it; humans did the writing. That is self-evident and needs no justification.

5. Science is not the book of nature; creation is its "book." Science is a hermeneutic that interprets what Galileo called the "book of God's works."

6. The notion of some YErs that the Bible reveals more about nature than nature itself is inexplicable. Nature is a legitimate source for

---

54. For example, a strange but common idiom today is the phrase "very unique." It was used on TV recently about a Picasso ceramic where the owner stated it was "very unique" since there was only 500 of them made. Unique means "one of a kind." A thing is either one of a kind or it is not. It cannot be *very* one of a kind nor can a thing be more one of a kind than another one of a kind. Most of the time, this phrase does not even refer to something unique. Instead, it usually means *rare* or unusual. Society accepts this sort of "misuse" because, over time, it becomes clear how people are using it, which is the point of language in the first place. Ironically, the misuse of phrases is not "very unique." Over a thousand years of biblical texts, words can change in use without the modern reader realizing it.

discovering things about God, which Christianity calls general revelation.

7. The human presence permeates the composition of the Bible. There is no such human presence in the construction of the universe. Therefore, the Bible is less a product of God than the universe. These are indisputable facts.

8. Scholars in both Judaism and Christianity agree that the Exodus from Egypt is the signature event in the OT since God reveals himself as Redeemer.

9. All human language belongs to the human family and is intrinsic to human nature; human language is always "man's word." The Bible is God's word translated into man's *words*.

10. ANE language and imagery make extensive use of metaphor, allness statements, and hyperbole easily overlooked by modern readers.

11. "To argue that the Bible is authoritative, but to be unable to come to anything like agreement on what it says (even with those who share an evangelical commitment [to inerrancy]) is self-defeating." – D. A. Carson, a conservative Evangelical scholar

PART II: THE NATURE OF GOD IN THE SIX-DAY WAR

54

4.
IT'S ALL IN A "DAY'S" WORK

Whenever "day" is modified by a number [in the Bible], like the second day or six days, it can only mean a true solar day.
—John Morris (ICR)[55]

The word *day* in Genesis 1 refers to six 24-hour days. Every time it appears with "evening and morning or with a number like "sixth day," it refers to a 24-hour day.
—Terry Mortenson[56]

A major premise for YEC is that whenever biblical Hebrew uses the word *day*" with a numeral such as "day 1" or the "second day," it must be interpreted as a literal twenty-four hours. Since numbered days in the Bible are always literal, the assumption is God must have labored through a strict twenty-four-hour six-day schedule followed by a twenty-four-hour day of rest. Additionally, YErs believe the refrain "evening and morning" divides each day into the basic two twelve-hour daytime/nighttime cycle we experience today and is always twenty-four hours.

Evenings and Mornings

We now know that "evening" cannot mean *nighttime* and "morning" cannot mean *daytime*. Neither can the expression "evening and morning" refer to twenty-four hours. Instead, evening and morning refer to the entire night period only. This distinction is revealing. The mistake was encouraged by a mistranslation in the King James Version and the Latin Vulgate, influencing countless people. The KJV says, "The evening and the morning *were* the [nth] day." The grammatical mistake is in treating evening and morning as one event. Still, with this mistranslation, "evening and morning" literally exclude *afternoon* and, therefore, is less than twenty-four hours.

The Christian Standard Bible translates it; "There was *an* evening, and there was *a* morning." That says something different. Evening and morning are two separate events—an evening *and* a morning. C. John Collins, the MIT professor of Old Testament Literature and linguistics, writes:

> [Evening and morning are two] successive events, *each* denoted by the verb (*wayehi*, "and there was")... the [KJV] compresses the two events [as

---

55. J. D. Morris, *Does the Phrase "Evening and Morning" Help Define "Day"? Acts & Facts, 2007*, 36 (4).

56. Dr. Terry Mortenson, "Six Literal Days," April 1, 2010, AiG website.

if] the evening *plus* the morning were a day... the structure of the account shows us that *our author has presented God as if he were a craftsman going about his workweek.* This comes out from the structure of the account, the six workdays followed by a Sabbath. It also comes out from the refrain, "and there was evening, and there was morning, the nth day." The order... is crucial: it is evening followed by morning. This means that any effort to find ["evening and morning" alone] as defining the days runs counter to the author's own presentation. *Evening and morning bracket the night, and this is the time of daily rest for the worker.*[57] (Emphasis mine)

In other words, the evening ends the workday and begins the night, while the morning ends the night and begins the next workday. God only works during the daylight portion of the day in the story, while "evening and morning" describes the night's start and finish when God is supposedly retired. Here, God's "work schedule" is a human's work schedule based on human limitations that begins when morning arrives (so one can see) and ends when evening arrives because it is too dark to work.

Creation week is presented as if Yahweh works a Hebrew workweek, with daylight shifts, and a Sabbath rest, which cannot be literal. The Sabbath was an earthly sign of the covenant and a reminder of who freed them from bondage. The point is not to show the origins of the Hebrew workweek with its sunrise and sunset since the sun did not exist for the first four days. Israel's workweek was a creative or literary way of announcing to the ANE that *their* covenant deity is the Creator who freed them from forced labor, *seven days a week* in Egypt. An *unending* Sabbath rest alerts the reader to the figurative vehicle.

Interestingly, the Hebrew roots for evening and morning are "blurry" and "clear," respectively. These terms are deliberate. They suggest that focusing on our surroundings is too blurry at sundown to continue the workday. Things clear up at sunrise, so a rested person may begin a new shift properly. Ironically, the words *sunrise* and *sunset* do not work since the sun does not exist until the fourth day; therefore, *blurry and clear* are better descriptions for developing an orderly creation. The point is that decreasing and increasing vision due to light sources is a human experience; it cannot be God's experience. Therefore, these references to God are anthropomorphic and must be figurative.

The refrain, "evening and morning" (blurry and clear), may also provide *forward movement* from the darkened formlessness at the start of day one to a bright well-ordered (very good) world by the end of day six. Each day in the sequence gets more transparent and ordered for life as the narrative proceeds. YErs are preoccupied with time while the author focuses on developing

---

57. C. John Collins, *Genesis 1–4: A Linguistic, Literary and Theological Commentary* (P&R Publishing, New Jersey, 2006), Kindle edition, Location 886–887. C. John Collins is professor of Old Testament at Covenant Theological Seminary in St Louis, Missouri. He earned degrees from MIT, Faith Evangelical Lutheran Seminary, and the University of Liverpool.

conditions that climax in divine rest; YErs seem more concerned about what day it is.

God calls the creation "very good" at the end of day six. On the seventh day, the refrain "evening and morning" is conspicuously absent. Day seven does not end as the six days do, so the reader is left with an open-ended day *and week* since sundown was to complete both the Sabbath *and the week*. In this case, the notable omission of the statement, *"There was an evening, and there was a morning,"* intends a definite point—this is not an ordinary week, yet, the YE movement seems more concerned about the hours in a day instead of the point: Israel's God alone is the creator who transcends the universe and has an eternal plan for humanity, not a weekly one.

Furthermore, calendar days (therefore chronological ones) began and ended at sunset, not sunrise or morning. Only the workday organized for labor starts in the morning at dawn. The week also closes at sunset ending the weekly Sabbath in Israel, and a new week begins. No literate Israelite would miss that. Of course, this isn't an *ordinary* week; it is a *divine* week, which is no earthly week except for literary purposes. The author is saying that the divine week did not end, that it has a theological point, not to mention a psychological impact on the children of Israel. Therefore, if this seventh day is not ordinary, then the week is not an ordinary week. A similar example of a theological idea created by omission is in Hebrews 7:3, where Melchizedek is "given" eternal existence simply because Genesis omits recording his birth, genealogy, and death in a book where birth records and genealogies are critical proofs of ancestral origins. None of this is coincidental.

The language in Genesis presents God as a Hebrew "craftsman" who forms cosmic materials in the rough into a well-functioning world. "Evening" ends the shift, and "morning" starts a new one. God has nights off and a seventh-day Sabbath—on a literal Genesis.

With six *literal* days, a strange thing occurs; God *paces* Himself.

While YErs insist that the refrain "evening and morning" means a literal twenty-four hours, they also claim that the lack of it on day seven is still twenty-four hours. Why? It just is. The author meticulously chooses his words yet abruptly drops the "evening and morning the [nth] day" refrain on day seven, leaving the "day" without end. That means nothing to YErs since all roads lead to YEC.

It certainly appears that the transcendent God follows a craftsman's workweek *for six days*, but an unending seventh day awakens the reader that this is the Hebrew God, not a Hebrew craftsman. The Hebrew day, most notably the Sabbath, ends at sundown, and so must the week. That does not occur on this seventh day of creation. Therefore, *this is no ordinary Sabbath or week since an ordinary week ends ordinarily, i.e., at sunset ending the seventh day when a new week begins.* YErs are inconsistent on day seven.[58]

But what could a literal workday say about God? First, it means God rises in the morning and retires at night. What could He be doing at night? Moses does not say. Perhaps God was planning the next day's words, relaxing, or just waiting in the dark with the angels. Why would the Almighty do any of that? He does not since He is infinite and unaffected by time/space, light, and darkness.

The YE reading has God sitting in darkness, waiting for the sun to come up. Doesn't God know the sun is always up and down every moment on a globe? Of course. But the author does not seem to be aware of that. God would have to be stationary in a specific spot on earth for sunrise and sundown to be relevant or useful for governing a daily schedule. It's as if the author anticipates the Holy of Holies in Jerusalem, where they thought God dwelt. That is a low view of God if taken literally.

Moreover, the ancient Hebrews needed regular rest at night to recover physically from daily work. God does not rest at "night" or on weekends. Night, sunrise, sunset, and weekends are meaningless for Him, though they may have literary usefulness. C. John Collins provides further insight into the language by sighting Psalm 104 (a recounting of creation). Verse 23 says, "When the sun rises [morning] man goes out to his work, and to his labor, *until the evening.*" Interestingly, the subject of Psalm 104 is the creation and echoes Genesis 1. Yet it points out that man works this way because humans are part of the created order. God is not part of the created order, especially while creating the created order. That is a critical point in Genesis. Language cannot dictate the nature of God. Therefore, God only appears to put in a human workday with "evenings and mornings." One must have the insight to interpret soundly, and literalism doesn't get us there.

I have met YErs who are sure that the days of creation must be literal simply because they are of the twenty-four-hour "variety". Yet taking the word "day" figuratively is the same as taking a twenty-four-hour day figuratively! For instance, Todd Beall writes, "Bruce Waltke views the six days of Genesis 1 as our twenty-four hour days, but then [Waltke] adds "they are metaphorical representations of reality beyond human comprehension and imitation."[59]

---

58 It is remarkable how YEC dismisses the importance of the seventh day of creation.

59. Terry Mortenson and Thane H. Ury, *Coming to Grips with Genesis* (Master Books, Green Forest, Arkansas, 2008), p. 150. "Waltke received a Th.M. and Th.D. from Dallas Theological Seminary and a PhD from Harvard University. He served as president of the Evangelical Theological Society, was on the translation committee of the New American Standard Bible and the New International Version, and is an honorary member of the committee responsible for Today's New International Version." YErs have tried to ruin his reputation because he accepted theistic evolution. See *Wikipedia* article "Bruce K. Waltke."

Beall implies that if the language uses six ordinary days, it cannot be figurative even if the scene is God acting like a man. However, authors are not in the habit of alerting their readers that "the following sentence is figurative." Authors expect their readers to "get it."

On YEC, the nature of God submits to the literal meaning of words.

The question is not, "Does the *wording* describe earthly days?" Of course it does.[60] The real question must be, "Is God earthbound, and do words determine His nature?" Can an infinite Almighty God, immaterial, without body, spaceless and timeless, be limited in time-space to a common human work schedule, at a spot on the earth, governed by day and night—literally speaking? Would God be in the universe while creating it? Or would He transcend it? Worse yet, would God, as Paul says, who "lives in unapproachable light," wait around in darkness every night for sunrise? In a *literary* ANE context, He could. But in a *literal* sense, knowing what we know about the earth is contradictory.

Here is the point: *God's nature decides how to interpret the words*

Does God organize "His time" like humans? Does He work by the hour or use space and light to work? Is the literal day theory consistent with historic Christian thought on the unlimited attributes of God?— obviously not. If YErs insist that God chose each word and that all must be true in *every sense*, then these questions are fair and critical in the SDWC. Otherwise, we must conclude that words can dictate the nature of God.

It is contradictory to say that God created the universe from within the universe. So how long did it take God to create time as understood in the ANE? A few "days," apparently. It is a bit much to insist that God could be on a clock like ours at any time, especially before the completed solar system when twenty-four-hour days first appear.

How much space did God need to work? The book of Hebrews says that God made all things in the universe without anything in the universe, namely time, space, and matter—the universe's content (Hebrews 11:3). That raises questions. Was there no light until God said, "Let there be light"? That means Genesis 1:1 was not the creation of the universe but a heading anticipating the creation as it unfolds through the chapter. There would be no sun, moon, and stars if there were no light. There would be no heat without the sun and stars not created until day four. Does no warmth mean the waters in verse two were frozen? The author doesn't seem to care about that. But the ancients did not believe the primordial waters were frozen because they had no concept of outer

---

60. Many people read commentaries that confirm that the language in the creation account describes twenty-four-hour days. They fail to realize the nature of language is not the final arbiter in interpreting God's action. Rather, the nature of the actor determines the nature of the action. The question is not "Does the account describe twenty-four-hour days?" but "Should these days be taken literally?" For YEC, taking the words literally is their main contribution to the subject.

space absent of all heat. So we have in Genesis an account of creation envisioned by ancient Israel and not lessons in physics.

Genesis says God made the sun, moon, and stars (heavens) on day four. That casts doubt on whether God created the heavens in verse one. That would make Genesis 1:1 what many scholars think it is—a heading for Genesis chapter 1 and not necessarily God's first creative act chronologically. Think of it. If God created the heavens and the earth in verse 1, why is the earth not formed in verse 2, and there is no light at the beginning of verse 3? Indeed, why is the act of creating the heavens and earth made explicit in the rest of the chapter?

Literalism creates more problems than it solves. Did God need to create light first to see what he was doing? The Jewish Talmud *seems* to say so: "'Let there be light' in particular is like the case of a king who wishes to build a palace, but the site was in darkness. What did he do? He kindled lamps and torches to see where to lay the foundations."[61] This analogy is a literary license, according to the Talmud.

Note the word "*like*." While the wording of Genesis presents God as a human king, the Talmud says it is only an analogy. God is not a man of any kind. So what exactly was this light? We can only speculate.[62]

Some say the light was the Big Bang. Others say it was the sun "incognito," i.e., God makes the sun and perhaps the moon and stars without mentioning them because they couldn't be seen through all the supposed cloud cover. That creates problems on day four when God explicitly makes the sun, moon, and stars. The author says nothing about clouds. In ancient Judaism, some believed the light on the first day allowed God to see the entire universe. However, once he created the sun, moon, and stars, he discarded the first light, not needing it anymore.[63]

Some suggest the division of day and night could refer to the creation of time, which is intriguing because it attempts to think like a person of the ANE. That would confirm that verse one is a chapter heading and not the first creative act since the actual beginning would be on "Let there be light," when time supposedly begins. But why is the light on day one called "good," while the

61. Umberto Cassuto, *A Commentary on the Book of Genesis* (Varna Books, 2005), p. 25. The king analogy is quoted from the Talmud Bereshith Rabba III, 1.

62. Other ANE creation accounts state that light was the first thing to emerge from the primordial waters. Egyptian cosmogony states that Ra (sun god of Egypt) was the first out of the watery deep. "Apep, the god of chaos was Ra's greatest enemy. He supposedly tries to swallow Ra as the sun god entered the underworld, causing the sun to set. When he spat Ra out [at sunrise] after not succeeding in his quest [to swallow Ra during the night], the sun rose again." In this way, the struggle between chaos and order is recounted daily in Egypt by sunrise and sunset. See https://www.gods-and-goddesses.com/, December 18, 2019.

63. See the work of James L. Kugel, Rowan A. Greer, *Early Biblical Interpretation (Library of Early Christianity)*, January 1, 1986.

dark of night is not called good? Genesis 1:3 says, "God saw the light was good," and that is all. In the ANE, light itself was good, but darkness held terrors that we do not regularly experience today until our car breaks down late at night in a strange place or the middle of nowhere, far away from home. If we lived with that anxiety every day, we would dread the darkness.

Why is only half of it good if day and night meant time? Moreover, no moon or stars govern the night on day one. This puzzle suggests that primordial darkness and light on days 1-4 were not associated with the sun, moon, and stars since they did not exist until day four. In other words, daytime and nighttime referred to limited allocations of the two phenomena until the earth was complete.

Light and darkness in Genesis 1:3 refer to the general creation of the phenomena in the universe, apart from sunrise and sunset that don't occur until day four. Isaiah 45:7 quotes God, saying, "I form light and create darkness; I make peace and create evil, I Yahweh make all things." This verse is a parallelism. Here light and darkness are synonymous with *peace and evil,* or the idea may be *order and disorder.* Whatever the case, the dualism in Genesis 1:2–3 is not limited to light and darkness but includes a formless and uninhabitable world moving incrementally toward a suitable habitat for humanity, not achieved until day six.

Still, others say that the light radiates from God Himself throughout the universe, as in Revelation 21:23. That is problematic since the complete phrase in Genesis is, "*And God said*, Let there be light." The words, "And God said," is a refrain introducing God's creative action in each of the six days.[64] God's radiance is not a created thing or something turned on and off when "needed," at least not literally. Besides, God's brilliance in Revelation 21:23–26 eliminates all darkness and all need for lights of any kind.

In the ANE of which Genesis was a part, light shines throughout the entire universe during the "daytime" as experienced on earth. During the dark period of Genesis 1:3, before there was light, the whole universe was in darkness, and since there was no light, you might think, no heat. But with the sun entering the *underworld* at sunset and then emerging at sunrise (in the east), the sun's courses distribute darkness and light separately over the entire earth *and universe.* Light and darkness do not appear simultaneously anywhere in a three-tiered universe but are entirely separate when the sun is in the sky during the day and detached in the underworld at night.

In other words, when the sun set into the underworld, darkness came to the "entire universe," which everyone could supposedly see in a dome-shaped sky. Their universe was limited by what they could see with their unaided eyes. When the sun emerged from the underworld, the entire universe lit up again;

---

64. First Timothy 6:16 says, "[God] who alone is immortal and *who lives in unapproachable light,* whom no one has seen or can see."

it was morning, starting a new workday on all the earth. Even so, the Bible does not teach a three-tiered universe any more than it teaches that emotions reside in the bowels or that sperm is all that is needed to conceive a child. Instead, these were common assumptions of the day—the author simply assumes a three-tiered universe for the reader, meaning our God made the world we know. Revealing a solar system is not within the Bible's purposes or scope.[65] We know the universe does not have its own days and weeks. It is too vast, more than the ancients could have imagined. Should the universe have days, they could not be twenty-four hours. It is not the role of scripture to argue for these things.

God's self-disclosure is the Bible's agenda, and that was gradual.

At any rate, the source of the first light remains mysterious because the pool of interpretive options is too large, and the text says so little. Since the first three days contain an unknown light source, and the earth is still under construction, we cannot be sure whether the author is thinking of literal or earthly days. Of course, one can choose one interpretation over another, but that would be an opinion unworthy of a reform movement that charges those of another view with compromising the faith. That should not need to be stated.

The author assumes his audience knows enough about this light that he does not explain it, supporting the idea that light had existence apart from lit objects was a common assumption in the ANE. Idiomatic obstacles confront us throughout the biblical narratives, suggesting that we should draw general conclusions and not overstate passing references.

Augustine seems to agree. He insisted that some biblical passages are open to diverse interpretations and not wedded to prevailing theories. Otherwise, the Bible becomes the prisoner of what may prove false in the future. Augustine wrote:

> In matters that are so obscure and far beyond our vision, we find in Holy Scripture passages, which can be interpreted in very different ways *without prejudice to the faith* we have received. In such cases, we should not rush in headlong and so firmly take our stand on one side that, if further progress in the search for truth justly undermines our position, we too fall with it.[66]

The irony is that YErs insist we should not use science to interpret creation since it was a miracle, yet they search for their own "scientific" proof they

---

65. There is simple no evidence to the contrary. The Jews did not know the earth was round any earlier than the third century BC when the Greeks discovered it using mathematics. Even then, it took many decades to become known. The Bible neither teaches nor assumes a globe.

66. Adapted from his 2009 Gifford Lectures, published as "A Fine-Tuned Universe: The Quest for God in Science and Theology" by Allister McGrath (Westminster, John Knox). Allister McGrath is Professor of Theology, Ministry, and Education at King's College, London, and holds a doctor of philosophy in molecular biophysics, a DD in Systematic Theology, and a third doctor of literature for Science and religion awarded from Oxford University.

call "Creation Science" for their biblical interpretations. They believe it is better to begin with their understanding of the Bible and search for a validating science than to start with a validated science to check their interpretation of scripture. That is not science but apologetics. It is using science for the sole purpose of defending one's own religious tradition. Literalizing the scripture as a basis for science had led to problems before Christianity helped develop modern science (a geocentric universe being one example). But science and the Bible are very different resources, have different purposes, and do not depend on each other.

Science and scripture are not sources for the same kinds of knowledge. It is the position of historical Christianity not to infuse scripture with *any* science. Mostly fringe groups are the exception to this. On the popular level, we find YEC using their unique presuppositions and claims to treat scripture in a way that is not part of historic Christian thought, the least of which is literalizing Genesis, which Christians are free to do. *It is the excesses of the movement that departs from Christianity. Reading science into scripture is one of them. Furthermore, as Augustine implied, if the science is validated, the scripture is figurative if it appears to disagree because Christians believe that God is responsible for both, though God is more responsible for the creation than the Bible since He alone is Creator; the Bible includes human authors.* YEC has little use for Augustine except where they use him to support their exclusive distinctive.

The Bible is not definitive on the age of the earth or science in general, nor does it take a stand on any scientific theory. That is a sign in favor of inspiration. That means the Bible assumes an authentic world without committing to all the specifics of that world. The scriptures do not impose a view of the cosmos on the reader, only that God created it. The opinions on nature at the time play no significant role in revelation. God is the revelation, not pre-sin vegetarianism among animals. According to Augustine, ever-changing and developing scientific knowledge does not represent a vital role in the Genesis account. YErs proudly declare that science changes, but God's word does not. That is why we do not use the Bible as an ever-changing science. Bible references related to "science" are ancillary, vague, or suggestive of the times and not a special revelation. Special revelation is a divine manifest, not a natural one:

> By special revelation, we mean God's manifestation of Himself to particular persons at definite times and places, enabling those persons to enter into a relationship with him... [Revelation expresses] the idea of uncovering what is concealed...especially the idea of manifesting.[67]

Special revelation makes God's nature and purposes apparent when once hidden.

---

67. Millard Erickson, *Christian Theology* (Baker Book House, Grand Rapids MI, 1985), pp. 175–176.

That's why insisting the ancient "science" that may be in scripture is *a special revelation* is contradictory. God's creation is not hidden. It is there for all to observe. Therefore, nature contains *general revelation* that all people are capable of exploring with God-given faculties for doing so. Special revelation is in God's self-disclosure as the Creator, Revelator, and Perfecter of our faith, not discoveries in the human project called "science" or determining the age of the earth or universe.

The Bible often presents God metaphorically. For instance, God appears to "keep the Sabbath," *sealing* the Hebraic connection to the Creator. Yet, we understand that God does not literally "rest" to refresh Himself from labor; though the Bible says that, it cannot mean it.

YErs are likely to interpret this "rest" figuratively, too, and rightly so. A refreshing rest-bit would limit God to a human-like body and mind with similar needs and behavior.[68]

However, this sets a trap for YErs.

If God does not take time to rest like a man, then it follows that He does not take time to labor like a man. It is inconsistent to interpret the effect (rest) figuratively while interpreting the cause (labor) literally. "Labor" or "work" literally means expending energy, i.e., the rapid activation of atoms that produce heat and sweat called kinetic energy. God does not labor or work this way. So how exactly does God do something? Answer any way you like; the truth is we do not know how God "works." We know that He does not expend energy on a daily basis that needs replenishing at night and on Saturdays. When applied to God, literal rest and labor deny His limitless attributes.

It is easy to fall into traps establishing the nature of God with ancient idioms. Still, we can avoid pitfalls knowing the setting described in Genesis might have been a pattern recognizable to the author and his original audience to serve important religious purposes. *Israel's common workweek with the Sabbath shows that Egypt's gods who enslaved them were defeated. It's a way of saying the "work" of creation was not by pagan creators that made humans slaves, but by Yahweh who*

---

68. Substituting the word *rest* for *ceased* may not be much better. God does not start and stop (cease) any more than he labors and rests. These are behaviors of a limited creature governed by time. God simply is. He is unchanging. If Augustine was right, that God created the universe instantly, i.e., without time, His creation nonetheless continues *unceasing* since even now, many things, including living creatures, continuously come into existence.

created humanity free with an eternal Sabbath.[69] Similarly, this book uses the Six-Day War between Arabs and Israelis in "67" (and militant YE Reform) as a metaphor for the "battle" over six days in Genesis.

In the first century AD, the Jewish historian, Josephus, wrote, "God created not with hands, *not with toil,* not with assistants, of whom he had no need… He *willed it,* and so [all things] were made in all their beauty."[70] By Josephus' time, there was the concept of creation *ex-nihilo* (out of nothing), so Josephus' audience (educated people) did not take those relevant parts of Genesis literally. That is, God did not work like humans or "try." Infinite Deity does not work at something and is thrilled to find His labor turned out "pretty good." Even according to a literal Genesis, God did not "work." He only spoke words and very few of them. That is not labor that justifies rest, even for a human. All the accomplishments feel like work because they are in context to a workweek (a literary device) in which only humans in all creation participate.

Furthermore, God did not fashion Adam with His "hands." God has no hands. No assistants, whether angelic or earthly, were involved. Thus, "work" is inconsistent with creation out of nothing. God did not lift anything or push or pull anything; He did not sweat or exercise Himself. *God did not wear out— God does not actually labor any more than He rests. Therefore, "work" and "rest" must be figurative in connection with God, and so must a workweek. The workweek was ideal for a Judaic vision of creation since it included a Sabbath, their symbol of freedom, while pagan gods made man slaves.*

Christian theology has always agreed with Josephus. We accept some of the language of Genesis figuratively without being unjustifiably dogmatic on what it means besides the obvious: God created the heavens and the earth. Josephus speaks eloquently of God's nature in context to the creation, but he is not quoting Genesis; he reflects the understanding of God's nature relative to the creation in first-century Judaism. Yet Genesis 2:2–3 significantly highlights *work:*

---

69. As in "Six days you shall work but the seventh day is a Sabbath of rest." It was common in the ANE to mimic gods involved in cosmic origins, particularly in the tribal calendar, during festivals. For Israel, organizing the story of creation into an earthly workweek was a *weekly reminder* of their origins that connected them to the true God. A similar thing may be intended by adding clean and unclean animals in the flood account. The Egyptians, for example, while they mimicked their cosmogony annually with festivals during harvest and the change of seasons, *they also mimicked their cosmology, daily.* The first thing created in Egyptian cosmogony was the sun or sun god Ra who emerged from the darkened deep. Every day in Egyptian life, Ra sunk into the underworld at sundown only to emerge at sunrise victorious after a night of struggle with the forces of darkness. The night was dangerous but with the hope that Ra would return in the morning. Sunrise was an everyday reminder of Ra's victory over the underworld. For Israel, the Sabbath was a weekly sign of the Creator's favor (see Exodus 31:13, 17).

70. Josephus, *Against Apion* 2:192—this quote reflects the nature of God as understood in the late Second Temple period (516 BC–AD 70).

By the seventh day God had finished the *work* he had been *doing*; so on the seventh day, he rested from all his *work*. Then God blessed the seventh day and made it holy because, on it, he rested from all the *work* of creating that he *had done*.

"Labor" is prominent in the account; you cannot miss it, so it is intentional. It repeatedly states that the seventh day of rest (an essential Hebrew concept) resulted from God's labor. Yet, this cannot be literal since these are physical attributes as we saw. Moses is giving God a Hebrew *literary context* for theological purposes. The language is stylistic. In other words, it means that Creation is the work of a divine "craftsman," Israel's covenant deity. Words cannot dictate God's essential nature; we will develop this idea further.

The activity in Genesis 1 sits within the work experience of a Hebrew artisan, including a Sabbath. That may be obvious, yet that alone suggests a figurative presentation of divine action. Since God does not spend Himself in the form of energy that needs restoring through rest, a one-to-one correspondence between all these words and reality is not possible.

God does not labor except in an analogous sense:

So then, there is still awaiting a full and complete Sabbath-rest reserved for the [true] people of God; For he who has once entered [God's] rest also has ceased from [the weariness and pain] of human labors, just as God rested from those labors peculiarly His own. (Hebrews 4:8–10)

There is an infinite difference between human labor and *"those labors peculiarly [God's] own."* Human labor and divine labor are only analogous. The author of Hebrews is an Alexandrian, skilled in allegory and cognizant of the ontological differences between human and divine nature. He is not about to explain what God's labors actually are, except to say they are "peculiarly his own," whatever that means.

Furthermore, if the seventh day of Creation is not twenty-four hours, then the corresponding six days should be figurative, too, because unending "rest" does not correspond to temporal "labors" that amount to merely speaking one, two, or three sentences each day. Therefore, the *divine nature* of the six days of creation and the eternal rest beginning on the seventh day are linked together and cannot be an ordinary week since God's nature is what links them.

Thus, God's nature governs the interpretation of Genesis.

5.
THE "COMMON" HEBREW WORKWEEK

You would think that workdays and workweeks are simple enough to measure, but it can get complicated. The nature of a workday often depends on the kind of worker and work. For example, a "day's work" for a firefighter has traditionally been a literal twenty-four hours. Firefighters work in twenty-four-hour blocks because fires and other emergencies do not follow the clock. So a work*week* for a firefighter is usually three twenty-four-hour days or seventy-two hours. Twenty-four hours equals a day, but seventy-two hours does not equal a week. We call it a workweek anyway. We mean seventy-two hours *per* week. We do not say it that way because we don't have to; people get it.

A day's work and a week's work for teachers, bankers, farmers, construction workers, Special Forces, and the president vary significantly. If people say they work "twenty-four-seven," they do not mean it literally, despite the explicit wording—"twenty-four hours a day, seven days a week." We call all these work-*weeks,* but we mean it loosely.

Is it a work*day* if you work the *night* shift?

If a man works the night shift five times a week, how many *days* a week does he work? Should we say none because he works at night? Words can be "versatile" and tricky. A *day* to an alien from another planet will depend on the time-space it inhabits relative to ours. The ancients could not have understood relativity. They thought the whole universe experienced days as the earth does; sunrise here was sunrise everywhere. Their universe was the *visible* universe from where they sat. We speak of the "visible universe" too, but we see with telescopes, particularly ones that orbit the earth. They had only their naked eyes.

We will fill in the blanks where we have an incomplete picture. That's what people did centuries ago regarding the age of the earth. They could only consider what they knew of history, which was meager. They knew nothing of prehistory, not having archeological finds that we are fortunate to have. They could not comprehend the vastness of the universe or the dimensions of the earth. Filling in the blanks is simple enough unless the blanks are 3,000 years old about a workweek that is not human or even alien from another planet but a "workweek" by one *not of this universe.* And so, the laborious infighting over the word *day* trivializes the transcendent grandeur of the Creator. How could anyone possibly capture the actual creation event with human language?

Even if every other instance in the Bible, where "day" carries a numeral is literal, the six days of Genesis can still be figurative. A unique interpretation may be justified if the circumstances are one of a kind. C. John Collins argues "that the Creation week is indeed a unique one, in that it is God's 'workweek.'" That means that though the sequence does, in fact, matter to the author's presentation, it is another question just how strongly the author is asserting the exact sequence as a historical matter."[71]

The Creation week is one of a kind.

It is a divine "workweek." How different is a divine "day" and "workweek" compared to human ones? No different, say YErs. God and humans are the same on this in YEC. Yet the Bible says, "A day is as a thousand years to God and a thousand years is as a day." That is a Hebraic way of saying that time is meaningless when applied to God.

God transcends time. He is beyond space. He does not have a body that might surface at coordinates in time-space or on the earth's surface. By necessity, a divine day and a human day are as different as God's nature is from human nature. No amount of words can change that. Therefore, YErs must justify limiting God's infinite attributes to the finite meaning of the words in Genesis.

That cannot be done.

The days in Genesis, taken literally, place the Divine Being in time *and space*.[72] It reads as if God's being is at a workstation *somewhere* on earth. For ancient Israel, that "somewhere" was the land of Israel. So the author places God on the ground where sunrise and sundown are visible in order to carve out the workday. Or perhaps God stepped down on top of the world, calling out "Let there be" commands from the North Pole. But, of course, that does not work since day and night are six months each at the North Pole.[73]

All ANE cosmogonies place their gods in their tribal lands. Yet we know that God does not exist in a material dimension except in a *literary* sense. If Shakespeare wrote himself into his plays, there may be some of Shakespeare's traits in his written character but only as a literary device, not the living, breathing person known as William Shakespeare. Indeed, it is infinitely different to represent God in literature. God became human and lived with us because words about God and His plans are not enough.

Isaiah 66:1 reads, "This is what the Lord says: Heaven is my throne, and the earth is my footstool. So do you think you can build a house for me? Do I

---

71. C. John Collins, *Genesis 1–4: A Linguistic, Literary, and Theological Commentary* (2006), Kindle Edition, Location 852.

72. People ask, "Is it not possible for God to work a week like humans do?" That is like asking, "Is it possible for God to take the subway?" By that, I do not mean, "Is God present to the subway but rather can God's being be said to take the subway? That is not possible because it is a contradiction to transport infinite being by way of finite space. Here is the point: for an infinite God, a literal workweek is no more possible than taking the subway.

73. Likely, Jerusalem is where the action takes place in Genesis 1, since ANE worldviews were tribal. Even today, Israel calls itself "The land of creation." This further supports the figurative nature of the narrative since there could be no humanly devised geographical borders during creation not to mention the contradiction of God operating in time and space while creating time-space and its contents.

need a place to rest" (NCV)? This verse ends with rhetorical questions which caution against a literal interpretation of day seven of creation: "Do I need a place to rest?" Resting requires a place. Not only is there no place for God to rest; there is no *need,* nor is it even *possible* for Him to be at rest because He is not a physical being. It is an ontological contradiction for God to rest to restore His *unlimited* being.

Scholars like John Walton and N. T. Wright think that the seven days of Genesis suggest the dedication of a cosmic temple. The ANE cultures expected their deities to live and rest while humans served them; the temple was the place for that interaction. Similarly, Babylon's temple dedication took seven days, ending in a festival dedicated to Marduk, whose *image* or icon stands at rest in the temple. Scholars think this may be the idea behind the Garden of Eden and God's image in the form of humanity in relationship with God characterized by Sabbath rest.[74]

In any case, the words *throne* and *footstool* are obvious metaphors that serve theological purposes. Such metaphors give perspective to ancient Israel on Yahweh's relationship with the world. The words "*heaven* and *earth*" mean the universe, as the ancients expressed it. The throne/footstool metaphor is Yahweh saying that He is no mere tribal deity limited to tribal land. Yet, today, people still want to place Him on earth and in time and space, watching the sun go down.

There is no place on the earth or anywhere in the universe where God would or could sit, stand, or rest. There is no time when God rests, as in the evenings or on weekends. God is not like a human or a bird that literally "hovers," as it appears to say of the Spirit of God in Genesis 1:2.[75]

In Genesis 1, God *seems* to operate in a cosmic workshop. God has no need for material housing or structures to work in and no need for tools, materials, or schedules from which to work. There was dark formlessness, so God began by "turning on a light." Turning on a light is only natural—at least for us. God "saw" the light in Genesis 1:4. However, God does not see as we see. We see things through our eyeballs into a brain when light reflects off a surface. God does not have eyeballs with sockets in the front of His head that absorb photons.

No language that gives God body can be literal.

To whom was God talking when he said, "Let there be light," or when he "uttered" all the other questions if we insist on word-for-word literalism? If he answers prays this way, our requests would have to wait until sunrise when

---

74. John Walton, *The Lost World of Genesis One: Ancient Cosmology and the Origins Debate* (InterVarsity Press, Downers Grove, Illinois, 2010), p. 87.

75. See Deuteronomy 4:14–19 and Matthew 23:37. Commentaries point out that the Hebrew for the Spirit *"moved"* over the face of the waters is similar to the idea of a mother bird hovering over her chicks. Obviously, these are figures of speech, even if the word only refers to physical wind.

God opens for business unless it is the Sabbath, during which he might have to remain closed.

Obviously, God did not speak Hebrew. Yet, that is "as written." Did God create sound waves with His speech? He would need a vocal apparatus for making sounds, which further needs space for sound waves to travel to creatures with cone-shaped receptacles called ears. God had not created those things yet. Where would these sound waves go? Of course, this line of questioning is absurd since it assumes God was in bodily form or that he does things as we do.

There is a saying: Michelangelo's Sistine Chapel are works of art, not photorealistic paintings.[76] Similarly, the author of Genesis paints God artistically with his language and the ideas available to him. Many scholars note that Genesis 1 is masterful in a literary and theological sense, not in an irrelevant scientific one.

God made time and is, therefore, timeless. Why would God use time as an organizing principle for Himself? He needs no time to will something into existence, including a universe, especially at a timeless point "when" time did not exist. If God can say, "Let there be light," and there was, then God can say, "Let there be the universe," and there it would be. He would not need to do the human thing—work piecemeal every day; "let there be land;" "let there be air;" "let there be water;" seeds; plants, fish, animals, etc. Of course, God made those things *without the help of time, which is something He also made.*

God does not work by the hour as literalists think. God transcends the sun, moon, and stars; he does not rely on them to get to work on time. Humans need light, space, and time to work. That is likely why Augustine concluded that God made *all things instantly.* To be honest, we have no idea *how* God "did it." In that respect, Genesis sheds no light, nor could it.

An ancient man worked by sunlight and stopped work at sundown. Humans need to refresh both mind and body every night. Nighttime also presents dangers for humans. Accidents occur at night, especially working outdoors in Israel's varied geography with its countless rocks, hills, mountains, and crevices. Predators that come out at night have excellent night vision and are on the prowl. The night creates real risks, particularly with primitive technology and no significant outdoor lighting. Better to avoid the dark if you are human. What does a literal Genesis say about God?

---

76. In fairness to the author of Genesis, there may not have been the language for an infinite, *nonbodily,* and personal God known in his day. There is evidence (we will see later) that the same may be true of our concept of creation *ex nihilo.* Those ideas developed gradually from the time of the prophets, the Intertestamental period, through the New Testament. Even so, it is remarkable to compare the transcendence of God in Genesis to the extreme imminence of the gods of ANE myth, which is evidence of divine inspiration not divine dictation. Later developments on God's nature rule out the possibility that God wrote Genesis 1. He knows His nature and would reveal it gradually until the Incarnation.

That God avoids the dark too.

That leads to the curious question, how much of the *action* in Genesis 1 is literal? Perhaps none but 1:1, "God created the heavens and earth," which may be a generalized statement or heading. Whatever the case, Genesis 1:1 does not *explain* how God created but only that he did create. We say God "created" the universe from nothing. Yet *nothing* is impossible to explain if *everything* arose from "*it*"—"it" meaning not anything.

So what is nothing?

Nothing is what you have if there is no universe—no time, space, or matter/energy. But nothing is not something you can *have,* especially since, in that case, there is nothing to have and no one to have it because you would not exist. Nothing would. So what have we said? Well, *not nothing.*

Even the word *nothing* is greater than *actual* nothing because the word *nothing* is something. The word *nothing* is a *thing* that symbolizes not anything. Therefore, the symbol is greater than what it represents. How can that be? It just can, which illustrates the inadequacy of human language, where artificial quandaries can arise with mere words. We can know that no human language can capture divine creativity in action in any literal way. Nothing can, and nothing did.

And I do mean *nothing.*

The Hebrew notion of work and Sabbath rest in Genesis 1 creates a theological link from the Creator to Israel's calling where God introduces the Sabbath (Exodus 16:23). The Sabbath was a weekly sign of the covenant. Genesis 1 anticipates even telegraphs the coming of the children of Israel. The *literary* use of a recognizable Israelite workweek says, "The God of Israel is the *craftsman* of all things." But, of course, God is not a *man* of any kind, *crafts* or otherwise.

Did Moses understand that as the sun goes down, it also rises? Apparently not, since Genesis 1 has God working only during the daylight portions of the day. I ask again, what happened at night? God appears to stay in one place at night, waiting for the sun to appear. How else could God see what he was doing?

The author likely thought that the entire universe was dark at sundown. His was a three-tiered universe where the earth is like an irregular disk, and the universe is dome-shaped above it as the day and night skies move overhead. They believed the sun sank into the underworld at night. God would "naturally" wait until daylight (morning) to continue His work. That would be the normal thing to do – for humans only. Picture the words, "Heaven is His throne, and the earth is His footstool" in a three-tiered universe. God sits on high and rests His feet on earth. It's a metaphor but an interesting one. A throne in heaven looking down at the earth at night meant everything was dark except the moon and stars. Their job was to shed light over the entire earth (disk) when the sun disappeared into the underworld. Craftsmen did not work during the night as a rule.

So exactly *where was it* an evening, and *where was it* a morning, for six 24-hour days? Remember, we are assuming that Moses wrote Genesis. What was in his mind about where to place God? A work schedule planned by the sun for God at a suggested location like Jerusalem cannot be literal.[77]

If God was above the earth, then sunrise and sunset could *not* interrupt His creative activity unless the earth was considered a flat disk and part of a three-tiered universe. In such a universe, the sun disappeared from the whole earth at night. Today we know the sun perpetually rises and sets somewhere because the earth is a sphere with no hard edges, and the sun is very far away, so God would not experience day and night, let alone be governed by them even from above earth because He's omnipresent. The writer does not seem to be aware of these facts. And YErs have not been aware that the writer is unaware of those facts.

The Almighty cannot be earthbound. That is reducing God by humanizing Him.

The ANE idea of a three-tiered universe meant that the sun left the entire sky at sundown and returned to the sky at sunrise. *There was no sky below the earth in the three-tiered universe.* Instead, the sun traveled at night through the underworld, Shoal in Hebrew. The ancients had no concept of people living below the land they occupied on the other side of a globe. They believed Shoal, the abode of the dead or the underworld, was "down there" and more waters below that. In Egypt, the sun (Ra) battled the underworld at night and rose victoriously every morning. People living on the other side of a globe would be unthinkable to the Israelites since Shoal would then be *"up there"* (in relation to Jerusalem) for those people. They lived with the confident belief that one could fall off the edge of the earth.

The sun neither rises nor sets since it is 93 million miles from the earth from God's perspective. The Creator of the universe would know that. If the Genesis language applied to Him literally, it restricts God to time and place and, worse, to a personal three-tiered understanding of the universe. Already, we can see how literalism might deny the attributes of God. Figurative language does not limit God; therefore, it is a better interpretive choice for Genesis 1.

Some believe God condescended to human behavior by imitating a Hebrew craftsman in the act of creation.[78] But this contradicts the critical revelation in Genesis 1—that God transcends nature. In contrast, pagan gods were

---

77. In the account, God operates from a spot on earth at certain times. In the mind of the original readers that spot would be in Israel, likely Jerusalem. The author does not refer to Israel explicitly since it would not exist at the beginning of creation. These ideas are theological, not literal history.

78. The notion that God was setting an example for humans to work a full week is weak. Why would God, who is not human, show humans human behavior? Are humans incapable of figuring out their need to work? This appears more like an attempt to equate literalism with inerrancy, i.e., if it is not literal it is error.

products of the universe and continuous with nature's courses. Pagan deities were human-like: they copulated, ate, and were limited in location (sea gods, storm gods, sun and moon gods, and most of all, *tribal* gods). Only Israel came to know one unlimited God whose personal being transcends *all nature,* including human nature (Exodus 20:4). Yahweh was nothing like pagan deities.

Multiple gods from within the universe necessarily varied since the phenomenon associated with them varied. Unlike other ANE creation accounts, Genesis 1 argues against God's continuity with nature and its forces. Besides, it is counterintuitive for God to condescend by adopting human behavior before humans existed and during His definitive Almighty act—creating the universe from nothing. Whatever happened to "I believe in God, the Father *Almighty, Creator* of heaven and earth?"[79]

YErs have an anthropomorphic view of the God of Creation—six literal days, from sunrise to sunset, one created object at a time, and self-evaluating craftsmanship—all in a day's work. Is God like a painter who paints a portrait after a certain length of time and then sits back to admire it as if He was happy to see it turn out well?

Thomas Aquinas said that *origination* (First Cause) is not the most significant aspect of creation. It's not only *that creation began* for Aquinas, but *how it continues to exist* that makes God Creator. Of course, the Bible tells us the universe began by God. But God's creative activity is defined most by continually grounding the universe in existence, without which the universe ceases to exist whether it began or not. In that sense, creation does not need a beginning for God to be Creator (though it certainly appears to have one), nor has it ever literally ended (or ceased), nor will it end. Every day, galaxies are forming, stars are born, and so are millions of living creatures, including human babies, while God sustains all that exists. In other words, according to Aquinas, an eternally

---

79. Today, we adapt Bible stories for kids. Those stories often remain with us virtually unchanged in adulthood because most of us do not devote a lifetime to serious study. However, Genesis was not a children's story. Genesis 1 is a highly stylized cosmology at home in the ANE, and its theology was unique for the day in that it showed God is not part of the universe. It is more reasonable that Genesis 1 uses unavoidable anthropomorphisms (see chapters 8-9) than that God adopted human limitations during his supreme act of creation *ex-nihilo.*

created universe by an eternal Creator is every bit creation as a chronological one.[80]

Some note that the narrative describes God ordering things into existence with mere verbal commands and that no human could do that. Of course, no human could create anything by verbal command or a universe by any other means. That misses the point.[81]

God orders things into existence by *decree or volition, i.e., expressing a desire.* The narrative in Genesis gives God a "voice" similar to a human king. Human kings get things done by command. They order their subjects. That is literary composition. Unlike some pagan deities, Genesis shows that nature submits to God through repetitious and blunt phrasing, "And God said... And it was so." The language simply affirms that all things are subject to Elohim and no one else.[82]

Bill T. Arnold, Director of Hebrew studies at Asbury University, helps contextualize the point:

> God's method of creation—divine fiat, or spoken word—is known else-where in the ancient world... Similarly, in the Memphite theology of

---

80. In "Creation, Cosmology, and the Insights of Thomas Aquinas," William E. Carroll writes, "Creation is not primarily some distant event; rather, it is the on-going complete causing of the existence of all that is. At this very moment, were God not causing all that is to exist, there would be nothing at all. Creation concerns first of all the origin (source of being) of the universe, not its temporal beginning. Thomas [Aquinas] thought that...the universe had a temporal beginning, but for him there is no contradiction in the notion of an eternal, created universe: for were the universe to be without a beginning it still would have an origin, it still would be [eternally] created, it still would depend upon God for its very existence.

"It was the genius of Thomas Aquinas to distinguish between creation understood philosophically with no reference to temporality and creation understood theologically, which included, among other things, the recognition that the universe does have an absolute temporal beginning." Dr. William E. Carroll, on February 21, 2012, Biologos website.

81. In Genesis, God does not create *everything* by simple command. The *earth* brings forth plants and animals. God makes Adam from the ground. He forms Eve by surgically removing a rib from Adam while under anesthesia. The imagery is simple and beautiful in its literary power. Reading it literally or detaching it from its ANE context robs the story of its power and mastery.

82. The ANE cosmologies we are familiar with describe a world of chaos, an untamed world against which the gods struggled. Genesis depicts God at ease and in complete control. He can order everything because he rules all. ANE creation accounts were not like that.

Egypt, the god Ptah creates...by the word of his mouth. Like a king issuing a decree, the creative orders are given and fulfilled.[83]

Of course, "king" is also symbolic. God does not wear a literal crown on a head He does not have. Who would crown Him? Why would he crown Himself? It is clear that the writing skills and cultural context of Genesis require interpretive skills and training few have. It is common to underestimate the biblical writers' capability as if they wrote words without insight or imagination or that all one must do to understand scripture is simply read the words.[84]

Summary

1. Taking the word *day* figuratively is the same as taking a twenty-four-hour day figuratively.

2. The expression "*evening and morning*" serves as "bookends" for the nighttime only. In other words, *God works only during the daylight* portion of the day at creation.

3. The actions of a transcendent God are impossible to explain in literal terms.

4. By necessity, a divine day and a human day are as different as God's nature is from homo sapien nature.

5. YErs must justify limiting God's attributes to the finite meaning of words.

6. There is no time when God actually rests, let alone in the evenings or weekends.

---

83. Bill T. Arnold, *Genesis (The New Cambridge Bible Commentary)*, 2009. Since the Israelites lived in Egypt for centuries and Moses was likely educated there, it is reasonable to assume some influence remained in Israel's view of the world. Ptah, the supreme god in the Egyptian pantheon, creates by his word. Ptah even makes man "*according to his image and according to his likeness*" and breathes life into his nostrils. The Babylonian Lord Marduk also creates a star by fiat. But in ANE myth the verbal commands are magic or incantations. There are similarities and dissimilarities with ANE literature. The similarities place Genesis in the ANE world. The differences indicate where the revelation might lay. Bill T. Arnold is the Paul S. Amos Professor of Old Testament Interpretation at Asbury University. He has also served as Vice President of Academic Affairs/Provost, Director of Postgraduate Studies, Chair of the Area of Biblical Studies and Director of Hebrew Studies.

84. Consider the significant education a Constitutional Scholar needs to be expert on constitutional law. You would think that a very short document written little more than two hundred years ago, in our own language, no less, and at an early stage of our own culture would be easy enough for anyone in America to understand. Yet the cultural setting, with the political, social, judicial, philosophical, theological, historical, linguistic, and scientific worldview of the founders and the American colonies must be mastered before these very few pages could be properly understood. The Declaration of Independence requires the same diligence. How much more the Bible?

7. If God does not take time to rest a body He does not have, then He does not take time to labor with one either. It is inconsistent to interpret the effect (rest) figuratively and the cause (work) literally. Therefore, the unending seventh day of creation corrects the notion that the days are literal.

8. In Genesis, God *appears* to operate in a workstation on earth. There was darkness, so God began by "turning on a light" or lamp because people did so in ancient Israel.

9. Just where was it an evening, and where was it morning for six literal days on a globe? In a three-tiered universe, the evening brought darkness everywhere in the universe, and daytime brought light everywhere. Evening and morning are meaningless to God and cannot influence His actions.

10. The nature of God *always* governs interpretation.

11. The *nature* of the six days and the rest on day seven are linked by more than words. God's nature links them and governs the interpretation of Creation week.

6.
BUT THE DAYS ARE NUMBERED

Insisting that numbered days in Genesis must be literal because numbered days are always literal is arguing in a circle—it must be because it always is, no exceptions. Mere definitions of terms do not dictate whether authors used those words literally or figuratively. How words correspond to their references determines that. Is this "numbered days rule" legitimate in Hebrew grammar or an arbitrary YE rule? It turns out that there are instances in the Bible where days accompanied by a numeral are figurative.

Here is a fresh look at the much-analyzed Hosea 6:1–2:

Come; let us return to the Lord. He has torn us to pieces but he will heal us; he has injured us but he will bind our wounds. After *two days,* he will revive us; on the *third day,* he will restore us that we may live in his presence.

The context is the exile of Judah into Babylonian captivity in the sixth century BC. Jeremiah predicted that God would bring the captives back after seventy years. Hosea describes God's actions in the future when he restores the nation of Judah to the land. The numerals "two" and "third" modify the word *day.* Christianity generally sees these verses as anticipating Christ's resurrection (on the third day) and an ultimate fulfillment at the general resurrection—both are figurative interpretations. In any case, the essential elements of Hosea 6:2, for our purposes, are twofold: an infinite God's actions and time displacement.

1. God's action is the focus in Hosea, as in Genesis, plus

2. Hosea describes three divine "days" in displaced time—the prophetic future. In Genesis, the time displacement is the primordial past.

In Hosea, God's actions and time displacement are the same ingredients in all seven days of creation. The action is divine, and the numbered days are set in the primeval past.

Finite days refer to limited persons, not a timeless God. The reason numbered days are so often ordinary days is that they almost always refer to humans or human activity. In the rare moments when days involve God, they are figurative. Time binds humans expressed by earthly days. God is not so bound.

Hosea 6:2, rightly understood, is a corrective to the ad hoc YEC hermeneutic regarding numbered days. These numbered days in Hosea are clearly not twenty-four hours in length. Yet some YErs have an odd explanation for Hosea 6:2:

Some say that Hosea 6:2 is an exception to this [that all Hebrew uses of "day" with a numeral are literally 24-hour days]... However, the Hebrew idiomatic expression used, "After two days...in the third day," *meaning "in a short time,"* makes sense only if "day" is understood in its normal sense.[85]

Admittedly, this comment is unclear. It appears to mean that the days in Hosea 6:2 are figurative ("a short time") only because we must *first* understand the word *day* literally. How this helps the YE case is uncertain. James J. S. Johnson of the Institute of Creation Research (ICR) says a similar thing:

Before any use of metaphoric speaking [about the word day] can be "figuratively" stretched...the underlying literal meaning must be accurately recognized."[86]

Johnson's comment is unclear, too; it suggests an oddity—that authors (or interpreters) who use a word in the figurative sense must first show that they "accurately recognize" the word's literal meaning. This is a naked assertion, not an argument.

Curious reasoning develops when people invest their central identity in a peculiar doctrinal distinctive; they seem impervious to any opposing idea. Zealots that draw conclusions indiscriminately hang on to them with the same indiscretion. The point is to hang on to them, not reassess them. That tendency confuses stubbornness with faithfulness and can lead to rigidity. However, oddities and rigidity in YEC are not why the earth is old. It means YErs have not made the case that numbered days are always literal or must be literal in Genesis 1. Why the need for arbitrary rules? Ad hoc regulations are a symptom of a weak case.

The figurative sense of a word assumes there is a literal sense. Johnson means one must accurately recognize the literal meaning when using a word figuratively. In the argument, as vague as it is, Johnson appears to break his own rule by using the phrase "figuratively stretched" without explaining how words are *"literally shrunk."*

The above logic seems to say that the word "day" accompanied by a numeral is always literal, even when it is figurative. Whatever the authors meant by these quotes, the vagueness or confusion alone shows how quick their instinct is to protect a cherished distinctive while lacking minimal clarity.[87]

Figurative interpretation is a legitimate option, especially when literalism creates correspondence problems. Does the language correspond to the reality

---

85. "Six Days or Millions of Years," by Ken Ham (AIG website). The title itself is a false choice.

86. See ICR website, article "Genesis Compromise of the Bible," James J. A. Johnson JD. Th.D.

87. To be fair, the tendency to defend cherished distinctives on shaky ground is hardly limited to fundamentalists or people of faith. The inclination is especially noticeable in partisan politics, ideologically driven newsrooms, and institutions of learning that amount to little more than indoctrination classes. Living in a bubble controlled by such things as "in speak," political correctness, and peer pressure can produce the most absurd trains of thought even in the academy and in so-called "settled science."

to which it refers? The question is *not*, "Does the language refer to twenty-four-hour days," but "does the nature of God correspond to a slavishly literal interpretation of Genesis? I do not use the word *slavish* gratuitously. What could be more slavish than insisting upon a "one-to-one correspondence" between each word and reality?[88]

In the ANE, people mimicked the acts of the gods in their cultic practices. Are we to assume that Moses would reverse this practice by having the true God mimic man in His Almighty act of creation? What is the justification for such a reversal? The literal definition of words is no justification.

In Daniel, there are several instances where a number modifies the word *day* and is figurative. For example, Daniel 10:12–13 says, "Do not fear, Daniel, for from the *first day* that you set your mind to gain understanding and to humble yourself before your God, your words have been heard, and I have come because of your words."

"From the *first day*" obviously means that God heard him when Daniel first set his mind to gain understanding and humbled Himself. What kind of day it was is meaningless. So is interpreting this to mean "from the *first twenty-four hours, y*our words have been heard."

Notice verse 13:

> But the prince of the kingdom of Persia opposed me *twenty-one days*. So Michael, one of the chief princes [in heaven], came to help me, and I left him there with the prince of the kingdom of Persia, and have come to help you understand what is to happen to *your people* at the end of days. *For there is a further vision for those days.* (NRSV; emphasis mine)

---

88. I disagree with the idea that there were four *literal* meanings in the single word *yom* (day) in the limited Hebrew vocabulary of the Bible. The four being: daylight, daytime, eon, and the standard twenty-four hours so that Moses could have literally meant day as in "eon" each "day" of creation week. Eons do not begin at sunup and end at sundown, not literally, that is. A limited vocabulary means that many terms may have to do extra duty when translated into modern languages. That does not mean the original word has multiple literal meanings but that each idea that yom stands for has its own literal usage apart from the literal meaning of yom. A similar word, *starlight*, does not literally mean "a star." It literally means the light from a star. The word *daylight* (and *daytime*) does not literally refer to "a day" but to *the lit portion of a literal day,* accompanied by a numeral or not. We would not say that the word *nighttime* is a literal use of the word *day,* simply because "night" is the other half of a literal day. I may work five nights a week and be entitled to say "five *days* a week," but that only refers to a portion of each of five *days* in a given week, not five literal days or daytimes per week. "Nighttime" is simply a synonym for *the dark of a day* as daytime is for the light of a day. Claiming multiple literal meanings for the word *day* seems like an attempt to smuggle in *literalism,* unnecessarily. The SDWC is not only about what Genesis literally says but what it *meant* and how Christianity might apply Old Covenant concepts to Church life. The two are often not the same. Finally, it seems contradictory to say "day" literally means twenty-four hours but can also literally mean *not twenty-four hours.* Neither literal nor figurative interpretation is superior to the other so we should justify either one in its context.

These twenty-one days were part of a vision about the end time. Daniel often uses numbered days as symbolic imagery. Michael is battling the King of Persia (or perhaps some counterpart in the heavenly realm) for "twenty-one days," which is 3x7, two numbers known to have symbolic significance in Judaism.

Notice Daniel 12:11 says, "From the time that the regular burnt offering is taken away and the abomination that desolates is set up, there shall be *one thousand two hundred ninety days.*"

Daniel 12:12 also says, "Happy are those who persevere and attain the *thousand three hundred thirty-five days"* (emphasis mine).

Some have interpreted these verses with the so-called "day for a year principle." That is, 1290 "days" are supposed to be 1290 years into the future when someone will fulfill the "abomination of desolation" typified by Antiochus Epiphanies (who set up Jupiter's image in the Holy Place in Jerusalem, desecrating the sanctuary). Jesus linked this event to a future fulfillment in Matthew 24:14-16 when he said, "Therefore when you see the 'abomination of desolation,' spoken by Daniel the prophet, standing in the holy place (whoever reads, let him understand), then let those who are in Judea flee to the mountains."

The 1,290 days, to some, represent 1,290 years or longer. Whatever the correct interpretation is, these numbered days are not literal. Daniel is an example of Jewish apocalyptic literature (as is the book of Revelation) loaded with symbolic imagery about the end times.

God's relationship *with time* is different from humans *in time.* "One day is as a thousand years to God and a thousand years is as a day."[89] That does not mean one day to God is actually a thousand years, which misses the point. Time is meaningless when affixed to God's attributes.[90]

YErs say since these are prophetic or future references using numbered days; therefore, they do not count in their "rule of numbered days." First, that is an admission that numbered days do not *always* refer to a literal twenty-four hours. Secondly, we might equally make up our own rule that "whenever God is the reference with numbered days, it is always figurative." Thirdly, it is an arbitrary assertion that *future* numbered days can be figurative, but *past* numbered days must be literal. Psalm 90:4 clarifies this, "For a thousand years in your sight are like yesterday when it is past." Here, the nonliteral use of time (yesterday) applied to God refers to the past.

Time itself includes past, present, and future. It is artificial to maintain that numbered days for the present and past tenses must be twenty-four hours, but numbered days for the primordial past are figurative. Can there be any

---

89. Psalm 90:4; 1 Peter 3:8.

90. Jehovah's Witnesses, for example, interpret the days of creation as a thousand years each because the Bible says "a day is as a thousand years to God" and *vice versa.*

doubt that YErs force these "rules?" YE zealots assume no exceptions to their rules because there can be none for their ideas to survive. Some YErs claim the conservative Old Testament scholar Walter Kaiser as one of their own on numbered days, but in an interview on the John Ankerberg show, on October 2, 2013, Kaiser addresses this YE Reform Movement "rule":

> Well, John, that's a very common objection you hear frequently [in YEC], but there is no rule in the Hebrew grammar. I mean, *you have to invent that rule for just this situation.* The other thing is, yes, there does occur a case in which you have *yom* used along with an ordinal or even a cardinal number: one. One, it's the same word for both the cardinal and the ordinal. The difference between cardinal and ordinals is, between one, two, three, four, and first, second, third, fourth. So, Zechariah 14:7 has a *yom echad.* It's "one day." And there it's talking, again, about the *yom Yahweh,* "the day of the Lord," which is a future day covering all of the eschatological events. So I don't think you can make that rule... I don't think it'll work.

Young's Literal Translation on Zechariah 14:7-8 says,

> And there hath been *one day,* It is known to Jehovah, *not day nor night,* And it hath been at evening-time — there is light. And it hath come to pass, in that day, Go forth do living waters from Jerusalem, Half of them unto the eastern sea, And half of them unto the western sea, In summer and in winter it is.

The Hebrews knew God's days were not the same as human days.

Jesus and Numbered Days

The most striking example of numbered days in the Bible that affects both the Old and New Testaments is when Jesus predicted his resurrection in the most explicit terms. The Pharisees wanted a sign showing Jesus was the Messiah. Jesus said his only sign would be that of the prophet Jonah: "For as Jonah was *three days and three nights* in the belly of the huge fish, so will the Son of Man be three days and three nights in the heart of the earth" (Matthew 12:40).

Can any biblical reference to numbered days be more explicit? These are Jesus's words guaranteeing his identity. Here, it is not just three *days* but also three *nights.* That is more explicit than "evening and morning." How do we reckon these days? There is a numeral "3" before the word "day" and a "3" preceding the word "night" in the same sentence. Must the expression "3 days" alone equal seventy-two hours? YErs wouldn't say that; what would we do with the "3" nights?

You might expect YErs would at least conclude that this double set of threes together refers to seventy-two hours. You would be wrong. YErs say Jesus's words do not mean "3" days and "3" nights, but "1" day and "2" nights!

Here is how Paul F. Taylor explains Jesus's words: "Jesus was indeed crucified on a Friday but that the Jewish method of counting days was not the same as ours."[91]

Think about that.

The *"Jewish method of counting days was not the same as ours?"* What have we been talking about, if not the Jewish method of counting days? The YE presupposition is that whenever a number accompanies the word "day" in the Hebrew Scriptures, it *always* (not sometimes, not even most of the time, but *always*) means twenty-four hours. Where would these Jews get a different method of counting days? Who told them they could "mess with the rules?" How can we trust the rest of the Bible if they could change that?

Seriously.

Are we to assume that for over a thousand years, Jews knew that every time a numeral accompanies the word *day*, it is *always* a literal twenty-four hours, yet as soon as the Messiah comes, and in a most crucial statement, they take up a method unfamiliar to anyone else? Why would they do that? Where is the evidence they did that?

This quote of Jesus is in Matthew, who wrote for a Jewish audience and likely wrote in Aramaic—a language related to Hebrew. Matthew quotes Jonah's Old Testament example when people supposedly "knew the rules." Was Jonah in the great fish for one day and two nights? Look at it again, "And Jonah was in the belly of the fish *three days and three nights*" (Jonah 1:17).

Was Jesus lying?

Would Jesus confuse Jonah's story to fit an unintelligible numbering system that the Jews and the Bible authors never used before? Did Jesus not know the difference between a "1," a "2," and a "3"? *Jesus did not think that numbered days should always be literal in his day or Jonah's.*

YErs agree that Jesus was in the grave from Friday sunset to sunrise the following Sunday, i.e., one day and two nights. In this case, numbered days do not seem to be a big deal to Jesus (or YErs, for that matter). He said, "3 *days* and 3 nights." The cognitive dissonance is tangible since YEC hurriedly claims Jesus as a disciple.

So what do we make of this apparent contradiction in Jesus's time in the tomb? First, the number "3" is significant in Judaism. It indicates divine providence. Secondly, the emphasis in Jesus's phrase is on the repeated number "3," not on the "days" and "nights." Jesus was *dead* for parts of *3 calendar days*: Friday, Saturday, and Sunday (a set of threes); Then *rose* after one day and two nights: another set of threes. The double use of the number three emphasizes, even overemphasizing, God's hand in Jesus's life and work. Remember,

---

91. Paul F. Taylor, "Three Days and Three Nights," June 29, 2009, AiG website.

the primary purpose of the Bible is God's self-disclosure in Christ, not how *long* Jesus was in the tomb *exactly,* or even less on how old the earth happens to be.

Similarly, Genesis states that it rained during the flood for forty days and forty nights and that Moses fasted forty days and forty nights (Genesis 7:4, 12; Exodus 34:28). In these two examples, the word day is twelve hours, not twenty-four hours each. Like the number three, in "3 days and 3 nights," the number forty is also providential in Judaism. The number forty is a theological reference indicating God's involvement and not necessarily the precise time duration.[92] Maybe forty days and nights were precise, but that cannot be certain since a similar formula put Jesus in the tomb for only one day and two nights. These observations on the numbers three and forty are closer to Jewish thought than the slanted assertion that "every time a number is attached to the word *day,* it always means a literal twenty-four hours," as if God's nature must submit to the literal meaning of words.

It does not matter how long Jesus was in the grave. He rose; the tomb was empty. God resurrected him. Neither does it matter how many days God took to create, if any. He made all things visible and invisible in Almighty fashion, making any theory on the earth's age irrelevant.

A major pillar for YEC has fallen.

There is no rule that numbered days must be twenty-four hours each.

---

92. In the Babylonian flood story, it rained six days and six nights, reflecting Babylonian theology. Exact chronology is not the point in either account. Many fundamentalists have a hard time with observations like this because it lacks the legalistic view of scripture that often governs their presuppositions. Among reformists, it's about who believes in words more than concepts.

7.
"MYTHS" ABOUT GENRE

If [Genesis] is a literal historical account, there is a one-to-one correspondence
between words and reality.[93]
—Stephen W. Boyd

Myth is not fiction: it consists of facts that are continually repeated and can be
observed over and over again.
—Carl Jung

Of course, identifying the genre of any document is an essential part of interpreting. Writing is an art form. Poetry is more artistic than prose, which is more artistic than history; which is more creative than theoretical physics; which is more artistic than mathematics; and that is more artistic than reality. While identifying the genre can be essential, too much reliance on it can be misleading, depending on how one appeals to it.

Scholars have long puzzled over the precise genre of Genesis 1. Its artistic style in the original text appears unique and striking. Suggested genres have been all over the map. Is it myth, saga, poetry, prose, allegory, a hymn, legend, narrative, history, science, or some hybrid like mytho-history? Or could it be an unidentified lost genre? On balance, the answer seems to be "yes." The genre of Genesis 1 may be challenging, but that shall not deter us. Here is why:

1. The nature of God remains the same, no matter the genre, and

2. The nature of God takes precedent and must govern interpretation.

Without these two fundamental principles, the intended revelation fades since it loses sight of God's nature and the purposes of scripture— God's self-disclosure, whose high point is the Incarnation.

Despite the historic quest for the genre of Genesis 1 or Genesis 1–11, YErs have no doubts. They are sure that all of Genesis is in the genre of a "literal historical narrative." Everything it says about God binds His attributes. As Stephen W. Boyd says, there is a *one-to-one correspondence* between words and reality throughout Genesis. By that, YErs mean that Genesis 1–11, in particular, is a set of strict literal, historical, chronological, and scientific facts that God

---

93. See Terry Mortenson and Thane H. Ury, *Coming to Grips with Genesis: Biblical Authority and the Age of the Earth,* specifically the essay of Boyd in chapter 6. Boyd is confusing the philosophical definition of a true statement where words are said, have a one-to-one correspondence to reality, with the genre of Genesis and the intentions of the author. This is not argument or evidence but imagination.

wrote. YErs base this claim on the clearer genre of Genesis 12–50 that gives us the patriarchal narratives of Abraham, Isaac, and Jacob.

The YE claim is since the patriarchal narratives are "literal history," we must accept Genesis 1–11 as precise history because they are in the same book. YE evangelist Terry Mortensen writes:

> Genesis 1–11 unmistakably has the literary characteristics of biblical historical narrative just as do Genesis 12–50, Exodus, Joshua, Judges, Acts, and the Gospel accounts of the virgin birth, crucifixion, and resurrection of Jesus, as Chapters 6 and 8 in *Coming to Grips with Genesis* demonstrate."

In chapter 6 of *Coming to Grips with Genesis*, Stephen W. Boyd makes the following claim:

> Is Genesis 1–11 to be interpreted differently from Genesis 12–50... and the rest of the OT? In other words, [should] a *unique hermeneutic* be used for these chapters, since they are not "history." This permits scholars to treat Genesis 1–11 figuratively...but the remainder of Genesis (the accounts of Abraham, Isaac, Jacob, and Joseph) as historical. Unfortunately for this interpretation, such a distinction between Genesis 1–11 and 12–50 will not hold up under scrutiny.[94]

Here, Boyd claims to be consistent, though the content of chapters 1–11 is radically different from chapters 12–50, as the most cursory reading will show.

Also, Boyd's use of "a unique hermeneutic" is prejudicial. Unique means one of a kind. Except for the truly unique example is the "God wrote it word for word with a one-to-one correspondence to reality" genre of YEC, the most often suggested genres by widely recognized scholars for Genesis 1-11 are not one of a kind since they are found elsewhere in scripture and ANE literature in general. Even the historical-grammatical hermeneutic does not reject figurative interpretation, which can have a historical context but can also uncover figurative intent. It is not the *hermeneutic* that is unique in professional scholarship but the *genre* of Genesis 1 itself.

Note that Boyd uses near legalistic language, i.e., one needs a "permit" to interpret scripture figuratively. He assumes that historical narrative does not *"permit"* significant figurative language. Does that mean "the shot heard around the world" was actually heard around the world? What temperature was the Cold War? Language does not behave as YErs assert.

The YEC claim is this: if a significant part of a book is in a particular genre, the entire book must be in the same genre. But in the interest of corresponding to reality, reality refuses to be that simple.

On this, YEC presumes several things:

---

94. Terry Mortenson, Thane H. Ury, *Coming to Grips with Genesis* (Kindle edition, 2013), pp. 143–145.

1. A single work cannot employ more than one genre.

2. A book cannot contain other literary forms apart from its genre.

3. Genesis is not a compilation of more than one work.

4. The ancients had the same concerns about historiography that moderns do.

5. Genre determines the nature of God.

6. Moses was familiar with all these rules!

Genesis 1–11 is very different from chapters 12–50. Genesis 1–11 speeds through thousands of years of *primeval stories* paralleled in Egyptian, Mesopotamian, Canaanite, and other ANE literature. This rapid flow comes to a screeching halt in chapter 12, which begins the Patriarchal Narratives, leading to the Exodus, none of which parallels anything in ANE literature. Boyd does not account for this.

The contrast between Genesis 1–11 and 12–50 is among the most striking in Scripture.

What is lacking in these YE assessments is familiarity with or an appreciation of ANE literature, where multiple genres and literary forms end up in a single work. For example, both prologue and epilogue, in the book of Job, are prose narratives while the body of his story is poetry. The literary composition of Job is an "ABA" type. The two "As" that begin and end the work are of one genre, while "B" in the body of the work is in a different genre.

Multiple genres in a single work were common in the ANE. Similarly, both prologue and epilogue in the Hammurabi law code are in poetry, but the interior law code is ANE legalese. Incidentally, the book of Job and Hammurabi's code are earlier works than Genesis, so we know this ABA form in the use of genre existed during Moses's time. Additionally, the book of Daniel begins and ends in Hebrew, while the middle chapters are in Aramaic.

A genre can be broader in scope than many literary forms, so one genre does not rule out the use of other literary forms *however brief*, that may be figurative. A historical narrative may contain poetic elements, figures of speech, parables, hymns, allegory, proverbs, liturgical elements, and even apocalyptic. Poetry can also contain literal and historical references (see Psalm 7, 104; Job 41; Isaiah 27).

Narratives often include figures of speech of various kinds. The gospels are examples of first-century Roman biography. Yet we know that the gospels contain numerous literary forms: hymns, parallelisms, chiasms, proverbs, parables, allegory, hyperbole, creeds, Jewish apocalyptic, etc. John's gospel is high theology and philosophical and known to set aside chronology for important theological purposes.[95]

Genesis 1 contains multiple literary forms such as chiasm, at least one parallelism, versets, refrains, leitwort (repeated word), symmetry, architectural design, and near-constant plays on words difficult to translate well. Here are some examples of wordplay in Genesis not always translated literally:

- Let the waters *swarm* with *swarms*,
- Fill the sky with *flying* things that *fly*,
- The *lights* should be for *lights*
- The earth *vegetates* with *vegetation*
- The man's (adam's) name was Adam (man)

According to Bill T. Arnold, a most interesting example of wordplay is the poetic twist in Genesis 3:1:

> The serpent is "crafty" (or "shrewd," *'ārûm*), indeed more so than any other animal (3:1). The term has been chosen as a deliberate wordplay on the description of the humans as "naked" in the previous verse (*ărûm-mîm* in 2:25). The idea is that the nude humans have been duped by the shrewd serpent; they want to be shrewd (v. 6), but in the end, they are only nude (v. 7).[96]

This amount of wordplay (and many other literary forms) in a short document section shows that the author favors artistry over strict data in a so-called "one-to-one correspondence" between words and reality. Artistry and poetry do not translate well. Their "sound" is muted, though the concepts may come through. So there can be various literary forms and devices in one book or one chapter of the Bible. YErs repeatedly seek to limit all other interpretations with arbitrary rules so that one is stuck with literalism. That is a highly suspicious approach. Intellectual honesty requires people not to make up rules on the road to truth.

I hesitate to say YErs are dishonest because my experience in the former WCG is that sincere people can believe mistakes and even contradictory things without seeing them. Some still cannot see mistakes when pointed out

---

95. The gospel of John throws many YE presumptions of the Bible into question. John is unlike the synoptic gospels (Matthew, Mark, and Luke) to the extent that the tensions between them are considerable. There are no parables in John. John records long speeches of Jesus that are unique. There are explicit claims to the deity of Jesus and his messiahship. There are significant chronological differences in John, examples being: an alternative day for the Last Supper, the feeding of the 5,000, and the clearing out of the temple merchants to name a few. It is evident that a consistent chronology was subordinate to John's theological purposes and that he was not lying.

96. Bill T. Arnold, *Genesis (New Cambridge Bible Commentary)* (Cambridge University Press, New York, New York), Kindle edition, location 1907, 2009, location 1909.

in the most explicit terms. We can sincerely believe the absurd, especially when surrounded by others that do. I do not doubt that some YErs honestly cannot see any cognitive dissonance. They are zealous. Good reasons to abandon their distinctives do not register. There is no patience for intellectual honesty when people are motivated by suspicion and assume God has given them an exclusive mandate with the special knowledge He gave them. Many fundamentalists see what other Christians call *intellectual honesty* as weak and compromising, which is decidedly unchristian.

Many scholars (secular and otherwise) believe the artistic elegance that characterizes the first chapter of Genesis is a masterpiece of ancient literary composition. That is a description not often used of wooden literalism. Genesis is not the modern work that YErs assume it is. By comparison, writing in a strictly literal or academic style is staid and sterile, not ancient.

There are other artistic elements in Genesis.[97] Genesis 1 contains regular rhythmic movement with repeated refrains: "And God said," "let there be," "and it was so," and "it was good," "an evening and a morning," "the nth day." Literal historical narratives do not behave this way. In addition to movement, repeated refrains create suspense and expectation. In Genesis, they seem to lead somewhere other than God created everything, which was already stated explicitly in verse one. Numerological elements are constant in Genesis, especially in chapter one.

Genesis 1 is unlike any strict, literal, historical narrative we know.

It is Figurative, Literally Speaking

Figurative expressions in any gene are always words we might take literally. One could believe it rains real cats and dogs, and the moon smells of green cheese. What else is there to take figuratively other than words with a literal usage? So how can we know the *days* of creation are figurative? We can see that words by themselves are not enough to determine that. Words can go either way. Authors may use the same words differently, no matter the genre.

Out of frustration, YErs ask, "If God wanted to convey six literal days, what *words* would He use?" The implication is that words are enough, and the assumption is that Genesis 1 obviously uses words literally; therefore, we have

---

97. YErs are quick to dismiss any poetry or artistic language in Genesis especially chapter 1. In YEC, poetry undermines literalism. But if Genesis 1 were a poem or hymn, that would not rule out literal references in the passages. Miriam wrote a hymn about the Exodus and Mary, Mother of Jesus, wrote a hymn about her experiences. Many poetic and hymnic works contain ideas that are literally true and historical. Our "Star-Spangled Banner" is a hymn or anthem with historical elements and lyrically crafted for the purposes of eliciting pride in a people. While the SSB has historical value, it is unapologetically one-sided. Other ANE cosmogonies were myths, legends, and epics, but Genesis is different enough that scholars are cautious singling out a form that captures the whole. Genesis 1–11 is significantly different from Chapters 12–50 in form and texture.

six literal twenty-four-hour days, six-thousand years ago. But is it really that simple? Even the *word* figurative can be literal. If we use a word *figuratively*, then it is figurative, literally.

Since taking the word day figuratively is the same as taking a twenty-four-hour day figuratively, YErs have not made their case. The Bible nowhere uses the expression "twenty-four-hour day." The phrase "literal twenty-four hours" is an oxymoron since hours do not literally exist but are a contrivance invented by humans. Biblical authors used the simple word *day* for both figurative and literal senses no matter how they described those days. Word choices alone do not determine whether the author means them literally or not. So how can we be sure one way or another?

How words correspond to their references indicate the usage. For example, take the sentence "Life is a bowl of cherries." These individual words—*life*, *bowl*, and *cherries*—mean something entirely different from the sentence. We might ask, "If God wanted to convey that He exists in a burning bush or is a real lion in Judah, what words would He *use*?" As if individual words are all that matters. It would be like an ancient person watching a modern person using a cell phone. They hear a person's voice through the speaker; they can see a video of a person moving on the phone's screen. You are not likely able to explain it satisfactorily. "Well, you see, Late Bronze Age person, our voices and pictures travel through the sky from this device to billions of other devices...blah, blah, blah." You must explain that the person is not really in the phone. Humans can't exist in a phone as God doesn't live in a burning bush or even the Temple in Jerusalem!

So *how do we know* it cannot be that God lives in a burning bush?

The words do not tell us *how*. Instead, we instinctively know there is low correspondence between the nature of God and bushes, lions, bread, doves, etc. One must be quite slow to take any of those figures of speech literally.[98] Low correspondence tells us those are figurative, like the low-level correspondence between rain and house pets. The central issues in the SDWC are less about the words than the attributes of God that expose the inadequacy of words. That is the brutal truth for YEC reformists that think words are more fundamental than the nature of God. The plain language of a limited being fails when referencing *infinite incorporeal Being*. That is basic to biblical interpretation. We do not even know what "infinite incorporeal Being" means. Those are the words we have, but they do not grasp reality.

Metaphor is unavoidable when describing God because incorporeal life does not correspond to anything in our reality. For that reason, many people do not believe that a spiritual realm can exist. They insist there is no "evidence."

---

98. My first real foray into reading the Bible was the book of Revelation. Being a fifteen year old who knew nothing of scripture, I took it all literally. I was relieved to find out later very little of it is literal.

They mean physical evidence, which is a category error since incorporeality means *not physical*. Conceptual evidence or abstract argument is the corresponding evidence for incorporeality, which is not much but enough to make a plausible case. When there is no concrete language to describe the real thing, metaphor is unavoidable, even if the author is unaware of using it.

We know ANE cultures thought and spoke metaphorically more than modern cultures, especially in the West. Ancient literature and histories show us this. However, since the Enlightenment, Western culture puts a higher value on literalness or factual data (science and history) and devalues poetry, fiction, intellectual fiction, philosophy, and theology as sources of truth.

The irony is that theology and revelation are much more metaphorical than the science or academic history that YErs want Genesis to model. We know literature, especially ANE literature is far more open to interpretation.[99] Additionally, theological interpretation is not literal historical narrative nor relies on it. Using narrative simply as a vehicle for theology is a legitimate practice in any age, especially in ANE cultures such as ancient Israel. In other words, the theology in an ancient narrative, particularly the intensely stylistic Genesis 1, is more about what it meant conceptually than what it says with individual words. The *theology* of a narrative is in its meaning, not simple wording only. On the other hand, historiography employs critical methods such as Criteria for Authenticity not fully appreciated before the Enlightenment.[100]

Kenton L. Sparks, a specialist in Old Testament history and language, observes:

> One result of [the Enlightenment] was that truth was no longer conceived in figurative and poetic or religious terms but in historical terms... In the English-speaking world, this Enlightenment-era tendency is no better illustrated than by the influential Scottish historian Thomas Carlyle (1795–1881). Carlyle believed that there were in fact two basic genres of writing, "Reality" (meaning history) and "Fiction." He invited his readers to realize "how impressive the smallest historical fact may become, as contrasted with the grandest fictitious event;" indeed, Carlyle went as far as saying that fiction "partakes of the nature of lying." This

---

99. Even the American Constitution and Declaration of Independence are subject to endless scrutiny.

100. It was not until the fifteenth century that modern historiography was born. Only later did this kind of history become a widely read literary genre. For the Criteria of Authenticity applied to the gospels, See William Lane Craig, *Reasonable Faith: Christian Truth and Apologetics* (Crossway Books, Wheaton Illinois, 2008), Kindle edition, location 9317.

Enlightenment tendency toward historicism tended to undermine biblical authority.[101]

Ironically, what tended to "undermine biblical authority" was not figurative interpretation associated with theology but a rigid "historicism." Historicism can lead to prejudice against metaphors— calling them "partakers of lying"—as does YE literalism. Literalism constrains the biblical authors to the dictionary meaning of words instead of liberating the theological ideas they intended to communicate. You can see this in atheists who, like YErs, read Genesis with the same wooden literalism, which they also use to their advantage.

The point is that the Enlightenment spawned a prejudice against any writing as a source of knowledge that is not strictly historical, factual, or scientific. A similar idea behind YEC, namely, *what is not a historical fact in a given narrative is a lie,* is a decidedly modern prejudice unintelligible to the ancients. At issue is *how* biblical authors communicated, not current biases about how those authors should communicate.

Before the scientific era, storytelling, tales, myth, legends, and poetry were far more common and revered forms of literature that ANE scribes habitually used to convey truth, mainly profound truths. Those kinds of literary forms we now relegate to the popular culture. Ancient Israel was no exception in the use of these forms. However, Israel was exceptional in its theology spoken through these literary forms and not through science.[102]

Metaphors still find their way into scientific literature more than moderns are willing to admit. Werner Heisenberg said, "Quantum theory provides us with a striking illustration... we can only speak of in images and parables." In a more recent *New York Times* interview, Michael Ruse, the British-born philosopher of science, stated:

> Science interprets the world through experience, and just like poets, metaphor is the key to the whole enterprise. Everything is metaphorical, the "struggle" for existence, natural "selection," "division" of labor, genetic "code," and "arms races" between "competing" species.

These are metaphors, such as anthropomorphisms, that even modern science uses because relentless literalism in any literature is not realistic or sustainable.

---

101. Kenton L. Sparks, *God's Word in Human Words: An Evangelical Appropriation of Critical Biblical Scholarship.* The irony is that biblical literalists have bought into this unwittingly.

102. Consider *Aesop's Fables, The Iliad, The City of God, Chaucer's Canterbury Tales, Shakespeare,* and *Dante's Inferno;* the great period of novels, like *The Brothers Karamazov, Pilgrim's Progress, Don Quixote,* and *Gulliver's Travels.* Such literature still exists today, but with scientism, few take them as a serious source of knowledge like they once did.

Of course, pagan myths contained errors, but errors were not what made them myths. Myth was often religious art in an epical form that may correspond to other types of religious art in visual forms like the Sistine Chapel or images of Michael the Archangel in battle or the "Stations of the Cross" on Church reliefs in Catholicism. These teach religious beliefs in pictures, also called *pictorial myth*. God does not look nor behave as it appears on the Sistine Chapel's ceiling, something Michelangelo knew. We do not mind that because a real message stands behind the artistic medium. The artistry is visual and memorable for those who appreciate fine art and the illiterate who learn from its story.

Today, we have historical novels and films *based* on true stories. When those writers dedicate themselves to historical accuracy, they still must fill in gaps when existing facts are inadequate or seem disconnected. Adjustments are necessary to avoid confusing the audience. The priority is the main storyline; the second is communicating coherently in the confined space that a specific genre or medium may offer.

The same story in a play, a film, or a book flows much differently. There would necessarily be inconsistencies with some details if each medium told the same story. We see minor inconsistencies even when the genre is the same, such as in the four gospels. Clarity in the time and space available may require leaving out some details in one genre or offering fictional yet reasonable details in another to make the story flow coherently while all *essential truths* remain intact. That is the human condition even in historical narrative. We cannot see all. Filling in missing details is like replacing a link in a chain with an alloy or even rope if it gets the job done. Telling the truth inside a story is the point.

Empiricism and rationalism valued historical fact above the more artistic forms of literature, especially theology, myth, and ancient literature, like the Bible. That is why atheists are happy to read Genesis 1 literally as YErs do. Atheists and YErs have allowed a modern prejudice to influence their appreciation of religious truth rich in metaphorical, figurative, and symbolic forms in all its genres. Stories give a community meaning and connectedness—a shared identity. Figurative language, such as metaphor, is not a lie or empty speech, nor is it inferior to literal usage.

Metaphor is a profound vehicle for meaning.

Scholars have long demonstrated that the Hebrew of Genesis 1 is highly stylized with figurative elements, despite the narrative feel that modern translations give it.[103]

---

103. See, e.g., Adele Berlin, *Poetics and Interpretation of Biblical Narrative* (Sheffield: Almond Press, 1983). Genesis 1 has extensive parallel patterning: the repeated "and God said" and "it was evening and morning the x day" for each of the six days, and much more." Berlin was also sighted in *Reading Genesis 1–2: An Evangelical Conversation* by Richard Averback, Todd Beall, C. John Collins, Jud Davis, Victor P. Hamilton, Tremper III Longman, Kenneth J. Turner, John Walton, and J. Daryl Charles.

Notice the Manual of Catholic Theology, circa 1898:

> The best Catholic authorities...[tell us] that the whole act of creation [was] only one instant of time, and that the division of it into six days is a way of presenting to the reader the order according to the connection of causes rather than the order according to the intervals of time (St. Aug., De Gen. ad Lit., 1. V.). such is the opinion of St. Augustine, and St. Thomas thinks it highly probable (I., q. 66, a.i.)... These and similar considerations, quite independently of natural science, have induced the theologians of all times to allow a very free interpretation of the six days.[104]

The "order...of causes" refers to secondary causes flowing from an instantaneous creation, or any other creation set in motion. Nature, or God's operations, necessarily develops. Genesis 1 is how the ANE (not just the Hebrews) saw these causes—the need for water, air, soil, domesticated animals, and seed for food. Evolution is the best explanation science offers about natural causes, evidenced by the development of species, which Christians are free to take or leave.

Our world develops dramatically under any theory of origins.

This Manuel of Catholic Theology says that many Catholic theologians *of all times "allow a very free interpretation of the six days."* In other words, since Augustine (AD 354–430), theologians of every generation have allowed for a figurative understanding of the six days and did so *"quite independently of natural science."* The phrases *"allow* a very free interpretation of the six days" and *"allowed* for the days to be figurative" means that even if past theologians believed the days might be literal, they also knew the days *could be figurative.*[105] That underscores my main thesis: *while a literal six-day creation may or may not be a mistaken opinion of Genesis, it is only an opinion. Therefore, the Young Earth Reform Movement is excessive and has a distorted view of Christianity.*

Earlier theologians did not insist that the six days of Genesis were literal because biblical authority or God's integrity depended on it. They were well-acquainted with allegory, metaphor, symbolism, typology, and *theology,* which they applied freely to Genesis. They understood that theological truth is not

---

104. From *A Manual of Catholic Theology: Based on Dogmatik (Complete in Two Volumes),* 1898, Chapter IV. Most theologians, centuries ago, considered the earth young by today's estimates. Before the scientific era, there were two choices people were aware of—a universe that began or one that always existed. The more popular view in the world until the middle of the twentieth century was a universe eternal in the past. The Big Bang Theory raises doubts about a past eternal universe and the Steady State Model.

105. The *Wikipedia* article "Young Earth Creationism" says, "A number of prominent early Church Fathers and Christian writers, including Origen and Augustine who were convinced the days were not ordinary. Several early Jews also followed an allegorical interpretation of Genesis, including most notably Philo (*On the Creation,* III.13)."

dependent on nor inferior to literalism. If anything, many of the best theologians thought literalism in Genesis 1 was simplistic and not attentive to the details that point away from literalism.

Sometimes theological truths are not intended to be historically accurate. For example, is it true that Jesus is the Lamb of God? Christians say, of course, it is true. But in what way is it true? Think beyond figurative vs. literal for the moment. Think of what *kind* of truth it is. "Lamb of God" is true theologically. It is interpretive.

Figurative language can create theological awareness.

The expression *Lamb of God* makes sense in a world where people sacrificed to their gods—animals, even human sacrifice. Historically, Jesus was not a sacrifice in any cultic sense, which required selecting a spotless animal (rarely a human) by a priesthood and laying it upon an altar. Jesus certainly was not a four-footed lamb. The "Lamb of God" metaphor removes any association with a literal human sacrifice. Jesus was not a human or child *sacrifice,* not factually, but theologically speaking, the result is similar but better, genuine reconciliation with God.

The historical facts are these: The Romans tried Jesus for sedition and executed him on a hill outside the city walls. The historical context involves other figures: Pilate, Caiaphas, Judas, Herod Antipas, Joseph of Arimathea, and the twelve disciples. No one offered Jesus upon an altar, and the Romans and Jews did not consider the theological import of this execution. Only after the resurrection did the disciples understand the significance of Jesus as the Lamb of God. That is how they explained the unexpected events surrounding the crucifixion of the Jewish Messiah. The historical facts regarding the events were immediate and easy to see; the theological arguments needed time to develop.

By definition, historical data is verifiable or subject to the *Criteria of Authenticity* used by independent historians. Theological truth can stand above any factual data in science or history because it is conceptual. Theology says something about God and his purposes. The crucifixion was not an abstraction but a concrete event. Jesus as the "Lamb of God" is an abstract idea, not a verifiable fact. Theologians may establish some ideas using abstract reasoning when that is all they have. One believes or rejects such concepts on intellectual grounds since they cannot be falsifiable using observation and experience.

The truth behind this theological concept of the Lamb of God is special revelation, meaning it is not detectable but revealed. Though "Lamb of God" is not an empirical fact, it is better than that; it is an essential revelation in Christianity. Therefore, it is misguided to assert that scripture—in our case, Genesis, must be historical or scientific data to be true theologically. One does not necessarily follow the other.

In the ANE, historical facts may be irrelevant to spiritual or theological truths for a given author. Not all the facts or accurate chronology were available to an ancient author. The chronology of events was one of the first things to go if it got in the way of an author's theological or philosophical imperatives. That is why Jesus's statement on "three days and three nights" in the tomb (Matthew 12:40) is not precise or completely factual. It is a theological claim to his messiahship pivoting on the providential use of the number three. The gospels differ on the chronological day the Romans crucified Jesus (the fourteenth or fifteenth of Nisan). That does not alter the historical truths of the death, burial, and resurrection of Jesus or the theological truths that he is the Lamb of God and our High Priest (which is a contradiction if meant literally since High Priests did not sacrifice themselves).

We believe Jesus's resurrection is a historical fact, but the crucial *meaning* of the resurrection for the identity of Jesus and the world's hope is *theological*. We get this meaning from the New Testament writers who witnessed Jesus and experienced the Holy Spirit. They tell us what God was saying to their generation with the cross and resurrection. The resurrection confirms the things we read about Jesus. God's plan is not mere history; it transcends history in that it was conceived before the world began, before history, and continues post-history. Today, God's plan drives history until it comes to an end, i.e., when this universe ends. We can better understand the writer's intentions by making distinctions such as historical facts relative to theological truth.

Augustine wrote, *"In the beginning [God] created only the germs [seeds] or causes of life which were afterward developed in gradual course."* [106] Countless secondary causes operate in the universe, but Christianity accepts that the First Cause has set the parameters and trajectory of secondary causality according to a plan.[107]

Augustine also said, "At least we know that the [Genesis creation day] is different from the ordinary day with which we are familiar."[108] *"At least we know"* is another way of saying, *"One thing we know for sure."* That is quite a bold statement—too bold for YEC. There are good reasons why Augustine thought the six days were figurative. Augustine would have recognized the humanizing of God (anthropomorphism) in Genesis. *He was a bishop and theologian of the first rank. Human traits applied to God can only be metaphors. And since the Bible has no authority over God, Genesis does not dictate His nature.*

Furthermore, *the science* of Augustine's day informed him that the days of Genesis had to be figurative. Origen before him said that only a simpleton

---

106. *"The Literal Interpretation of Genesis"* 5:2 (AD 408).

107. By "First Cause," I am not referring to a *temporal* first cause where the first created thing (e.g., the singularity) causes the second thing (the Big Bang). Instead, it's an ontological First Cause or the *efficient cause*. In this case, God is the uncreated, transcendent, necessary cause of all contingent things.

108. Augustine, *The Literal Interpretation of Genesis*, 5:2 (AD 408).

would think there were literal days before day four when God reportedly created the sun, moon, and stars.[109]

By Augustine's time, the educated classes knew the earth was a sphere with perpetual sunrise and sunset, so an unlimited God guided by sunup and sundown (especially in a three-tiered universe) had to be metaphorical. It is metaphorical when we use the same terms for ourselves in that the sun still does not go up and down. We follow the sun visually. *God does not follow the sun at all.*

God's nature and practical science informed Augustine that the days of creation were figurative. Yet, YErs claim Augustine was one of them because he reasoned that the earth was thousands of years old and not extremely old or eternal in the past as most in his day thought. But since he knew the six days of Genesis were figurative, and YEC depends on the six days being literal, there must be more to Augustine's speculation on earth's age than creation week. Archeology, geology, paleontology, prehistory, and most histories like those found in ANE tablets were unavailable in Augustine's day. His main argument was against the prevailing view that the earth was eternal in the past *and* what he knew of history being several thousand years, he drew his conclusion as speculation.[110]

Today, it does not matter how old Augustine estimated the earth to be since figurative days throw all estimates into speculation when using biblical data alone. Since Augustine considered the earth thousands of years old and the days of creation were figurative, he did not use the six days to determine the earth's age. He simply had no data to assume anything beyond the basic construct of known history; the prehistoric was unknown to him and not a subject for the Bible. Contrary to YE assumptions, Christianity does not depend on Augustine for the age of the earth. It doesn't need to. Because Augustine believed God created the universe instantly and that the six days were figurative, which rules out using the Bible to date creation. Christians do not use modern science to

---

109. The notion that the sun was created on day one but only became visible on day four seems arbitrary. There is nothing in the text to warrant it. That would imply that God and spiritual beings experienced obstructed vision since no other life existed, which is absurd.

110. YErs want to claim Augustine as their own because, while insisting the earth has not always existed as pagans believed, he speculated that the earth was in the tens of thousands of years old. He did not base that on literal days in Genesis but on his knowledge of knowable history, which we now know was very limited. Even so, he was hardly preoccupied with the age of the earth nor did he think the Bible's credibility depended on it, though the going theory was not an old earth but *an eternal universe.* You must search long and hard to find references to the age of the earth in his works. This means he was not a YEr with the theological baggage. He was not a YE evangelist preaching a Young Earth gospel. He did not think the age of the earth was the key to all biblical doctrine nor did he think it possible for God to lie. Can you imagine Augustine saying, "A young earth may be necessary for indirect salvation"? Or "A young earth is the key to reforming the pagan culture"? Or "If the earth is old, God has lied to us"? Such messaging proclaimed by Christians would have been disturbing in Augustine's day as they should be today.

discredit the Bible; they use it to correct misusing scripture as a science book. Science confirms Augustine's remarkable interpretive skills, which showed the six days are figurative without modern science. YEC falsely charges Christians with rejecting biblical authority for science, when real science liberates the Bible from losing its authority. Thanks to science, we know that the earth goes around the sun. We have learned to recognize phenomenological language in scripture and our own experience, thanks partly to science done by Christians.

The testimony of the best theologians and scholars on the nature of God, the Bible's purposes, prehistoric data, ANE literature, and science provides multiple streams of evidence that the days of Genesis are figurative. Here is the point: If Augustine is correct that the days of creation are figurative, then we cannot determine the earth's age from the Bible alone. That means genealogies in Genesis used to date the earth, at best, only go back to the first modern humans and not the initial creation. The lineages are undoubtedly relevant to the history of Israel but not necessarily meant for the entire human race of Africa, Asia, and the Americas.

Furthermore, genealogies in the ANE tradition of extremely long lifespans up to 936 years with missing generations cannot establish a date for the first humans. In other words, we do not see from the Bible where modern humans fit in the succession of cause and effect since the initial creation. That was not the author's purpose, which was exclusively theological. A list of who begat who may have historical significance, e.g., who sired whom, in rough order, but does not make Genesis 1-11 an entirely literal history in the conventional sense. YErs insist on a literal interpretation of the six days, not as a possibility but as a brute fact, because they cannot establish a young universe any other way. Therefore, on YEC, the earth's age depends solely on one interpretation among many of Genesis 1.

Why should all this led to conflict?

Presenting God in literature is forgiving compared to discerning God's nature with theological precision. Today's issues in Genesis are theological more than scientific and literary more than literal. Not that science or history is irrelevant, but they are not the point. The early Genesis literature expresses the cosmology and theology in the Late Bronze and Early Iron Ages language. Prose, poetry, narrative, and even myth are not true or false intrinsically; they are genres. They communicate truth differently. Like the book of Revelation, Jewish apocalyptic is an example of a genre similar to myth. It is heavily symbolic, not lies.

Ultimately, the key to interpreting Genesis is more about the nature of God than the nature of words. The critical point is to avoid limiting God to the literary world of the ancient tribal culture that encountered him. Instead, we should ask, "What is this culture trying to tell us about God that harmonizes with what we know about His attributes?"

How does a *literal* workweek speak to the nature of God?

It would mean God organizes His time, beginning each workday at sunrise and ending at sundown. He uses light to view his workspace. He avoids working at night. He evaluates his work as he "goes along." Finally, God ends the week with time off.

That sounds suspiciously like my dad.

The one-to-one correspondence "genre," asserted by Stephen W. Boyd and others, confuses the association of words to a *genre* with words and their *referent*. The language is figurative when there is low correspondence between words and their referent. For example, when scripture refers to God as a lion, the remote similarity between God and a lion makes it absurd as anything but metaphor. In an exceedingly narrow sense, God is like a lion— "powerful and majestic." When the level of correspondence is between God and the human person, the metaphors are not as obvious. God is more like a human than a lion. But let's be honest, not by much.

We are far more like a lion than God is like a human. Both lions and humans have bodies; we walk, run, eat, produce offspring, die—I could go on. Biblical authors go out of their way to warn against confusing human nature with God's nature. We want to believe God is like us in ways that cannot be. By contrast, there is little concern in the Bible about confusing God's nature with animal nature though that happened too.

While it is true that Genesis 2–3 is overtly anthropomorphic and less so in chapter 1, nonetheless, the level of correspondence between God and human nature in all three chapters is only a matter of degree.

The Invisible, Visible

"Because he saw Him, who is invisible."

"Language about God is something like the language of poetry," not that the genre is poetry necessarily. A skilled poet tries to express a vision of the world that is hard to put into words for most people. For a spiritual vision, prose does not have the same facility.[111]

Like the poet, a spiritual writer tries to elicit a particular response with their art. Language about God, worship, liturgy, and prayer are similar. A vision about God expresses a way of seeing the world when encountering God's mysterious presence. For example, the work of the Spirit is a mystery because it is invisible— "The wind blows wherever it pleases. You hear its sound, but you cannot tell where it comes from or where it is going. So is everyone born of the spirit" (John 3:8). The analogy of wind attempts to envision the mystery. That

---

111. Keith Ward was helpful on this point. See Keith Ward, *What Do We Mean By 'God'? A Little Book of Guidance* (2010). I paraphrase him here to some extent.

is why "wind" and "spirit" are the same words in biblical languages. Spiritual language should reflect the mystery.[112]

An example of prose or "historical narrative" with a poetic flair is Hebrews 11:28: "By faith [Moses] left Egypt, not fearing the Pharaoh's anger; he persevered *because he saw him who is invisible.*" Taken "as written," this is contradictory as in the *invisible, visible.* The author heightens the value of faith poetically by using the idea of "seeing" in two ways—one with eyes and one with the "eyes" of faith. This double use of "seeing" is not an equivocation because the author's meaning is clear; the mind's eye can "see" in a way that the eyes of the body cannot. First-century Jews would be well acquainted with this kind of language.

Faith brings perseverance because people with faith see God beyond the circumstances. Faith and its sister, hope, are necessary kinds of vision that, without it, one has a corresponding sort of blindness—by faith Moses "saw." Real faith is not blind; faithlessness toward God always is.

God sees with limitless sight and not by natural light reflected off a surface.

The author could have used a literal phrase, "Moses trusted God, so he persevered." But anybody can say that. This story was extraordinary and required a similar way to express it. The power of a new and effective way of expressing something of value is immeasurable. Literalism is not synonymous with truth or with God's Word.

Indeed, Moses *saw* Him who is invisible.

Authors cannot express how God exists in reality because they cannot see God as He is. Spiritual vision is all we have until our transformation. Wooden literalism is lifeless like a dead tree—it covers up a spiritually live vision— "the spirit gives life." Remember when Jesus said we must eat his flesh and drink his blood? John continued: "When many of his disciples heard it, they said, "This teaching is difficult; who can accept it?" But Jesus said to them, "Does this offend you? *The words that I have spoken to you are spirit and life.*"

That is to say, Jesus's words were visionary.

Elevated language in scripture is often evidence that the author or someone he writes about had an experience with God. Such language can also encourage the reader to perceive God's presence. Thus, Moses saw the invisible, and Jesus spoke words that were spiritual, metaphorical, theological, or call it what you will—*those critical words were not literal.*

It is evident that the Bible, especially Genesis, is loaded with anthropomorphic imagery, the subject of the next chapter.

---

112. God's spiritual work in each believer does not require a specific length of time since the life spans of believers vary widely, from the thief on the cross, to the Apostle John. "Length" of life has more to do with this life then the next since the spiritual realm "in us" or without us is not governed by time-space.

Summary

1. Genre does not dictate the nature of God.

2. Taking the word *day* figuratively is the same as taking a twenty-four-hour day figuratively.

3. Words are the same whether used literally or figuratively.

4. Word meanings can change depending on the nature of the subject.

5. All genres are artistic.

6. Poetry can be literal. Prose, historical narrative, and even scientific literature may contain metaphors and other literary devices.

7. Prejudice toward figurative speech is a product of modernity.

8. Many of the best theologians allowed a free interpretation of the days of Genesis.

9. Details about God's actions expressed in words must be analogous.

10. If any day of creation is figurative, we cannot determine the earth's age from the Bible.

11. If we cannot include Genesis 1:1–2 on day one, then the age of the universe and earth is undetermined in the Bible.

12. Numbers 10 and 11 also show the genealogies in Genesis 5 do not help the case for a young earth.

8.
GOD AND ANTHROPOMORPHISMS
PART 1[113]

No one has seen God at any time...You have neither heard His voice at any
time nor seen His face (nature).
—John 1:18; 5:37 (NMB)

Wanting to bridge the gap between the infinite and the finite, YE evangelist Steven W. Boyd does not recognize the contradiction in his question when
he asks, "If God could speak literally about creating Adam and Eve...why can't
God speak of literal events on literal days of creation in a way that we can readily
understand?"[114] A simple question demands a simple answer: God cannot do the
intrinsically impossible. So there are a few things wrong with Boyd's question.

First, Boyd *begs the question* since the words "If God could speak literally about creating Adam and Eve" assume that God *spoke literally* about creating Adam and Eve. For instance, Moses says God made Adam and Eve (in
Genesis 2), but He does so in overt anthropomorphic imagery, namely, God
"handmade" or molded them out of dust. Deities making humans out of the
dust, soil, blood, and body parts like ribs was common in the ANE. It is easier
to understand that the original humans came from something.

Boyd himself acknowledges anthropomorphisms in chapter 2. Christians
have always believed God created the universe out of nothing. If that is true, then
creating Adam from clay and Eve from a rib is not literal but literary for theological *ideas that motivated the author*. Therefore, God did not speak about *how*
He created Adam and Eve, not literally. Of course, Christians are free to take
these stories literally, but an artificial reform movement over that is senseless.

Secondly, the context of Boyd's question is Genesis 1, the only place we
find the six days that he wants to take literally. Yet, *how* God created humans is
not stated in Genesis 1. Any explicit "how" language is in chapter 2, where God
formed Adam from clay like a potter, then "breathed" into Adam's nostrils as
a paramedic administering CPR. God performed surgery with some kind of
anesthesia to form Eve from Adam's side. The clay/potter imagery fits nicely
into the broader ANE worldview about the creation of humans, but it is hardly
literal, nor is that creation out of nothing.

---

113. Some anthropomorphisms are more obvious than others are. In Genesis, God is pictured
speaking out loud in Hebrew at the beginning of time, seeing with light, working the daylight
portion of the day while avoiding evening hours, crafting, resting, breathing, walking in the cool
of the day, searching, manufacturing clothing, repenting, enjoying the aroma of "barbeque."
Details like these make God humanlike, which must be metaphoric.

114. *Coming to Grips with Genesis*, page 160.

Boyd goes on, *"Then why can't [God] speak literally* about literal days" (as if God would be concerned with speaking literally about literal days)? That amounts to saying, "If God spoke literally, then why can't he 'speak literally' some more?" Yet God did not write Genesis or narrate it in order to speak literally about days, nor did He "speak literally" about creative techniques regarding Adam and Eve in Genesis 2. That reads too much into the story.

Boyd acknowledges some of God's actions in Genesis 2–3 are anthropomorphic but does not grant *any* anthropomorphic imagery in Genesis 1. Again, the author of Genesis does not describe *how* God made humans in chapter 1 but only that he did make them. The names "Adam and Eve" do not appear until chapter 2. That means we do not have a literal Adam and Eve mentioned in Genesis 1; humans are there, but not specific ones. We simply assume the humans in Genesis 1 are the same in Genesis 2, and they may be. Yet Adam's firstborn, Cain, found a wife in a different land. That throws some doubt on how many humans were there in Genesis 1–4, particularly if more than one author is responsible for these chapters at different times, which is plausible. Historical, Textual, Source, and Literary criticisms suggest more than one author.[115]

But that is not for this book.

Boyd's argument hinges on Chapter 1, not Chapter 2. Genesis 1 says that God created humans on day six, not how he made them, literally or otherwise. Furthermore, if in Genesis 1, God creates humans from nothing, which Christians have come to believe, it contradicts a literal interpretation of chapter 2, where God *forms* Adam and Eve out of clay and rib. Genesis 1:24 says the land (soil) produced all creatures that live on the ground. So God does not make the animals *ex-nihilo,* according to Genesis 1. Verse 26 says that God created humans, not *how* He made them but *that* He made them.

It is not until chapter 2 that we meet God, the humanlike Potter/Surgeon/EMT.

---

115. For example, the applicable names for God are different in chapter 1 then chapter 2. The older title "Elohim" is used in chapter 1. "Yahweh Elohim" is used in chapter 2 despite Exodus 6:3 that says, "I appeared to Abraham, Isaac, and Jacob as [Elohim], but by my name [Yahweh] *I did not make myself known."* Genesis 4:26 says, *"At that time people began to call on the name of [Yahweh]."* It would seem that later author(s) wrote *or edited* Genesis 2 and other uses of the name "Yahweh" throughout Genesis and seems to be an inconsistency. However, for Umberto Cassuto, who rejected this "Documentary Hypothesis," it becomes especially striking in the first chapters of Genesis. Genesis 1 uses the name "Elohim" since it is describing God's creation of the universe. Genesis 2, however, uses the unique combination "Yahweh Elohim." Yahweh is the covenant name for the Hebrew God. *Cassuto acknowledges that the Documentary Hypothesis is based on some valid observations.* But he made three crucial counter-arguments. The different names of God, for Cassuto, are not necessarily evidence of separate sources. Instead, they are used to call attention to different attributes and activities of God. But that does not resolve the inconsistencies. See Umberto Cassuto, *The Documentary Hypothesis*, Kindle edition.

Therefore, the mistaken premise of Boyd's question (if God could speak literally, which He does not do) spoils his follow-up plea—"Then why can't God speak literally about literal events on literal days we can readily understand." Boyd knows that anthropomorphisms are present in Genesis but denies them altogether during the six days, exposing an inconsistency.

All of Genesis 1 needs to be literal if YEC is to survive.

As we have seen, anthropomorphic pictures can be subtle or overt, with low or high correspondence to the realities they represent. There is no limit to how low corresponding representations can be with God since He is unlimited, and there is none like Him. The greatest person we can conceive is still lower than God in corresponding attributes since our language and imagination necessarily falls short of the Absolute.

Thirdly, and more importantly, Boyd's question contains a contradiction regarding the nature of God. The one thing omnipotence cannot do is perform nonsense. God cannot create a square circle. He cannot create an infinite object that is finite at the same time *and* in the same way. Therefore, God cannot explain in literal and "easy to understand language" what is beyond our ability to comprehend in any language.

That is the point.

He is the Creator; we are the creature. If God explained how He performed what is incomprehensible to us in the information age, how much more out of place would it be for tribal people of the Late Bronze Age? Think about this YE contradiction.

YErs insist that creation was an absolute miracle, as all Christians do. However, miracles, by definition, are unexplainable. Therefore, *"explaining the miracle"* of creation is contradictory, particularly if that phrase is literal. You can state that a miracle occurred, but you cannot explain it in any human language, let alone language *"we can readily understand."*

Every YEr has experienced the wonder of creation: the birth of a baby, a spectacular sunset, an intense starry night, the Grand Canyon, earth from 30,000 feet, the most impressive wildlife up close, an orchid under ultra-magnification, or a caterpillar reborn a monarch. There are no adequate words to express many wonders of creation in literal terms, such as "the caterpillar grew into a butterfly."

"Yes, I can see that, thank you very much." However, that is no explanation of metamorphosis, which is a simplistic example compared to the wonder of the universe.

Poets have tried to capture the awe and beauty of creation. The loves and the mysteries of life are an endless pursuit for artists. Yet YErs demand we understand the Almighty's acts of creating inexpressible beauty and complexity

THE SIX DAY WAR IN CREATIONISM

in flat terms. "God made that on day such and such." Wooden literalness is not "wondrous" or what the author is getting at in his ANE context.

For many YErs, God is not the primary revelation or focus; *the days are.*

Explanations are limited to explainable things. We can know some things about God but cannot *explain* Him. We can say God is infinite, though that is not an explanation; it only helps manage our limitations. No languages comprehendible to us explain *the hows* of God's actions in any literal sense. We *relate* to God primarily by an inner communion or union of spirit, not through words only. The *primary* purpose of prayer, for example, is not about finding the right words; it is about finding a connection. God does not use words when He communes with us in real-time.

We relate to the natural world primarily through empirical data and sensory information to work within the possibilities it offers. But the difference between God's nature and the natural world is that no empirical data can explain God's nature and workings (John 3:8). Romans 11:35 says, "How impossible it is for us to understand [God's] decisions *and his methods.*" (TLB). You might as well explain how man landed on the moon to a baboon. Truthfully, the gulf between God and us is infinitely vaster than between a man and a baboon. DNA has informed us of that.

Face it: there is no *Nature of God for Dummies.*

YErs acknowledge that the Creation event is an absolute miracle, not explainable by science nor any *natural* explanation. Yet they demand the simplest literal explanation, and why? YErs appear motivated more by preserving their distinctives. One cannot require a literal and basic explanation for a miraculous claim and remain cogent. If the Creation is beyond our comprehension, then it is beyond words—how much more is the Creator?

My point is this: *how* God created, meaning any "mechanism" He used for the initial creation, is beyond the biblical data and indeed out of our reach today. The act of creation is not only about its mechanisms; It's primarily about the power that grounds existence. Like the age-old question, "Why is there something rather than nothing?" *Nothing* has no explanation, while all things have an explanation for their existence, at least theoretically. Evolution shows that physical states cause other physical states, but it does not explain *existence*; and particle physics doesn't show *why* things have existence, only *that* they exist and *how* they behave; their continuous existence remains unexplained.

Additionally, YErs claim theistic evolution, intelligent design, and progressive creation are inferior explanations (or lies from the devil) because they simply acknowledge observable natural processes. Natural processes are all we can see after the initial creation, no matter how one believes that happened. YErs insist on a simple, literal explanation for how creation unfolded so that anyone can understand it, yet they reject reasonable ones offered for secondary causes that we can clearly see. People will inevitably deny plain enough answers to protect a distinctive as the hill to die on.

Empirical data is the literal information that the book of nature provides. Oddly, many YErs reject the "book of nature" because it contradicts *how they read* biblical literature, yet they insist that nature and the Bible cannot contradict, so nature itself must submit to YEC. They would rather have words about God's handiwork, which could be literal or figurative, than the actual evidence that witnesses to God's handiwork.

Words *tell*, empirical data *shows*.

The value in biblical texts is what they mean, not just what they say, which is why scholars take seriously ANE literature that sheds light on biblical texts. On the one hand, the value of empirical data collected from nature is that it's verifiable. On the other hand, like most literature, biblical literature can be more open to interpretation since there are shades of meaning in theological and philosophical concepts that develop over centuries and across diverse cultures. The task of recovering the sense of those texts and how to apply them in the modern age can be daunting. *Theologians and biblical scholars do not use science to correct Genesis; they can show that science may confirm someone like Augustine's ideas that the six days are figurative and creation was instantaneous, which also shows that the Bishop's ideas were not only legitimate but without the aid of modern science. Augustine's example is one of many where purely rational thought can lead to the same conclusions as science.* [116]

Ironically, the Big Bang Theory, Evolutionary Creationism, and Intelligent Design come closer to Boyd's wishes for literalness than any other "*explanation*" of "how." [117] Even so, those theories only describe what we can see. They do not explain why those mechanisms exist, why some are constant, or why conditions

---

116. Stephen Hawking once remarked that Augustine was the first person to understand time in the modern sense 1500 years before Einstein.

117. I am not advocating Evolutionary Creationism or Progressive Creationism in this book because theology is primary and science is not my emphasis here. However, I reject two competing views: (1) That *blind undirected* macroevolution is a brute fact; and (2) Macroevolution is necessarily atheistic. Evolutionary Creationism is the belief that God continually causes and sustains nature's existence, and processes such as evolution, which is God's operation in the diversity of species. God's person operating cannot be seen but His affects can be noticed like humans operating on the surface of Mars taking photos, collecting rocks and doing experiments, but from earth. We see the effects of our operations. An important motivation in YEC is to remove evolutionary theory and deep age from the culture in the belief that those ideas are atheistic, anti-Christian, and anti-Scripture, which makes a good slogan for the unsuspecting but is self-evidently false. Many theists accept evolution and the vast majority of Christians believe the overwhelming evidence that the earth is old, "literalism" notwithstanding. Science is not used to contradict Genesis among practicing Christians but it can affirm theologians like Augustine who insisted that God created the universe instantly, that the six days of Genesis 1 are figurative or that the earth revolves around the sun despite the phenomenological language of scripture. For the best defense of Evolutionary Creationism, See Biologos.com.

arose for them to work. More importantly, no mechanism explains the initial creation of the universe despite attempts to do so. The singularity before the Big Bang does not appear to have a trail that led to its appearance in the face of grand assumptions that substitute nothing for something like quantum tunneling or fluctuations in quantum vacuums, which, of course, are not *nothing*. The singularity appears to have come from nothing. That is not to say it did come from nothing, but that is how it looks. Suggestions like String Theory and M Theory are speculative without any evidence.

The only way to communicate an infinite God's movements to any human is through figurative or theological language, often with anthropomorphic imagery. Humans are the only persons we comprehend. Figures of speech help ease the tension between God's eternal nature and the *limits* of human thought expressed in concrete language.

The "Sensitive," Non-Sensory God

In Genesis, God treats the first humans with sensitivity, even after they disobey Him. God is decidedly personal and offers humans tranquility (implied by the seventh-day rest). There is communion in the Garden between God and humans.[118] God loves us, and He is worthy of our love.

The author of Genesis goes out of his way to present one Almighty God delighting in His creation, especially humans. All creation is a stage for the union of divinity and humanity. Humans are one creature that is personal, rational, and capable of being the vice-regents for God on earth.

On this planet, only humans can connect with God. We can apprehend Him in spirit and commune with Him, but we cannot comprehend God, unlike the anthropomorphic pagan deities. Knowing things about God is not *comprehending* Him.

Among all ANE gods, Yahweh values this personal communion most.

Consequently, there is a trade-off to presenting God in such personal terms. The personhood we are familiar with is human. We have no adequate language for "persons" of a different reality, let alone a language for the ground of all existence. God is not a person in the same way we are persons. Werner Heisenberg said, *"The reality we can put into words is never reality itself."* That's especially true of ultimate reality. Persons, in our experience, are individuals of discrete quantity and quality. We are packets of personhood.

The Trinity doctrine does not teach that God is three *individuals* or *separate* persons. That is polytheism. The "persons" of the Trinity are *distinct*,

---

118. The Old Testament hints at the metaphysical idea behind Divine Rest. The New Testament develops the concept in the light of Christ. Christ ties rest for the soul to himself and to the ultimate meaning of the Sabbath command (compare Matthew 11:28–30, 12:1–14; and Hebrews chapters 3 and 4).

not separate beings. Distinctions are possible without separation. "Separation" imposes onto the Trinity what theologians since Augustine have called *extension in space*, denying its omnipresence. Instead of being omnipresent, separateness and spatial extension limit God to three finite and measurable dimensions (see Acts 17). Extension in space means where one person ends, another begins. Infinite personhood does not end or begin. Therefore, the three infinites must be one "singularity."

Consider an *analogy* (and this is only an analogy) by adding three infinities:

1. All *even* numbers, plus.

2. All *odd* numbers, plus.

3. All *whole* numbers.

These three *distinct* infinities equal a single infinite.[119] The point is these three are distinct, i.e., they are identifiable. Still, they are not separate from each other in any way, nor are the quantities "three" and "one" coherent, relative to infinity. Therefore, our language betrays our limitations. So it is with God's attributes. His attributes are limitless, yet we can only identify them with the limitations inherent in our thought and language. Therefore, God's infinite attributes are not countable.

Yet we have no other terminology available to us.

In our limited understanding, God's love is "*distinct*" from His goodness, which is "*distinct*" from His patience because we identify them according to the same attributes in ourselves. All these attributes are infinite in God, having no beginning or end in time or space; they must be simple, meaning one as in a singularity. None of God's attributes can be a separate and finite quantity from His other attributes. A God without limitations cannot have a finite attribute. A divine attribute cannot leave off where another begins. All God's attributes are unbounded and, therefore, one, like a singularity. Divisions mean limitations

---

119. The analogy is strengthened by the fact that an infinite series is a *potential infinite* not an actual infinite so that even here, we have a case where three *potential* infinites are distinct but not separate. How much more true might oneness be with three actual infinites that are not in series?

and sections where one-part ends, another begins. That is the nature of *our* personhood. Hence, God must be one, infinite, and indivisible.[120]

We can personally relate to God through a communion of Spirit. This kind of relationship is more intimate than talking or sharing a social life between separate persons, which we shall be able to do with the glorified Jesus, who is both God and Man. The humanity in the Incarnate Son connects our need for socializing with an incorporeal God, especially in the transfigured state when our union with God is more comprehensive.

There are no limits whatsoever in God.[121]

Humans developed languages to communicate with other humans. The limits of our nature determine the limits of our language. Human language is "earth speak." God's nature and His speech are nothing like ours. We speak and write one word at a time: we plan, work, build, create, breathe, rest, draw conclusions, and teach these things to other humans. Humans enjoy themselves and a job well done. God does not do these things, at least not *as we do*. We rule our property or home, but God is sovereign over all things visible and invisible, including our homes and lives, over which he has given us stewardship.

We describe things according to our experiences in the natural world. God transcends the natural world, though Genesis gives Him human ways and human emotional responses. Scripture may present God as though he *exists*

---

120. According to the divine simplicity of Thomas Aquinas, all God's properties are identical to each other and indistinguishable. For example, God's essence and existence are identical. Aquinas's view of divine simplicity is essential to his Christology in that all that proceeds from God is God and not parts or separations of God; otherwise, we have divisions in God's nature with the Incarnation. Therefore, when Jesus says he proceeded from the Father, He cannot be a separate part of the divine. All that proceeds from God, whether from His essence or His existence (being), must be God. Therefore, God's essence is existence. This concept may be related in the burning bush where God identified Himself as the "I am that I am" or perhaps "I am existence." Thomas's view has been somewhat controversial in recent decades. Many Protestant theologians have a more limited view of divine simplicity that some label "Personalism." Orthodox Churches tend to agree with Aquinas.

121. Protestants (myself being one) may have more difficulty identifying with classical theism because of our greater devotion to biblical authority, which can lead to a more literal view of scripture than is sometimes warranted. Instead of recognizing the anthropomorphic pictures in the Bible and theophanies (no one has seen God nor can see Him), we look for what we call the "biblical view" which can be little more than our view on the Bible. There is nothing wrong with having a view on the Bible—we cannot help that. However, the Bible is a collection of books from different authors; it does not have a single unified view on the nature of God throughout its pages. For example, the Old Testament view of *one God* is different from the New Testament revelation of one God in *Father, Son, and Holy Spirit*. Yet we know there can be only one God. The purpose of Theology Proper is to determine what must be and what cannot be true about the nature of God, not what interpretation of the Bible we prefer. For example, since God created the universe, the content of which is time, space, and matter, so Theology Proper tells us that God cannot be temporal, spatial, or material, even if the Bible presents Him as humanlike or with anthropomorphisms. All those kinds of biblical references must be figurative.

inside the universe or in time/space, which cannot be if meant literally. By becoming human, God really entered this world. He lived in it! He had not entered this world in a literal sense before the Incarnation. Yet, the infinite God impacts our world and is "present" to it, without existing *in* or being *of* the universe. For example, we exist in a three-dimensional world but can relate to a two-dimensional space. Recall that artists paint the impression of a three-dimensional portrait on a two-dimensional canvas, yet all this actually takes place in three dimensions.

In Genesis, God enjoys the aroma of ancient "barbecue" (Genesis 8:20). Really?

No, not really.

In Genesis, God is not "*as written*" in "word for word" fashion, as YErs claim. Instead, there is a thread on the nature of God woven throughout the scripture gradually. It runs through the Pentateuch to the Second Temple period, the New Testament, and the Councils of Nicaea (fourth century AD). Even so, metaphors for God in human and animal imagery abound in scripture. At the same time, there are severe warnings in the Bible about humanizing God. We must reconcile all that.

We cannot help but talk about God or even think about Him without imposing limits upon his attributes. We lack experience with the infinite. We also lack the literal language to describe things that are beyond our five senses. Contrary to popular myth, our imagination has limits. God has none. The best we can do is recognize this when we speak. While none can comprehend God, it is possible to be less wrong about Him. We can appreciate God to the extent our limited nature allows, which is sufficient.[122]

Out of necessity, authors must resort to descriptions of God in human form or what literary and biblical scholars call "anthropomorphisms." The *Encyclopedia Judaica* gives insights into the anthropomorphisms in the Hebrew Bible:

> Anthropomorphism is a normal phenomenon in all primitive...religions. Yet at the same time, it is accepted as a major axiom of Judaism, from the biblical period onward, that no material representation of the Deity is possible or permissible... In every instance, it should be asked whether the expression is an actual, naively concrete personification of God, or a fresh and vital form of religious awareness resorting to corporeal imagery, or an allegorical expression.

---

122. Many theologians have concluded that all language about God is figurative or abstracted from metaphor out of necessity since human language is naturally finite and inexact. Whatever the case, God's creative acts are well beyond the details of the creation account in Genesis. That makes warring over those details futile.

The phrase "naively concrete personification of God" means believing that sensory language about God literally portrays His being. The Apostle Paul says in Acts 17:29–30 that God once overlooked such naiveté but now requires all to repent. Paul says now we all must stop making God in our image or *imaginings*. That is, not just in statuary but in space such as occupying a room in a temple (the Holy of Holies) made by man as they did in the ANE—"The God who made the world...does not live in temples built by human hands" (v. 24). God's nature is central to all understanding since errors about God naturally lead to mistakes about the things of God.

Notice the phrase *"corporeal imagery"* in the *Encyclopedia Judaica*. God is incorporeal. We are corporeal. Once we see this, John's words make sense, "No one has seen God at any time, nor heard his voice"—that is, no one has experienced those things literally. The Bible also says, "No one can see God and live," meaning to see in the literal sense. Paul is equally emphatic in 1 Timothy 6:16, "[God] who alone is immortal and who lives in unapproachable light, *whom no one has seen or can see*" (emphasis mine).

An anthropomorphic view of God affects one's theology regarding other matters related to God. The most striking example is the suggestion that God is a liar if the earth is old. Would God be a sinner if he disagreed with something in the Bible? YErs say yes. *It is possible to have so high a view of the Bible that it leads to a low view of God.*

More subtle human characteristics given to God throughout the Bible (especially Genesis 1) are often anthropomorphisms gone undetected; examples are "Let there be light" and the resulting "God *saw* it was good." At first glance, this seems perfectly reasonable. Yet photons bombarding the surface of an object do not enable God to see. You may say this train of thought overthinks it or overstates the point. But YEC claims that Genesis has a one-to-one correspondence from words to reality; that is, every word in Genesis 1 must be literal, and scientifically and historically accurate.

Even in Genesis 1, the ancient Hebrews were less concerned about metaphysics[123] than the moral authority of Elohim:

> The Hebrews attained at an early period, a belief in God as the Creator and sustainer of the universe, but their interest in metaphysics did not go beyond this. It is in their moral idea of God that we shall find anticipations

---

123. By "metaphysics," I mean contemporary *Analytical Metaphysics* (AM) that seeks to uncover and discover fundamental features of the universe, such as elements of existence. AM respects science but is not limited by it. For example, things that exist are made possible by power or powers that can bring them about. If parents alone give their children existence how is it that children continue to exist after parents die? Parents have the power that God/nature *necessarily* gives them to bring children into existence. If we apply that to everything in the universe, there must be a power that brings all things about, which is what omnipotence means. Thus, God is a metaphysical answer to existence.

of the Incarnation. It is also remarkable that, although the sense of the... transcendency of God grew with time, the Jews in the later periods [still] did not shrink from strongly anthropomorphic expressions.[124]

The exact nature of God's being is not the focus in Genesis 1. There is no attempt to explain God's incorporeality or His attributes. Genesis 1 is a story. Since incorporeality is not detectable by any of the five senses, it is not captured adequately with words. God does not see, hear, smell, touch, or taste as we do. How He does things, we cannot tell. Therefore, sensory descriptions of God are necessarily figurative—*any* sensory description.

The language is figurative when God talks aloud, moves around, accomplishes something one step at a time, reacts to circumstances, or anything similar. In other words, the language accommodates our sensibilities with the kind of descriptions a limited person can understand to get a point across.

People ask, "Can't God physically manifest Himself?" God created time, space, matter, and energy; therefore, he can impact them. Nonetheless, God *impacts* the physical universe without being part of it. God "appears" in this world by physical *representations* of His Being, called *theophanies*, not by actually entering this world. Similarly, we can impact the surface of Mars with mechanisms that represent us: the rover, cameras, hydraulics, robots, etc. Theophanies are manufactured *corporeal* images for our sake. God personally enters the universe *only by Incarnation*, which has happened only once (see chapter 39).

The Infinite and the Finite

If God created us in his own image, we have more than reciprocated.
—Voltaire

There are Christians that believe God has a body similar to ours. It is a shock for some to discover that God has no bodily features. God is something like infinite will, consciousness, and mind without body. But He is only similar to those related properties we can understand in our human nature. We cannot help but think of God as humanlike.

Jesus said God is Spirit—not *a spirit* but Spirit, which means "without body" (John 4:24). He does not possess the weakness inherent in any composite set of parts, including body parts. The more moving parts in anything, the more susceptible it is to break down. God is pure simplicity meaning not constructed, and not as some think means simplistic. God cannot be touched, seen, or heard; he is pure incorporeality. We cannot relate to that reality without Him condescending to us with physical representations that can be felt, seen, heard, etc. Becoming human in Christ was the ultimate outreach.

---

124. *Dictionary of the Bible edited by James Hastings* (four volumes in one), "Incarnation" (Delmarva Publications, Harrington DE., 2014), Kindle Edition, Locations 55522-55547, www.DelmarvaPublications.com.

No words can bridge the gulf between a bodily creature's actions and that of immaterial unlimited "being" who does not act in steps but simply is. As C. S. Lewis wrote, "If we talk at all about things which are not perceived by the senses, we are forced to use language metaphorically."[125]

One's choice of hermeneutic or genre cannot alter that fact.

Lewis excels in language usage. He says metaphors are necessary to discuss anything imperceptible to the five senses. God is the ultimate imperceptible. Lewis illustrates his point with the phrase "grasping a point." You cannot grasp a point of an argument literally; our minds do not have hands, and arguments do not have sharp tips. Try saying the same thing with other words, such as "I get your point" or "I follow you." Those statements are not factual, but they are true in another sense. Some people can be suspicious of metaphor and figurative subplots in the Bible because they have difficulty distinguishing the *superficial* and *irrelevant* falsehood from the deeper truths. Yet, the Bible is teeming with such language.

Lewis distinguishes between *true concepts* from the imaginative way authors express them, which can be false if taken literally, like *grasping* a point. Overlooking such distinctions leads to confusion. God is not sensory or a composite of *moving parts* with hands, eyes, lungs, feet, tongue, standing, sitting, walking, etc. Therefore, all earthly language about God's actions and speech that involve such parts are inescapably figurative, even the words "God raised Jesus from the dead."

"Raising" is how we see it since Jesus got up from the tomb. Spatial transference in the upward direction is not the intended meaning. A body can be raised that way and remain dead. We could say that Jesus *went* from death to life. Yet the word *went* implies travel. There is no actual traveling from death to life. That is just human talk.

Enough said.

Keith Ward, Regius Professor of Divinity at Oxford, wrote:

All our words are about finite things...God is not just one thing among other things... When we use a word for something, like a table or a chair, we use that word to pick out something which is different from other things, *which marks out the limits of the thing*, which refers to a finite reality. So none of our words can apply properly to God. If God is infinite, and if all our words must apply to finite things, then none of our words are going to describe God *properly. We cannot have words, which are exact*

---

125. C. S. Lewis, *Miracles (Collected Letters of C. S. Lewis).*

descriptions of God; nor can we have pictures which are exact representations of God.[126] (emphasis mine)

Notice it: we cannot have photos of God. We know that much, yet we say, "Pictures are worth a thousand words." So what makes fundamentalists think that *words* provide an accurate picture of God? Just as we cannot have a photo of God's likeness, we cannot have a satisfactory description of God in words. Abstract expressions like "God is love" and "God is righteousness" may be true in principle (i.e., God is clearly loving), but we cannot know what it means to *be* love or to *be* righteousness. Those are attributes with which God is infinitely endowed.

By contrast, we can understand Jesus because he was human and because he shares our finite nature. He speaks our language. The Incarnation was necessary for God to relate to us in ways we can understand and where words fall short. Our glorification *in Christ* will bring a more comprehensive union with God. We will know much more about God by fully sharing in the glorified Christ.

G. B. Caird, the distinguished Professor of Exegesis at Oxford, wrote:

We have no other language besides metaphor with which to speak about God. Abstract terms such as "righteousness," appear to be an exception to this rule, but on closer examination they are found to be abstracted from metaphors.[127]

Thomas Aquinas seems to confirm this idea:

We must think of God as wise, good, and beautiful, and though these terms do not apply to God as we understand them; in some sense God really is wise, good, and beautiful.[128]

Aquinas' words "in some sense" imply God's transcendence while giving our inadequacies away. We may know what a righteous *human* is, but our knowledge and experience prevent us from identifying the fullness of God's righteousness. Divine "righteousness" is infinite. God is really beyond righteous. When we think of someone honest, we think of someone who chooses to tell the truth, someone who is "godly." God does not *choose* to tell the truth; He

---

126. Keith Ward, *What Do We Mean By 'God'?* SPCK (Great Britain, 2015), p. 5. "Keith Ward is a philosopher, theologian, and scholar. He was a canon of Christ Church, Oxford until 2003. Comparative theology and the relationship between science and religion are two of his main topics of interest. He was Regius Professor of Divinity at the University of Oxford from 1991 to 2004. He is a fellow of the British Academy and a priest of the Church of England." ("Keith Ward," *Wikipedia*.)

127. G. B. Caird, *The Language and Imagery of the Bible* (Westminster Press, Philadelphia), p. 174.

128. Thomas Aquinas, *Summa Theologia*, 1a, Question 13.

is truth. Saying "God is righteous" is like saying righteousness is righteous—it is the distinction without a distinction.

Literal references to God come more easily when put in the negative.

We can say God is infinite, meaning *not finite*. We comprehend "*finite*," but the infinite escapes us; we can only speak of it theoretically. God is timeless, spaceless, and immaterial, and while accurate, these are all in the negative and do not resolve the puzzle as to what God is or how He operates. Other statements about God in the negative are "God is not a lion" or "God is not a tree." These are literally true but not worth saying. Better negations are "God is not like a man" and "God does not have human nature," which are worth mentioning because we tend to project our nature onto Him.

Positive statements like "God is truth" and "God is love" are not entirely explainable in literal terms. We believe God is personal, yet not a person in the same way we are. He is "*infinite personhood*," whatever that may mean, so God largely remains a puzzlement. Fortunately, we can know God's nature positively (as opposed to negatively) to some extent; otherwise, God would not bother to reveal Himself. The glorified state we shall share with Jesus destines us to understand God much more. Paul wrote, "For now we see only a reflection as in a mirror; *then we shall see face to face*. Now I know in part; then I shall know fully, even as I am fully known" (1 Corinthians 13:12). This likely refers to the glorified Christ, not the infinite God.

Realistically, we understand God according to our capacity, so God became human to maximize that capacity, which must be sufficient in this universe. We can know God apart from language, in a union of spirit or communion with God. We tend to think that language is the fullest expression of knowing. Not likely: The Apostle Paul wrote, "Likewise the Spirit helps us in our weakness; for we do not know how to pray as we ought, but that very Spirit intercedes with sighs too deep for words" (Romans 8:26). Even so, our capacity to understand God to the extent possible is sufficient for God's purposes. Keith Ward puts it this way:

> God cannot transcend all human concepts, since then nothing at all could be said of God; not even that God exists. Some concepts must apply to God in a literal sense, or we would literally not know what we were talking about. And it does seem that among the things we must say literally of God, are such things as God knows all things, God cares about

the good of creatures and God freely gives good things to those who love him.[129]

In historical Christianity, humans can know God in three ways:

1. Positive assertions—Observing God's impact on the creation and people's lives.
2. Negative assertions—What God is not and does not.
3. Personal experiences—Union or contact with God.

As we have seen, describing God in human terms is necessarily metaphorical *in any genre.* Therefore, the real issues in the SDWC are not about biblical authority or the nature of words. It is not even about a *high view* of scripture. The issues land squarely on the nature of God.

Ending the SDWC is restoring the higher view of God.

Anthropomorphisms are useful when understood figuratively and if they express an underlining truth in a meaningful way. Judaism, Catholicism, Orthodoxy, and most Protestantism have learned this, though many laypersons, especially among Protestantism, have not. Evangelicals take some anthropomorphic pictures of God literally due to a "high view" of the Bible. We should have a high view of the Bible but not to the extent that it reduces God.

The responsibility for developing the concepts on the nature of God fell to Christian thinkers before the Protestant Era. Their task was to piece together what amounts to hints of the Trinity in the Bible. Those hints were a foundation for a sound Trinitarian theology of God. Given the New Testament revelation of Father, Son, and Holy Spirit, it became necessary to develop a sound doctrine on God's oneness. Protestants have inherited the Trinity doctrine. As a result, Catholics and the Orthodox are less vulnerable to confusing anthropomorphisms with God's true nature. An overly literal reading of God in scriptures containing anthropomorphisms leads to confusion about Him, to which fundamentalists are particularly vulnerable.

---

129. See *By Faith and Reason: The Essential Keith Ward,* edited by Roberto Sirvent, Wm Curtis Holtzen, Darton, Longman and Todd Ltd. (London. 2012, Kindle edition), location 1154. It is true that God knows "all things" since he created all things. We do not really apprehend what "knowing all things" means since we are not party to all the things there are. Nonetheless, we can understand that God does know them. What kind of "knowing" does God possess that we do not? He also knows all things that are possible in the universes He purposely created with those possibilities. In other words, we are using references we comprehend about matters that are largely incomprehensible and, therefore, not fully expressed in the literal sense. We know in part as Paul says in 1 Corinthians 13:9. Our knowledge of God, even where correct, is incomplete and significantly analogous. My main point is that describing God's actions, words, and personality necessarily requires metaphoric language and *not* that it is impossible to know anything about God.

The Bible is so full of anthropomorphisms that it is easy to lose sight of their figurative sense. "As written" is an insufficient interpretive method for scripture that describes God in any detail that implies sensory perception, e.g., seeing, hearing, or distinguishing details from broader attributes.

As C. S. Lewis said, there is a distinction between the concepts authors have in mind that are true and the imaginative way they express them. Interpreting a figure of speech *prima facia* is a mistake, like literally "grasping a point" or giving God body parts or any other anthropomorphic imagery like God laboring from sunrise to sunset, six days a week, and resting on the Sabbath. God may be presented this way in literature but not in reality.

Because of limited vocabulary: imagery, metaphor, allegory, types, and symbols were especially prevalent in ancient literature. The Incarnation is the only condition where we frame God in human terms because the Logos or Word *became* human (John 1:14). Even so, we should proceed with caution.

Jesus was a historical figure, objectively speaking. Theologically speaking, we believe the Logos was in the stream of human history as the man Jesus. Technically, Almighty God has no biographical history like the mythical gods of the ANE. God has no history as we understand history, or the way history applies to us. The biography (or history) of any god is mythology. Yahweh was not born, nor did he emerge from within the universe where history is made. God is not subject to the stream of secondary causes or events that create history. Yahweh impacts history and the people of history; that is, his Spirit is immanent to ours. God's relationship to history is teleological, not ontological.

By contrast, most pagan gods had a history or biography precisely because they were products of the universe. They were born, and many could die. History is of the universe and within it. God is not.

Consider Shakespeare's characters who have a life of their own in a world of their own. Without Shakespeare, they could not exist like we cannot exist without God. Shakespeare, the living person, transcends the world in his literature, yet he is immanent to it and intimate with it. If he wrote himself in his works, it would not be the person we know as Shakespeare but a literary representation of him. Shakespeare's relationship to his works is creative (he authors them), not ontological, i.e., he does not experience existence in his books. Similarly, scientists impact the surface of Mars with testing and mechanical operations (rovers, cameras, drones, experiments, etc.) But they do not exist on Mars, living and breathing on the planet. God is present to history. Yahweh is a God *of* history; He has operational discretion with history's trajectory, but history cannot contain God's essence or existence. God transcends all things, including history.[130]

---

130. In a similar way, God as Creator is an operational attribute. He creates. He does not find His existence in nature. His essence does not exist in a finite reality except in the Incarnation when God enters history, literally, by becoming human, that is, by being born of a woman.

On the other hand, *Jesus is God in history because he was from heaven and existed on earth.* We accept the miracles associated with him, especially the resurrection and ascension, which were historical events.

Jesus has a natural history or biography; he was human with a beginning at birth, an end at death on a cross, and a life in-between, making a literal history. We call him Jesus of Nazareth, meaning Jesus from Nazareth (a city in time-space). We do not say "God from anywhere in this universe" but rather God *in heaven,* meaning His nature transcends all things in an ontological sense. Notice a fresh translation of John 1:1–14:

> Through him the cosmos came to be, and the cosmos did not recognize him. He came to those things that were his own, and they who were his own did not accept him. But as many as did accept him, to them he gave the power to become God's children—to those having faith in his name, Those born not from blood, nor from a man's desire, but of God. And the Logos became flesh and pitched a tent among us, and we saw his glory, glory as of the Father's only one, full of grace and truth.[131]

Here, David Bentley Hart translates "world" as *cosmos,* the Greek term for the universe. Notice that the Logos created the cosmos, then later *entered* it when he became human. It is reasonable to assume that being literally *in* the cosmos, one must be part *of* the cosmos, i.e., composed of things in this universe. God Almighty is not *part of* this universe; His nature transcends it.

On the other hand, an Incarnation changes the conversation. In historical Christian thought, the Logos really entered the world and so entered history as Jesus of Nazareth. There is a difference between the transcendent God's impact on history and the Logos entering history as Jesus.[132]

Whatever the genre, Almighty God does not have any bodily parts, like eyeballs that depend on sunlight, vocal cords to speak audibly, cone-shaped ears to capture sound waves, a nose to smell barbeque, or lungs that breathe, etc. God is Spirit. John's gospel is explicit; "No one has seen God at any time, nor heard his voice"—not Moses, not Abraham, not even Adam and Eve.

William Lane Craig observes, "Augustine worried that a literalistic interpretation of the Genesis creation story would invite the mockery of unbelievers and thus prove to be an obstacle to saving faith. In his Literal Commentary on Genesis, [Augustine] writes:"

"Certainly, if the bodily things [attributed to God] mentioned here could not in any way at all be taken in a bodily sense that accorded with

---

131. David Bentley Hart, *The New Testament: A Translation* (Yale University Press, New Haven, and London, 2017) p. 169.

132. This may seem like splitting hairs but it prevents unnecessary mistakes, like calling theophanies in the Old Testament, incarnations. Imagine the absurdity of doing the same scholarly work on "The Historical Yahweh" as on the historical Jesus.

truth, what other course would we have but to understand them as spoken figuratively, rather than impiously to find fault with holy scripture?" (8.1.4; CSEL 28:1, 232).

Craig adds, "Augustine's principle… that any text which, taken literally, implies falsehood or impurity should be interpreted figuratively was widely accepted in both Western and Eastern exegesis through the Middle Ages." (Richard Swinburne, "Authority of Scripture, Tradition, and the Church," in The Oxford Handbook of Philosophical Theology, ed. Thomas P. Flint and Michael C. Rea [Oxford: Oxford University Press, 2011], 16).[133]

YEC invites finding "fault with holy scriptures" because the nature of God (per Augustine) *could not in any way at all be taken in a bodily sense that accorded with truth.* Therefore, the YEC's claim that their theological *system* is historical Christian thought is false. Augustine's principle is the historical one. There never was a requirement in the history of the Church to take Genesis literally or to take bodily parts attached to God literally.

God is beyond any human imagery—*any* human imagery, including YEC.

133. William Lane Craig, "In Quest of the Historical Adam: A Biblical and Scientific Exploration," Wm. B. Eerdmans Publishing Co. Grand Rapids Michigan 49546, 2021, 57. For illuminating discussion, see Gavin R. Ortlund, Retrieving Augustine's Doctrine of Creation: Ancient Wisdom for Current Controversy (Downers Grove, IL: IVP Academic, 2020)."

9.
GOD AND ANTHROPOMORPHISMS
PART 2: THE LOW VIEW OF GOD

The fossil record is a graveyard full of…carnivory, suffering, and death … If God had called [that world] "very good," then He either had a cruel sense of irony or didn't know what He was talking about, or worse, he is a liar.
—Dr. Elizabeth Mitchell (AiG)

With the cool, calm calculus of the Tasmanian Devil, Elizabeth Mitchell tears into God for allegedly calling the prehistoric worlds "very good." Mitchell's language is incendiary. She really wants people to take YEC seriously. She failed. To her, God might have a *cruel sense of irony*," or He may be ignorant or worse, *"a liar."* Mitchell happens to blunder here. God did not call the prehistoric world "very good."

She did.

The arrival of modern humans was long after the prehistoric worlds were extinct when God called the resulting world of *modern humans* "very good." God arranged the world for the coming of humanity when the Genesis account of creation ends. Before that, things were in various stages of *good*—without the modifier "very." Today, we know that several prehistoric worlds had long since passed before the advent of Homo Sapiens. All of pre-human history seems prepared for our arrival. Even the original handbook of fundamentalism, written in the early twentieth century, recognized this:

> Geology is felt only to have expanded our ideas of the vastness and marvel of the *Creator's operations through the aeons of time* during which the world, with its teeming populations of fishes, birds, reptiles, mammals, *was preparing for man's abode*-when the mountains were being upheaved, the valleys being scooped out, and veins of precious metals being inlaid into the crust of the earth.[134] (emphasis mine)

The unfinished world was not "very good" since it was not optimal for our flourishing. But those prehistoric worlds were still *good* for some things. For example, the multiple layers of primordial worlds that teemed with life that we see buried in the earth provided a treasure trove of resources such as numerous energy reserves, vast reservoirs of fresh water, precious stones, and metals requiring eons to develop. Of course, Moses would know nothing of those prehistoric worlds, but YErs do. Consequently, it is disingenuous to suggest God is a liar because He might call the prehistoric world good in its context.

---

134. R. A. Torrey, A. C. Dixon, editors, *The Fundamentals, 90 Essays* (1910–1915), Kindle Edition, location 4455 (2013).

God as Liar

A sure sign of naive anthropomorphism is Elizabeth Mitchell suggesting a circumstance where God would be stupid (*"not know what he was talking about"*) or a liar. The flimsier the instance, the more complete the naiveté. This strange impulse among YErs is naïve because it maintains an unreasonably high view of scripture at the expense of a low view of God. God *cannot* lie. Christians should know this. To think otherwise is adolescent— "You lied to me!"

How then do we know that God *cannot* lie? Some might say because "the Bible says so." The Bible does say so: "It is impossible for God to lie" (Hebrews 6:18). Nonetheless, because "the Bible says so" is not the *reason* God cannot lie. The reverse is true: the Bible says so *because* God cannot lie. People like Abraham, who did not have a Bible, learned this.[135]

But how?

A person who lies does so for personal gain, self-protection, or, at best, to protect someone else. Those are impossible motivations for an omnipotent, all-knowing, and eternal God to lie to creatures He has made. The way to know God cannot lie is twofold: by *appreciating* God's nature intellectually and by personally experiencing God's character.

Biblical authors knew by experience that God *would* not lie. Note Numbers 23:19, "God is not human, that he should lie, [or] change his mind. Does he speak and then not act? Does he promise and not fulfill?" These rhetorical questions come from people who had experienced a God that is not human-like and would not be untruthful.

Unlike Elizabeth Mitchell, biblical writers also knew God is all-powerful, all-knowing, and all good and *could* not lie. Sadly, it is possible to call God a liar or accuse someone else of calling God a liar over a simple disagreement on a nonessential. We might look upon Christians who use this tactic with a certain amount of skepticism. They are using a tactic, perhaps reverse psychology, but at God's expense—"If you disagree with us, *you* call God a liar."

Frankly, YEC is not worth it.

Christianity has always defined God's attributes in absolute terms. God has no limits of any kind. Yes, God cannot do the intrinsically impossible, such as creating a married bachelor or a square circle, which are inherently illogical. However, being unable to do the contradictory only sounds like a limitation due to the inadequacies of finite human language. In short, lying denies God's attributes.

Therefore, it is intrinsically impossible for God to lie.

---

135. The pagan pantheons of Abraham's day contained decidedly anthropomorphic gods, some of which were deceptive and perverted. Pagan gods could age and younger gods could defeat them. They could lie and did so and much worse. All this makes Abraham's unswerving faith more noteworthy.

And it is not that God always *chooses* to tell the truth. He is truth. There is no possible world where God could be a liar. The "God is a liar" pretense has nothing to do with errors in cosmology or the age of the earth and certainly not biblical authority; it is about *naive suppositions* on both the nature of God and the Bible. This strange YE eccentricity makes the Bible equal to God, or worse, it subordinates God to the Bible. Isn't it thoughtless for a believer to entertain the possibilities when God might lie? Why would any Christian want to do that?

Christians also believe that Jesus was without sin, such as lying. Yet that does not stop the pretense. Ken Ham writes, "Belief in evolution implies that one does not accept the clear teaching of Jesus and that he was...a liar." And this: "The issue is...can we trust scripture and was Jesus a liar?" And again, "If [the earth is old], then it would undermine the gospel, which a professing Christian claims to believe. The point is that the entire Bible stands or falls on Christ's truthfulness."[136]

All the "liar rhetoric" by YErs really means is that the entire Bible and God Himself stand or fall on YEC. Notice that an OEr is only a "professing Christian that claims to believe [the Gospel]." In other words, your belief in the gospel is questionable if you believe the earth is old. We look more carefully at the connection between YEC and the gospel in "Part V."

Call this rationale what you like; it is not good.

Does the purity of the gospel depend on a young earth? YEC says yes on one side of their mouth, but when called out on that, YErs backpedal and assure people the gospel does not depend on a young earth.[137] Backpedaling on something self-evident is telling in itself. But do YErs really believe if evolution is true, Jesus is a liar, or if the earth is old, God is a liar? Then their faith would depend on a literal Genesis. That does not a Christian make. If "natural explanations" show how God operates in the creation, then "natural explanations" will not be atheistic and should not threaten one's faith. God created nature. Nature does not exist by itself. Instead, those explanations reveal how God operates in the world.

---

136. Bodie Hodge, "Jesus Devastates an Old Earth," January 25, 2018, AiG website.

137. Ken Ham, "Does the Gospel Depend on a Young Earth?" January 1, 2010; November 10, 2013, AiG website. Consider this: Why was there a need to write such an article if the line between the gospel and their nonessential distinctive was clear?

It is possible for the earth to be old and for God to develop life with what we call evolution, while neither God nor His Son is capable of lying.[138] Consequently, many YErs cannot navigate simple questions such as, "If evolution is true, was Jesus lying?" Or is God a liar if YEC is mistaken? As an experiment, I asked a Young Earth group on Facebook the following questions: "If the earth is old, is God a liar, or is the Bible unreliable?"

As of this writing, over a thousand people commented. Except for comments in the single digits that said "yes," the Bible would be unreliable; or "no," it would remain reliable. Almost all evaded the question by refusing to consider the word *if*, using a variation of, "The earth is old, *and* the Bible is reliable."

I pointed out the question is contingent on the words *if* and *then*: "*If* this, *then* what about that?" Almost all comments avoided the "if" in the question like this: "The Bible is reliable because the earth is young" or "The earth is young because the Bible is true." More than a few resented the question as a trick question. To them, the earth cannot be old. Evading the question so strenuously implies the answer: one cannot help but think, for some of them, if the earth is old, God *is* a liar, and the Bible is unreliable. Their faith appears to depend on six literal days. They could not summon Nancy Reagan and "*Just say no.*" This YE attitude shows a severe weakness and naivete in theology.

Keith Ward observes:

Jesus was the finite manifestation of the infinite God, the human "image of the invisible God" (Col. 1:15). He was incapable of sin, though he would feel all those things that incline humans to sin. He would feel the pains that humans feel; he would act in ways limited by the capacities of a human body; and he would be bounded in knowledge by what he experienced and learned in his own culture... Yet what Jesus wills is what God wills in a human mind.[139]

What kind of journey are people traveling who believe God is lying if YEC happens to be wrong? They are saying that YEC cannot be wrong. That is hardly historic Christian teaching. Yet they think God can lie. What kind of Christians think *they* are infallible about something they know almost nothing about or what God did and when? Augustine said, "In matters that are *so obscure*

---

138. I agree with classical Christology that Jesus *could* not lie because He was God made human and because lying is not intrinsic to human nature in its unfallen state. Rather, lying is evidence of contaminated human nature. Jesus's human nature was not fallen. More importantly, Jesus's divinity rules out lying. How one defines or rejects the theology of the fall does not alter this view since the will of Jesus *was* the will of God within the confines of human nature. Keith Ward finishes the thought: "[Jesus's] consciousness could never fall away from God, or rebel against God, or set itself in opposition to God. For it would be God's own consciousness. It would be what things looked like to God from a particular human point of view." See Keith Ward, *The Word of God: The Bible after Modern Scholarship* (SPCK London, 2010), p. 81.

139. Keith Ward, *The Word of God: The Bible after Modern Scholarship* (SPCK London, 2010), p. 82.

and far beyond our vision, we find in Holy Scripture passages which can be interpreted in diverse ways without prejudice to the faith we have received."[140] There are few *obscure* passages beyond our vision than those written in the first or second millennium BC in an ANE language from a lost culture about the primordial past.

If the Bible contains lies, they must be human lies. If the Bible contains mistakes, then literalists have misunderstood the nature of the Bible. The onus is on us either way. It is not a sign of credibility or faithfulness when Christians have so high a view of scripture that effectively reduces God.

The God is a liar delusion comes from people who firmly believe God has spoken to them personally. He brought them into the chamber of truth, and they must be faithful to their privileged place in God's inner circle at all costs. Reformists are not open to rethinking. God has already spoken to them; if it is not true, *God lied.* They have already done all the thinking they are willing to do. The war is on.

Their mission is to reform you.

It Is Personal

Awake, Lord. Why do you sleep? Rouse yourself. Do not reject us forever.
—Psalm 44:23

God is personal and present, but not in the way we are. He is not *physically* or proximately present, meaning His presence is not material, so it is not in time or space. Most of us have thought at one time that God is right there next to us or that He is "up there," but we cannot see Him. But He is not *there, anywhere,* strictly speaking. God is the one reference where "There is no there, *there,"* and it would be true since there isn't any spatial kind of "there" "where" He would occupy. Therefore, God is not material and not in any location in any visible or invisible way.

In reality, God makes us present to Him "in spirit." The expression "in spirit" describes a different dimension where the human spirit and the Holy Spirit have some union. All spirit is necessarily a different reality than the physical realm. In other words, our bodies are in time and space, but spirit is not. The connection is analogous to a TV screen picking up a worldwide broadcast. God communicates to us through spiritual means in a similar way.

Anthropomorphisms make God seem "up close and personal" in the human sense. The human presence is the only kind of tangible presence we know. Anthropomorphism is the primary way to communicate with each other about a personal God. Otherwise, we could not say very much about God. We could not say much about God's plan or His work in the world through the

---

140. Allister McGrath, 2009 Gifford Lectures, published as "A Fine-Tuned Universe: The Quest for God in Science and Theology" (Westminster, John Knox).

Church without describing Him in terms we readily understand: "God spoke to me," "God opened doors for the Gospel," "God *carried* me through," or the extreme, "God *wrote the Bible.*"

Note the verbs. Descriptions of God in actions like these are often anthropomorphic. Other acts of God, such as creating the universe, and judging Sodom and Gomorrah, are closer to literal statements about God's activities, even if God had Sodom and Gomorrah destroyed through an agent without doing it Himself. God's actions are about His operations in the universe, whether through nature, mediation, or human agency. Like a King, God orders His subjects to carry out His will. Even human kings rarely fill their own orders. The king's role is to cast the vision. That's what makes them kings.

While our anthropomorphisms fall short of reality, they have practical usefulness. Unlike the impersonal, austere, and sometimes twisted pagan deities, Yahweh is a "lover." In the Hebrew Bible, God is like a "husband" and Israel a "bride." God is quoted saying:

> I came by again and saw you, saw that you were ready for love and a lover. I took care of you, dressed you, and protected you. I promised you my love and entered the covenant of marriage with you. I, God, the Master, gave my word. You became mine. (Ezekiel 16:8 MSG)

That is about as personal as our language gets. But is it accurate?

Yes and no. It is not literally true or historically accurate, i.e., Israel neither married Yahweh nor became His lover. Nonetheless, that extraordinary language highlights Yahweh's uniqueness, who, unlike pagan gods, did not have a consort. Yahweh is not sexual. This language is doubtless metaphorical. Yet the language of lovers elevates humanity's worth beyond anything known in the pagan near east. Humans are God's "consort"—not physically but *metaphysically.*

The imagery of husband and wife is even more potent in the New Testament. The fulfillment of God's plan appears as a metaphysical "wedding" between the Incarnate Christ and the glorified Church (see Revelation 19:7, 9). This metaphor represents a necessary step in the union of all things to God since Jesus is one with God, and the marriage of the Lamb draws humans into a comprehensive union with God through or in Christ. The Gospel is to spread to the human family as a wedding invitation goes out to all the families (Matthew 24:14). Everyone is invited. Weddings in Jewish custom brought two families together as one. This Hebrew imagery of the first century AD represents cosmic events in the spiritual union of divinity and humanity.

There are several other relational metaphors in the New Testament. God is Father to every Christian by a spiritual rebirth and to all humans by physical birth in creation. However, God heightened that relationship by adopting Christians as children in His family for eternity (Romans 8:15). Jesus is also called our Captain, High Priest, and Master. He calls us "friends."

We are "betrothed" to Him, and at the same time, He is our Brother. Why so many terms?

No single word fully expresses our intimacy with God, so all are used. But, of course, it is unreasonable to take these relations literally. Biblical authors describe our relationship to God with a myriad of human terms that, at face value, are absurd. All authors expect their intended audience to "get it" without having to explain the metaphors.

The point of this language is to show that God is intimate and personal. Our relationship with Him is without adequate description, illustrating that God's personhood is unlike any person we comprehend. Consequently, metaphors are indispensable and cautionary. *Figurative does not mean false; instead, it suggests resemblance.* The love of God for His simple created creatures is beyond any love we know. Therefore, we cannot express it fully. Biblical authors such as Ezekiel used language that expresses the highest love we know with an ancient kind of romanticism—God is a lover.

According to Genesis, God's opening creative act was, "Let there be light." God does not speak like us in a language like Hebrew, which is especially absurd when there were no Hebrews or the Canaanite precursors to what we call the Hebrew language. There were no humans at all. God does not have a voice box, larynx, tongue, or lungs that "breathed" into Adam. He can make Himself known to us without sound or written words, which is the nature of spiritual unions.

God does not see with eyeballs in front of a skull. God's vision does not depend on reflected light. He "sees" every sub-particle in the universe at once. Proverbs 15:3 says, *"The eyes of the Lord are everywhere, keeping watch on the wicked, and the good."* His "eyes" are not *eyes* fixated in place. Human eyes are like real estate—location, location, location. God is not located in one place to witness the sun going down or rising. God's "eyes" are universal, which means they are not eyes.

God does not experience evening and morning as we do. Time, space, and matter are in His grasp and under His influence, not the other way around. Though God is beyond everything we can name, think, or understand, God's being does not sit beside the world, looking at it from the outside. Instead, He is operating upon everything in every moment. "The God who made the world and everything in it is the Lord of heaven and earth... 'For in him we live and move and have our being.' In the past, God overlooked such ignorance, but now he commands all people everywhere to repent" (Acts 17:24–29).

Moreover, God is present to us more than we are to each other. But the word *presence* is earthbound and inadequate because we understand it in a three-dimensional sense. Nonetheless, *presence* is the best word our language provides us. Though God is without time or space, He is in the immaterial substance of those whose bodies are in time and space, that is, spiritually.

God impacts our world without existing in it or His essence occupying it. "To occupy" is a spatial term, meaning to occupy space. Only matter—i.e., solids, liquids, gases, and plasma—extend in space. That cannot apply to incorporeality. Nonetheless, God impacts everything. How? By not being limited by anything.

Since God sees all things all the time, there would be no dark side of the moon for Him. The moon's *dark side* has meaning only for creatures who need light to bounce off the surface of objects to observe them. God does not speak one word at a time. God hears all our prayers simultaneously without ears and answers them at once, and nobody hears a thing. Veteran Christians ought to know all these things. Of course, God did not say, "Let there be light" in Hebrew or any other human language, yet God is not without speech of any kind. So what is an ancient author to do?

The author expresses it in the only way available to him—imaginatively.

Denying Anthropomorphisms

In an attempt to neutralize the anthropomorphisms in Genesis 1, Todd Beall writes:

> Yet even understanding the occasional use of anthropomorphic language [in scripture], how does that relate to our understanding of the days of Genesis 1? Anthropomorphisms *usually* take the form of a *body part or organ or movement to describe God's actions*, but they *never* take the form of a unit of time such as a day."[141] (emphasis mine)

Note some interesting things in this statement.

Beall's phrases "Yet even" and "the occasional use of" appear to mean *even if* there were a few anthropomorphisms, here or there, in scripture, etc. Beall seems to believe he is being generous by accepting the "occasional" anthropomorphism despite the *extensive* use of them in Genesis and throughout the Bible. Anthropomorphisms are unavoidable when they take on the form of—notice Beall's own words, *"movement to describe God's actions."* A human's movements and actions do not occur in a vacuum; they only occur in time-space. A daily schedule of activity for God described in Hebraic terms, meaning between sunup and sundown, complete with labor and Sabbatical rest, is decidedly anthropomorphic.

Beall asserts another YE rule that *only* body parts are used in anthropomorphisms while inserting the ambiguous *"usually."* In other words, Beall is claiming that since anthropomorphic images *usually* employ body parts, they can *"never* take the form of a unit of time." What about "Father Time" or "Old

141. Coming to Grips with Genesis," p. 159.

Man time," and "time will tell"? Shakespeare's Sonnet 19 is a personification of time.[142]

Beall once again does not think through his YE presuppositions. Beall believes interpreters anthropomorphized the days when the point is that days anthropomorphize God as in one of His names—the "Ancient of Days" (Daniel 7:9, 13, 22). God is not ancient, and He has no days. "Ancient of Days" is a Hebraism. Beall commits a factual error since *no one personifies the days of Genesis.*

It is anthropomorphic to use days to govern God's behavior or mimic human actions during the day. To further anthropomorphize God in the narrative, the author ends the first six days of creating with God saying, in today's vernacular, "That's pretty good." The point here is that twenty-four-hour days rule earthly creatures, i.e., their *daily activities.* That is not possible with God. Remember, Genesis says the sun *rules* the day and the moon the night. So are we to believe that God creates the sun and moon and then *regulates Himself by* them? Beall's use of *"usually and never"* exposes his mistake on what the author anthropomorphizes: i.e., God, not time.

Furthermore, authors do personify *time* as: "Father Time," "hands of time," "running out of time," "the day that time stood still," "time heals all wounds," and "these are crazy times." A literal reading of Genesis 1 humanizes God in how the author organizes "God's time" as a limited craftsman in his daily labor. God sees the sunrise—time to go to "work," which consists of speaking a few words in His case. When God sees the sun go down, it is time to end his day. That illustrates finitude, not unlimited being.

Some of the movements given to God in Genesis 1 are humanlike because they operate in time-space governance and because much of God's "supplied perspective" on time is that of a human. God is up at dawn and retires at night when the sun enters the underworld. On the actual earth, sunrise and sunset are continuous, so God does not need to stop His activity at some localized sunset. God appears to perceive the world as a three-tiered universe. The sun sets under the earth for six nights, singling God to end his day, limiting him to a place, and point in time, the only way to experience sunrise and sunset in our universe.

Sunrise and sunset were essential in Jewish theology since they governed the liturgy of weekly and annual Sabbaths. In a literary sense, the author presents Elohim as the Hebrew God when he places Him inside the Hebrew

---

142. "Devouring Time" is his name, and he wears down all creatures. But the poet draws a line between his lover and time. He will not allow "Devouring Time" to carve his artwork on his love's aging face. He writes:

I forbid thee one most heinous crime...
Do thy worst old Time: despite thy wrong,
My love shall *in my verse* ever live young.

The poet says that time shall stand still for "my love," through his verse.

workweek. Such figurative language and figures of speech are rhetorical devices that can make arguments more persuasive; it presses the point, making it stick in readers' minds, enabling them to empathize with the characters and drive readers to think differently about the issues.[143]

With the ordinary Hebrew workweek, the author argues that Yahweh Elohim is the real God of creation and, more importantly, the Creator is the focus of daily life in Israel. He has a purpose for all humanity. Using Israel's ordinary workweek metaphorically is far more persuasive and dramatic than just stating the point bluntly, e.g., "Our God is the true God." Okay, that's it then. Well, no, that is not it.

He might have aged a week if God actually experienced sunrise and sunset. The Jewish consciousness of sunrise and sunset is in the musical *Fiddler on the Roof*:

Sunrise sunset,

Sunrise sunset,

Swiftly fly the years,

One season following another,

Laden with happiness and tears.[144]

God is not Jewish. In the ANE, the earth was a large piece of land surrounded by oceans with irregular mountains and valleys and not a sphere. People believed at sunset that the entire universe was without sunlight. At night, the sun entered the underworld and "rose" in the opposite end of the universe (the east). We know the sun is neither east nor west since it is millions of miles away, and the earth is an imperceptible sphere relative to billions of lightyears across a universe. East and west are human perceptions of reality. If one knew nothing of astronomy, sunlight and darkness would appear to come and go in the whole universe.

The author of Genesis did not know any of this, which a careful reading shows.

We know that the earth's rotation *continuously* distributes day and night upon the earth and only as a finite creature perceives it. Night on earth is not night above or beyond our world. It can never be nighttime for God. Genesis states that God created day and night, so He does not live, move, or have His being in them.

---

143. Lindsay Kramer, "What is Rhetoric, and Why is it Important," January 26, 2022, Writing Tips from Grammarly.

144. Music by Jerry Bock, lyrics by Sheldon Harnick. The play is an adaptation of a series of stories by Sholem Aleichem, written in Yiddish, between 1894 and 1914 about Jewish life in a village in the Pale of Settlement of Imperial Russia at the turn of the twentieth century.

We understand that "day and night" are metaphors for time's passage and happen to be relative. A day's length varies on every planet throughout the universe without considering any light and darkness between solar systems and galaxies. Day and night (days, in other words) are meaningless to God's nature when taken literally (see 2 Peter 3:8).

Nahum Sarna writes:

Nowhere [in the ANE] is this brought out more forcefully than in the Hebrew Genesis account. Here we find no physical link between the world of humanity and the world of the divine. There is no natural connection between the Creator and his handiwork... The God of Creation is eternally existent, removed from all corporeality, and independent of time and space.[145]

God transcends "*all corporeality.*"

Sarna sees any subtle or unavoidable anthropomorphisms that human language may impose on an author in such a context and concludes: "There is no *natural connection* between the Creator and his handiwork." Therefore, the days of Genesis orient *humans* to the story and not God to the days of the week. Granted, Genesis 1 is less anthropomorphic than chapters 2–3 because it intends to capture God's full transcendence that differentiates Him from ANE gods. Nonetheless, as we have seen, Genesis 1 is not without anthropomorphic pictures.

The gods of the ANE were continuous with the universe; they operated within it. Hence, they were part of the universe. They had a geographical locus. Yahweh is not geographical and did not live in the Holy of Holies, or any temple, even Eden.

Jesus said:

Believe me, a time is coming when you will worship the Father neither on this mountain nor in Jerusalem...a time is coming and has now come when the true worshipers will worship the Father in the Spirit and in truth, for they are the kind of worshipers the Father seeks. God is spirit, and his worshipers must worship in the Spirit and in truth (John 4:21–24; emphasis mine).

A geographical God is the sort of ignorance that Paul says God no longer overlooks (Acts 17:24, 30). According to Paul, references to God in time-space, e.g., living in a temple location, must be metaphoric or ignorant. These include anthropomorphism, mediations using angels, and theophanies. One example is God, who did not voice the Law given at Mt. Sinai as written. Instead, according to Stephen in Acts, God delivered the Law through angels: "You [Jews]

---

145. Nahum M. Sarna, *Understanding Genesis (The Heritage of Biblical Israel)* (Varda Books, Skokie Illinois, 1966), p. 11.

have received *the law that was given through angels* but have not obeyed it" (Acts 7:53–56; see also Hebrews 2:2).

YEC minimizes God's nature. YErs confuse their commitment to literalism with faithfulness but minimizing God's attributes is not faithfulness. The YE priority is elevating a doctrinal distinctive based solely on their understanding of scripture when the ultimate purpose of the Bible is God's self-disclosure, not six literal days, the historicity of Genesis 1–11, or the Bible's self-disclosure. Revelation is more than accumulating factual data or propositions forged from the Bible.

Beall's argument looks like this:

Premise 1: Anthropomorphisms in scripture are "usually" body parts.

Premise 2: Scripture "never" uses anthropomorphisms for days or time.

Conclusion: Therefore, God labored during six literal days.

Premise 1 is not accounted for in Beall's conclusion that says nothing about body parts. The first premise is also irrelevant, and the word *usually* is ambiguous. The anthropomorphisms in chapter 1 may be subtler than those in chapter 2; nonetheless, it takes body parts to perform many of the tasks described in Genesis 1. For example, audible speech in a material universe requires sound waves, a larynx, and a tongue to create them. It is justified only when a bodily creature's ears are around to receive sound waves. Vision requires eyes connected to a brain to perceive light reflected off objects.[146]

Other anthropomorphisms include God evaluating His work, the work/rest cycle, and more, conforming to a craftsman's skilled labor. *The clearest and more literal statement is in Genesis 1:1: "God created the heavens and the earth." The rest of the chapter animates that point by creating a seven-day narrative with theological and religious purposes, namely Hebraizing creation and its creator.*

Genesis 2 adds *personal touches* to show that God's prime interest in creation is intimacy with humans. There you find God has "hands" for planting seeds and forming Adam, "breath" for breathing life in him, a "surgical" procedure on Adam to make Eve, "feet" for walking in the cool of the day, "sowing" garments to cover their nakedness, savoring the aroma of barbeque, and so on. The personal touch shows that God is imminent as a Father in addition to being transcendent as a Creator.

We have already seen Premise 2 as an assumption without justification because authors can anthropomorphize time, such as "Father Time." We saw

---

146. The expression "And God saw that it was good" loses all meaning if taken literally. It assumes God realizes he did a good job once He completes something as a human artisan might. Instead, the work is good because it is suitable for His crowning jewel, the humans He is about to create, and not for God's self-esteem or His reputation as a builder. The language implies God has something special in mind for humankind.

one of God's names is *"The Ancient of Days."* He is not called the *"Ancient of Twenty-Four-Hour Days."*

More importantly, time is not the object of anthropomorphisms in Genesis 1. Instead, *time provides a context and a vehicle for anthropomorphism.* God does not expend energy in the form of labor, nor does He recoup energy resting at night and on Saturdays, and since literal work and rest require body parts operating in time-space, it must be figurative.

Denying legitimate anthropomorphisms also denies God's attributes.

Beall's conclusion is hopeless, yet he is confident because he has words interpreted literally.

YErs believe an instant creation that continuously unfolds, illustrated by the singularity/Big Bang dynamic, reduces God's greatness and denies His Word. Yet that dynamic shows God grounds the universe and its subsequent unfolding. Compare that to creating things one at a time by taking six daytime shifts, retiring at night, and a day off. A developing world like ours is in a continuous unfolding state. That is to say, creating continues. An embryo is a new creation given everything it needs to develop dramatically, then replicate. This happens within nature's laws that God sustains continuously. Could the cosmic singularity be similar? Might the singularity be something of an embryonic universe?

According to YEC reasoning, people today are not special creations because God did not make us "by hand." But since He made the first human by hand, we are somehow "grandfathered in." Yet, contrary to that reasoning, YErs do believe God created each of us despite our development that *evolves* from conception, gestation, and birth.

A human and a universe continue to develop after birth and until death. We don't usually think of a God of the gaps in the womb or that God is making adjustments since genetic disabilities occur. Jesus said, "Neither this man nor his parents sinned, but this happened so that the works of God might be displayed in him" (John 9:3). That does not say God allows every birth anomaly to reveal His works. But in this particular case, Jesus was to use this man's circumstance to identify the Messiah, the Son of God.

A superior creative act is to make humans that procreate rather than make them one at a time in assembly-line fashion. Jesus's human nature was born naturally—that is, by conception, gestation, and birth, even given the Incarnation. The nature of a physical creature is that it must replicate to continue. Are YErs saying that Jesus's body is inferior to Adam's? Do they think Jesus's body was lower than Adam's because Jesus was born of a woman? They wouldn't say that.

God did not work for billions of years, six days, or any time at all.

Time and the universe seem to exist simultaneously and so developed. Per Augustine, the universe came at once like a "singularity" when God seeded it. Time, space, and matter/energy depend on each other for existence. Like cells depend on all their parts to exist, the universe could not be created one section at a time, as YEC and ANE cosmology asserts. The universe is too fine-tuned and interdependent for that. It must develop like a human at conception, i.e., all together as one.

Think about it.

Were you made one section at a time? Or did you grow at once? You began on the cellular level, and everything needed to be you residing in *that cell* made it a personal singularity. By analogy, the universe was "born" and continues to grow. Christianity teaches that God upholds and sustains all things continuously; otherwise, nothing could exist. Aquinas, and others before him, considered contingent existence a metaphysical phenomenon that must depend on the self-existent as an essential aspect of creation.

The notion that God *literally* rested or *ceased* to create after day six is not quite right. Many get around an eternal all-powerful God needing rest by using the term "ceased" instead. He just stopped. But that solves one problem and creates another. Of course, God does not tire. Yet, starting and stopping, otherwise called motion, is Newtonian physics regarding material things. The thing that ceased is the account of the beginning, as told in Genesis, not to comment literally on God's ongoing creative acts. The universe appears finished or static, and there was no reason to think otherwise in the Late Bronze Age even up until the 1960s, which scientific consensus claimed. Instead, God's rest in Genesis is a theological statement with profound meaning we explore in chapters 29-30.

God neither rests *nor ceases* in reality.

So why does Genesis present creation as finished? Because that is how it appeared to the author. God saw no need to correct *irrelevant and harmless* assumptions that are authentic for the day instead of forcing an author to write something no one understood. An authentic account with irrelevant misunderstandings has more integrity than a contrived account that secures useless facts.

The Genesis account could not be about the actual state of the universe. It's about Israel's God. The universe looked static to all people until Edwin Hubble discovered an expanding universe in the late 1920s. That was a shock. The CMB found in the 1960s was a further shock and sealed the deep age of the universe. Like the sun that appears to rise and set, the creation seems settled. The language in Genesis is phenomenological or observational, not scientific.

To believe otherwise is not realistic or necessary.

The Bible says in several places that the earth does not move. Why? Because that is how it feels. Their so-called "science" was experiential, not analytical. What ceased in the story is evident throughout Genesis 1. What God ceased to create on day two, God already made on day one; what ceased on day three, God already created on days one and two; and so on. What God created on day eight was not made during "Creation Week," nor is it mentioned in Genesis; yet new life, stars, and galaxies continue to come into existence. The creation *account* in Genesis ceased in its literary setting, but all creating did not end. You and I are proof of that.

Jesus said, "My Father *is always at his work* to this very day, and I too am working" (John 5:17). God's chief work is creation and redemption, which have to do with creating. The first creation is about this universe; redemption is about *recreating* the universe anew. God never ceases. Besides, creation is not *only*, or even primarily, about how things began but how they can exist and continue to exist. God sustains the universe by upholding it or being its ground for existence, and He is imminent in that occupation.

A creation that unfolds over time does not mean God needed extra time. On the contrary, God wanted a dynamic, expanding universe. It is developing now and will throughout eternity in a new heaven and earth. Furthermore, God wanted us to emerge from within an environment suitable for our flourishing, which gives us a connection to the universe and meaningful identity. The secondary causes in the universe are like the developing life of a human embryo — both are spectacular.

God underwrites our creation at conception *and* upholds our development afterward. It is not that everything that happens is God's will, but God willed the range of possibilities available in this universe, so the outcome is ultimately within His will and according to plan. Conception is the creation of a living being. God ordained a biological process, yet biology is not the cause of life. Indeed, God created us in Almighty fashion *with biology*.

While secondary causes result from an unfolding creation, YErs believe the Big Bang is the devil's plan to deceive the world into rejecting six literal days even though people like Augustine rejected six literal days long ago and knew nothing of the Big Bang.

Nonetheless, consider three ideas:

1. Presenting God literally in and under time-space denies His necessary attributes. Time and space are created things and cannot be controlling factors looking over God's shoulders.

2. Taking no time to create the universe, suggested by the Big Bang, is consistent with God's attributes. That is why Augustine proposed an instant creation with the "seeds for life" gradually unfolding. In any case, time is irrelevant to initial creation except as a created thing since God is timeless and spaceless.

3. The Big Bang theory says that an infinitesimal and infinitely dense point of light and heat was an "embryonic" universe called the singularity. A perfect calculus between expansion and gravity created and spread all time-space and matter/energy in this universe. As far as the theory goes, the singularity came from nothing since nothing in

the universe had yet to exist. Some scientists suggest the possibility that the singularity was not physical. Yet the universe was every bit in existence as a human is at conception. Both develop. This process (a finished product from a seedling) has a divine signature. That is not to say the Big Bang must be a brute fact; it means that the Big Bang is not the devil's plan to destroy the Bible. Instead, it shows the universe had a beginning—a major victory for Christian thought.

Literalism on point 1—that God was governed by the flow of time when He created time—or worse, "*while*" He created time—is incoherent. Number 2 is consistent with God's attributes and is an infinitely grander creation event than the literalized "paint by numbers" concept in YEC, where God manufactures us like carmakers make cars or a kind of cosmic Giuseppe assembling a race of animated clay Pinocchios.

Instead, God made us through a natural process that He also created to give us genuine identity.

Notice this YE declaration: "Man was directly handmade by God."[147] "Handmade" in YE circles is supposed to be a more impressive creative act, but the opposite is true. First, we have the well-known biblical phrase, *"Not made with hands,"* which contrasts God's creative action with that of humans (2 Corinthians 5:1). God does not hand-make anything since he has no hands. Human beings are not a piece of furniture. One primary distinction between modern humans and hominids is self-awareness, i.e., personal awareness and identity, higher abstract reasoning power, and language. God wanted our identity to be genuine. Our natural birth into an actual world with continuity and history gives our identity an authentic context and personal authenticity.

Being manufactured does not.

Furthermore, Christians see themselves as participating in the creation of their children. We *procreate*. We understand that God makes this possible. We believe God created us through this natural process, which is superior to assembling us with manufactured parts, including "batteries." Predestination is compatible with the Big Bang, too. Indeed, the ingredients for life were already in the mysterious singularity billions of years before we arrived, as Augustine suggested. God appears to have seeded (predestined?) most if not everything in the singularity. The Big Bang unleashed it all.

Here is what I'm getting at. God became human and laid down his life, *not* for something He manufactured, any more than a manufacturer would lay down his life for a car or a robot. God is infinitely greater than us than our superiority over robots. We do not consider our children manufactured. However, in a natural or genuine world, ordained by God, parents would sacrifice themselves

---

147. See the online Doctrinal Statement of Justin Peters Ministries on the subject "Man."

for the sake of their children, whom they *procreated* because children are genuine persons. We do not have that kind of love for manufactured things.

No matter how sophisticated a manufactured thing is, laying down one's life for it is not love but obsession.

God chose a way to create free will beings from a natural living process into a real world, thereby increasing our worth. We were not "manufactured." A certain amount of randomness is necessary for each of us to be unique, or we would all be exactly the same, even more than so-called "identical twins." Each of us is a distinct person in our own right, not products in an inventory. In that way, we are like God. Far from diminishing our status as legitimate persons, God saw our birth within the natural world He also created for our "incubation." It is this realism out of nothing that makes creation an absolute miracle.

God sacrificed His unique Son not for manufactured objects but for a real family. Jesus Christ is the "firstborn" of a *new kind of family*— *the union of God and Man.* Our familial relationship with God is now in Christ and dependent on him (see Galatians 6:10; Ephesians 3:15; 1 Thessalonians 4:10; Hebrews 2:11; 1 Peter 2:17; 1 Peter 5:9).

If "forming" Adam from clay as an adult is a superior creative act than to be born "of a woman," then was Jesus in some sense inferior to the biblical Adam? Do YErs ever stop and consider that Jesus (the new and better "Adam") had to be born through a natural process to be fully human, participate in the flow of history, to be genuine? If Adam was an immediate adult, he had no development from childhood, no guidance, or the formation necessary to be an experienced adult human. Just because the Bible words it that way doesn't make it literal.

The superior intelligence often assigned to Adam by fundamentalists could not include experiences vital for making sound judgments. If God created Adam with built-in knowledge and experiences, God would be more responsible for Adam's actions. If *all humans* "inherited" sin and biological death through Adam, would not the righteousness of Christ that removes sin also remove natural death for *all humans*?

Yet, it is appointed to all humans to die the natural death of the body— "People are destined to die once" (Hebrews 9:27). *Destined* is a strong word; it implies that God ordained natural death. 1 Corinthians 15:45-48 says, "So it is written: "The first man Adam became a living being," the last Adam, a life-giving spirit... *The first man was of the dust of the earth*; the second man is of heaven. As was the earthly man, so are those who are of the earth."* Paul adds, *"For this perishable body must put on imperishability, and this mortal body must put on immortality."* verse 53, (NRSV). Adam was not a superior being among humans but was the same as we are, or we could not be his descendants. DNA proves we are all related.

1 Corinthians 15: 45-48, 53 is definitive: Adam died as all mortals must.

The first Adam was of the earth, mortal, natural, made of dust; the New Adam is of heaven and spiritual (1 Corinthians 15:42–49). "So will it be with the resurrection of the dead. The body that is sown is perishable, it is raised imperishable...it is sown a natural body, it is raised a spiritual body." (1 Corinthians 15:42–44). According to Paul, a natural death for the natural body seems to be unrelated to sin. The first death is also temporal or of the body and must undergo an ontological transformation into a new kind of body in a new order. The point is that dogmatic literalizing can lead to oddities.

Perhaps the New Adam did lift the curse. He became a "curse" for us and solved the only relevant curse—spiritual death or eternal destruction: "Christ redeemed us from the curse of the law by becoming a curse for us, for it is written: "Cursed is everyone who is hung on a pole" (Galatians 3:13). And there are these statements of Jesus: "Very truly I tell you, whoever hears my word and believes him who sent me has eternal life and will not be judged but *has crossed over from death to life*" (John 5:24); "But here is the bread that comes down from heaven, which anyone may eat *and not die*" (John 6:50).

Notice Luke 9:27 says, "there are certain of those here standing, who shall not taste of death till they may see the reign of God" (Young's Literal Translation). This language, especially in John 5:54 on not dying, is an idiom similar to Genesis, where God says to the first couple, "In the day that you eat of it, you *shall certainly die*." It is similar but in reverse—Jesus says believers *surely won't die,* that is, until glory in the kingdom when we shed the bodies we currently possess. The sense in these two expressions is the opposite of what appears to happen. That suggests spiritual life is the referent in both cases, not biological life.

The following deductive argument sums up the last two chapters:

1. All anthropomorphic pictures of God are figurative.
2. The Hebrew workweek for God with daily labor and nightly rest followed by a Sabbatical rest is anthropomorphic.[148]
3. Therefore, this Hebrew "workweek" for God is figurative.

The genre of Genesis is not the only consideration in determining whether the six days are literal or figurative. This detail is vital to hermeneutics— *God's essential nature is unaffected by the genre.* Still, this does not mean the earth is old. Nonetheless, it does mean that Genesis 1 is more figurative than YErs are willing to admit, and that the earth's age is indeterminate from the Bible. Consequently, the genealogies of Genesis 5 are no help to YEC.

God is utterly beyond human nature. Words cannot narrow the gulf that exists between God and humanity. C. S. Lewis wrote:

---

148 And since an unending 7th day supports Hebrews 3-4 and Augustine's claim that the days are not literal.

Man, after all, is the highest of the things we meet in sensuous experience...it is not unreasonable to suppose that we are less unlike [God] than anything else we know. No doubt, we are unspeakably different from Him; to that extent, all man-like images [of God] are false.[149]

Notice Lewis's compound negative language— *"not unreasonable...*that we are *less unlike"*—eloquently or unartfully (take your pick) demonstrates the difficulty of comparing the nature of God to ourselves with words. Scripture warns us about using anything to represent God, including human attributes, except in a figurative sense.

The figurative sense that words carry is critical to biblical passages describing God in detail.

Today, we think of ourselves as more sophisticated than the ancients; we would never worship a graven image. But we are in a spiritual age, i.e., we worship God in spirit and truth. We understand that God resides in our conscience, so idolatry becomes more sophisticated than worshipping hand-carved images. As Lewis wrote above, *"All man-like images of God are false,"* whether carved from wood, stone, or *words.*

---

149. C. S. Lewis, *Miracles,* revised edition (2009), p. 118.

10.
GOD IN THE ANCIENT NEAR EAST

Scripture is our only credible source of information about Creation...
God Himself was the only eyewitness to the event.
We can either believe what he says or reject it.
—John MacArthur[150]

YEC presupposes that Genesis 1–2 is God's personal creation account. God was *there* at the beginning, and Genesis 1 is a virtual excerpt from His "diary" given directly to Moses. As MacArthur stated, *"We can either believe what he says or reject it."* In other words, arguing against YEC is arguing against God. With this claim, YErs attempt to bind their interpretation on Christians. Yet Genesis has curious similarities to other ANE literature, including some that go unnoticed by all sides in the SDWC.

Interestingly, ANE and Jewish traditions appear in the Genesis account that did not exist at the beginning of time. So the question then becomes, If the creation is God's story in His own words about what happened in real-time, how could it contain ANE and Jewish traditions that did not exist until an untold number of centuries later?

What to make of this, and how do YErs answer?

Students of the Old Testament know that significant differences exist between ANE accounts of creation with the Genesis account. Skeptics of the Bible overstate the similarities while many YErs *dismiss* them entirely. Some similarities are striking.

Pagan creation stories can include the number "six," which was significant in Mesopotamia. The Babylonians, for instance, considered it a perfect number. Six is divisible by all its parts. Thus, six equals two threes, three twos, six ones, and one six. The divisions within the number six come full circle. Consequently, the Babylonians based their numbering system not on ten as ours, but sixty or six.

The Hebrew and Babylonian flood stories differ in how many days it rained—forty days and forty nights in the Hebrew account—six days and nights of rain in the Babylonian version. "Forty" is repeated twice for emphasis (*forty* days and *forty* nights). Forty is a significant number in Judaism, indicating God's providence and a time of testing. The Babylonian flood story says it rained for *six* days *and six* nights; that account repeats the number six for similar theological reasons. In both versions, fountains of the deep burst open, engulfing the

---

150. *Coming to Grips with Genesis*, p. 12.

surface, and "floodgates" from above the skies released their waters, filling the valleys up to the mountaintops.

Chaos returned as Nahum Sarna writes:

> The very word *mabbul*, translated "Flood," is now recognized as having denoted originally the heavenly, or upper, part of the cosmic ocean. "The fountains of the great deep" are none other than the primeval sea. In other words, the Deluge is directly connected with Creation. It is, in fact, the exact reversal of it. The two halves of the primordial waters of chaos which God separated as a primary stage in the creative process, were in danger of reuniting. To the Bible, the Flood is a cosmic catastrophe.[151]

The author connects the deluge with the waters at creation, and animals play a significant part in both events. Noah is something of a new Adam, and all life gets a new beginning. Food distribution repeats but with explicit permission to consume animal flesh—the mandate to "Be fruitful, and multiply, and replenish the earth" repeats.

Sarna's significant point is that *"The very word mabbul, translated "Flood," is now recognized as having denoted originally the heavenly, or upper, part of the cosmic ocean."* It signifies the upper waters *beyond* the day and night skies, not something *in* the sky like clouds. YErs are reluctant to admit any ANE comparisons with Genesis. At the same time, many YErs overemphasize a *six-day creation 6,000 years ago* and virtually ignore or dismiss the importance of the seventh day.

Besides Yahweh, the seventh day is the only significant theological difference among other ANE creation accounts. The exclusive focus on the number six gives YEC a Babylonian numerical twist (*six days, 6,000 years ago*) when the prime revelation of creation week is the true God (Yahweh Elohim) and His plan found in the meaning of the seventh day (see chapters 29-30). That alienates the YE position on creation week from the biblical record. Without elevating the seventh day to its proper place, YEC fails to rise above what Babylonian reference points to which the author of Genesis 1 alludes and to appreciate the theological significance of *seven* days.

In Genesis 1, the six days are in two blocks of threes: days one to three and days four to six. The first three days prepare water, sky, and land; the next three days fill those spaces with suitable life forms. The number three shows up in a parallel of twos, and twos are in a parallel of threes.[152] Any commentary

---

151. Nahum M. Sarna, *Understanding Genesis (The Heritage of Biblical Israel)*, Jewish Theological Seminary (New York, Varda Books, Skokie, Illinois, 1966), p. 55.

152. Another example that reinforces the number six is that *three times,* God separates (divides) parts of the creation in twos: light from darkness, the dividing of the upper and lower waters makes room for the sky or expanse, and the separating of land from sea. Three separations into two are more sixes.

would show that the construction of the six days in Genesis revolves around the number six and its numerological characteristics. This literary form gives the Genesis account symmetry similar to architectural designs of the ancient world.[153]

The seventh day is the foundation for the structure, as in a building like a temple. At the risk of overstating it, Genesis 1:1 is like a capstone.

When God created the heavens and earth

Day 1	Creation of Light separates The darkness	Day 4	Creation of luminaries that carry the light
Day 2	Separation of waters from sky	Day 5	Creation of marine life and birds
Day 3	Land (earth) is separated from waters	Day 6	Creation of land animals and humans

God rests on the seventh day and sanctifies it

God's nature sits beyond creation and six days. Besides Yahweh and the highly theological 7th day suggestive of God's plan, the six days are at home in virtually any other ANE creation account. The 7th day separates Genesis from other accounts because it uniquely identifies Yahweh by pointing to His covenant people. The creation account appears to "rest" on the 7th day. The six days served their purpose and are now in the background, and the significance of the number seven dominates the entire account in ways not apparent at first glance in English.

---

153. Similar literary structures of an architectural design are in the Psalms. Bruce Waltke has analyzed Psalm 44, a prayer fashioned after the design structure of a ziggurat (a Babylonian stepped pyramid probably referred to as the Tower of Babel in Genesis 11:4). Waltke lays out this stunning design in the Psalm:

"The symmetry of [Psalm 44] shows that there...are actually *ten lines* of *Hebrew* poetry [not in English] within verses 1–8. Then in verses 9–16, we have *eight lines* of Hebrew poetry. We then have *six lines* in the protest from verses 17–22. [Next] the petition gives us *four lines* of Hebrew poetry. *Thus, we have ten lines, eight lines, six lines, and four lines. I don't think that this is accidental... I see serenity and composure in the shape of a ziggurat; like a step pyramid. The ten lines represent that higher part of the walls made up of the larger base and then the eight lines represent a smaller section of the walls on top of the first section and the again the next six and four lines represent smaller section on top of each other.* So the Psalm rises up like a ziggurat, and only when the poet has come to the top most flight does he raise up his prayer to God in a climactic moment representing [his] petition at the end. This is an overall outline of the Psalm."

This literary ziggurat built on ten, eight, six, and four lines from foundation to peak with a petition sent up to God [as a capstone]. This is a Psalm of Lament over captivity in Babylon in the lamentable form of a Babylonian ziggurat. Waltke says, "A sense of symmetry is pervasive in the Bible. The authors of the psalms crafted their compositions very carefully. They were heirs of an ancient art (in many details showing that they had inherited a poetic tradition that goes back hundreds of years), and they developed it to a state of high sophistication. Their works must be carefully studied and pondered."

The Babylonian creation account *Enuma Elish* has seven tablets: six refer to creation. The seventh tablet refers to the rest and repose of the gods after creating humans. It is not clear that the tablets represent days though the activities in each roughly line up with the days of Genesis in the minds of scholars. However, in Enuma Elish, the number seven is not prominent. The number six, as with YEC, is *most* pronounced in Babylonian literature.

The narrative of Genesis 1:1 through 2:3 carefully fits into a highly structured section within Genesis, the Pentateuch, and in the context of Israel's covenantal and religious life. Bruce Waltke, professor of Old Testament and biblical Hebrew, writes:

> Narrative is literature, consisting of both story (event) and plot (a creative representation of the event)... Meir Sternberg validates that three... principles are at work in all biblical narrative: historiographic, ideological, and aesthetic [history, theology, and artistry]. The first and last must be held in tension.[154]

Extensive artistic techniques alert the reader that more is happening than meets the eye. Waltke quotes the esteemed literary theorist, Northrop Frye, saying, "Symmetry, in any narrative, *always means that historical content is being subordinated to the [creative] demands of design and form*" (emphasis mine).[155]

Scholars have long pointed out that biblical authors did not put a high priority on strict literalism or precise chronologies. Their intention was primarily to elevate the subject matter and aid memorization in an oral society. For instance, the gospels were in the genre of first-century Roman biography. They sometimes sublimate chronology in favor of theological imperatives.

Was Jesus' sermon on the mount, as in Matthew, or a sermon on the plain as in Luke? It could be both, some suppose. But Matthew chose the Mount to show that Jesus supersedes Moses and Sinai – *"you have heard it said by them of old... but I say to you."* He presented Jesus to his Jewish readers as the New Moses.

The genre of John's gospel is also Roman biography, yet chronology plays a lesser role. Theological and Christological considerations were of greater value, particularly in John. Historical exactitude was subordinate to providing theological grounds for the identity of Jesus in John's gospel.

The ancients thought more in metaphorical terms than we do today. Lacking the tools for analytics, they depended more on imagination. That did not make the ancients stupid. Albert Einstein wrote, "Imagination is more important than knowledge. Knowledge is limited. It is the language of the soul."

---

154. Bruce K. Waltke and Charles Yu, *An Old Testament Theology* (Zondervan, Grand Rapids, Michigan, 2007), Kindle Edition, Location 4626.

155. Northrop Frye, *The Great Code: The Bible and Literature* (Toronto: Penguin, 1987), p. 43.

Strict literalism is rationalistic and generally lacks the expressiveness found in biblical literature. The author of Genesis 1 has assembled this chapter in striking creative detail. Much is not translatable. For example, verse one contains seven words in Hebrew (the number varies widely in translation). The Hebrew reads from right to left:

בְּרֵאשִׁית בָּרָא אֱלֹהִים אֵת הַשָּׁמַיִם וְאֵת הָאָרֶץ

("Beginning created God the heavens and earth")

There are several multiples of seven in this verse alone. Each letter in Hebrew also stands for a numerical value. For instance, adding the numeric value of the three nouns— God, Heaven, and Earth equal 777. The word for "the" underlined in the middle of the verse contains two letters (the first and last letters of the Hebrew alphabet) that provide a "conduit" for both halves of the verse; that is, each word to the immediate left and right contains five letters, adding up to *seven* in each direction, counting the two-letter conduit. Verse two has fourteen or 7x2 words and so on.

Of the keywords in 1:1— "God," "heaven," and "earth,"— "God" occurs thirty-five times (7x5), and heaven and earth appear 21 times each throughout the creation account (Genesis 1:1-2:3). "Living things" and the word "good" occur seven times. The repetition of a word seven times is a literary device often used by ancient writers, called *leitwort,* meaning "repeated word." In the *seventh* paragraph, which deals with the *seventh day,* the following *three* sentences (three for emphasis) occur, each consisting of *seven words,* and in the middle of each sentence contains the expression *the seventh day.* The literary scholar Umberto Cassuto notes this abundance of sevens:

> "And on *The Seventh Day* God finished His work which He had done, and He rested on *The Seventh Day* from all His work which He had done. So God blessed *The Seventh Day* and hallowed it." (Genesis 2:3)

This passage is not wordiness or poor writing; it is deliberate. It is a poetic device called *chiasm.* Cassuto continues:

> "The words in the seventh paragraph total thirty-five—five times seven. To suppose that all this is a mere coincidence is not possible. This numerical symmetry is, as it were, the golden thread that binds together all the parts of the section and serves as a convincing proof of its unity against the view of those—and they comprise the majority of modern commentators—who consider that our section is not a unity but was formed by the fusion of two different accounts, or as the result of the adaptation and elaboration of a shorter earlier version."[156]

---

156. See *"A Commentary on the Book of Genesis: from Adam to Noah* (Umberto Cassuto Biblical Commentaries 1)" by Umberto Cassuto, Israel Abrahams, 1989, page 14.

It hardly seems possible that God would employ numerous ANE and Hebrew literary devices upon reporting his work when no such literature existed. The notion that God wrote this or chose the exact wording for Moses is not worthy of serious consideration. Nothing in Genesis suggests that.

Throughout Genesis, many literary devices are both Hebraic and ANE in origin. That places Genesis in its ANE context and not at the beginning of time.

Spasms of Chiasms

Chiasms are a poetic device that fills the Bible and is common in virtually all ancient cultures, not just ANE cultures. Genesis 2:1-4 is one chiastic structure, but it is not the only one in Genesis, not by a long shot.

So what is a chiasm?

A chiasm is a literary device that lists parts of a story or idea in a particular order and then repeats the order *in reverse* to close the thought or narrative. The chiastic structure has two main variants:

1. A, B, B, A

2. A, B, *C*, B, A

Number 1 takes a step forward from A to B, then reverses the order, giving it the characteristic symmetry. The second variant adds the author's chosen focal point in the middle of the structure, represented by the letter "*C*." That structure notifies the ancient reader of the essential point the author is making. Genesis 2:1–4 is an example of the second variant where the author emphasizes his main point: *God rested on the seventh day from all His labor.* The author overemphasizes the sabbatical rest to make clear that the Creator of the universe is no other than the God of the Hebrews. *That is the reason for the weekly structure chosen by the author, which is purely theological.*

The seventh day of Creation has implications far beyond the Israelite mimicry of this day in their daily life (see chapter 29). Sabbatical rest is an identifying marker of Yahweh Elohim. The seventh day distinguishes Genesis from all other ANE creation accounts because we learn that God invited humans to join His rest, whereas pagan deities enslaved humans so that the gods could rest.

Ironically, what God creates in the first six days makes Genesis similar to other cosmogonies of the ANE. This emphasis on the seventh day and the overwhelming use of the number seven set the narrative apart from all other ANE creation accounts. The number seven and day seven were central to the author's vision of creation. It links the Hebrews to the true God with their unique identifying institution: the Sabbath. The Israelite Sabbath was *analogous to or symbolic* of the seventh day of Creation and a sign of Israel's covenant (see Exodus 31:13). The creation account is not merely a covenantal story about the origins of ancient Israel; it is also a universal story for all people since God's real rest is for all creation, as we shall see.

Genesis 2:1–4 is not likely a matter-of-fact account at the beginning of time, thousands of years before Israel received the Sabbath. It was common in the ANE to link covenants to a festival commemorating origins, as with the winter festival in Babylon dedicated to Marduk.[157] Moreover, the Sabbath command sits in the middle of the Ten Commandments, which was the core of the covenant. Thus, the creation week with a Hebraic seventh day may be an anachronism projected back to the beginning, not as a factual detail but as an essential theological point, namely that Israel's covenantal deity, Yahweh, is Creator of heaven and earth and that His rest is for *all universes.*

Biblical chiasm can be as short as a two-line symmetry or as long as the author wishes. For example, Gordon Wenham has analyzed the flood narrative in Genesis 6–9, showing that it is essentially an elaborate chiasm. Based on an earlier study of the grammatical structure by F. I. Andersen and Wenham illustrated the chiastic form of the flood narrative in the following table.

The Chiastic Structure of the Genesis Flood Narrative

A: Noah and his sons (Gen 6:10)

B: All life on earth (6:13a)

C: Curse on earth (6:13b)

D: Flood announced (6:7)

E: Ark (6:14–16)

F: All living creatures (6:17–20)

G: Food (6:21)

H: Animals in man's hands (7:2–3)

I: Entering the Ark (7:13–16)

J: Waters increase (7:17–20)

X: God remembers Noah (8:1)

J: Waters decrease (8:13–14)

I: Exiting the Ark (8:15–19)

H: Animals (9:2, 3)

G: Food (9:3, 4)

F: All living creatures (9:10a)

---

157. "The feast celebrated the triumph of Marduk, the patron deity of Babylon, over the forces of Chaos, symbolized in later times by the mythological sea monster Tiamat. The battle between Marduk and Chaos lasts 12 days, as does the festival of Zagmuk." See Wikipedia article "Zagmuk."

E: Ark (9:10b)

D: No flood in the future (9:11)

C: Blessing on earth (9:12–17)

B: All life on earth (9:16)

A: Noah and his sons (9:18, 19a)

You can see that the chiastic structure governs the exact sequence of events and is not likely or needs to be strictly precise. Strict chronologies study historical records that establish dates of past events in their order. In Genesis, biblical genealogies are oral traditions about ancestral origins and simply display a general order of birthing to establish a pedigree. The birth order may or may not be correct; there are missing generations in biblical genealogies and variations of the same generations, which is not at issue since the point is ancestry. Biblical genealogies are not strictly chronologies intended to date anything.

More importantly, the story's focal point for the author is not flood geology or even the flood itself. Instead, where X marks the spot, the focus is an all-important redemptive principle: God remembers Noah. In so doing, God remembers humanity; Noah becomes something of a "new Adam."

Again, the point is God's self-disclosure, not flood geology.

In his commentary on Genesis, Nahum Sarna writes, "Noah received the same divine blessing as Adam: "be fertile and increase" (1:28, 9:1). Just as genealogical lists follow the Creation story, so the "Table of Nations" expressing fulfillment of the blessing comes after the flood story. The lineage of all nations is traced back to a common ancestor, Noah... is an unparalleled notion in the world picture of any people in ancient times. Its comprehensiveness and universality prefigure the idea of the brotherhood of man."

The universal treatment of the flood is not about covering a globe the author knew nothing about but anticipates covering the world's sin. The New Testament tells us the flood was a universal baptism: "This water symbolizes baptism that now saves you also" (1 Peter 3:19–21). In that way, "God so loved the world," not the globe (John 3:16).

That sentiment makes Noah relevant to Israel's self-identity in the author's day—God also remembered Abraham and his children in Egyptian slavery. They were saved too by water that covered sin symbolized by the Egyptian army when the Red Sea closed. Remembrance is a constant theme throughout the Scriptures and finds its ultimate expression in, "Do this in remembrance of me." God remembers everything he promised with Jesus and invites us to celebrate by remembering him.

The point is, in the worst circumstances, God remembers His people. It is not judgment only but redemption that separates the Noachian flood from other ANE flood accounts. The pagan explanation said the gods brought the flood because of the noise made by humans in newly developed cities. But

Genesis says it was a deep decline into moral degradation. The former is arbitrary and childish; a holy Creator can justify the latter.[158]

Chiasms show up often in Genesis.

The chiastic structure on day three flows like this:

A. And God said, "Let the *waters under the heavens be gathered together* into one place,

    B. and let the *dry land* appear." And it was so.

    B. God called the *dry land* Earth,

A. The *waters that were gathered together* he called "seas," And God saw that it was good. (Genesis 1:9–10 ESV)

The first and last lines of this chiasm labeled "A" open and close the thought like a ribbon. It begins with, "And God said" and closes with "And God saw." Genesis 2:3 is also this way.

The number of chiasms in the book of Genesis alone are too numerous to list here. But you might try to google "chiasms in Genesis" or the Bible, even the NT, and you will soon be "swimming in a swarm of chiasms."

There are chiastic structures on day four, day seven, and the generations in Genesis, beginning with chapter 2:4. The chiasms are obvious in Hebrew but somewhat camouflaged in translation. For example, here is the chiasm on 2:4 based on Young's Literal Translation:

A. These (are) (the) generations of the heavens and the earth

    B. in their creation

    B. in (the) day of making

A. (by) the Lord God of earth and heavens.

Note the reverse order from heavens and earth to earth and heavens in the first and last lines labeled A that tie the chiasm like a bow.

---

158. Nahum Sarna observes: "In the Bible, the Flood is a cosmic catastrophe. This explains why Genesis, *unlike* the Mesopotamian versions, is completely silent about the city in which the hero lived and why reference is repeatedly made to "man's wickedness on earth" (6:5), to the fact that "the earth" became corrupt, the earth was filled with injustice . . . all flesh had corrupted its ways on earth (11f.), and God decided to put an end to "all flesh," "to destroy them with the earth'" (11:13)... Now this kind of universalistic terminology, and this concept of the Flood as a returning to primeval chaos, has profound moral implications... For it means that in biblical theology human wickedness, the inhumanity of man to man, undermines the very foundations of society. The pillars, upon which rests the permanence of all earthly relationships, totter and collapse, bringing ruin and disaster to mankind. This idea is one of the dominant themes of scripture and runs like a thread of scarlet throughout its literature." Of course, language like "the very foundations of earth tottering and collapsing" is figurative. Nahum M. Sarna, *Understanding Genesis (The Heritage of Biblical Israel)*, Jewish Theological Seminary (New York, Varda Books, Skokie, Illinois, 1966), 55.

The point is not to list all the possible artistic and literary devices in the Bible (there are too many). Instead, the fact is that the genre of Genesis 1 is not one we are familiar with or ever use.

To insist that Genesis 1 is like modern historical documents is (ironically) out of touch with its historical context. The author carefully selected every word in Genesis 1, *even some individual letters,* not as history but in an artistic way to emphasize religious ideas.[159]

Literary forms can aid memory in the oral society of ancient Israel. It also elevated the language, added mystery, and made its focal point more vivid. The author makes conscious, specific, and artistic choices intuitive to his immediate audience but not necessarily to us. This creation account is a thoroughly Hebraic story set in the ANE. Therefore, it is not, nor could it be, a report from God in His own words.[160]

The narrative is in the third person, "And God said" and "God saw," not "I said" or "I saw."[161]

All this is not to say that the earth is old. It does mean that God did not write this. Nor could Genesis 1—a unique stylistic piece about *prehistory* with numerous literary forms—be like the modern piece of academic history claimed by YEC. Genesis 1 is neither like strict history nor does it intend to be. Genesis is the theology of origins for the covenant people, Israel, in the Late Bronze Age. How could it be like a meticulous history?

In addition to idiom and artistic forms, ANE customs and traditions in Genesis 1–2 were not relevant at the beginning of time, not the least of which is the Hebrew language. The six and seven numerologies reflect ANE and Jewish mentality that could not have originated at creation. It is impossible that God personally used non-existent ANE and Hebraic numerology and worldviews to express Himself at creation. Genesis 1 presents a transcendent God as an ANE author might describe Him without a modern or more sophisticated language. While the anthropomorphisms are subtle in chapter 1, the idea that it's God's personal report in ANE and Hebraic idioms is an anthropomorphic bridge too far.

---

159. For example, Gerald Schroeder writes of an interesting Jewish tradition that speculates on the purpose of the first letter in the book of Genesis (the Bet). The Bet (ב) is closed off on the right hand side. It looks like a backward *C* and since Hebrew reads from right to left, the bet signifies that which went before Genesis 1:1 is "closed-off" to human understanding—an astonishing idea if true. On this point, see *"Genesis and the Big Bang," "The Hidden Face of God,"* and *"God According to God: A Physicist Proves We've Been Wrong about God All Along."*

160. Some believe chiasms must be of divine origin because there are so many in the Bible. However, chiasm was common in virtually all ancient literature, especially in oral societies. *The ILiad* is one example. *The Quran* contains chiasms. Even *Paradise Lost, Beowulf,* and countless other works, including the *Book of Mormon,* make use of this literary device. Chiasm is a human invention.

161. Interestingly, an earlier creation account in Job 38–39, *God speaks in the first person.*

Since God was there, the notion goes only He can precisely describe what happened. However, that assumes it was *necessary* to "precisely describe what happened." Who says? It makes more sense that Moses conveyed recognizable ideas in his day to present a revelation of the Hebrew God as he understood Him and not a science lesson."[162]

The next chapter shows that even gardens like Eden were an ANE concept.

---

162. Since *literalism* is a product of the rationalism and empiricism that emerged from the Enlightenment period, no such philosophical position was likely in ancient Israel that could govern their literature.

11.
ANCIENT NEAR EAST LITERATURE AND GENESIS PART 1

Until the nineteenth century, the Bible was the only significant body of literature from the world of ancient Israel. Before that, Christians assumed every tone, tenor, and idiom of the Old Testament was the same style and grammar of divine revelation. However, when massive discoveries revealed older literature from the ANE with similar stories, some with phrases near word for word the same as biblical texts, the *Bible's uniqueness* needed to be narrowly defined.

For example, stories such as *The Paradise Myth of Enki and Ninhursag*, *The Dispute between the Shepherd God and the Farmer God*, *The Deluge, and the Epic of Gilgamesh* (3200–1700 BC) belong to ancient Sumerian mythology concerned primarily with creation, agriculture, the building of cities, and the flood. The universe emerged from the primordial waters in ANE literature and virtually all other ancient literature. The gods were born in the universe. The gods formed man out of clay or soil (one mixed with "divine" blood) to till the ground for the gods.[163]

One remarkable Sumerian story of the third millennium BC is of a mythical place called "Dilmun." It was a paradise where humans raised domesticated animals and served the gods. Dilmun was a place said to be "pure, clean, and full of light." Animals we think of as predators were vegetarian, e.g., "The lions kill not," "the wolves snatch not the lambs," and "unknown is the wild dog devouring the kid." There is no sickness or old age in Dilhum. It is a place where childbirth is painless and quick, with a nine-day gestation instead of nine months culminating in labor.

Enki, the main character in Dilhum, commits a sinful act. He eyes eight plants in a marsh and sets out to "know their heart" (i.e., eat them). The two-faced god Isimud brings the fruit to Enki, who eats it. The goddess Ninhursag, primarily responsible for creating the plants, promptly *curses* Enki, who is to die, never seeing the goddess's favored eyes again.

Dilhum is an example of a mythological paradise in the ANE.

The following story is reminiscent of Cain and Abel called *The Dispute between the Shepherd God and the Farmer God*. It is a fanciful and less violent story than Cain and Abel. *The Deluge* and *Epic of Gilgamesh* follow. These texts

---

163. In Greek mythology, Zeus commissions Prometheus and Epimetheus to create Man (males only) out of clay. After one generation of males, Zeus instructs Hephaestus to create the first female. Her name was Pandora. Interestingly, her intense curiosity unleashed evils in the world, not totally unlike Eve.

have interesting similarities to Genesis. Nonetheless, substantial differences may indicate the biblical author's purposes.[164]

We know these ANE myths and others like them were familiar to the Greeks and undoubtedly to the author of Genesis. He is not dependent on them (there are too many differences) but recasts some ideas behind them for Israel's covenantal setting but without the pagan mythology. Rejecting the pagan mythology for a narrative about Yahweh is expected of a Hebrew author. However, removing the myth for theological purposes can give the stories a more "matter-of-fact" feel or the *impression* of history. But the same ideas (when they are the same) presented in different genres are of the same ideas still. If the concepts are figurative in one genre (say waters above and below the expanse), they are also figurative in another. The *meaning* of the ideas behind these stories is what the modern reader seeks.

Various covenants played a central role in God's relationship with humans throughout the book of Genesis. Covenants like these were common forms of agreement in the ANE. A well-known example is the covenant at Sinai modeled after the *suzerainty* covenants of the day. A comparison of ANE literature with Genesis reveals differences that may point us to special revelation and away from some of the *common assumptions* throughout the ANE captured in the Bible that, before extensive archeological discoveries, were thought to be special revelation, including the idea that creation took days or stages with the division of large segments of the universe, all ANE ideas.

While Genesis is unique, it *remains* ANE literature. YErs practically deny this because if Genesis is ANE literature, it would be less inspired, i.e., not God's word-for-word report. Yet, a simple comparison of the literature shows that scripture such as Genesis is documentary evidence of an ANE people: the Hebrews. Archeological discoveries confirm that stories about creation, paradise, echoes of Cain and Abel, and flood accounts were common among Israel's

---

164. For all these ANE texts translated and annotated, see Ancient Near Eastern Texts Related to the Old Testament, by Pritchard, pages 37–38. See also *The Ancient Near Eastern Treaties and the Old Testament* by The Rev. J. A. Thompson, MA, PhD London, (Tyndale Press © The Tyndale Press, December 1964), p. 7. Thompson says, "The structure and subject-matter of some of the Psalms can be paralleled in the literature at Ugarit. The wisdom literature of the Old Testament has numerous parallels in the ancient Near East; some of the laws of the Pentateuch have parallels in the Hammurabi Code and elsewhere; the Old Testament story of the flood has certain points of contact with the Babylonian flood stories; indeed, examples could be multiplied." There are, of course, important differences showing the Bible's independence.

neighbors. This is a fact. Some comparisons of similar stories are mere echoes, while others are too similar to be coincidental.[165]

There is no denying it; Genesis fits into a broader context.

There are similarities and differences between Genesis and ANE literature that are striking.

Various stories and myths from Mesopotamia, Canaan, and Egypt provide Genesis with a literary, historical, and theological context. The vast array of these myths tells of the creation of gods, heavenly bodies, animals, humans, gardens, temples, and cities. Sometimes the origins of gods (theogony) and heaven and earth (cosmogony) are indistinguishable. The gods represented forces that governed people's lives, such as rain in due season, love and fertility, and fate. That is to say, the sun, moon, and stars were gods; the sky, earth, sea, wind, and weather were associated with gods or were gods themselves, as were other powerful and mysterious phenomena such as sexuality. Myth is a sacred narrative of the origins of gods, their battles, and the blurring of the lines between gods and physical phenomena. Genesis avoids any origin of Yahweh (there is none), confrontation with deities at creation, and animism. Therefore, Genesis is not in the form of myth in the classical sense, though it may sometimes be a reaction to surrounding pagan myths.

Common assumptions between Israel and her neighbors regarding the *general composition of the cosmos,* even aspects of its formation, clearly existed. The similarities help us understand confusing statements in Genesis like "formless and void," "waters above and below the expanse," and the significance of naming, not to mention mystical trees, serpents, and garden paradises. However, the *differences* with Genesis will help point us to revelation. The ANE literature that many YErs dismiss provides a context that focuses on the Bible's unique claims. To understate or overstate the similarities are both mistakes.

A simple comparison illustrates the point.

If one places any ANE cosmogony, including Genesis, alongside twenty-first-century cosmology, one cannot help but notice the stark differences between the two and the substantial similarities between Genesis and ANE literature. The comparison shows that *Genesis belongs to the category of ANE literature.* It is not hard to see how similarities between Israel and her neighbors may appear in their literature.

---

165. Fundamentalists like YErs believe earlier ANE accounts of similar stories found in the Bible were false versions of the true stories that the Israelites corrected. But that goes against the common sense principle that an account closer to an event is likely to be more reliable than a much later version. Islam, for example, revised biblical stories in the Koran some 600-1000 years later, which could hardly be seen as more reliable objectively. Furthermore, ANE cosmogonies are different from histories in that they are mythological (not meant as literal history). Genesis takes up the stories and recasts them for a new monotheistic theology in Israel.

The centuries of Egyptian slavery would have influenced the children of Israel in profound ways. Egypt was an advanced empire where Moses received an education (Acts 7:22). A royal education in Egypt might include writing, mathematics, language and literature, cosmogony, technology, warfare, architecture, agriculture, economics, and general education. The Israel of Moses's day was partly a product of Egyptian, Mesopotamian, and Canaanite influences, which explains why they continually returned to those influences, especially in the northern kingdom of Israel.

More telling is the conquest of Canaan under Joshua, forty years after the Exodus. Joshua himself says, "Throw away the gods your ancestors worshiped *beyond the Euphrates River and in Egypt and* serve [Yahweh]" (Joshua 24:14; emphasis mine). Beyond the Euphrates River in Mesopotamia, Abraham and his significant entourage had worshiped before settling in Canaan.

Even after the Exodus, the covenant at Mt. Sinai, the forty years of wandering, miracle after miracle, at the moment of knocking on Canaan's door, Egyptian and Mesopotamian religious ideas lingered among the Israelites. Joshua's command lends historical credibility to the scripture since it was an embarrassing snapshot of Israel's spiritual condition, even among the generation allowed to enter the land forty years after the Exodus.

The three most significant influences on ancient Israel were Mesopotamia, Egypt, and Canaan.

Bill T. Arnold observes:

The Mesopotamian materials are helpful for understanding the broader worldview, although they have fewer direct parallels than the Egyptian. The Epic of Atra-ḫasis can be dated to around 1700 BCE, although its original composition may have been centuries earlier. *The reason this text is of such great interest is the way it presents the sequence of events from the Creation of humankind to its near extinction in the flood.* The Babylonian Epic of Creation (better known by the Akkadian title, Enuma Elish) was probably composed around the eleventh century BCE, although there have been precursors... Fragments of the Sumerian Eridu Genesis have been preserved in various versions from approximately 1600 BCE. *It puts in sequence the Creation of humanity; the institution of kingship, the first cities, and a great flood in a way reminiscent of Genesis.*[166] (emphasis mine)

The influence of the Baal cult of Canaan on the Israelites was next.

The Northern Kingdom of Israel continued in the Baal cult until the Assyrians took them into captivity around 734 BC. Furthermore, since Israel's neighbors could influence her religious concepts, how much more might

---

166. Bill T. Arnold, *Genesis (The New Cambridge Bible Commentary)*, Kindle Edition, location 1235.

general ideas regarding the cosmos be circulating, especially those from more technically advanced societies like Egypt and Babylon?

At the beginning of ANE creation myths, there is nothing but a formless, dark, watery deep. There were no governing principles or functioning structures in the formlessness that could support human life. The pagans believed the pre-creation watery world gave birth to the gods. The gods usually fought each other for dominance over the cosmos. Eventually, a created order emerged out of the chaos. Genesis includes the waters but avoids the birth of any gods or large-scale chaos. Elohim is before the beginning and uncreated.

In ANE cosmology, this "formless deep," sometimes called a void or an abyss,[167] typically contained the material from which an ordered world arose. Creation in the ANE meant developing an ordered universe out of the disordered deep. In many of these cultures, people believed that at some point, the forces preserving the new order could weaken, and the world could lapse into disorder, as in Noah's flood or Jeremiah's allegorical description of the Babylonian invasion of Judah in Jeremiah 4:23–26.

Mesopotamia

The epic Enuma Elish (*e-nu-ma e-lish*) comes to us from the Assyrian library of Assurbanipal (c. 630 BC) in Mesopotamia. The British Archeologist Austen Henry Layard discovered the tablets in 1849. However, precursors of the epic myth go back to the early second millennium BC from Sumer, written in Akkadian. A priest of Marduk called Berossus recorded Babylonian history and myths for the Greeks around 290 BC. He played a similar role as Josephus, who wrote *A History of the Jews* for the Romans in the first century AD.

Enuma Elish begins with the familiar watery deep—what some scholars call the *World Ocean*— a primeval cosmic ocean usually referred to as "waters" (often salt and fresh water). Authors of the ANE personified these waters as gods in the form of mythical sea monsters. In the case of *Enuma Elish*, the characters were the gods Apsu and Tiamat.[168]

Apsu is the Babylonian male deity of primordial freshwater, and Tiamat is the sea dragon goddess of saltwater. The primordial deep in the ANE was a darkened, unwieldy void preexisting the created order. Sea monsters went by various names like Tiamat, Rahab, Leviathan, Lotan, Yam, and the Greco/Roman myths of Neptune and Poseidon. Genesis 1:2–7 parts from personifying the waters by not naming them, though elsewhere, the Bible preserves the mythology for poetic purposes (see Psalm 74:13–1; 89:8-11; Isaiah 51:9; Job

---

167. Egyptian records sometimes call the primordial waters a "limitless deep"—that is, an abyss.

168. Umberto Cassuto and Israel Abraham, *A Commentary on the Book of Genesis Part I: From Adam to Noah* (Varda Books, Skokie, Illinois, USA, 2005), p. 22.

26:10–14). Mythical language on origins is similar to apocalyptic language on end-times. Neither one is a set of lies since both are mainly symbolic.

The waters commingled, meaning they "copulated" and could give birth to almost anything in other ANE versions. In *Enuma Elish*, the first thing birthed from the waters was a new generation of gods. Besides magic, seeds in soil and birthing were the ways living things came into existence in the ANE. Genesis 2:19 says, "So the Lord *took some soil* and made animals and birds" (CEV).

The gods usually *split* open the primeval waters to create an expanse (meaning the day and night skies) that sometimes exposed material the gods could use to form objects, creatures, dry land, or celestial and terrestrial bodies. In Greek mythology, Zeus, like Baal, was god of the skies, Hades was god of the underworld (Sheol), while Poseidon was god of the sea. There was a remarkable similarity throughout the ancient world on essential cosmological elements. That is true of most generations since humanity often moves forward in rough unison, even without much, if any, continental connections.

In ANE cosmologies, the material that formed the earth was sometimes the clay and silt deposits (typical of river systems found in Mesopotamia and Egypt) in the primordial waters. The ancients believed wetlands or ocean floors were necessary to hold up a body of water so that the world ocean was not simply water but oceans.

Moreover, the gods could use silt deposits and clay to give form and function to the earth or even to something on its surface like plants, animals, and humans. The wetland or silt may not be the entire earth hidden in the depths, but the material that formed the earth as God does in Genesis 1:9–10: "God said, "I command the water under the sky to come together in one place, so there will be *dry ground*. God called the dry ground 'land'" (CEV). Giving it an *official* name "land" or "earth" after separating the waters indicates a new creation, i.e., a radical change from the nameless, formlessness in verse 2, where the earth is mentioned but not officially named, meaning there was more to come.

John Walton observes that in the ANE, the earth came from deposits in the waters:

> Creation often begins with that which emerges from the waters—whether a deity or land (e.g., the Egyptian Primeval Hillock). These primeval waters are designated the "nonexistent" in Egyptian texts... The god Atum is said to have developed "out of the Flood, out of the

Waters, out of darkness, out of lostness." The Waters [are] the "father of the gods."[169]

Nearly every aspect of creation in paganism relates to animism. Many forces of nature appeared to have a life force. Miller and Soden write:

All the elements and forces that a human being might encounter in this [ANE] world are not impersonal matter and energy but the forms and wills of living beings—beings that surpass the merely human scale, but are godlike.[170]

Contrary to popular opinion, Israel rejected animism. Their only deity, Yahweh, transcends the creation that He alone made and that, apart from biological life, other created things were inanimate. The biblical text revealed a clear and dramatic departure from animism.

Enuma Elish (EE) is one of the better-known creation stories extant during the Exodus. Some form of EE would have been familiar to the educated classes in Israel. The opening statement in Enuma Elish is similar to Genesis 1:1–2:

When on high the heaven had *not been named, Firm ground* below had not been *called by name,* [Nothing] but primordial Apsu, *their begetter,* And [Tiamat who] *bore* them all, [existed] *Their waters* commingling as a single body.[171]

Like Genesis, EE begins with heaven and earth, but in this case, two gods in place of Elohim. Not having names means heaven and earth did not yet exist. Only Apsu (freshwater male) and Tiamat (saltwater female) existed as only Elohim, and as we shall see, perhaps the darkened deep existed in the beginning. However, Apsu and Tiamat were mere animating forces behind the waters and not self-existent beings in their own right, both "killed" in the myth. EE begins by referring to a creative ordering named "heaven and earth" that had not yet started, which indicates where the narrative is leading. Therefore, the waters are a pre-creation condition in EE. Does this mean that the waters in Genesis 1:2 were necessarily pre-creation conditions? No. But it is not reasonable to dismiss the possibility outright since Genesis seems to leave the possibility open.

The waters are personified as the gods Apsu and Tiamat but not yet *called* heaven (celestial bodies) and earth (firm ground). The "firm ground" was not the "planet" earth but merely "dry land" as in Genesis 1:9. There was no concept

---

169. John Walton, *The Lost World of Genesis One: Ancient Cosmology and the Origins Debate (The Lost World Series)* (InterVarsity Press, Downers Grove, IL, 2010), p. 31. See also *Coffin Texts,* Spell 76, Translation by James Allen, in Context of Scripture 1.6, ed. W. Hallo and K. L. Younger (Leiden: Brill, 1997), pp. 10, 16.

170. Johnny V. Miller and John M. Soden, *In the Beginning We Misunderstood: Interpreting Genesis 1 in Its Original Context* (Kregel Digital Publications, 2012), p. 79.

171. See *The Academy of Ancient Texts,* online.

of the world as a globe in the ANE. The writings and illustrations in Egypt and Mesopotamia make that clear. EE's opening point is that only waters existed since they had names.

Again, the word *earth* in Genesis 1:2 often just meant "land" or, in this case, an ocean floor that large bodies of water are known to have. The ancients believed something had to hold up the pre-creation waters like any other body of water; otherwise, it would just fall. So verse 2 could mean, "Now the earth [land] was formless and empty [uncreated], darkness was over the surface of the deep, and the Spirit (wind) of God was hovering over the [primordial] waters."[172]

The earth was formless and dark, without its final shape or function, meaning God had not formed it yet. The land received its solid form and function (as soil for crops) and an official name on day three: *"God called the dry ground 'land'"* (Genesis 1:10). Land (earth) was a new development. Wetlands were used in some ANE creation stories to develop the firm or dry ground, usually with divine winds that dried the wetlands. *Enuma Elish* is a similar example where *north winds* divided the waters and exposed those wetlands to open air. In many ANE creation accounts, the primordial waters preexisted simultaneously with the wind as it appears in Genesis 1:1–5, right before the account of creation begins on day one:

> In the beginning God created the heavens and the earth. Now the earth was formless and empty, darkness was over the surface of the deep, and the Spirit [wind] of God was hovering over the waters.
>
> And God said, "Let there be light," and there was light. God saw that the light was good, and he separated the light from the darkness. God called the light "day," and the darkness he called "night." And there was evening, and there was morning—the first day.

When the Israelites crossed the Red Sea, also called the Reed Sea, God sent an *east wind* to divide it, so the people crossed on dry land. Notice "The Lord sent a strong east wind that blew all night until there was dry land where the water had been." This action was evidence that Yahweh was the Creator who did a similar thing with the waters at creation. As a result, the sea opened up, creating an expanse, so the Israelites walked through on dry land with a wall of water on each side. That reassured the Israelites that Yahweh was indeed God. He separated the waters in half as in Genesis, where the separation of the primeval waters allowed dry land to form the earth as the ancients understood it.

Why a north wind in EE and an east wind during the Exodus? Because a north wind toward Babylon came from the gods of their fathers in northern Mesopotamia. An east wind toward Egypt was from Canaan. That meant

---

172. If not uncreated, the earth was certainly unfinished since the rest of the chapter proceeds to describe its creation as well as the heavens.

the God of Abraham, Isaac, and Jacob, the patriarchs that came to Egypt from Canaan, where the Israelites were now headed, had sent the east wind.

In both cases, divine wind divides waters in half. That is not a coincidence.

The wind firmed up the ground in EE, Exodus, and Genesis. God created humans free in Genesis and provided dry land to walk in freedom in Exodus. The Bronze Age was not aware of a globe. Earth was the dry land in which they lived and grew the food necessary for habitation, which was the point of the narrative. They had no idea how big the earth was or its actual shape. The ancients believed the earth rested on the ocean; Shoal was below that (see Fig. 2). Undoubtedly, the ancients conceived the earth as very small by our calculations. Even at the time of Christopher Columbus, when Europeans believed the world was round, they expected India to be a short trip due west.

The heavens resulted when the gods separated the waters by wind and war. That left waters beyond the sky and waters below the sky:

> Then God said, "Let there be a space [sky] to separate the water *into two parts.*" So God made the space and *separated the water.* Some water was above [the sky], and some were below [the sky]. God named that space "sky." There was evening, and then there was morning. This was the second day (Genesis 1:6–8 ERV).

Psalms 24:2 and 136:6 say (respectively), "For he established [the earth] *on* the waters," and he *"spread out the earth upon* the waters." The land rests on water indicated by surrounding oceans, underground seas, lakes, and springs seemed to confirm that water surrounded the land on all sides: above, underneath, and below that, *the great deep.* It is as if the exposed silt from the primeval waters spread out and dried to create soil, making "earth" as the ancients conceived it. The "earth" mentioned in the account appears to be just the land usable for growing food. The land referred to may not always include mountains, deserts, or oceans since they were obstacles to growing food in a world in the early stages of agriculture.

Notice what it says in Genesis:

> Then God said, "Let the earth [soil] grow grass, plants that make grain, and fruit trees. The fruit trees will make fruit with seeds in it. And each plant will make its own kind of seed. Let these plants grow on the earth [soil]." And it happened. The earth grew grass and plants that made grain. And it grew trees that made fruit with seeds in it. Every plant made its own kind of seeds. (Genesis 1:11–12 ERV)

Here the earth is simply the land for growing food. Any place that could not produce food was something else. For example, in the Messianic Age, the prophets say that the mountains shall be made low, and the deserts and wilderness shall blossom; the rough or rugged terrain shall be made smooth, and the oceans removed (Isaiah 35:1, 40:4-5; Revelation 21:1). Theirs was a world that did not efficiently use soil as does our modern world. We also see mountains and oceans, even some desserts, as beautiful places with abundant resources. The ancient Israelite imagined a world in the Messianic Age where the surface was entirely fertile soil. That was the ideal world for the ancient Israelites because there would be plenty (of food) with minimal work.

All those changes in the Messianic Age relieve people's burdens without the technology to deal with nature's challenges. The depiction of wild animals in the Millennial Age is of particular predators turned vegetarian, not that carnivory is necessarily evil. Certain predators will no longer threaten farm animals that also threaten livelihoods (Isaiah 65:25). These Messianic images are not likely literal, i.e., they do not present the new heaven or the new earth in actuality. Instead, they are saying that life under the Messiah shall be the most blessed world Israel could conceive—*the idyllic agrarian society led by Israel.* That was their best concept of utopia. But agriculture will not be part of the spiritual new heavens and new earth. The point is the utopia, but it won't be agrarian or earthly; it won't be the great hunting ground in the sky nor the Marxist/Socialist victory of the proletariat over the bourgeoisie.

A new heaven and earth is the union of divinity and humanity through Christ (Ephesians 1:10).

The universe of the ANE consisted of vast water *beyond* the skies. The day and night skies contained space with air, birds, clouds, sun, moon, and stars. The waters below the skies bordered the landmasses and pooled below the earth's surface. That included seas below the land. In the waters below, pillars held up the world over the waters. Most ancients believed the earth was a large disk resting on the waters below. Pillars, metaphorical or literal, held up the earth to prevent it from sinking into the great deep. "For the pillars of the earth are the Lord's, and *he hath set the world upon them*" (1 Samuel 2:8; emphasis mine). And "He shakes the earth from its place and makes its pillars tremble (Job 9:6; see figure 1, the three-tiered universe).[173]

The heavens and earth emerged from this primeval deep by a supreme deity or deities in most cultures throughout the ancient world. Indeed, EE went through various iterations, from early Sumerian and Assyrian gods to Babylonian and Neo-Babylonian versions, with Marduk as the supreme deity. However one might interpret "the earth," dry land, waters above and below the expanse, and skies in all these passages, the lack of clarity alone rules out any legitimate *reform movement* over opinions regarding these ancient references.

The dense mythological language bogs the modern reader down upon first meeting EE. The story is about the origins of gods, heaven and earth, humans, and especially Marduk, who became the supreme deity in Babylon. EE

---

173. Pillars may be symbolic for whatever way God held up the earth. Still, waters were thought to be below the earth.

flows much differently than Genesis because it is an epic. Genesis 1 is crisp, to the point, and absent of mythological imagery, although the two trees and the talking serpent are said to echo myth.

Mythological imagery does occur elsewhere in Scripture, and some verses relate directly to Genesis 1 (see Psalm 74, 104, 89:9–13; Job 41; Isaiah 27:1). Consequently, some linguistic scholars think that the garden of Eden story might have as its source a more ancient Hebrew epic lost to us that can be inferred elsewhere in the OT, specifically Isaiah 27:1 and Ezekiel 28:11–19, 31:8–18.

The textual scholar Umberto Cassuto writes on Ezekiel 28:11–19 (see also note 152):

> All this testifies to the fact that in a remote period of antiquity, there was an Israelite saga that related how the cherub —or one of the cherubs— who dwelt in the garden of Eden, upon the top of the mountain of God, which was as high as the heavens, sinned in his pride against God, and as a punishment for his transgression he was driven out from the garden of Eden and cast down to the earth. *It may be that the word earth occurs here in the sense of Sheol [abode of the dead], in which sense it is also found in Akkadian.* This saga, therefore, belongs to the cycle of legends concerning the angels who were hurled down from Heaven... [in] the episode of the sons of God and the daughters of man (vi 1–4). The prophet [Ezekiel] alludes to this tradition and uses it as a poetic parable for the downfall of the king of Tyre. The Torah, on the other hand, seeks to refine and purify the tradition.[174] (emphasis mine)

(The italicized sentence shows another way the word *earth* was used in the ANE to mean Sheol.) Yet, there is no evidence that "earth" meant a globe.

According to Cassuto, Ezekiel shows traces of a more ancient Eden epic or saga in Israel connected to what Ezekiel calls *"the garden of God"* (a phrase found nowhere else in scripture) and the fall of the angels who sinned with the "daughters of men" in Genesis 6. Later biblical and Talmudic sources may have reinterpreted the fall of the angels as the fall of humans. Perhaps two falls mirrored each other—one heavenly, the other earthly. None of this is clear.

Relying on literalism is easy enough when reading a modern text written recently. However, reading about primeval concepts from the Late Bronze Age based on sources (written or oral) centuries earlier is exceptionally challenging.

EE reads more like Jewish Apocalyptic with sea monsters, beasts, and no doubt, extensive symbolism. EE is not apocalyptic; it is a mythological treatment in theogony and cosmogony. This type of language is "mythological" if it refers to the beginning of time and "apocalyptic" refers to the end of times. One

---

174. Umberto Cassuto and Israel Abraham, "A Commentary on the Book of Genesis: From Adam to Noah," *Umberto Cassuto Biblical Commentaries 1* (Varda Books, 2005), pp. 81–82.

is cosmological, the other eschatological. There is nothing wrong, nefarious, or deceptive about using such language. Jewish apocalyptic, like myth, asserts truths, but no one but a novice reads such literature literally; the apocalypse of John, popularly known as the book of Revelation, is a case in point.[175]

We know that the imagery in Jewish apocalyptic, equally bizarre as mythology, is not literal though it refers to future events related to the present. Our extensive knowledge of Israelite history, theology, and literature tells us that apocalyptic is dramatic end-time imagery that Israelites knew was purposely symbolic. Our understanding of other ANE religious ideas is not so complete that we can be sure how literal their respective audiences took their mythologies. A critical comment recorded near the time of Alexander the Great by Berossus, priest of Bel in Babylon, who preserved substantial portions of EE in his history of Babylon, states that EE was an *allegory*.[176]

Interestingly, Berossus also preserved a ten-generation genealogy of Babylonian kings listed before their own flood story, not unlike the ten generations of patriarchs from Adam to Noah that YErs use to date the universe. Like Genesis, the lifespans of these kings were extraordinarily long. However, the total life span of the ten Babylonian kings is a combined 435,000 years. This Babylon list is similar to an older Sumerian king list with a combined lifespan of over 240,000 years. Some kings supposedly reigned in Mesopotamian cities such as Eridug and Alulim for 28,800 years. The Babylonians did not mean these numbers literally. The point was establishing a dynastic pedigree or legitimacy and not providing factual chronologies, genealogies, or histories. Egyptian king lists were even more outrageous.[177]

The Genesis list is far tamer but served a similar purpose—legitimacy. Such long-life spans illustrated the legendary status of kings as semi-deities, namely that they were in the image of the gods. The specific number of years selected for each king would have held significance. The life spans were based on the Babylonian numerical system and divisible by sixty and therefore had no real value other than theological.[178]

There is evidence that the more modest yet unusually long-life spans in Genesis and their specific number of years also have theological significance. The number ten is in keeping with Mesopotamian lists and biblical references: the Ten Commandments, the ten plagues of Egypt, the tithe, the ten-horned beasts in Daniel and Revelation, etc. The ten generations from Adam's royal line produced Kings David, Solomon, and Hezekiah through Seth. This line

---

175. There are countless stories of people new to the Bible that read John's Revelation, assuming it is literal. Reading ancient myth the same way is likely a similar mistake.

176. See *Wikipedia*, "Berossus."

177. See *Wikipedia*, "The Sumerian King Lists."

178. Ibid., specifically the subtitle "Antediluvian rulers."

would bear the Messiah, whose rulership has no end. These genealogies were not chronologies, strictly speaking. They could not date anything, nor could they establish the age of the earth. Instead, they help trace the ancestry of the promised one as Luke wrote: Jesus was the Son of David, and the Son of Seth, Son of Adam, the Son of God (Luke 3:38). Such long life spans mean divine purpose and are not necessarily literal.

Genesis is not twenty-first-century literature. It is ANE literature likely written or edited around the time of the Babylonian king list. That does not mean Genesis depends on Babylonian literature, but that ideas and idioms can appear shared among similar cultures and times. Many of the long ages in Genesis are in multiples of sixty. The list of patriarchs or kings (Abraham is called a king) begins in Genesis 5:2: "When God created mankind, he made them in the likeness of God. He created them male and female and blessed them. And he named them 'Mankind' when they were created." The list of ten patriarchs follows. Their ages are extreme not only in the total number of years but also in the ages when they and their wives could have children:

- Adam and Eve had a son at 130 years and many more until age 930.

- Seth had Enosh at 105 and lived to 912.

- Enosh became a father at 90 and lived to 905.

- Jared became a father at 162 and died at 910.

- When Methuselah had lived 187 years, he became the father of Lamech.

- Lamech had a son at 182 years. His name was Noah.

- After Noah was 500 years old, he became the father of Shem, Ham, and Japheth. (vv. 3–32)

Unusual life spans, not to mention virility, continued after the flood:

Two years after the flood, when Shem was 100 years old, he became the father of Arphaxad. And after he became the father of Arphaxad, Shem lived 500 years and had other sons and daughters... Arphaxad lived 403 years and had other sons and daughters... Shelah lived 403 years and had other sons and daughters. Eber lived 430 years and had other sons and daughters. (Genesis 11:10–32)

Nahor was Abraham's grandfather and died "young" at 119. Yet, he had sons and daughters late in life. Even Abraham's father, Terah, sired him at age seventy and at least two other children after that and lived 205 years and died.

The point of all this is Abraham's puzzling statement in Genesis 17:17. Upon hearing that God would give him and Sarah a son at one hundred and ninety years old, respectively, this happened: "Abraham bowed with his face to the ground and thought, 'I am almost a hundred years old. How can I become a father? And Sarah is ninety. How can she have a child?' So he started laughing" (CEV).

This statement is odd given Abraham's ancestry if all the details of his forefathers are literal. In other words, if we take the extreme ages in Abraham's generations at face value instead of theologically, their promised son would be entirely reasonable at Abraham and Sarah's ages. The miracle would be limited to their fertility, not their age. The rest of the story shows that the miracle included their ages and the healing of Sarah's barrenness. Instead, Abraham's reaction focuses on their ages exclusively.

Abraham's reaction implies that the extraordinary lifespans of previous generations of patriarchs mean something other than a one-to-one correspondence to reality to which Abraham seemed oblivious. It was not reasonable for Abraham to react this way otherwise. Furthermore, Shem would still be alive during Abraham's life. That would mean other generations between Shem and Abraham were still active, hundreds of years old.

The target audience would likely understand the apparent inconsistency as idiomatic and that the extreme ages of Abraham's ancestry expressed something other than actual age. They represent the divine stamp on the Messiah's lineage—a concept likely known to the writer and readers of Genesis. The most extraordinary thought would be if the extreme ages before Abraham were well-known to be figurative that God would choose to perform the real thing in Abraham and Sarah. As C. S. Lewis said of Christ, "myth became fact." [179]

If ancient myths were allegory, are similar stories in Genesis somehow symbolic? Probably, but not necessarily. YEC's insistence that the similarities in stories written long before the Bible suggest that some faint memory about the beginning lingered in the pagan world is an arbitrary assertion if carried beyond speculation since records written closer to the event are much more likely to be accurate than competitive stories written many centuries later. Today's example is the Quran, written about one thousand years after the Old Testament. Yet, Muslims insist that the Quran's retelling of biblical stories corrects the original author's witness. Why do they believe that? The Quran (or Allah) told them so. That is convenient but not convincing. Muslims must provide evidence that justifies overturning the original stories with more credible versions. Otherwise, theirs are just partisan opinions.

The YEC claim that some faint memory about the creation events lingered in the pagan world is forced and counterintuitive. Why do all the ANE stories largely agree or make the same mistakes? It is more believable that primordial accounts are a combination of observation, oral traditions, and speculation precisely because there were no eyewitnesses alive for the writings that

---

179. C. S. Lewis, edited by Walter Hooper, *God in the Dock: Essays on Theology and Ethics* (William B. Eerdmans Publishing Co. Grand Rapids, Michigan, 1970), Location 686.

survived. The insistence that Genesis chapters 1-2 must be eyewitness testimony is an unwarranted belief. All the ancients attempted to explain the world and their people's place in it. What matters most is the theological explanations of their speculations, which differ most from Genesis. The Bible's advance is in theology, stripping the mythology from the stories to the bare-boned historical point that Yahweh and He alone is the Creator of heaven and earth.

The notion that mytho-history or myth itself in the Bible somehow rejects divine inspiration is to misunderstand myth and divine inspiration. God can inspire in any genre. The genre does not determine God's nature nor His will, which are constant. The uncertainty about many statements throughout Genesis demands *modesty* in drawing hard conclusions other than theological ones, such as one God created heaven and earth and has a plan for his creation that especially involves humans even though we go astray. The ancients were not literalists. Recounting their world and origins was a highly metaphorical conversation. But modesty is not what we have in the SDWC.

In ANE literature, the first word or phrase serves as the title for a book. *Enuma Elish,* which means "When on high," is how it begins. *Genesis* means *origins* in Greek and comes from the first word in the Septuagint. The Hebrew word for Genesis is *Bereshith.* We'll see that *bereshith* is translated variously: "In the beginning," "The beginning *of*," "When God began," or "In the beginning *when.*" These variants make the most familiar verse, Genesis 1:1, less clear. We address this in chapter 13.

At the start of EE, the phrases "the heaven had *not been named*" and "*firm ground* below had not been *called by name*" are another way of saying heaven and earth did not yet exist. Things that functioned in an identifiable way received names in the ANE—e.g., "Adam" means earthling, made of earth, "Eve" means mother of all living, and "earth" means the land, its primary function being food production. There was no functioning heaven and earth at the beginning of EE or Genesis, and the act of naming could carry a special significance. Chapter 14 looks more closely at the ANE concept of naming.

The creation of the gods in EE begins *when* the mythological characters Apsu and Tiamat combine their primeval waters to birth new generations of gods. Some of the younger gods assassinate Apsu in an attempted takeover. Tiamat is furious, as tempestuous waters are want be, and soon, war erupts among the gods over dominance and the right to establish a world order.

A council of gods commissions Marduk, the god of Storms, to defeat Tiamat and earn supreme rulership. After Marduk slays Tiamat, a north wind splits her body in half *"like a shellfish,"* which opens up the heavens, leaving waters above the sky like a ceiling to *"not allow her waters to escape* and establishes the earth on her waters below the sky."[180] That is the Babylonian version of the creation of heaven and earth, aka "sky and firm ground."

The *elements* are similar in Genesis 1, a wind or Spirit of Elohim (verse 2), an expanse of sky divides the waters, which leaves waters above and below the expanse (verses 6–8). The immediate difference in the Babylonian account is the genre; it is epical and mythical. The deities involved are the most significant dissimilarity.

Scholars point out that the Hebrew word for "waters" or "deep" in Genesis 1:2 is *tehom*, a Hebrew word with a possible etymology distantly related to but not synonymous with the Akkadian, "Tiamat," the goddess of the deep. However, while formless and void, the darkened depths of Genesis are simply deep waters without animism or mythological imagery. So the waters are not a challenge to the God of Israel.

The significant similarity with the ANE world is not whether the waters were gods or serpents or that there was a chaotic struggle; rather, it is *the very existence of those primordial waters in the first place that we know did not exist as described.* Nahum Sarna writes, "Just as Apsu and Tiamat, the two oceans, existed before all things, so in Genesis, the existence of water is taken for granted."[181]

These waters did not really exist as presented. They are understandably speculative.

The division of primal waters was fundamental to cosmology in the ANE. It is useless to deny the concept of a primeval watery deep in the Genesis account. Genesis 1:2 is an explicit reference to this concept. Tiamat's character in the Babylonian myth is associated with later biblical references: Rahab (Egyptian) and Leviathan (Canaanite; see also Isaiah 51:9).[182]

The Bible elsewhere explicitly addresses the mythological versions of primeval waters and the multiheaded sea dragon called Leviathan. These are analogous to the Egyptian sea monster Rahab, the Phoenician sea serpent Yam, the Ugaritic Lotan, or even the later Greek and Roman gods of the sea, Poseidon and Neptune.

Psalm 74:13–17 states:

It was [Yahweh] who split open the sea by his power; you broke *the heads of the monster in the waters.* It was you who crushed *the heads of*

---

180. Edited by James B. Prichard *Ancient Near Eastern Texts: Related to the Old Testament* (Princeton University Press, 1969), p. 67.

181. Nahum M. Sarna, *Understanding Genesis (The Heritage of Biblical Israel)* (1966), p. 13.

182. See Michael D. Coogan, *The Old Testament: A Historical and Literary Introduction to the Hebrew Scriptures* (New York: Oxford University Press, 2014), pp. 34–40, ISBN 978-0-19-994661-7. Rahab, Tiamat, and Leviathan are Egyptian, Babylonian, and Canaanite versions (respectively) of a similar myth.

Leviathan... you established the sun and moon. It was you who set all the boundaries of the earth; you made both summer and winter. (emphasis mine)

Psalm 89:8–11 repeats this idea here in the Expanded Version with its notes in brackets:

Lord God All-Powerful [Almighty; of Heaven's Armies; of hosts], who is like you...? You rule the ·mighty [raging; surging] sea and calm the stormy [rising] waves. *You crushed the Rahab [a sea monster, representing chaos (Job 26:12; Isaiah 51:9].* The skies [heavens] and the earth belong to you. You made the world and everything in it. (Expanded Version)

Note the creation is the setting for this battle: Heaven and earth belong to Yahweh. "You made the world and everything in it." Job 26:10–14 adds:

He marks out the horizon on the face of the waters for a boundary between light and darkness. The pillars of *the heavens* quake, aghast at his rebuke. By his power he churned up the sea; by his wisdom he *cut Rahab to pieces.* By his breath the skies became fair; his hand *pierced the gliding serpent...* Who then can understand the thunder of his power? (emphasis mine)

The primeval waters are rehearsed in these two scripture sections in mythological language absent in Genesis. There are variations in the details, mainly because the texts we have from all ANE sources come from different centuries and peoples. The ANE sea monster goes by various names: Rahab (Egyptian), Leviathan (Canaan), and Tiamat (Mesopotamian).

These verses seem to connect sea myth with creation. In Psalm 89:8–11, the victory over the raging sea appears to create the heavens (skies) and the earth: *"You crushed Rahab... You made the world and everything in it. The skies and the earth* belong to you." And Job 26:12–14, "By his wisdom *he cut Rahab to pieces. By his breath, the skies became fair."* Whatever the case may be, is there any doubt that these biblical references capture common ANE concepts?

The point is that Genesis 1 contains some assumptions shared throughout the ANE but lacks the kind of mythology surrounding pagan deities who were products of the universe and embodied natural phenomena. ANE mythology *does* show up in Scripture, as we have seen in Job, Psalms, Isaiah, and elsewhere showing an awareness among biblical authors of those myths. Still, biblical authors appear to use myth only as a backdrop for poetic imagery and metaphor.

In Genesis, the watery deep in 1:2 has no name. It is not alive nor a finished creation.

The darkened deep was amorphous and uninhabitable. The author mentions the "earth" in verse 2, but is it the finished earth or the materials that would become the earth? Could these be the conditions before God created the heavens and the earth? (We examine that question in chapter 13.) The spectacle is a formless void or a dark abyss, meaning "earth" was not the finished earth since it was formless inside an abyss. In other ANE accounts, it was a mound of sediment. That may imply that here the word "earth" could mean the generic: "world," the pre-creation state of the cosmos, and not necessarily an entirely created earth engulfed by waters.

Young's Literal Translation renders Genesis 1:1, "In the beginning of God's preparing the heavens and the earth—the earth had existed waste and void." In other words, according to a literal translation, Genesis 1:2 may have been the formless world before God created anything. That is how the world of the author understood cosmology. That does not mean Israel had to see the cosmos in the same way, yet the language of Genesis certainly supports that view.

It is fascinating that Moses assumes his original audience knows the references from a broader ANE worldview since he does not bother to clarify them. Since floods routinely deposited sediment into the Tigris and Euphrates river systems mentioned in the Garden of Eden (Genesis 2:10–14), the Mesopotamians envisioned sediment in the primeval waters that formed a basis for establishing what EE calls "firm ground." In other words, the gods used sedimentary deposits already in the primordial waters to create an "earth."

The point is that the Hebrew word for "earth" (*aretz*) has several possible meanings. "Earth" in Genesis 1:2 could also mean *ground, land or dirt, clay or silt* as a starter for creating the earth that God was beginning to form and not the finished earth covered by water sitting alone in the universe. That is not to say the creation happened precisely this way; instead, *that may be how the author designs the ANE story of creation for the covenant people of Israel.*

Additionally, suppose Genesis 1:1 is a heading for the chapter (as many scholars believe). In that case, God does not actually create anything until he declares, "Let there be light" *in* verse three. However, that may not be certain because of some ambiguity in verse one. Think of the primeval waters as analogous to an abyss or a "black hole," or as John Walton writes:

> Nearly all the creation accounts of the ancient world start their story with no operating system in place [only waters]. Egyptian texts suggest a kind of singularity where nothing is separated out and all is inert and undifferentiated.[183]

ANE gods appear to have drawn the heavens and the earth out of the watery abyss. That process brought orderly conditions for life, before which nature's systems were nonexistent or inoperative. At a minimum, chaos means

---

183. John H. Walton, *The Lost World of Genesis* (InterVarsity Press, Downers Grove, Il, 2010), p. 31. Walton cites one Sumerian text that refers to the time of darkness, heaven and earth were still joined together and nothing had been created, not even the gods—Walton quoting *Cuneiform Studies in Honor of Samuel Noah Kramer*, ed. B. Eichler et.al. (Neukirchen-Vluyn: Butzon & Bcrker, 1976), pp. 125–133.

nothing more than disordered, dysfunctional, uninhabitable, and untamed. Think of experiencing multiple tsunamis on a marsh in absolute darkness. The ancients believed the darkened deep was something like that.

"Chaos" in ANE accounts invariably includes a struggle for supremacy among the gods absent in Genesis, where only one God exists. Not yet ordered for life is better said for Genesis 1:2 than the ANE idea of violence and chaos. As we saw earlier, the ANE myths accompanying disorder are found elsewhere in scripture but for poetic purposes. Even there, Yahweh is victorious, effortlessly.

Other surviving ANE cosmologies include the Syrian, Assyrian, Hittite, and Ugaritic versions. Ugarit was a coastal city in northwest Syria with a language earlier than and related to Hebrew. Hundreds of tablets discovered at Ugarit contain Canaanite mythologies, such as the *Baal Cycle*, Anath, Yam of the sea, and Mot of the underworld.

These records are significant not because Genesis is dependent on them but because they provide a broader context into the world of the ancient Israelites. They show similar language usage, idioms, and how people generally viewed the cosmos and the spiritual world. ANE records help illuminate biblical revelation, especially in how the two differ. They also help fill in the blanks for us since biblical authors wrote for readers who already knew the landscape. Contrary to the YE notion that some faint memory about the creation events lingered in the pagan world, the special revelation in Genesis could not come from the similarities with ANE literature but where it departs from the broader landscape of the ANE.

The similarities between Genesis and other ANE literature reveal common assumptions that cannot be special revelation. Israel's experiences with the natural world were similar to their contemporaries. Israel's knowledge and use of natural resources were on the same plane as the surrounding cultures. Where *correct*, those shared assumptions about nature are not anti-*special revelation* but *general revelation*, available to all. However, their theologies were radically different.

Enuma Elish is significant because it is well-preserved and well-documented, with similarities and dissimilarities to Genesis. At the time of Judah's captivity in Babylon, Enuma Elisha's presence makes it significant for its impact on the Hebrew captives. Many scholars see Genesis as a competing creation account against Babylonian mythology.

Most scholars believe Genesis 1–11 first appeared at this time.

Linguistic evidence suggests this because some terms and concepts fit more during the time of the Exile than in the Late Bronze Age. Indeed, Genesis likely received editing sometime around the Babylonian deportation and after the Jews returned to Jerusalem seventy years later. At that time, they established a new form of Judaism (Second Temple Judaism) in the light of the return.

Why did God let the chosen people go from the Promised Land back into captivity? The early chapters of Genesis seem to show how that could happen, beginning with the "exile" of humans from Eden due to unfaithfulness. God exiled the first humans from the garden and now the covenant people from Judah.[184]

According to the Noachian flood narrative, God released "chaos" using the primeval waters above the heavens and the deep below the earth with rain for forty days and forty nights. God also confused language at a tower called Babel [Babylon]. Those stories and others find counterparts in Mesopotamian literature. But biblical authors radically reinterpret them to primarily reflect the covenantal relationship between God and Israel.

Furthermore, the Babylonian origin of EE is significant because Abraham was from Ur of the Chaldeans in the Mesopotamian region associated with Babylon and so a worshipper of other gods at the time of his calling. Abraham's migration to Canaan and Israel's later Exodus from Egypt and settlement in Canaan with its vital trade routes connecting Egypt and Mesopotamia with Israel caught in between, assured that many ideas would flow in and out of the region.

The notion that the biblical authors were unaffected by such influences is unrealistic and unnecessary because those realities are the context. There can be no doubt that Genesis contains some common assumptions with the ANE. How else could Genesis be relevant in its own time?

Upon discovering EE in the Iraqi city of Mosul (1875), the similarities with Genesis seem striking at first. Not only is the "sound" of the language

---

184. It is hard to appreciate how devastating and theologically perplexing was the Jewish experience of enslavement in Babylon. God delivered them from captivity in Egypt and now they were right back in a similar predicament. Furthermore, the gods were gods of their respective lands. If a pagan people defeated another people, and took them into slavery, it was a defeat of one god by another. Psalm 137 captures this idea: "By the rivers of Babylon, we sat and wept when we remembered Zion...for there our captors asked us for songs, our tormentors demanded songs of joy; they said, 'Sing us one of the songs of Zion.' How can we sing the songs of [Yahweh] while in a foreign land? Happy is the one who repays [Babylon] according to what you have done to us. Happy is the one who seizes your infants and dashes them against the rocks."

The last two sentences have disturbed Christians for centuries because it appears to advocate barbarism. Consequently, it is often interpreted figuratively—Babylon being a type of sin or the birthplace of sin, which will be destroyed. But this is likely a parallelism; the thought is that the Babylonians seized Hebrew babies and smashed them against rocks, i.e., *"What you have done to us."* The same will happen to them. It is like saying what goes around comes around. The Persians saw to that.

To their credit, the Jews as a whole did not abandon Yahweh for Marduk but concluded that they were responsible for their calamity. They had broken covenant with God. Covenant, fall, exile, and redemption is a constant sequence in the Hebrew Scriptures from Genesis on and for good reason.

similar to parts of the OT, but the *order* of creation is similar in Genesis 1. Here is a comparison of the two accounts drawn up by Alexander Heidel, who has influenced many scholars:[185]

Enuma Elish and Genesis

Divine spirit and matter are coeternal and coexistent	Divine spirit creates cosmic matter and exists independent of it.
Primeval chaos; (Tiamat) enveloped in darkness	The earth is a desolate waste, with darkness covering the deep (*tehom*)
Light emanates from the gods	Light created
The Creation of the firmament	The Creation of the firmament
The Creation of dry land	The Creation of dry land
The Creation of luminaries	The Creation of luminaries
The Creation of man	The Creation of man
The gods rest and celebrate	God rests and blesses the seventh day

This order of creation in EE is not as obvious as Heidel's display. EE is elaborate mythology with brief biographical sketches of the Babylonian pantheon. The order of creation is almost incidental to the story and can get lost in the epic, though it is of primary importance to students of the Bible.

Six tablets are dedicated to each stage of the creation, and a seventh tablet features the resultant rest and festivities for the gods, especially Marduk. The similarities of six plus one in both creation accounts are not likely coincidental. The numbers six and seven are present in each account, but the number seven is central in Genesis. In other words, the setting for creation was the framework of a divine week explicitly presented in Genesis and implicitly (at best) in EE. And because of the Sabbath (which can mean "week"), the weekly cycle was central to religious life in Israel, and it provided a more vivid theological vehicle for the creation story for the Israelites. It makes a case for the Hebrew God as the sole Creator against pagan deities.

EE's main storyline is how Marduk became the supreme deity in Babylon by defeating Tiamat, the *sea dragon goddess*. He then divides her carcass into two, creating a firmament or expanse with waters above and below the expanse. A similar division of waters in heaven and earth runs all through the Scriptures: In the last book of the Bible, it says, "I saw *in heaven...standing beside the sea,* those who had been victorious over the *beast* and its image and over the number of its name" (Revelation 15:1–3; emphasis mine).

---

185. Alexander Heidel, *The Babylonian Genesis: The Story of Creation,* p. 129.

One distinction between Mesopotamia, Egypt, and Israel's geography is their primary watering sources for crops. In Mesopotamia and Egypt, irrigation came primarily from rivers like the Euphrates, Tigris, and Nile River systems. That is, *from waters below the sky*. In Israel, crops received water from above the heavens (i.e., above the sun, moon, and stars), which they experienced as rain released by God in due season. They understood drought was nothing less than God withholding water from His "storehouses." Today, we know rain is condensed moisture within our atmosphere and not from a storehouse of water beyond the stars that opens and closes.[186]

According to a previous agreement, a council of deities declares Marduk all-powerful. The mythological language is so dense that you might miss the creation if you read the story literally. By contrast, Genesis is crisp, deliberate, and to the point without dense imagery.

Another order of creation in both accounts is side by side in the following table:

Enuma Elish	Genesis
When on high	When God created
Tiamat—primeval waters	*"tehom"* – Hebrew for "the deep"
Marduk injects wind in Tiamat's face	A wind from God over the face of "the deep"
Marduk splits Tiamat's waters in half, creating an expanse	God divides the waters above the heavens and below the earth, creating an expanse
Land and ocean separated	Water receives boundaries, establishing land
Creation of Sun, Moon, and stars	Creation of luminaries
Creation of animals and man	Creation of animals and man
Rest for the gods	God rests

The openings in EE and Genesis begin similarly. The ANE idea of primeval waters in Genesis is undeniable. However, Genesis 1 treats the waters as merely physical. The waters split above and below the expanse. It is too much to ask the modern reader to accept these waters as an actual explanation of either a pre-creation or initial creation condition. The waters in Genesis say more about God than they do the creation. Turbulent waters represented violence and chaos in the ANE. They were formidable threats to orderliness. In Genesis, God puts the waters in their place without incident. He doesn't need any help.

---

186. Peter Leithart, "The Firmament, Part I–III," YouTube.com.

What stands out in Genesis 1 is God's nature, not the universe's configuration. Bluntly speaking, modern science has uncovered much more *general revelation* about the universe with its trillions of stars, galaxies, black holes, quasars, nebulae, supernovas, dark matter and energy, quantum physics—need I go on? However, science cannot tell us anything about essential knowledge— God's nature and purposes—so we have the Bible. Genesis does not claim to be a revelation in its cosmology, which is too similar to other ANE accounts to be special revelation. It does claim to reveal the Creator of all.

Israel's theology stood out more in the ANE than her cosmology did.

Biblical authors knew of Tiamat, the monster of the deep, and recognized her as a myth. In scripture, a sea monster appears several times elsewhere as a mythical creature named Rahab and Leviathan. The texts refer to these creatures only to praise Yahweh for crushing them. The book of Genesis is not that kind of literature; it is about Yahweh's role in origins.

After dividing the waters and exposing the sky and the land, the heavenly bodies are next in EE. Unfortunately, the verses in this Babylonian epic relating to the sun did not survive the ravages of time. Concerning the moon, we read:

[Marduk] caused [the moon] to shine" he gave brightness to the moon; he set it over the night; he made it the adornment of the night *for the fixing of the days*" (Tablet V, lines 12–13). *He also made the stars* (one by fiat).[187]

The Genesis account also says the sun and moon (called greater and lesser lights) *"serve as signs to mark sacred times, and days... He also made the stars."* You can see that the concepts and even the tempo are similar. The missing fragment regarding the sun's creation would be crucial since the sun was a primary deity in Babylon. No doubt, the creation of the sun would have complemented that of the moon as in Genesis.

The Babylonian account has the sun, moon, and stars as gods since humans depended on them for life and appeared alive by their intentional movements. Though the Genesis account does say the luminaries "rule" the night and day, "rule" here is meant figuratively, i.e., anthropomorphically, since the luminaries are not named and simply serve functions. The sun and moon are not *living rulers* in Genesis.[188]

The most significant similarity between the two accounts is the order of creation and some details. While this order is not exact, it is too close to be coincidental. Similarities are bound to show up among people in the same world.

---

187. Umberto Cassuto and Israel Abrahams, "A Commentary on the Book of Genesis: Part 1 from Adam to Noah" (*Umberto Cassuto Biblical Commentaries 1*), (Varda Books, Skokie Illinois, 2005), p. 43.

188. Ibid. This seems obvious to us but at the time people might believe the sun and moon were alive.

This is common sense.

In an attempt to dismiss the similarities, Todd Beall writes:

To argue that Moses or whoever wrote Gen. 1–11 was *so immersed* in the ANE world that it caused him to write in the way of other ANE literature is to deny the *uniqueness of the biblical record*. Certainly, God could have directed Moses to write in this way, but he was under no obligation to do so.[189]

Notice the contradiction: "*God could have* directed Moses to write in *this way*." What way? He states it: the way that "*denies the uniqueness of the biblical record*." Really? Could God have directed Moses to deny the uniqueness of the biblical record? In other words, God *could have* misdirected us, but Beall says, "He was under no obligation to do so."

Furthermore, God is not prejudiced against ANE literature as Beall is since He inspired the book of Job about a Gentile from an unknown land in "the east," which always means east of Israel, i.e., Mesopotamia or pre-Zoroastrian Persia. Job's rare and unusual words are linguistic support for its composition centuries before Genesis and placed in the middle Bronze of the Patriarchal Period.

How much did Beall think this through? There was no "unique biblical record" to deny when Genesis was written. Any of the first entries into what would become the Bible would have been unique on its face. Yet, when the author sat down to write, it is unlikely he was conscious of writing "the Bible." Besides, it is not just the unique parts of ANE creation accounts that are critical; the similarities are too.

Confronting the YE Reform Movement claims and arguments is necessary with the historic Christian understanding of God's nature, the Bible's purposes, and the Christian Mission. C. S. Lewis wrote that many of today's ideas about God were trotted out centuries ago and rejected by the best theologians. Among those ideas are anthropomorphic views of God, rejection of inspiration for some form of dictation of the Bible or confusing inspiration with dictation, and mixed priorities concerning the Church's primary mission, all of which lead to confusion and conflict among Christians.

Beall says Moses was not "*so immersed*" in the ANE. This is pejorative. Moses was born in the ANE and educated in the greatest empire of that day— Egypt. Did he refuse to learn anything in class? Moses was a general, fighting against Israel's surrounding enemies. Where did he learn weapons technology, military strategy, and combat? He was multilingual, a prophet, writer, and

---

189. Richard Averback, Todd Beall, C. John Collins, Jud Davis, Victor P. Hamilton, Tremper III Longman, Kenneth J. Turner, John Walton, J. Daryl Charles, Richard Averback, *Reading Genesis 1–2: An Evangelical Conversation.*

administrator. Who taught him languages? Moses was not "dipped" in the ANE. *He was a product of it.*

If biblical authors detached themselves from their world, they could say *nothing* meaningful to it. Beall's use of the phrase "so immersed" in the ANE is prejudicial. Paul was all things to all men. He quoted pagan poets. Paul brilliantly divided a council of Pharisees and Sadducees by siding with the Pharisees (Acts 23:6–7). He knew their philosophical positions and exploited them. The idea that biblical authors cannot use nor even accept concepts from the world they interacted with is nonsense.

Beall adds James Atwell's voice to his. Atwell (an OE Anglican and Dean of Winchester) wrote that the shared order of creation between EE and Genesis is *"not striking."* What did he mean by that? Atwell does correct overstating the similarities, and so do I. He does not deny them. Neither do I. Atwell concludes that it "does no more than *witness to a general ANE background* to both accounts." *That is my point.* Beall denies a shared ANE background with Israel. In the absence of anything striking, Atwell nonetheless says something significant: the similarities *"witness to a general ANE background to both accounts."*[190] One witness is from the Bible and a similar one from Babylon.

Something struck.

That should be particularly striking to any one-to-one correspondence-to-reality person. There are indeed more differences than similarities between EE and Genesis. Besides being pagan theology, EE is an epical myth. It is much larger than Genesis. Much space in EE refers to the primeval battles between the gods (myth), their origins (theogony), and the universe's origins or cosmogony.

By removing the dense mythology, EE shrinks to expose a more evident order of creation.

You could take creation week from Genesis and spread it across the length and breadth of a demythologized creation week in EE, and a similar order of creation appears. In other words, an EE without the mythological language makes the similarities with Genesis more noticeable.

Nonetheless, the theological differences far outweigh the cosmological similarities, so most scholars doubt any dependence either way. Cosmological similarities and parallels do not necessitate a kinship in literary roots. The oral exchange of ideas between cultures is often at play. My point is that the *shared ideas* in cosmology between Israel and her neighbors are not special revelation. That fact exposes another blunder of YErs like Beall, who believe any shared ideas between Genesis and other ANE cultures deny the biblical record's uniqueness.

---

190. Terry Mortenson, Thane H. Ury, *Coming to Grips with Genesis.*

All the talk about waters and the sky, the sun, moon, and stars, at least on their face, are not special revelation but are simply observation-based. There is a sky, a sun, a moon, stars, and water—all of which are obvious without a Bible. Of course, there was no Bible. The *theology* of Genesis is the revelation, and *Yahweh makes the biblical record unique; the observable universe does not.*

The absence of dense, overtly religious, and mythological language in Genesis gives it a more matter-of-fact account of similar primordial stories that were speculative explanations in the ANE similar to the tendencies of all other ancient cultures. Otherwise, plugging in Yahweh's name in similar dense storylines with mythological language, would confuse Yahweh and His purposes with other deities who created the same sectors of the universe in their ways for other purposes. Genesis presents Yahweh as Creator in comparatively rational terms, as a craftsman going about his daily work.

Enuma Elish is older than Genesis, and its Sumerian sources are much older. So, where did the peoples of Mesopotamia get their similarities with Genesis? How would pagan idol worshippers know about waters above the expanse and below the earth and the general order of creation if that knowledge was special revelation?[191]

YErs are so worried about traces of ANE custom and tradition influencing biblical writers; they fail to see that assuming God superintended each word of the Bible, they place ANE assumptions in God's pen. The point is that ANE assumptions in the Bible mean *God did not write it.* The Hebrews in the ANE wrote it word-for-word — inspired, not forced. Their scribes also copied every word numerous times.

These are indisputable facts.

The nature and purposes of ANE gods generally provide the essential differences between Genesis and ANE literature. The simple *order* of creation is how ancient people conceived the natural world. A flourishing world needs light, water, air, celestial bodies for navigation and special days (in the ANE), soil, marine life, plants, birds, and animals. These divisions in nature are observable in everyday experience and do not need a scientific background or special revelation. Therefore, understanding the natural world is available to all and must be general revelation. God's self-disclosure, which is not discoverable, is special

---

191. Some YErs assert that some knowledge was passed down from Adam that remained with all cultures. "The existence of other creation myths actually lends strength to our case rather than weakening it. It shows that other cultures knew the truth of creation, but their stories have been altered from the correct biblical version over the centuries." See "Genesis: the True Creation Account," AiG website. However, it is simply asking too much to believe the elaborate pagan stories all got everything so wrong but in very similar ways, and in concert with an animist view of nature and its gods to the attending mythological creatures, yet happened to retain the order and elements of creation and floods that were common in major river systems. It is more reasonable that the ancients simply saw the visible world in a similar way. See John N. Oswalt, *The Bible Among the Myths* (2009).

revelation. YErs think the phrase *"after their kind"* is a revelation. But do we really need Moses to tell us that animals produce more animals like themselves?

Ken Ham writes on Enuma Elish, "Creation from preexisting matter is not creation at all." According to Ham, if God uses existing matter to create something, He commits "creation fraud." Ham does not mean to call God a fraud, yet his words amount to just that. God makes several things from existing matter in the Genesis story, including plants, birds, animals, and Adam and Eve.

Note Genesis 1:24, And God said, "Let *the land produce* living creatures according to their kinds: the livestock, the creatures that move along the ground, and the wild animals, each according to its kind." And it was so (emphasis mine).

Genesis 2:19 adds, "Now the Lord God had formed out of the ground all the wild animals and all the birds in the sky." According to Genesis, this was not the creation of creatures from nothing but out of *the ground*. Either the soil produced animals like a crop, or, more likely, God forms creatures out of resources in the ground like a craftsman. Given the text of Genesis, if creation ex-nihilo is to survive, then an instant creation with the "seeds of life" unfolding gradually (per Augustine) must be the case so that all that emerges has its origins from nothing. We will examine what "nothing" may mean later.

What we have is storytelling with implications for us to unpack.

The point is that God does not say, "Let there be living creatures, and it was so." That suggests that living creatures were not instant creations from nothing. For all we know, the concept of absolute "nothing," namely no time, space, or matter/energy, was not in people's consciousness in the Late Bronze Age. The concept of *absolute nothing* does not seem to occur to any of the ancients. In fact, with or without an efficient first cause, it is impossible to envision something from absolute nothing.

Throughout the ANE, the creation emerged from the darkened, disordered deep where wind also existed. Hence, creation was about bringing order to the deep. Separating the waters using wind opened up a sky (heaven); sometimes gods use sediment from within the deep to form the material to make the earth or some similar scenario.

There were ANE gods that reportedly created by fiat, such as Ptah and Marduk. Elohim explicitly wills light to appear; the heavenly bodies and marine life also come from His stated desires. Psalm 33:6, 9 says, "By the word of the Lord the heavens were made, their starry host by the breath of his mouth... For he spoke, and it came to be."

This verse says God made the heavens or the starry hosts by command, whereas Marduk only makes a single star by fiat. That is another way Genesis purposely positions Elohim as superior to Marduk. Elohim "separates" the waters and then "gathers the waters." But Genesis does not say God *made* the waters. The first day of creation does not appear to begin until the formula for creative acts is given in verse three, *"And God said, 'Let there be light.'"* If God created by His word, initiated by His commands, as recorded in the six days of creation, the formless deep was implicitly pre-creation. For until verse three, God said nothing.

Today, we believe God made all things out of nothing, *but we do not get this from a literal reading of Genesis.* The soil participates in creating the things the ancients believed depended on the soil—plants, land animals, including birds, and humans. According to Genesis, God makes all those things from the ground. The heavenly bodies and marine life had no connection to the soil, so God created them by fiat, which is not likely coincidental.

The concept of creation ex-nihilo came much later when better knowledge of God's nature in relationship to the cosmos developed. An infinite God does not exist within a finite space such as this universe. New efforts in theology and philosophy led to the realization that God is without time, space, and matter/energy—the universe's contents.

Furthermore, God does not create the universe from within the universe. He does not take time to create time. "By faith we understand that the worlds were prepared by the word of God, *so that what is seen was made from things that are not visible*" (Hebrews 11:3, NRSV). The author of Hebrews is conscious of living by faith and not by sight. If God made *all visible things*, then it follows that he made them from things invisible.

Historically, Christian theology understands that God created everything in the universe from *nothing in the universe.* But YErs believe that everything made was a *special creation* from absolute nothing and that God made everything in segments or one at a time. But that does not match the "one-to-one correspondence to reality" YErs impose upon Genesis. In Genesis, God made many things from the ground, including Adam.

Besides, Hebrews 11:3 does not say God made everything from nothing. It says, "What is seen was made *from things* [not from *no things*] but things that are invisible." Invisible things exist. What are those invisible things? We do not know, or I do not know. John Lennox, the Oxford mathematician, and Christian Apologist said, "I do not believe the universe came from nothing; I believe it came from God, but that God is not physical."[192]

I could say, "God prepared all things by His Word," and stop there. Hebrews 11:3 does not stop there. God used things (plural) that were not visible. Spoken words are not visible, so some believe they might be candidates for *things* God could use to create. But words are not exactly building blocks. He exercises the power of his will by command or desire. But invisible things must be things that exist, or they could not be *things.* Being invisible is still being, and being is something, not nothing. The author of Hebrews would have been

---

192. "God, Science & the Big Questions: Leading Christian Thinkers Respond to the New Atheists," reasonablefaith.org, YouTube clip.

well-acquainted with these distinctions since he was likely from the highly philosophical school in Alexandria, Egypt.

When we say God made all things by His Word and at the same time insist that He made all things from nothing, we cannot mean His Word is nothing. Furthermore, creating everything *by* His Word is not the same as creating everything *out of His words.* For example, a king could command the building of a temple. As a result, kings got credit for building projects they did not personally build, such as Herod's Temple. Yet the king's servants make temples out of things, not out of commands, so they build or create *by the king's authority.*

So what does "ex nihilo" mean that is compatible with Hebrews 11:3? The idea of "nothing" in ex-*nihilo* means that whatever the invisible "things" God used could not come from *this universe,* such as time, space, or matter/energy. Strangely enough, the pre-Big Bang singularity, or its origin, seems to confirm this.[193]

A literal interpretation of Genesis does not.

According to Christian cosmology, the universe's cause was not a *material* cause (nothing material existed) but an *efficient* cause (agency), i.e., God creates ex-nihilo and sustains all other causes in operation. The ANE gods created things by various means, including procreation, the use of blood ("life is in the blood"), and from the land or soil as in days three and six of Genesis.

Ancient people believed that life came from those three things: sex, blood, and soil. Note Genesis 2:7, "The Lord God formed the human from *the topsoil of the fertile land* and blew life's breath into his nostrils" (CEB). Their experiences with nature told them how life begins—observation again. We see all three methods (sex, blood, and soil) in ancient creation myths.

For instance, the *Song of the Hoe* (pickax), also called *The Creation of the Pickax,* a Sumerian creation myth from the late third millennium BC, speaks of flesh produced from the soil.[194]

Denis Lamoureaux, Professor of Science and Religion at the University of Alberta, writes:

> The [ANE] Hymn to E'engura states that "humans broke through the earth's surface like plants." In the Sumerian text KAR 4, the gods plant

---

193. I do not mean the *singularity* that birthed the Big Bang is in the Bible but only that the biblical language does not contradict the nature of the *singularity* that according to physics was not time, space, matter, or the laws of physics—all of which came afterward with the Big Bang. The Bible does not rule out the singularity and Big Bang. It simply does not address them, which should encourage believers.

194. See John Skinner, *A Critical and Exegetical Commentary on Genesis* (New York, Charles Scribner's Sons, 1910, Kindle Edition), Location 1911. On Genesis 2:19, it says, like plants (v. 12) the animals are "boldly said to be produced by the earth, their bodies being part of the earth's substance."

the seeds of humans into the earth and people later "sprout from the ground like barley..." (Interestingly, this sprouting mechanism seems to be the creative process used in Genesis 1:24, where God commands, "Let the land produce living creatures." The Hebrew verb translated "produce" is yaşa' and it is the same verb used in Genesis 1:12: "The land produced vegetation." With regard to the [craftsmanship] of making humans, it appears in Atrahasis where a goddess mixes clay and the blood of a slain god to fashion seven males and seven females. In Enki and Ninmah, an intoxicated divine being uses earth to make imperfect human beings. And in Gilgamesh, a pinch of clay is used to create a man.[195]

If Genesis 1:24 said, "Let the land produce *barley*," the soil's reference would be obvious. But when it says, *"Let the land produce animals,"* the soil does not register. Why? Because we are not people of the ANE. Genesis 1:24 implies that God uses the same life-giving attribute of soil, for it clearly says the land produced not just the vegetation *but all the land animals:* perhaps a whole crop of them? We can't go that far because it is not that clear. But it does not say that God created Adam and Eve from nothing. Instead, God specifically forms Adam with dust, dirt, clay, or soil (which is not clear either).

The author chooses a creative technique to create Adam and Eve for two reasons: first, the author is interested in an intimate relationship between God and man after the impersonal and sweeping decrees of chapter 1; and second, the Hebrews would have been familiar with creating from clay or soil—a common idea in the ANE.

The account of Adam's creation in Genesis 2 was special in the story, not because God formed him from nothing or by command but by God's intentional and personal act of forming *a particular man* and infusing him with an animating "breath." An irony is that this special act is figurative because God has no hands or lungs. Nonetheless, whatever way "hands" and "breathe" correspond to God's genuine attributes, then that is how He really did it.

God infuses us with the animating spirit that comes from Him, not literal breath from His lungs. We still do not know how God brought everything into existence beyond the natural processes we can observe that He also created. How they exist and how they got there is unknown. Natural methods are not Mother Nature acting but God's operations or what some call nature's mechanisms that He upholds and sustains to carry out His desires.

Here is the point: Christians believe the universe came from nothing in the universe, including time and space. Nature then takes its course in time-space through secondary causes or cause and effect and the laws of physics. We believe God sustains and upholds cause and effect since nature is not self-existent.

195. Denis Lamoureux, John H. Walton, C. John Collins, William D. Barrick, Gregory A. Boyd, Philip G. Ryken, Ardel B. Caneday, Matthew Barrett, Stanley N. Gundry, *Four Views on the Historical Adam (Counterpoints: Bible and Theology).* page 57

This understanding clarifies historical Christian cosmogony, which allows various theories on the mechanism for creation. Of course, YErs do not accept this flexibility. They know their beliefs are correct, which is inconsistent since believing is not the same as knowing. In other words, they cannot *know* these things; they can only *believe* their opinions about biblical literature, which can be figurative or literal. Yet those who disagree are called "compromisers." That is not how opinions work. That treats Genesis like a legal document, not a creative narrative.

We have already seen that Augustine and Aquinas believed secondary causes were instrumental in the creation. Indeed, secondary causes continue today as new things form: each new generation of life, new stars, and galaxies result from secondary causes sustained by God. Stars are developing throughout the universe at this moment. Even in conceiving, the competition for life continues. One sperm cell defeats millions of others to fertilize an egg. "*The losers die.*"

Even human conception is "in tooth and claw."

Is this drama in human conception also the result of the fall? Suppose God intended that one sperm would comfortably make its way to the egg in perfect harmony until Adam sinned. Indeed, it would be a strange act if the Creator then contrived the massacre of between forty million to 1.2 billion sperm cells in every ejaculate of every male creature throughout time. That mass slaughter of spermatozoa may approach the number of stars in the universe.

You might say a sperm cell does not qualify as a life form. A sperm cell represents half a human, which would be worth more than microbes or many insects. Without sperm, there would be no humans. *Sperm determines the gender and, to a large extent, the specific person* different from the other millions of spermatozoa that perished. The egg is singular and remains the same, no matter the sperm. Like millions of salmon swimming upstream, life may be a race toward a goal. Salmon sacrifice their lives, racing upstream to create many more lives, as the Apostle Paul declared, "I have finished the race" (2 Timothy 4:7). Everything in the universe seems to speak this "language" (see chapter 26).[196]

Furthermore, the Hebrew word *bara,* a divine act of creation (not necessarily from nothing) applied to marine life, suggests God created them by fiat. However, Moses does not use *bara* about plants, animals, birds, or humans. Instead of *bara* "to create," he uses the word *asah* "to make" or "produce," no

---

196. The assault of millions of sperm invading the vagina has been compared to US troops landing at Normandy on D-Day, where many perished to achieve a goal. The odd truth is that the vagina contains acids and antibodies that treat sperm like invading cells, killing the vast majority of them so that millions of sperm are necessary for one to succeed. It is not easy to come to grips with the stark realities of the God revealed in creation. Neither does evolution give a satisfactory answer since it is hardly intuitive that evolutionary processes should create such complex obstacles to reproduction.

doubt because the land does the producing. Genesis states that God orders the land to produce (*asah*) every living thing on land. Does this mean God did not create all things out of nothing? The answer would be "yes," if the Genesis account is literal.

Interestingly, God does not say to Adam, "From *nothing* you came and to *nothing* you shall return," but rather, "You will...go back to the soil from which you were formed. *You were made from soil, and you will become soil again*" (Genesis 3:19 GNT) [197]

YErs do not take Genesis literally. That is, they literally don't.

The revelation in Genesis is not in the fact of creation widely believed in the ANE, nor was it the schedule employed in creating or the chronological sequence of created things or whatever methods were conceivable at the time. Instead, the revelation is the disclosure of the God of Israel, who is solely responsible for a universe that He transcends.

He also has eternal purposes for it.

---

197. God says Adam was made from the soil and will return to the soil. There is no heaven or hell, or immortal soul mentioned. Those concepts, like creation from nothing, developed later. So is this passage literal, or unclear, or what? Furthermore, "return to the soil" was simple observation at the time of writing and not a scientific explanation of our atoms breaking apart into the ground. People lived with death all around them. They could see that corpses wither and become soil.

(Figure 1: One of the seven Enuma Elish Tablets on Creation from Babylon)

12.
ANCIENT NEAR EAST LITERATURE AND GENESIS PART 2

We saw similarities between the Mesopotamian myth EE and Genesis, including references to a watery deep before specific creative acts. Those waters are separated to create an expanse between heaven and earth. The number of tablets in EE (seven) corresponds to the number of days of the Genesis creation. Each tablet appears to correspond roughly to the seven days of creation. The biblical evidence in the SDWC is theological. Genesis does not teach science in the modern sense; there is no scientific method found in its pages. We tend to read our science into the story. ANE creation accounts are about correctly identifying God (of the Hebrews) or the gods (of the pagans) and everyone's place in the cosmos.

Canaan and Egypt

Among the Canaanites, Yam (the mythical sea monster) and Baal-Hadad are Tiamat and Marduk's equivalents. They fight a similar battle. Baal, the storm god, defeats Yam by bludgeoning, while Marduk kills Tiamat and separates her carcass (waters), creating the heavens and earth by injecting an expanse of wind into her that becomes the sky. In Syrian mythology, the storm god, Hadad (the Syrian equivalent to the Canaanite Baal-Hadad), defeats the serpent, *Těmtum*, found on Syrian seals of the eighteenth to sixteenth century BC, was the equivalent to Tiamat. These shared ideas are in the genre of myth.

The gods most likely to lead the Israelites into idolatry were Canaanite, and Baal worship, more than any other system competed with Yahweh. The climax of that struggle is in 1 Kings 18. Four hundred and fifty prophets of Baal versus the lone prophet of Yahweh, Elijah, meet in a showdown to determine which one is the true God.

According to Canaanite mythology, Baal was the son of El, the chief god. Abraham worshipped an "El," who later became associated with Elohim. Baal was more powerful than El in the Ugaritic Baal Cycle dated around the Exodus. Since Baal defeated Yam, the god of the sea in the Canaanite pantheon, he would have power over the waters. Baal was a storm god often depicted holding a lightning bolt. Interestingly, the prophets are quick to give Yahweh credit for defeating the sea (Psalm 74:12–14; Job 26:12; Isaiah 51:9).

> Awake, as in days gone by, as in generations of old. Was it not you who cut Rahab to pieces, who pierced that [sea] monster through? Was it not you who dried up the sea, the waters of the great deep, who made a road in the depths of the sea so that the redeemed might cross over? (Isaiah 51:9).

Dividing the Red Sea calls to mind the division of waters at creation. That's what gods did in the ANE. The miracle in 2 Kings occurred when most of Israel's northern kingdom abandoned Yahweh for Baal. Yahweh had just exposed Baal as a fraud in 1 Kings 18 when Baal failed to light a dry fire for a unique offering that could prove the Canaanite deity is the true God. When it was Yahweh's turn, Elijah soaked the wood for the sacrifice and flooded the area around the site with water, calling on Yahweh to ignite the wood, which he did instantly, likely with a bolt of lightning, thus defeating Baal. "When all the people saw this, they fell prostrate and cried, '[Yahweh]—he is God. [Yahweh]—he is God.'" The Master of the seas is the one who created them, Yahweh, and not the storm god of Canaanite mythology. Yahweh does not carry around lightning bolts, but He used them since water, lightning, and storms were a fascination in the ANE.

Bill Arnold observes:

> The West Semitic background for Genesis 1 may be reflected in the Ugaritic Baal Cycle, in which the storm-god Baal defeats Yam, the sea-god, and Mot, the underworld-god in order to secure kingship. Dated to the fourteenth century BCE, it tells of Baal's struggle for supremacy in the West Semitic pantheon and of his right to succeed the chief older deity, El. It has been proposed that Genesis 1 should be read as a demythologized Canaanite [refutation] assuming the wind of 1:2 is related to the wind Baal used against the sea monster in the Baal Cycle, and that těhôm ("deep") has Canaanite mythological origins.[198]

A Leviathan-like sea monster appears throughout the ANE and goes by different names according to the languages spoken and the deities worshiped. For example, at Ugarit, the fifth tablet in the *Poems of Baal and Anath*, the sea monster's name is Lotan, meaning *"coiled," "the wriggling serpent,"* and the *"mighty one with seven heads"* is the biblical Leviathan.[199]

In Genesis 1:2, the author does not present the waters in mythological terms. In other words, they are not given names and status as gods or identified as sea serpents. Instead, they are simply the primordial waters, a common belief in the ANE but without mythological language. The pre-creation waters are analogous to a singularity where nothing is differentiated, yet everything a universe needs except life is inside. The relatively easy way God handles the waters is the author's way of treating them as inanimate.

The serpent in Eden (Genesis 3:1) serves a similar purpose in causing trouble and curses, but he does not appear to be a sea serpent (as in Revelation) but a wild beast from the wilderness as far as the story goes. Notice Isaiah 27:1,

---

198. "Genesis," *New Cambridge Bible Commentary,* Location 1238.

199. The notion that Leviathan is a dinosaur is without foundation. See James B. Prichard, *Ancient Near Eastern Texts: Related to the Old Testament* (Princeton University Press, 1969), pp. 137–138. See also C. Uehlinger, "Leviathan," *Dictionary of Deities and Demons in the Bible,* 2nd ed. (Grand Rapids: Wm. B. Eerdmans Publishing, 1999), pp. 511–515.

"In that day, the Lord will punish with his sword... Leviathan the *gliding serpent*, Leviathan the *coiling serpent*; [Yahweh] will slay the *monster of the sea.*"[200]

The book of Revelation reflects this ancient concept:

Then war broke out in heaven. Michael and his angels fought against the dragon, and the dragon and his angels fought back. But he was not strong enough, and they lost their place in heaven. The great dragon was hurled down—*that ancient serpent* called the devil, or Satan, who leads the whole world astray... But woe to the earth *and the sea,* because the devil has gone down to you. He is filled with fury, because he knows that his time is short." Then from his mouth *the serpent spewed water like a river,* to overtake the woman and sweep her away *with the torrent.* (Revelation 12:7–15)

(Note that the earth and sea are differentiated. For us, the earth includes the sea).

This verse is in the symbolism of Jewish apocalyptic, as is the rest of Revelation. Jewish apocalyptic is like mythology but applies to the end time. Mythology is about origins. Determining the truth that apocalyptic literature represents is not our purpose.

A Leviathan-type sea monster is a mythological character throughout the ANE. Such mythological references in the Bible are poetic or symbolic in similar ways to monsters that appear in apocalyptic literature like Daniel, Revelation, and various parts of scripture.

In Psalm 74, the multiheaded Leviathan is referred to by name:

But God is my King from long ago... It was you who split open the sea by your power; you broke *the heads of the monster in the waters.* It was you who crushed *the heads of Leviathan* and gave it as food to the creatures of the desert. (Psalm 74:12–14)

Psalm 74 uses the division of primeval waters in mythological terms (Leviathan) to describe splitting the sea and crushing Pharaoh and his armies. A sea monster is symbolic of disorder and evil, God's enemies. The final use of the symbol is Revelation 12:3, "Then a second sign appeared in heaven, ominous, foreboding: a great red dragon, with seven crowned heads and ten horns." That is a reference to Satan in the guise of Leviathan. Read the same verse from the Expanded Bible, just as it reads:

Then another wonder...appeared in heaven: There was a giant red dragon with seven heads [reminiscent of the many-headed Leviathan representing evil and chaos, here representing Satan [Psalm 74:14; Isaiah 27:1; Daniel 7:1–9] and seven crowns [diadems; royal crowns] on each head. (EXB)

---

200. Leviathan is obviously the mythical sea monster, not a dinosaur.

Dangerous waters attached to rivers can symbolize Egypt/Pharaoh and Satan. For example, the Nile irrigates Egyptian farmland yet can destroy infrastructure through torrential floods. In Canaan, rainfall was the only consistent way to water crops. Since rain came from the waters above the expanse, it appeared to come directly from God.

The myths of Marduk defeating Tiamat, Hadad defeating Lotan, Ra defeating Apep, and Atum defeating Nehebkau are ANE examples of the struggle against chaos, disorder, or the case of later biblical references when Yahweh defeats Leviathan. Again, the mythological language is absent in Genesis but found in some poetic and apocalyptic literature of the Bible.[201]

It is essential to distinguish between the primordial waters as a natural phenomenon and the mythology surrounding them. In pagan mythology, the gods continued to struggle against the forces of chaos seen in the waters, which helped explain the cycle of good seasons and bad, triumph and tragedy. We noticed that the Egyptian sun god Ra followed his course in the sky westward daily. At night, he entered the underworld only to struggle with the darkened deep, then rose triumphantly in the east each morning. The Egyptian myth of a deity defeating disorder played out daily with sunrise and sunset.

As late as AD 98, the Roman historian Tacitus states that the edge of the world is the sea north of the land of the Swedes [the Arctic], "where nature stops." There the sun sinks *into the sea at night*. Tacitus believed one could hear the sun rising from the waters at dawn! The Roman author Pliny the Elder said, "There, twice in every twenty-four hours, the ocean's vast tide sweeps in a flood over a large stretch of land and hides Nature's everlasting controversy about whether this region belongs to the land or the sea." The ancients seemed to think that the oceans and the land competed for space. A victory for the land would be order, while a water world is disorder.[202]

We must face the fact that Genesis, written many centuries earlier than the Roman Empire, is the product of a world we do not understand very well. Understanding the Bible is not the same as knowing the words in Hebrew and looking them up in a lexicon. That is no different than looking up an English word in a dictionary. It doesn't explain the concepts behind the words or the context. No matter who we are—Catholic, Protestant, Orthodox, Jew, scholar, or layperson—it is likely that we do not understand the scripture as well as we might think. We have simply unearthed countless puzzle pieces that still give us an incomplete picture of the Bible's settings.

---

201. An important distinction between ancient mythology and apocalyptic is that the former is about origins and the latter is about the end-times. This might indicate that pagans knew their myths were symbolic as Israelites knew apocalyptic is symbolic.

202. We can relate to a land/ocean "competition" from a local perspective as hurricanes threaten coastal areas and can change them. Even so, a modern, secular eschatology is found in climate change zealots. Climate change issues are real but the hysteria is not.

The ancient world feared that disorder could engulf the world by return-ing to pre-creation conditions. Storms, tsunamis, hurricanes, typhoons, and river floods were a terrifying reminder of potential chaos. So the gods must be pleased with humans if they are to escape a water world. Noah's flood is descrip-tive of a return to the primal disorder where the waters above the heavens rained down, and the fountains under the earth burst open (Genesis 7:11–12). Other flood narratives say a similar thing.

A literal translation of Deuteronomy 5:8 indicates this: "Thou dost not make to thee a graven image, any similitude which [is] in the heavens above, and which [is] *in the earth beneath, and which [is] in the waters under the earth*" (YLT; emphasis mine). Waters under the earth may not be the oceans we are familiar with, but ocean waters (the Great Deep) below the earth's position. Technically, oceans are on the earth, not under it. Tombs and temples through-out the ANE confirm this (see figure 2).

The primordial waters seem analogous to our understanding of space that holds everything in suspension. The ancients did not conceive of unbounded empty space. Instead, objects in the universe, including the gods, were birthed not in space but from the primeval waters. This concept seems to be the general idea throughout the ANE, with some details varying among cultures.

Nonetheless, the Israelites believed that chaos, disorder, and desolation come from breaking the covenant, not that Yahweh lost to evil forces. Yahweh never struggles.

> The Lord reigns [He is] robed in majesty and armed with strength; indeed, *the world is established, firm and secure.* Your throne was estab-lished long ago; you are from all eternity. The seas have lifted up, Lord, the seas have lifted up their voice; *the seas have lifted up their pounding waves. Mightier than the thunder of the great waters, mightier than the breakers of the sea—the Lord on high is mighty.* (Psalm 93:1–3)

When Job felt cut off by God's wrath, he said, "Am I the sea, or the mon-ster of the deep, that you put me under guard?" (Job 7:12). Job tended toward hyperbole. Who wouldn't under the same circumstances? But his hyperbole is not ours. We are far removed from the ancient concept of the cosmic deep.

Scholars have noted that Egyptian creation stories share similarities with Genesis on specifics, while EE offers broader similarities. Bill T. Arnold at Asbury University writes:

> The Egyptian material offers several interesting parallels with Genesis 1, including the belief in a creator god who made the universe *by verbal fiat.* The so-called Memphite Theology is preserved on a monumental inscription placed in the temple of the god Ptah at Memphis, probably composed during the thirteenth century BCE. In this text, Ptah creates by divine word and was "satisfied" (or "rested") after his work. Even more striking is the Instruction of Merikare, which [declares] that the deity

subdued chaos (or "the water monster"), created heaven and earth for the sake of humanity, *breathed life into their nostrils, created them according to his image, and according to his likeness,* and finally, that he created for them plants and animals, fish and fowl for food.[203]

Various pantheons and theological systems existed throughout ancient Egypt's rich and complex history. In the "Instruction of King Merikarē," the sun god is the creator of humans in his likenesses. Atum commanded the creation of plants and animal life; the sun god Ra emerged from the waters and formed man in his image; *Khnum fashioned man with clay on a potter's wheel with his breath, giving life to the image.* In other accounts, man springs from the tears of Atum (the sun).[204]

In Enuma Elish, we saw the splitting of Tiamat's body, opening the sky and establishing firm ground. The tombs in the Valley of the Kings of Egypt, seen by millions, picture a similar view of the cosmos, complete with a female body arched over the universe in a dome *shape* where she gives birth to the heavenly bodies. Above her are the gods' dwelling place and a king's place in the afterlife, where they travel in boats on the waters above the sky. Another female body below the sky lies in a semi-flat or reclining position to represent the irregularities in the earth's surface with its mountains and valleys (see figure 3).

Somewhere below the earth's surface is the netherworld or Shoal, and below that, more waters.[205]

Dissimilarity and Common Assumptions in the ANE

All ANE cosmologies, including Genesis, exhibit some common assumptions about the cosmos and life's necessities on earth. While Genesis is similar to the rest of ANE literature, the dissimilarities are more significant. The lack of ANE mythology, the divine rest in the form of a quasi-Hebrew Sabbath,[206] the unique style of Genesis 1, and especially the nature of Israel's God contribute to the profound differences between ANE literature and Genesis. The similarities become more apparent when stripping the ANE accounts of mythological language about gods and monsters.

---

203. "Genesis," *New Cambridge Bible Commentary* (Kindle edition), location 1217.

204. See Johnny V. Miller, John M. Soden, *In the Beginning... We Misunderstood: Interpreting Genesis 1 in Its Original Context* (Kregel Publications, Grand Rapids Michigan, 2012), page 79.

205. There is no reason to believe that a correct understanding of the cosmos is necessary for divine inspiration since God did not compose the Bible and since the make-up of the cosmos is not the subject of divine revelation. Rather, God's self-disclosure is the Bible's focus. `

206. The seventh day in Genesis is never called "the Sabbath." It does not end with a necessary sundown that completes the Israelite Sabbath, which is a shadow of God's eternal rest in Christ (Colossians 2:16-17; Hebrews 3-4).

Genesis is revolutionary in its theology but *not* for the necessities of life as understood in the ANE: water, light, air, land, food, seeds, animals, and daily work. In contrast, Genesis reveals Yahweh as One *Almighty* God who cares for and about the human family and transcends the created order. Instead of endowing a select group of kings and nobles with a divine image as most pagan gods did, Yahweh created *all humans* in his image, male and female. According to Genesis, everything else in the heavens and earth is inanimate except for living creatures.

While God upholds the universe, his nature sets him apart from it. Pagan deities generally emerged from within the universe and occupied the same space, time, and matter as the creation. Pagan gods were imminent but could be impersonal as nature itself. They were humanlike with character flaws, and many could grow old and die.

The first chapters of the Bible show God is transcendent *and personal,* but he is not creaturely, i.e., moving, laboring, or resting in this world, except for literary purposes. Literary devices cannot establish God's nature. God is not another thing in the universe or an individual alongside other individuals on earth or anywhere else. Genesis 1–3 illustrates two different perspectives on how humans may experience God in two creation accounts set side by side. First, Genesis 1 presents God as transcendent, but in chapters 2–3, God is immanent, even intimate, which is much easier for the ancient writers to describe than absolute transcendence. In both these ways, the children of Israel and all people can experience God.

Scholars recognize Genesis 1 for its mastery of the language. It is a highly stylized and efficient use of ancient Hebrew. Genesis avoids the superstitious animism, widespread in the ancient world to present one God outside the primeval waters, i.e., outside the universe.

The pagans used incantation, magic, sexual arousal, and performing certain ceremonies at festivals in hopes of moving the gods to increase fertility. They hoped to stimulate the gods to fertilize the crops, breed domestic animals, and multiply successful childbirth. The festivals of Israel celebrated the blessings already given with thanksgiving, while the winter festivals among the pagans attempted to arouse the gods for a bountiful harvest.

For Yahweh, religious festivals were meaningful only in celebrating a genuine fellowship with God by a holy people. Festivals dedicated to God by a religious class that oppresses the poor and the innocent were self-indulgent parties. Their religious pretense was the worst hypocrisy. This moral concern in Yahweh essentially separates Him from ANE deities. Israel's religious practices affected most aspects of daily life: worship, relationships, work, time management, diet, dress, and a social structure that recognized in all humans the dignity of God's image, if in a primitive way.

Most ANE cosmogonies state that light emerged first out of the darkened deep. For example, Ra, the sun god of Egypt, divided the light from the darkness at the beginning of his creative activity. In Genesis, light also comes first, but the author does not identify it. God simply says, "Let there be light...and there was." However, that was mere light, not *a light*, i.e., not a lit object—just light. The ancients believed that light existed independently, not necessarily bound to objects like the sun, moon, stars, or even a lamp. Umberto Cassuto writes:

> According to [the ANE view], the sun is not the cause of daytime, for [daytime was believed to exist] without the [sun]. This is an empirical concept based on the observation that light pervades the atmosphere even before sunrise and also after sundown. Although *we know* that this light emanates from the sun only, nevertheless it is a fact that there is daylight even when the sun is not visible in the sky. This then is the meaning of the verse: that just as at the beginning and at the end of every day there is light without sun, so throughout those first three days God caused light to shine...from some other source without recourse to the sun; but when he created the luminaries he handed over to them the task of separation, that is, he commanded that the one should serve by day and the others should serve at night, and thus they would all become signs for distinguishing the two periods of time. In addition, the sun's light would naturally augment the already-existing daylight.[207]

The idea here is that the sun disappeared into *the underworld* after sundown, so these ancients believed the sun left the universe. We know there is residual light from the sun after sunset and before sunrise because it doesn't leave the universe, whereas the ancients saw such light as independent from the sun or anything else. That seems to be how the ANE and the author of Genesis treat the first light. The making of lights on day four is too explicit (and day one too vague) to take it any other way than that the sun, moon, and stars did not exist until the fourth day. Johnny V. Miller and John M. Soden write, "Since Atum, Amun, and Ra are all connected with the sun, light was then in existence, even though the sun itself had not yet risen." In other words, light existed before the creation of the sun.[208]

God once asked Job, "Do you know where the light comes from or what the source of darkness is?" (Job 38:19). That was one of several rhetorical questions in the dialogue. Job does not know where the source of light is in the

---

207. Umberto Cassuto and Israel Abrahams, "A Commentary on the Book of Genesis: from Adam to Noah," *Umberto Cassuto Biblical Commentaries 1* (Varda Books, 2005), p. 44.

208. Johnny V. Miller, John M. Soden, *In the Beginning... We Misunderstood: Interpreting Genesis 1 in Its Original Context* (Kregel Electronic Publications, 2012), p. 78.

universe. Therefore, the obvious answer to us, "the sun," or even God's radiance, would be wrong.[209]

To the Bronze Age Hebrews, the sun merely carried light like a lamp. Yet this is a world where the sun was, even more, the dominant source of light to people without floodlights, light bulbs, or streetlights. It would not occur to Job that a simple lamp like the sun is responsible for all the light he experienced in the universe, even a universe as relatively tiny as Job's universe. The implication is that light exists of its own beyond the objects that carry it. Light itself was a thing.

The claim that God made the sun on the first day claims more than is said. God's said, "Let there be light," not *a light* or a luminary to govern the day as explicitly stated on day four. Furthermore, there could be no sun, moon, or stars without light, otherwise known as the heavens. This claim contradicts the assumption that God made the universe in Genesis 1:1. If the heavens existed from verse one, then light existed, but the transcendent statement "Let there be light" suggested the actual beginning of the creation that was merely announced or anticipated in verse one.

The assumption that the heavens were meant by "Let there be light" is reading between the lines on day one and ignoring the obvious on day four. To read modern science into the Bible—whether mainstream or YE science— is a hermeneutical method called *concordism*. Concordism is making scripture accord with science. That is not necessary. Light of itself was a thing on its own in the ANE, and the sun was something that held light. This account is an authentic ANE story in the Hebrew tradition inspired but not written by Israel's God.

Examples of *concordism* are reading into scripture such modern ideas as a sun-centered solar system, the earth as a globe, or the YE theory of flood geology in the late Bronze Age. Some OECs read the Big Bang into the words, "Let there be light," even though the BB was unheard of until the twentieth century.[210] Even Einstein was not ready for the Big Bang until the end of his life—to his regret. *Nonetheless, YErs are correct to say that we should not read billions of years into Genesis or read evolution between the lines. There is no reasonable way to establish these modern ideas from texts too vague to support them. More importantly, the history of Israel shows no trace of these concepts.*

The mining of scripture for *modern* scientific nuggets hidden in the text is an artificial attempt to imbue a kind of supernatural "sleight of hand" in the

---

209. Physics tells us that the primary reason the sky is dark at night is not the setting of the sun. Instead, the visible stars whose light has had time to reach earth is not sufficient to replace the light of the sun. When enough time elapses for all starlight in the universe to reach us, there would be a perpetual day sky.

210. There were ideas that were precursors of the BB, e.g., Augustine's instant creation with seeds of life.

Bible as if God slipped hidden messages to assure present-day devotees that He inspired the Scriptures or even wrote them. That is more like a Nostradamus-like fascination than faith in the God of the Bible. It is unnecessary for the Bible to be something it is not or for the authors to be people they were not, nor does God need to be "clever" to prove Himself.[211]

God seems satisfied to accommodate the historical context at every point in the life of ancient Israel. His revelation unfolds as human knowledge progresses, which is true today. Revelations did not stop with the book of Revelation. The following words of Jesus reflect this divine sensitivity toward human progress: "There is so much more I would like to say to you, but it's more than you can grasp at this moment" (John 16:12 TPT). Jesus then promised that the Holy Spirit should come and enlighten the developing Church.

God's revelation increases to the degree that humans can receive it. Parents do not feed babies foods when they are not ready, nor do they feed them faster than they can swallow. The Apostle Paul's words in Galatians 4:4 are decisive: "When the set time had fully come, God sent his Son."

Premier scholars are not concordists for good reasons. The Bible is not a book of science. It is not interested in science since nothing recognizable as science appears in the text (talking about things in nature is not science). What would happen if modern science or YE science turns out to be wrong, and people used those opinions to interpret the scriptures or evangelize? (See chapter 15, *Past Presumptions and the Bible*,). Whatever the world's current view, every generation seems to read their understanding into the Bible, from geocentrism to heliocentrism, special creation, evolution, or some combination. The Bible has been an all-you-can-eat buffet for science, and every generation digs in.

It is a blessing and a stroke of inspiration that any "science" associated with creation is incidental and uncommitted in the Bible. The Old Testament form-critical scholar, Hermann Gunkel, wrote:

Eden is the beginning of theology and of philosophy. It is no wonder that special emphasis has been laid upon these features and that every generation, since Genesis, has been known [to] read into it its own deepest thoughts.[212]

Most elements in the Creation account: a watery deep, the separation of light from darkness, sky from land, land from waters, and the origin of luminaries,

---

211. It is remarkable that the Bible comes from a nonscientific world, yet, it allows any age for the earth and universe simply by not addressing the subject directly. Because the Bible allows for something, does not mean we should draw that "something" from the text. It simply means that humans are free to make discoveries that are outside the purposes of scripture.

212. Hermann Gunkel, *The Legends of Genesis: The Biblical Saga and History* (Kindle edition), Location 263.

birds, fish, animals, and humans created last are standard components of origins throughout the ANE. Nonetheless, there is "some assembly required."

Those elements were commonly understood, like our idea of knowledge in the public domain. The gods, theologies, and theogonies in ANE creation accounts were pagan. Still, the world's visible contents, such as water, light, air, land, seed, plants, birds, and animals, and their essential functions were observable to all. Even a daily order of creation ending in rest for the gods was not unique to Israel, as we saw with Enuma Elish.

Their intimate connection with nature informed the ancients that specific things were necessary for the world to function well. It was evident that some things had to develop with a rudimentary order, not in our scientific sense but in a practical and commonsense way. The people of the ANE made assumptions according to their only tool for observation, their naked eyes. That fact has enormous implications for determining just what Genesis reveals.

For example, John C. Collins writes:

Some suggest that the word 'kind' is roughly equivalent to "species" and that the text is opposed to any notion of new species developing from old ones...the term [kind] is not as technical as "species"; it means something like "category" or "variety," and its basis for classification is *appearance*. [The text] simply says that these first plants bore their fruit according to their kinds and that the first animals were according to their kinds. This does not say that these are the only "kinds" that ever were or could be.[213]

Ancient peoples built cities and large communities near water sources like rivers and lakes because they recognized fundamental interconnections in their environment. How order originated was the question they thought to answer. We do too. Through the ages, uneducated and educated alike perceived a law in nature (Natural Law) that governs the essential way things are. What organizing power or powers established this order? Order in nature was apparent throughout the ANE, but who was responsible for it? And what was its purpose?

Quenching thirst is vital to all living things and a preoccupation in arid climates. The power of water to give life or destroy it has been a stark reality for humanity throughout time. Egypt had the Nile; Canaan had the Jordan and Sea of Galilee; Mesopotamia had the Tigris and Euphrates river systems that made stable life possible. Water sources make agriculture possible and provide various plant life suitable for food and trees for building projects. An abundance of water and plants ensures a large variety of marine life and land animals that, in turn, provide food, tools, clothing, and trade opportunities. Abundant water sources allowed agriculture and the domestication of animals to create a regular food supply, meat, dairy, and clothing supplies. With reliable water sources,

---

213. C. John Collins, *Genesis 1–4: A Linguistic, Literary, and Theological Commentary* (P&R Publishing, New Jersey, 2006, Kindle edition), Location 665.

clans grew into villages, which turned into towns, cities, and states where cooperation, trade, and ideas could flourish, and, as it turned out, evil did too.

The ancients lived fully aware of these connections.

Summary

The climax of many ANE creation accounts is building a great temple in a garden setting. Such was a place of rest for the gods and the center of cultic worship and servitude of human beings. Bill Arnold observes:

> Both the Enuma Elish [Mesopotamia] and the Ugaritic Baal Cycle [Canaan] close their creation accounts in cultic dramas, in the building of great temples, and in the case of Enuma Elish, specifically as a place of "rest." Likewise, in the Memphite theology of ancient Egypt, the god Ptah rested after creating everything. At the conclusion of each of these, the cultic drama gives reason for the preeminence of a deity, of a temple, or of a specific cultic feature of life or worship. Similarly, at the conclusion of Gen 1:1–2:3, we have... explaining the origins of an important Israelite cultic concept—the Sabbath.[214]

It so happens that the divine rest in Genesis is permanent as the unending 7th day at creation suggests, and Hebrews 4:4-6 supports:

> Then somewhere he said this about *the seventh day of creation: God rested on the seventh day from all his works.* But again, in the passage above, God said, *They will never enter my rest.* Therefore, it's left open for some to enter [that rest], and the ones who had the good news preached to them before didn't enter because of disobedience. (CEB)

The book of Hebrews explains that the divine rest at creation is an ongoing offer for all to enter fellowship with God, described as rest or peace. Jesus is the source of that rest as it says at Advent, *"Glory to God in the highest, And on earth peace, goodwill toward men."* (Luke 2:14 NKJV), and *"Come to Me, all you who labor and are heavy laden, and I will give you rest"* (Matthew 11:28). The theological and significant difference with God's rest is that God shares it with all humans. It is not a selfish rest supplied by human servitude as in pagan myths. That is the point of the creation account in Genesis, not literal days or the age of the earth.

These ancient stories account for the origins of the heavens and earth as understood in the day. They also introduce gods and account for the origins of any cultic associated with them. However, basic human needs would be no special revelation in ancient Israel or among the pagan nations around them. *Do we really need a special revelation from God telling us that life requires water, light, air, soil, and food? Wouldn't thirst, suffocating, and hunger convince us? Do*

---

214. "Genesis," *New Cambridge Bible Commentary*, Location 1563–1569.

we need special knowledge from God that things develop naturally? These essential elements for life known to all are pliable and moldable enough to fit into any ANE account of origins—and they do.

The Genesis account starts a narrative about God's sovereignty over the world and human history. Nahum Sarna writes:

> The Bible opens with the account of creation, not so much because its primary purpose is to describe the process of cosmogony... [It] ensures that there is a divine purpose behind creation that works itself out on the human scene—*unlike other ANE creation accounts.*[215]

God is neither a product of the universe nor an object in it. Similarly, God is Lord of history, not a character governed by history any more than Shakespeare is a character in Macbeth or Hamlet, even if he is identified and speaks in the text to alert the reader where the story is heading. Shakespeare does not live inside a book, except in a literary sense. As Shakespeare is sovereign over the characters in his plays, God is the Sovereign of all that plays out in world history. Yet, unlike other deities of the ANE, God entered the limitations of history with the birth of Jesus.

It was time to announce God's active and open "takeover" of the universe.

---

215. Nahum M. Sarna, *Understanding Genesis (The Heritage of Biblical Israel)* (Varda books, Skokie Illinois, 1966), pp. 8–9.

13.
WHERE THE REVELATION LAY

[Israel's] whole history is one of failure to live up to the light recorded in their
own literature. Thus, we are forced to pay serious attention to the Hebrews'
claims to have gotten their views by special revelation...
Their view of God and of the world is unparalleled elsewhere.
If they did not get [their view] from the source they claim,
no other good candidates present themselves.
—John Oswalt[216]

The theological differences between Genesis and other ANE literature
indicate where special revelation is likely to be. Unlike the surrounding pantheons, Yahweh stands out because He is without origin in a book about origins. Only Yahweh transcends all things; He is holy like no other. He freely and
intentionally created a spectacular world with a divine purpose for humanity's
benefit—unlike the gods in other ANE creation accounts. Hebrew *culture* and
assumptions about the world are not revelations. *Instead, the gradual unfolding of God's self-revelation and His purposes are the essentials of special revelation.
Frankly, all sides in the SDWC seem to miss this.*

In Genesis, God did not "respond" to any threat from the forces of
nature, nor does He compete with other deities.[217] There can be no doubt that
conditions were unsuitable for life in Genesis 1:1–3ff; otherwise, the rest of
the account would be redundant, even unnecessary. Isolating Genesis 1:1 may
give the impression of a complete universe, but that is inconsistent with what
follows. Taken in isolation, Genesis 1:1 suggests God created the entire universe
at once, yet the rest of the chapter accounts for God's creation of the universe
in stages. Which is it? These and other reasons that will become clear have led
scholars to conclude that Genesis 1:1 is a summary verse or heading introducing
the subject. These are real possibilities.

---

216. John N. Oswalt, *The Bible Among the Myths: Unique Revelation or Just Ancient Literature?
(Ancient Context, Ancient Faith)* (2009), p. 148.

217. The absence of other gods in Genesis 1 is curious. If Genesis 1 was written before Mt. Sinai,
when other gods were taken for granted— *"You shall have no other gods before me"*—why no
mention of them? This implies that Genesis 1 was written or edited at the time of the prophets
(or shortly after) when Yahweh was the only God— *"I am God and there is no other"* (Isaiah
46:9). This is just one observation that lends some support for Genesis 1 first appearing sometime
around the exile to confront the Babylonian worldview in Enuma Elish, especially considering
the Jews in Babylon would have been reeducated along Babylonian lines. Perhaps that compelled
Judaism to address this challenge with a new cosmogony of their own or a reshaped version of an
existing one.

There was a similar expanse (firmament or sky) in other ANE cosmogonies, with waters above and below an expanse that included the sun, moon, and stars. The sky appears shaped like a blue dome over the land occupied by any observer. Below the expanse (sky) were the land and waters below the earth created over days in ANE accounts.

We noted that commonly understood elements of the cosmos could not be a revelation; however, *pagan cultures* considered nature's forces as competing powers that had some control over people's lives. Miller and Soden write, "All the elements and forces that a human being might encounter in [that] world are...forms and wills of living beings—beings that surpass the merely human scale, and are therefore gods."[218]

Genesis clarifies that God is the sole commander of nature, which is passive before Him. The sun, moon, and stars are mere lights, not gods, nor are they animated. They were physical objects and functionaries only. All other elements—sky, water, land, etc.—were inanimate physical objects. The pagans, on the other hand, interpreted them with some form of primitive *animism*. The rejection of this universal superstition in Israel (or at least in the Bible) was unique and nothing less than extraordinary. Yahweh prohibited worshipping any created thing, including the sun, moon, and stars that were part of every ancient pantheon (Deuteronomy 17:2–3). That is one reason the Western intellectual tradition generally revered the Bible for centuries because of its unparalleled theological sophistication in a primitive world.[219]

Judaism was unique with its departure from animism until Christianity, and Judeo/Christianity was alone until Islam, and they were alone until Christianity helped bring modern science into the world. The differences with other ANE literature point us to revelation. It is not the created elements themselves but the nature of those elements and their Creator that is revealing. Pagan gods were part of an animistic world. Yahweh is the only deity in the ANE that created a natural order as we might understand it, yet He utterly transcends it.

God's nature, by contrast, demonstrates the contingent nature of everything else.

In pagan creation stories, the gods created humans and enslaved them to ensure rest and repose for themselves. *Israel's primary conflict with pagan theology was not with the observable world nor how many days it took to create it and certainly not the things made on which day but who did it, what He wanted, and how we fit in His plans? That is what special revelation, the Bible, and the mission*

---

218. Miller and Soden, *In the Beginning We Misunderstood: Interpreting Genesis 1 in Its Original Context* (Kregel Electronic Publications, 2012), p. 79.

219. It is disingenuous to expect scripture to compete in all respects with modern advances. The superstitious view among some fundamentalists that God wrote the Bible (as opposed to inspired it), and therefore, it should be perfect on science, history and chronology, is the catalyst for such misunderstanding.

of the Church are all about—God's self-disclosure. God revealed Himself in a world the Israelites understood, including some common cosmological speculations shared with their ANE neighbors. How else could He be recognizable or relatable? God's revelation in a recognizable context is called *condescension,* the Incarnation being its ultimate revelation. Yahweh always stands out in contrast to the world where He reveals Himself.

Genesis is like God revealing Himself for the first time in today's world if the whole world had no knowledge of God but maintained our commonly understood science in the public domain. With today's physics and biology, a modern Moses writing a contemporary Genesis might credit God for the Big Bang and evolution and reject materialism. The purpose would not be to confirm the Big Bang or evolution (neither one would be a revelation) but to reveal God as responsible for all that is and assure the world that life has meaning. People would consider today's atheistic or materialistic worldview with the same Big Bang and unguided evolution for what it is—a myth.

Moses essentially reworks a cosmogony typical of his day but in the Hebrew tradition. Genesis is in contrast to the Mesopotamian, Canaanite, and Egyptian traditions. In other words, the similar features in both pagan cosmologies and Genesis are relevant to the author because they provide the language of shared assumptions that create a setting to display God's transcendent nature in contrast to the misguided polytheism of the day.

For how could any human possibly comprehend or explain in what manner God created the universe, especially those who have no conception of a universe like ours? Why would that be relevant in the Late Bronze Age? YEC's driving force is less about the Creator and more about how long creation took and how long ago it took place. We have to ask: "Is it Christ and him crucified? Or is it the unique YE distinctive that gives YErs their identity?"

We have been comparing gods in the ANE with Elohim (the Almighty) of Genesis 1. The creation account in Genesis was not about methods or mechanisms of creation, nor was it a reaction to chaos, but a manifestation of His will. As the story goes, He forms creatures from the soil and humans similarly, "by hand" from earth or clay like a potter. God makes a *very good* world for benevolent reasons, not for the selfish motives of many pagan deities.

The gods of the ANE were quasi-physical creatures with special powers. So physical were they that ANE creation myths always invoke procreation. Nahum Sarna puts it this way:

> In polytheistic mythologies, creation is always expressed in terms of procreation. Apparently, paganism was unable to conceive of any primal creative force other than in terms of sex. It will be remembered that in Enuma Elish, Apsu and Tiamat represent respectively the male and female powers, which through the "commingling of their waters" gave birth to the first generation of gods. The sex element existed before the cosmos came

into being and all the gods were themselves creatures of sex. On the other hand, the Creator in Genesis is uniquely without any female counterpart and the very association of sex with God is utterly alien to the religion of the Bible. When, in fact, Genesis (1:27; 5:2) informs us that "male and female he created them," that God Himself created sexual differentiation, it is more than likely that we are dealing with an intended protest against such pagan notions.[220]

The emphasis on the Creator who made "male and female" and is not Himself sexual is another concept in Jewish theology contrasted in Genesis with other pagan accounts where the gods were hypersexual.

Note how different Yahweh is.

Note how significant these differences are to our appreciation of biblical revelation—having nothing to do with days but everything to do with God's self-disclosure. How different the Bible is from other ANE texts. You can see why ritual prostitution (hetero, homo, and bestial) was part of pagan worship. Pagan gods generally came into existence through sexual means and governed a mythical world that reflects their origins and nature. By stimulating the gods' procreative forces through ritual prostitution, worshippers sought to invoke their deities to "fertilize" the crops, and livestock, and bless human procreation. In Genesis, indeed, throughout the Bible, "gender and its accompanying sexual activity is an attribute of creation, *but it plays no part at all in the production of creation.*"[221]

How would we know all this unless we were familiar with the ANE world to view Israel in her context? How else might a revelation come to light unless it stood out in the day? *Undoubtedly, the ANE context provides immediate help and perspective on idioms and assumptions unfamiliar to us. Otherwise, all we have are our assumptions projected onto scripture. Without this background, we can become sidetracked from the relevant theology by incidentals: what God made on which day or how many days did creation take? Those are not "techniques" used by God to create a universe. They make up a vehicle for the story designed for the Hebrew people.*

To illustrate this point, we have centuries of concerted effort focused on the waters above and below the earth, as if they were a mystery given to Moses. In reality, it was an ANE concept about primeval conditions familiar to someone like Moses, who would have learned fundamental cosmology in Egypt. Pagans believed similar things, not because they were pagan or because they all received the same special revelation about waters above and below the earth, but

220. N. Sarna, *Understanding Genesis (The Heritage of Biblical Israel)*, p. 12.

221. John N. Oswalt, *The Bible among the Myths: Unique Revelation or Just Ancient Literature?* (Zondervan, 2009), p. 71.

because the world appeared that way to humans in the ANE. The blue in the sky seemed like water suspended beyond the stars.[222]

The missing point in the SDWC is that divided waters did not exist except as a phenomenological perception like sundown and sunrise. Therefore, the waters above and below the earth (however interpreted) are culturally specific, and part of the author's storyline for his original audience but are incidental to special revelation.

Bill T. Arnold states:

That which comes immediately prior to a text assists most in our interpretation. Genesis 1 is the only passage of the biblical canon without such an immediately preceding context [therefore]... The ancient Near Eastern background for Genesis 1 is even more important than usual in the process of interpretation.[223]

The context of Genesis 1 is not the beginning of time *but Israel's life situation at the time of writing*. While Genesis includes a common assumption about waters above and below the sky, there is no god or goddess of water, no biographies of the gods, or titanic battle for control over tempestuous sea monsters. God simply commands light to exist and separates it from the darkness. He orders the waters to separate so that the sky appears, followed by the separation of land and sea. The top half of the waters are suspended above the stars in an arch creating the marine blue, domed-shaped sky visible to all people.

The gods (or, in Israel's case, God) were to release the waters in judicious amounts in the form of seasonal rains. Otherwise, the upper waters remained locked up in cosmic "*storehouses*." Only the gods knew the exact nature of the storehouses. The bottom half became the waters "below the expanse" (sky), sometimes adding "waters below the earth" (Exodus 20:4 NRSV). The waters "below the earth" seem to be below the earth itself, not merely below the earth's surface like underground springs; nor does "below the earth" appear to mean in the sea, which is on the earth's surface. There was no concept of a globe at the time. To the best of our knowledge, theirs was a three-tiered universe surrounded by water. This worldview is no criticism of these people. Their knowledge was observation-based, not a scientific analysis, which was impossible to achieve and unimportant then.

---

222. The blue in the sky looks like a sea of water suspended beyond the sky and the stars. It is not likely we can know exactly how the ancients interpreted the heavens.

223. "Genesis," *The New Cambridge Bible Commentary,* Kindle edition, location 1143.

Figure 2: A depiction of the three-tiered universe

Lightning, rain, and the wind are said to come from God's "storehouses" through the "windows" of heaven (Psalm 135:7). Authors pictured these storehouses with windows that released the weather. See Job 37:9: From God's upper "chambers" comes the tempest."

Psalm 104:3 says, He "lays the beams of his upper chambers on their waters." And verse 13 says that God "waters the mountains from his upper chambers." Or Job 38:22, "Have you entered the storehouses of the snow, or have you seen the storehouses of the hail, which I have reserved for the time of trouble?" If those storehouses were clouds, the answer might be "yes."

These ideas regarding storehouses of water were not new and undoubtedly incorrect scientifically but acceptable metaphorically; therefore, they cannot be the divine revelation intended in Genesis. Notice the author assumes his readers were already familiar with "*the* deep" and "*the* waters above and below" by abruptly mentioning them with the definite article "*the*" with no explanation. These were not revelations to the original audience that did not need an explanation of those expressions while they have baffled modern readers. Like the rest of the Bible, Genesis had a direct and specific audience that was not us. That is why much of it can be unclear. Nonetheless, the Bible was *preserved* for us, now requiring due diligence to unlock its complex messaging. That is common sense.

The Bible is a record from various times in one nation's history, safeguarded for our benefit. Many Christians believe that scripture speaks directly to them with little or no regard for the author and his intended audience. However, reading the Bible is more like reading other people's mail. Unknown and incidental references are inevitable. So we must deal with "divided waters," mysterious trees, talking serpents, and where Cain got his wife, not to mention cryptic references to giants and the "sons of God with the daughters of men." We could go on and on. For whatever reason, "abrupt" inserts like these presented little problem for the author's intended readers but stump us, even startle us.

There were reasons why the ancients used language like "storehouses" of water in the form of rain, snow, and hail suspended above the sky. Those waters came down intermittently, accompanied by cloud cover. They had to be up there to come down here. Since waters come down from the sky on rare occasions in the Middle East, something must hold and release them. There must be a storehouse for each type: rain, snow, hail, with their clouds. The essential "door" of those storehouses "opened" during the rainy seasons, aka, the Lord gives "rain in due season." There appeared to be a rationale or intentionality to the cycles since they produced a harvest that sustained life. Even today, most farmers are awed by this natural process.

The idea of storehouses was a technology understandable in the ANE since they collected grain in storehouses, trapped water in cisterns, and diverted water from elevations for irrigation. Humanly constructed storehouses were for collecting things that sustained life. Divine storehouses or windows in heaven were a way of referring to something that was otherwise unknowable—how does all that water stay up there, and what language and technology were available to them to explain it?[224]

We tend to explain mysterious things with known things, too. For example, in Newton's day, the most advanced technology was a complex machine. People thought of the universe as a highly sophisticated machine that operates on its own, logically, so Deism flourished. Today, we compare the human brain to the most advanced computer. Some people believe that computers may eventually be able to think just like people with an emergent consciousness so that "living" robots could fully replace people— a myth in waiting.

As stated earlier, the waters above appeared to create a marine blue sky shaped like a dome. The Hebrew word for the firmament is *Shu*, meaning a

---

224. The waters above cannot refer to clouds that are intermittent and scarce in arid climates. The point was, where did the rain come from? As if it was stored. When there are no clouds in the sky, which was often in the ANE, the clouds have returned to their storehouses. I am open to the possibility that the ancients knew there were no literal storehouses with doors in the heavens. Today, we use language like the sky having a "low *ceiling*." In EE, Marduk holds up the waters of heaven with Tiamat's ribcage. The ribcage is obvious symbolism for some kind of barrier or obstruction for the waters. However, it is difficult to establish exactly what they meant from so little documentation that exists. *Storehouses* or *windows* seem to be the most obvious answer.

hammered-out shell, which gets much attention. Here is an example from Miller and Soden:

> They viewed the sky as a void between themselves and a great ocean of water above it, with the lights of the sun, moon, and stars in between, [with boats] sailing on the surface of that ocean. *That sky ocean was held back by Shu (the atmosphere)*. In Genesis 1:6–7, the ocean of "waters above" are held back by a "firmament" (KJV) or "expanse" (ESV), which Job portrays as *"hard as a cast metal mirror"* (Job 37:18). God merely refers to their perception of reality without explanation or contradiction.[225] (emphasis mine)

Now notice the language in the flood account.

"And God made a wind blow over the earth, and the waters subsided; the fountains of the deep and the windows of the heavens were closed, the rain from the heavens was restrained, and the waters gradually receded from the earth. (Genesis 8:1–3)"

It does not say the rain ended but rather "restrained," also translated "held back." Young's Literal Translations says:

> And God causeth a wind to pass over the earth, and the waters subside, and closed are the fountains of the deep and the network of the heavens, and restrained is the shower from the heavens. And turn back [are] the waters from off the earth, going on and returning. (YLT)

The Almighty showed His power over the waters when he released them and particularly when he restrained them:

1. Divine wind controls the waters.
2. Fountains of the deep (waters below the earth) were closed.
3. The windows of the heavens were closed, holding back the rains.

This language is reminiscent of how God treated the waters in Genesis 1. When the windows holding back the "waters above" open up, they fall to the earth as rain, snow, and hail, with the accompanying clouds. In this case, the windows opened wide to destroy or cleanse the earth instead of water's usual life-giving purpose.

The blue waters above appeared held up or suspended. Otherwise, the blue in the sky (mistaken for waters) would fall all at once. Some commentators focus on the dome's material composition as if the ancients believed it to be a real hammered-out shell. The idea of Job's "cast metal mirror" may have been a tangible way of describing how it appeared and functioned, not that the ancients necessarily believed an actual hard reflective shell existed. Then again,

---

225. Miller and Soden, *In the Beginning, We Misunderstood: Interpreting Genesis 1 in Its Original Context*, p. 90.

they may have taken this literally. A similar idea is when Marduk holds up the heavens with Tiamat's ribs or torso. Another analogy for this dome might be a bead of water on a rose petal that becomes dome-shaped because of surface tension or cohesion. Surface tension acts as an invisible barrier. People of the ANE were intimately aware of waters' characteristics since they had a preoccupation with capturing it in an arid climate.

Even today, when we speak of a low "ceiling" in the atmosphere, we imply higher ceilings. A ceiling is just a way of describing a lack of visibility. Future archeologists may wonder what we meant by a moving ceiling in the sky three thousand years from now. The book of Job also says in 38:37, "Who can tip over the *water jars* of the heavens?" i.e., in times of drought. "Jars," "storehouses," and "windows" all serve the same purpose, the containment of the waters above with the potential for release. We might call them "dams." The intended meaning may be the resulting containment of the waters *in the language and mentality* of the Late Bronze Age and not the actual means of that containment.

Good interpretation is not just reading words; it seeks to understand how authors use them.

The ancients knew water also came from under the earth's surface; they dug wells to extract it. The oceans that we are familiar with were, to them, the waters on the sides of the "earth," i.e., the waters God separated from the land (Genesis 1:9–10). The "earth" ended at the ocean shore. Major landmasses beyond vast and seemly "unending" oceans like the Atlantic may have been as baffling as discovering another world. There was no more earth or "another earth" (as understood in the ANE) beyond the "great" oceans.

The separating of materials in creation so noticeable in Genesis is how many ANE people thought order came into an otherwise undifferentiated watery deep. Initially, the primeval waters were like a singularity that needed separating to release its internal elements; each release builds a part of the universe and receives a function. Like Ra of Egypt, a sun god was one of the first things to emerge from the watery deep in most ANE mythology. In turn, the first thing God creates is light. That light (as we saw earlier) was not a person or even a bright object but light itself to counterbalance the existing darkness.

Separating materials for creation is not too different from a building project at a construction site today. The work begins at daylight. The ground is prepared and leveled; workers *separate* materials into sections: lumber, bricks, metals, cement, etc. These materials are prepared and *cut* to fit a function. The Hebrew word for "create" (*ba'ra*) at its root means to "cut" or "separate." Thus, God separates light from darkness, upper waters from lower waters, and land from the sea.

The ancients envisioned the construction of the universe in terms familiar to them. The notion that the simple ANE concepts in Genesis were special revelation is nothing more than an impulse without foundation. Separating the elements—light, waters, sky, land from the sea that all ANE cosmogonies assumed—prepared each construction site to receive life forms. Even in Christendom, the Word, the divine Logos, is this cosmic "carpenter."[226]

Everyone knows that humans need water, land, and air to live. Humans need light to work and darkness for sleep. How it all got here and in working order was the mystery. Darkness and waters or never-ending tsunamis are a way of describing a nonfunctioning uninhabitable world. Waters are the dominant feature on the earth's surface and, next to air, most critical for all life, but freshwater is scarce in arid climates and would be a preoccupation in the ANE.

Most importantly, waters are amorphous, unstable, and uncontrollable, especially in the raging form of tsunamis. We cannot take residence in the sea. It is hostile to creatures that get their oxygen from the air. Many of the beasts that live in the oceans are bizarre. Its erratic and powerful nature makes it volatile. We belong on the land. We use expressions like, "He has his feet *on the ground*," describing a stable person. Water can be either life-giving or the most destructive force in the world when unleashed.

The concept of *absolute* nothing may not have been in people's consciousness of the ANE. Everywhere we look, there is something. No one has ever seen *nothing*. Close your eyes, and you can still see something. The ancients believed the created order had a beginning out of something chaotic, disordered, or uninhabitable. The best candidate for an uncreated and unorganized something may have been water in an amorphous uncontrollable state since so much life depends on it.

The created order was the gods' work, many of whom emerged from the deep. Otherwise, the ancients would have had to navigate through something like this: absolute nothing, then gods, then the war breaks out among the gods, the victors create, then order. The origin of the gods would then be nonsensical. Aristotle found the concept of absolute nothingness disturbing. It was Aristotle who first said, "Nature abhors a vacuum." It is doubtful that the ANE's intellectual currents seriously considered that *absolutely nothing* existed before the *created order*.

Something necessary for life, such as water, is potentially dangerous and might conceivably produce a world with chaos and order or good and evil like our world. This concept of cosmic waters is similar to how moderns first considered space. We now know space is an expandable low-energy field or like "fabric." "Space" is not empty. It contains things, quantum fields, dark energy, and different types of cosmic radiation. There is no such thing as nothing in this universe. Primeval waters like space are like a canvas for creation.

---

226. A good example of language barriers is that last sentence. By abruptly injecting the terms, *the Logos,* and *this carpenter,* I'm assuming you know the references without explanation whereas the ancient Israelites would be completely at a loss by them.

There was no word for *creation ex-nihilo* (out of nothing) in Hebrew.[227]

Although a writer could assemble the idea of *ex-nihilo* with more than one word by saying, "God created everything that exists without anything that exists." Similar language appears in the New Testament (Hebrews 11:3). It is hard to see how this metaphysical concept would have occurred to the minds of those in the late Bronze Age. It is reasonable that the ancients considered something disordered in perpetual existence before a created order rather than absolutely nothing. In any case, formlessness or an abyss may have been their equivalent of nothing, that is, nothing functional for life, which for them might as well be nothing.

Scholarship in Christianity and Judaism suggests that the opening of Genesis should read, "In the beginning *of* God creating" or "*When* God began to create" or "*The beginning of* God creating the heavens and earth." If correct, this possibility adds uncertainty to interpreting this first passage because we may be dealing with a *dependent* clause needing more information to complete the thought, or perhaps the first verse is a heading for what follows.

The text is unclear on these points.

The traditional wording, "In the beginning, God created the heavens and the earth," is a complete thought or *independent* clause and, as such, could function as a chapter heading. If the dependent clause is correct, the thought finishes with "and the earth *had been* a formless void, and darkness covered the face of the deep." In other words, the "earth" or world was already a formless deep when God began to create.[228]

Some think the Hebrew connector, *waw* (meaning *and* or *now*), lends credence to an independent clause and a general or introductory statement that often begins an important treatise.

Even if Genesis 1:1 is an independent clause, it still might be an introductory statement. ANE stories often read like this as Umberto Cassuto writes:

> It follows, therefore, that the first verse is an independent sentence that constitutes a formal introduction to the entire section, and expresses at the outset, with majestic brevity...at the commencement of time, in the remotest past that the human mind can conceive, God created the heavens and the earth. How he created them will be related in detail further

---

227. Contrary to popular belief, *"bara"* in Hebrew does not mean creation out of nothing. Bara is the divine act of creation, what God uses to create is irrelevant.

228. John Walton states that, to people in the ANE, material things had no existence without a proper function. The identity of a thing emerges when obtaining form and function. While some scholars think Walton overstates the case (I tend to agree), but the idea has some merit as we have seen.

on [in the Chapter]. Following the principle that one should 'first state the general proposition and then specify the particulars.'[229]

According to Cassuto, Genesis 1:1 is not a self-contained creative act but a statement about what is to follow. It is like saying, "Here is what happened: In the beginning, God created the heavens and earth, now the world *had been* a formless darkened deep, and the Spirit of God moved across the surface of the waters, and [God began by saying] 'Let there be light.'"

And so, the Spirit or wind from God approaches the darkened formlessness, and "let there be light" was the first creative act when God made the heavens and earth. To seal the idea, Genesis 2:1 explicitly states that "the creation of the heavens and the earth and everything in them was completed" (NLT), and not before. Perhaps God did not create the heavens and the earth in Genesis 1:1, which may serve as a heading.

Genesis leaves open the possibility so prevalent in the ANE that creation began with a preexisting "formlessness" characterized by a "darkened deep." Young's Literal Translation says, "In the beginning of God's preparing the heavens and the earth—the earth *hath existed* waste and void, and darkness on the face of the deep." Here, the "earth" may simply mean the *world*, though, throughout the ANE, the earth came out of the primordial deep. The great rabbis of Medieval Judaism say, "*bereshith*" (the first word of the Bible) never means "in the beginning" but "*the beginning of.*" A paraphrase of Genesis 1:1-3 may read like this:

> "In the beginning, when God created the heavens and earth, and the earth had not been formed, and darkness covered the surface of the deep, the wind of God hovered over the waters, then God said, "Let there be light, and there was light."[230]

This literal translation of Genesis 1:1 is consistent with ANE assumptions and, more importantly, the Hebrew grammar and syntax. Those two facts make this translation a real possibility. Hebrew specialists generally agree on this. Nonetheless, many scholars do not dismiss the traditional translation and still consider it optional because the intended meaning is not clear enough to speak dogmatically.

---

229. Umberto Cassuto and Israel Abrahams, "A Commentary on the Book of Genesis: from Adam to Noah," *Umberto Cassuto Biblical Commentaries 1* (Varda Books, Skokie Illinois, 2005), p. 20.

230. *The Soncino Chumash, The Five Books of Moses with Haphtaroth* translates the verse, "In the beginning of God's creating the heaven and earth, the earth was without form and void...when the Spirit [Wind] of God hovered over the face of the waters, God said, 'Let there be light.'" Furthermore, it says "this translation is necessary because the Hebrew *reshith* never means 'in the beginning' but 'the beginning of' (compare Genesis 10:10 and Jeremiah 26:1)." This indicates that we have read Genesis 1 with modern eyes and not the eyes of the author. The many purposes of scholarship include the unearthing of discrepancies like this one.

That is the point.

A war or movement over unclear possibilities is unhealthy. Feeling certain is not evidence for certainty, which is an impossible bar to climb here. That means giving the appropriate options in translation their due is necessary. To make matters worse, 2 Peter 3:5 says, "By the word of God, the heavens existed long ago, and an earth was formed *out of water and by means of water*." Peter suggests the heavens existed first, then the earth was formed, not out of nothing, but out of water. For Peter, it appears that God made the heavens before he made the earth. How long before, he does not say.

Moreover, according to Peter, God did not make the earth when He made the waters. On the contrary, God formed the earth "*by means of water*." For Peter, the waters were first, then the earth. As we have seen, this was the general idea in the ANE but is hardly clear to us today.

Note the things Peter says:

1. "The heavens existed "long ago." He gives no specific age, but it's old.

2. God formed the earth after He made the heavens. However, in Genesis, the heavens are made on day four.

3. The earth was formed out of *existing water*, the same waters of Noah's flood.

Note: Peter then says, "*By these waters also* the world of that time was deluged and destroyed" (2 Peter 3:6). That generation ignored the fact that primordial waters existed and God created the earth "*by means of*" the same waters that God separated and restrained until the flood when they were released. The idea is that without God's grace, those waters could return.

YErs already go off the rails at Genesis 1:1 in that they dogmatically reject the literal translation, which deserves real consideration, "In the beginning of God creating the heavens and earth, the earth hath existed waste and void" (Young's Literal Translation). None of this tells us how old the earth is; it does mean four things:

1. The literal translation supports the Hebrew grammar no less than the traditional reading.

2. Though we believe creation ex-nihilo includes all things, that is not clear from Genesis alone. That idea developed over several centuries.

3. Yahweh is the revelation. The ancient Israelites were already familiar with many concepts in Genesis that would not have been a revelation to them or the ANE world.

4. The Bible is unclear about the age of the earth.

From the book *Genesis 1–2: An Evangelical Conversation,* we read:

Genesis 1:2 begins with a [*waw*] disjunctive on the noun "earth" ("*Now* the earth was formless and empty") and continues with two more such clauses through the end of the verse: "*and* darkness was over the surface of the deep, *and* the Spirit of God was hovering over the waters. [And God said]..." At that time, "the earth was formless and empty." This is a common way to start a narrative account in Hebrew: first the circumstantial information, and then the action begins.

Compare, for example, Gen 3:1 ("*Now* the serpent was more crafty than any beast of the field which the Lord God had made, *and he said*") and 16:1–2 ("*Now* Sarai the wife of Abram had not borne children to him... *and Sarai said* to Abram"). All the major units in Gen 1 begin with "and/ then God said" (1:3, 6, etc.). Days 1 and 2 as well as 4 and 5 have only one such unit. Day 3 has two units, and day 6 has three. Day 7 is arranged quite differently.

So, what does v. one accomplish here? I take it to be an independent clause serving as a title announcing the subject of Gen 1, not the actual beginning of God's creation work in the Chapter. It does not fall within the "and God said" units as do all the other action units in the Chapter.

Instead, it offers a first glimpse at the whole of creation as ˋstarting point for the account, and around which the story is shaped so that the ancient Israelites would know that their God, and their God alone, created their world. The expression "the heavens and the earth" at the end of v. 1 is a merismus; that is, the two opposite parts refer to the whole of the created order. It has the effect of setting Gen 1:1–2:3 off as a sort of prologue to the remainder of [the book of] Genesis.[231] (emphasis mine)

Like EE, Genesis opens intending to create the heavens and earth. Though God appears to have created them immediately, He then proceeds to create them as the chapter progresses. In Genesis 1:2, the only reference to what exists before God's creative acts is a formless world of dark waters, again like EE. Genesis 2:1 seems to confirm that the heavens and earth were not created in verse 1 when at the end of six days, it says, "Thus the heavens and the earth were finished, and all the host of them" (AMPB). Then God rests on the seventh day. If God completed the creation of heaven and earth in six days, what are we to make of Genesis 1:1?

Comparing Genesis 3:1 to Genesis 1:2 is illuminating, "Now the [blank] was." Chapter 3:1 opens with, *"Now the serpent was."* Here, YErs accept the time-lapse inherent in the *waw* disjunctive (now) since it enables them to distance Genesis 3:1 from the Fall. Otherwise, they would have the Fall occurring on the sixth day, ending with God's "very good" evaluation, followed by a

---

231. Richard Averback, Todd Beall, C. John Collins, Jud Davis, Victor P. Hamilton, Tremper III Longman, Kenneth J. Turner, John Walton, J. Daryl Charles, Richard Averbeck, Todd S Beall, C John Collins, Victor P Hamilton, *Reading Genesis 1–2: An Evangelical Conversation.*

peaceful Sabbath, a non sequitur. YErs acknowledge an indefinite time-lapse here because not only is it grammatically correct but also because it is useful to them. To dismiss outright the same usage of the *waw* on Genesis 1:2, so close to 3:1, is inconsistent.

Of course, one is free to prefer one interpretation over another, but that is a far cry from the excesses of the YE Reform Movement should you happen to choose the wrong option:

1. You are calling God a liar.

2. You have ruined every doctrine in the Bible.

3. You are undermining the Christian faith.

Since "the heavens and earth" in Genesis 1:1 mean the entire created order, God's following creative acts would be redundant. If all this is strict chronology, as YErs insist, why backpedal and account for the Creation sector by sector of the universe after God created it? More likely, we have a heading in verse one that prepares the reader for what follows, and we have a formless deep that God begins to address. I do not presume to have definitive answers. Dogmatism on most of this is not credible.

Umberto Cassuto observes:

In v. 1 the heavens come first, because in referring to the two parts of the universe together, the more important part must be given precedence; but when the Bible proceeds to describe the work of creation in detail, the earth...is mentioned first, whereas the heavens are dealt [with second].[232]

Verse 1 may be a way of saying, "This is what happened when God began to create the heavens and the earth. There was a formless world." Catholics and Orthodox might quote *The Wisdom of Solomon 11:17*: "For your all-powerful hand, which created the cosmos *out of formless matter.*"

Formless matter is what we have in Genesis 1:2.

This analysis supports the literal translation of Genesis 1:1-2 mentioned earlier. "Formless matter" may be the closest the ANE mind came to describing "nothing" or pre-creation conditions. John Walton writes that the ancients believed things only exist if they have form and function. If something lacked form and function, it had no identity in reality. In any case, the literal translation

---

232. Umberto Cassuto and Israel Abrahams, *A Commentary on the Book of Genesis: from Adam to Noah* (Varda Books Skokie, Illinois, 2005), p. 21.

is a real possibility, throwing any chronology, particularly any age of the earth, into serious doubt.[233]

The New Revised Standard Version attempts to preserve both translations with "In the beginning when..." followed by an explanatory note. My point is not to settle the translation issue but to show that dogmatism over Genesis 1 is unjustified because the context far removes us from the scene. Wisdom should temper any excessive claims that lead to warring factions among Christians over some objectively questionable and unknowable conclusions.

All attempts to explain the first chapter of the Bible apart from its theology are speculative. Today we understand God created all things visible and invisible from nothing, not by a literal Genesis that says God used the earth, water, dust, or rib to make things. The concept of ex nihilo was developed and refined over many centuries. In a language more familiar in Christian theology, first voiced in 2 Maccabees 7:28, "Look at the heaven and the earth and see everything that is in them, and recognize that God did not make them out of *things that existed*. And in the same way the human race came into being" (NRSV).

This concept is a development on creation since Genesis, which explicitly states something different: God made plants, animals, and humans from *"things that existed"*—"And God said, *'Let the land produce living creatures'*" (Genesis 1:24). YErs often ignore this and state that God's verbal commands created everything except humans. They insist on a literal interpretation of the highly anthropomorphic imagery of God making humans from dust. However, contrary to that, God made Eve from a body part donated by Adam. Yet later, God says that both were made of dust and shall return to dust (Genesis 3:19). At best, the literal meaning is inconsistent; that is why scholars seek other explanations than literalism.

By New Testament times, traces of creation *ex nihilo* had shown up in the second temple period. The philosophical influence of Hellenism may have provided the language to express it. We tend to read our theology into Genesis instead of measuring Old Testament theology against the ANE backdrop and how the New Testament treats the Old to notice meaningful theological differences.

As far as we know, the ancients did not think of the earth as a globe before the middle of the first millennium BC. Even then, the idea took centuries to spread. We call "sky blue," what the ancients considered "marine blue" as water also appears blue on earth. The blue in the sky looks like water suspended

---

233. The *Soncino Chumash, The Five Books of Moses with Haphtaroth* literally translates the verse, "In the beginning of God's creating the heaven and earth [the earth had been]...this translation is necessary because the Hebrew *reshith* never means 'in the beginning' but 'the beginning of' (compare Genesis 10:10 and Jeremiah 26:1)."

beyond the transparent sky with its sun, moon, and stars *inside*, just like all other ANE cultures with which we are familiar.

At sunrise, we can see early stars in the sky that appear in front of the blue background. It is the same blue color as the waters on the earth. It is sometimes hard to tell where the sky ends and the sea begins at the horizon. There is little difference between the blue in the sky and its reflection on a lake. Therefore, the waters above appeared suspended beyond everything visible in the day and night skies. The ancients would describe that suspension in a relatable way— storehouses, windows, etc.

The ancients seemed to think our oceans were on the sides of the "earth" and "separate" from it. Below the earth (land) was "Shoal" (hades in Greek), the place of the dead. Another "great deep" was below Shoal. "You shall not make for yourself an idol, whether in the form of anything that is in heaven above or that is on the earth beneath or that is in the water *under the earth*" (Exodus 20:4 NRSV). Deities of the sea supposedly lurked in the waters beneath. This view of the heavens and earth is the so-called "three-tiered universe" that included:

1. The heavens above (sun, moon, and stars),

2. The earth (land) is a disk with irregular surface features resting on ocean waters.

3. And an underworld below the earth is where (Shoal) existed. "For all of them are handed over to death, *to the world below*; along with all mortals, with those who go down to the Pit" (Ezekiel 31:14).

There were waters above and below this three-tiered universe (see figure 3).

Notice Psalm 148:1–5, an exhortation of praise to God. It adds to the idea of the waters above the heavens or skies:

> Praise the Lord. Praise the Lord from the heavens; praise him in the heights. Praise him, all his angels; praise him, all his host. Praise him, sun and moon; praise him, all you shining stars. Praise him, *you highest heavens, and you waters above the heavens.* Let them praise the name of the Lord, for he commanded and they were created. (NRSV; emphasis mine)

This Psalm exhorts the creation to praise God, including the most powerful thing known to the ancients—the mighty ocean waters. Verse 4 says, "waters that are *above* the heavens." It hardly seems reasonable to dismiss this ANE view of the world in exchange for a thick band of clouds fixed over the earth. Clouds come and go. Clouds block the heavens (sun, moon, and stars). Besides, "clouds" and "rain" were words readily available to the author; as Genesis 2:5 tells us, "*the Lord God had not sent rain on the earth* and there was no [man] to work the ground." How does the Lord God send rain on the earth? *By way of clouds.* That had not occurred before the creation of Adam and Eve in 2:7. That seems to make an unnecessary, cumbersome and vague phrase, *"waters that are above the sky* (Genesis 1:7), especially in a chapter with exceptionally efficient use of language. Clouds are not above the sky; they are *in the sky*, so is rain, but to the ancients, rain and clouds originated from the "storehouses" and were part of the waters above the skies, i.e., beyond the stars as they understood them.[234]

Psalm 104:2 adds, "[The Lord] stretches out the heavens like a tent and lays the beams of his *upper chambers on their waters*" (emphasis mine). Nahum Sarna makes a significant point about the upper waters in connection to the flood—*mabbul* in Hebrew: "The very word *mabbul*, translated 'Flood,' is now recognized as having denoted the heavenly, or upper, part of the cosmic ocean originally."[235]

In Enuma Elish, Marduk divides the waters mentioned in the fourth tablet but does not create the clouds and the celestial bodies until tablet 5. Marduk then places the heavenly bodies and clouds below the upper waters. This is ANE cosmogony.

The stunning discovery of a 144-foot ship in the pyramid at Giza in 1954 helps illustrate the ANE concept of the upper waters:

> [The Khufu ship] is of the type known as a "solar barge," a ritual vessel to carry the resurrected king with the sun god Ra across the heavens. However, it bears some signs of having been used...that Khufu Himself used it as a "pilgrimage ship" to visit holy places [during his lifetime] and that it was then buried for him to use in the afterlife.[236]

Figures 3 and 4 below depict a scene (top left and right-hand corner) of a king sailing the upper waters in the afterlife with Ra.

---

234. An objection to the idea of "storehouses" or "windows" is that water would be dumped in the form of flooding and not as rain or snow and hail. That objection exaggerates the idea from an analogy to at utterly wooden literalism. Clouds come from the "storehouse" and rain comes from the clouds.

235. Nahum M. Sarna, *Understanding Genesis (The Heritage of Biblical Israel)* (Varda Books, Skokie Illinois, 1966), p. 11.

236. See *Wikipedia* article "Khufu Ship."

Figure 3: The three-tiered universe depicted in Heliopolis, Egypt

In figure 3 above, the female body (a Tiamat-like figure) arched in a dome shape separates the waters above the starry heavens. Note the boats on waters above the stars, where the gods live, and where kings travel in the afterlife. Her body contains the stars that, in other Egyptian depictions, are birthed through her vaginal canal. Under her belly is the sun, and above her left shin, the half-moon and a star. The female body below the expanse is in an irregular reclining position to depict the mountains and valleys on the earth's surface. Note that the sun, moon, and *stars are under the waters above*, where the boats sail in the afterlife.

Below is figure 4, another of many depictions of the three-tiered universe from ancient Egypt.

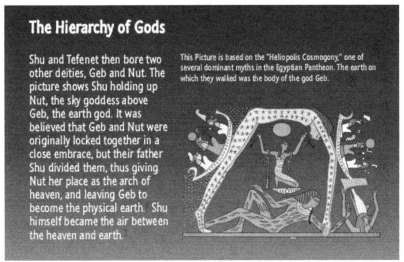

Comparing Psalm 148:3–4 (the highest heavens) with verses 7–8 (earthbound phenomenon), differentiate the waters above the skies with atmospheric precipitation over the earth. Here is how the Psalmist differentiates the divided waters:

Waters above

Praise him, sun and moon; praise him, all you shining stars.

Praise him, you highest heavens, and you waters above the heavens.

Waters below

Praise the Lord *from the earth, you sea monsters and all deeps, fire and hail, snow and frost, stormy wind fulfilling his command.* (Psalm 148:6–7)

Here, precipitation (hail, snow, frost, and storms) is part of the earthly realm below the heavens and where sea monsters live. When precipitation is visible, it is no longer above the sky/heavens where people believe rain and clouds originated. "Storehouses" of rain, snow, and hail, thought to be beyond the day and night skies, were "opened" judiciously to provide precipitation upon the earth as God's provision.

Rainfall was critical in Canaan, where rivers were not significant irrigation sources like Mesopotamia and Egypt. Canaan and Israel depended on rain in due season and cisterns (another kind of storehouse) to trap the rain. They could not rely on Nile-like or Tigris and Euphrates river systems for irrigation.

The "storehouses" and "fountains" of water above and below the expanse opened in Noah's day. *All the fountains of the great deep* were burst open, *and the sky's windows opened.* The rain was *on the earth* for forty days and forty nights. The opened windows of heaven released all *the waters above*, not just rainfall. The idea is obvious. The primordial waters above collapsed and returned to their original condition. God, who held them back, now released them all. Disorder returned. That is how the ancients in the Near East understood their world.

On the function of primeval waters in the ANE, John Walton writes:

Creation often begins with that which emerges from the waters—whether a deity or land (e.g., the Egyptian Primeval Hillock). These primeval waters are designated the "nonexistent" in Egyptian texts... The god Atum is said to have developed "*out of the Flood*, out of the Waters, out of darkness, out of lostness.[237]

As understood throughout the ANE and in Israel, these waters do not exist. Therefore, they cannot be a revelation, *at least not in a literal sense.* Instead, they exemplify phenomenological language on how the ancients observed their world. For instance, many ancients assumed seas or oceans existed on the moon. The dark portions are the same color as the blue sky if you look at the moon in

---

237. John Walton, *The Lost World of Genesis One: Ancient Cosmology and the Origins Debate (The Lost World Series)* (InterVarsity Press, Downers Grove, Illinois, 2010), p. 31.

the daytime. If one thinks the blue sky indicates water, it follows that the same blue on the moon is more water.

When Neil Armstrong landed the lunar module on the Sea of Tranquility, people wondered why NASA and news reporters called that piece of land the *Sea of Tranquility*. That is the English translation of the Latin *Mare Tranquillitatis*. Mare means "sea," of course. Early astronomers thought the dark portions of the moon were waters as late as the seventeenth century AD. During the day, the moon's dark surface areas were marine blue as the sky, lakes, oceans, and rivers. It is perfectly reasonable for the ancients to assume that the same nautical blue was likely water.

Today, we know that the blue on the moon is an electromagnetic effect in the earth's atmosphere, which creates an *atmospheric coloration* and not a continuation of waters on the moon or above the sky. The ancients could not know this, nor should they be expected to. So the *scientific concept* of an *atmosphere* projected anachronistically into the ANE is unacceptable.

There is no way to interpret Genesis successfully without understanding the common assumptions that expose the theological differences where the revelation is. Since the sun, moon, and stars are noticeably inside what we call the "blue in the sky," it *appeared* to the ancients that "blue waters" were beyond those stars. Take time to look at a blue sky and notice that the blue does not block the sun, the moon, and stars as seen during the day. Clouds block them all, so they were the closest objects in the expanse that the ancients could see. Therefore, waters above the heavens cannot be clouds.

That God would be concerned about revealing the earth's shape or other scientific data—wonders He likely delights in seeing us discover on our own—is inexplicable. He made us able to explore our world. God does not even name the animals; He left that to us, so they belong to us as gifts. God reveals wonders we cannot discover that are vital to salvation, discipleship, and evangelism. We are on our own for the rest, which is a beautiful thing. God's nature and purposes are special revelations.

Physics, biology, and "flood geology" are not in the game.

WHERE THE REVELATION LAY PART 2

A name by any other name

There are ANE and Hebrew customs and traditions in the Creation account. Those customs existed in ancient Israel but did not exist when God created the world, nor do many continue to exist today. If Genesis 1 were a precise word-for-word historical and chronological report by God given to Moses, then why would God inject customs and traditions that could not exist at the dawn of time? Some peculiarities of the narrative only make sense in the author's time but make no sense at the beginning of time.

For example, giving a name to a person, place, or thing in ANE tradition can show dominance or authority over the thing named. According to ANE tradition, naming could even create something that had not existed. Naming customs in the ANE bordered on superstition. At some point in Israelite history, to utter the divine name "Yahweh" became forbidden for fear of accidentally misusing it. Some ancients thought they might influence or even control a god by using its name.

You will remember that Pharaoh Necho of Egypt removed Jehoahaz, king of Judah, replacing him with the king's son, the vassal prince, Eliakim, whose name the Pharaoh changed into "Jehoiakim," exercising control. Necho promptly levied tribute from Judah, taking further control (2 Kings 23:33–35).

An example of naming that creates something is Jacob, who "created" a new place by calling it Bethel, where there was unknown ground before. It was the same piece of ground but now a recognizable place. Therefore, the reasoning goes that Jacob created Bethel from a wilderness (formless) landscape by giving it a name. These naming customs are ANE ideas and incidental to special revelation. Incidentals are relevant to the extent they provide insight into that world and make it easier to recognize where special revelation lay. Such customs are from the Bronze Age, and their relevance must stay in the Bronze Age.

After wrestling with the "angel," God changes Jacob's name to "Israel," meaning "struggles with God." The name change indicates a relational change—a real relational development. Jacob officially belongs to Yahweh and will worship Him, as will Jacob's descendants, and God will bless them appropriately.

Since later biblical authors continued to use the name Jacob, as in the "house of Jacob," so the name "Israel" is Jacob by another name. This new name, "wrestles" or "struggles with God," foresaw the tumultuous relationship between God and the Israelites. The point is that naming things took on a significance in Moses' day that is foreign to us today and, more importantly, a significance upon which God would not depend when *"writing His diary" on the creation*.[238]

As God creates, He names the light "day," the darkness, "night," and the heavens "sky." He calls the waters "seas." He calls the dry land "earth," meaning they now exist with an identity.[239] Notice God calls only the *dry land* "earth." The oceans are not included as part of the "earth" since they are not land, and ocean floors are unusable or, we might say, "dark and formless." The reference is specifically to the terra firma, not the earth *as a planet*.

From John Walton, we saw that creation in ANE societies begins with what emerges from the primeval waters—whether a deity or land (e.g., the Egyptian Primeval Hillock of the first creation). Land that is wetland or silt was in the waters before *"earth's"* creation, known in the ANE as firm ground or dry land. This concept supports the idea that the "earth" mentioned in Genesis 1:2 is not the finished product.

Mud was the material thought to form the earth into a disk. The "disk" is how scholars think the ancients conceived the earth's shape, based on both writings and depictions in art. But ancient tribes thought of the earth as their land and all lands they knew of and might live on or grow food. They could not have understood the vastness of earth beyond the oceans. Bill Arnold confirms this: "Heaven [is] the domed sky created in Genesis 1:6–7 and earth being the land inhabited by humans and animals created in verses 9–10."[240]

God fills heaven (sky) with *"the heavens"* (plural), meaning the contents of the sky—sun, moon, and stars, verses 14–19. Similarly, God appropriately fills the other sectors of this three-tiered universe—marine life in the oceans and animals inland. Elohim alone separates the three main sections and fills them in this Hebrew version of the creation story. In most ANE versions, there is a pantheon involved. The three tiers (sections) were the same in these versions and, therefore, not revelatory in Genesis. The universe's boundaries were the waters beyond the heavens and below the earth. Beyond the universe was God's heavenly dwelling, uncreated like Him.

God brings things into existence and has power over them, highlighted by the ANE custom of naming. Note again the opening lines of Enuma Elish:

When on high the heaven had *not been named*,

---

238. The objection to this could be that God gave Moses the actual story but let him put it into idioms the people could understand. But this is a roundabout way of saying that Moses wrote the account, and it must be interpreted, which we already knew. Besides, it is presumptuous to assume that Moses could improve on God's inspiration or that God could not muster the right words Himself. Besides, any changes Moses could make would diminish the perfect Word of God.

239. It is important to remember that when the author of Genesis uses the word *earth*, he means the known land. A global earth was unknown and so it is absurd to suggest he is referring to something he knows nothing about.

240. Bill T. Arnold, "Genesis," *New Cambridge Bible Commentary* (2009), location 1249.

Firm ground below [netherworld] had not been *called by name*,

[Nothing existed] but primordial Apsu, their begetter,

(And) Mummu-Tiamat, she who bore them all,

Their waters commingling as a single body...

Uncalled by name, their destinies undetermined-

Then it was that the gods were formed within them.

Lahmu and Lahamu were brought forth, *by name they were called.*[241]

Bill T. Arnold comments:

> The opening lines of the Babylonian creation epic myth Enuma Elish, *equate naming something with its existence*, showing that naming is often determinative of existence. It says, 'When on high no name was given to heaven, Nor below was the netherworld called by name'... A few lines later, the epic describes the primordial period when only Absu and Tiamat existed. 'When no gods at all had been brought forth, None called by names, no destinies ordained, Then were the gods formed within these two. Lahmu and Lahamu [the first gods born] were brought forth, Were called by name.' Many other examples illustrate that throughout the ancient world, naming and existence were often equated.[242]

Naming a thing affirmed its existence in the ANE. It gives identity to something at the discretion of the one doing the naming. According to Bill Arnold, "names were seen as a 'hypostasis;' that is, the very essence of a thing."[243] This concept is strange to us, which is often my point about ANE ideas reflected in the Bible. There can be no casual reading of these texts if comprehending them is the goal.

While the ancients thought this way, God did not. It may seem inexplicable that something like a place may not exist unless it has a name. But think of it like being lost. When lost, it is common for us to feel like we are in the *"middle of nowhere?"* There is no such place as "nowhere." Yet, the lack of an organizing reference is disorienting. *Nowhere* is *somewhere* we do not recognize until we give it a reference point. In ancient times, there was far less "discovered" territory and little or no mapped landmasses. Getting lost was common and dangerous. Names added a reference point to the terrain. One reference point now connects to other reference points; only then do we know *where* we are, even though the place has not changed. It was *perceptions* that changed. Such perceptions are not reality but can seem to be.

---

241. See *The Academy of Ancient Texts* online.

242. Arnold, Genesis, TNCBC (Kindle), location 1385–1390.

243. Ibid. This ANE idea is "Platonic."

The wilderness beyond known territory would have been foreboding to the much less adventurous. Columbus traversed the Atlantic and announced that many new lands existed on the other side of the globe. This discovery astonished Europeans, almost like finding a new earth. We even named it *The New World*. "New" implies coming into existence, but this phrase is an idiomatic expression, having nothing to do with newly *formed* lands or worlds. The ancients appear to have not always made these distinctions. Perhaps they did more than we realize, but that is not always clear.

In ANE literature, unfamiliar territory and amorphous primordial waters were surreal without a name that indicated a familiar function or identity. Recall riding your bike beyond familiar places at six years old. The further you went, the more alienated you felt, even though you recognized similar kinds of trees, streets, houses, people, grass, and the sky. The clouds looked the same. You still did not know where you were. The fear was that if you went too far, you might not find your way back. If you just went straight, you could always go straight back.

Perhaps you once dreamt of walking home from school and turning a recognizable corner to find nothing was as it should be. You felt disoriented. You may have awakened at that point. Multiply that a hundredfold in ancient times with dangers all around, with life and death on the line by wild animals and unknown marauders that could spring on you at any moment because you are in no identifiable place; you knew you did not belong. Your imagination might take over in a world where you have virtually no power and few reference points. The ancients lived in that kind of world.

Curiously, God refrains from naming the sun and moon on day four. The author only describes their functions as "greater" and "lesser lights." Moses has God conspicuously abstaining from calling them the "sun" and the "moon."

Why is that?

Scholars have noticed that the Hebrew words for "sun" and "moon" are similar to the Canaanite names for their sun and moon gods. The author seems conscious of avoiding confusion for those who might conclude that the sun and moon are something more than functionaries. It might even be a dig at pagan accounts where the sun and moon have a personal identity.

Here is Arnold again:

> The sun and moon were the most important gods of the pantheons in the Ancient Near East. The use of "greater light" and "lesser light" [in Genesis] avoids the words for sun and moon (šemeš and yārēaḥ, respectively), *which could have been taken for the names of the Canaanite deities, Shemesh and Yarikh.* These great subjects that were worshiped in the ancient world, have instead become physical objects [in Genesis]. Ancient religion was usually chained to the natural rhythms of time, irrevocably associated with the personification of Sun, Moon, and Stars.

But these personified powers have been "demoted in Genesis to mere artifacts, lamps rising and setting on command of the One Creator.[244] (emphasis mine)

There was already a tendency to believe that the sun and moon were alive because they seemed to move on their own—a major characteristic of livings things in general—indicative of expressions like "living waters," meaning moving waters compared to stagnant ones.[245]

Despite Moses' concerns, he uses the anthropomorphic term "governs" for the greater and lesser lights, i.e., the greater light *rules* the day. The lesser light *rules* the night, meaning they dominate the sky visually. Yet they do not take this role for themselves as lords but only receive it as a function from the Creator. The ancient Hebrew readers could interpret anthropomorphic imagery in objects well enough. But the apparent power of naming impacted them significantly, especially in some ANE creation accounts when gods officially existed when named.

Here is the thing: it is implausible that Genesis is the word-for-word divine description of the actual creation. Could the custom or superstition regarding naming influence God during His transcendent act of creating the universe? That would mean that a superstition surrounding naming originated with God, which is impossible. Doesn't it make more sense that the author prepares his document in ways his readers can identify?

Todd Beall asks a similar question but with a different outcome:

Certainly, God could have directed Moses to write in this way, but he was under no obligation to do so. In fact, ironically it is the Creation account that would have had to be supernaturally revealed (whether passed on orally or directly given) to Moses, since no human was alive to witness the acts of the first five days. Why would God have used ANE myths to reveal his truth to Moses concerning this unique event?[246]

---

244. Bill T. Arnold, "Genesis," *New Cambridge Bible Commentary* (Cambridge University Press, 2009), Kindle edition, location 1444.

245. Even today, the native inhabitance along the Amazon River believes the high tides of the "Pororoca" (meaning "great roar") *is alive and angry*. Some high tides rise up to four meters high and travel up to 800 km inland, upstream on the Amazon River. These waves begin where the Amazon meets the Atlantic Ocean. When the conditions are right, the force of the waters called a "tidal bore" makes a roaring sound that can be heard *ten miles away*. The Bible and ANE literature often refer to waters that "roar." Scripture says that God laughs at the "roaring" of an "angry" sea. God does not think this way; ANE people thought this way, not unlike some people along the Amazon River do today.

246. Richard Averback, Todd Beall, C. John Collins, Jud Davis, Victor P. Hamilton, Tremper III Longman, Kenneth J. Turner, John Walton, J. Daryl Charles, Richard Averbeck, Chapter Two: A Literal Approach by Todd Beal, *Reading Genesis 1–2: An Evangelical Conversation* (Hendrickson Publishers Marketing, LLC, Peabody, Massachusetts, 2013), p. 142.

The right question is not, "Why would God have used ANE myths?"—Genesis avoids mythology, as we have seen, but *"Does the author employ some common assumptions about the observable world?"* We are not talking about pagan mythology but *ANE cosmology* shared by the Hebrews. Beall does not distinguish between the two. All ANE cultures had similar creation accounts that connected their gods with their tribal origins.

Moses wrote on a subject recognizable in his time but from a Hebraic point of view, namely the revelation of Yahweh without mythology. The objects in a creation account that all can see (water, sky, animals, humans, sun, moon, and stars) were not the revelation; neither were days since other ANE accounts included them. How they got here and what happened was a matter of speculation. The God or gods (always tribal) and their motivations were the attempted revelation. Beall unintentionally makes my point. Since God was not a product of ANE culture, He *would not have written it the way we have it.*

The author(s) was a product of the ANE, and he wrote it for a real ANE people—the Hebrews.

Interestingly, Jewish traditions show up throughout the account; not the least was an explicit seventh-day rest (see chapter 10 on the number seven in Genesis 1). Other festivals are implied, such as on day four: "And God said, 'Let there be lights in the dome of the sky to separate the day from the night; and let them be for signs and for seasons and for days and years'" (Genesis 1:14). The Jubilee Bible reads, "And let them be for signs and for appointed times and for days and years." Coincidently, Enuma Elish has Marduk creating the heavenly bodies for similar reasons—"for the fixing of the days."

More than lights and the four seasons, the sun, moon, and stars are for signs, festival days, and yearly festivals. They are lamps or signposts that mark out when the sacred festivals of Israel arrived. For example, the Sabbath began at sundown. The priests were diligent in determining the moment of sunset by observing the *first star* that appeared in the sky at dusk. Sighting the first star officially began the Sabbath. So not only did the sun mark the beginning and end of each Sabbath, but so did the stars.

The moon's role in the festivals is prominent since Israel celebrated each new moon, most notably the new moon "announcing" the feast of Trumpets (see Leviticus 23:23–25). There were weekly, yearly, or annual Sabbaths, land Sabbaths, and the Year of Jubilee that helped fill out the biblical calendar we know as the Jewish sacred calendar.

The *seasons* in Genesis 1:14 likely refer specifically to the festivals of Passover, the Feast of First Fruits (Pentecost), and the Feast of Succoth or Tabernacles because they coincide with the harvest seasons, as Bill T. Arnold writes:

> The great lamps are also to become signs and seasons throughout the years, which implies more than simply establishing the pattern of the

four seasons. It seems likely this also refers to the special functions of the sun and moon in the sacred seasons of the worship of Yahweh, especially as defined in Leviticus 23 (where the word translated in [Genesis 1:14] as "seasons," *mô 'ădîm,* is translated "appointed festivals," and see Ps 104: 19).[247]

The Hebrew word for seasons in Genesis 1:14 is *mo'adim.* Throughout Leviticus 23, this word appears concerning Israel's appointed festivals, consistently translated as "festivals." Psalm 104:19 rehearses creation, saying, "He made the moon to mark the festivals, the sun knows when to set" (CSB).

No doubt, the author of Genesis writes for the covenant people of Israel and not a real-time play-by-play analysis of the beginning supplied by God. Face it, Creation week even ends with a Hebraic-like Sabbath, identifying Elohim as Yahweh, the Hebrew God. The irony is that the festivals and Sabbath days in Israel are a shadow of Christ in Christianity (Colossians 2:16–17), which could not be true of the divine seventh day of Creation. We will see that the nature of the seventh-day rest in Genesis and the weekly Sabbath in Israel are different.

The fact remains that Israel's festivals cannot be *why* God created the sun, moon, and stars. If that were true, we would not need them anymore now that the festivals are retired; the light on day one (whatever that was) should be sufficient for the daily cycle. In ancient Israel, the sun, moon, and the star's primary function served the festivals. This function is decidedly a theological and covenantal purpose of the heavenly bodies. Our understanding of stars stretched across billions of light-years is well beyond anything understood in biblical times.

The Hebrews demoted the heavenly bodies from gods in a pantheon to mere objects serving as signposts for the festivals. These heavenly bodies served humans in ancient Israel, while humans served them in paganism. *The celestial body's primary purpose in Genesis 1 is not physics or astronomy but their covenantal role in ancient Israel. In other words, besides light, the purpose of creating the sun, moon, and stars in Genesis 1 was their role in the covenant, not scientific.*

Also, on day four, Moses singled out the stars grammatically. Genesis 1:16 reads, "God made two great lights—the greater light to govern the day and the lesser light to govern the night. He *also made the stars.*" The author treats the stars separately partly because they are tiny and numerous. But there may also be a veiled purpose for giving the stars their own space in the narrative. God made the stars and knows them all, even by name, according to Psalm 147:4. This focus on the stars may reinforce the unconditional promise God made to Abraham: *"I will make your descendants as numerous as the stars in the sky"*

---

247. Bill T. Arnold, "Genesis," *New Cambridge Bible Commentary* (Cambridge University Press, 2009), Kindle edition, location 1435.

(Genesis 15:5). Granted, this is vague, but the children of Abraham did not likely miss it.

Genesis is no lesson in physics, nor should it be.

At any rate, the heavenly bodies are not ceremonial candles in the sky. Therefore, Moses writes directly to Israel's covenant people within an ANE context. This context creates serious doubt that Genesis 1 is precisely what God did, how He did it, and what He "said" when He did it. Its primary purpose and inspiration was covenantal.

Another Jewish concept unique in the ANE where gods are sexual, Yahweh is genderless. Since God created the cosmos, he must transcend it, including the creaturely property of males and females. The early chapters of Genesis overemphasize this by insisting that males and females are not an extension of God's nature (Genesis 1:27, 1:27, 5:2, 6:19, 7:3, 7:9, 7:16). That was a Hebraic concept foreign to the ANE.

Therefore, it is incoherent and insulting for Israelite priests to incorporate sexual behavior in the temple cult to stimulate Yahweh into procreative activity. God's indignation over temple prostitution was not divine prudishness (he created sex) but the fleshly nature it projected onto Him. All these theological differences should assure any Christian that this initial glimpse of Yahweh given in Genesis against the crude ANE backdrop is, in fact, its revelation. The God of Israel was radically new and stood alone among ANE deities that have long since disappeared. Only Yahweh continues.

The narrative is clearly in Moses' hands.

Summary

The two accounts of creation in Genesis 1 and 2 set the stage for *two promises* God made to Abraham: (1) That God would create a diverse nation of Abraham's direct descendants (the twelve tribes of Israel); and (2) that God would bless the rest of the world through his descendants that came to include the Church (cp. Genesis 22:18; Galatians 3:16). The calling and election of Abraham's descendants seen in the Exodus and the Sinai covenant is the culmination of all covenants found in Genesis.

Nahum Sarna writes, "The theme of creation, important as it is in the [Hebrew] Bible, is nevertheless only introductory to what is its central motif, namely, the Exodus from Egypt. That event was the basis for the covenant with Israel."[248]

A "literal Genesis" is not the foundation of God's plan or the key to all biblical doctrine, nor does the Gospel depend on it. A figurative view of Genesis does not convict God of lying. Genesis does have a specific place in Old Testament theology, which gives it a historical connection to New Testament theology through a series of progressive steps. The Genesis account does not confine biblical theology to the primordial past; it merely has its beginnings.

Genesis is an example of God's Word to an ancient tribal people with groundbreaking theology, morality, wisdom, grace, philosophy, and promises of hope. It is genuine and, therefore, grounded in a real-life situation.

Sarna observes:

> The biblical writers had their own literary idiom. Therefore we must not confuse the idiom with the idea, the metaphor with the reality behind it. The two have to be disentangled [and] must be translated into the idiom of our own day. The biblical narrative has to be viewed against the background of the world out of which it grew and against which it reacted. A comparison with Near Eastern cosmogonies shows...the materials used have been transformed, so as to become the vehicle for the transmission of completely new ideas.[249]

The *language and idiom* of Genesis and even Jewish tradition, including the cosmos' design, place it squarely in the ANE around the early first and late second millennium BC. The revelation cannot be in the underlying construct of the cosmos that the Israelites understood, which is very similar to the general ANE worldview.

The theology in Genesis is the clear standout, not "science."

In "Part III," we take a closer look at the nature and purposes of the Bible in the SDWC.

---

248. Sarna was Jewish and did not accept Jesus or the New Testament. Yet he still did not place the creation at the top of the list of events in the [Hebrew] Bible. For Jews, their salvation and election at the Exodus is the single most important event in history. It is their life, death, resurrection, and ascension. It gives them identity and their lives meaning. For Christians, it is the life, death, resurrection, and ascension of Jesus that are the events of greatest importance. It is not clear what the most important event is in YEC.

249. Ibid., p. 5. On literalism, Sarnia says, "The literalistic approach serves to direct attention to those aspects of the narrative that reflect the time and place of its composition, while it tends to obscure the elements that are meaningful and enduring, thus distorting the biblical message and destroying its relevancy [for today]."

PART III:
THE PURPOSES OF
THE BIBLE AND THE
SIXTH-DAY WAR

15.
PAST PRESUPPOSITIONS AND THE BIBLE

It is too absurd to say that some men might have traversed the whole wide ocean,
and crossed from this side of the world to the other that even the inhabitants of
that distant region are descended from that first man [Adam].
— St. Augustine (A thousand years before Columbus)

We know the earth is a globe, and lands on the other side need evangelizing. We take it for granted that the earth revolves around the sun. We know that
foreign lands on the other side of the globe and the orbit of planets around the
sun are not threatening ideas, nor do they present theological conundrums.[250]

It was not always this way.

By Augustine's day (AD 354–430), the Greco-Roman world's educated
classes had long since known the earth was round. Since its inception, the
Church accepted the earth as a sphere, contrary to popular myth. The lunar
eclipse casts earth's round shadow on the moon, and the masts of ships sinking
into the sea at the horizon revealed a curvature. That made convincing evidence
that the earth—like the sun and moon—is indeed round.

The Bible does not define the earth's geometry. It assumes the ANE view
of the three-tiered universe described earlier. Theologians of the past could have
questioned the authority of the Bible after discovering that the earth is round.
They did not think that way. They were always aware of and skilled in symbolic and figurative interpretation, especially phenomenological language. They
also knew that incidental comments throughout scripture were not necessarily revelations.

Church leaders of the past treated the Bible figuratively if it contra-
dicted the obvious, not because they compromised biblical authority; instead,
they believed that inspired scripture would not include an obvious error on
a cultural incidental. Unfortunately, what seems evident about nature today
might become wrong tomorrow. Scripture and information found in nature
treat truth differently. Conceptual truths and empirical data are much different. Ancient literature is far more versatile with concepts and metaphors than
empirical data because of the lack of advanced instrumentation to discover and
collect data. The discovery that the earth was round did not result in theological
puzzles, initially.

---

250. A surprising number of people today genuinely believe the universe revolves around the
earth daily. They are geocentrists. The arguments they employ are similar to YEC: literalism,
biblical authority and the authority of the pre-Copernican Church. Everyone was a geocentrist.
It doesn't matter.

That changed.

Not Anticipating the Antipodes

It became clear that global geography presented the possibility of lands on the opposite side of the world called the "antipodes." People believed "new" lands existed not yet discovered in Augustine's day. New landmasses suggested new plants, creatures, and people—a separate creation, perhaps. Sounds silly today, but the antipodes presented real social problems for the world and theological issues in Judaism and Christianity. This challenge is not too different from finding creatures similar to us on another planet.

For millennia, the "earth" was the land surrounded by ocean boundaries. If there was land beyond the vast oceans, it was like another earth or another *"terra firma."* People thought, *What if we discover "people" not descended from Adam?* Jews and Christians firmly believed the Garden of Eden was in Mesopotamia, and humans spread from there. Could the Eden story in Genesis 2–3 be more about Israel's ancestral origins while Genesis 1 was about humanity's origins? Unlike Genesis 2–3, Genesis 1 contains no geographical references except "earth." Perhaps there was a Gentile or generic Adam (Mankind) in chapter 1 and a Hebrew ancestral Adam (man) in chapter 2. That seems unlikely, but it may be possible.

There was no record of anyone successfully navigating a global voyage to or from the antipodes. Even the term "new lands" is relative. Maybe they were "old lands." Suddenly, new possibilities created theological disputes and challenges to accepted history.[251]

The discoveries caused riddles for biblical interpretation. But, a misunderstanding of the Bible's purposes created dilemmas. For instance, some Christians concluded that Adam's descendants could not have populated regions on the other side of the globe for two reasons: (1) The biblical origins of humanity in the ANE; and (2) the lack of known navigational advances necessary to sail to the other side of the world that could transport Adam's descendants.

The Roman world's assumptions and that of the Church of the fourth and fifth centuries AD were that humanity's descendants originally inhabited Mesopotamia and spread into Africa, Europe, and Asia. They were unaware of humans migrating along a land bridge connecting Asia to North America after an Ice Age. People also sailed along the western shores of the Americas over several thousand years. Recent discoveries suggest island hopping in the Pacific, where the adventurous may have sailed along Central and South American coastal regions.

---

251. Paradigm shifts of that magnitude create dilemmas for many disciplines and institutions, not just theology. New competitors, unknown in character, may present potential threats or upheavals to a familiar order. Christianity's predicament was not unique.

The traditional assumptions on Genesis did not prepare the Church for these discoveries. None of this is unusual. People do not know what they did not know until they know it. What we do with new knowledge is another matter. As Soren Kierkegaard said, "Life can only be understood backwards, but it must be lived forward."

Some Christians had the strange notion that a second death and resurrection of Christ had to occur in the antipodes since these new populations could not be of Adam's lineage. Long-held assumptions led to rigid and ad hoc explanations that today seem absurd. Confusion over major worldview shifts is what we would expect in the human experience. Some possible theological solutions were more like thought experiments to navigate murky waters.

Some thought God might have created humans in the antipodes independent of Adam and Eve. To most people, Christ's death and resurrection, as understood in Paul's letter to the Romans, only applied to Adam's descendants. They believed that if there were "humanlike creatures" in other hemispheres, they could not bear the image of God. That assumes God's image transmits through reproduction, a rather naturalistic explanation for a spiritual attribute.[252]

People did what people usually do during times of rapid change—overreact at first, settle down in time, and eventually reach some clarity. Depending on the extent of the seismic shift, the process could take centuries. Theologians in Augustine's day were moving through rapid paradigm shifts. There were advances in the Trinity, Christology, free will, and original sin. All this occurred while the Roman Empire fell and eventually disintegrated into smaller competing states that still reverberate today.

By the end of Augustine's day, the Ancient Near East and even the Roman Empire had shrunk. They were not nearly the "whole" world anymore. We experience similar changes in our perspective when engineers create more powerful telescopes, reminding us of our tiny place in the universe. A stunning example of this is the *Voyager* spacecraft as it left the interior of our solar system. It relayed pictures of our solar system where the sun is small but visible. Jupiter and Saturn are much smaller and barely noticeable. However, the earth is undetectable except as the tiniest speck, unrecognizable as a planetary body or a distant star. Even when pointed out, it is hard to spot. It took astronomers to find it.

Those pictures from *Voyager* demonstrate that the earth and planets revolve around the sun. Despite this, there are organizations passionately dedicated to an earth-centered (geocentric) universe. An actual snapshot of the sun-centered solar system still does not convince them. Nonetheless, they are marginalized, having no influence. YEC will likely be around for a long time, but it is going the way of the geocentric universe.

---

252. To this day, most Christians are not clear on what God's image is exactly.

Better vision helps correct misunderstandings humans inevitably make. Since there is a progression of revelation in the Bible, we do not expect Old Testament writers to understand the cross or resurrection of Jesus or even the person of Jesus as the Incarnate Son. Their knowledge of God and His purposes needed gradual development with time and the help of seismic experiences, all of which happened. As a truth-teller, God's integrity has nothing to do with the way humans see their world or the cosmos at any given point in time, so the accusation that God lied to us because the earth is old is degrading to Him, and sadly, that assertion is for a nonessential.

Some Christians who could not adjust to the new worldview hindered evangelism. For example, some thought newly discovered natives from Ferdinand Magellan's voyages in the sixteenth century might not be Adam's descendants. Evangelistic efforts suffered in those lands initially. Some Christians believed the Bible indicated that these "people" were descendants of creatures created before Adam and Eve, which, surprisingly enough, was before Darwin. Most Christians were eager to organize missions to these lands putting the Gospel first and setting aside other presuppositions. In time, we either solve riddles or quit looking at them by returning to the mission.

In general, theological assumptions about Adam and Eve and Creation contributed to the mistreatment of native populations when colonial powers landed on their shores. To be sure, lusts for gold and political power were primary motivators for expansion. Nonetheless, legalistic theological assumptions made it easier to justify the accompanying excesses.

Ironically, science tells us that all humans are related genetically, something Christianity has always maintained. Past and present, Africans, Asians, red, brown, and white races are all one family. This science sounds like biblical theology. DNA demonstrates the unity of humanity, as does an original pair. We might say that Adam and Eve are the ANE's only way of expressing what we call human DNA, i.e., that we are one family.

How advanced people are technologically or theologically cannot determine inclusion in the human family; *neither can ancient genealogical records of a single line be the determinant.*[253] Today, the paradigm shift is toward DNA. For example, if recent developments in Neanderthal DNA are correct, they are full members of the human family biologically. In other words, the Bible is not the tool to determine whether newly discovered people are human. That is now a question for genomics. An oddity in YEC is that many think Neanderthals descended from Noah together with hominins like Homo Erectus, Homo Habilis, Heidelbergensis, and others. DNA and carbon 14 dating consistently show that those creatures predate modern humans of the third millennium B.C., the time of Noah's flood. Some YErs

---

253. The genealogies in scripture are to identify the covenant people and the Messiah to come from them, not to age the earth or define which humans are in God's image.

believe Australopithecus boarded the Ark. Those are extravagant prices to pay for literalism.

Genomics and molecular biology are nothing more than observing God's coherent way of developing living organisms using the natural processes He ordained, whether scientists credit God or not. We do not judge engineers for not giving God credit for tolerances they discover or techniques for using nature's resources efficiently; we just want to know if their math is correct. Like science, engineering is neither religious nor irreligious. Scientists and engineers are not supposed to be a priestly class. Similarly, the age of the earth is an empirical question, not a religious one.

That is just a fact.

The fundamentalist's idea that the further you go back in Church history, the purer Christian doctrines are (e.g., on the earth's age) is provably false. Jesus told the disciples the Holy Spirit would lead the Church into necessary truths. This work of the Spirit has been a gradual process. The earliest Church, for example, refused to accept uncircumcised Gentiles into the fellowship until after Peter's vision of Acts 10, yet *Gentiles were known to be descendants of Adam.*

The early Church required circumcision of Gentile converts until the Acts 15 conference. The Hebrew Bible teaches and requires circumcision *explicitly*, even upon the pain of death (Exodus 4:24–26; Genesis 17:14). First-century Jewish Christians considered it arbitrary to disregard clear and consistent scripture texts. Christianity required a new view of scriptural authority. After the conference of Acts 15, disputes among Jewish Christians continued (Galatians 2:12). Christianity would have remained Jewish or died on the vine if the early Church had taken a literalist view of scripture or the useless one-to-one correspondence to reality fiction.

Even after Peter's vision, it took the Church years of struggle to understand its full implications because they needed to adjust to a counterintuitive fact: A human named Jesus has more authority than the Bible. Matthew 28:18 says, "Then Jesus came to them and said, '*All authority* in heaven and on earth has been given to me.'"[254] Of course, Jesus has more authority than the Bible. He is the Son of God. He discontinued many Old Testament prescriptions and principles, such as perpetuating "the sins of the father" upon the children:

> As he went along, [Jesus] saw a man blind from birth. His disciples asked him, "Rabbi, who sinned, this man or his parents, that he was born blind?"

---

254. The New Testament goes out of its way to show that Jesus has greater authority than Moses. This has to include teachings as well as status. It would be absurd to claim Jesus's superiority to Moses in everything but teaching authority. Let's face it: the New Testament has authority over the Old Testament. The Law indeed came through Moses, *but* grace and truth came through Jesus Christ (John 1:17).

"Neither this man nor his parents sinned," said Jesus, "but this happened so that the works of God might be displayed in him." (John 9:1–3)

The disciples assumed two possible causes for the man's blindness: the man or his parents. That was a false choice. The answer was neither. Presuppositions are often subconscious, perhaps forgotten, or taken for granted. They mold our response to what draws our attention. No one is immune to our false assumptions, so we should reassess them.

Christians should welcome new perceptions awakened by discoveries in archeology, science, or language but carefully evaluate them. Correcting cherished beliefs should not be done in haste or forgetting why they became treasured in the first place. It takes courage to turn our backs on something we identified with or have loved. But we must turn our backs; otherwise, maintaining a fiction shown to be fiction in "service" to God is a betrayal of one's soul.

Our identities transcend our opinions, and personal responsibility should not lay powerless in the face of our presuppositions. Our character is at stake. When seriously threatened or during a crisis, our real identity emerges. We find out who our real friends are, who we are, and whether we will change to get along or refuse to change in the face of overwhelming evidence.[255] It is better to experience discomfort by surrendering to truth than to suffer more later.

Overzealous and rigid Christians, if fortunate, will eventually experience a crisis of faith, which may be God's way of softening us—"The Lord disciplines the one he loves, and he chastens everyone he accepts as his son" (Hebrews 12:6). Past generations could not know the things we take for granted, like humans in God's image inhabiting landmasses around the world or that the earth is spherical and not the geographical center of the universe.

For centuries, the Bible was the source of knowledge on topics addressed almost nowhere else, such as pre-history, astronomy, genetics, and geography: not just morality and religious practice. People would search its depths for answers about most anything. They still do. The tendency was to "fill in the blanks" or clarify where the Bible may not be clear with whatever

---

255. John Stuart Mill wrote, "So long as an opinion is strongly rooted in the feelings, it gains rather than loosens stability by a [preponderance of evidence] against it. For if it was accepted as a result of argument, the refutation of the argument might shake [one's] conviction; when it rests solely on feeling. The worst it fares in argumentative contest, the more persuaded its adherents are that their feelings must have some deep ground, which arguments do not reach; and while the feeling remains, it is always throwing up fresh entrenchments of arguments to repair any breech made in the old."

In other words, when the reason for one's opinion is defeated, another reason takes its place and still another when that reason is defeated so that reasons shift continually to maintain the opinion. A tip-off that this is happening is the logical absurdity in an argument that is entirely missed by its proponents.

seemed reasonable. There was nowhere else to go on some things. "Fills" that were suggestions at first became certainties over time. The Bible may seem compromised by the discoveries in geography and astronomy when, in reality, the new information revealed a blind spot in biblical interpretation we could not have anticipated.

We did not anticipate the antipodes.

The unforeseen misapplication of the Bible's purposes produced havoc for centuries. We dealt with the implications only after humans living on the other side of the globe became indisputable. People had depended on the Bible to inform them on matters not relevant to its purposes. Those are errors made by believers, not by biblical authors who could not possibly know about people on the other side of the earth that they did not even realize was a globe. Nor could they understand how future generations would misuse their work.

Our mistakes impose unreasonable expectations upon the Bible and trivialize its most profound wisdom. Biblical authors are not responsible for our misuses, and neither is God. These authors wrote to specific audiences with specific needs at particular times and places mostly alien to us, even when the overarching lessons may be universal. The Bible's wisdom often lies in overarching lessons, not six literal days in Genesis.

Should we adopt "biblical" engineering, medicine, construction, farming, and weaponry because they were "God-breathed?" Honestly, we uncover our narrow views when enlightened and not before. It is common for humans to close their minds to realities in full view, especially with passions over religion, politics, and love. Evangelism can lose its perspective until the Church's mission comes back into clear focus and the Gospel's preeminence reemerges to meet the demands of a "new" world.

Humans in God's image inhabited the antipodes.

Asking if they were descendants of Adam was not the right question. If we were to find persons like ourselves on another planet that are not human but have self-awareness, are endowed with the faculty of reason, use complex languages, and exhibit an awareness of God, they would bear His image and receive His love. They are in God's image, no matter their pedigree.

The New Testament cautions against those "wasting their time on senseless stories and endless lists of ancestors. Such things only cause arguments. They don't help anyone do God's work that can only be done by faith... There are some who have given up these for nothing but empty talk... But they don't know what they are talking about, even though they think they do" (1 Timothy 1:4–7 CEV).

Let the reader decide if these verses in any way describe the SDWC.

Paul places, side-by-side, spending one's time on stories and genealogies. These are not a set of Christian presuppositions. Unlike Judaism, Christianity does not care if someone is a gentile or alien. It took hundreds of years for some Christians to get used to the idea that their presuppositions about the world and the Bible, by extension, had to change. We still have a ways to go.

The key is in the Bible's purpose: to reveal God's nature and will through the Logos Incarnate.

16.
CURRENT PRESUPPOSITIONS AND THE BIBLE

The Bible tells how to go to heaven, *not how the heavens go.*
—Galileo

The Bible does not just teach us how to go to heaven but also
how the heavens go.[256]
—Steven W. Boyd, YE Evangelist

General opinions on the nature and purposes of the Bible vary widely. On one end are many fundamentalists who say God "wrote" the Bible word-for-word, and therefore, it is accurate in every sense as God is. Inspiration amounts to dictation for these believers in that God uses human authors as a quill to write each word as He wishes. On the other end of the spectrum are *unbelievers* who say the Bible is wholly a human product with some literary and historical value but spoiled by superstition, flights of fancy, and primitive delusions.

As with many sharply contested opinions, the truth lies somewhere in between.

The Problem

Most Christians, including myself, believe God is the inspiration for the Bible. The three main branches of Christianity officially state that the Bible is the inspired Word of God. However, while Christians consider the Bible the Word of God, Christianity does not claim the Bible is the *words* of God, except where the authors quote God directly, which is rare. The problem is that if God wrote the Bible, He did not inspire it. Why? Inspirations do not write.

Someone or something inspires writers to write.

Many scholars say the Bible is the Word of God translated into the words of men. Biblical authors attempt to translate God's will or actions that have inspired them into words. Something is always lost in translation, especially from the perfect word of infinite being through an imperfect language. God's personal "language" is not any finite human language. But that is what we have, and it is beautiful, despite—or perhaps because of—the fragileness of human speech. God is not afraid to use us in our frailty.

Moreover, Christians mean different things by the "Word of God." Catholics, Orthodox, Protestants, and fundamentalists rely on different Bibles

---

256. Terry Mortenson, Thane H., eds., *Coming to Grips with Genesis* (Master Books, 2008), Kindle edition, location 4737.

containing various books from alternate manuscripts when referring to scripture. These variants are common knowledge throughout Christianity. That should not disturb Christians who understand the human contribution to the scripture's composition, transmission, and canonization. However, those that believe God selected and preserved every word perfectly are vulnerable. Scholarship has made it so.[257]

Many Christians believe their religious tradition is the most faithful to the Bible and that the Bible version they chose is more accurate to their tradition: there's circular reasoning somewhere in there. Across Christendom, believers disagree on what the Bible is, what the Bible means, its role in the Church, methods of interpreting it, and the degree of reliability inherent in it. There are significant differing opinions on biblical teachings, even among those claiming that the Bible is clear, infallible, or without error, known as *inerrancy*.

For example, some say the scriptures were without any error when originally composed. YErs, among others, fall into this camp. Others will note that the original *writings* are not with us today, so the claim is impossible to verify. Inerrancy becomes a matter of faith for these believers.[258]

Others say the Bible is inerrant only in matters of *"faith and practice"* or only on what it *"affirms and teaches,"* which is to say the Bible is *not* inerrant. That is because the referent, "the Bible," refers to the whole, not selected portions of it. If any part of the Bible is errant, then we cannot claim the inerrancy of the whole though we may believe it to be so. Therefore, claims of inerrancy must be more modest or reduced in scope, which we have already seen in the different definitions of inerrancy. Otherwise, any book is inerrant if part of it is without error. The claim that God superintended *every word of the Bible* while applying inerrancy in a limited way is self-defeating.

Furthermore, some note that even if the Bible is inerrant, we are not. In other words, our fallible interpretations would inevitably make errors, not recognizing the Bible's inerrant meaning. A helpful question would be, is the Bible, in fact, *identical* to the Word of God? Is it the *perfect* Word of God that exists in eternity with God himself? The answer should be evident since the Word of God existed long before there was a Bible. At best, the Bible would be an abbreviation of God's Word limited, in its scope, where just the word *limited* is a clue. Did God select every word in the Bible to avoid *any* human error, in effect

---

257. Remember Augustine's words, *"Wherever truth may be found, it belongs to our Master."* Scholarship is a source for truth and a tool for the Church. We would not have a Bible in our languages without it.

258. It is true that textual criticism helps uncover the original text of the Bible. While useful, and at times invaluable, this is far from having the original text. Ask yourself, what would you rather have? The originals or a helpful reconstruction? Besides, if God required perfection in the writing, why allow imperfection in the copying and editing, unless the copying and editing offered a more inspired document than the original, which would be inconsistent on God's part?

writing it himself? YErs and fundamentalists say yes because that is what they think inspiration means—control over every word. It has never meant that in the history of Christian thought.

However, if humans get any credit for writing the books of the Bible, would God be the author of their mistakes, including scientific ones? For example, God knows that human conception requires sperm and egg. He also knows that emotions do not reside in the bowels. Anatomy and biology were hardly exact sciences or sciences at all in the biblical period. God could have prevented those mistakes. Why didn't He? Because it was not necessary, and more importantly, because He would not assume authorship to Himself.

Even Jesus did not write; he left that to his imperfect disciples!

Nobody denies the human authorship of the Bible, even when they insist that God wrote it. Just ask such a person, "Who wrote the Psalms of David?" That question answers itself. Why are fundamentalists concerned about giving Moses authorship of the Pentateuch or that the right men wrote the gospels and epistles rather than no-named individuals? All Christians recognize the authority of human authorship. If God micromanages each word, then the human author does not matter. All words would be the same. Yet, human authorship does matter, especially to fundamentalists, because the right author lends authority.

Luke gives us a more reasonable glimpse into inspiration when he wrote:

Many have undertaken to draw up an account of the things that have been fulfilled among us, just as they were handed down to us by those who from the first were eyewitnesses and servants of the word [of Jesus]. With this in mind, since *I myself* have carefully investigated everything from the beginning, *I too decided* to write an orderly account for you, most excellent Theophilus, so that you may know the certainty of the things you have been taught. (Luke 1:1–4; emphasis added)

Luke's preface gives insight into how many biblical authors approached their work. The messaging begins with an inspired person, a prophet, or a disciple, then follows an elaborate process like any conscientious writer. The following is a breakdown of Luke's process:

- "Many have undertaken to write"—the sources.
- "Just as they were handed down"—respecting the chain of custody.
- "From the first eyewitnesses"—disciples or insiders.
- "I have carefully investigated"—questioned key people and compiled the evidence.
- "I too decided to write an account"—the will to authorship.
- "For you... Theophilus"—the audience.

"*I decided to write*," says Luke. It was a personal choice. Of course, he acts on inspiration throughout this process. Nonetheless, the writer does not cease to be a fully engaged human. His motivation is to disclose God's nature and purposes revealed in the person of Christ.

Ideas began with preaching a message from God preserved and spread initially through oral tradition. Throughout the life of a prophet or evangelist, professional scribes recorded excerpts of oral tradition and teachings. After a prophet or evangelist's death, his disciples compiled all the sources, papyri, and parchments containing his teachings and speeches. Then authors and scribes edit and organize the material into a cohesive whole for specific purposes. As needs arose, they adapted the source material for a particular audience that needed the message in real-time. In Luke's case, the audience was, as far as we know, one person—Theophilus. Undoubtedly, Theophilus was a center of influence that affected a larger population, yet Luke appears to have written the book specifically for him.

Luke could not think he was adding to the canon of scripture or that the whole world would cherish his work or even read it. He did not know if some of his sources were to become books of the Bible. He was in the thick of it, on the front lines, trying to make a difference for the movement. The mission remained the same, and YEC had nothing to do with it. Luke did not merely sit and write as God funneled words in his head.

What did Luke say he did?

He did his homework; he interviewed relevant principles, researched, compiled the sources, and *wrote the book*. His unique skill, style, and perspective as an author appear in the text. Medical terms are evident in Luke's writing since he was a physician. His process was not unique. It is what writers do and how they do it. Why go through all that if God has planned every word? Truthfully, the more Luke puts effort and planning into his work, the more credit he deserves. Christians have always been willing to give him and other biblical authors credit.

Why commission humans to write in a nonhuman way? Human frailty and human error are not sins. Living with mistakes is the occupation of every human, even with an inerrant Bible. Mistakes do not thwart the Word of God. Human frailty does not deny the inspiration of God. If there are mistakes in the Bible, they are human, and we can adapt.

Some believe the Bible *contains* the Word of God or a Word *from* God. The Word for all time is the mission of Jesus called the Gospel. That leads to a question: Is the Bible the word in the same way Christ is *the Word*? (John 1:1–14). In John, the Greek word *Logos* does not mean a *literal word*. John's first description of the Word is not linguistic, but "in him was life and the life was the light of men, and the light in the darkness did shine, and the darkness did not perceive it" (John 1:4–5). *Logos* was a philosophical term for reason, meaning, or wisdom, especially in speech. Logos is where we get the English word *logic*. Christ is, in some sense, the expression or communication of divine reason, i.e., he is special revelation. A person could be deaf, a child, an infant, a senile adult, and the mentally disabled, yet none are turned away due to cognitive deficiencies. All can receive the light. So Logos does not exclusively mean "words" or human language. Logos grounds this universe, not with words but *as* "the Word." Being "the Word" is a metaphor for what it is all about.

The Logos, the Word, is it.

YErs identify the Bible as "the perfect Word of God." That seems to be the YE definition of the Bible. There are other possible definitions. "What is the Bible?" is also a question of *identification*. In other words, how do we identify the Word of God in any medium? There is a law that identifies something as that unique thing.

The *law of identity* states that all things true of one object must also be true of another to be *identical*. If anything, anything at all is different between the two; they cannot be identical. Is anything true of *God's perfect and eternal Word* that is not true of the Bible? Or is the Bible *identical* to God's "perfect and eternal Word?" Are humans even capable of composing, creating, arranging, copying, and preserving God's perfect and eternal Word even under inspiration? These questions underscore the problem.

Just what is "the perfect Word of God?"

We believe that God created the world by the Word of God. But what does that mean? In Young's Literal Translation, Hebrews 11:3 says, "By faith we understand that the worlds were prepared *by a saying* of God, so that what is seen was made from things that are not visible."[259] John identifies Jesus as this Perfect Word, "In the beginning was the Word and the Word was with God and the Word was God... Through him, all things were made... The Word became flesh" (John 1:1–4). John calls the Word "Him," not *"it."*

John says that all things came into existence through the Logos (the divine, reasoned speech). The words of God in the creation account are not commands but express the will or desires of the Creator: "Let there be light;" not, "There shall be light." This distinction is essential because expressing one's desires does not need a listener to hear them while commands do.[260] We would not say that God created the universe with the Bible or the words in the Bible. The Bible is not the Logos, which means it is not *The Word* in the same sense. At least we know that the divine speech in John and the Bible are not identical.

---

259. The word *prepared* in Young's Literal Translation is similar to the word *bara* in Genesis, which can also mean "prepared."

260. Francesca Aran Murphy, Troy A. Srefano, eds., *The Oxford Handbook of Christology* (Oxford University Press, Oxford England, 2015), Kindle edition, location 473.

The point is that the expression "Word of God" can mean different things, so equivocating may run rampant.

Adding the modifier *perfect* to the Word of God is superfluous. It should go without saying that when God speaks, it is perfect in context because His actual speech proceeds from He who is perfect. But YErs use this superfluous statement to equivocate on the "Word of God." There is a difference between the perfect Word that proceeds from God—the Logos—and inspired words written by men. Adding the superfluous modifies *perfect and eternal* to the "Word of God" (meaning the Bible) and attempts to equate it with literal thoughts of God generated in words. Doing so implies a piousness earned solely by being Young Earth Creationists.

We believe God can and does "speak" through the Bible's pages, yet the Bible is, in fact, a thing in this world. God's Word is independent of any*thing, including paper and ink.* God "speaks" through many things: creation, events, other people, our conscience, dreams, visions, Balaam's ass (Numbers 22:21–34), and no doubt different ways in which we are not aware. Are all these things the inerrant Word of God? No, because each is a medium through a third party. God's perfect and eternal Word proceeds directly from Him to the receiver without translation, medium, or any imperfect third party like the Old Testament books written by Hebrew authors. The Bible records messages from God to the prophets. Are those prophets equal to God's own eternal, perfect Word?:

> "At different times and in various ways, God's voice came to our ancestors through the *Hebrew* prophets. *But in these last days, it has come to us through His Son...through whom all worlds were made* (Hebrews 1:1-2, The Voice) [the Son is the radiance of God's glory and the exact representation of his being who] sustains all that exists through the power *of His Word".* (Hebrews 1:3 NIV)

The power of God's Word is Christ through whom *"all worlds were made."* Christ is the Word or Logos generated from the Godhead as thought generated from mind. One might think human language is more precise than nature, events, or dreams, yet we believe a picture can be "worth a thousand words." Words alone did not convince the Apostle Paul on the road to Damascus, nor were words enough for Jesus's brother, James. It took an *event,* the resurrection, to convince those two that Jesus was indeed the Messiah, the Son of God.

The Christ events are the power of God's Word translated into actions.

Romans 1:16, "For I am not ashamed of the Gospel of Christ, for it is *the power of Go*d. that brings salvation to everyone who believes."

1 Corinthians 1:18, "Christ is the Power and Wisdom of God. *For the message of the cross is... the power of God."*

Christ's gospel is the power of God to effect salvation. The meaning is not simply the words about the cross or the Gospel but the deeds that produced the words. Without deeds, the words are empty. In fact, without the resurrection, the cross is empty—"And if Christ has not been raised, your *faith is futile*; you are still in your sins" (1 Corinthians 15:17).

Notice 1 Corinthians 4:20: "For the kingdom of God *is not in word* but in power." Here, "word" means human language. The kingdom is a reality; words are not. It is not that words are unimportant, but they are not the most important.

There are essential differences in how the phrase "*the Word of God*" is used by Christians, sometimes with no regard to those differences. It makes no sense for anyone to say, "*In the beginning was the Bible, and the Bible was with God, and the Bible was God.*" Most importantly, John says that the Word became flesh and lived among us. The Bible remains a book.

The Son of God, in some sense, is *the* Word of God. He is also God and man. Since it would be idolatry to equate the Bible with God, the Word, meaning the Logos, is quite different from "the word," meaning the Bible. Nonetheless, Christians use the expressions "*the Word*" and "*the Bible*," expecting them to be identical. Such equivocations create confusing conversations and serious mistakes when the terms go undefined.

The Godhead speaks in our universe through the Logos (Word). Jesus said of Himself, "I proceeded (came forth) from God [out of His very presence]" (John 8:42, 15:26 AMPC). The Logos proceeds from the Godhead as words or thoughts flow from a personal being. How can that be?

We have no idea.

It has something to do with infinite being. At a minimum, it means the Incarnate Christ is God's perfect and eternal expression of His Word, not the Bible. Or are Christians prepared to say the Bible is equal to God Incarnate? If not, how is it inferior? There are things true of the eternal, perfect Word of God that are not true of the Bible. The Bible is not eternal. It did not exist 3500 years ago. Humans canonized it in two stages, approximately 1,600–1,900 years ago. The Word (Logos) is spirit and can join with our consciousness personally; a book cannot. God's eternal, perfect Word proceeds *directly* from God's being into another person's consciousness and is *indirectly* translated through other means like human authors, a quill, ink, and words on a page. Words are symbols. God's eternal Word makes a direct connection without symbols—without words.

For example, Jeremiah said God writes His law in our hearts by His Spirit (Jeremiah 31:33). That does not mean God writes the Bible or anything else on our hearts; it means the Spirit of God influences us from within. The Spirit inspires us. When Jesus *breathed* on the disciples and said, "Receive the Holy Spirit," he illustrated inspiration, which means *inbreathing* (John 20:22). This inbreathing also leads to rebirth. This divine breath was not about words or even breath; it could be about life, influence, and transformation. The disciples were ready for the indwelling Spirit, where He communes with us by a shared spirit or consciousness (Romans 8:16).

The eternal Word of God is the revelation of Christ, succinctly stated in the Gospel.

No doubt many words in the Bible, or the thoughts behind them, will endure forever. But human language is finite. The words of the Bible bear witness to Christ, who is the revelation, and who is eternal. The Bible predicts the Messiah, traces his human ancestry, and puts his birth in context to Israel's history in the Gentile world of Egypt, Assyria, Babylon, Persia, Greece, and Rome. It establishes dual nature in the name *"Jesus Christ,"* who is both a world figure and a cosmic presence—the Messiah and the Son of Man spoken of by Daniel (Daniel 7:13; Matthew 26:64).

The "perfect" and "eternal" Word of God and the Bible are linked but not *identical*. The Bible is the words of men under God's influence, not his thumb. The Bible is the Word of God as it discloses the nature and purposes of God that culminated in the Incarnation. God's perfect Word is *His* Word, not the words of imperfect men *about* His Word. God's Word is infinitely more than the Bible.

People use expressions like "the Word of God" loosely. When YErs refer to the Bible as the Word of God on the one hand and the perfect Word of God on the other, they use the referent "Word of God" in two different ways. They do something similar with the initial creation. God calls it "very good," but YEC corrects the record with "perfect."

Divine perfection is in the necessity of God's being, not in the contingent objects He creates. Consequently, perfection in us will come from God's union with humanity so that we partake of His nature as 2 Peter 1:4 says, *"You may participate in the divine nature."* In other words, God perfects us by infusing Himself into our being as an act of grace, not for sheer modification of our behavior. That is why our efforts do not amount to much; they are not about us having the power to perfect ourselves; instead, our efforts demonstrate our willingness and desire to be infused like a bride on her honeymoon who desires her groom.

God's perfect and eternal Word does not sift through human strainers called "authors" and remain unaltered any more than God becoming human continued, in every respect, unaltered. Something is lost in translation. The human element makes the loss unavoidable.

Yet, the Bible is not simply the words of men unaffected by divine guidance.

The Hebrew Bible was a world-changing advancement in God's self-disclosure. Yahweh's personhood was unknown. Enslaved Israelites claimed He revealed Himself to them. Out of nowhere, they defeated the Egyptians on the way out of slavery with Yahweh's help. If Israel made up Yahweh and His covenant to satisfy some psychological needs, why did they struggle so much to be faithful to Him? Why not attribute false righteousness to themselves like pagan societies generally did?

When punished for infidelity, why did the Jewish nation not do the customary thing and turn to the gods of the people who conquered them? Why not accept the conquering Babylonian pantheon with Marduk as the reigning Most High God? Instead, the Jews did a strange thing. They turned to Yahweh in repentance when in captivity. Jeremiah relays God's word in the moment, saying to the Jewish captives, "Seek the peace and prosperity of [Babylon] to which I have carried you into exile. Pray to the Lord for them because if [Babylon] prospers, you too will prosper" (Jeremiah 29:7). That is the unprecedented practice of praying for one's enemies (Matthew 5:44). This divine decree is remarkable; why not pray for freedom if prayer works? They understood that the Lord chastens those He loves and was now chastening them (Deuteronomy 8:5). That was a revelation they were not likely to make up.

Why does Yahweh alone endure among all ANE gods of the great empires?

More importantly, the Hebrew Scriptures contain the extraordinary promises and prophecies of the Messiah recorded hundreds of years before their fulfillment in the Christ events—the life, death, resurrection, and ascension of Jesus. With written promises fulfilled a thousand years later, and other promises that will unfold throughout eternity, we are dealing with something beyond history and someone who has all things in His grasp.

It is truly remarkable that the Old Testament's Jewish stewards faithfully preserved the Messianic passages referring to Christ, yet they rejected Him. Jesus both fulfilled Old Testament prophecy so Jews might receive Him but fulfilled them in unexpected ways so they might reject Him. Even that was prophesied.

The consistent focus on the coming of Christ throughout the Bible, both in explicit and enigmatic terms, indicates a reality beyond human powers and human language itself. The living Word was to come in person. Human words, even those of the Bible, are too limiting to express God's ultimate self-revelation. To see Christ face-to-face, we must receive him in our conscience and *share in His glory* by a resurrection (1 Corinthians 13:12; 1 John 3:2). We must acquire a state of being beyond this world to see Him who is beyond this world.

Promises and prophecies by themselves are given in *words*, human words. History is about events put into words, not the events themselves. However, to enter history, become its point, exit history, and then enter it a second time is something else. That is to *be* the Word, the Logos.

The reality of God's Word is Christ. That is why placing all importance on literalism can be misleading. Words alone cannot provide everything God has to say: thus, the Incarnation. Words cannot always say things well. We often say, "I don't have the words" or "There are no words." Words are often inadequate for the most profound human experiences. There is nothing more profound than God and the things of God.

The Bible is not the Logos. It contains traces of the Logos.

As the moon reflects sunlight, the Bible reflects the Son's Light. Neither the Bible nor the moon is the source of the light they reflect. This metaphor is not a low view of the Bible but places the Bible in perspective to God. This comparison is a corrective to a fanciful opinion of scripture outside its essential purposes.

The Bible is an Israelite record of God's revelation to the nation as they understood it. Scripture is His Word translated into "earth speak," often in various forms and received in progressive stages until fully exposed at the fullness of time—the coming of Christ. The Bible contains an eternal Word from God, and it's not the age of the earth; it's the Gospel.

However, the Bible generally is not the *words* of God Himself, except where authors quote him directly. *The Word* of God given to the world *is the life, death, resurrection, and ascension of the Incarnate Son* and his intentions for heaven and earth. This message finds its way in the Bible, written in the *words* of men.

Jesus said: "How foolish you are, and how slow to believe all that the prophets have spoken. Did not the Messiah have to suffer these things and then enter his glory? And beginning with Moses and all the prophets, he explained to them what was said in all the Scriptures concerning Himself" (Luke 24:25–28).

Men wrote the Bible beginning with "Moses and all the prophets."

There are five reasons why all Christians should stop saying, "God wrote the Bible:"

1. It is misleading.

2. It leads to other errors.

3. Unbelievers know better if some Christians do not.

4. It denies the biblical view of inspiration and replaces it with dictation.

5. It is self-evidently false.

The "God wrote the Bible" fantasy is the fundamentalist's transubstantiation in that they both deny the obvious. But the former is less persuasive than the latter from a biblical perspective. At least Jesus said, "This is my body," and "This is my blood," but scripture never says anything like, "God wrote the Bible." Instead of adding words and concepts not found in scripture, Christians should use the scriptural terms "God-inspired," not God wrote, or "moved by the Holy Spirit," not "written by the Holy Spirit." The Bible is a unique record from a single nation that follows their religious development from the Bronze Age through the first century AD—over one thousand years. God's purposes unfold throughout its pages. We know of no other people with so long a continuous and progressive record that makes sense of God's presence in the world. Moreover, by New Testament times, that record blossomed into the witness for God *to all people*. The revelation to Israel in both Old and New Testament stands apart from all other worldviews.[261]

The biblical authors witness to that revelation within the authentic context of tribal life in ancient Israel. We can see that later authors began to interpret earlier authors within the pages of the Bible that *they* penned at later stages. Later generations looked for reoccurring patterns from previous times that might help explain perplexing events of their day.[262]

After the exile in Babylon, scholars and historians refer to Judaism as Second Temple Judaism. It developed interpretive methods to apply or link earlier events recorded in the scriptures to current events. As a result, some past events seem to anticipate current ones, showing a pattern that repeats itself with an increasing sense of destiny.

Such patterns point to providence and continuity. The theological applications of Noah's flood are versatile. Moses gets rescued in a basket (ark in Hebrew), saving him when tossed into the Nile River. The ancients understood well that water could be chaotic, destructive, and life-giving. The Hebrew word *ark*, generally translated as "basket" by which Moses escapes, appears only twice in scripture—here and Noah's Ark. The dividing of waters in Genesis 1 and the unleashing of those same waters upon Noah's generation anticipated the dividing of the Reed Sea that protected God's people and engulfed the Egyptian army.

There is an allusion to Noah's Ark in this story of baby Moses. Moses' "ark" also foreshadowed the dividing of the Reed Sea, where it says in Exodus 2:3-4, "She got an [*ark*] for him, and coated it with *tar and pitch*. She then placed the child (Moses) in it and put it *among the reeds* [alluding to the Reed Sea]." Peter equates the flood to baptism in the New Testament, and the Church is like an ark (1 Peter 3:19–22).

---

261. See John N. Oswalt, *The Bible among the Myths: Unique Revelation or Just Ancient Literature?* For a comparison of the ANE worldview and Old Testament revelation.

262. A prime example of this is the return of the Jews from exile in Babylon. The generation of Ezra and Nehemiah began a tradition of interpreting scripture in the light of catastrophic experiences despite being God's chosen people. Thanks to Jeremiah, they recognized their failure to keep covenant with Yahweh. Few captives would have survived to remember what life was like in Israel before the exile. The books of Moses were now in an older Hebrew dialect with idioms different from that experienced in the seventy years of exile in Babylon. In addition, the exiles came back speaking Aramaic. The Law of Moses needed interpreting for new circumstances, which required a professional class of interpreters to apply a legal framework for renewed life upon the return. The need for trained interpreters is truer today due to the distance of time and all that that means. Postexilic interpretive tradition called the *Second Temple Hermeneutic* would have ramifications on the New Testament's authors who interpreted the Old Testament in the light of the life, death, resurrection, and ascension of Jesus.

Remember that tar and pitch played prominently in the construction of Noah's Ark. In addition, many scholars think the "Red Sea" is likely better translated as *Reed Sea*. Patterns in stories like these are virtually a traditional element of biblical literature. Only through significant experience in the biblical text will that become obvious.

These repeated patterns with God's work in Israel's life would make sense to the Hebrews because God's work was this way since creation. Reoccurring patterns ("And God said," "and it was so," and "evenings and mornings," etc.) or cycles like rainy seasons, harvest, sunrise, and sundown, winter, spring, summer, and fall are observable and reliable for planning communal life. God works the same way in nature and scripture to provide stability in social and religious life. The two books of God's Word and works were noticeable even in ancient Israel's unscientific world.

Notice again that the seminal event in the Old Testament is the Exodus from Egypt. On Passover evening, God instructs the Israelites to sacrifice a lamb and apply its blood to their doorposts. That ensured the death angel (symbol of judgment) would *pass over* their homes, saving their firstborn. Since the firstborn sons inherited the house, he represented the household and future generations. Passing over all the Hebrew firstborn sons ensured the salvation of the house of Israel. The symbolism or type anticipates Jesus, God's firstborn who is also the New Testament Passover Lamb—the Lamb of God—whose shed blood saves the *Jew first* (God's firstborn among the nations), then the Gentile.

God's "sacrifice" of an animal to cover Adam and Eve's nakedness at the fall of man is the earliest story with a faint whisper of this pattern. Likewise, the Day of Atonement covered the people's sins, symbolized by a goat's blood (Leviticus 16). These patterns and linguistic similarities lead some scholars to believe the Garden of Eden story was either *composed or edited* during or soon after the exile into Babylon, a time known as the Second Temple Period.[263]

The Bible is a *literary* cooperative between God and humans, a union of God's purposes and the experiences of a wide variety of human authors from

---

263. The "Second Temple" refers to the temple built after the return from Babylonian exile. The Second Temple Period begins with this event and continues through the destruction of the Second Temple (that became Herod's temple) in AD 70. This period is significant since a Second Temple hermeneutic developed in Judaism to make sense of events in their day by finding antecedents in the now ancient writings of scripture. The exile of Adam and Eve from Eden was analogous to the Babylonian exile—an event the kingdom of Judah experienced. Typological patterns in scripture helped explain current circumstances. The reason for the exile was similar to the reason Adam and Eve were banished into the "cursed" field—disobedience, i.e., breaking an agreement. Here is the point: as a highly trained rabbi, the Second Temple Hermeneutic of the Rabbis was also Paul's method. *Except the events that mattered to Paul for interpreting all scripture were the Christ events. For Paul, and therefore Christianity, the Christ events interpret Old Testament scripture, not the other way around.*

Moses to John. The human impact on the Bible is undeniable. Minimizing either its human output or the divine stamp is a cross-eyed view of scripture.[264]

Current Presumptions

Past presumptions about the Bible have led to mistakes in interpreting, even absurd conclusions. What are current presumptions relevant to age/earth controversies? Here is a partial list:

1. *God wrote Genesis.* What people probably mean by this is that God micromanaged the Bible down to every word and detail. Humans amount to being a pen in God's hand. Inspiration is dictation. Therefore, the Bible cannot contain *any* mistakes on any subject *"it addresses."* Each word is a result of a miraculous act of God. This idea is not worth our time if taken literally. Writing is a human endeavor, yet even the God/Man Jesus *did not leave any writing.*

2. *Comprehensiveness*: The Bible *clearly* teaches God's will about all issues relevant to the Christian life.

3. *Reading is studying*: The best way to understand biblical texts is by simply reading them in their plain and literal sense. Poetry and predictive prophecy are exceptions.

4. *"Scripture by itself"*: One can understand the significance of any given biblical text without reliance on other sources of authority or knowledge. That especially applies to ANE literature, scientific sources, and biblical scholarship.

5. *Internal harmony*: All Bible-related passages on any subject fit together into a unified, consistent body of instruction about right and wrong beliefs and behaviors.

6. *Universal applicability*: What the biblical authors taught God's people at any point in history remains universally valid for all Christians at every other time *unless explicitly revoked by subsequent scriptural teaching.*

7. *"Fully" understanding the Bible/Gospel depends on believing in six literal days.*

The reasoning goes:

1. God "superintended" every word in the Bible.

2. God cannot make any mistakes.

3. Therefore, the Bible cannot make any mistakes.

---

264. In a similar way, Christ the Word is also divine and human. The difficulty for Christology is accounting for his divine authority and his subordination as a man.

The conclusion follows *only* if the premises are true.[265]

Premise 1 is a vague assertion with the word *superintended*. If the word *superintended* means God micromanaged or selected each word of the Bible to convey absolute truth, then the claim has no foundation. It comes primarily from misunderstanding or *mistranslating* verses such as 2 Timothy 3:16 in the following way: "Every Scripture has been *written* by the Holy Spirit, the breath of God" (TPT). The phrase "written by the Holy Spirit" is not in the text and is a serious mistranslation. The ASV says, "Every scripture inspired of God is also profitable for teaching, for reproof, for correction, for instruction which is in righteousness." *The Word Biblical Commentary on 2 Timothy 3:16 says, "God-breathed refers to the source of influence, not the method." That means God influences but doesn't write.*

Inspiration does not override the free will of the author but influences it. It does not make the writer perfect, like God. Free will allows error, or there is no free will. God cannot give us free will and prevent us from doing anything against His will. The degree to which God's inspiration affects the author, down to each word, is unknowable but is self-evidently not absolute. Fundamentalists risk confusing God's authority with their authority for claims they make when appealing to scripture in this way.

Premise 2 is true—God makes no mistakes, yet the conclusion (therefore, the Bible cannot make any mistakes) does not follow from premise 2. The issue is not: does God *make* mistakes, but does God *allow* mistakes? It does not follow that if God is actively involved with humans, they can make no mistakes. That claim does not bear out even in scripture. Adam was "God-breathed." Jesus breathed on the disciples and said, "Receive the Holy Spirit." Neither Adam nor the disciples were flawless as a result. The Holy Spirit simply moved the authors of scripture to write and elevated their awareness.

The Holy Spirit lives in every Christian. He moves us all according to the gifts he has given us and his calling to specific service. *No Christian perfectly executes the services God calls them to perform despite being inspired by the Holy Spirit.* That is not to say that our calling is the same kind as the authors of scripture, only that none is perfect in their calling. Even during the most critical periods in their service to God, all the righteous persons of faith faltered.

God operates with the universe continuously since he must ground it and sustain its existence. Every realm God has created has flaws, not because God is flawed but because only God is perfect in the absolute. He allows freedom of thought to humans and some random movement in the created order.

---

265. While Christians instinctively refer to the Bible as the Word of God, we rarely say "the Bible is the *words* of God." That is partly because the phrase does not roll off the tongue so easily but also because we know humans wrote the words themselves.

Perfection for humans in the biblical sense is to be sin-free, not error-free. Human perfecting takes a special act of God's grace that Christians believe is coming. The creature cannot be omniscient nor omnipotent; it can be all the Creator intends it to be, the only kind of perfection available to a contingent being. Only the Creator of humans can inform us of what it means to be fully human (demonstrated in Jesus), and only God can create that in us. God's plan is not merely to reward good people and punish bad ones; it is finishing what he started—us.

A math book may be error-free, but a large body of ancient literature with numerous genres is not math. Inspiration does not make human authors all-knowing nor guarantees an error-free brain trust among them. The claim that every human who wrote a part of the Bible was inerrant is a matter of faith. Even if the Bible is without error, we can only allege it. We cannot prove it since it takes an error-free mind to recognize and prove it.

Therefore, we can only believe the Bible is error-free. Here is the thing. Believing in the Bible is not equal to believing in God because of the most obvious fact—*humans* wrote the Bible. That means that faith in the Bible, regardless of what one thinks the Bible is, must also include trust in all who brought its many books to the world—writers, compilers, copyists, canonizes, and translators. They are not comparable to God.

Consider just one of these: the translators critical to making the Bible assessable to the masses. How many of them do fundamentalists trust, word for word? The answer is none. Some only trust the KJV as the most accurate. Nonetheless, it has to be less reliable than the original writings that we do not even possess. That means any translation fundamentalists use cannot have the one-to-one correspondence to reality YErs feign. This observation is not an indictment of the Bible or its translations but the exaggerated emphasis on wooden literalism or the one-to-one correspondence claim of YEC.

Why would God ensure perfect writers but allow imperfect compilers, editors, copyists, canonizes, and translators? Were those involved in the transmission of the Bible equally inspired as those involved in its composition? For inerrancy to be meaningful, it seems necessary that those responsible for each level in the process be inerrant. Otherwise, we must be able to track down every mistake in the process and know how to correct them perfectly, which is not serious.

Furthermore, a few verses in the New Testament about the Septuagint Old Testament appear to fundamentalists to assert inerrancy. The Septuagint Greek version of the OT is hardly inerrant. It is generally considered inferior to the Hebrew Masoretic text, not developed until centuries later. Few, if any, in the early Church either used or could read the Hebrew text. The Jews spoke Aramaic, not Hebrew. There is no way the Septuagint—the scripture of choice in the early Church—was inerrant. At the time, the Apocrypha and Pseudepigrapha were also part of Holy Writ. An official canon of either the Old or New Testament did not exist, nor was a list of writings in universal agreement.[266]

We have seen that biblical authors exposed their ideas about anatomy and reproductive biology, which God allowed since those ideas have nothing to do with his word. The copying errors we find in our oldest manuscripts are trivial compared to the actual revelation of God Incarnate. He allowed errors in copying and translating scripture too. Fallen or flawed humans wrote, copied, transmitted, canonized, translated, and interpreted the Bible. Our interpretations are imperfect. Like the poor, flaws will always be with us. Only God is without any error. The Bible is not God, nor are its words equal to God's own Words.

An evangelical might think it is difficult to *exaggerate* the Bible's importance, but YErs have managed to do it. When John said "the Word was God," he was not referring to the Bible. Nor does Hebrews 1:3 refer to the Bible when it says, "The Son is the radiance of God's glory and the exact representation of his being, sustaining all things by *his powerful word*."

Some fundamentalists revere the Bible as the object of their faith. YErs even subjugate God before their understanding of the Bible, saying, "If the earth is old, God is a liar." God and YEC must agree, or He's a deceiver. YErs judge God with the Bible. There are no words for the deficiency of this YE notion.

Why did Jesus not write the book, "The Gospel According to Jesus?" Would that clear up any confusion? Not likely. The point of Jesus's coming in person demonstrates the inadequacy of words. Coming in person and accomplishing deeds says so much more. Knowing the way people do obeisance to a written text, Jesus would not add fuel to the fire since we would revere his text over his person. Six-day warriors already subordinate God to the authority of the Bible. But worse, some YErs subordinate God to *their authority* on scripture by calling Him a liar if He disagrees, misunderstanding the Bible's purposes and God's nature. These YErs assume God is somehow accountable to their beliefs regarding the Bible, that *their* interpretation of scripture is inerrant so that even God must be a YEr or a deceiver. The historical Church has learned that the real purpose of scripture—God's self-disclosure in Christ—provides a corrective for abusing others with the Bible.

In reality, God exists independently of all things, including the scripture.

God exists even if the Bible is unreliable or merely a set of ancient documents. The Bible is not equal to God in any way, nor is it equivalent to His

---

266. A common mistake today is to assume New Testament writers always meant "the Bible" when they referred to "scripture." The word *scriptures* simply meant *writings (grapha)* and could refer to any writings. "The writings" for the early Church were Jewish theological works. "The Law, the Prophets, and the Writings," some of the Apocrypha, Pseudepigrapha, and Jewish Christian writings that were produced by the Church. They were not all a canonized or official Bible.

"eternal, perfect Word," a phrase that fundamentalists belabor with a proverbial fist in the air. There is too much content in the Bible once binding "forever" that is no longer applicable (Exodus 12:14; Leviticus 10:9, 23:14, 21, 23; Numbers 10:8, 18:23; Deuteronomy 4:40; 2 Kings 17:37). Prescriptions like these are not the eternal word of God but temporal rules for a tribal people of the ANE. Those words are in the Bible, they may have metaphorical applications, but they were of temporal relevance only. That is not a low view of the Bible.

It is a higher view of God— "the Most High."

Since the Bible is a compilation of humanly composed works inspired by the Spirit (yes), its accuracy is not equal to God's, nor can it be. No human language is capable of communicating divine perfection. That should be obvious. The Bible is an inanimate object, a book, or a library of books written in imperfect human language by some great and flawed individuals. That helps ensure the Bible is genuine. The Bible finds inspiration from heaven but is of the earth. Events in the history of ancient Israel are in the Bible's record. The New Testament presents a "New Israel," a spiritual body that shares in Israel's promises.[267]

Put another way, God "underwrites" the book, but the text itself is in the hands of human beings. It must be so because the Bible is the written testimony of the covenant people and their encounters with God. *The Bible is not God's testimony about His experiences with humans.* Jesus is God's testimony.

Despite Stephen W. Boyd's backward view of Galileo's proverb, the Bible does not tell us how the heavens go. Galileo's words were, "The Bible tells how to go to heaven, not how the heavens go"— Galileo's most profound observation.

---

267. As the apostle to the Gentiles wrote, "I do not want you to be ignorant of this mystery, brothers and sisters, so that you may not be conceited: Israel has experienced a hardening in part *until* the full number of the Gentiles has come in, and in this way *all Israel will be saved.* As it is written: 'The deliverer will come from Zion; he will turn godlessness away from Jacob'" (Romans 11:25–26).

17.
APPEARANCES OF AGE AND OTHER SIGHTINGS

While accusing Old Earthers of calling God a liar, some YErs presume God created the universe with countless *appearances* of extreme age that are illusions. It is hard to see the integrity in that presumption. That is also an admission that the evidence for an old earth is significant; otherwise, there would not be "countless appearances" of extreme age.

Why would God create galaxies in the middle of a collision? This phenomenon naturally takes hundreds of thousands, perhaps millions of years, to reach the point where known collisions happen to be in the process. Did God create them that way? Or did he shove them together as soon as Adam and Eve sinned? Why would he do that?

Isn't it more reasonable that galaxies in collision billions of light-years away are part of an unfolding natural order that God created, particularly if the Big Bang was His preferred choice to begin a universe? The Hubble Deep Field reveals that early galaxies, over 13 billion years ago, were still in the process of forming. They are much looser and less developed than older galaxies. The brand-new James Webb telescope has already discovered a galaxy whose light is 13.5 billion years old. That places it about 300 million years after the Big Bang. Astronomers expect to peer even further toward the beginning. The young universe was densely populated with countless galaxies very close together and expanding at extreme speeds when some collisions were inevitable, even helpful in creating massive galaxies. The place in the sky chosen by astronomers for the Deep Field view was the size of a grain of sand against the night sky. It appears to have no celestial bodies in that space. It turns out there are thousands of galaxies, stars, and nebulae in view, suggesting a far more populated early universe.

How can a universe inconceivably vast in space be so infinitesimally small in time? The Big Bang model says the universe began infinitesimally small and has expanded for 13.8 billion years. That is a coherent model based on empirical evidence, unlike YEC. God has impressed us all with the incomprehensible vastness of space. Why should YErs despise the unfathomable length of time created by someone whose name is *The Ancient of Days?* That name doesn't have the same impact in a six-thousand-year-old universe (there are trees older than that).

For instance, the bristlecone pines found in the Sierra Nevada are the oldest living trees at six-thousand years old. The dead trees lying beside them are almost twice as old. Francis Collins writes: "The ages of the dead trees were calibrated by comparing rings from the end of their lives to the early rings of trees still living. For example, a tree from 11,800 years ago lived 6,000 years and then died. Its last 200 rings can be calibrated with the first 200 rings of a living tree that is currently 6,000 years old."[268] That means the dead tree on the ground was alive 11,800 years ago.

"Similarly, lakebeds accumulate sediments with seasonal variations: minerals in spring, pollen and plant material in summer and fall. This creates distinguishable annual layers that can be counted on the bottom of lakes, just like counting tree rings or candles on a child's birthday cake." Collins continues:

> Scientists have found lakebeds with layers as old as thirty-five thousand years. The seasonal ice rings in glaciers provide another example. The ice rings form through the accumulation of years of falling snow, and we can distinguish seasonal differences—such as increased dust and larger ice crystals in summer—that allow the age to be determined. Scientists have drilled ice cores deep into the glaciers and found ice that is 123,000 years old in Greenland, and as old as 740,000 years in Antarctica."[269]

Space-time is likely one thing, or at least they are interdependent. As one goes, so goes the other in this universe. The geometry of space-time demands that the presence of matter must occupy space in time. That *is our reality*.

The philosopher of mathematics, David Berlinski, writes:

> We locate an event in terms of both *where* it took place and *when* it took place. [For example] *Where* was JFK assassinated? Three numbers provide the answer (longitude, latitude, and height). [On *when* only] one number is sufficient. To have grasped this much is to have grasped everything.[270]

The Creation event is a space-time event; it seems they must come into existence simultaneously. If the universe spreads because space expands (which it does), space must take time along for the ride. The definition of space in the dictionary is fascinating, e.g., "Space: *a period of time; also: its duration*" (2018 *Merriam Webster, Inc.*). No matter where it is, space must be in time or cannot have a location; that is, in space or time. That's not to say time and space are identical because objects can stand still in space, whereas time does not stand still, as far as we know. Of course, the question arises, does anything really standstill if it is aging?

Nonetheless, the extreme vastness of space in an expanding universe like ours, during a severe limitation in time, is contradictory—all *wheres* need

---

268. Karl W. Giberson, Francis S. Collins, "The Language of Science and Faith: Straight Answers to Genuine Questions," (Inter Varsity Press, Downers Grove, IL), 2011, Kindle edition, location 755. Additionally, some clonal colony trees where a tree or tree system can clone itself through successive generations are estimated to be as much as eighty thousand years old—e.g., *the Pando*, a Quaking Aspen in the Fishlake National Forest of Utah.

269. Ibid. Location 755.

270 . David Berlinski, *The Devil's Delusion: Atheism and its Scientific Pretensions* (Basic Books, New York, 2009), p. 74.

whens. Note that we measure space in light-*years.* The spread of 13.8 billion spatial units (light-years), which YErs tend to accept, necessitates 13.8 billion corresponding chronological units or events to account for the spread. Therefore, God did not make this universe unimaginably vast as it unfolds in space while infinitesimally brief. Time and space seem too integrated for that development.

Why create a young universe cloaked by so many "appearances" of deep time? Spatial extension betrays the pretense. If deep time is mere appearance, should not the corresponding deep space be mere appearance also? If not, why not? Why would God confuse rational beings like us so that we could not trust our senses in a world supposedly designed, especially for us? This reasoning goes against what we know about creation.

The Cosmological Principle states that the universe's properties are the same for all observers everywhere in physics. The same physical laws apply throughout the universe. In essence, this tells us that the cosmos is knowable and is playing fair with us.[271] Otherwise, there could be no place for science. The YE notion that God does not play fair with a knowable universe or that most appearances are misleading sounds like Richard Dawkins's "appearance of design" argument. In both cases, appearances are deceiving.[272]

We have discovered hundreds of impact craters on earth. Countless other impacts during the solar system's *Heavy Bombardment Period,* evidenced on the moon and Mars, have disappeared through erosion, tectonics, and volcanic activity. In addition, there were calderas and volcanic activity, massive flooding and tsunamis, ice ages, climate disasters, five mass extinctions, and other catastrophic events worldwide. They indicate extreme age since not all these catastrophes could have occurred on the earth if they were merely 6,000-plus years old. The worldwide destruction of the dinosaurs is just one of five known mass extinction events in the geological record.

A YE difficulty is that "acts of God" killed far more animals in mass extinctions than carnivore species that merely eat to survive. YErs claim that God killed almost all the animals in the flood, including those living in vast areas of the globe where there were no humans supposedly. If killing animals is

---

271. William C. Keel, *The Road to Galaxy Formation (2nd ed.)* (Springer-Praxis, 2007. ISBN 978-3-540-72534-3), p. 2.

272. Richard Dawkins, author of *The God Delusion* asserts that the universe does not have actual design but only *apparent design,* even if it is very apparent. If that is true, then why is it delusional to believe in a Designer? Is it irrational "to call it as one sees it?" Such beliefs may turn out wrong, but they are hardly delusional.

evil, a mass extinction event otherwise called an act of God would be against innocent animals.[273]

Even Jesus sent two-thousand swine off a bank to their deaths to make a point (Mark 5:1–11). Several mass extinctions, impact craters, and countless widespread catastrophes are hard to explain if they all happened within the last six thousand years. Admittedly, being hard to explain is not proof. Even so, it remains hard to explain.

The thousands of impact craters alone on and below the earth's surface have left scars, not unlike the moon, but the earth's surface covers almost all of them. In June 2015, a team of international scientists discovered an impact crater under the icecap in the Hiawatha National Park in Northwest Greenland. This crater is massive; it is bigger across than Washington DC or Paris, France. Initially, scientists suggested a recent impact in geological time (13000 years ago) that lies nearly a thousand feet under the ice, which means the impact was before the advent of the Ice Age and, therefore, long before the flood. However, two laboratories in Denmark and Sweden, using different dating methods, now arrived at the same conclusion. The crater is much older—58 million years, to be exact. [274]

The earth's ever-changing surface and overgrowth masks impact craters that the bare and static lunar surface exposes. Our planet's much larger size would mean four times more surface area to catch several times the meteors and asteroids. Craters deep under the earth's surface had to occur a very long time ago.

It is unreasonable to assert that all these events or the vast majority occurred in a single year during Noah's flood. Archeological evidence for civilizations worldwide shows a smoother and continuous occupation through the time of the flood asserted in YEC. If sin brought numerous and complete upheavals of catastrophes that happened at once, including tsunamis, thousands of impact craters, mass extinctions, volcanos, calderas, earthquakes, etc.,

---

273 . Since creatures of earth reproduce, the Ark was a tool for preserving them. YE absolute morality on all death and killing is not biblical since reproduction has always been the way physical (mortal) creatures perpetuate themselves, i.e., through their genes.

274. David Bressen, "A Late Paleocene Age for Greenland's Hiawatha Impact Structure," Forbes Science, March 9, 2022, explains crystals of the mineral zircon contained in the rock were dated using uranium-lead dating. The uranium isotopes start decaying as zircon crystallizes, transforming into lead isotopes at a steady and predictable rate. The technique pointed to a date of about 58 million years ago. The grains of sand were heated with a laser, and the researchers measured the release of argon gas, which is produced from the decay of the rare but naturally occurring radioactive isotope of potassium, known as k-40. "The half-life of k-40 is exceptionally long (1,250 million years) which makes it ideal for dating deep-time geological events like the age of the Hiawatha asteroid," scientists said. The technique affirmed a similar time frame for the meteor strike.

then a significant break would occur in all civilizations *simultaneously*. There is no evidence of that, and the evidence we do have contradicts it.

Languages, cities, and cultures would suddenly be lost, and new ones would have slowly emerged generations later and should be evident everywhere. However, the evidence shows a continuous development of cultures and languages throughout the same period. Written languages developed gradually, and some can be traced unbroken before and after the flood.[275] New city structures around the world would coincide. There should be a treasure trove of worldwide archeological confirmation of *simultaneous* destruction and reconstruction. But there is none.

Besides, the deluge is not associated with meteors. According to YErs, the tens of thousands of meteorites crashing into the earth are part of a curse declared six thousand years ago. We are familiar with many global catastrophes that must have happened every year if our planet was only thousands of years old; what do YErs say about those things? Whatever their answer, it has one imperative in mind—preserving an earth several thousand years old. Note this unusual answer on the AiG website: "Science cannot actually determine the age of the earth. Age is not a substance that can be measured by scientific means."

Francis Collins writes, "If you believe that there are true statements that can be made—as almost all Christians do—then the age of the earth has a correct value to be determined by honestly sorting through all the relevant data."[276] Not by pretending the evidence doesn't exist.

Anything that exists in a finite world *must* be measurable. The opposite: timelessness is not measurable because it lacks *length*. Therefore, as Augustine saw so long ago, time is of the physical universe. He was the first to argue that linear time is part of the created order and that God created space and time together.[277]

Things in a finite universe are measurable by definition.

Science has confirmed that the contents of the physical universe include time. Therefore, are YErs saying that time or age is unrecognizable within a

275. For example, there is no break in the continuous development of cuneiform and Egyptian hieroglyphics in the archeological record at any time in Sumerian and Egyptian history, which precedes the flood and continues unbroken during and after the flood period. If all Egyptian and Mesopotamian civilization were wiped out, a new language and people would have emerged. But that is not what we find in the archeological record.

276. Francis S. Collins and Karl W. Giberson, "The Language of Science and Faith: Straight Answers to Genuine Questions," (Inter Varsity Press, Downers Grove, IL), 2011, Kindle edition, location 661.

277. Stephen Hawkins credited Augustine as the first person to understand time 1,600 years before Einstein. Augustine drew his conclusion by theological and intellectual inquiry without the mathematical tools that assisted Einstein. See *A Brief History of Time* by Stephen Hawkins.

temporal world? How would we recognize our world as *temporal*? Are YErs saying the Bible is the only dating device for the whole universe? If we cannot determine age, why do YErs go through tortuous means to prove the earth is young with their unique brand of "science?" If science can't measure age, where do they get the word *young*?

The Bible does not say the earth is young; it says it is old but does not say how old. "Old" could mean six-thousand years old. YErs believe the universe only *"appears"* old. How does *old* appear? How do they determine mere appearance? "Apparently," the Bible tells them so.

Tree rings measure time. YErs say God created trees all at once, yet they only appeared old, i.e., God created mature trees with a corresponding set of tree rings yet would only be as old as it took to create them—instantly, that is. That gives YEC the premise for a universe with the appearance of extraordinary age but is, *in reality*, inexplicably young.

Truth does not seem to correspond *to reality* in a YE universe.

Each tree ring is a record of an annual weather pattern. Seasons with heavy rainfall leave wider rings than years of drought. Rings give the tree a history. It is even possible to do a chemical analysis of the air and moisture surrounding a tree from the tree rings of a given year. YErs believe God made trees instantly, complete with tree rings. Why would God create a tree with a detailed "written" history in tree rings?

Think about that.

If God instantly created a tree with a hundred tree rings, would its rings be fake? Would fake tree rings mean an artificial tree? The essential part of a tree, its trunk, is virtually all rings? If they were real tree rings, God would have created a real tree with a hundred *honest* rings. In that case, God would have created a literal 100-year-old tree, not a new one. YErs prefer to think that is what God would do. But then the tree would not be young but a hundred years old, no matter how long it took God to create it. It was instant "outside" the universe where God exists, but 100 years inside this universe. If it were an authentic tree of this world, its age would need to be a hundred years old. Otherwise, we are talking about magic.

God does not do magic.

Why should God create nature and its processes only to manipulate it unnaturally? The carelessness in maintaining an exclusive distinctive and literalism at all costs is where the casualties are, such as misunderstanding God's nature and the purposes of the Bible. What matters most to enthusiasts is their conclusions, *not how they got there*. I've been there too. At least the case for Evolutionary Creationism, whether true or not, describes a God that instantly creates nature and its processes and sustains their existence while His creation does what temporal things must do—develop.

Age is the measurement of time, and time is the measurement of change. If we cannot measure age, then all the talk of evening and morning, six literal days, and thousands versus millions of years are pointless.

So if the deep age of the universe is so obvious, why do YErs not believe it? Because they have words. Words they take literally. Because they think God wrote the words and meant them literally, only YErs know how old the earth is though they cannot verify it with evidence.

And all evidence that exists points to deep age.

18.
THE LONGEST "DAY"

Adam was the most intelligent man that ever lived. God made him with a perfect
brain and a perfect memory. It wouldn't take him long to think of the names [of
all the animals] and to then remember which animal was which! He had plenty
of intelligence and plenty of time to name them all in one day!
—Ken Ham

The Bible says Adam named all land animals, including birds. We have
seen that "naming" had special significance in the ANE. Naming could show
ownership, rulership, or dominance. It is natural to name our animals, but
we do so for identification and sentimental reasons. There is more going on
with Adam.

What would naming mean to our author?

It is hard to see the relevance of literally naming all the animals beyond
the ANE idea that giving things a name shows rulership or ownership. The nar-
ration has already stated as much. How would Adam preserve all those names
for posterity? Some actually believe the names we use for animals today are the
ones Adam selected. This kind of understanding is childlike (not in a good way)
because it assumes the author (YErs say is God) is concerned about such things
or that future generations are not allowed to name their animals since God
commissioned Adam for the task.

Naming the animals in the story has little to do with *the names of the ani-*
mals. Scripture does not identify the names given by Adam, which is odd if the
names chosen were the point. The theological importance is in the *act of naming*
and not the names themselves.

Note that Adam is said to name all the animals on the earth (land):
domestic, wild animals, and birds (Genesis 2:19–20). YErs believe Adam named
all the prehistoric animals too since they do not think dinosaurs and countless
other animals were prehistoric but created on the sixth day, several thousand
years ago. That would include all those of the four or five mass extinctions in

the fossil record and, no doubt, many extinct animals not yet discovered.[278] It did not matter when these extinctions occurred. They were massive. *And if the earth is six thousand years old, we would have to account for all global extinctions being recent even though they occur at widely separated geological strata that contain divergent flora and fauna.*

Naming things sets humans apart from all other creatures. Animals do not give names to other things or even to themselves. Since Adam represented humankind, the naming sequence may simply be an ANE way for the narrator to show that humans rule the animals by the will of God. Because of Adam's dominant place in the world, he was free to begin owning and managing any of the animals, and not necessarily that he accomplished naming countless creatures within several hours on a single day.[279]

All the attempts by YErs to reduce the number of animals Adam named are predictable. Who can blame them? If Adam called all animals by name, he would need every minute of the 930 years of his life for that alone. Some say Adam only named the overall "kinds." However, the "kinds" were already named: cattle, wild beasts, four-footed beasts, creepy-crawlers, insects, and birds. These are categories, not names of creatures.

Furthermore, YErs are literalists. What happened to the "one-to-one correspondence of words to reality" claim? More to the point: *What happened to the YEC idea of biblical authority?*[280] Genesis 2:20 says Adam gave names "to *all*

---

278. There are currently some 6.5 million species of animals on land in the world. Many more millions, perhaps billions, have gone extinct. Scientists estimate that some five billion species have gone extinct since the beginning of life on earth. If they all existed at the time of Adam, are YErs still prepared to assert that Adam not only named them all but named them all during the daylight portion of the sixth day? He could not count that high in that short of time. Consequently, most YErs reduce "all animals on the earth" to a much smaller number taken from a local population. This YE inconsistency goes unnoticed by YErs, yet they rail against those who consider the flood, also said to cover "all the earth," to be local or widespread. Nonetheless, they say that *"all the animals of the earth"* means a local selection of animals from a limited area because the alternative is absurd.

279. The ANE idea of the power in naming is not so farfetched. Consider the 2016 presidential campaign when Donald Trump made an art form out of eviscerating his political opponents by "renaming" them. The examples are memorable—"Low Energy Jeb" for Jeb Bush and "Pocahontas" for Elizabeth Warren, and newsrooms are renamed "Fake News." CNN is now FNN—the "Fake News Network." These "new names" had a devastating effect and continued to stick. Naming effects perceptions.

280. Compare YE treatment of both the flood narrative and the naming sequence. YErs press the absolute literal language describing the flood, but the language regarding naming of animals they loosely interpret. The reasons are obvious. An absolute global flood is necessary to dismiss all the fossil and geological records that demonstrate extreme age of the earth. YErs reinterpret the naming of *all animals and birds* in a few hours, reducing their numbers to a manageable level because a literal view is impossible to maintain and unimportant because YEC is not dependent on naming *all* the animals. This is further evidence that literalism has nothing to do with biblical authority.

the livestock, *all* the birds and *all* the wild animals." All of them? That is what it says verbatim. So what were their names? We don't have but a few.

So Adam could not find a suitable helper. The point here is that humans are not just another animal since there was no complementary helpmate among them. Animals would become Adam's property, but he needed more than property, more than an animal. He needed someone like himself. Nonetheless, a painstaking search for a helper in every animal in twelve hours would be crushing.

If meant literally, there was not enough time during the sixth day, let alone the daylight portion of the day, to complete the naming sequence, not to mention all the other activities recorded in Genesis 2:4–25. There is little reason to think the sixth day is the subject here since almost nothing is the same between the creation accounts of chapters 1 and 2. There are no creation "days" or "weeks" in the "second" creation account recorded in 2:4–25. Perhaps chapters 1 and 2 are two creation stories written at separate times by different authors and preserved for posterity. The two narratives are telling us complementary or alternative details. A simple reading of the two chapters shows the order of created things is different. There is no attention to the days of the week. Some people deny the inconsistencies to preserve a view of the Bible, namely that the authors concerned themselves with inerrant historical and scientific precision over the theological truths they intended to pass on.

YEC must assert that all events mentioned in Genesis 2:4–25 occurred on the sixth day of chapter one; otherwise, it challenges the chronological order necessary to maintain YEC. However, chapter 2 does not refer to any time references—days, weeks, months, or years. The chronology of events in chapter 2, put alongside chapter 1, is hardly clear or precise. For example, God appears to create the animals and birds *before* humans in Genesis 1. In Genesis 2, God creates at least some animals *after* Adam. God created an unspecified number (we assume a pair) of humans at once in Genesis 1, but in chapter 2, he makes a single human first. God forms Eve *after* Adam names all the animals while failing to find a complimentary helper.[281]

God plants the Garden and transports Adam into it over an unspecified time frame:

> Then the Lord God formed a man from the dust of the ground and breathed into his nostrils the breath of life, and the man became a living being. Now the Lord God had planted a garden in the east, in Eden; and there he put the man he had formed. The Lord God made all kinds of

---

281. We saw earlier that some ancients believed life generates from the soil, not just plants and foliage but animals and humans. The text in Genesis 1:24 says, "Let the ground [soil] produced the animals." It might mean God made them *with* soil as he did Adam in chapter 2 or that He grew them *from* the soil as a "crop" of living creatures. The ambiguity presents problems for YEC, which depends on too much happening in a single day's activities.

trees *grow out of the ground*—trees that were pleasing to the eye and good for food. In the middle of the garden was the tree of life and the tree of the knowledge of good and evil. (Genesis 2:8–9; emphasis mine)

The phrase "Now the Lord God had planted a garden"[282] (v. 8) allows any length of time between planting the garden and Adam's arrival (v. 15). There is a second time-lapse—the maturing of trees for food. From the moment God planted the garden to placing Adam in the garden to keep it, there is an unspecified length of time. Note that all kinds of trees had time to *"grow out of the ground"* (v. 9) and bear fruit. *The words "grow out" do not make sense unless the trees did indeed grow. They were not created mature but needed to become mature to provide food for the new human arrivals. Picking apart all the details and arguing for them is outside the spirit of storytelling.* This story is not a deposition in a court case. If one side of the SDWC chooses specific details, the other uses additional details to push back. That misses the point.

"So the Lord *took some soil* and made animals and birds" (Genesis 2:19 CEV).

Here the animals and birds came from the ground, i.e., the existing soil, and not from nothing. "Then God brought all the animals and birds *the ground produced* (v. 19) to Adam to name them and find a suitable helper in the Garden. Genesis 2:8 says, "And the *Lord God planted a garden* in Eden to the east. And he *placed* there the human he had fashioned." According to the story, Adam started outside the Garden and was alone when God placed him there. The time lapse between each creation seems unimportant to the author. The implication is the Garden must have grown enough that Adam needed help managing it. As it says in verse 9, "And the Lord God *caused to sprout from the soil every tree.*" Sprouts are young shoots that start as seedlings. This sequence of events presents insurmountable problems for YErs who take it literally. It takes time for *every tree to sprout* after planting.

There is no explanation of how God creates animals from the ground or a human from another's body part. Why the "body part method?" Wouldn't Eve then have Adam's DNA? The author's chosen literary methods convey theological ideas, not biological ones or the actual processes during creation, unless we want Moses to reject the creation of all things out of nothing.[283] Chemically speaking, we all come from the same stuff in the ground. Yet, *Genesis is not about*

---

282. This phrase is in the same form as Genesis 1:2, "Now the earth had been formless and void;" and Genesis 3:1, "Now the serpent was craftier than any of the wild beasts of the field." There is an unspecified time-lapse.

283. Either God created all things out of nothing or out of things: water, soil, dust, ribs, etc. Christianity has always chosen creation ex-nihilo (out of nothing). That preserves God's transcendence over nature and not a dependence on it like pagan deities, which trumps wooden literalism.

the ground or biology. Genesis is about God's intentions as the author could under-stand them.

Most YErs believe Adam had up to twenty-four hours to name all the animals. But we have already seen that all the activities were during the day-light portion of each day. Perhaps chapter 2 diverges from the work schedule of chapter 1 since it is different in almost every other respect. Nonetheless, it is unreasonable to assume Adam stayed up all night processing the animal king-dom before Eve arrived to keep on a "YEC schedule."

In Genesis 1:26, we assume God made two humans, male and female. There is no reason to think otherwise. However, in keeping with literal analysis, an *unspecified* number of humans ("humankind;" v. 27 NRSV) appear on day six. God creates an untold number of each species of animal. In the Akkadian Epic of Atrahasis, Nintur and Enki used flesh and blood to fashion clay into *seven male and seven female embryos*. After nine months, a crop of humanity was born from them.[284] Perhaps the total number created was irrelevant to the author. We cannot impose these numbers on Genesis 1.

The natural assumption is that in Genesis 1, God created a single pair of humans, animal pairs on land, and pairs of sea creatures. That appears validated in chapter 2 by naming Adam and Eve. However, when God banishes Cain for murdering his brother, he fears someone will kill him. Who did Cain fear? The author complicates matters further when Cain finds a wife in another land. Where could Cain's wife have come? At the same time, Cain begins to build a city after his firstborn Enoch arrives? Did he build a city by himself? Were there other humans created besides Adam's family? If not, was Cain's wife a sister or cousin? It doesn't seem to matter because the author doesn't tell us. Therefore, the chronology doesn't matter. In a few short verses, we have gone from Cain murdering Abel, his mysterious wife, his exile, his siring of a large family with many grandchildren and great-grandchildren, cousins, aunts, and uncles, etc., and helped build a city he named after his son Enoch.

After Cain's saga, Adam and Eve's next child in the story is Seth. There is a significant time-lapse the author does not explain throughout Genesis chapter four. We do not have a chronology or details to fill in the blanks. Many have attempted to solve the mystery without satisfaction. We have Cain's wife, a fruitful family, a building project, and metallurgy are more mysteries in the text that should keep us leery of dogmatic, literalized conclusions. We also know that humans were here long before agriculture, which made possible cities, and metallurgy that replaced a long period of stone tools. The author and readers seem unconcerned about these "anomalies" because they were not anomalies to them or they did not know how to explain them, nor did it matter, because this was about God's intentions, not YEC.

---

284. See Pritchard, *Ancient Near Eastern Texts Related to the Old Testament* (Princeton University Press, New Jersey, 1969), pp. 99–100.

In half a day, supposedly, God creates all the animals, plants the Garden, forms Adam from clay, and gives Adam the exhausting task of naming all the animals while searching them for an ultimate helper to do his work in the Garden. He does not find one.

In the name of literalism, how thoroughly did he look?

Adam could find no helper among all the birds or the domestic and wild animals. Did Adam have a set of suitability standards? How else could he "screen each prospect?" Maybe he moved quickly, looking for a good first impression assigning names as he went along—"Horse, thank you for coming. Next!" All the animals failed to meet his requirements. Evidently, Adam had time during an astonishing array of activities to get seriously lonely or discouraged, so God said something out of character in the tranquil world of day six.

"This is not good."

Forget *very good* or just plain good; this was emphatically *not good*. During the naming of the animals, which YErs say took *all day*, God said things were *not good*. Were they not good for twenty-four hours? Perhaps this is too literal. The phrase "not good" is blunt compared to *omitting* anything labeled "good" that we saw on day two. Adam was deeply disappointed and felt alone in the world since he could not find a complementary partner.

YErs say all these activities occurred on Adam's first day of life in a world that was six days old.

In the day that the Lord God made the earth and the heavens, *when no plant of the field was yet in the earth and no herb of the field had yet sprung up—for the Lord God had not caused it to rain upon the earth,* and there was no one to till the ground;... And the Lord God planted a garden in Eden, in the east; and there he put the man whom he had formed. *Out of the ground the Lord God made to grow every tree* that is pleasant to the sight and good for food. (Genesis 2:4-9, NRSV)

In human experience, stimulating activity is usually an antidote to loneliness, especially on the first day of life for an otherwise "perfect human being." It is unlikely Adam could feel loneliness if he had never known companionship. How would he know he was lonely? He was only alive for a day. That question would be inappropriate if this is storytelling but not if understood verbatim.

You would think everything in Adam's experience must have been new and wondrous to him. However, he got discouraged enough to feel in want within half a day of life. It is conceivable that coming up empty searching for a partner suggests that naming was mainly about identifying a helper and not necessarily about identifying every animal. Interestingly, Adam's first act after God creates a woman is to name her.

Genesis tells us God put Adam under "anesthesia" for what appears to us as an ordinary surgical procedure. The need for anesthesia indicates that Adam was an ordinary human, that the operation took some time, and that cutting, healing, and pain were applicable in this "perfect" world. The man loses a rib in exchange for his soon-to-be bride, which seemed like a fair exchange at the time. YEC's demands mean all the above activities occurred during the *daylight* portion of the sixth day until sundown, declaring a Sabbath. Trying to cram all these events into a single day feels like *"fast-forward."* The pace, supernatural elements like the two trees, and this narrative's vivid imagery make it more storytelling than historiography.

Chapter 3:1 begins, "Now the serpent was craftier than any of the wild animals the Lord God had made." The expression *"Now the serpent was"* allows for a passage of time at an unknown length. Indeed, it is not likely that Eve's temptation occurred on the sixth day when God created her. Otherwise, the fall would have happened on the day that ended with everything being *very good.* So if the reader thinks chronologically, as YErs do, Genesis 3:1 would be an undisclosed interval or "gap" of time. On what day the serpent tempted Eve, whether the eighth day or a day much later, is irrelevant because the author does not specify. Chronology is not the point in the story he's telling.

Interestingly, the same expression occurs earlier in chapter 1:2, *"Now the earth was..."* Many commentators point to the same kind of gap between Genesis 1:1 and the first day of creation, which starts in verse 3 when the author opens day one with his daily introductory announcement, "And God said." If Genesis 1 is a strict chronology, there is the same gap in time as in 3:1 without a specified length. Nonetheless, YEC must be inconsistent with this to maintain itself. Therefore, YErs insist there is no gap in Genesis 1:2 (*Now the earth was*) while there must be a gap in chapter 3:1 (*Now the serpent was*) to maintain their doctrinal distinctive.

John C. Collins observes:

[Genesis 1:3] gives us the first *wayyiqtol* [God *"said"*]... In fact, each of the other workdays begins with the same wayyiqtol verb: that is, each workday begins with God saying something, in each case expressing a wish [or command]. It follows from this that we should expect the first workday to begin with God's speech in Genesis 1:3, and this makes good sense in view of the clause types. Since the backbone of a narrative, as we have already discussed, uses the wayyiqtol, and since Genesis 1:1-2 does not use the wayyiqtol, *we conclude that these verses [1 and 2] stand outside the main stream of the narrative.* The most common usage of the clause types that we find in verses 1–2 is to provide background material for the narrative. More specifically, the perfect of verse 1 ("created") may be either an event that precedes the main storyline or else a summary of the entire pericope; the stative clauses of verse 2 describe the conditions as the first day gets under way.[285]

It seems certain that the dramatic "Let there be light" in verse 3 was God's opening act in this story of creation. Quoting God in the Bible is no trivial thing. It had to be sobering and momentous to a Hebrew author to quote God since it was a sensitive matter in Israel just to speak His name. By contrast, Genesis 1:1–2 is the author's opening statement.

Nothing after Genesis 2:4 refers to the sixth day or any other "day," presumably because the author was not interested in which day it was. Fundamentalists assume the sixth day in Genesis 2:7ff to harmonize the accounts chronologically, something the author is unconscious of since questions about chronology in chapter 2 are unanswered. The length of time for all the activities in Genesis 2 is undeterminable, so how important was it for the author to maintain the sixth day? Clearly, it is not as crucial to the biblical author as in YEC.

Genesis 2:4ff is simply a change in the narrative with a different focal point from chapter 1. Chapter 1 is about God's relation to the created order, while chapter 2 focuses on God's relationship with the human family, which is the continued focus throughout scripture. YErs and many other Christians attempt to harmonize the two accounts instead of understanding what their differences may mean.

Devotion to an exclusive distinctive can obscure the revelation. For instance, the two ways humans may experience God are already noticeable in the opening chapters of the Bible—God's transcendence in chapter 1 and His imminence, especially in chapters 2–4. The change in focus funnels the narrative toward the human race and intimacy with God and, more importantly, to a special carve-out of the race, the children of Israel.

Genesis begins the story of God and humanity in general, and in chapter 12 onward, God and Israel specifically. Genesis 2 prepares the reader for God's covenantal relationship with Abraham that peaks at Mt. Sinai. For example, the different uses of the divine names: "Elohim" (God Almighty) in chapter 1 addresses the cosmos, and "Yahweh" in chapter 2 addresses humans in a Garden. The author's choice of the name Yahweh is significant. It shows that the God of creation is the same God that appeared to Moses in the burning bush—the God of Abraham, Isaac, and Jacob—and revealed His covenant at Sinai (Exodus 3:6, 14).

Yahweh is the God of the covenant. The striking introduction of Yahweh's name in Genesis 2 may imply that Adam was the ancestral beginning of the Israelite tribes. Of course, Adam is the ancestor of all humans, (Cain's narrative

285. C. John Collins, *Genesis 1–4: A Linguistic, Literary, And Theological Commentary* (P&R Publishing, Phillipsburg, New Jersey, 2009), Kindle edition, Location 508–509.

notwithstanding) but the author makes us conscious of the origins of God's involvement with the covenant people.

This switch of names from Elohim to Yahweh may not initially be significant to the modern reader. The original readers would find this use of divine names striking. Names mattered in the ANE, as we have seen. Genesis is an Old Covenant document written to the covenant people of Israel *in their time and their context,* not the beginning of time.

Some interpreters believe the two creation accounts in Genesis are contradictory with unresolved tensions. But it is unreasonable to assume that biblical authors and editors had the same scruples regarding strict history or chronology when theological imperatives dominate their objectives. In other words, there might be inconsistencies on some levels while being consistent on more critical theological matters. Others think the opening chapters of Genesis offer two distinct revelations that are complementary. Namely, God is both the *transcendent* Creator of the universe in chapter 1 and the *intimate* Lord and Father of each of us in chapters 2–4.

On this, Bill T. Arnold explains:

> [Cosmic and ancestral origins] work in concentric circles, drawing the reader ever closer to an understanding of God's relationship first with the cosmos generally, and then with God's chosen people, Israel. The ancestral narratives, in particular, the accounts of Abraham, Isaac, and Jacob, including the story of Joseph embedded near the conclusion, provide an essential ideological foundation for what follows in Exodus, Leviticus, Numbers, and Deuteronomy (e.g., Exod 2:24; Deut 1:8; 34:4). The saving acts of Yahweh on Israel's behalf (the plagues of Egypt, the miraculous crossing of the Sea of Reeds), and the covenant at Mount Sinai were based on the ancestral covenant and its intentions for the nation Israel.[286]

Genesis 1–11 shows God called the world into being and that "all the nations" (represented by the seventy in chapter 10) should be faithful to their Creator. They turn out to be unfaithful to an alarming degree. God's judgment falls on the human race, though a righteous line began with Seth and continues in Noah (see Genesis 5). The importance of genealogies is not to establish the age of the earth nor the sister idea of providing a chronology of the world. The author's interest is pedigree. We know these genealogies are missing some generations and contain no identifying markers leading to dates within the confines of scripture, which indicate that they are not chronologies in the conventional sense. Rather, the genealogies establish an ancestral thread—a pedigree of righteous patriarchs and kings that ultimately led to the Messiah, which is a theological purpose (Luke 3:23, 34–38).

---

286. Bill T. Arnold, "Genesis," *New Cambridge Bible Commentary* (Kindle), location 418.

The first eleven chapters cover an arrangement of pre-history in the near east, with large swaths of time covered in very brief strokes. That type of treatment is not usually associated with the strict history YEC asserts.

Genesis 1–11 focuses on the strain between God and humans and the seeds of tension that later grew between Israel and her neighbors. It is like history because it presents events that determine or even alter our story's trajectory. But it does so by tracing current circumstances (in the author's day) backward to their origins. Genesis answers the "who-are-we-and-how-did-we-get-here" questions for the people of Israel. Just who is Yahweh among the gods? God has no pedigree. Humans do, and so do the gods. The author records an oral history of ancestral origins for theological purposes.

The attempts to preserve a literal six-day creation through both accounts assume an unrealistically long sixth day in chapter 2. It forces a harmony to which the author seems oblivious. The complex variations between the two creation accounts in Genesis 1 and 2 are theological. Consistent and precise tracing of the chronology of creation could not be a priority if the same author wrote both accounts since the chronology is unclear. These chapters tell us important matters between God and the universe and between God and humans. Forced or contrived harmony distracts the reader from the author's real intentions.

Chapter 2 does not itemize events on the sixth day, let alone the daylight portion. The author is not interested in the day since he is silent on it. Protecting the sixth day is a YE preoccupation. The author appears occupied with other issues. Besides, how does keeping the sixth day intact in chapter 2 affect the story's essential theology or moral lesson? Wouldn't the author let us know if maintaining a consciousness of the sixth day had any theological importance?

Genesis takes the reader on a journey with the God of creation who chose to reveal Himself to Abraham and his descendants. The earlier covenants led not to Noah's Ark or flood geology but *through* Noah's Ark to the covenantal promises to the Patriarchs and the ultimate covenant at Mt. Sinai. Therefore, the religious theme in Genesis is the origins and establishment of *covenant theology* for Israel and the world. Interestingly, the Pentateuch ends anticipating the *new covenant*: "The Lord your *God will circumcise your hearts* and the hearts of your descendants, so that you may love him with all your heart and with all your soul, and live" (compare Deuteronomy 30:6 and Jeremiah 31:33).

All other motivations in Genesis are subordinate to the covenants of promise.

Genesis begins to answer thematic questions like Who is God? Who are we? Does God care? Why were we chosen? And why are things the way they are? Genesis tells us that we are not accidents, nor are we incidental or a means to an end like humans in other ANE creation accounts. God chose Israel as a special people and delivered them in a historical rescue from slavery. That showed Yahweh is unlike the more detached deities of the nations who created humans to enslave them so the gods could rest. The answers to those thematic questions are the same, no matter our understanding of the earth's age or waters above and below the heavens.

Whatever the *key* to reforming the Church and culture, it cannot be unique to any particular generation like today's YErs. Such a key must be for all ages and cultures because all humanity shares the same need for redemption because of sin, not mistakes in cosmology or imperfect knowledge of the Bible or accepting an old earth or evolution but because of moral degradation that leads to the depravity that Genesis indicts.

The focus in Genesis is clearly not YEC or any ageism of the universe.

Adam Who?

According to Genesis, sin did *not* enter the human family through the man Adam but through the *people* adam. 1 Timothy 2:14 says, "It was Eve and not Adam who was first deceived and fell into sin" (Phillips). The word adam is often a genus throughout the Bible, referring to all humanity. Genesis 5:2 explicitly states, "Male and female he created *them*, and he blessed *them* and *named them "Adam"* when *they* were created" (emphasis mine).[287]

Adam may refer to a "man" or "mankind," depending on the grammatical support. It comes from the word *adama,* meaning dirt or soil. *Adam* can refer to an individual, like Adam, or a category, like *the adam* (with the definite article)—male or female—and therefore *humankind.* The Greek word *anthropos* carries the same meaning. When we say sin first entered the human family through Adam, it must include Eve; otherwise, we have an odd historical mistake if taken at face value.

According to the NT, humans were not the first to introduce our world to sin. The "serpent" was a deceiver from the beginning (John 8:44; 2 Corinthians 11:3; 1 John 3:8). Furthermore, if the serpent in Genesis is literal, then a wild animal from the field that God made was the first earthly creature to sin (see Genesis 3:1). A literal reading of Genesis says the animal kingdom sinned before humans did. According to literalists, "animal sin" should cause animal death even before humans sinned. But consistency is not a hallmark of the SDWC.

Fundamentalists believe this animal walked on all fours until it became a deceiver. Surprisingly, God cursed the serpent, not with death (since YEC claims all animals had eternal life); instead, this creature received alterations

---

287. Adam is a genus in the way Caesar is a genus when Jesus says, "Render to Caesar the things that are Caesar's." This reference could not only refer to the current Caesar when Jesus spoke but all other Caesars; otherwise, at Tiberius Caesar's death, the principle would no longer apply. Obviously, this principle applies to all Caesars and all analogous positions among humans that serve both God and the state, or in the modern vocabulary, *Church and State.* Adam is both an individual and a literary device referring to all humanity.

in its physiology and diet. It now crawls on its belly and consumes dust, i.e., according to the story. So there were two sinners on the earth before Adam sinned. The sequence is; serpent sins → Eve sins → Adam sins. But can animals talk, reason, and deceive? Can they be admonished verbally for tricking humans who, according to YEC, were more brilliant than today's humans?

Technically, the man Adam did not sin first. However, there is a corporate sense in the word *adam* used far more often in the Bible. We instinctively think of the word *adam* as referring to an individual because the Bible does use it that way and because the focus on characters helps popularize stories. However, the word *adam* refers to an individual an unexpectedly few times.

Richard S. Hess, professor of Semitic languages, writes that of the *thirty-five occurrences* of "adam" in Genesis 1–5, *only five occurrences* clearly refer to a personal name, all without the definite article (Genesis 4:25, 5:1a, 3, 4, 5). Twenty-two instances have the definite article, which never attests to a personal name in Hebrew. The other instances [refer] to all people, including males and females. Hess concludes, "I believe that the definite article in all but Genesis 1:27 and 4:1 is used to designate the *archetypal* individual. In these examples, everything that this archetypal individual does, he performs as a representative for all humanity."[288]

The point is not that Genesis rules out Adam as an individual, but in the story, the person Adam mostly stands in for all humanity (*adam*).[289] It is legitimate and would have been common to refer to humankind as *adam* in biblical times. Before Eve, Adam *was* all humanity. It turns out that Adam's spiritual condition is valid for all, not because of genetics *but because our internal perfecting is in the same stage as his: unfinished.* We are in Adam because we are the same kind of creature: earthly.

We still must eat from a tree of life, whatever that means.

Eve came from Adam's side, further illustrating the categorical archetype. To insist that "Adam" is to be isolated to an individual *exclusively* misses too much since the representative man includes the first man and other created humans at the time. Whether Eve was the only other created human, as it appears, or there was the possibility of others existing that we are unaware of and that Cain may have encountered after being banished. The representative men: Adam and the New Adam, i.e., the earthly man and the heavenly Man, are

---

288. Richard S. Hess, J. A. Emerton in VTSup XLI, ed., "Splitting the Adam: The Usage of "Adam" in Genesis 1–5," *Studies in the Pentateuch* (Leiden: Brill, 1990), 1–15. Quoted in Four Views on the Historical Adam (Counterpoints: Bible and Theology) (Zondervan, Grand Rapids, Michigan, 2013), Kindle location 1578–1560. Richard S. Hess is professor of Old Testament and Semitic languages at Denver Seminary. Formerly, he taught at Roehampton Institute in London.

289. The debate among some scholars on the historical Adam does not affect the purposes of this book one way or the other.

the spiritual focus since both the fall and salvation happen to include all who are "*in* or *of* each man."

To theological categories, "*in Adam*" and "*in Christ*" means sharing the same spiritual nature of humans—earthly in the first Adam and heavenly in the second Adam. Paul wrote:

> As was the earthly man, so are those who are of the earth; and as is the heavenly man, so also are those who are of heaven. And just as we have borne the image of the earthly man, so shall we bear the image of the heavenly man. (1 Corinthians 15:48–49)

It is the archetypal or representative Adam and his earthly nature we inherit *that reinforces universal sin, not his individual identity*. YErs insist that we must believe Adam is a historical individual to understand universal sin. So the *theological* question becomes, "Why should Adam's sin transfer to all of us if Adam was simply an individual?" How does that work since the "*sins of the father are not visited upon the children*" (see Ezekiel 18:19–20), but the earthly nature is. It is not Adam's historic individuality but his place as the representative of humankind that his sin characterizes the race. The apples do not fall far from the tree—Adam's human nature is the tree. This is not historiography or genetics; it is theology. We are, by nature, *in Adam* or perhaps "adamkind."

Lange's Critical commentary adds:

> Paul evidently views the human race as an organic unit. Adam and Christ sustain a central and universal relation, similar to that which the root has to the tree and its branches. Adam was not merely an individual... and his transgression was not an isolated act... So it is with Christ. He calls Himself emphatically *the* (not a) Son of Man... Christ has gained far more for us than Adam lost— namely, eternal [union] with God, in the place of the temporary union of untried innocence. The resurrection of humanity in Christ is the glorious solution of the dark tragedy of the disastrous fall of humanity in Adam. In view of the greater merit of Christ and the paradise in heaven... It is God's infinite wisdom and mercy alone, which overrules the fall of man for [God's] own glory.[290]

For centuries, Christian and Jewish theologians have shown that the reference "Adam" is universal by way of simple grammar and because *adam* means "man" or "mankind." Even the word *man* in Hebrew and Greek can refer to an individual or all humanity—male and female—today's political correctness notwithstanding. Therefore, *Adam* can refer to an individual, but it most often refers to the human race.

---

290. John Peter Lange, translated by Charles F, Schaeffer (1866) and edited by Phillip Schaff, *Lange's Critical, Doctrinal, and Homiletical, Commentary on the Holy Scriptures* (Volume 7—Acts to 2 Corinthians) (Delmarva Publications, 2014), Kindle location 55713.

Of course, the first human or humans were not Hebrew. They could not speak Hebrew. Therefore, the first man could not have had a Jewish name pronounced or spelled A-d-a-m. The author of Genesis purposely chooses a generic Hebrew word for humanity to serve as an archetype. Furthermore, "Adam" is not likely a transliteration of the first human's actual name because of the variants of *adam* in biblical Hebrew, such as *adama* (soil). *Adam* is clearly a Hebrew word. Thus, the Hebrew name "Adam" is a literary designation that appears relatively late in human history (1200–700 BC). Therefore, we cannot reasonably conclude that "Adam" was the *first human's real name*. In that sense, we can safely say that the *name "Adam"* is not historical.[291] That conclusion alone does not prove there was no first couple. It means that the name Adam is not history but theology.

Consider another example among many where a theological interpretation is not factual. When Paul says our *baptism* is a sharing of the death, burial, and resurrection of Christ, he is presenting a theological way of looking at baptism and not a factual description. Paul's interpretation of baptism helps illustrate our place in the *body of Christ*, which is also a theological reference to the Church since the Church is not Christ's physical body. Humans work and act through the body. Similarly, through the Church, Christ acts in the world.

Paul's reference to Adam's universal role in our earthly condition is a theological way to introduce the heavenly origin of Christ for a New Humanity. All humans are born Adam (human), that is, in one earthly family. Similarly, all Christians are reborn into the new Adam—one heavenly family.

I am not addressing the historicity of "Adam," which is beyond the scope of this book. The relevant point is that the universality of sin through the original humans, no matter how many lived, two or twenty-thousand is theological. This point needs only one thing, a single race of sinners. Adam's everyman archetypal place in biblical theology makes his sin indicative of the entire race.

We all fall.

Christians are the "body" of Adam in one way and the body of Christ in another.

---

291. This is hardly controversial or unique in scripture. Even Jesus's name was never pronounced "Geezuz" in Hebrew, Aramaic, or Greek when he walked the earth. Names change as stories move from one language to another and one century to another. See Denis Lamoureux, John H. Walton, C. John Collins, William D. Barrick, Gregory A. Boyd, Philip G. Ryken, *Four Views on the Historical Adam (Counterpoints: Bible and Theology)*.

19.
THE GENESIS "FOUNDATION"

God's salvation plan rests on the foundation laid in the Genesis creation
account. *An* old earth *undermines* every major doctrine of the Bible.
—Ken Ham[292]

A clear theological thread begins the journey in Genesis from creation,
showing the covenantal roots from Adam to Noah to Abraham, Isaac, and
Jacob, which led to the Sinai covenant spoken to ancient Israel.

C. John Collins writes:

The Mosaic covenant carries forward the covenants made with the patriarchs. The pattern we find is that each successive covenant builds on
(rather than replaces) those before it... [And] provides a setting in which
they are to be realized. Hence later writers speak of God's "covenants"
(for example, Wis. 18:22; Sir. 44:12, 18; 2 Macc. 8:15; Rom. 9:4; Eph.
2:12), seeing all of them as applicable.[293]

Genesis is foremost a book written to the covenant people, Israel. The
author's *most crucial point* is not to explain the universe's structure or even its
contents. Everyone in the ANE could see those things. The focus is on origins,
especially the covenants between the Creator and humanity and Yahweh and
Israel. Genesis reveals why God elected Abraham's children from all the nations.
The language must be intentional and immediate for an authentic audience to
satisfy the covenantal needs at the time. Therefore, it is more appropriate to
interpret their ideas within their context before applying them to our context.
The driving force in Genesis is to set the stage for God's covenant with Israel and
not set the table for future generations of creationists of any type.

Look at Ken Ham's extraordinary statement again: "God's *salvation plan*
rests on the foundation laid in the Genesis creation account. An old earth undermines *every major doctrine of the Bible.*" These two sentences are disjointed. Note
that Ham blurs the theological importance of Genesis with the *earth's age* as if
they are the same thing. He nonetheless assumes that one necessarily follows the
other with no such connection.

First, Ham refers to the "Genesis creation account" in general. The second sentence imposes a specific reference to "age" as if age is what makes the
Genesis creation account foundational, indeed, foundational for "*every major
doctrine of the Bible.*" Note the powerful yet unclear terms: "salvation plan,"

---

292. Ken Ham, "The Necessity for Believing in Six Literal Days," December 1, 1995, AiG website.

293. C. John Collins, *Genesis 1–4: A Linguistic, Literary, And Theological Commentary* (P&R
Publishing, New Jersey, 2006), Kindle edition, location 428–433.

"rests," "foundation," "laid," "every major doctrine"—all aimed at the YEC distinctive. That's a lot of power for a nonessential. In the proper context, these are potent terms, but Ham chains them to YEC with no clear conceptual links.[294]

For instance, Ham, who carries a large megaphone for YEC, says God's plan "rests" upon a foundation. What foundation? The one laid in the Genesis creation account. Which one is that exactly? If we are honest, Ham's "foundation" is the "six literal days" foundation. But six literal days is one of many interpretations of Genesis through the centuries. A literal *Genesis* is not a foundation for anything in the Bible, let alone the entire Bible; instead, it is the foundation for only one thing, YEC. The fact is the first creation is temporal from its beginning:

> In the beginning, Lord, you laid the *foundations* of the earth, and the heavens are the work of your hands. *They will perish*, but you remain; *they will all wear out* like a garment. *You will roll them up* like a robe; like a garment *they will be changed*. But you remain the same, and your years will never end. (Hebrews 1:10–12)

Whatever foundation that YEC claims about six literal days rests on sand. The original creation has temporal usefulness, like our physical bodies. So it is with the material elements in this universe that cannot endure: days being one of them.

> Then I saw a new heaven and a new earth, for the first heaven and the first earth *had passed way*... Never again will night appear, and no one who lives there will ever need a lamp or the sun. The Lord God will be their light, and they will rule forever. (Revelation 21:1, 22:5 CEV).

The new universe shall be the transfiguration of this cosmos, taken out of this space and time, like our bodies. There will be no days in the new heaven and earth.

YErs insist that the earth's age is not really the issue; they insist *biblical authority* is the issue.

If the age of the earth is not the point, why focus on it incessantly? *If the age of the earth is a non-issue, then the so-called "real issue" (biblical authority) cannot be about the non-issue (the age of the earth).* A thing cannot be about, *not the thing.* In other words, the YEC argument on the "real issue" can be assembled: If we let *YE* = young earth, *I* = the issue, *BA* = biblical authority, then the *form* of this YEC argument looks like this:

If *YE* ≠ *I, while BA* = *I, then a YE* ≠ *BA.*

---

294. Naturally, YErs would strongly object to classifying these terms as unrelated. In another context, there may even be some way to understand the terms if defined properly. However, the unique YEC linkage fails. It is impossible for the physics of creation or when it occurred to be the grounds for God's plan of salvation in Christ or the key to all biblical doctrine since God's plan was determined before creation. The creation rests on God's plan, not the other way around.

Spelled out, it reads:

4. If a Young Earth is not equated with the issue, and

5. Biblical authority is equated with the issue, then

6. Biblical authority is not equated with a Young Earth.

Therefore, according to YE logic, the earth's age has nothing to do with biblical authority, but YE rhetoric says the opposite. Of course, YEC and biblical authority are not synonyms. They are separate issues, established independently. Nonetheless, there is no justification for the movement without attaching it to something critical like "biblical authority" that is satisfied if you accept YEC. That is why the age of the earth is, in fact, only a YEC issue.

We saw earlier that the systematic theologian Norman Geisler, one of the framers of the Chicago Statement on Biblical Inerrancy, a most conservative group, wrote:

> The founders and framers of the contemporary inerrancy movement (ICBI)...*explicitly rejected the Young Earth view* as being essential to belief in [biblical] inerrancy.

YErs are simply not experts in biblical authority or inerrancy.

Again, we have cognitive dissonance at the heart of an issue. Remember this statement: "The Lord has raised up *creation ministries around the world to call the Church back to the authority of God's Word in Genesis.*"[295] All Christians believe God is Creator. What sets apart YErs is not their belief in creation or that God is Creator but only that they are *Young Earth Creationists. If the earth's age has nothing to do with biblical authority while accepting a young earth means "accepting the authority of God's Word in Genesis,"* then we have nonsense. That *reinforces the idea that a young earth is what everyone knows it is—a nonessential.*

In the hands of some YE evangelists, it has become a *nonsensical* nonessential. The charge that anything less than a literal interpretation of Genesis 1 compromises the faith and all biblical teaching is entirely arbitrary. This confusion comes from the mistaken presupposition that God had to write Genesis because no one else was there at creation to account for it; furthermore, when God writes, He is a literalist.

No one had to be there at the beginning to write Genesis.

I wonder, did the Babylonians believe that Marduk wrote *Enuma Elish*? Did the Canaanites believe Baal wrote any tablets at Ugarit? Everyone knew in Egypt who wrote in hieroglyphics. Those gods were far more anthropomorphic. If God were ever to write scripture, Jesus would have done it. No one in the ANE believed the gods wrote books. Muslims, Mormons, and Christian

---

295. Ken Ham, "The Enemy Within," August 9, 2003, article on AiG website.

fundamentalists believe God wrote their scriptures. Historically, Christianity has never claimed such a thing. The Holy Spirit moved the biblical authors to write, meaning "God-breathed" or inspiration, *not dictation*.

The act of writing would be an indignity for a god since the task always fell to a hired servant called an *amanuensis*. Furthermore, an amanuensis, often a slave, took dictation from the author. Biblical authors were not amanuenses; they hired them as an architect hires builders to compose their books. Biblical authors rarely did physical writing because it was painstaking and time-consuming work; it required specialized training.

Even the Rabbinic scholar, Paul, who rarely wrote, was perhaps the most capable of physical writing among biblical authors. Notice, "I, Tertius, *who wrote down this letter*, greet you in the Lord" (Romans 16:22). Tertius fulfilled the role of an amanuensis for Paul. On one rare occasion, Paul did handwrite an "IOU" in Philemon 1:19, where he states emphatically: "*I, Paul, am writing this with my own hand. I will pay it back—not to mention that you owe me your very self*." If Paul had written all his letters by hand, he would not take considerable time and effort to point out the obvious. The fundamentalist view that God used writers as amanuenses is not the historic Christian view. That is dictation, which Christianity has always rejected.

Thus, another YEC presupposition falls.

God did not write the Bible or dictate the words. He did not manipulate the authors. The notion that *biblical authority* comes from treating a story literally, even when referring to the primeval past, is nothing more than claiming *personal authority* on one's opinion.

Since YEC is *far more* than the simple belief in a young earth, no Christians have been *Young Earth Creationists* until the modern movement. The *ism* in YEC is the belief that YEC is the key to everything: animals with eternal life, dinosaurs on the Ark, all biblical doctrines: the Gospel, the Atonement, the cross, reforming the Church and culture, branding the faith, defining sin, *and worst of all, it is the key to determining if God and Jesus are liars*. How YErs read Genesis is what they think God meant when *He wrote it*. All that is a fantasy for a group of people who believe that something they acknowledge is nonessential is an all-encompassing essential.

All Christians see the origins of the human condition *represented* in the Genesis story; in the moral of the story, God is the Creator who made us in His image, and despite God's profound interest in us, we have turned away from Him. Our condition is serious, but there is hope. The identity of that hope would not appear for a thousand years.

Genesis begins to offer hope for humanity with the covenant promises that crescendo at Mt. Sinai— a national and ethnic agreement with Abraham's descendants. Yet, the Sinai covenant was temporal (see 2 Corinthians 3:13). At the right time and beyond expectations, the divine Logos fulfilled all covenantal promises from Abraham to Sinai, from Sinai to David, to a new covenant *for all nations,* ratified in the Christ events: the life, death, resurrection, and ascension of the Logos Incarnate. Christ has superseded any "foundation" in Genesis or anywhere else in scripture.

For any doctrine to be the foundation of God's plan and the key to all major tenants of the Bible, we should expect *explicit* references throughout Scripture. It should be the prime motif of scripture. Indeed, it would be the most important of truths.

Biblical authors often praise God's creative works, yet they never include statements on the earth's age or the importance of *dating* the beginning, let alone base all biblical doctrine on such things. When Jesus and Paul refer to the Creation, it is never to establish anything like YEC.[296]

How could biblical authors continuously fail to explicitly state what many YErs say is the foundation upon which God's plan rests? Biblical authors did not fail at this since it is not believable that a young earth or even the book of Genesis is, in fact, the foundation upon which God's salvation plan rests, whatever "rests" means.

John 1 trumps Genesis 1—"In the beginning was the Word." Christians should know that Christ is the foundation of all God's plans without qualification. The Old Testament repeatedly predicts and promises the Messiah, from where he would be born to how he would die and why. The New Testament explicitly and repeatedly identifies Jesus of Nazareth as the One "by whom, for whom, and through whom all things exist." He is the beginning and the end, the Alpha and Omega (Revelation 22:12–13). Only Jesus is *the foundation,* and Chief Cornerstone taught repeatedly, explicitly, and without fail throughout scripture. Indeed, the Apostle Paul wrote, "Jesus Christ Himself is the foundation. *No one can make another one*" (1 Corinthians 3:11).

According to YE theology, the Creation is *the signature event* explaining the entire Bible when, in reality, it is not the signature event in the Old Testament or even the Pentateuch. Scholars in both Judaism and Christianity agree that the Exodus from Egypt is the Hebrew Bible's signature event. The primary kind of history in the Bible is *redemptive history;* it cannot possibly be geological history. The scripture contains records of what God has done for His people. It is also predictive of what he intends to do for all creation. It is not a scientific, historiographic, or systematic presentation.[297]

Genesis sets the stage for the theology of election and redemption in the Exodus and Sinai Covenant. God divides the waters at Creation and the

---

296. See chapter 23: "Scriptures Not as Written" on Mark 10:6, Divorce and Remarriage.

297. Redemptive history is highly selective and theological, which has nothing to do with science or modern historiography. In fact, the overarching genre of the Bible may very well be redemptive history.

Exodus, linking Israel's national deity to the Creator of the universe, who also defeats pagan gods in both events. For instance, the ten plagues are assaults on the gods of Egypt. The Exodus grounds redemptive history, which is a theology of history. However, to best understand Genesis, it helps to know the pagan myths in the ANE to see how Genesis asserts God's sovereignty over other gods. The similarities between Genesis and ANE creation accounts where Yahweh replaces all other deities establishes His superiority.

Redemptive history is God's plan before the world began now acted out from creation to the present with the death, burial, and resurrection of Jesus as its pulse. It is salvation history planned and predicted in the past, unfolding in the present, and continuous through time. Unlike other accounts, redemptive history is theological or soteriological truth in progress. [298] It is not the arrested facts of a history book. It is a history that never stands still in that as it unfolds, the Christ events reinterpret it.

The entry into Egyptian slavery, the election of Israel, the Passover, the Exodus from Egypt, and the entry into the promised land amount to a "death, burial, and resurrection" of the children of Israel personified in Joseph, the favored son of Jacob. Entering the Promised Land is a type of paradise: milk and honey, vines and fig trees, etc. Luke 9:30–32 conveys this idea as it says in the New American Bible Revised Edition with verse numbers and footnotes preserved below:

> Behold, two men were conversing with [Jesus], Moses and Elijah,[a] who appeared in glory and spoke of *his exodus* [b] that he was going to accomplish in Jerusalem. Peter and his companions had been overcome by sleep, but becoming fully awake, they saw his glory and the two men standing with him.

Footnotes as published

9:30—Moses and Elijah: the two figures represent the Old Testament law and the prophets. At the end of this episode, the heavenly voice will identify Jesus as the one to be listened to now (Lk. 9:35).

9:31—His exodus that he was going to accomplish in Jerusalem: Luke identifies the subject of the conversation as the exodus of Jesus, a reference to the death, resurrection, and ascension of Jesus that will take place in Jerusalem, the city of destiny (see Lk. 9:51). *The mention of exodus, however, also calls to mind the Israelite Exodus from Egypt to the Promised Land.* (emphasis mine)

The language of Christianity—salvation, deliverance from the *"slavery of sin,"* "rest" in Christ—has its roots in Judaism and has entered the Christian

---

298. Soteriology examines salvation, which includes the entire scope of biblical salvation. It includes election, calling, deliverance, regeneration, sanctification, and glorification, which are all grounded in the Incarnation. It also includes God's plan determined before the creation, providing salvation in human history, and perfecting salvation throughout eternity future.

conversation. Christ is not only a New Adam; He is the New Moses, affects a New Exodus, and leads a new Israel to the New Jerusalem in the New Heavens and New Earth. That is how the Jewish Church of the first century AD understood Jesus and his work. Whenever we use this language, we should remember that the Incarnation, *i.e., the identity of Christ*, radically interprets the focal point of the Hebrew Bible.[299]

Jews in Christ's day still considered themselves in exile in their own land. The occupation gave rise to a passionate prayer for deliverance. The Jews expected a deliverer more like Moses (see Deuteronomy 18:15; Acts 7:37–38). Jesus chose the Passover/Exodus time—the coming out of slavery in Egypt (a type of slavery to sin) secured by the lamb's blood on the doorposts and unleavened bread that symbolizes sin's removal—to show he fulfills them.

The giving of the Holy Spirit came on the day of Pentecost, and Christ is our atonement. In addition, the Feast of Trumpets announces his return; the Feast of Tabernacles symbolizes his Messianic kingdom so that the Feasts of Israel have significant theological connections to Christianity (far more than a literal Genesis does). Still, the festivals have no covenantal obligations for the Christian calendar because they are typological. Observing them today looks back at the ritual instead of looking forward to the reality as ancient Israel did (Colossians 2:16–17).

Christ is the reality.

Church history reflects this by the abandonment of Israel's Feast days and the Israelite Sabbath for days reflecting the Christ of the New Testament, not because the Feasts of Israel lack typology with Christ but because being in Christ, the typology has run its course. The Israelite Sabbath of Exodus 20 was only a type of the divine rest at creation that continues through time. The weekly Sabbath in Israel *will not participate in the new creation.* There will not be sunrise and sunset in the New Jerusalem (Revelation 22:5). Eternal rest (we understand is in Christ) is what the divine seventh day of Creation meant: it is unending, *not temporal or weekly.*[300]

YErs cannot accept that the seventh day of Creation is endless without the critical refrain "evening and morning, the 7th day." That refrain ends each of the first six days, and YErs claim it proves a twenty for hour day. *If the seventh day does not end, the week does not end; therefore, the six days are not literal.*

Christ's life, death, resurrection, and ascension are more than the signature events of the Bible. They are the signature events in this reality. Scripture is

---

299. At the time the New Testament was written, Christianity was still part of Judaism and shared a common language on theological issues. The challenge for Christian thought has been determining to what extent the substantial Jewishness in its language should be interpreted.

300. YErs do not understand that if the seventh day of creation is unending, creation week is unending. In other words, the six days are unending and, therefore, not literal.

not *the* revelation: scripture records witnesses *to revelation,* God's self-disclosure that eventually culminated in Jesus. A Christian who misses this or conflates *the signature events* as something other than the Christ events is misguided. Trustworthy witnesses must be allowed to speak of their own free will. All the accolades YErs give to the six literal days of Genesis would be better applied to the "three days and three nights" in the tomb, though even they were not literally three days and three nights.

With all the discussion through the centuries since Augustine, whether Genesis 1 is figurative or literal on the six days, plus our recent controversies, it is evident that the Bible is not *explicit* on age/earth questions. It is, however, clear that Christ is the foundation of all biblical understanding in Christianity. Luther's belief that the plain sense of scripture should be apparent to most people is much more complicated since he knew nothing of ANE literature, archeology, and advanced scholarship. If only the "plain sense" of scripture was clear to the tens of thousands of Protestant denominations in controversy—and growing.

The different theories on the creation and the disagreements on many other doctrines in Protestantism illustrate a real problem. The following observation by D. A. Carson on the issues related to biblical interpretation among like-minded Evangelicals demonstrates the problem:

> I speak to *those with a high view of Scripture*: it is very distressing to contemplate how many differences there are among us as to what Scripture actually says... The fact remains that among those who believe the canonical sixty-six books are nothing less than the Word of God written, there is a *disturbing array* of mutually incompatible theological opinions.[301] (Emphasis mine)

The many differences of opinion on *"what Scripture actually says"* make it more challenging to determine what scripture *means.* Even so, the "disturbing array" of contrary opinions on age/earth issues is no proof that the earth is old. It does show that *age/earth issues cannot be "the foundation upon which God's plan rests,"* as YErs assert. Neither could it be the key to all biblical teaching, biblical authority, or the integrity of God. Christian Smith goes further:

> That evangelicals, all claiming a common biblical norm, are reading contradictory theological formulations on many of the major issues they are addressing suggests the problematic nature of their...understanding of theological interpretation. To argue that the Bible is authoritative, but to be unable to come to anything like agreement on what it says (even

---

301. See D.A. Carson, *Exegetical Fallacies*; I am not sure an array of "mutually incompatible theological opinions" should be so disturbing, except to those that believe the Bible should be clear and explicit in all matters it addresses. Real life, in a world of good and evil, is not so simple. See also Christian Smith, *The Bible Made Impossible: Why Biblicism Is Not a Truly Evangelical Reading of Scripture* for another treatment of this phenomenon.

with those who share an evangelical commitment [to inerrancy]) is self-defeating.[302]

More importantly, the *"disturbing array* of mutually incompatible theological opinions" of serious-minded and devoted adherents to biblical inerrancy suggests that the Bible is not a simplistic oracle that tells us exactly what we need to know in all subjects that it addresses. That is not a criticism of scripture; instead, that is the nature of philosophical and theological literature. It is highly interpretive. Every line is not a legal statement. In fact, very little of scripture is law under the New Covenant. My point is that the *foundational truths* of the Bible, its essential purposes, are God's purposes in Christ and their fulfillment. Everything else, to one degree or another, is ancillary.

YEC organizations like those at CGI and AiG devote themselves and their resources to the literal interpretation of Genesis 1-11. For them, Genesis 1 provides the key to all reform and the foundation upon which God's plan rests. Let's see it again:

> *A literal Genesis* is the key to reforming the Church and reclaiming our culture... *God's salvation plan rests* on the *foundation* laid in the Genesis creation account. *Foremost* is that allowing these days to be long periods of time *undermines* the *foundations of the message of the Cross.*[303]

This quote is saying an old earth threatens the Gospel.

Apparently, you can't teach an *old earth* new tricks.

Notice the equivocation on the word *foundation.* It could mean the beginning of a process (its origin or *founding*) or the basis upon which something exists or establishes a thing. Genesis 1-3 is the *founding* of the world and the *beginning* of what unfolds. That is obvious. For something to be foundational to creation, it must be necessary. For instance, the fundamentals in Genesis are only One God, who creates the universe with purposes that focus on the human family. Things went wrong between God and humans. This Creator happens to be the God of Israel who elects and saves. These actual fundamentals do not depend on the definition of the word day or the meaning of "evening and morning," how many days the Creation took or how long ago it occurred.

None of the actual fundamental ideas in Genesis has anything to do with YEC.

---

302. Christian Smith, *The Bible Made Impossible: Why Biblicism Is Not a Truly Evangelical Reading of Scripture* (Brazos Press, Baker Publishing Group, Grand Rapids, Michigan, E-book edition, 2012), p. 52. See also Peter Enns, *Inspiration and Incarnation: Evangelicals and the Problem of the Old Testament* (Grand Rapids: Baker Academic, 2005), pp. 71–112. "The presence of theological diversity does not mean that [the Bible] lacks integrity or trustworthiness. It means that we must recognize that the data of scripture lead us to [think] differently [on] how scripture has integrity or is worthy of trust. Scripture may indeed 'lack integrity' if we impose upon it standards that have little in common with how the Bible itself behaves."

303. Ken Ham, "The Necessity for Believing in Six Literal Days," December 1, 1995, AiG website.

No matter how hard YErs try to attach their distinctive to something important like biblical authority or conspiracies to compromise the faith, a lying God, YE evangelism, or the meaning of sin, it is obvious that YEC is neither foundational nor fundamental.

The view that *six literal days* are the grounds for all truth in nature and the Bible is a "roll-your-eyes" exaggeration. The beginning of God's plan and its foundation can only be the Logos, the Lord Jesus Christ (John 1:1, 14). Even the famed theoretical physicist Werner Heisenberg said, "The first gulp from the glass of natural sciences will turn you into an atheist but at the bottom of the glass God is waiting for you." In other words, Logos grounds science. Unfortunately, YErs took the first gulp and retreated.

To suggest any other foundation of *God's plan* in addition to Christ is not a Christian concept. It is adding to the Word we preach—the Gospel. The Logos is foundational. Furthermore, the foundation for the message of the cross is John 3:16, "For God so loved the world that he gave his one and only Son, that whoever believes in him shall not perish but have eternal life." It is not easy to miss this one. It sums up redemptive history; it does not sum up YEC.

Missing this comes from a devotion to something other than the foundation.

20.
HIDING BEHIND "BIBLICAL AUTHORITY"

> We talk about creation/evolution, the fossil record, and the age of the earth...
> But we really are a Biblical Authority Ministry.
> —Ken Ham[304]

YErs do not like the label "Young Earth Creationist." So they insist that the issue is not really the age of the earth; it is about "biblical authority." They do so because the age of the earth is too trivial to attach so much weight to it. On the one hand, the Bible is central, particularly in Evangelical Christianity. On the other hand, YErs define biblical authority with YEC.

It is simply absurd that the quality of one's faith is in how old they think the earth is, so YErs try to hide behind something that sounds very serious— thus the YE "biblical authority" myth. They might as well call themselves a "Bible-believing ministry" or a "truth-telling ministry," or a "no lying ministry," which says nothing. That is similar to a "bait and switch" like Jehovah's witnesses saying "we're biblical authority witnesses." A Matthew 25 ministry is a biblical authority ministry, too. By that tactic, any Bible-based ministry is switchable to a "biblical authority ministry."

These terms are not interchangeable, or Judaism, keepers of the Old Testament, would be a biblical authority ministry too. Paul wrote, "The Jews were entrusted with the oracles of God (Roman 3:2). Therefore, the "biblical authority" label is a meaningless and gratuitous misdirection away from the feeble priority of a young earth. The "biblical authority ministry" in YEC is another YE misnomer.

Because YErs sometimes shy away from "too much" focus on the age of the earth and dislike the title "Young Earth Creationists," it indicates their cognitive dissonance with their most identifiable distinctive. These are *Young Earth* Creationists, not *Biblical Authority* Creationists. YErs are who and what they are. In reality, they are about the age of the earth, including the baggage that comes with it (see *Young Earth Missionary Trips* in chapter 35). Hiding behind a vague abstraction like "biblical authority ministry" implies their YE distinctive is too weak to stand on its own.

Furthermore, the earth's age is neither biblical nor theological by nature. No statement, focus, nor concern on the age of the earth appears in the Bible. You cannot find age-earth evangelists or YE prophets in scripture as we have in YEC. There is no religious or biblical component to accepting the geology of

---

304. Ken Ham, *The Authority Crisis in the Church: Science or the Bible*, DVD, see AiG website.

any age of the earth. That is because the earth's age is a scientific issue based on empirical data, and that is all it is. That is a fact.

Facts are verifiable by independent analysts who would draw similar conclusions: Washington DC is the capital of the United States, $2 + 2 = 4$, etc. Naturalistic conclusions that are not verifiable are opinions. YEC is not a biblical authority ministry; it's a "biblical *opinions* ministry," and everybody's got one. The earth may be young, but that is not a fact. If it were a fact, YErs would have a reliable way to verify the earth's age by dating it. It should be easy if the world is only six thousand years old and the universe is the same age. They ought to give us a date based on data. None is forthcoming. No amount of feigned authority, haranguing, accusing, threatening, or warnings can alter that.

Some Catholics boil down all their conflict with Protestants to one issue—authority; in this case, papal authority, including the Church hierarchy and teaching arm or magisterium. For Roman Catholics, the Church claims authority regarding scripture since it asserts that the Roman Catholic Church wrote, compiled, and canonized it. That claim is not entirely so since the earliest Church was Jewish, born out of Judaism and Jerusalem. What became Christianity wasn't separate from Judaism until the end of the first century, when the Greek scriptures were complete. Judaism may have a higher claim to the New Testament than the Roman Church, which did not exist despite their claims. The name *Roman* Catholic distances itself from their contention as 1st-century Jewish Christian writers. The earliest Church was a Jewish sect. Nonetheless, centuries later, the Catholic Church was instrumental in compiling and canonizing scripture. That is no small thing.

Non-Catholics do not accept the papacy or its magisterium and do not recognize Catholic authority over the Bible. If the Bible and the papacy conflict, there is protest. Yet Protestants can use the Bible as a "literary papacy" against others, and some do. Leaders determine what the Bible's central truths mean for its members in most Protestant denominations. That is authority. The difference is the ease with which new denominations split away under the umbrella of biblical authority or conscience if there is enough disagreement between denominational leaders and members. There are strengths and weaknesses in both Catholic and Protestant applications of authority.[305]

Too many YErs go a step further by co-opting the infallibility of scripture in the service of their personal authority. They warn others, label them compromisers, and at times ruin careers and the reputations of Evangelical scholars and

---

305. In Catholicism, there is more discipline and uniformity in biblical interpretation but less freedom of opinion. A level of unity is maintained but the potential for abuses of authority may be greater. The freedom in Protestantism leads to factions and instability, but with the clear conscience of free will. In the Age of Reason, where all humans are seen as capable of exercising their faculties, freedom of conscience is favored.

theologians.[306] They justify themselves by one thing—their *perceived* authority hidden behind the *claim* of biblical authority. It is precarious to confuse one's opinion with God's opinion. That claim leads to excesses; it is legalistic and dictatorial. Anyone can be mistaken, particularly in interpreting primordial events and obscure cosmologies.

Besides, what value is an infallible nonessential.

Fundamentalists assert the authority of their tradition in the belief that they trust the Bible more or that God has given them better insight. While others pay lip service to the Scriptures, fundamentalists believe they are better, more faithful Christians uncompromised by the world, etc. YErs believe God has given them a mandate among denominations. The so-called "biblical authority ministry" is nothing but a "YE authority ministry."

Because YErs don't like the descriptive "Young Earth Creationist," they prefer to hide behind the ambiguous "biblical creationists." It is easier to defend an ambiguity than a clearly stated position. This ambiguity lets YErs claim to believe the Bible when others don't. Cults do the same thing; Jehovah's Witnesses and Yahweh groups insist on the deity's "biblical name." Seventh Day Adventists keep the "biblical day" of rest. Geocentrists believe in the "biblical universe." All Christian groups believe their unique distinctives are biblical, but they don't usually run from their descriptive. Catholics believe in the "biblical bread and wine"— Christ's literal body and blood. "Biblical creationist" is another meaningless YE phrase.

Some fundamentalists are like Old Testament prophets. They hold watch over spiritual Israel and *warn* them: "Son of man: I have made you a *watchman* for the house of Israel; therefore you shall hear a word from My mouth and warn them for Me" (Ezekiel 33:7).

Isaiah wrote, "Cry aloud, spare not; Lift up your voice like a trumpet; Tell My people their [sins], and the house of Jacob their sins" (Isaiah 58:1 NKJV).

The prophets received a word from God, usually in the moment. They carried that message to the people. Today, the Message, the Word, is the Gospel. The Word is out so that everyone can hear. Notice what Paul wrote to the Church in Rome, "The word is near you; it is in your mouth and in your heart," that is, the message concerning faith that we proclaim" (Romans 10:8). YErs, on the other hand, spare not and lift their voices like trumpets to show God's people "six literal days."

But *the word* in Christianity is this: "Lift up your voice and show the people, *My Son.*"

---

306. I've been called an atheist, apostate, humanist, gnostic, conspirator, can "insurrectionist" and "Russian agent" be far behind. Most accusers don't seem to know what those philosophies even mean and especially how they apply. Those accusations are nothing more than flares launched to throw off someone they hope know even less about Gnosticism, humanism, etc.

The Bible Was Made for Man, Not Man for the Bible

Christianity has not confused inspiration with dictation historically. There have been Jews who believed that God created the Torah before creating the heavens and earth, perhaps equating Torah with Wisdom's personification in Proverbs 8.[307] Many Muslims believe the Koran is incarnate from heaven and has eternally existed as is, then dictated to Muhammed, word for word. Mormons believe Joseph Smith received the book of Mormon similarly. However, the Bible *is not* transcendent in Christianity.

God is.

Believing that "God wrote the Bible" is superstition; it does not make one a better Christian, nor is it a high view of the Bible because it is false. The Bible often sites who the authors are of the respective documents. They are always human. Biblical authors wrote a genuine record of their times. That was their calling because of who they were. If God told them to write something specific, then only that is dictation. Their literary forms and styles are indicative of each period and author. The scripture is not a divine contrivance; it is an authentic record of Israel's encounter with Yahweh during various periods.

God does not contrive.

However, such authenticity is uncomfortable for some, perhaps understandably so. Without a personal experience with God, humans tend to cling to markers for security—for Catholics, it is the Pope; for Protestants, the Bible. These can become anchors of security and authority psychologically.[308]

The term *bible* is not a word used in the Bible for what *we* call "the Bible." No agreed-upon canon existed in biblical times. The five books of Moses were the only universally accepted books among the Jews and Samaritans until the late first century, but their respective texts differed. The Septuagint was not a single book called the Bible. It was a collection of Hebrew writings translated into Greek and included many books not part of today's Bibles, Jewish or Christian.

The Law, the Prophets, and the Writings were the three main divisions of the Hebrew scriptures of the first century AD (Luke 24:44). When the New Testament refers to "scripture" (*grapha* in Greek), meaning "writing" without a modifier, it could refer to *any* written document. Today, the English-speaking world uses the word *Bible* and *scripture* synonymously. They also refer to the "Hebrew" and "Greek" Testaments, regardless of the various canonical lists.

In the Old Testament, the "Word of God" refers to divine promises, commands, or oral messages given to the prophets, written down later, then

---

307. "Incarnation," *Hastings Dictionary of the Bible*, states, "The doctrine of the Divine Wisdom as set forth in the Books of Proverbs (Pro. 8:22, Wis. 7: 23-25; Wis. 8: 1 etc.) personifies Wisdom almost to the point of ascribing to it separate existence."

308. The primary authority in the Eastern Orthodox Church is the Bible as interpreted by the seven ecumenical councils of the Imperial Roman Church that occurred from AD 325–787.

collected and edited. In the New Testament, the Word of God is the Gospel itself, which Christians are to proclaim. The phrase "the Word of God" is not a technical term for a single book called the Bible."[309] Calling the Bible "the Word of God" is an expression we use in Church life that we understand in perspective. The Bible is a cooperative undertaking between God and men and not solely the work of either. Therefore, the Bible is critical to understanding Judaism and Christianity, its roots, beginnings, founding, central teachings, Mission, and message.

For Christians today:

1. The word we proclaim is the Gospel;

2. *The Word* is the divine Logos that communicates God's will;

3. The Bible is mainly a collection of *witnesses* to God's workings in Israel on behalf of the world (see Hebrews 12:1).

Yes, the Bible is an incalculable blessing, a gift inspired by God. But it can be misused, misunderstood, and can become a new law, analogous to the role the books of Moses once played, or worse, a tool for neo-Pharisaism. *Jesus's words regarding the Sabbath can be adapted to the scriptures. He said, "The Sabbath was made for man, not man for the Sabbath (Mark 2:7);" and so, "The Bible was made for man, not man for the Bible." In other words, the Bible is not our master; Jesus is. We cannot serve two masters equally. One must be subordinate to the other. The Bible is subordinate to Jesus and cannot be equal to him in any way.*

Oxford Professor Keith Ward describes divine inspiration this way:

[Inspiration] is a kind of divine guidance, a raising of the mind and heart to a greater sensitivity to divine presence and purpose, with an increase in the ability to express in memorable ways the insights such sensitivity brings...It does not overrule the unique personal styles and interests of human persons. But it does shape them to a deeper insight and more meaningful form of expression.[310]

This definition of inspiration is a reasonable attempt to describe something mystical. To what extent God may have injected thoughts into the minds of biblical authors is impossible to know. For example, *The Fundamentals,* the book considered to be the founding document that launched Christian fundamentalism, though its purpose was to lay down the core beliefs in Christianity, some of which today's fundamentalists reject. It states that God allows or can inspire people to write their own opinions:

---

309. John Goldingay, *Models for Scripture* (Wm. B. Eerdmans Publishing Co. Grand Rapids, Michigan, 1994).

310. See Roberto Sirvent and Wm. Curtis Holtzen, *By Faith and Reason: The Essential Keith Ward* (Darton, Longman and Todd Ltd, London. 2012), Kindle edition, page 129.

Ecclesiastes is a case in point, which on the supposition of its Solomonic authorship, is giving us a history of his search for happiness "under the sun." Some statements in that book are only partially true while others are altogether false; therefore, it cannot mean that Solomon was inspired as he tried this or that experiment to find what no man has been able to find outside of God. But it means that his language is inspired as he records the various feelings and opinions which possessed him in the pursuit.[311]

Solomon is like other biblical authors: inspired by the Holy Spirit to write, so he did. God expects us to be mature to sort out a masterpiece in ancient "existential" philosophy on the futility of life, such as Ecclesiastes.

Ecclesiastes preserves a fatalistic view of human mortality as Solomon wrote:

Surely the fate of human beings is like that of the animals; the same fate awaits them both: As one dies, so dies the other. All have the same breath; humans have no advantage over animals. Everything is meaningless. (Ecclesiastes 3:19).

The Bible is not for lightweights.

In what sense is the book of Ecclesiastes what YErs would call "God's eternal, perfect Word?" Is it God's eternal, perfect Word as John 3:16 is? "God so loved the world that He gave his one and only Son." It is disjointed to say that God caused every word of an author's *opinion* in Ecclesiastes, then calling it God's eternal, perfect Word. The problem with fundamentalism is the presupposition that God wrote the Bible; for them, inspiration is not inspiration but *dictation*. Many YErs don't know the difference. *There is no real difference between God writing every word and causing every word in the Bible to be written, which are both versions of dictation. Inspiration is not dictation of any kind.*[312]

Interestingly, those early fundamentalist scholars were not YErs. They accepted mainstream geology on the earth's age, giving no aid and comfort to YEC. Notice: "But things, as in the case of astronomy, are now better understood, and few are disquieted in reading their Bibles because it is made certain that *the world is immensely older than the 6,000 years*" (emphasis mine).[313]

---

311. R. A. Torrey, A. C. Dixon, *The Fundamentals (90 Essays)* (1910–1915), Kindle Edition, location 4828 (2013). The idea is that errors in the Bible cannot be attributed to God but to humans as in the case of Solomon's Ecclesiastes or characters that lie like the devil. God either wanted or allowed them to be written.

312. This does not rule out the occasional divine dictation to a prophet in special circumstances. Here the exception proves the rule. God did not make certain the Bible's every word came by force.

313. *The Fundamentals (90 Essays)*, R. A. Torrey, A. C. Dixon, editors (1910–1915), Kindle Edition, location 4455 (2013). These fundamentalists were conservative scholars, theologians, and pastors of the early twentieth century.

Almost everything we see in scripture is a record of several things: stories and narratives, events, wisdom, national history, prophetic messages, theological development, praise, and liturgy. We know God used flawed humans to write the books of the Bible. God used imperfect humans to make copies of the texts through the centuries. God used fallen humans to finalize the canon of Scripture. Most importantly, all humans that interpret the text are flawed.

What other kinds of humans are there?

A good father is sincerely interested in tutoring and nurturing his children toward success. A wise father helps his children with their homework; He *does not do their homework for them.* We believe the Holy Spirit inspired and moved humans to write the Bible's books—the Spirit did not do their homework for them.

We are Christians. No one else but Jews accept any part of the Bible as inspired. It seems that Christ expects us to meet the challenge from the world of *unbelievers* and not to dedicate ourselves to fighting Christians over nonessentials, especially in a popular culture that grows more hostile to Christianity every day.

Biblical authors did not give up their free will, creativity, or even subjectivity, in the process. Christianity has always believed that the Bible is a genuine project involving God and humans. The governing term in the last sentence is "genuine." The human element makes the project subordinate to God, not equal to Him.

If we disagree with science, we should still not assume our scientific presuppositions are in the Bible but offer a better scientific explanation. Most scientists are not authoritative on spiritual matters, nor are biblical authors authoritative on physics or biochemistry. Why would they be?

21.
WHAT THEN IS BIBLICAL AUTHORITY?

The BIBLE, I say, the BIBLE only, is the religion of Protestants!
—William Chillingworth (1602–1644)

Some Christians see Chillingworth's words as *bibliolatry*. Bibliolatry is what the term suggests—making an idol out of the Bible. Fundamentalists that believe bibliolatry is impossible are likely flirting with it. That level of reverence and glory reserved for God is idolatry if applied to anything else.

No Christian intends to worship the Bible. Even so, any *thing* can become an idol.

The reverence and glorification of scripture can cross a line. God is the only eternal perfection. God's eternal and perfect word proceeds from Him without a filter. Since the Bible is *handwritten*, it is an object of human civilization, even while divine inspiration has underwritten it. In other words, *the Bible is God's word filtered through human agents and retold in stories, events, laws, proverbs, and songs—all of which are earthly experiences.* The Bible has a beginning. God does not; neither does God's *eternal* word.

There are eternal truths in Scripture. But not everything in it is eternally true. For example, the old covenant and most of its laws were temporary since much of it had symbolic value that pointed to the future Christ incarnate. The entire Old Testament is grounded in the first covenant and its prescriptions. Yet, "If there had been nothing wrong with that first covenant, *no place would have been sought for another*" (Hebrews 8:7). The temple services could not redeem the sinner; they could only symbolize it. "For this reason [the law] can never, by the same sacrifices repeated endlessly year after year, make perfect those who draw near to worship" (Hebrews 10:1). Paul wrote, "With regard to a religious festival, a New Moon celebration or a Sabbath day. These are a shadow of the things that were to come; *the reality, however, is found in Christ*" (Colossians 2:16-17). Therefore, not everything in the Old Testament is eternal truth, nor was it meant to be.

Scripture commanded circumcision, Sabbath-keeping, and a sacrificial system; it suggests folk medicine like taking wine for your stomach's sake, customs like wearing a veil, casting lots, and many other things that had a place at one time but no longer. Those customs and temporal prescriptions were not the eternal, perfect Word written by God.

My point is that the Bible is God's word in general because it carries the Word of God given in Israel's history. God's presence inspired and influenced men to write at various times and places (Hebrews 1:1-3). The many authors of scripture witnessed to matters based on a word from God. The Bible points us to God's self-disclosure that culminates in Jesus—the "eternal Word." I reject the notion that this train of thought is a low view of the Bible. Instead, it frees the fundamentalist to attain a higher view of God. It places the Bible properly in relationship to God and humans.

I am not aware of Christians that bow down and worship the Bible. Years ago, I occasionally studied the Bible on my knees. It was an act of worship directed toward God, not the Bible, hoping a humble spirit might help me better understand what I was reading. But one does not have to bow down or worship a thing for it to be an idol. Money can be an idol, yet people do not have to bow down or worship it for it to be so. It becomes idolatry when something replaces or competes with God's rightful place in the world or our lives.

The Bible is not, as Chillingworth described it, a religion, nor is it the object of our faith. It is an irreplaceable tool in our walk of faith that is in spirit. It contains eternal truths and special revelation. In Christianity, God is one being in three limitless persons, not four: God the Father, God the Son, and God the Holy Spirit, but there is no *"God the Holy Bible."*

Making a thing equal to God *in any way* is idolatry.

The secular state can replace God, and political parties are like a church with an ideology analogous to a theology for the secular-minded. They have a doctrinal statement of beliefs called a "platform." The global threat of climate change is their eschatology; their hope in global governance by an oligarchy to bring in some utopia, which is their version of the Messianic Kingdom. Statism is the worst fundamentalism in that it has the power to make laws and enforce them with enough power to avoid accountability standards. But people do not have to bow down and worship or pray to the state in the traditional sense to be idolatrous. It is an overstatement to insist that the entire Bible is God's eternal, perfect Word for the simple reason humans participated in its composition and preservation. The Bible cannot equal God in knowledge, authority, or anything else. Insisting on that flirts with bibliolatry.[314]

There is no such thing as a "biblical authority ministry."

The Bible is not the message; it contains the message, which is the Gospel. It is silly to hear some fundamentalists attempt to "expose" other Christians by reading a verse in scripture (sometimes obscure) that they understand differently. "So and so is a false teacher" because he follows some ancillary "chapter and verse" differently. These fundamentalists think they have authority on any verse because they have a "higher view" of Scripture. A high view of scripture does not inoculate one from serious mistakes. An idolatrous view of scripture guarantees it.

The Bible is not the message; it is a primary medium for the message.

---

314. A discussion on bibliolatry would not be necessary if Christians did not insist that God wrote the Bible.

The early Church got its message from Jesus and his disciples, centered on Christ's life, death, resurrection, and ascension. That message was not explicit in the Old Testament scriptures they possessed. After the crucifixion and resurrection, the disciples could look back on several passages that they could interpret in the light of what happened. The Christ events and teachings that the disciples preserved and transcribed produced the New Testament documents. Nonetheless, the New Testament came filtered through the disciple's experience so that we might relate to God through the human Jesus.

The New Testament contains the primary sources for the *good news* of Christ. The Old Testament contains the sources for the Old Covenant with the promise of a new one. A preoccupation with the medium loses the message; as Paul said, "The letter kills." Evangelicals, especially fundamentalists, are vulnerable when a good thing, love of the Scriptures, becomes the master of one's life and a weapon to accuse others. The Bible is not the master; it points to him. Nor is scripture a weapon for Christians to brandish at each other but a sword to wield upon oneself (Hebrews 4:12).

In some circles, the Bible has become the religion, the judge, and the Savior. Worse yet, an opinion on the Scriptures has become the Judge and Savior. Jesus said, "You search the scriptures because in them you think you have eternal life" (John 5:39). The scriptures do not give us eternal life; it is not earned by obeisance to them. Life is in a person—Jesus said to some of the searchers of scripture in his day, "You refuse to come to me to have life" (v. 40).

The Bible can be an idol by elevating it to divine status, as some think devotion to Mary does. Bibliolatry is practically an unspeakable subject in Protestantism because the Bible often plays a role similar to the papacy in Catholicism— the primary authority in Church life. The Bible has become a shield in Protestantism against the papacy's authority. It is effective for that purpose.

The Bible introduces us to Christ, but the real authority lies *in Him*. He said, "*All authority in heaven and on earth has been given to me*" (Matthew 28:18). Therefore, the real authority in our lives is Christ living in us. He is in heaven so that he can be in us. The Bible is a blessing and a critical *source* of theological truth. But Jesus is truth. A "real relationship" with Christ remains the hallmark of Evangelicalism—or it should be. Christ in us is "the hope of glory" (Colossians 1:27). He is the Word *beyond* words.

Some YErs find their authority in six literal days because they have no authority in anything else. When YErs claim that any other interpretation of Genesis compromises the faith, they telegraph a strange legalism. They believe the Bible *requires* YEC for the soundest of faith, an uncompromised faith. That is faith in a chapter—Chapter 1 of the Bible—and worse, it's building a *reform movement* on a one-dimensional wooden interpretation.

The famous Galileo affair created tension between the Copernican theory of a sun-centered universe and the widespread geocentric view of the Ptolemaic model based on Aristotle. Neither the Church, Judaism, Islam, nor scientists were ready to accept heliocentrism due to insufficient data. Galileo knew he lacked the data when he backed down before the Inquisition. It took another generation for enough new data to overturn the Ptolemaic/geocentric model. The everyday language of the biblical authors assumes the earth-centered model. In the Late Bronze Age, Israel had no other information except their observations without the technological advances we enjoy. That is hardly relevant since the purpose of the Bible has nothing to do with Ptolemy or Galileo.

Regarding the theological basis for the tension between science and scripture, two Popes addressed whether speaking of a thing's appearance conflicts with its actual nature (i.e., the setting of a sun that does not move), otherwise called *phenomenological language*. In other words, would phenomenological language compel one to admit an error in Scripture? Both insisted it would not. Pope Leo XIII (1878–1903) wrote:

> St. Augustine warns us, "not to assert what is not known as if known." If dissension should arise between [the Bible and science], St. Augustine said, "Whatever [the theologian] can really demonstrate to be true of physical nature, *we must show to be capable of reconciliation with our Scriptures*; and whatever they assert in their treatises which is contrary to the Scriptures, we must either prove it as well as we can to be entirely false, or *we must, without the smallest hesitation, believe it to be so*...the Holy Ghost did not intend to teach men these things (that is to say, the essential nature of the things of the visible universe), things in no way profitable unto salvation." Hence they did not seek to penetrate the secrets of nature, but rather described and dealt with things in more or less figurative language, or in terms which were commonly used at the time, and which in many instances are in daily use to this day, even by the most eminent men of science. Ordinary speech primarily and properly describes what comes under the senses; and somewhat in the same way *the sacred writers... "went by what [appeared to their senses]," or put down what God, speaking to men, signified, in the way men could understand and were accustomed to.*[315] (emphasis mine)

The wisdom here of Pope Leo the XIII on the Bible exceeds too many of our Evangelical pastors. It is a more insightful way to understand the scripture with explanatory scope and power back in the nineteenth century.

In the end, Christian faith, saving faith, is in a person, Jesus Christ. Only He personifies the faith because only He has the words of eternal life. Peter said, "Lord, to whom shall we go? You have the words of eternal life" (John 6:68).

---

315. Pope Leo XIII, *Providentissimus Deus* 18 (Encyclical 1893).

Yet, Peter had the Old Testament scriptures, including the book of Genesis. Peter's inspired words were not a reference to biblical authority but to the personal authority of Jesus that we proclaim:

> That which was from the beginning, which we have *heard*, which we have *seen* with our eyes, which we have looked at and our hands have *touched*— this we proclaim concerning the Word of life. The life appeared; we have seen it and testify to it, and we proclaim to you the eternal life, *which was with the Father and has appeared to us.* We proclaim to you what we have seen and heard, so that you also may have fellowship with us. And our fellowship is with the Father and with his Son, Jesus Christ. (1 John 1:1-3)

Note the sensory experiences with Christ: heard, seen, and touched. The incarnation makes possible *"fellowship with the Father and with His Son,"* symbolized by the seventh day of Creation.

Jesus is the Word of Life (1 John 1:1–3): "To whom or what shall we go?"

A few words on a single point anywhere in the Bible is all that is necessary for some to label someone else as a false teacher, though there is agreement on everything else. It is a way for some pastors to gain authority over others by misdirecting biblical authority toward themselves. That is not biblical authority. It is the authority of words backed up by a dictionary projected onto a tradition. Some of these leaders steal sheep from one flock to another. They use the Bible to judge each other because they believe God will use the Bible to judge the world. They have taken it upon themselves to start the judgment early.

God is not a Christian. He does not read His Bible daily or post scriptures on a refrigerator. Acts 17:31 says Christ and his saints will judge with *justice*. Judging does not mean quoting scripture or looking up verses in Genesis or elsewhere to condemn or justify. We should not assume that the Bible contains all the authority of a Messianic "Justice Department," and all we have to do is read it *as written.* That is not an authoritative view of God, the Word, and the mission.

"Authority" is exercised in two ways:

1. As a right to command others.

2. Citing recognized sources or standards, such as textbooks, law, or a specialist in a field, in defense of an opinion or action: *credibility.*

The primary difference between the two is that the first is hierarchical. The second way concerns credibility, i.e., a qualified opinion or a recognized standard.

Christians use the Bible as an authority in both ways. When Christians appeal to the Bible's authority, they usually mean its inherent right as inspired scripture to command belief and adherence. In many traditions, the Bible is either the infallible or the inerrant Word of God. Every Christian tradition accepts the Bible as credible and authentic; otherwise, we are not dealing with Christians in any historical sense. Therefore, the Bible acts as a rule for Christians. We know that overstated rules can lead to authoritarianism, which is the abuse of or preoccupation with authority and is a means to an end, also called legalism.

Far less of the Bible expresses this kind of hierarchical authority considering the primary genres of Scripture: narrative or story, law and prescription, psalter or worship, wisdom literature, mystical experience as in visions and prophetic utterances, history, Roman biography or gospels, letters, sermons, apocalyptic, and others. Some people have treated all scripture as if its law. It is not. Most laws in scripture applied to national life in Israel. All its genres have one overriding direction: God's self-disclosure culminating in the Incarnation.

Defining the Bible in authoritarian terms is legalism. It is the "*if-the-Bible-says-it-you-better-believe-it*" warning. It is better to say, "If the Bible says it, then take it to heart, but remember, you may not understand it very well." The Bible is a gift, not a curse like the law could be: "Christ redeemed us from the curse of the law by becoming a curse for us, for it is written: 'Cursed is everyone who is hung on a pole'" (Galatians 3:13). That is the only curse the new Adam brought to the new covenant.

It should be a lesson for all Christians that the Law no longer carries the kind of authority it once had, most notably for the Jews. It is strange to treat Genesis legalistically—remember Henry Morris' rant: "Christians who flirt with less-than-literal readings of [Genesis] are also flirting with theological disaster. [Christians must] either...believe God's Word all the way or not at all."[316]

It is safe to say that God will not judge the world this way.

Many Christians accept biblical teachings without question. This sense of authority is subjective, and not everyone among Christians accepts the Bible without *any* question. Christians want (or should want) some assurance that the Bible is credible if they give it a healthy authority in their lives. The question is, "In what sense is the Bible authoritative in our lives?"

Opinions vary.

Claiming the Bible is authoritative because scripture says so will not do since the average person knows this is begging the question or arguing in a circle. Todd Beall argues that God superintended or directed the words of scripture when he writes, *"First and foremost, the Bible claims to be the authoritative Word of God. This means that God superintended and directed what was to be written."*[317]

---

316. Henry M. Morris, *The Origin and History of the Earth* (2000), pp. 229–231.

317. Todd Beall, *Coming to Grips with Genesis*, page 142.

Beall loses credibility because he begs the question. That is, he argues that the Bible is authoritative because the Bible says it is authoritative. The argument looks like this:

1. If the Bible claims to be the authoritative word of God, it therefore is.

2. The Bible claims to be the authoritative word of God.

3. Therefore, the Bible is the authoritative word of God.

Premise 1 is false. The Bible may be God's authoritative word, but it is not by virtue of one of its authors making a claim, especially since none of the authors knew what the Bible canon would be. When the Bible refers to "the word" or "Word of God," the meaning depends on the context (see (Matthew 4:4,7,10, John 1:1-3,14, Acts 6:7, Hebrews 1:3). Equivocations in interpreting the phrase abound. Canonization was hundreds of years in the future. Premise 2: Can the Bible claim to be the authoritative Word of God without a canon?[318]

Most Christians quote verses such as John 10:35, "the scripture cannot be broken" (meaning "set aside" or dismissed). That cannot refer to the Old Testament, the Old Testament's religion, or the old covenant prescriptions since Jesus ended (set aside) most of them. The Jews themselves have abandoned the sacrificial system and all the temple services. John 10:35 refers to the specific words God Himself spoke, "I said, 'You are gods. You are all sons of the Most High.'" The entire Hebrew canon, which was not complete or fully accepted as we have it today, could not be the referent.

On 2 Timothy 3:16, "All scripture is God-breathed" should be "All writing *that is* God-breathed is profitable, etc." (see discussion in chapter 16, subheading **"Current Presumptions"**). Additionally, those references are to the Hebrew Bible. The New Testament developed much later. *The ultimate authority in the New Testament is not scripture; it is Christ. Oddly, such a statement is threatening to some Christians. The Bible's considerable authority must be held in perspective to the person of Christ. How can one do that thinking God actually wrote the Bible?*

Beall's conclusion in his argument above, namely, "the Bible is the authoritative word of God," does not follow Premise 2. The point is that arguing

---

318. The Old Testament canon was completed around AD 90–100: See L. M. McDonald, J. A. Sanders, *Introduction: The Canon Debate* (Hendrickson Publishers, 2002), p. 4. The New Testament canon evolved over several centuries. "The first Council that accepted the present Catholic canon (the Council of Trent of 1546) may have been the Synod of Hippo Regius, held in North Africa in 393. A brief summary was read and accepted by the Council of Carthage (397) and also the Council of Carthage (419). These Councils took place under the authority of St. Augustine (354–430), who regarded the canon as already closed." However, debate and changes were to continue through the Reformation period: See *Wikipedia* article "Biblical Canon."

in a circle to establish an exclusive distinctive is disqualifying. Would God be the author of a fallacy? Most people know that asserting biblical authority is unsuitable for evangelizing unbelievers. Unbelievers must first believe God exists to take the Bible seriously and accept that Jesus was who he said he was. Somewhere in that process, a person can honestly assess the scriptures to inform their faith in God. Their faith does not begin or end with accepting the Bible; it begins with meeting Jesus.

The Bible points us to Jesus, but we meet him in our conscience.

In a parable about the word, Jesus said, "But the seed falling on good soil refers to someone who *hears the word and understands it*. This is the one who produces a crop, yielding a hundred, sixty or thirty times what was sown" (Matthew 13:23). Others heard the word and received it with joy but were shallow in understanding. They fell away. *Therefore, understanding begins God's work in us.* "*For we are God's handiwork, created in Christ Jesus to do good works*, which God prepared in advance for us to do" (Ephesians 2:10). *God's redemptive work began before the Bible in the life of Noah and especially Abraham. The Bible does not produce the "crop." God does.*

Many Christians justify the Bible's authority by appealing to its credibility—the second definition of authority. They attempt to do so rationally and with common sense where possible. By rationally, I do not mean scientifically, since the Bible is not a science book; it just isn't. Instead, they approach the Bible with attention to scholarship, criteria of authenticity, as well as reverence, depending on one's ability and opportunity to learn.[319] They approach the Bible with even-handedness and a sense of personal responsibility to understand. They hope to dialogue with unbelievers open to the Gospel and the existence of the God of scripture. Both Jesus and Paul made a point to reason with people.

This second view of authority includes faith in that it *believes* the Bible has a rational basis for its teachings and seeks it out. Indeed, any use of reason in any discipline demonstrates one's faith in reason's reliability. Nonetheless, this second view of authority is more objective since it *seeks* an open and intellectually honest approach, namely to verify, as much as possible, the *credibility* of the Bible. That is no easy task, and there will be mistakes along the way.

Nonetheless, it is the best way forward in seeking biblical understanding. This idea is similar to Anselm and Aquinas's scholasticism, whose motto was "*faith seeking understanding.*" Faith should give one the confidence to seek and find sound reasons for their beliefs. Avoiding critical analysis is not faith; it is what it sounds like—*avoidance.*

---

319. By opportunity, I mean the freedom to study the Bible seriously for several years. Most people do not have the luxury of time. Consequently, most Christians depend on others (teachers and pastors) and will read scripture more for devotional reasons, which also has its place in Church life.

Faith and reason are not like matter and antimatter; they don't annihilate each other, nor are they like oil and water but work together. Faith or trust comes from experiencing God, and reason comes from a mastery of the arguments for God. The cumulative case made with experience and argument lends credibility to God's existence. Each has some slight weight, but together, they are weighty.

Sound Christian faith is never absent of reason but rather a belief that the existence of God is more plausible than not. Faith and reason are more like electrons and protons orbiting a nucleus. In this case, the nucleus is the Word—the Incarnate Christ. Christians operating out of one concept of authority or another can and do clash. There is a spectrum of opinions on biblical authority in the world, with absolute authority on one end, no authority on the other, and various levels of credibility in between. Inanimate objects do not have authority—not literally, that is. Only persons have authority.[320]

When biblical authors speak of supreme or final authority, it is about God or the person of Jesus. Appeals to authority by biblical authors usually give reasons behind those appeals. We may not identify with those reasons. Nonetheless, they are not arbitrary.[321]

Books are inanimate objects; their authority resides in their authors and the interpreter's skill that may reference them. That is true for any book or document. The authority of writers and interpreters naturally varies. Ask yourself, "Which authors have greater authority: Moses or Amos; Isaiah, Jeremiah, and Ezekiel; or Zechariah, Zephaniah, and Habakkuk; John and Paul or James and Jude? Just ask yourself which Bible books we could get by without and which are indispensable? For example, how critical is Paul's letter to Philemon compared to Timothy's letters or the epistles to the Romans or Ephesians?[322]

My point is only that the books of the Bible vary widely in their impact on Church life and Christian thought. Martin Luther thought very little of James's letter at one time, calling it "an epistle of straw." Others say James provides a corrective for antinomianism that overstates Paul's concept of law and grace.

---

320. The concept of sovereignty in Constitutional Law is similar in principle. In the first Supreme Court decision of 1783 by Justice James Wilson wrote, "In the Constitution of the United States, the term *sovereign*, is totally unknown. Rather, Wilson characterized the individual free man as an original sovereign. The states were mere aggregations of individuals: a collection of original sovereigns... The sovereign, when traced to his source, must be found in the [individual]." See Randy E. Barnett, Josh Blackman, Wolters Kluwer, *An Introduction to Constitutional Law: 100 Supreme Court Cases Everyone Should Know* (New York, 2020), p. 3. The Bible is a collection of books by free and authoritative authors. The authority of the whole of scripture comes partly from the authority vested in the individual parts as well as divine authority.

321. Goldingay, *Models of Scripture*, p. 94.

322. Personally, I think the letter to Philemon is extraordinary.

In the hands of the novice, the Bible has little authority. Consider that a book is inanimate. It needs a person to interpret it, without which it cannot contribute anything. But when you hear an insightful and knowledgeable interpreter illuminate the Scriptures in a way that clarifies matters that have always puzzled you, the power of the interpreter *and* the author resonate. That is likely the Holy Spirit at work.

Authority ultimately resides in persons.

Since we tend to use language loosely in everyday conversation, the time comes when we must clearly define common phrases like "biblical authority" to avoid being misled, not that biblical authority itself is misleading. In common usage, biblical authority is an umbrella term for Old and New Testament prescriptions. In a serious study, it becomes necessary to define our terms precisely and understand the unique way individual authors contribute to biblical authority and what level of authority their work has in the Church's life and work.

In Catholicism, Ecclesiastical leadership is the overriding authority. Church authority is primarily in the papacy—an ecclesiastical system governed by the bishop of Rome, the pope. All ecclesiastics represent the pope, the Vicar of Christ, the supreme leader of the Church on the earth—a rather heady authority.

It is more precise to say that authority is vested in persons or authors than in books. We casually give credit to the book, but we mean the author. That is a critical distinction. Biblical authors are authoritative. Their biography sheds light on their work. That is why scholars constantly refer to authorship, even when unsure of the author. They can profile an unknown author by a work's unique content.

They seek to match the author to the document. An author's works reflect who they were in life. Books cannot make decisions; they do not draw conclusions; they cannot make demands; only *authors do these things. The rhetoric of fundamentalists denies this.*

Fundamentalists refer to the Bible almost as if it's a person who authored itself or a written record of God's actual voice. Yet, they strenuously object when scholars suggest that the author of John's Gospel may not have been the Apostle John (one of many such possibilities). *Why? Because suggesting another author weakens its authority.* The failure to make proper distinctions like where the authority lies leads to cognitive dissonance like "God wrote the Bible but don't mess with the 'right' human authors." If God wrote the Bible or "superintended every word," the human author should not matter. We value the human author because he counts; we trust him. God's choice of who to inspire identifies an author with the credibility to do the writing. If the words were not their own, there was no need for credibility.

In Protestant theology, no single tradition on biblical interpretation has authority over another. There is the freedom to disagree or *protest* as many do, perhaps too many. Where it counts, disagreement is necessary.[323] The premise of Protestantism is the freedom to protest based on conscience. Consequently, there are many denominations and growing, for good or ill.

So, how credible are biblical authors? Only they can have authority on their life situations and their understanding of the God they experienced. *When biblical authors speak of God and events, it can only be on terms they can comprehend through their experiences. They are reliable for their purposes even if incidental references like how nature works in the microscopic and telescopic worlds were unknowable. Therefore, because those worlds are unrelated to the Bible's purposes—God's self-disclosure, His plan in the Incarnation and its implications—primitive "scientific" and cultural landscapes must not be divine revelations.*

Not all of God's words or the words from others in the Bible are a divine revelation, e.g., "You are a stiffnecked people;" or "Jacob loved Rachel." The first was already clear to the reader and not divine revelation though spoken by God; the second is a simple observation from the author or just a known fact central to the story.

Authors shared their experiences as messengers and witnesses for God to a particular generation at a specific time and place. Their authority does not go far beyond that. They are authoritative and credible about how *they* experienced God as witnesses in a trial. They imparted wisdom and vision inspired by God. Their view of the universe accurately stated how *they* perceived it, not how *all people* should perceive it. The purposes of scripture do not lie in subordinate places that simply supply the *context* for a revelation and not necessarily the *content* of a revelation. Biblical revelation is decidedly not a scientific explanation of the sky and earth.

God allowed authors freedom of conscience too. Each biblical author has authority or *credibility* all their own. That is why conservatives want to maintain that Moses wrote the entire Pentateuch, Solomon wrote Proverbs, or the Apostle John wrote Revelation. We all admit the particular human author matters. But matters for what? Credibility. Yet, no specific human would matter if all the words were God's or God superintended each word. In that case, the text would remain the same if a child wrote it.

Keith Ward writes:

Christians can accept the Bible as a record of...human discernments of God, gradually being developed within a community of worship and prayer that culminates in a disclosure of God in the person of Jesus. *We should trust the Bible because it points us to Christ*, and Christ is known in

---

323. As I write, it appears the United Methodist Church will not remain "united" because of irreconcilable differences on same-sex issues. The wide diversity within the denomination was impressive until the unity collapsed, which likely began years ago.

the community of the Church as the living presence and power of God, which enters into and transforms our lives.

Here is where the Bible is most authoritative and worthy of our trust. Ward continues:

> Christ becomes the test of biblical truth. If we bear that firmly in mind, we can say that the formation of the Bible is inspired by God, in that *God gradually led human minds* to new perceptions that were unknown to them, to lead to the culminating revelation of God in Jesus Christ.[324]

Note the words *"Christ becomes the test of biblical truth."* Christ is the living Word. The Gospel is the Word proclaimed. No Christian should confuse this with anything like the age of the earth or an impersonal abstraction like "biblical authority." Yet YErs say a literal Genesis is a test of biblical authority, and to think otherwise is calling God a liar.

We can see that knowledge of God and the things of God grew through the pages of the Bible, especially from the close of the Old Testament period through the New Testament. Ward continues:

> *If there was [nothing lacking anywhere] in the Bible, it could not point to a greater fulfilment in Christ.* If there were no diversity in the Bible, it would not represent the richness and variety of human encounters with God in Christ. *If there were no development in the Bible, Jesus could not be seen as a new and decisive revelation of God.* If there were no truth in the Bible, we would not know what Jesus was and taught.[325] (emphasis mine)

Hebrews 8:6–7 confirms Ward's point on this:

> But in fact, the ministry Jesus has received is as superior to [the OT priesthood] as the covenant of which he is mediator is superior to the old one since the new covenant is established on *better promises. For if there had been nothing wrong with that first covenant, no place would have been sought for another.* (emphasis mine)

Ward eloquently states, "It is through the Bible, as it is understood in the believing community of the Church, that we come to a living consciousness of God through Christ. Because of that, the Bible has an irreplaceable authority for the Church." Here is the point to this entire line of reasoning as Ward concludes:

> Christ stands over the Bible as the living Spirit stands over the written law, and he provides the standard by which each stage of biblical revelation is to be allocated to its proper place in the long and checkered

---

324. Keith Ward, *The Word of God: The Bible after Modern Scholarship* (SPCK London, 2010), p. 41.

325. Ibid.

history of the reception of [God's] self-disclosure by the prophets of the Hebrews.[326]

It is not possible to overstate the importance and centrality of Christ, who is the divine Logos, and *The* Word. Authority always resides in a person. "Biblical authority" is no different. It can only refer to the credibility of human authors who received inspiration to write. They are the witnesses preserved for us. The Gospel is the word today and should not share the limelight or take a back seat to tradition or nonessential distinctives. YErs project less the authority of *the Word* than they do the *authority of words*.

In such hands, the Bible loses authority, and there is no hiding behind that.

---

326. Ibid.

22.
NO INTERPRETING ALLOWED

[Many] Christians...profess to believe the Bible, [but] they fail to accept Genesis 1–2 *as written*. [They tell themselves] one can accept the rest of the Bible as written yet reject the doctrine of a recent six-day creation. Unfortunately, accepting an old earth logically undermines the *entire* Bible.[327]
—Jake Hebert PhD

No one takes the *entire* Bible "as written," not even Jake Herbert, Ph.D. The notion that accepting an old earth "logically undermines the entire Bible" is itself illogical. Who knows what *"logically undermines the entire Bible"* means.

Slogans attempt to persuade people when repeating them as mantras, while the concepts behind them are often expressionistic. In reality, an older earth undermines the entire YEC platform and nothing else. I suppose if one's religious center revolves around a six-thousand-year-old universe, any threat to that would feel like undermining everything you hold dear.

YErs assure us that we can believe in an old earth and still be Christian. Well, thank you very much. How can you believe in something that "logically undermines the *entire* Bible" and be a Christian? That notion *does* undermine the Bible. We marginalize the Bible if we undercut it "entirely" yet claim to be a Christian. Just how consequential is the Bible under those YE circumstances?

Many YErs not only believe the Bible is the *Word* of God, they think it is the *words of God,* every one of them. Consequently, YErs claim to read the Bible *"as written."* To many YErs, this "as written" slogan means something like reading the written word, at face value, according to the "plain reading" of the text *without interpreting it.* But all words are symbols and need interpreting. Every translated word adds a new layer of interpretation.

It gets more complicated with Jesus, whose Aramaic was translated into the Koine Greek of the New Testament and then translated into English. We are interpreting an interpretation of an interpretation. Even if one could read the original words in Hebrew and Greek, interpreting them is unavoidable. All words symbolize their referent, as numbers symbolize quantities. Reading is interpreting; we either read poorly or more or less well. Even so, the message can get through.

So what exactly do YErs mean by "as written?"

Do they mean as written in the original text? Do they mean the same thing as those who read the US Constitution "as written?" Not to be confused with

---

327. Jake Hebert PhD, *Genesis Compromise Unravels the Bible* (2016), from the Institute of Creation Research (ICR) website.

originalists concerned with the Constitution's original intent. YErs are not orig-inalists; they are textualists with strict adherence to the text that pushes toward literalism. Unlike the Bible, we have the original version of the Constitution *as it was written*. We do not have the original scriptures. Do YEs mean *as written* in later copies or manuscripts of scripture or *as written* in their favorite translation of a particular manuscript, which is merely a personal preference?

Perhaps by "as written," YErs mean *literal,* while "not as written" means *figurative*. If so, why not use the standard terms "literal" and "figurative?" How do YErs read the following words of Jesus, "You must eat my flesh and drink my blood?" Indeed, *not as written*. Why the insistence on "as written"? Could it be because "figurative" is too interpretive for their favorite verses? Interpreting suggests a choice in determining the meaning. "As written" appears to cloak interpreting. It implies a single choice, which means no choice since real choice requires at least two. Fundamentalists believe one is only to read the text in its ordinary and prima facial meaning: there's no interpreting allowed.

YE apologist Todd Beall asks a revealing question: "Should [a Christian] develop...an apologetic system *evidentially* by human reasoning, and then move to special revelation or *presuppositionally* starting from special revelation?"[328]

YErs adopt an apologetic similar to *presuppositionalism.* Presuppositionalism inherently begs the question, which assumes something is true in order to prove it. The primary presuppositions are the existence of God and the infallibility or inerrancy of the Bible. For Christian presuppositional-ists, the content of scripture serves as the ultimate set of presuppositions.

YE apologists regard not just the Bible but their interpretations of the Bible as *axioms*. Most importantly, this tactic means that the YE interpretation of Genesis 1 needs no defense. For YErs, their opinions are self-evident truths. That questions how much objective evidence and reasoning go into their unique distinctives. Here is an example of this YE philosophical position:

> When explaining their beliefs, Christians often feel they must first prove the Bible or prove the existence of God. This approach reveals that they do not yet understand the Bible's approach, known as *presuppositional apologetics*. If we start off believing the Bible is the Word of God (2 Timothy 3:16; Psalm 18:30; Proverbs 30:5), then *we use it as our axiom.* An axiom (often used in logic) is a proposition *that is not susceptible to proof or disproof; its truth is assumed.* The Bible takes this stance, assuming God's existence to be true and not something to be proven (Genesis 1:1; Exodus 3:14; Revelation 1:8).[329]

---

328. See *Coming to Grips with Genesis,* specifically the essay by Todd Beall. This view is called *Presuppositionalism* or presuppositional apologetics in contrast to classical apologetics and evidential apologetics.

329. David Wright, "What Is 'Presuppositional' Apologetics?" October 1, 2007, Last featured February 7, 2010, on AiG website.

An *axiom* in logic is self-evident; presuppositions are not self-evidently true but supposedly so. The proof of an axiom is in its own statement, not that no proof exists. Examples of such axioms are A = A and A ≠ negative A. An example of A = A is "all bachelors are unmarried men," which is the same as saying unmarried men are unmarried men since all bachelors are unmarried men; thus, A = A. Axioms are universally valid. YEC is not. The target for apologetics is the unbeliever or the believer who cannot cope with attacks on their faith (1 Peter 3:15).

Obviously, creating the universe in six days some six thousand years ago is not an axiom. They are opinions from debatable interpretations of rather obscure language about the primordial past. These are hardly the ingredients for axiom, nor are they self-evident. They are merely interpretive claims of YEC masquerading as axioms, which is question-begging. Of course, biblical authors assumed the existence of God. Everybody did.

Some apologetic questions in Genesis were "Who was the supreme God?" and "How many are there?" Every religion had its pantheon. That was the paradigm. Additionally, biblical authors who already believed Yahweh was God wrote to the covenant people. Still, it took many years of convincing with spectacular miracles that helped establish that Yahweh is God alone. Heroes in the Bible found themselves repeatedly proving Yahweh when challenged by unbelievers.

For example, Elijah uses a creative apologetic long after entering the Promised Land. He asked Yahweh for some unusual miracles to prove He is God and not Baal, the Canaanite deity. A popular Baal cult in Israel's northern kingdom significantly outnumbered Yahweh worship (see 1 Kings 18:19–40). The apologetic Elijah used was hardly *presuppositional*. Instead, he employed miracle after miracle, even the absurd miracle like *setting water on fire*. Upon convincing 400 prophets of Baal, Elijah promptly rested his case by having them executed.

Elijah was oblivious to presuppositionalism.

Suppose you are involved in the discipline of classical apologetics. You understand that it combines Christian theology, natural theology, and the *tools* of philosophy to present a rational defense for the Christian faith *to unbelievers* (see 1 Peter 3:15). It can go where the evidence leads if done correctly instead of the YEC approach of going where their presuppositions lead.

The YE apologetic begins by claiming their conclusions are axioms and looking for evidence supporting them. But if their conclusions are axioms, there would be no need for evidence. And what would prevent other creationists from adopting the same apologetic, creating a stand-off? They would then fight it out by making a case for the "best axioms," which is contradictory since classical apologists know axioms are true. This sort of presuppositionalism is more muddied thought from YErs. Apologetics means making a reasoned defense, not asserting axioms where they don't exist.

Furthermore, the claim to presuppositionalism is an admission that YErs have not made their case with a reasonable defense; if they could, they would, instead of asserting that they don't have to. We have seen that thus far, YErs have not made their case. Their "settled theology" is worse than the "settled science" they condemn. Reasoning itself is unnecessary and considered deceptive to overzealous fundamentalists. Is that a model for investigating and arriving at the truth when reasoning is the faculty for doing so? Or is it a model for preserving a private distinctive aimed at the choir?

Ideally, Christian apologists draw inferences to the best explanation of existing sources of evidence on the overwhelming number of matters that are not self-evident in Scripture. This interpretive method has never been rejected in Church history. Theologians and philosophers also rely on deductive arguments for a disciplined treatment of concepts. The quality of work depends on one's mastery of available tools, as in any discipline.

YErs like Beall begin with what he calls presuppositions, but what are really conclusions. What is the difference? Conclusions result from reasoning, usually coming at the end of an argument or train of thought. Presuppositions are assumptions before a case begins and before argumentation. Assumptions alone are not a defense, which means they are not apologetics by themselves.[330]

On one side, classical apologetics draws conclusions with all the tools available to biblical interpretation, philosophy, and science, seeking a sound train of thought. On the other hand, YEC accepts their conclusions from the literature based on the literal meaning of words. They claim those words are noninterpretive, yet they build a train of thought on them. A literal view *is* an act of interpreting.

It is unclear how one interprets Genesis literally or arrives at young earthism from the Bible absent all reason. The Bible nowhere tells us the age of the earth, so YEC strings scriptures together, making connections in an elaborate attempt to date the universe. Since the Bible is not interested in dating the earth or universe, YErs have to string many verses together to draw their conclusions, which is reasoning. It may be flawed reasoning, but it is reasoning. How can one understand special revelation without reasoning? Reasoning is a tool or *faculty* of the mind for thinking clearly and arriving at the truth; it is not a presupposition or axiom.

Beall's simple argument appears to be this:

1. Apologetics can begin with *either* reasoning or special revelation.

2. Apologetics should *not* begin with reasoning.

---

330. YE evangelists do attempt to convert nonbelievers but their primary audience, where they are much more likely to gain followers, is other Christians. This is clearly not Christian evangelism but YE evangelism with a YE gospel.

3. Therefore, an apologetic should begin with special revelation.

Beall begins with this reasoning to say we should *not* start with reasoning. Yet he *concludes* that we can and indeed must receive special revelation without "human reason." The fact is that "concluding" is the result of reasoning. He uses the word *human* as in "human reasoning," in a pejorative sense as if another kind of reasoning is available to us.[331]

Some fundamentalists adopt the *secular view* that reason and faith are either in tension or incompatible. On the contrary, historical Christianity says the two are harmonious and essential to human nature. Faith continues where reason has run its course. Reason cannot "prove" what is beyond itself; however, things we cannot know, we can believe, disbelieve, or neither, which are exercises in cognitive choice.[332]

Does life emerge from non-life? The theory of *abiogenesis* is the creation of organic molecules by forces other than living organisms, which may have led to the origin of life. It is "chemical evolution." There is no natural selection or random mutations with abiogenesis, only chemical reactions. Things are not looking good for that theory. Without God, one must *believe* this non-sentient planet could give rise to so much sentience all by itself. A multiverse is an object of faith in science because physicists know there is no empirical evidence possible for a multiverse. The theoretical physicist Sabine Hossenfelder says, "This does not mean the multiverse cannot exist," but that *"science does not tell us anything about universes we cannot observe; therefore, claiming that they exist is not science... Do not confuse the multiverse with science because it is not."* Another universe outside our own is unobservable because the laws of its physics are separated from ours by spacelessness, timelessness, and without matter and energy between universes, meaning we have no sensory apparatus to reach it. As Hossenfelder says, "That is not to say the multiverse does not exist." But only that embracing it is a matter of faith, at least as much as believing in God.[333]

---

331. Human reason is not a substitute for so-called "divine reason." Reason is a process for arriving at truth. God does not "arrive" at the truth. He is truth and the absolute source of it. Humans have no choice but to use their God-given faculties to *arrive* at the truth. Special revelation is no exception to this.

332. Faith merely means belief and/or trust. Disbelief is the other side of the two sided coin we call "faith." Both belief and disbelief imply what is to the contrary. If one believes Jesus is the unique Son of God, then they do not believe Muhammed is his messenger. The reverse is also true: Muhammed cannot be God's messenger if Jesus is the unique son of God. In other words, "beliefs" imply "counter beliefs" and vice-versa.

333. Sabine Hossenfelder, "Why the Multiverse is Religion, not Science," July 9, 2019, YouTube. This does not mean the multiverse cannot exist but that "science does not tell us anything about universes we cannot observe, therefore, claiming that they exist is not science... Do not confuse the multiverse with science because it is not." Sabine Hossenfelder (born 18 September 1976) is a German author and theoretical physicist who researches quantum gravity. She is a research fellow at the Frankfurt Institute for Advanced Studies.

The Nobel Laureate, Roger Penrose, says the multiverse is not even a theory but a mere "collection of ideas."[334] But that does not prevent people from having faith in it. Personally, I *hope* a multiverse exists though there is no evidence to believe it. Christian faith requires some evidence that there are good reasons to believe. Unlike faith, *hope* does not require evidence. Another Nobel Laureate, Stephen Weinberg, seemed to embarrass Richard Dawkins by relegating the multiverse to speculation. Weinberg added that no one has "constructed a theory" that might show the multiverse is "mathematically realized."[335]

Christians believe saving faith is God-given; so is reason. The relationship between faith and reason is not too different from the relationship between the "two books"—the "book" of nature and the book of scripture. Faith accepts that God made the world and made it intelligible so that rational beings can discover things about it and its Creator. That is why Christians founded the project of modern science. They had *faith* that the universe was *rational*. Reason is the only intrinsic faculty we possess to understand the universe and special revelation to the extent possible. Faith does not explain or prove special revelation. Instead, faith leads to *accepting* revelation. Faith, at some point, is necessary for a rational creature that is not all-knowing or all-powerful.

True, our powers of reason are imperfect, but so is everything else about us, including our faith and ability to comprehend or simply identify special revelation. Sound reasoning ensures fewer mistakes than presuppositionalism; it does not eliminate errors. Nothing does. It is also true that reason alone does not bring the devotion that faith brings. Nevertheless, reason can aid faith by helping us determine what *deserves* our devotion.

One of Jesus's names is Reason—*Logos*. Logos is one of the richest words in any language. Peter Kreeft, Professor Emeritus at Boston College, wrote recently:

> [Logos] has at least three fundamental meanings: (1) essence, nature, structure, meaning, *order*, intelligibility, formula, form, law, or cause (real reason); (2) mind, *thought*, truth, intelligence, understanding, *reason, knowledge, science, or explanation*; and (3) word, speech, language, discourse, communication, revelation."[336]

Quite a word!

Notice that (1) is metaphysical, (2) is epistemological, and (3) is linguistic. Logos literally means *reasoned speech*. But it often includes intelligibility,

---

334. See YouTube clip "Roger Penrose debunks M-theory on Christian Radio," September 29, 2010.

335. See YouTube clip, "Atheist's Blind Faith—Richard Dawkins and Stephen Weinberg—God or the Multiverse?" July 2, 2011.

336. Peter Kreeft, *Socrates' Children: The 100 Greatest Philosophers, Volume I: Ancient Philosophers* (St. Augustine Press, South Bend Indiana, 2019), p. 60.

meaning, thought, wisdom, and enlightenment. Christ the Logos is the rationale behind existence. "The true light that gives light to everyone was coming
into the world" (John 1:9). The Logos enlightens the world, including the
world of science (John 1:3–5). Without the Logos present in the cosmos and
communicating to us, we could not comprehend it. So special revelation does
begin and end with Logos (reason).

Special revelation is Logos in communication.

It is popular in some religious circles to denigrate "human" reason as if we
have a choice whether or not to use it. Notice that people criticize reason when
it undermines their cause or interferes with issues that have become inflamed.
Jesus often reasoned with the Pharisees and Sadducees by cross-examining them.
Paul reasoned with the Jews in the synagogues and debated Gentiles and other
Christians as a matter of course. What did they argue? They reasoned back and
forth about *special revelation*—the resurrection of God Incarnate—the Messiah
and what he means for life in this world and the next.

If an argument seems to work, most people will use it; thus, Beall's contradiction when he first reasons that we should not reason first. If YErs were
confident in their case, they would not require opponents to first agree with all
their presuppositions and pretend they are axioms. That is not teaching; it is
indoctrination. No fair-minded or confident person would insist on this.

Doesn't it make more sense that God created us to think well and not do
all our thinking for us? He is like a good father who wants his children to make
wise choices when not looking over their shoulders. Our free will enables us to
cooperate with God and embrace Him in spirit, not merely to do what He says
when He says it and how He says it. God rejects sycophants: just ask Job's three
friends who took up the case for God against Job as yes men. So "The Lord] said
to Eliphaz the Teammate, I am angry with you and your two friends because
you have not spoken the truth about me, as my servant Job has." Respecting God's
person at the expense of justice is a sin.[337]

Free will, which includes thinking for ourselves, is so important that,
given God's mercy, He has allowed indescribable suffering on the principle—
from Job's suffering to that of Jesus. God does not answer Job until Jesus. The
cross and redemption are God's "apologetic" of free will and suffering. Since
God allows the *malady*, He supplies the *remedy*.

The Apostle Paul wrote:

Where there is knowledge, it will pass away... When I was a child, I talked
like a child, I thought like a child, I reasoned like a child. When I became

---

337. Job 42:7-8 continues, "So now take seven bulls and seven rams and go to my servant Job
and sacrifice a burnt offering for yourselves. My servant Job will pray for you, and I will accept his
prayer and not deal with you according to your folly." *Those three friends fought for God against Job
with conventional or (dare I say) fundamentalist theology and they were wrong.*

a man, I put the ways of childhood behind me. For now we see only a reflection as in a mirror; then we shall see face to face. Now I know in part; then I shall know fully, even as I am fully known. (1 Corinthians 13:9–13)

Verse 9 in the Amplified New Testament says, "For our knowledge is fragmentary (incomplete and imperfect), and our prophecy (our teaching) is fragmentary (incomplete and imperfect)."

Paul says in this life, there is no perfect knowledge about God or the Bible or even in the Bible (Paul wrote part of it.), only a perfect God. God is not using force on us, nor does he want mindless obedience. Therefore, reasoning is not just necessary; it is unavoidable. The choice is not between reason and non-reason but between reasoning well or poorly. When Paul became an adult, he reasoned like an adult. He also became skilled through education, training, and preparation. He is one of the more brilliant thinkers in history, yet he only knew in part even under divine inspiration.

It is safe to say God prepared Saul all through his life. Few, if any at the time, could comprehend the finer points of Christianity so quickly—the twelve certainly did not. It took an educated and thoroughly prepared person to develop Christianity's theological and philosophical grounds.

The question for YEC is, why did God not channel all the truths, word for word, that Paul possessed into the heads of the twelve as YErs believe God did to Moses? Why did God not provide the one-to-one correspondence "mind meld" on the twelve to produce the New Testament? God does not seem to do things that way; he does not think like a YEr or anyone else for that matter.

Paul was an exceptionally well-educated scholar, philosopher, theologian, and Rabbi from Tarsus— "no ordinary city" (Acts 21:39). He learned at the feet of Gamaliel, the grandson of Hillel the Great—the two most outstanding scholars in the annals of first-century Judaism. This brilliant man, the chief destroyer of Christianity, came to believe God raised his archenemy, Jesus of Nazareth, from the dead. He claimed to have seen him. The rabbi/philosopher from Tarsus was a fitting choice to meet the Greco/Roman world's educated classes, including Rabbinic Judaism's challenges. He was no fundamentalist. The best educated had to take Paul of Tarsus seriously. That made him dangerous.

Paul's unique role turned out to be crucial. The book of Acts preserves a critical conflict in the early Church that illustrates the point. The twelve apostles, particularly Peter and James, the brother of Jesus, did not admit uncircumcised Gentiles into the Church unless they became circumcised according to the Law. As a result, a dispute broke out between Peter, James, and Paul, regarding whether specific biblical prescriptions for religious life applied to Gentiles. You can read about it in Acts 15 and Galatians 2:8–17.

Paul understood the theological implications of Jesus's life, death, resurrection, and ascension. He articulated them in ways the disciples who knew

Jesus could not, though they walked with him before and after his resurrection. Paul was not a layman; nothing against laypeople—God chose them twelve to one. Real scholars are rare, yet many fundamentalists behave as if they are one or know better than scholars. It is the age-old conflict between ideological schooling and systematic or disciplined education.

Theologians develop Christian doctrine and dogma with reason despite its limits, but we *embrace* doctrines by faith. There is no conflict with this distinction. For example, we consider the doctrine of the Trinity special revelation; yet, at the same time, it is not an *a priori* gift; the Bible does not teach it explicitly. Philosophical reasoning and terminology gave the three Cappadocians: Basil the Great, Gregory of Nyssa, and Gregory of Nazianzus of the fourth century AD, the Trinitarian language we possess today—one God in three "persons" (Gk. *hypostases*).[338] Add to that the development of the two natures of Christ, free will, and other issues partly or ambiguously found in scripture that required exceptional skill from some of the most brilliant theologians to develop.[339]

Since we only see in part, some Christian doctrines are, to some extent, fluid, which is one reason why we have so many denominations. Christian doctrines develop through both revelation and human reasoning. It could not be any other way. What we call special revelation seldom comes in neat and complete packages. The history of Christian thought is just that: *thought*—a lot of thinking and rethinking over centuries of construction and reconstruction.

The classic case is the Trinity; it was both a philosophical and theological concept drawn from hints found in Scripture. Those hints require reasoning to comprehend and faith to believe. Contrary to popular belief, the Bible does not teach the Trinity *doctrine*. While there are *three* in scripture (Father, Son, and

---

338. See Allister McGrath, *Historical Theology* (Oxford: Blackwell Publishers, 1998), pp. 22–66. Greek philosophers and intellectuals challenged the early fathers in the second and third centuries regarding the Christian arguments against polytheism; yet the Church asserted three divinities: the Father, Son, and Holy Spirit. The Church had to address the inconsistency for both evangelism and the integrity of Christian thought. The three Cappadocians made major contributions to the definition of the Trinity stated at the Council of Nicaea in 325 and finalized at the First Council of Constantinople in 381. See *Wikipedia* on the "Three Cappadocians." My point is that the Trinity developed over centuries of highly focused and masterful reasoning. Yet, few Christian theologians would deny that the Trinity doctrine is one of the greatest examples of special revelation in Christian thought. In other words, special revelation needs reasoning to be understood.

339. A major confusion on the Trinity is the use of the word *person* (*hypostasis* in Greek). The word *person* in English, as in a living *person*, is a concrete noun. "Hypostasis" is an abstract, highly philosophical term used in Hebrews 1:3, which means something like essence or a basis of reality or ground of being. The difficulty is in translating the term hypostasis into English that has no equivalent upon which the doctrine heavily depends.

Holy Spirit) and *one* God in scripture, there is no "one God in three persons" anywhere in scripture.[340]

The Trinity doctrine is dogma in Christianity, partly because it appears sound theologically but cannot be *proven,* not because we should avoid reason in developing it. Indeed, it did take centuries to reason out, the doctrine that is. We do understand the *doctrine* of the Trinity. We have yet to comprehend the Trinity Himself.

All this is a matter of record. Without reason, we could not recognize what special revelation says, let alone what it means. Accepting special revelation does not absolve anyone from reasoning soundly. Beall's *reason versus revelation* is a false choice.

Reason sets humans apart from beasts. Without reasoning, we could not be the vice-regents on earth as God's imagers (see Genesis 1:27–28). Reason enables us to relate to God. It is a gift of God. What would we use in its place—the blank stare of a lesser primate? It is the lack of sound reasoning that contributes to the SDWC. Undoubtedly, faith and reason are necessary for Christian apologetics from beginning to end.

The lack of critical thought has led to one primary presupposition in YEC: Christian scholars and theologians are *complicit* with atheistic scientists on the age of the earth and threaten to dislodge all the biblical doctrines they hold dear.

It does not faze YErs that their literal interpretation of Genesis happens to be compatible with the atheists' interpretation of Genesis. Many atheists avoid a figurative interpretation of Genesis because they underestimate the sophistication of biblical authors. Atheists are happy to interpret Genesis with the same wooden literalism of YEC. Ideologies make strange bedfellows, indeed. A further irony is that atheists charge all Christianity of preferring blind faith to reason, often fueled by a loud fringe group of fundamentalists.

Hyperbole and Overstatements

Hyperbole and overstatements are figures of speech found throughout the ANE and the Bible. Exaggeration can stir emotions like happiness, romance, inspiration, laughter, anger, sadness, or feigned "barbarism" such as "If your eye offends you, pluck it out." Statements like "forever," "throughout all your generations," and, as we will see, "the whole earth," and "all nations under heaven" must be considered hyperbole.

Jesus famously said, "You must eat my flesh and drink my blood." Some Catholics claim to take those words literally, thus Transubstantiation. At the

---

340. The text of 1 John 5:7-8 is used to claim scriptural proof of the Trinity doctrine. The evidence is decidedly against its authenticity, but is a later gloss. See Bruce Metzger, Textual Commentary, 2nd ed., pp. 647–649.

same time, Catholics insist that Transubstantiation is not *cannibalism*. Those two thoughts contradict. Transubstantiation is not cannibalism, but Jesus's statement cannot be both literal *and* not about cannibalism.

The words "eat my flesh and drink my blood" would promote cannibalism if meant literally. Therefore, even Catholicism takes those words of Jesus figuratively, despite the claim of some Catholics. Nobody can seriously take these words "as written." Augustine said (paraphrasing), "If the scripture promotes barbarism, it must be figurative."

In Acts 2:1, 5, we have a typical allness statement in the Bible. Luke writes, "When the day of Pentecost had come...there were devout Jews *from every nation under heaven* living in Jerusalem" (emphasis mine).

"Every" nation under heaven? Well, not literally.

We know Jews did not live in *every* nation under heaven (the sky). On the surface, it could mean something like "as far as the eye can see" or the known world in a theological sense or the sense it has in Genesis 10. Today, we speak of Montana as "big sky country." Yet the sky is no bigger in Montana than anyone's backyard. *"Every nation under heaven"* is a Hebrew idiom. In early Judaism, "every nation under heaven" refers to the seventy Gentile nations in Genesis 10. They represent the rest of the world in which the Jews interacted. *"Under heaven"* adds hyperbole on top of the nonliteral *allness* statement *"every nation."*

We often use words impressionistically to capture feelings as artists use color and strokes to make impressions on a canvas. Impressionism is an example of information delivered through visual arts and literature too. Note *Webster's Second Edition* on "impressionism:" "[Impressionism is] the depiction (as *in literature* or scene, or emotion, or character) of details intended to achieve a vividness or effectiveness more *by evoking subjective and sensory impressions than by recreating an objective reality*." (emphasis mine)

In that sense, its intention is in the impression it makes and not the exact words it uses or in any attempt to recreate objective reality or, for that matter, a one-to-one correspondence to reality. That is the nature of some forms of literature, especially ancient ones. YEC's obsession with the dictionary definition of words is misplaced.

Montana's sky looks wider, so we say it idiomatically because it feels right. The impression (big sky country) gives you a better sense of what is unique about Montana. Biblical authors were quite familiar with the idea of "impressionism," though they didn't use the term. Some Christians find it hard to accept that most biblical literary styles were common throughout the ANE. Impressionism makes the content less clear for people who want the Bible to be a rulebook that should be easy to understand but without beauty.

We also know that every nation where Jews lived was not in Jerusalem on that day of Pentecost. Luke lists just sixteen countries and territories from Persia in the east to Spain in the west, corresponding to the landmass associated with the table of nations in Genesis 10. These seventy nations *represented* the whole world through seventy ancestral lineages (wherever they may spread), not unlike Adam, who could represent all humankind no matter where the race spread. That is how Judaism understood or referred to the ethnic makeup of the world. This Jewish view of the world can be disturbing to Christians if they believe the Jewish perspective is God's view of the world. But it should be more upsetting to think God has an ANE or Jewish worldview.

Many gentile nations existed by the first century AD in Africa, North and South America, the Far East, Australia, and many other places, including island nations in the Pacific and different oceans unknown when Luke wrote. Again, we have biblical testimony *as written,* which needs significant interpretation to avoid confusing facts with the idiom.

Luke notes that Jews came to Jerusalem from the Gentile nations *in every direction,* as seen from the land of Israel. Perhaps that is what he meant by *"under heaven"* (the sky). It was just an expression, similar to "Jews and Gentiles," which covers everyone in the world no matter where they live, limited only by the user's concept of the world.

For people in first-century Judaism, the whole world was tiny compared to the world we know and could not possibly mean the same thing we mean by the entire *planet.* This is a fact. The Roman historian Livy (first century BC), commenting on the war between Carthage and Rome, states that the stakes were nothing less than "the rule of law over the *whole world and for all time."*[341] The kings of empires such as Assyria, Babylon, Egypt, Persia, and Greece considered themselves kings of the "whole world."[342] Of course, the world was as large or small as their experience informed them. The Bible, an eclectic group of diverse authors, can only reflect this; otherwise, it would not make sense to its original audience.

The words and their dictionary meanings are not the only relevant matter in scripture. The *thoughts* of the author are what his words can only represent. An English translation is two steps away from the words of the author. Ancient thoughts are always, to some extent, buried in the past. We cannot read authors' minds, and the changing world of word meanings shows that identical words uttered centuries or only decades later begs misunderstanding.

A modern example of a radical change in the meaning of a word is *"apocalypse."* This word is from Greek, meaning "to reveal." "Apo," meaning "un" and "calypse," meaning "cover"—combined, it means to uncover or reveal. Yet most English dictionaries say apocalypse means "the end of the world." The dirty little secret is that dictionaries do not simply define words; they show how people *use*

---

341. Livy, *The Punic Wars.*

342. For example, Ashurbanipal wrote that he was "king of the world" on a cuneiform tablet from his library at Nineveh (seventh century BC) found by Henry Layard in 1849.

words. The term *apocalypse* has lost meaning through decades of misuse except in scholarly circles, which is an excellent reason to listen to scholars.

Since the Bible covers centuries of massive change, interpreting it is far more complicated than reading words and looking them up in a lexicon. Cultural and linguistic modifications must be traced, like the variations in pottery art help archeologists identify times and places.

According to G. B. Caird, hyperbole is habitual among Semitic people, ancient and modern. He recounts the experience of T. E. Lawrence, the historical figure portrayed in the cinematic film *Lawrence of Arabia*. Lawrence lived in the Middle East during WWI and was particularly interested in Semitic people, specifically their speech and thought patterns, making a lasting impression on him. He wrote:

> Semites had no halve-tones in their register of vision. They were a people of black and white... They knew only truth and untruth, belief and unbelief, without our [Western] hesitating retinue of finer shades... Their thoughts were at ease only in extremes. They inhabited [exaggeration] by choice...but they never compromised.[343]

Caird comments on this outlook in people of the Middle East: *"It could equally well have been written about the ancient Hebrew."* My ancestors come from that part of the world. Growing up in Michigan has also exposed me to nationals from all over the Middle East. The stark dualism reflected in the Semitic idiom Lawrence and Caird identify is still evident.

The contrast between love and hate, light and darkness, good and evil, truth and falsehood, which are so prominent particularly in the Dead Sea Scrolls and in the writings of the Apostle John, came from their shared cultural background in the tribal Old Testament. One perfect example is the contrast between "love and hate" in scripture. The Israelites used one or the other to express a simple preference, such as "Jacob loved Rachel more than Leah." However, Moses comments on this statement, "When the Lord saw that *Jacob hated Leah,* he opened her womb: but Rachel was barren" (Genesis 29:31).

What do you think? Did Jacob *hate* Leah? Or did he love her less than he loved Rachel? We find the same idiom more than once in Jesus' teachings: "If any man come to me and *hate not* his father, and mother, and wife, and children, and brethren, and sisters, yea, and his own life also, he cannot be my disciple" (Luke 14:26; emphasis mine).

"No man can serve two masters: for either he will *hate the one, and love the other*; or else he will hold to the one, and despise the other" (Matthew 6:24; emphasis mine).

---

343. G. B. Caird, *The Language and Imagery of the Bible* (Westminster Press, Philadelphia, Pennsylvania, 1980), p. 110.

"Anyone who loves his life loses it, and anyone *who hates his life* in this world will keep it unto life eternal" (John 12:25; emphasis mine).

Yet Jesus also said to "love your neighbor as yourself." Something has to give. Idiomatic language like this has caused untold confusion for the casual reader. Hate in the Bible can simply mean to love less by comparison. So what does *as written* mean here in this historical narrative?

Nothing whatsoever.

A more subtle example of hyperbole is Jesus's answer to a comment from Phillip. Phillip said, "Lord, show us the Father, and that will be enough for us" (John 14:8–9). Jesus answered, "Don't you know me, Phillip? Anyone who has seen me has seen the Father. How can you say, 'Show us the Father?' So is Jesus the Father? No.

The Son is not saying he is the Father, though reading it a certain way seems to say that. Jesus likely means the full extent of God's self-revelation is in him. We cannot see God. We get the fullest revelation of the Father in Jesus of Nazareth, who is God's corporeal presence in this universe. Only corporeality is visible in this world. Humans cannot see God, except to the degree they see the Incarnate Son. Of course, we have yet to see the Son fully. The statement, "Anyone who has seen me has seen the Father," is a kind of hyperbole that Jesus makes clear when he adds in verse 10, "Believe that I am in the Father and that the Father is in me." In our glorified state, we may see God in Christ *most* fully.

Notice another allness statement common in the Bible: 2 Chronicles 9:22–23 says, "King Solomon was greater in riches and wisdom than *all the other kings of the earth. All the kings of the earth* sought audience with Solomon to hear the wisdom God had put in his heart."

If this is literal, kings of the Americas, the African continent, Eskimos, China, India, the South Seas, Japan, etc.—came to visit Solomon. Again, *"all the earth"* may refer to the seventy Gentile nations in Genesis 10. That was a theological way of referring to the world. To no small extent, ethnicity was how the ANE saw the world, i.e., tribal.

Hyperbole was characteristic throughout the ANE, especially when praising heroes. Donald Trump engages in hyperbole as a matter of course. Everything is fantastic, the greatest that has ever been *"by far."* "No one has seen anything like (fill in the blank)."

Modern ears bristle at that kind of hyperbole, and it should. Excessive overstatement feels like lying to some people. Of course, it is not lying, strictly speaking, but such language makes it easy to criticize and difficult to defend. Constant overuse of hyperbolic statements diminishes their impact. Today, we tune out such overuse, but not so in ancient times. Such hyperbole makes a person more vulnerable to misunderstanding.

Similarly, if the Bible says it, we want to believe it must be true in every respect and may not notice any hyperbole that our biases may find inappropriate. Some think God would never talk that way or allow biblical authors to write that way. Yet how we believe the authors should write is irrelevant. The point is to understand how the author and readers thought and not just how a dictionary defines their words. Their cultural perspectives fill in when terms and concepts are unclear to us.

Praise language for heroes in ancient times was hardly strict literalism or pure fact. It was not enough to say Solomon was very wise or wiser than other kings in living memory; the way moderns might say it since we believe there is always someone better or wiser. If you know Solomon's story, you realize he made some serious and foolish mistakes. There is no way to measure the full extent of *net wisdom* in one's choices when measured against foolish ones. No doubt, Solomon was exceptional. Let the times of Solomon say it the way *they* said it.

Most YErs are practicing hyperbolists. We saw Henry Morris's "If the earth is old, God has lied to us;" and the musings of Jake Herbert Ph.D. when he wrote, "An old earth *logically undermines the entire Bible.*" There is Ken Ham's "An old earth undermines *every major doctrine* of the Bible." And who can forget Elizabeth Mitchell's frenzy? If the earth is old, "[God] either had a cruel sense of irony or didn't know what he was talking about, or worse, he is a liar."

What is most interesting is that YErs do not seem to recognize any of this as hyperbole.

They believe those statements are literal too. Human language is a funny thing. It means different things to different people and at various times. Not enough people make a clear distinction between *literal* and *figurative.* We cannot always trust the language usage of others for consistency with our use of the same language. People often say, "I know," when they mean "*I believe*" or "I believe" when they actually *know.* This is not a serious issue unless being precise is necessary for the discussion or if a lack of precision creates misunderstandings as it often does. The reality is that people use words inconsistently, and over time, word usage changes.

Consider the modern phrase "In order to form a *more perfect* union" in the US Constitution. Untrained critics who opine on the American founders point out that something "perfect" cannot become *more perfect* (my grammar checker is flagging that phrase now). Supposedly, this phrase in the Constitution was bad English or poor thought. However, the word *perfect* at the time and in the King James Version of the Bible meant "*fully mature*" (a phrase my grammar checker does not flag). Thus, *perfect* at that time did not always carry the absolute meaning it does today, while "maturity" does vary in degrees.[344]

As I write, politicians and the new media in Washington are debating the meaning of "misdemeanors" and "bribery" in the Constitution. Those terms had different usages at the time. Yet, during the first impeachment proceedings against Donald Trump, it was politically expedient to equivocate. At the time, "misdemeanors" in the Constitution were not minor crimes against property or persons as they are today, but high crimes defined in the Constitution as treason or bribery against U.S. sovereignty. It can also be theologically expedient to equivocate on words such as "foundation," "compromise," "day," "the Word of God," "myth," "very good," "perfect," etc.

Here is the thing: The Constitution is a relatively recent and short document written in our language, from our history, early in our cultural development. Unlike the Bible, we have the original Constitution and Declaration of Independence *as they were written*. We have the rough draft from Thomas Jefferson. There are not thousands of variant versions or diverse fragments of the Constitution floating around. We even have commentary on the documents in other types of literature from people at the time, including those who helped influence the founding documents. We know who wrote the founding documents and why. We have a good idea of how the Declaration and Constitution developed and the philosophical grounds for the concepts contained in them through the writings of Aristotle, the Magna Carta, Montesquieu, John Locke, Thomas Hobbes, and Francis Bacon, and the Roman philosopher and statesman, Cicero.

To be a constitutional scholar requires many years of study to master its content with its legal, historical, political, and cultural context. Really? Does a small and comparatively simple document like our Constitution require scholarship and specialists to understand it correctly? Yes, it does.

And there is no end of disagreement over how to interpret it.

Biblical authors began to write over three thousand years ago. Some undoubtedly used older written and oral sources now lost to us. The Bible is a library of ancient documents about varied life experiences from lost cultures that we have only begun to understand. Its subject matter includes theology, law, history, philosophy, poetry, wisdom, military strategy, changing custom and tradition, politics, commerce and trade, dynastic succession and rule, social norms and complexities, technology, engineering, and the massive changes

---

344. The use of *perfect* in the KJV (AD 1611) means mature or complete as in Jesus's words to become perfect as your Father in heaven is perfect, which is unreasonable if perfect is meant in the absolute. This same Jesus said there is only One who is good (Matthew 19:17). Adam and Eve, and the creation may have been perfect in the sense that it was complete with the arrival of humans but not in the absolute sense that we associate with the word *perfect*. Therefore, the use of the term can be misleading.

from the Bronze Ages through the Iron Age to the Greco-Roman Period. What are the *odds* that interpreting the Bible is so easy that anyone can master it simply by reading it?

Eight billion to one!

23.
SCRIPTURES *NOT* AS WRITTEN

> But I am afraid that just as Eve was deceived by the serpent's cunning,
> your minds may somehow be led astray from your sincere
> and pure devotion to Christ.
> —2 Corinthians 11:3

YEC claims that Jesus and Paul take Genesis literally when they quote it for theological support. By that reasoning, Paul's quote above means we are dealing with an actual animal, a talking serpent, and at the same time, it is a spirit named Satan. Both cannot be literal since A ≠ not A. Instead, Paul quotes the story, allowing for its literary form. The apostle does not take the time to explain that the serpent is symbolic, not only because it was unnecessary but because that would likely disrespect his reader's intelligence. It likely never occurred to Paul to explain the symbolism.

The YE community is quick to recruit Jesus as a disciple by quoting Mark 10:6:

> It was because your hearts were hard that Moses wrote you this law, [the Writ of Divorce] Jesus replied. But at the beginning of creation God 'made them male and female. For this reason a man will leave his father and mother and be united to his wife, and the two will become one flesh. So they are no longer two, but one flesh. Therefore what God has joined together, let no one separate.

It is easy to confuse a referent when looking for something other than the point. Of course, any of us can do that; God knows I have. Judge for yourself if YErs take Mark 10:6 out of context when Ken Ham writes, "From this passage, we see that Jesus clearly taught that the Creation was young."

"Jesus clearly taught that the Creation was young"? From this passage? By that reasoning, Paul "clearly" taught that Satan was a real reptile when he wrote, "Eve was deceived by the *serpent's* cunning" (2 Corinthians 11:3). You can see how the YE distinctive causes them to jump on the words "beginning of creation" as if Jesus's point was that God made Adam and Eve at the *beginning of time.* Jesus refers to the creation of the human race at the beginning of the Hebrew Scriptures.

Listen, humans were the point of creation. Everything God created until humans arrived was to establish a home for our flourishing. The beginning of creation ends at humanity's arrival. That is how the author tells it. The author is not interested in YE matters or how long God prepared the ground for our arrival. And because time is not meaningful when applied to God, creation would still be in its beginning stages, no matter how much time elapsed between "Let there be light" and humanity's eventual arrival. The advent of modern humans completed the story of creation and the extent of "the beginning" as Genesis presents it.[345]

Only after God made humans was the Creation called "very good." That singled its completion. We could say that humans were the last thing created at the beginning of this world. That is true, no matter when humanity emerged in the process. In other words, humans arrived at the end of the beginning of the world we know, not at the beginning of time, whether the beginning of time was six days earlier or 13.8 billion years ago.

Furthermore, there is no marriage or divorce without humans, which was the subject. It helps to keep the referents straight. Upon respecting Jesus's point, you can see that the advent of humans was when the subject of divorce and remarriage became *relevant* or even possible. Matthew's account adds some clarity (note the pronouns):

> Some Pharisees...asked, "Is it lawful for a man to divorce his wife for any and every reason?" "Haven't you read," he replied, *"that at the beginning the Creator 'made them male and female,'* ... "Why then," they asked, "did Moses command that a man give his wife a certificate of divorce and send her away?" Jesus replied, *"Moses* permitted *you* to divorce your wives because your hearts were hard. *But it was not this way from the beginning.* (Matthew 19:1–10; emphasis mine)

YErs jump on phrases like "at the beginning" and "from the beginning," assuming they must refer to the beginning of time. That is because they are YErs, which amounts to begging the question. It is beside Jesus's point to claim the phrase refers to the beginning of time. The "beginning" here is that of the human race, i.e., from the start, *"God created them "male and female"* —when divorce and remarriage were first an issue. Therefore, Jesus's reference to "the beginning" has no relevance to God's first act—"Let there be light" or dividing the waters. Instead, Jesus refers to *our beginning,* the beginning of *our* world, that God later called "very good." When humans arrived at the end of creation, marriage and divorce could occur, not before. Jesus says, 'from the *start,* God meant for humans to take mates for life.' It has always been thus.

Notice a similar reference to "the beginning." John 8:44, "You belong to your father, the devil...he was a murderer *from the beginning,* not holding to the truth, for there is no truth in him. When he lies, he speaks his native language, for he is a liar and the father of lies." The level of metaphor in this statement of Jesus is significant: e.g., "your father," "from the beginning," "his native language," and "the father of lies."

Furthermore, Jesus is not saying that the devil murdered anyone in the Garden of Eden, that he has been a pathological liar for six thousand years, that

---

345. The story of creation was complete in a literary sense, but without doubt, the creation of all living things, of stars, planets, galaxies, and other heavenly bodies continue to this day.

lying is his original language, or that he fathered anyone. The devil does not commit murder at the beginning of creation or before that. In this case, "from the beginning" is an expression that simply refers to the devil's beginning.

Lucifer's beginning was before the world's creation and before he became the devil. Iniquity was found in him sometime after his creation, so God changed his name. How much time elapsed between the events that transformed Lucifer's creation into becoming the devil? The devil's *"from the beginning"* had nothing to do with YEC. Likewise, Adam and Eve's origin is the beginning of *their* creation, not the beginning of time, space, and matter/energy. Besides, Satan is a sinner before Adam and Eve; therefore, sin was in the world "from the beginning," so choosing from a Tree of Good *and Evil* could make sense.

Did Paul think a literal serpent deceived Eve or was it a *literary* one? Simply because Paul recalls the passage does not mean the devil is a member of the animal kingdom. The result of Eve's experience with the devil is the apostle's point. But, of course, this is no concern unless we insist on a one-to-one correspondence between words and reality or that Satan was a literal reptile.

Another reference to *the beginning of the world* is Matthew 24:21, which says, "For then there will be great distress, unequaled *from the beginning of the world* until now—and never to be equaled again." If Noah's flood was a global catastrophe and Peter's prediction about universal destruction by fire are facts, then Jesus's words about the tribulation are hyperbole. Here the "beginning of the world" is a sweeping statement as in "the worst ever." YErs literalize any word they think will preserve their most cherished distinctive.

It does violence to the text to force modern YEC into Jesus's mouth.

As Written: When?

YEC says we should take the Bible "as written." But on which version of the Bible, "as written," do YErs depend? The original texts, as written by the authors, do not exist. And the copies and fragments we do have vary.[346] It was within God's power to prevent any variants, but that appears unnecessary to Him. There are thousands of variants if you include all words, sentences, paragraphs, and whole chapters among the manuscripts and fragments. Most variations are minor, but some do change the text's meaning. That should not be news to any Christian.

Nevertheless, the agreement between the thousands of manuscripts, copies, and fragments is remarkable and unprecedented in ancient literature. *It is as if God left enough room for reasonable people to see his hand in transmitting the text while ensuring genuine human participation in the process.*

---

346. It is true that textual criticism seeks to recover the *original text*, but while helpful and crucial at times, this is hardly the same as having the originals.

Most evangelicals believe the New Testament Church claimed their Scriptures were inerrant. The Septuagint was the scripture of choice for the New Testament Church. Yet we know it is full of errors; no doubt, new errors are waiting for discovery. There is a silver lining; we can detect most errors or inconsistencies when comparing the variants. There are verses and whole chapters in today's Bible versions (plural) that were not likely part of the original text. Known examples are the woman taken in adultery in John 8, and the two endings of Mark's gospel (a shorter and longer version) are in dispute. Many smaller and moderate fragments are questionable, even by conservative Evangelicals. The book of Job may be missing parts near the end of the debate with his friends. YErs ask, how can we possibly trust the rest of the Bible if we cannot trust in six literal days?

We manage.

We have always managed. It is likely that marginal notes by copyists eventually made their way into the text of the Bible. The purpose was to "clarify" misunderstandings when word meanings evolve or become obscure or when idioms, names of places, and titles inevitably change. That is the nature of books—we edit them. If copyists believed God wrote every word of Scripture, their changes and additions exceeded their authority. But then what user-friendliness is in our Bible's current form would be compromised. Things get out of hand with literalism.

Some verses in today's Bible were *not* in early manuscripts that first appeared as late as medieval times, which some translators choose to preserve. One example is 1 John 5:7, "For there are three that bear record in heaven, the Father, the Word, and the Holy Ghost: and these three are one."[347]

Furthermore, we cannot reasonably interpret many verses in scripture *"as written"* outside biblical poetry or apocalyptic. We have already seen such verses in the creation account alone:

1. God "speaking" Hebrew at the beginning of time.

2. God needed or even used natural light, i.e., God "saw."

3. God is "laboring" in shifts.

---

347. Most of these manuscripts originate from the sixteenth century; the earliest manuscript, Codex 221 (tenth century), includes the reading in a marginal note, which was added sometime after the original composition. Thus, *there is no sure evidence of this reading in any Greek manuscript until the 1500s*; each such reading was apparently composed after Erasmus' Greek New Testament was published in 1516. Indeed, the reading appears in *no Greek witness of any kind* (either manuscript, patristic, or Greek translation of some other version) *until AD 1215* (in a Greek translation of the Acts of the Lateran Council, a work originally written in Latin). This is all the more significant, since many a Greek Father would have loved such a reading, for it so succinctly affirms the doctrine of the Trinity. The reading seems to have arisen in a fourth-century Latin homily in which the text was allegorized to refer to members of the Trinity. From there, it made its way into copies of the Latin Vulgate of the Roman Catholic Church.

4. God "resting."

5. God physically "plants" a garden from seed.

6. God "breathing" into Adam's nostrils like an EMT.

7. God is a potter.

8. God "performs" surgery.

9. God "walks" in the cool of the day.

10. God "slays" an animal and "sows" garments to cover the couple's nakedness— an illusion of a priestly "sacrifice" that covers sin.

The *verbs* concerning God's actions often point to metaphor and analogy.

Did God need to post sentries blocking the tree of life to prevent Adam from "stealing" immortality? Should we take that reference "as written?" If we say "yes" and at the same time call it symbolic, then "as written," as YErs use the term, is meaningless. The cherubim guarding the tree of life represent justice and the impenetrable barrier between God and humans that sin creates, which is not written in the text since this is a theological interpretation of this ANE account. As temple guardians, similar Cherubim appear in other ANE literature; they also face east as in Eden. Therefore, this is ANE symbolism for a falling out between God and humans.

Exodus records a long narrative of the Law given at Mt. Sinai by God "personally." But here, the "as written" interpretation is inconsistent with the New Testament (and Rabbinic) interpretation of angelic mediation.[348] Which text do we take *as written?* Exodus, which says God spoke the words? *Or* the New Testament that says angels (messengers) spoke the words? No doubt YErs have YE "answers" to questions like this, but they likely involve words *not* as written.

Fundamentalists will insist they do not take the entire Bible literally, as when David wrote, "Trees clap their hands." Of course, only a fool would think trees applaud, no matter how the Bible puts it. No thoughtful critic of literalism refers to verses like that. YErs allow figurative interpretation for poetry, parables, some predictive prophecy, and no doubt apocalyptic literature. Anyone can do that much. Virtually everything else—historical books, narratives, law,

---

348. Five verses speak of the angel's role in giving the Law at Sinai. In the Old Testament, there are two verses (Deuteronomy 33:2; Psalm 68:17). In the New Testament Stephen refers to angels giving the Law at Sinai (Acts 7:53). In Galatians 3:19, Paul says the Law was ordained by angels in the hand of a mediator (Moses). The fifth verse is Hebrews 2:2, the Law was spoken by angels. What did the angels communicate here? Was it just the Ten Commandments or the whole legal dialogue at Sinai (cf. Exodus 19:1–Numbers 10:10)? The answer is the latter, the whole body of the Law. First, the Decalogue that was delivered at Sinai (Deuteronomy 33:2; Psalm 68:17). Second, in Stephen's critique of apostate Judaism, he mentions the angel's role in giving the Law. Stephen meant that Israel had broken all the Law and not just the Ten Commandments. Third, there is a comparison and contrast between the Old Testament law of Moses (not merely the Decalogue) and the new covenant or gospel of Christ (Galatians 3:19).

gospels, letters, and wisdom literature are supposedly literal, or in their words, meant "as written literal historical narrative" word for word. That is just not true. YErs do not take every verse in those genres literally though they claim to.

Here are some examples:

- "Destroy this temple, and in three days, I will raise it up."
- "Eat my flesh and drink my blood."
- "If your eye offends, you pluck it out."
- "If you do not hate your father and mother, etc., you cannot be my disciple."
- "This generation shall not pass."
- "God's back parts" in Exodus.
- "If you've seen me, you've seen the Father."
- "Some here will not see death."
- "In the day you eat of it, you shall surely die."
- "You must be born again."
- "Behold, I come quickly."
- "The last shall be first, and the first shall be last."

These passages are in books considered by YErs to be, as they say, "literal historical narrative." Yet YErs cannot take these statements and countless others *as written*. That is fine since innumerable passages like these are not meant *as written*. Their meaning requires wisdom to flush out.

But YErs go much further.

They claim that all Genesis 1–11 must be literal historical narratives because the ensuing Patriarchal narratives were literal and historical. These YErs appear to believe a book in scripture can only carry one genre. Stephen W. Boyd writes:

> To answer the question about the author's intention [in Genesis 1–11], it is necessary to expand the question to biblical narratives in general. How did authors of biblical narratives understand the events about which they wrote? Did authors of biblical narratives believe that they were referring to real events? If they did not, we are at a dead end yet again. But if they did—it can and will be argued—so does this text at the beginning of Genesis... if the text is a literal historical account, there is a one-to-one correspondence between words and reality.[349]

---

349. *Coming to Grips with Genesis,* page 168.

Boyd then uses the patriarchal narratives (chapters 12–50) as proof that Genesis 1–11 is literal, meaning "a one-to-one correspondence between words and reality." But why is it necessary to *"expand the question"* beyond chapters 1–11 to biblical narratives in general? Why leave the scene? Boyd does not seem to believe Genesis 1–11 can stand on its own as "literal historical narratives." Did the original readers of Genesis need to compare other biblical narratives to interpret Genesis 1–11? The quote above looks like a misdirection: *don't look here; look over there.* After all, Genesis 1–11 is radically different from Genesis 12–50. The first eleven chapters of Genesis have striking similarities to an abundance of ANE literature where the Patriarchal Narratives do not. That Genesis 1–11 is primordial or pre-history and singled out obsessively by YErs over what the stories may mean indicates a sharp distinction between the two sections. Genesis 1–11 is not the same literature or genre as chapters 12–50, i.e., *they are not Patriarchal Narratives of the Middle Bronze Age.*

Boyd asks and answers his own question: "How did authors of biblical narratives understand the events about which they wrote? Did authors of biblical narratives believe that they were referring to *real events*?" Since the answer must be yes for Boyd, *ipso facto,* the universe is six thousand years old. These questions are misleading because biblical authors can write about *real events* in figurative and theological language. Indeed, that is what they often did.

To sum up, Boyd says if figurative language enters the text, "we're stuck," we cannot know if the events really happened. Who are "we"? YECs. Or does Boyd mean that no one cannot know if creation really happened unless the six days are literal? No, he suggests we could not know earth's age and make progress with YEC as if that defines progress. *Common sense tells us that measuring the planet's age means measuring it.*

Theological reflections in the Bible about an event are not necessarily history, though they may contain history. For example, God created the heavens and the earth. Creation is an event described in various genres: science, myth, theology, poetry, or story form, otherwise known as narrative. As we have already seen, Genesis 1 is too stylistic and loaded with literary forms that do not behave like scientific literature or academic history. Nevertheless, God did create the heavens and the earth and everything in them, no matter what the genre is in Genesis 1. That is the historical fact and the "real event." We can speculate all we want about how God did it.

We have seen Christ as a sacrificial Lamb, yet the Bible says that Rome falsely executed him for treason against the empire. These two statements are different kinds. The latter is a historical fact, but the former is a theological interpretation; we distinguish between them. Facts are a subset of truth that is verifiable.

Theology is interpretive, not necessarily fact or empirical data. People confuse facts with truth as if something cannot be true unless it is a fact, which is neither true nor a fact. The facts are that the Romans executed Jesus for sedition on a hill outside Jerusalem. That is history void of theology since the Romans did not offer Jesus on an altar to any god. Nobody did in the literal sense. This theology helps illustrate why God allowed the execution of the Messiah, the Son of God. It expressed God's desire to redeem the world—*"For God so loved the world that he gave His Son."*

That is the fact.

You can distinguish theology from history in the patriarchal narratives when it comes to the nature of God. How does God act in the patriarchal narratives? Is God really *as written* in these narratives? Or is there some understanding of God in the late Bronze Age that biblical narrative accommodates?

Let's see.

After Abraham reportedly passed a test by offering up his son Isaac, God stops him in the act and says, *"Now I know* that you fear God for you have not withheld your son, your only son, from me." Why does the author quote God saying, *"Now* I know"? Is there a "one-to-one correspondence" between these words and reality? Did God not know the "end from the beginning?" And why "Now I know you fear *God"* and not *"Now I know you fear Me."* We now appear to have competing statements about God in the Bible that cancel each other out if taken literally:

> Remember the former things, those of long ago; I am God, and there is no other; I am God, and there is none like me. I make known the end from the beginning, from ancient times, what is still to come. I say, "My purpose will stand, and I will do all that I please." (Isaiah 46:9–10)

Either God can declare "the end from the beginning," or He cannot (or could not in Abraham's case). This episode has possible explanations, including the "as written" one. The problem with an *as-written* interpretation is obvious. God fails the test of omniscience. Predicting how Abraham would respond to this test should not be a challenge for God. *"Now* I know???" Was God wondering about this *before*? If literal, Moses makes this a *test for God* too, which Jesus said never to do (Matthew 4:7). Here, God's foreknowledge comes veiled with the words, "You have not withheld your son, *your only son,* from me," which anticipates the full extent of God's love when He did not withhold His Son—*His only Son*—from us.

God was not conducting an experiment to test His theory on Abraham. Frankly, *as written* will not do for this all-critical moment in a so-called "literal historical narrative" since it does not have the wooden "one-to-one correspondence" YErs demand. The sacrifice of Isaac is surely narrative, not poetry. The author's motive is to show the reader why God chose Abraham and his descendants in ways they could relate. It is not a lesson in God's attributes.

No literary form decides God's nature, especially language concerning His movements described in anthropomorphic terms. Literal activity refers to changes in kinetic energy expended bodily in space. God created the kinetic energy in both animate and inanimate bodies—that He does not possess. God's nature transcends such bodily (i.e., literal) movements, so they are out of the question for Him. How He acts without mechanisms, we cannot explain, except those He creates and sustains in nature that are operational, not ontological, concerning God. We could say God wills something, and it is so. However, the act of will alone is not explainable in mechanistic terms.

God knows all things knowable in any universe He creates. He determined all the knowable things that are possible in His creations. He must then be aware of them all and recognize them before and when they occur. God does not discover. He does not *now* know something he did not know *before*. He created the potential for all the possibilities that could actualize.

God knew *us* before we were born and that we would be in line with the faithful since Abraham (cp. Ephesians 1:5 and Galatians 3:29). Those words of God at the sacrifice of Isaac that *appear* to call into question God's foreknowledge require theological explanations that were not necessary at the time. Those explanations would become apparent in the fullness of time. This story had a purpose that did not include lessons in *Theology Proper* but lessons in *covenantal theology* more suitable for ancient Israel.

God's self-disclosure must continually unfold because understanding His infinite nature can never be fully met by a finite being. In other words, since we cannot know about God except by revelation, and what He reveals must be when we can receive it, God must gradually reveal Himself as we are able (John 16:12). Therefore, the further back in time we go, the more primitive the revelation.

Given that the Holy Spirit continues to lead the Church into greater understanding (John 14:26), we have learned more about God's nature since the canonization of Scripture, which provides new insight for interpreting the Creation story, which John 1:1-14 demonstrates. The mistake fundamentalists make with words on stone tablets is setting their interpretations in stone. There can never be progress in understanding if stone tablets remain in control. That is contrary to the New Testament understanding about reading the Old Testament that we interpret in the light of Christ (see 2 Corinthians 3:3–6):

> You show that you are a letter from Christ, the result of our ministry, written not with ink but with the Spirit of the living God, not on tablets of stone but on tablets of human hearts... He has made us competent as ministers of a new covenant—not of the letter but of the Spirit; for the letter kills, but the Spirit gives life.

There is more.

In Genesis 18:20–21, God decides to "check out" Sodom and Gomorrah to "verify rumors" He has "heard." Again, these are narratives, not poems, yet corporeal imagery characterizes the report. God "discovers" the rumors are true and decides to destroy the two cities of the plain. Abraham takes up the cause as an apologist for Sodom and Gomorrah in an attempt to "change God's mind," hoping to save Lot and his family.

Before the "Divine Bar," Abraham's defense was a series of leading questions that resulted in God sparing Lot and his family. The point here is that according to the story, God had to go *on-site* so he could "see" for Himself as if he is in bodily form and travels through space or that he cannot get a good look at His earthly "footstool" from His heavenly "throne" (Isaiah 66:1). So God enters negotiations with Abraham. He *reasons* with the man in a humanlike fashion (even God uses *human reasoning* if you take it all *as written*). Luckily for Lot, Abraham makes the case.

How should ANE cultures convey *religious truths?* YErs and atheists would say by scientific accuracy or through strict history. But the ancients did not think in a modern way. Besides, it is too confining for the theological and philosophical truths the author is making. The intended audience is tribal people in covenant with God in the late Bronze or early Iron Ages. Objective news reporting is sterile, restrictive, and often unnecessary for an ancient audience. Vivid stories are essential in an oral society because they make a lasting impression. They still do.

How can we be sure *what biblical authors meant* by their accounts? YErs assume that if figurative language and symbolism are present, the authors did not believe they were writing about real events. Would any accepted and recognized literary scholar say such a thing? It appears YEC lacks the imagination to understand the literature of these highly imaginative authors.

For example, forty-five years ago, a college professor challenged the historicity of Abraham in class. He simply gave us the arguments for and against the historical Abraham and let us draw our conclusions with suggested reading. Archeology has since given some credibility to the customs found in the patriarchal narratives. But what if Abraham was not a historical character? Say he was a composite of patriarchs; would there be no God of Abraham? More directly, if Abraham were not a historical person, would the Bible be uninspired?

For Christians, Abraham is called the "father" of the faithful. The definitive event in Abraham's life was a test suggesting he sacrifice his only son Isaac. At the time, an heir was vital to a wealthy person's legacy. Otherwise, one's life's work might go to a servant, or worse, broken up. Building a heritage from generation to generation was a way of preserving ancestral roots, ancestral gods, and the family house presented in the community. It determined blessings or curses for many generations. After carefully reading Genesis 22 and related scholarship, I discovered remarkable allusions to God's only Son in the story.

Genesis 22:2 sets up the location of Isaac's sacrifice, where we read, "Then God said, 'Take your son, *your only son,* whom you love—Isaac—and go to the region of *Moriah.* Sacrifice him there as a burnt offering *on a hill* I will show you.'" Comparisons between Isaac and Christ suggest that Abraham is symbolic of the Father, and Isaac is a type of the Son.

I've italicized the contacts between the two stories below:

Then God said, "Take your son, *your only son*, whom you love—Isaac—and go to the region of Moriah. Sacrifice him there as a burnt offering on a mountain, I will show you."

Early the next morning, Abraham got up and loaded his *donkey*. He took with him *two of his servants and his son Isaac*. When he had cut enough wood for the burnt offering, he set out for the place God had told him about. *On the third day,* Abraham looked up and saw *the place* in the distance. He said to his servants, "Stay here with the donkey while I and the boy go over there. We will worship and then we will come back to you."

Abraham took the wood for the burnt offering and placed it on his son Isaac, and he Himself carried the fire and the knife. As the two of them went on together, Isaac spoke up and said to his father Abraham, "Father? "Yes, my son?" Abraham replied.

"The fire and wood are here," Isaac said, "but where is the lamb for the burnt offering?"

Abraham answered, "*God Himself will provide the lamb* for the burnt offering, my son." And the two of them went on together.

When they reached *the place* God had told him about, Abraham built an altar there and arranged the wood on it. *He bound his son Isaac and laid him on the altar, on top of the wood.* Then he reached out his hand and took the knife to slay his son. But the angel of the Lord called out to him from heaven, *""Abraham! Abraham!"*

"Here I am," he replied. Do not lay a hand on the boy," he said. "Do not do anything to him. Now I know that you fear God, because you have not withheld from me your son, *your only son.*"

Abraham looked up and there in *a thicket he saw a ram* caught by its horns. He went over and took the ram and sacrificed it as a burnt offering instead of his son. *So Abraham called that place The Lord Will Provide.* And to this day it is said, "On the mountain of the Lord it will be provided."

You know the story. Isaac lives. Here is a list of similarities (some not obvious) with Christ's passion and resurrection:

1. They arrive at the *place* of sacrifice on a *donkey* (Jerusalem in both stories).

2. There are two "no-name" individuals next to Isaac; remember the two thieves?

3. Note the expression "*on the third day*" in both accounts.

4. Isaac carries his "cross," so to speak, carrying the wood used to sacrifice him.

5. God provides the *sacrifice* in both narratives.

6. Both Isaac and Jesus were bound and went as a lamb to the slaughter.

7. A voice twice cries out for Isaac's father, "Abraham! Abraham!"— Jesus twice cries out to his father, "Eli, Eli" (Matthew 27:46).

8. They reach "*the place.*" The expression adds drama to both stories. The place of Jesus's crucifixion was called "*The place of the skull.*" In other words, the exact place was not only significant in both, but they are virtually the same place. Since Isaac's offering was in "the region of Moriah," where Mt. Moriah later became the foundation for building Jerusalem. God indeed provided the same place in each event—Abraham called the place "*The Lord Will Provide*" (Genesis 22:14)

9. Isaac lays down in wrapping, like Jesus in the tomb, and both rise up alive.

The Islamic Dome of the Rock houses the peak of Mt. Moriah at the temple mount in old Jerusalem. Mohammed is said to have received the Quran there. There are several hills within the metropolitan area. The "Place of the Skull" (also called Golgotha) was a "mountain" (hill by western measurements) in the region of Moriah just outside the city gate in Jerusalem.[350]

The similarities in both stories are not perfect or exact—a point in favor of its authenticity. Too much exactness would make Jesus's story appear contrived. Most people are still unaware of these remarkable similarities. Thus both narratives stand on their own. The contexts and periods are very different. Yet, some of the similarities are striking and numerous enough to be more than coincidence.

A believer should recognize God's inspiration in both stories. Even *if* the details in the narrative were not historically accurate, it has prophetic power, and eternal truths built in that are divine signatures. If Abraham was a composite or archetypal character of the faithful, the stamp of divine revelation is still there. After all, the Word of God is foremost the revelation of Christ. Isaac was the birthright son through whom God intended to bless all nations (Jews and gentiles), again a type of Christ. In Abraham's story, we also have a revelation of Christ, the point of inspiration, and the subject of revelation.

Nonetheless, there are no good reasons to deny the historicity of Abraham.

Interestingly, in 1922, Sir Leonard Woolley discovered a massive burial site at Ur in southern Mesopotamia with sections dating around the patriarchal period

---

350. Biblical authors described geographic locations more "ambitiously" than we might. For example, what we call lakes they called "seas" (e.g., Sea of Galilee and the Dead Sea). The Mediterranean Sea is called the "Great Sea," and mountains are often just hills. The River Jordan, for the most part, is a stream. Simple expressions like these alone help illustrate the need for extensive experience in interpreting biblical references.

of Abraham, Isaac, and Jacob (2000–2500 BC), confirming the historical context preserved in the Abrahamic narratives. One of the most striking sections unearthed at Ur is the "Great Death Pit," some 2,000 burial sites. Sixteen are royal tombs of the same culture where Abraham grew up and worshipped. The royal tombs revealed significant *human sacrifice* of servants for the afterlife:

> More bodies or victims are buried often in separate chambers or, more commonly, in "death pits," an open sunken court. The amount of sacrificed bodies in one tomb can range from a small amount of six to between *seventy and eighty bodies*. The attendants are usually lying in neat rows within the death pits or chambers.

More surprising were two sculptures depicting a "Ram in a Thicket" (see figure 5):

> The discovery of two goat statues in PG 1237 are just two examples of polychrome sculpture at Ur. These objects, referred to as *"Rams in the Thicket"* by Woolley, were made of wood and covered in gold, silver, shell and lapis lazuli. *The Ram in a Thicket* uses gold for the tree, legs, and face of the goat, silver for the belly and parts of the base alongside pink and white mosaics.[351]

---

351. See "Ram in a Thicket," *Wikipedia.*

Figure 5: "Ram in a thicket" as displayed in the British Museum

With Isaac's feigned sacrifice and the provision of a sacrificial "ram in a thicket," the connection between the biblical story and worship at Ur seems to be that Abraham will abandon his old gods and reject human sacrifice in favor of worshipping Yahweh. In other words, the discoveries at Ur help solidify essential details in the biblical story for the historical period it claims to represent.

Additionally, the Nuzi tablets confirm other customs unique to the period, such as the incident of Rachel's theft of the household gods as described in Genesis 31 and the adoption of a servant in the absence of an heir was the law at the time. Consequently, we have some verification and authenticity for the historical setting of the biblical Patriarchs.[352]

Stephen Boyd offers this false choice:

So if the text is a *poetic metaphor*, it has nothing to say about scientific theories on origins, and therefore nothing about the age of the earth... if the text is a literal historical account, there is a one-to-one correspondence between words and reality.[353]

"Poetic metaphor" refers to metaphors in poetry, not metaphors in prose or narrative. Boyd's false choice is between what he calls "poetic metaphor" and his "literal historical account." Boyd overstates it further with his "one-to-one correspondence" proclamation. By that, he hopes to force upon the author a "*no metaphor zone*." Incidentally, there is no genre called "poetic metaphor." There is poetry as a genre that makes extensive use of metaphor. But "poetic metaphor (also called extended metaphor) in a poem is the *concrete object representing an abstract idea throughout the poem.*"[354]

The metaphors are the concrete ideas (days) that represent abstract ideas (creation). But no matter how metaphorical (or *theological*) the account may be, the real event in the story is not literal days or even creation *ex nihilo*, but that Israel's own, Yahweh Elohim, created the heavens and the earth.

Authors do not reserve metaphors for poetry only. There are also metaphors in prose, historical narratives, and scientific literature too. Boyd is attempting to set up a stark bifurcated choice of genres—either the words are a poem (his poetic metaphor), or they have a one-to-one correspondence to reality (his "literal historical narrative"). This claim is false all around because writers use metaphors in all literature. Indeed, it is challenging to avoid them.

Contrary to Boyd's claim, science and history also make extensive use of metaphor. We saw the British-born philosopher of science, Michael Ruse, saying, "Science interprets the world through experience, and just like poets, metaphor is the key to the whole enterprise. Everything is metaphorical, the 'struggle' for existence, natural 'selection,' 'division of labor,' genetic 'code,' and 'arms races' between competing species, etc."

There are countless other metaphors in science like "cutting edge" science and "wormholes," and regarding origins, there is the obvious "Big Bang" metaphor since it was not a literal explosion. By the way, the "Big Bang" is a

---

352. J. Bright, *History of Israel* (Westminster Press, Philadelphia, 1959; SCM, London, 1960). Bright says, "One is forced to the conclusion that the patriarchal narratives authentically reflect social customs at home in the second millennium rather than those of later Israel." Bright's conclusions were challenged by Thomas L. Thompson but affirmed by leading scholars, notably William F. Albright, E. A. Speiser, and Cyrus Gordon.

353. *Coming to Grips with Genesis*, pages 166–167.

354. Deviant Art Home Page, deviantart.com, 2020.

metaphor for a *real event*. Real events can carry metaphors; to think otherwise is odd. In Genesis, the real event is that God created the universe *while* He is in metaphor as a King, craftsman, potter, and surgeon.

Histories also contain metaphors.

Historians speak of the "course" of history as a river that flows. History is not conscious, yet we say it "repeats itself"—an anthropomorphism. The Battle of the Bulge was not a battle over a sprawling waistline or an aneurism. Martin Luther King Jr. said, "History is a great teacher." It is in one sense but not in another. There are "branches of history" with "roots" from the past. Historians describe the context of their subjects as a "landscape," and events can "sweep" an existing landscape away. History does not make progress; people do or do not.

History does not repeat itself. It has no self. Then there is the "march" of history. History has "highlights" and "lowlights." There are "alternative histories" of the same events even in the Bible with four gospels and Samuel, Kings, and Chronicles. *There could not be alternative histories in the Bible if all the words have a "one-to-one correspondence to reality."*

Giving an age to the earth or universe by ancient writers could only be a product of their observational scope, mythology, or speculation, which may be why biblical authors refrain from explicit statements about those things. Ironically, this restraint is evidence of inspiration, not the lack.

Now consider the book of Job. It is poetry and wisdom literature. In translation, its poetry is hardly noticeable to an untrained reader. A cursory reading of its pages reveals significant metaphors and figures of speech. Yet, Job comes across as a real person. That Job is poetry does not mean that no events in the story occurred. Why should it? He has a history, hometown and family, specific events in his life, many relationships, and a relationship with God.

Here is the point: What if Job were a composite character by a brilliant author? Could Job be a fictional character like a tale written that begins, "Once upon a time in the land of Uz?" Would the value of the book of Job be any less? Would the recorded events not seem real to all who suffer miserably while God seems disinterested? Job confronts the most perplexing questions common in the human condition.

Today, the problem of evil and suffering is still the most persuasive and enduring argument against God. The wise and those seeking wisdom have found answers and comfort in the masterpiece we call "Job," even if *he* never existed. In the end, there is no way to know if Job was a historical person. Therefore, *the question of historicity can have no bearing on the value of Job's story.*

The unverifiable history of an unknowable character takes nothing away from the universal truths found in the book. There are truths found in fictional narratives because truth is universal to the human condition. *Literary fiction* can be a vehicle for truth and not a synonym for lies. The Bible writers address many patterns of life common to humanity. The commonality makes the *lessons* authentic. Similarly, the serpent in Eden does not have to be literal or *historically accurate* to understand or believe the theological truth the author intends.

Isn't this obvious?[355]

Adam and Eve did what God expressly told them *not* to do. That is a regular pattern in the Bible and our collective human experience. Our universal experiences appear in the best fiction, like Shakespeare, Milton, and Dostoyevsky. YErs believe God is untrustworthy if he allows the author's imagination to express profound wisdom in a narrative. YErs seem to assume that the Bible's *historical records* cannot offer *both figurative and literal content*.

In YEC, biblical authors may only pick one.

---

355. One can only imagine "fundamentalists" at the time of *Aesop's Fables* struggling over the historicity of the tortoise and the hare.

24.
THE OLD TESTAMENT *NOT AS WRITTEN*

The Lord regretted that he had made human beings on the earth,
and his heart was deeply troubled.
—Genesis 6:6

For he chose us in him before the Creation of the
world to be holy and blameless in his sight.
—Ephesians 1:4

We have a contradiction above if the word *regret* is literal. God *does not* experience regret. Humans regret. God *cannot* repent, change His mind, or atone for Himself since he is perfect, all-knowing, and all-powerful. And this, despite Genesis 6, where it says God repents or regrets making humans. In contrast, the New Testament says God *predestined* Christ and the saints *before* the world's creation, which contradicts Genesis 6:6 if every word in both statements should be literal. For how could God regret (Genesis 6:6) creating a world that he knows he will save?

God was not surprised or thrown by human sin no matter what Genesis 6:6 might mean because the Godhead predestined Christ: "He was chosen before the creation of the world, but was revealed in these last times for [our] sake" (1 Peter 1:19–20). Our author did not know this.

God's plan always was to reveal Himself in human form. There could be no regrets. To miss this is to miss the implications of Christ Incarnate, disclosed for the first time at his resurrection. Therefore, there is no evidence that God revealed the Incarnation to Moses. The New Testament revelation takes precedent over the Old Testament revelation because it is the *fullness* of God's self-disclosure: *"For in Christ all the fullness of the Deity lives in bodily form"* (Colossians 2:9).

Remember that the periods represented through the books of the Bible cover more than a thousand years. In that context, idioms came and went, or worse, they lost their meaning over time so that future authors misunderstood them or used them differently in later pages of the Bible.

For instance, the word *soul* means something entirely different in Genesis than in the gospels. Yet the soul is central to Christian theology of human nature. In past Christian traditions, humans are bodies and souls, i.e., material and immaterial creatures— a philosophy called "substance dualism." Moreover, Christians generally believe that the soul continues in a disembodied state after death. It awaits the resurrection of a new body, only hinted at in the Hebrew Bible.

The concept of an immortal soul distinct from the body is not so apparent in Judaism before the Babylonian exile. The idea may have first entered Judaism through Zoroastrianism during the Exile. Hellenism likely provided the language for the soul's immortality in the post-exilic period.

According to Genesis 2:7, God made Adam from dust and breathed life into him, so he became a living soul that some compare to Ptah's creation of man in Egypt.[356] In other words, according to Genesis and indeed the Old Testament, humans do not have a soul; they *are* a soul. Souls are mortal in the Old Testament; they can die (Ezekiel 18:4, 20). Animals are souls in the Old Testament too. Genesis 2:19 says:

> And out of the ground the Lord God formed every beast of the field [as he did man] and every fowl of the air; and brought them unto the man to see what he would call them; and whatever the man called *every living soul,* that was its name." (JUB)

Interestingly, the ANE cultures seemed to view the soul apart from the body. For example, in ancient Egyptian religions, an individual comprises various physical and spiritual elements. Similar ideas appear in ancient Assyrian and Babylonian religions.[357]

Ecclesiastes preserves an extreme view of human mortality, "Surely the fate of human beings is like that of the animals; the same fate awaits them both: As one dies, so dies the other. All have the same breath; humans have no advantage over animals. Everything is meaningless" (Ecclesiastes 3:19), which leads to despair.

In the New Testament, James 5:20 says, "Let him know, that he which converts the sinner from the error of his way *shall save a soul from death*, and shall hide a multitude of sins" (KJV). It does not say, "Save his soul from hell, but 'death.'" Perhaps he means spiritual death. Perhaps he uses *soul* to mean "body," which might be unexpected for a Hellenistic Christian but understandable for a Jew or a Jewish Christian.

Even Paul, quoting Genesis 2:7, does not conserve the *mortal* soul view in 1 Corinthians 15:45, where it says, "And so it is written, the first man Adam was made a *living soul* [as opposed to a dead one]; the last Adam was made a

---

356. Bill T. Arnold, *Genesis (The New Cambridge Bible Commentary),* 2009, (Kindle edition), location 1217. Ptah, the supreme god in one Egyptian pantheon, creates by his word and makes man in his image and likeness, breathing life into his nostrils.

357. See "Found: An Ancient Monument to the Soul," *The New York Times*, 17 November 2008, Archived on April 24, 2009. The earliest known reference to an immaterial soul is from the eighth century BC. "In a mountainous kingdom in what is now southeastern Turkey, there lived in the eighth century BC a royal official, Kuttamuwa, who oversaw the completion of an inscribed stone monument, or stele, to be erected upon his death. The words instructed mourners to commemorate his life and afterlife with feasts *for my soul that is in this stele.*" See *Wikipedia* article, "Soul."

quickening spirit." Paul, quoting this passage, does not take it literally or as a theology for the soul by rejecting its immortality. He also wrote, "We...would prefer to be *away from the body* and at home with the Lord" (2 Corinthians 5:8). See also 2 Corinthians 12:2. Instead, Paul contrasts the earthly nature of Adam's descendants and the reborn community in Christ.

Some Christians use such verses to reject the soul's immortality. But Paul uses Genesis 2:7 to contrast Adam and Christ and, in doing so, snares a *mortal soul* reference. It is a mistake to assume Old Testament quotes in the New Testament mean the authors took those quotes literally or how we would take them today.[358]

Many YErs suppose that if Jesus and Paul quote Genesis, they do so as YE creationists. That is not possible. The subject for the Apostle Paul is the resurrected body of which Genesis says nothing. Despite what Genesis says about Adam and the soul, the immaterial substance in human nature that we call the "soul" is immortal for Paul, where he may also use the term *spirit*. Resurrection refers to the body. Glorification refers to body, soul, and spirit.

The use of the word "soul" throughout biblical literature shows how inept literalism can be, as the following quote demonstrates:

> The traditional concept of an immaterial and immortal soul distinct from the body was not found in Judaism before the Babylonian exile, but developed as a result of interaction with Persian and Hellenistic philosophies. Accordingly, the Hebrew word שֶׁפֶנ, *nephesh*, although translated as "soul" in some older English Bibles, actually has a meaning closer to "living being." *Nephesh* was rendered in the Septuagint as ψυχή (*psūchê*), the Greek word for *soul*. The New Testament also uses the word ψυχή, but with the Hebrew meaning and not the Greek. *The textual evidence indicates a multiplicity of perspectives on these issues including probable changes during the centuries in which the biblical corpus developed.*[359] (emphasis mine)

Genesis says nothing about a disembodied soul. According to a literal Genesis, God did not *give* Adam a soul; He turned Adam into one. After a long life, the "living soul" named Adam died. Do YErs take Genesis *as written* or with their one-to-one correspondence to reality regarding the soul? No. And why? Because the soul has nothing to do with the age of the earth.

---

358. It is unlikely that Moses, referring to "living soul" meant to contrast "mortal and immortal" but animate and inanimate in regard to Adam. Nonetheless, he clearly believed humans were mortal, *"For dust you are and to dust you shall return"* (Genesis 3:19). Also, the annexing of the tree of life was a statement on human mortality.

359. See "Soul," *Wikipedia* article.

Interpretive Challenges with New Testament Authors

We know that the New Testament writers did not interpret scripture as written. This is a fact. The Apostle Paul, for example, used rabbinic *methods* of interpretation to form a new Christian *message*. There are many examples of this. A striking less-known example that has gained exposure recently is Paul's commentary on Exodus 17:10 and Numbers 21:16, in 1 Corinthians 10:1–4:

> I do not want you to be unaware, brothers and sisters, that our ancestors were all under the cloud, and all passed through the sea, and all were baptized into Moses in the cloud and in the sea, and all ate the same spiritual food, and all drank the same spiritual drink. *For they drank from the spiritual rock that followed them, and the rock was Christ.* (NRSV, emphasis mine)

Were the Israelites really "baptized in the cloud and in the sea?" No, they did not get wet. That is a theological treatment of Old Testament events from a New Testament perspective. *Note that Paul applies a baptismal allegory within a historical narrative* against YEC "rules." But where did Paul get the idea that a supernatural rock *followed* the Israelites? Fundamentalists would say God inspired this interpretation for Paul, word for word. But, according to Paul, the rock was present over the entire forty years of wilderness wandering. This interpretation was decidedly not from a one-to-one correspondence to reality since the Bible says no such thing. So, where did Paul get the idea?

New Testament scholars point to Judaism, a Talmudic commentary in Tosefta, Sukka 3:11:

> And so *the* well *that was with the Israelites in the wilderness was a rock,* the size of a large round vessel, surging and gurgling upward, as from the mouth of its little flask, rising with them up onto the mountains, and going down with them into the valleys. *Wherever the Israelites would encamp, [the rock] made camp with them,* on a high place, opposite the entry of the Tent of Meeting.[360]

This highly creative description is typical of Rabbinic Midrashim.

Paul was a well-schooled Rabbi. The actual story mentions a rock that supplied water to the Israelites at the beginning of the wilderness wandering in Rephidim (Exodus 17:6). The next time the rock appears is at the end of the wandering, in the area called *Beer* forty years later (Numbers 21:16). Rabbinic interpreters surmised that this rock must have followed them up and down the hills and valleys for forty consecutive years. Maybe it did. Nonetheless, the Bible does not say that.

Jewish tradition said that.

---

360. Peter Enns, *Inspiration and Incarnation: Evangelicals and the Problem of the Old Testament, Second Edition* (Baker Academic Division of Baker Publishing Group, Grand Rapids, Michigan, 2015), p. 140.

The Bible says nothing about a moving well, but the place was called Beer, which means "well." Beer is likely north of the Arnon River in Amorite territory on the Jordan River's east side. The Bible pictures the Israelites going to this water-supplying rock located in Beer; the rock did not follow them in the story. Wells are stationary after all, so what is happening? A Jewish tradition developed into a theological interpretation of an Old Testament text.

The Apostle Paul appears to follow a fanciful Talmudic interpretation of a *moving rock but reinterprets it in Christ*. In other words, Paul interprets the scripture—or more accurately, a rabbinic tradition about the scripture—in the light of Christ. There is no need to figure it all out for our purposes except to say that the apostle is oblivious to an "as written" hermeneutic or any "one-to-one correspondence to reality" that YEC demand. Yet Paul's point is on a fundamental theological concept, in a "literal historical narrative."

Christ corresponds to reality for Paul; words do not.

Studying the New Testament's use of the Old Testament has puzzled Bible students for centuries. New Testament authors quote the Old Testament differently than it appears in the Hebrew Scriptures. The New Testament translations do not correspond to Old Testament wording. Why is that? Because New Testament authors usually quoted from the Greek version of the Old Testament, the Septuagint. Our Old Testament comes from the ninth century AD Masoretic Text, written in a new Hebrew form. The Septuagint and the Masoretic text are different "*as writtens.*"

More puzzling is how New Testament writers interpreted Old Testament passages. One famous text is "Out of Egypt, I called my son." Matthew treats this verse as a prophecy about Jesus's return from Egypt with his parents in Matthew 2:14–15. Matthew quoted Hosea 11:1, which refers to God calling Israel out of Egyptian slavery. Just the words, "I called out *my Son* from Egypt," would have stood out in the first-century Church. Instead, the Jewish Church reinterpreted "my Son" to mean "My only begotten Son."

This Hebrew interpretive vision of Matthew is not intuitive to us, and for a good reason. A direct connection between the two verses in their contexts is virtually unrecognizable. While their wording is similar, the meaning in each is different on its face. Instead, Matthew's interpretation was a Jewish thought process in service to Christianity. Christ is the revelation, not Jewish hermeneutical practice.[361]

Sometimes, New Testament writers paraphrase the text, perhaps from memory or another source. None of these issues is a big deal unless one insists

---

361. The hermeneutical methods of the first century in both Judaism and Christianity are not always synonymous with how Old Testament authors might have interpreted their own work. That did not matter in NT times since Christ ushered in a theological revolution. Nothing would be the same.

on reading scripture with word-for-word literalism or some blanket ill-defined "as written" rule. The New Testament Church, shaped by the Holy Spirit for interpreting, had no consciousness of such *ad hoc* rules.

One primary hermeneutic in Judaism during the Second Temple period was to interpret Old Testament stories in the light of current events and *vice versa*. This hermeneutic helped explain happenings in the present circumstances. The series of events that shaped first-century Judaism and its view of scripture were the exile into Babylon and the return during the Persian period, followed by the Greek and Roman occupations. Those events had a particular motif: divine commands given, divine commands broken, expulsion, or occupation. Versions of this theme appeared in Genesis: the Garden of Eden, Cain's expulsion into Nod, and a fall and redemption story like the flood. But there is also Egyptian slavery and freedom, wilderness wandering, the conquest of Canaan, the ups and downs during the Judges' period, Assyrian captivity, etc.

Past biblical narratives (ancient by the first century) and the prophets' message helped answer *why* Yahweh allowed the destruction of Jerusalem, the expulsion from Judah into Babylon, the desolation of the land, and subsequent occupations. Israel continuously failed to keep covenant with God. They saw the consequences.

By the first century, Judaism understood the expulsion from Eden, Abraham's call, the Passover and Exodus, the covenant at Sinai, the Davidic dynasty, the exile and return, and the Maccabean revolt, all in context to the coming Messianic rule. God's past moves seemed to give meaning to current circumstances and gave their hopes a new focus.

Jews were looking for a Messiah to restore Israel's rightful place in the created order. That would mean removing the Romans and installing the prophesied Messianic Age. They expected a Messiah that would be King with the Law in one hand and a sword in the other, the kind of Messiah that the prophets predicted. However, the type of Messiah God sent fulfilled the prophet's predictions in part—the part they understood least or not at all. For example, the future forgiveness of sins promised in those prophecies, which we now apply to Jesus, was for Israel, making her fit for the Messianic Age. That did not happen.

As written and as understood, biblical statements on the Messianic Age were not to be.

A similar hermeneutic appears in the New Testament, except that the current events used to interpret scripture were the life, death, resurrection, and ascension of Jesus. In no way could the Messianic Kingdom, not of this world, led by God Incarnate, be gleaned by reading the Old Testament "as written." The New Testament writers often do not interpret the Old Testament as written. Why not? That is because Jesus changed a theological landscape steeped in tribal Judaism (see 2 Corinthians 3:15). Jesus changed everything. All the world's writings are inadequate to detail God's will for all time. We needed God to show us *in person*, not just tell us in words.

Thus the Incarnation.

The truth is that later authors of the Bible, moved by the Holy Spirit, do not read older biblical texts "as written." That is because they wished to understand the troubling things God was doing or not doing in their day. They hoped to find answers in familiar patterns of the past written in the Bible. Don't we all?

James L. Kugel, Professor Emeritus at Harvard, writes:

> And so, it was this interpreted Bible—not just the stories, prophecies, and laws themselves, but these texts...that came to stand at the very center of *Judaism and Christianity*... Both religions had begun with basically the same interpreted Bible. *For both inherited an earlier, common set of traditions, general principles regarding how one ought to go about reading and interpreting the Bible as well as specific traditions concerning the meaning of individual passages, verses, and words.*[362] (emphasis mine)

One of the hard lessons the Israelites learned, as we must, is that God does not fit into any narrow theology. That does not stop any of us from reducing Him that way. A way to *avoid* boxing God is by setting systematic principles for best practices and accountability standards, as with any serious discipline. We need checks and balances alongside our truth-finding. The Bible, especially its high metaphorical content, requires careful deliberation. Krugel continues:

> Old Testament "prophecy provides the best example of *the projection of historical narratives onto a cosmic scale*, when it speaks of contemporaneous political dangers for Israel, in terms of judgement on the world (the 'Day of the Lord'), of the darkening of the powers of the heavens, and of a Davidic king who will return to lead a faithful remnant into a renewed world and to the true worship of God.[363]

According to Judaism, true worship in the future Messianic Age is the joy of keeping the covenant with Yahweh. The Messiah ensures that all temple services shall be according to covenant requirements. All male children shall be circumcised on the eighth day. The Gentiles will come to Jerusalem to learn the law and keep the Feast of Tabernacles (Isaiah 2:3; Zechariah 14:16). In reality, as Jesus told the woman of Samaria, true worshipers will not come to Jerusalem or any mountain but worship God in spirit and truth (John 4:21–24). God is Spirit, not an ANE deity housed in a temple on a mountain top.

This incident with the Samaritan woman seriously challenges much of the Old Testament, if taken literally, in that Jesus ended the old covenant

---

362. James L. Kugel, *Traditions of the Bible* (Harvard University Press, 2009), Kindle location 709. Kugel is Professor Emeritus in the Bible Department at Bar-Ilan University in Israel and Professor Emeritus of Classical and Modern Hebrew Literature at Harvard University.

363. Ibid.

obligations and its religion. Jesus's comments are not just figurative speech; they are revolutionary speech. And as the temple symbolized a heavenly place, the prophecies about religion in the Messianic Kingdom *symbolized* true worship. Still, the old covenant's literal language (as written) is what first-century Pharisees and Sadducees wanted to preserve. Those prophecies have real meaning (the whole world will know God), but they illustrate it symbolically. Old Testament authors could not have predicted who the Messiah would be or the revolutionary changes he would bring because the time wasn't right.

The *fullness of time* had not come. Matthew 13:16–17 says: "For truly I tell you, many prophets and righteous people longed to see what you see but did not see it, and to hear what you hear *but did not hear it*." Paul said, "When the fullness of time came, God sent His Son" (see Galatians 4:3–5; Ephesians 1:10). Christianity does not simply rely on "as written" hermeneutics, so the YE "as written" presupposition is meaningless.

Elaborate symbols, rituals, and geography would no longer characterize worship practices, as Keith Ward observes:

> These symbols were, Christians think, fulfilled in Jesus, and so they are tremendously important as pointers to future disclosures of God. But they were fulfilled in quite new and unexpected ways—for Jesus did not rule as a king in a Jerusalem palace, but was crucified on a hill outside the city walls. So, for Christians, the Hebrew Bible anticipates and points to fuller discernments of God, but often in very obscure [ways].[364]

The point is that the earlier books of the Bible, written in various genres and styles, are also interpreted variously by successive biblical writers. Thousands of variant copies, different manuscripts, and an endless stream of new translations attest to this. The Bible contains priceless guidance, but it is not *the guide*. That is the domain of the Holy Spirit. The Holy Spirit does not cease to be our personal and ultimate influence because He inspired scripture and inspires us.

---

364. Keith Ward, *The Word of God? The Bible after Modern Scholarship* (London, 2010), p. 40.

25.
THE LAW: NOT AS WRITTEN

> All language is inherently confined to the context in which it was given.
> What we say today is different than it would be 2,000 years from now. Today's
> ideas would be unfit for people 3,000 years ago. Eternal principles have to be
> adapted to new circumstances.
> —Ben Shapiro on the Torah

Consider Jesus's statement on the *Writ of Divorce* again. The irony in Jesus's point is that he and God disagreed with the Law of Moses! Therefore, God could not be the source of that writ. The implications of this extraordinary statement of Jesus appear lost on YErs and many Evangelicals.

The Writ of Divorce was Israelite law, not divine law.

This Writ was a *compromise* between Moses and the people's will outside God's will. If YErs are correct that God "superintended" each word of the Bible, then we might ask, "Did God let the hardness of people's hearts influence His better judgment when superintending every word of scripture?" Was the Writ God's "perfect, *holy*, and eternal Word?" Think, was it *holy*? Indeed, God was not intimidated by the people. But did He compromise? To be consistent and honest, YErs should answer that. Such fundamentalist confusion is where an extreme and absurd view of inspiration leads. It is less a faith in God than faith in the Bible. The Writ of Divorce was not God's law; its a human law.

Thomas Aquinas identified four types of law:

1. Eternal Law—that only God knows.

2. Divine Law—revealed by God in scripture.

3. Natural Law—a subset of divine law discoverable through reason:

   - Romans 1:20 ESV: "His eternal power and divine nature...is understood from what has been made."

   - Romans 2:14–15 ESV: "When Gentiles, who do not have the law, do by nature things required by the law, they are a law for themselves."

4. Human Law—made by humans

Jesus said that *the Writ of Divorce* found in the Bible is not God's word on the subject; it is not really Moses's word or even the people's word generally. It is the word of the hard-hearted among the people, probably elites, who were the most influential and could pressure Moses (the sort that confronted Jesus). This writ was not what YErs would call eternal, divine, perfect, holy, or even Natural

Law, but a poorly devised human law that crept into the scriptures. God allowed it, but it could not be a law that proceeds from Him despite being a law found in the Bible. Jesus corrects the record when prompted by the Pharisees who were testing him (Matthew 19:3).

Without this incident between Jesus and the Pharisees, we would not know of this Mosaic compromise that went unknown for a thousand years. This example raises the prospect of other Bible passages that contradict the YEC assumption that God superintended every word of scripture or that all words are God's words and must be truthful in every respect. God certainly disagreed with the Writ of Divorce, and Jesus knew it.

Is it any coincidence that Church governance in all Christian branches has struggled with administering divorce and remarriage? Perhaps this is due to inconsistencies between Moses, Jesus, and Paul, our hardness, and the sheer complications in marriages that no book or series of books could sort out. Jesus did not support the Writ because he would have given that law (in the Bible) an authority it does not have—that of putting the crowd's madness over God's will.

There is a similar example in Paul when his words are explicitly his own: "Here is what I say to other people. (This is my word, *not the Lord's).* Perhaps a Christian brother has a wife who is not a Christian. If she wants to stay with him, then he should not send her away" (1 Corinthians 7:12 WE).[365]

One wonders if there might be similar instances of this and the Writ in the Bible that have gone unidentified. Paul's admission is not a big deal, except for those who believe that biblical authors refrained from their personal opinions.

Paul speaks here, not with the authority of his office as an apostle but with an educated opinion and considerable experience.[366] Absent any precedent in the Bible or elsewhere to draw from, an opinion was necessary to address a unique problem. For instance, most of the time, clergy must use their judgment based on broad principles, experience, and education from the Bible and other sources. The Bible does not address every predicament humans may face. Judges must make countless discretionary rulings in an orderly society.

---

365. Paul's opinion seems to continue through verse 39. We may still believe Paul's opinion is God's word, but the *as written* interpretation would be, it is God's word that it is Paul's opinion, which is not saying anything.

366. Paul is not saying that his writings are the Bible except for this opinion. He could not have presumed his words would end up in scripture as he expected the Second Coming to be soon. Rather, he means the office he holds carries an administrative authority, assumed when writing officially to the Churches. Nonetheless, he could not in good conscience exercise that authority over an opinion outside the boundaries of his office. Jesus said a similar thing in Luke 10:13–14, "Someone in the crowd said to him, 'Teacher, tell my brother to divide the inheritance with me.' Jesus replied, 'Man, who appointed me a judge or an arbiter between you?'" There was a proper use of authority, even for Jesus.

THE SIX DAY WAR IN CREATIONISM

One might think the Mosaic Law would be exacting above all biblical genres. Some of it may be. Yet even with the Law, the meaning or usefulness eventually fades. For example, in Exodus 20:5–6 and Deuteronomy 5:6, there is the well-known divine declaration: "[I punish] the children for the sin of the parents to the third and fourth generation of those who hate me, but showing love to a thousand generations of those who love me and keep my commandments."

The second commandment bluntly states that one generation's actions, for good or ill, will affect how God deals with subsequent generations. Can we assume this commandment contains hyperbole, especially the words "a thousand generations?"[367] Laws are usually without embellishments, in our world at least, but the Semitic world was different. Whether this idea in the fourth commandment developed from observation of what we might identify as hereditary traits through generations is unknown, at least to me. However, Ezekiel 18 reassesses and reinterprets this law rationally.

Ezekiel comments on this law by saying, "The one [soul] who sins is the one who will die" (18:4). He then illustrates his point with three generations of Israelites: the first generation is righteous (meaning obedient to the Law); the second is violent (killers); the third generation is again righteous. Ezekiel states quite adamantly that a violent second generation does not benefit from the righteousness of the first, nor is the third generation punished for the second's violence. Then Ezekiel asks a pointed question as to why he sets aside the plain words of the law *as written*:

> Why does the son not share the guilt of his father? Since the son has done what is just and right and has been careful to keep all my decrees, he will surely live. The one who sins is the one who will die. The child will not share the guilt of the parent [contrary to the written letter], nor will the parent share the guilt of the child. The righteousness of the righteous will be credited to them, and the wickedness of the wicked will be charged against them. (Ezekiel 18:19–20)

If what we know as hereditary traits believed to be divine blessings and cursings misguided the ancients to judge others unfairly, we cannot say. Ezekiel simply uses common sense. Yes, parents shaped us both genetically and in how they raised us—what we call "nature and nurture." Nonetheless, adults are responsible *by law* for their actions. Perhaps Ezekiel saw an old idiom in the second commandment about "a thousand generations." If so, it is not the sort of idiom generally expected in legal codes where the language must be clear to administer the law consistently. After Ezekiel, it was much clearer.

---

367. People have used the number 1,000 throughout history as a metaphor or a way of saying "a very long time." The British Empire was to last a thousand years, same with the Third Reich. This may have been especially true in ancient times. A day is "as a thousand years" to God, and Jesus shall reign a thousand years. Neither of these is likely literal.

Laws develop specifically to address wrongs and injustices and promote the people's welfare. Naturally, many rules no longer speak directly to new generations when enough time elapses. One law from the 1800s prohibited tucking ice cream cones in the back pocket. Thieves lured horses with cones into backstreets or secluded areas to steal them. That law and many like it are still on the books in many states. Few pay attention to them, but there they are.

When laws begin to lose relevance, we may reinterpret them, replace them, or they might remain unenforced. Change is unavoidable as civilization, culture, technology, knowledge, and worldviews become more complex. There are good reasons why the Old Testament is *old*; it even predicted a new covenant (Jeremiah 31:31). Eternal truths do not age. Orthodox Judaism, for that matter, recognizes much of the Mosaic Law is irrelevant in practice.

Ezekiel was aware of the second commandment. He quotes it. His concern is with those who avoid responsibility for their actions or the actions of others. What was all that language about "the fourth and fifth generation of them that hate me?" Ezekiel treats it like a hyperbolic or idiomatic expression, which also attributes the anthropomorphic trait of "jealousy" to God in the same commandment.[368]

Enough time had gone by to see the injustice of applying that law *as written*. The irony is that *according to Exodus,* the Ten Commandments are something God wrote with His finger. Exodus singles out the Ten Commandments as unique because of God's direct authorship. This uniqueness implies that God did not write the rest of the Bible, which is self-evident anyway. Yet Ezekiel is confident enough to amend "God's writing" of the commandment. That is so unusual that one must wonder if Ezekiel believed God wrote down the command. At any rate, he did not take the "sins of the father" literally.

The *spirit* or intent of the Law covers what the *words* no longer can or ever could.

---

368. God's "jealousy" in the Bible first appears here in Exodus. Because of the importance of the Ten Commandments, the *jealousy of God* became part of the popular language about God. It appears about a dozen times in the Bible. What it cannot mean is that God actually feels jealousy in the ordinary manner it is used. "Jealousy" maybe how the Bible authors express God's rights due Him under the covenant when they are trampled on by the covenant people. They had no right to worship other gods or withhold agreed upon obligations. Yet, ultimately, God's rights are not as ours, which are endowed upon us from outside ourselves. Our rights are contingent on God or some law or agreed upon contract by a higher body. Here in Exodus, jealousy is related to God's right to be Israel's God and King for rescuing them out of slavery under Pharaoh and the Egyptian pantheon. Remember the Israelites at the time believed other gods existed. Gods were affiliated with a tribe, city-state, or empire. Surprisingly, Yahweh did not inform them at the time that he is alone as God in the universe. He says in Exodus, "You will have no other gods before me." Not "There are no other gods besides me." God appears not to have revealed this at Mt. Sinai. This distinction gives credibility to the text in that it is authentic to the time it purports to be. No later prophet making this story up would likely admit to other gods in competition with Yahweh. These scriptures are genuine to their times.

The law said plenty about justice, which helps put the language of the second commandment into perspective. Most people have enough common sense to see an injustice, but literalism can make those so inclined to abandon common sense when it is to their advantage. A well-known example is that the Pharisees would ease their farm animal's burdens on the Sabbath but resisted Jesus relieving the burdens of the sick and disabled on the Sabbath (Luke 13:15–17). The Pharisees had to know nothing was wrong with Jesus's healing ministry, but they could gratuitously apply the written law against him. Ezekiel teaches his generation not to hide behind the letter of the Law. That means all are personally responsible for handling the spirit of the Law justly.

Law, including that in the Bible, cannot address all possible abuses and misinterpretations because unintended consequences are unpredictable, inevitable, too numerous, and beside the point since amendments and new laws can address future abuses. The Law helps spell out acceptable behavior within society and the state, but conflict is inevitable with human nature. People are clever enough to find ways to circumvent a law's intent without violating the letter.

A balance between justice and mercy is the aim of interpreting laws, particularly in the Bible. That is what judges do when they exercise discretion. If all we needed were words *as written*, there would be little use for judges. Yet, early Christians radically reinterpreted the Law of Moses in the light of Christ, with apparently little regard for the written language. Why? Because Jesus is the Logos, the governing principle of the universe. Therefore, we understand scripture through him, who is the eternal Word.

Ezekiel's words regarding the sins of the fathers are instructive precisely because they illustrate the practical need to interpret scripture in light of a changing world, i.e., "You've heard it said of them of old...But I say unto you." When fundamentalists cry, "science changes, but the Bible doesn't change," it means the written words don't change. The Koran doesn't change either, nor does the Book of Mormon. That is the nature of written documents and why we must amend Laws, such as the Constitution and, yes, even the Hebrew Bible, where the Prophets and especially the New Testament amend the Mosaic Law.

Written words not changing can be a strength and a weakness. That is not a criticism of the Bible; it means human language is finite and limited, while God's Word is not. That is why the Bible and God's "eternal and perfect Word" are not identical. YEC equivocates on "God's eternal and perfect Word." Words may remain the same, but their meanings can change, and so can the context. But God never changes, and neither does His perfect and eternal Word, or it would neither be perfect nor eternal. That is why law cannot be the end-all and be-all of God's revelation. Law cannot be the grounds for a loving or familial relationship. But love defined by Jesus's words and actions endures forever. Jesus changed how we look at everything, especially scripture (2 Corinthians 3:13–18). Even the Ten Commandments are open to diverse handling depending on the circumstance. The human condition is too complicated, and the metaphysical nature of God's plan makes capturing aspects of it in a so-called one-to-one correspondence to *this* reality impossible. How much more out of reach is capturing the divine nature with words?

To acknowledge diversity in Scripture, Israel administered the law with justice and mercy. A reading of the same Law in Exodus and Deuteronomy shows diversity in the written language. The Ten Commandments listed in Exodus are not "word for word" the same as in Deuteronomy, and God wrote it once! As Moses said, "He wrote them on two stone tablets and gave them to me" (Deuteronomy 5:22).

Yet Exodus and Deuteronomy are not in word-for-word agreement!

I am aware of attempts to harmonize these references and other explanations to account for the differences so that *words not written must sort out those written.* We interpret rigid laws and reapply them to new circumstances. Not doing so is *legalism* or its stepsister, literalism.

That is what we have with the YE Reform Movement.

Taking the entire Bible and its meaning *as written*, or some YErs like to say "verbatim" (except poetry and some prophecy), is a practical impossibility. *Insisting on doing* so is a neo-Pharisaic approach to the scripture that becomes absurd in practice. It means not only interpreting the Bible literally but that the Bible we have is precisely *as written in its original form.*

Here are the facts:

1. The original scripts of the Bible have not survived.

2. The originals had no spaces between words, lower case letters, punctuation, paragraphs, periods, chapters, headings, or verse numbers. All these changes we now have are assumptions, though educated ones. Yet they can affect interpretation.

3. We have thousands of copies and fragments of scripture that vary.

4. Most variations are minor, but some do alter the meaning of the text, if only slightly.

5. Some words, verses, and whole chapters in our current manuscripts are absent in earlier versions and copies, making it near-certain that some were not in the original text.

6. Textual criticism has helped recover some of the original text, but not all is recoverable.[369]

7. New archeological discoveries continuously help scholars correct mistranslations unnoticed or unknowable previously. There are likely more mistranslations and variants to discover.

8. The Septuagint was the scripture of choice in the New Testament Church, yet we know it is full of inaccuracies.

None of this is a significant concern unless one thinks God wrote or supervised each word. If God micromanaged the written text, why not ensure the same perfection in the copying?

Seriously, why not?

Perfect copying would not be beyond God's powers and would seem necessary if word-for-word accuracy to His word choice over the human author was His will. Are we to believe the composition was perfect, but its transmission was flawed? Why the glaring inconsistency with thousands of words, many paragraphs, and whole chapters? Indeed, God was the inspiration for the Bible, but He did not write it. The Bible is an authentic set of books written by men inspired but not controlled by the Holy Spirit. That has explanatory power over any discrepancies.

So what does "as written" mean? It is a slogan to appeal to the choir. Henry Morris explained it: "Christians who flirt with less-than-literal readings of biblical texts are also flirting with theological disaster. [Christians must] either...believe God's Word all the way or not at all."[370] So if there is something in the Bible you do not take as written or if you flirt with "not as written-ness," then you might as well reject the whole thing. That's right; if you reject six literal days, you might as well reject Christ too.

That's telling them.

What going "all the way" with the Bible implies is unclear. Some biblical texts are metaphorical, some are literal, and we are not always sure which. Morris's thought confuses interpreting a biblical text figuratively with not

---

369. An example of textual criticism is the height of Goliath in 1 Samuel 17:4. The Masoretic text (that we use) compiled in the tenth century AD says Goliath was six cubits and a span, which is around 9.5 to 10 feet tall. English translations come from the Masoretic text so many Christians think Goliath was gargantuan. However, two older texts, the Septuagint (second century BC) and the Dead Sea Scrolls (third century BC), both say Goliath was four cubits and a span, making him between 6.5 to 7 feet tall— a height tall enough to play in the NBA. It is more reasonable to accept the two older texts than one that comes to us more than a thousand years later and that at some point earlier was likely a copyist error.

370. Henry M. Morris, *The Origin and History of the Earth* (2000), pp. 229–231. I also found this on a Facebook thread: "Why believe any of the Bible if you call part of it a lie?" So if you are not a YEr, you are calling God a liar.

believing it. This mistake is one that a recognized scholar would not make. For Morris, literal means true, and figurative means not just false but *"theological disaster."* And this man is revered in YEC circles.

Telling people that they are flirting with theological disaster does not say anything. It is hysteria. "As written" gives the *impression* of being faithful to the text. It is hardly that if the text is metaphorical, which it often is.

Notice this statement by Ken Ham: "Just because someone states they believe the Bible is inspired or authoritative does not mean they take it *as written.*" Ham concludes, "It's really a form of doublespeak." But taking the Bible "as written" is not the same as accepting biblical authority either. Atheists are more than happy to take Genesis "as written," as do YErs. And why not? "As written" is in their self-interest precisely because atheism rejects biblical authority. Note, too, according to Ham, interpreting scripture figuratively is not doublespeak *per se* but a *"form"* of doublespeak. The word *form* muddles the thought. For Ham, this is not your garden variety doublespeak. Instead, it comes from the ethereal place of forms.

It is unclear which "form" of doublespeak Ham refers to, nor does he tell us the doublespeak types. In any case, "doublespeak" is not the use of figurative language. Thus, an example is when one pretends people should always take the Bible "as written" when they often, by necessity, cannot; that *is doublespeak.* It is talking out of both sides of one's mouth.

Indeed, it is absurd to say that taking the Bible figuratively rejects biblical authority or doesn't take scripture seriously. When something doesn't add up in the Bible or people study to understand its symbolism, they take its authority seriously. Seasoned students of the Bible do not simply appreciate the Bible "as written." They comprehend its words "as meant," which is not always as written.

Yet, we are often puzzled by what the Bible means, so we work to determine what it means as far as we can tell. Three thousand years of experience shows we do not always know what the authors intended. Well-known biblical passages are often enigmatic, such as:

- On that day, you shall surely die.
- Cain's wife.
- Talking serpent.
- Tree of life and the tree of good and evil.
- Waters above and below the earth.
- Turn the other cheek.
- All Cretans are liars.
- This generation shall not pass.
- The unpardonable sin.

- Sodom and Gomorrah have it *easier* in the Judgment.
- Graves opened with the torn veil.
- I come quickly.
- Taking God's name in vain.
- God becoming a man.
- The Virgin birth.
- If you've seen me, you've seen the Father.
- The Father is greater than I.
- The earth was without form and void.
- The Writ of Divorce law was not God's will.
- Two different versions of the fourth commandment (Exodus 20/ Deuteronomy 5).
- To the third and fourth generations.
- To name a very few.

Though we have explanations of these passages, they are enigmatic and are explained with words not "as written." We look for meaning and understanding in biblical theology, not just word definitions. Words are symbols that assemble a thought. They are not the thought. Many varied opinions exist on many biblical subjects, even among those that consider the Bible inerrant. Those opinions often divide Christians. For example, Christians that claim the Bible's teachings are both clear and inerrant differ sharply on essential points of doctrine, including:

- Various theories on the Atonement.
- The proper form of baptism.
- Whether hell is an actual place of eternal torment
- The Eucharist/Lord's Supper/Real Presence.
- The millennium.
- The precise canon of Scripture.
- Predestination and election.
- Sabbath or Lord's Day.
- Law and Grace or the role of works in salvation.
- Which day was Jesus crucified?
- What does inerrancy mean?
- On the eschatology of the nation of Israel

- The nature of the Second Coming.

- Age of the earth.

- Use or abstinence from alcohol.

- Biblical Church government.

- Thousands of denominations and growing.

- Birth-control.

- Women's role in the Church

- Sexual preference/Same-sex marriage.

- Divorce and remarriage.

On and on it goes.

Inerrancy does not help sort out the differences. Most of these differences are among those who believe the Bible is either inerrant or infallible. Ironically, some believe the Bible is so clear that anyone can understand it. If Christians struggle to understand their own fundamental teachings, how will we reach unbelievers when engaging in ridiculous fights like the SDWC?

Much of the Old Testament (especially its 613 laws) may only be applicable figuratively for Church life because they pointed to a principle that may still be valid, like mixing theological fabrics instead of sewing materials. In general, the ancients thought and wrote in more metaphoric, artistic, and creative ways because it is more profound, memorable, and fitting for spiritual or religious literature. And since their languages were less developed, figurative speech could make up for less vocabulary and less precision than modern, more-detailed languages. Less vocabulary can mean less clarity in conveying thought. Add an alien culture that no longer exists when the ideas and metaphysical concepts lack our detailed terminology, making translation daunting. A prime example is the so-called "Christmas tree" passage that affected me as a teenager:

> For the customs of the people are vain: for one *cutteth a tree out of the forest,* the work of the hands of the workman, with the axe. They *deck it* with silver and with gold; *they fasten* it with nails and with hammers, *that it move not.* (Jeremiah 10:3-4)

This passage is from the KJV, a favorite among fundamentalists and the required version by fringe groups. The problem is not with this literary masterpiece but with its language caught in time. It misleads people not thoroughly versed in how it means what it says. Jeremiah knows nothing of the Christmas tree, nor is this a prophecy about paganism's eventual contamination of Christianity implanted in Jeremiah's head by God. You must admit that cutting a tree out of the forest, "decking" it with silver and gold (tinsel effectively), and fastening it to the floor sounds "Christmassy." Now, look at a version in today's English:

Their religion is worthless. They chop down a tree, carve the wood into an idol, cover it with silver and gold, and then nail it down so it won't fall over. An idol is no better than a scarecrow. It can't speak, and it has to be carried, because it can't walk. Why worship an idol that can't help or harm you?

Jeremiah condemned the worship of false gods carved out of wood and adorned splendidly. They are not alive and cannot hurt or help, so their worship is not worth anything. Yet, millions of people condemn Christmas as pagan idol worship because they think God is condemning it. Fundamentalists are also suspicious of scholarship that undermines their favorite translations and distinctives when the scholar's work is clarifying translation difficulties. Scholars are not obsessed with the Christmas tree.

Consider the importance of dreams in the ANE. Dreams can seem real or surreal and ridiculous. They may be symbolic of issues in our lives, so we interpret them. In ancient times, the mystery behind them suggested a transcendent source. God accommodated the human tendency to dwell on the importance of dreams by using them to communicate His will. These days, many people take their dreams seriously as if God or fate is telling them something.[371]

Some imagery we experience in our dreams is a short step away from the imagery in mythology and apocalyptic literature. All three can contain bizarre metaphoric images. For example, countless people have had a reoccurring nightmare of a looming wall of water threatening to overwhelm their world. Those "tsunamis" in our dreams can symbolize the chaos and challenges in life that engulf us.

The threatening sea is still with us.

The ancients lived well exposed to nature's elements, so their connection to nature's powers was vivid and profound. Lucid dreams can mimic what we might think of as a vision. Symbolic language added a conscious form of mystery for an author and his readers. It creates drama and is fitting for spirituality and heavenly themes. It is like adding an element of worship or mysticism into the text.

Origen, the well-known third-century theologian, captures this ancient view:

> For as a man consists of body, soul, and spirit. So in the same way does Scripture. These senses were the literal, the moral, and the allegorical; *the literal was the least significant,* the only one that a spiritually unenlightened mind could grasp, *and the only one that did not even exist for many biblical passages.* The moral sense was the "soul" of scripture, discerned by more spiritually advanced thinkers. *The allegorical sense was*

---

371. Even if God did not place an enlightening dream in one's mind, the fact that He created the phenomenon to deepen our psychology makes Him its source.

the highest, revealing theological insights that shone with a grandeur that overwhelmed the literal meaning of the passage to which the allegory was attached by the thinnest of exegetical cords. (emphasis mine)

Origen does not prove that Genesis 1 is an allegory. His comments seem overstated to me, but that may be a modern bias of my own. What is sure is that the ancients thought more like Origen than modern fundamentalists do. They prized the figurative sense as the depth of scripture because it was akin to the author's theological intent. It also illustrates that literalism was not all the rage in the pre-scientific era, as YEC assumes.

We know the Church fathers brought the Old Testament into the Christian canon, not as covenantal books for Christianity but because the Church could take the non-Christian elements figuratively. A prime example is Psalm 137:8–9:

> "Daughter Babylon...happy is the one who repays you...who seizes your infants and dashes them against the rocks."

This verse, understood literally, is not even acceptable by Old Testament standards, e.g., "Vengeance is mine says the Lord" (Deuteronomy 32:35; Romans 12:18–20). Nonetheless, Christianity accepted the Old Testament books because they contained the promises and prophecies of the Messiah, providing a context for the birth of Christianity. But the Church cannot possibly incorporate vast portions of the Old Testament into Church life "as written." YErs surely understand this.

Do YErs understand that they read Genesis figuratively when they infuse the Gospel and Christ into it? They do not seem to. They are proud to take Genesis as written or literally and to shun figures of speech under the mistaken impression that they are preserving biblical authority. Whenever we interpret an Old Testament passage with Christ or his Gospel, we are not treating that passage literally, even if the interpretation is true theologically. I agree that reading Christ into the Old Testament shows divine inspiration; call it biblical authority, assuming the context is warranted.

Nonetheless, a New Testament interpretation of an Old Testament passage does not mean we must take that Old Testament passage literally in its original context. A New Testament interpretation works whether the Old Testament passage was literal or not. Therefore, it is unmistakably false to claim that interpreting scripture figuratively, whether in prose narrative or poetry, is synonymous with compromising biblical authority.

Much of the Law does not apply to Jews anymore, let alone Christians. Judaism recognized this as early as the second century AD since many biblical laws and prohibitions intended to insulate Israel from Canaanite religious practices. Canaanite worship practices were extinct by the second century AD, rendering such laws irrelevant—times change. The Old Testament does not carry the same weight in the Church as it did in ancient Israel for obvious reasons.

Keith Ward writes:

While owing almost everything to its Jewish roots, Christian faith puts the whole Bible in a different light by claiming that Jesus of Nazareth both negates and fulfills the Hebrew Bible prophecies and expectations. He negates them by becoming the origin of a new religious set of institutions, the Christian Church, no longer bound by Jewish law, centered on him *as the decisive revelation* of God. He fulfills them by taking the main strands of Jewish prophecy, law, and wisdom, and bringing them to one focal point in his own person.[372]

Hebrews 1:1–3 sums it up:

In the past, God spoke to our ancestors through the prophets at many times and in various ways, but in these last days he has spoken to us by his Son, whom he appointed heir of all things, and through whom also he made the universe. The Son is the radiance of God's glory and the exact representation of his being, sustaining all things by his powerful word.

Christ is the Word, the message, and the revelation. Not everything in the Bible is an equal *revelation*. Christians who treat the Old Testament as equal revelation with the New Testament may not fully appreciate who Christ is and what he did. Old and New Testaments may be equally *inspired,* but inspiration and revelation are not the same things. Inspiration refers to the *source of influence* (the Holy Spirit), while revelation relates to the extent of *God's self-disclosure of both His person and His plans*. Hebrews says, "Christ is the exact representation of God's being and the radiance of God's glory." There is no brighter revelation possible in this universe than the Incarnate Christ.

According to the book of Hebrews, Moses mediated the Old Covenant, while the New Covenant came through the personal revelation of God's unique Son. Divine revelation may shed light with various intensities. In the New Testament, The Logos is the Light of the world: "In him was life, and that life was the light of all mankind. The light shines in the darkness, and the darkness has not [perceived] it" (John 1:4–5). Christ, the Logos, is the source of all enlightenment in this universe, including science, whether in scripture or not.

Old and New Testaments shine light, but the latter outshines the former.

---

372. Keith Ward, *The Word of God? The Bible after Modern Scholarship* (Great Britain, 2010), p. 9.

26.
THE NEW TESTAMENT "GENESIS"

So it is written: "The first man Adam became a living being;"
the last Adam, a life-giving spirit.
—1 Corinthians 15:45

The synoptic gospels establish Jesus' human nature. Mark is likely the earliest gospel and emphasizes Jesus' human nature more than the others. Matthew and Luke begin with the genealogies of Jesus and his birth.

John opens the fourth gospel with this:

In the beginning was the Word [Logos] and the Word was with God, and the Word was God. He was with God in the beginning. Through him all things were made; without him nothing was made that has been made. In him was life, and that life was the light of all mankind. The light shines in the darkness, and the darkness has not [perceived or] overcome it... *The Word became flesh* and made his dwelling among us.

The words "In the beginning" telegraph John's intentions to bring a new perspective on creation. He says, "Christ is the *reason* for the cosmos." The New Testament term "New Adam" applied to Jesus is not literal (how could it be). It is a theological way of saying we have a new *"in the beginning"* with the new reborn humanity and new creation.

John's gospel starts "before" the beginning with God and the Word (Logos). The result of this new beginning is a new creation in John 1:14, "The Word became flesh." That is the moment the New Adam arrived. John is not interested in *when* the Creation of the world occurred. He does not mention the animals, vegetarianism, even the first Adam, or any central role Adam may have had. Instead, he reveals that the Word or Logos is the reason for and the origin of all things. The universe was made for him, by him, and through him. The purpose of the creation is to infuse it with the Logos, i.e., with his light and life (John 1:4).

John concerns his readers with things unknowable to the author of Genesis or anyone else.

"Logos" was a philosophical term in the Greco/Roman world that carried more connotation than its literal meaning—"reasoned speech." We get the English word *logic* from "logos." It also carried the concept of thought and meaning. In everyday Jewish usage, it had the generic meaning of *"word,"* but theologically, it could refer to the Torah and Wisdom. In John, Judaism, and Hellenistic philosophies, the Logos imbued life and enlightenment into the world. John separates from all other philosophical systems by stating that Logos becomes human (John 1:14).[373]

John introduces a new "Let there be light," expressed by the Godhead who is Christ the Word. Like Genesis, the darkness in John is not good. John is clear about darkness being evil while veiled in Genesis by omitting the reference "good" to the darkness. The Logos makes the world intelligible. The true light that gives enlightenment to everyone entered the world. He made the world, and the world did not recognize him upon entering it. He came to his own, but his own did not receive him (John 1:9–11).

In the intertestamental period, there was little news about "the word of the Lord to a prophet saying." As a result, the voice of the prophets went dark. The period of the Prophets officially ended when John the Baptist handed the baton to Jesus. The transition inaugurated a new kind of Creation in the Gospel of John when God said, "Let there be *the* Light."

John continues, "Yet to all who did receive him, to those who believed in his name, he gave the right to become children of God—children born not of natural descent, nor of human decision or a husband's will, but born of God." So the first Adam is not relevant here.

The new creation is *"not of natural descent...or of a husband's will."* Therefore, genealogies are not relevant to newborn children of God. The natural world is temporal; the new is eternal. The first Adam does not appear in this "new beginning." Indeed, John intentionally avoids Adam with the phrase *"not of natural descent."* Notice, too, that this new beginning did not consider "a husband's will." Just as Joseph was irrelevant to the birth of Jesus, Adam does not contribute to a new humanity. The new creation began with a new human— "The Word became flesh."

There is nothing in this *"New Testament Genesis"* about any presuppositions of YEC—not a thing. There is no claim that the key to all truth is a "literal Genesis;" there is no dependence on the book of Genesis, only the faintest allusion to it, not even a nod to *six days*. For John, *the* truth, *the* word, and the meaning of all things arrived *in person*. It had not arrived this way on tablets of stones or words on a page.

The New Adam is a new beginning or a new *"In the beginning."*

There is no flood geology in John. There is no flood geology in Genesis, for that matter.[374] There is no "root" of the Gospel found in Moses's creation

---

373. Most Greco Roman philosophical systems and even Judaism would have tracked well with much of John's description of the Logos. The dividing line is verse 14 where the Logos becomes flesh. This was unacceptable on the radical dualism of the Hellenistic world when philosophers considered flesh evil and spirit good.

374. YErs warn people not to add anything to Genesis, especially science. Yet their "flood geology" does just that.

account, something unthinkable to John, who wrote, "For the law was given through Moses; [but] *grace and truth came through Jesus Christ*" (John 1:17). After this statement on Moses, John says, "*No one* has seen God *at any time* but the one and only Son."

So Moses never actually saw God when he received the Law, though the story *reads* that way in Exodus.[375] John sublimates Moses's authority (and, therefore, his writings) to Jesus' authority, who is the only human that has seen God. This critical distinction between humans and Jesus already puts him in a different category since no ordinary human can see God and live (Exodus 33:20).

Christians believe *Jesus* is the foundation upon which God's plan rests so that any other foundation does undermine *all* Christian doctrine, especially the Gospel. "For no one can lay any foundation other than the one already laid, which is Jesus Christ" (1 Corinthians 3:11).

Notice another allusion to Genesis in John: "He *breathed* on them and said, "Receive the Holy Spirit" (John 20:22). This act was a theological "upgrade" from a similar act in Genesis. When God created Adam, He "breathed into [him] the breath of life." In Genesis, that means *soulish life* or what we would call *biological life*. The Logos breathed a new kind of life into the disciples, creating souls reborn and a spiritual organism called the Church. John trumps the first Adam and so the first creation with this new creative act that began with the Incarnation. The Logos now infuses those who receive him with the breath of eternal life.

The "tree of life" has reopened.

The Logos or Word that "breathed" into Adam in Genesis *anticipated* a reality that "has come, is coming and is to come" through Jesus Christ. The type is a shadow of reality. God's finishing work in humanity *begins* in John 20:22. We can bury ourselves so deep in the Old Testament that we lose a Christian perspective. As I said in the Preface, I was a pastor in a Church with a Jewish Christian culture where very few members were Jewish. We observed the seventh-day Sabbath and the annual feast days of Israel but in a "Christian way." We saw Jesus in those practices and concluded they must be obligatory, especially since the author quotes God personally commanding them. But the fact is the Hebrew Scriptures, in general, suggest the Jesus Christ we came to know.

A suggestion is not the reality nor the revelation that enlightens it.

A careful study of John's gospel will yield many reflections of a "new genesis" or a new creation, the new commandments of Jesus (John 15:10–17), and a new exodus. Examples and reflections are a theology on rebirth in John 3; Jesus is the Bread of Life (Manna) come down from heaven that gives eternal

---

375. Moses was not allowed to see God's face (Exodus 33:20), which means he did not see God's real person or essence. Moses was allowed to see a theophany of God, which is a special representation of His presence.

sustenance; we have life more abundantly (John 10:10); Jesus is the vine (tree) of life (John 15:5). The word *"life"* appears in John forty-one times, while it appears only twenty-nine times in the much larger book of Genesis, which is about the origins of life.

Peter Enns offers this piece of advice:

A proper Christian understanding of the Creation narratives will follow the lead of the New Testament writers in seeing the Gospel as the culmination of the ancient message. Christians should not search through the Creation stories for scientific information they believe is important to see there. They should read it, as the New Testament writers did, as ancient stories *transformed in Christ*.[376]

Precisely. Christ the Logos transforms Genesis. Young earth creationism freezes us there.

In 2 Corinthians 3:2–3, Paul wrote, "You yourselves show that you are a letter of Christ, prepared by us, written not with ink but with the Spirit of the living God, not on tablets of stone but tablets of human hearts." God's Word is less a handwritten letter than the living Spirit creating Christ's likeness in the conscience of a Christian. That is union with God—direct communication—the most efficient kind. As Paul said, "The letter kills, but the Spirit gives life."

That is the language of Christianity. Paul further instructs the Corinthians to interpret Moses in the light of Christ and not Christianity in the light of Moses. Second Corinthians 3:13–18 says:

[Christians read the OT] not like Moses, who put a veil over his face to keep the people of Israel from gazing at the end of the glory that was being set aside... To this very day, when they hear the reading of the old covenant, the same veil is still there, since only in Christ is it set aside. Indeed, to this very day whenever Moses is read, a veil lies over their minds; but when one turns to the Lord, the veil is removed.

The "veil" refers to Moses's encounter with God in Exodus 34. Upon leaving the Lord's presence down Mt. Sinai, Moses' face was glowing from the experience. But Paul says the people were afraid, not of the glow but because the luminosity would fade in front of their eyes, indicating the temporary nature of the revelation and perhaps the fading presence of God. Paul says Moses "put a veil over his face to keep the Israelites from gazing *at the end of the glory [of the Old Covenant that] was being set aside*." Admittedly, Paul's interpretation does not easily derive from Exodus 34. This interpretive method is typical New Testament treatment of scripture in light of the Incarnation. Christ transformed biblical interpretation beyond literalism. That would be earth-shattering if understood by the "one to one," "as written," "word-for-word" crowd.

---

376. Peter Enns, *The Evolution of Adam: What the Bible Does and Doesn't Say about Human Origins* (Brazos Press, Grand Rapids Michigan, 2011), p. 75.

The decreasing "glow" or "glory" on Moses' face indicated that the revelation to Israel would give way to an internal enlightening by a new revelation with *"ever-increasing glory"* (2 Corinthians 3:18). The idea is that the old covenant's glory was only on the surface of Moses's face and fading, only to flicker out eventually. That glory seemed to be external and not internalized in the people. It is like the moon's glory compared to that of the sun. The moon has no light in itself but reflects the sun. Likewise, the Old Testament is a mere reflection of the Light Himself.

Paul finishes his point this way: "And we all, with *unveiled* faces reflecting the glory of the Lord, are being transformed into the same image from one degree of glory to another, which is from the Lord, who is the Spirit" (NET).

The idea seems to be that the old covenant under Moses was a reflection of the glory of God. Today, the Church is the body of Christ in our midst radiating ever-increasing glory in and through us, not merely reflecting *on us*. This radiance is a spiritual reality, not a physical one. "It is Christ *in us* the hope of glory" (Colossians 1:27). The scriptures tell us this, but nothing written can accomplish it.

In *The Bible Made Impossible,* Christopher Smith writes:

> The purpose, center, and interpretive key to scripture is Jesus Christ. It is embarrassing to have to write this, for it should be obvious to all Christians... Seeing Christ as central compels us to always try to make sense of everything we read in any part of scripture in light of our larger knowledge of who God is in Jesus Christ. We do not then read scripture devotionally to try to find tidbits there that are "meaningful to" or that "speak to" us, wherever we are in our personal subjective spiritual experiences. We do not read scripture as detached historians trying to judge its technical accuracy in recounting events. We do not read scripture as a vast collection of infallible propositions whose meanings and implications can be understood on their own particular terms. *We only, always, and everywhere read scripture in view of its real subject matter: Jesus Christ... That is, for Christians, Christ is the center, the inner reason [Logos] and the end of all of scripture...* "The law is only a shadow of the good things that are coming—not the realities themselves" (Hebrews 10:1; emphasis mine).[377]

The Evangelical Church needs fresh emphasis on Christ's personal authority, not merely in the hierarchical sense but as the authoritative source for truth through an intimate relationship. There is the temptation of substituting the personal influence of Christ for the written text, the Bible. Yet, the scripture subordinates itself when stating that Christ has *all authority* and is the

---

377. Christian Smith, *The Bible Made Impossible: Why Biblicism Is Not a Truly Evangelical Reading of Scripture"* (2012), p. 166.

personification of truth: "I am the way, the truth, and the life." That is not a low view of scripture but a high view of the Logos.

Jesus inaugurated the new creation by being the Firstborn from a resurrection. Being in Christ and the new humanity that the New Adam creates is Christianity. Being in Christ has nothing to do with a literal Genesis. Genesis is not "the key to reforming the Church and reclaiming our culture," no matter how one interprets it. God's salvation plan cannot possibly rest on the six literal days that Moses or someone else authored.

I try not to judge motives because they are hard to know and beside the point. Accusations of conspiracy, "compromise," being an "enemy of biblical authority" are red flags showing the lack of confidence that most extremists have in the merits of their case. A case has sufficient value, or it does not. If the case for an earth that is older lacks merit, then a confident and knowledgeable person will show why it lacks merit. But judging motives is a fool's errand. We all have believed things we were sure about but were mistaken.

Mistakes are what Jesus said of the poor; they will always be with us. Overcoming poverty requires education and a willingness to stop habits perpetuating the *poverty of understanding*. An excellent place to start is reassessing our presuppositions. The scripture tells us that wise people will accept correction; they do not take it upon themselves to correct everyone else.

But what kind of Christians call God a liar if the Bible means something unexpected?

27.
THE SLIPPERY SIDE OF THE SLOPE

*Foremost is that allowing these [six] days to be long periods of time
undermines the foundations of the message of the Cross... As soon as people allow
for millions of years for the fossil record the whole foundations of the Message of
the Cross and the Atonement have been destroyed.*[378]
—Ken Ham

With the kind of thoughtful reflection that accompanies panic, Ken
Ham gives the most important reason to believe the universe is six thousand
years old—because without it, *"the whole foundations of the message of the Cross
and the Atonement have been destroyed."* Fear is undoubtedly a motivating factor
in YEC, although justifying the fear is elusive.

With this, we have the *slippery slope argument.*

Slippery slopes can occur, but they make weak arguments. In YEC, what
is *foremost* in Genesis is not the revelation of one God that transcends nature or
the value he places on *all* humanity by making us in His image or the place we
hold in God's plan. Above all other considerations, what is "foremost to YErs"
is the twenty-four-hour day, six-day chronological sequence. Extremism often
results when nonessential distinctives become *foremost.*[379]

It is true that assuming the days of Genesis represent billions of years is
unacceptable; I agree with YEC on this. There is no evidence that ancient Israel
interpreted the days as eons, nor could the author know the universe is billions
of years old. That would not be a Late Bronze Age or Iron Age development.

But YEC assumes a false choice when it insists on only two basic interpretations of the six days in Genesis: six literal days or billions of years. The
point in this book is that Genesis is neither. The author is not interested in the
age of the earth. Though the account uses days, it is not about days. Genesis

---

378. Ken Ham, "The Necessity for Believing in Six Literal Days," December 1, 1995, AiG website.

379. Distinctives that identity a group are prone to extreme adherence since they are the reason
for the group's existence. Protecting distinctives becomes an imperative for the group's survival.
When a distinctive that is not essential to the Gospel is mixed into evangelism and both must
be accepted together, the Gospel is diluted. Other examples are: God's sacred name groups,
Sabbatarianism, Mormonism, Word Faith groups and the health wealth gospel, some (not
all) Charismatics and Pentecostals, radical environmentalism, and any group within the main
branches of Christianity that mix what belongs in discipleship training into accepting the Gospel.

has religious and theological priorities. Interpreting that injects billions of years into the text is concordism which most recognized scholars reject.[380]

Forcing the Bible to fit into a worldview outside itself does an injustice to its character. The Bible hardly needs another worldview to make points in its natural context. It does require a worldview from its day to be authentic. That also requires us to understand the changing worldviews represented throughout the Bible. The best we can deduce is that the Bible does not commit to any age or date of the universe regardless of the going theory on origins at any given time. The last part of the above Ham quote is objectionable: an old earth undermines "the foundations of the message [Gospel] of the Cross and the Atonement have been destroyed."

Foundations? What foundations? We know that the life of Jesus is the foundation for the *message of the cross,* the gospel, and atonement—for the creation and the new creation (John 1:1–3). How is the age of the earth any kind of foundation? Genesis and YEC are not the same things, no matter how much YErs try to make them appear so. Notice the strained and indirect wordiness. An old universe does not undermine the cross exactly; instead, it undermines:

1. The foundations of;
2. The message of;
3. The cross.

The undermining is three "degrees" removed from the cross.

Ham does not say which foundation he refers to or how many there are. So, again, we have a strong yet unclear YE assertion. The statement sounds terrible, whatever it means. The word *foremost* typically means "*of the highest priority.*" That is a signal to take the point seriously.

Okay, let's do that.

The destruction of the message, the cross, and the atonement (i.e., the Gospel) likely means that an old earth will lead people away from their need for atonement. They won't get that humans need redemption. You are not alone if the earth's age and the atonement seem disconnected.

YErs believe that the universe's deep age somehow removes universal sin, eliminating the need for atonement. YE evangelists believe that an older earth casts doubt on Christ's atoning work or, as Ham insists, *destroys it*. How is this

---

380. I am familiar with Gerald Schroeder's apologetic work on Genesis. Because of the relativity of time, the days of creation for Schroeder are both literal (from God's perspective) and billions of years each from ours. He actually assigns billions of years to each day "coincidently" arriving at the approximate age of the universe. Although there are many helpful points that Schroeder makes, especially in science, Hebrew idioms, and the understanding of Genesis from the great medieval philosophers of Judaism, in the opinion of many, his reinterpretation of the six days is not one of them.

destruction possible? Nobody knows, despite YEC's certainty and multiple attempts to explain it.

Stepping back, however, all Christian traditions agree that *modern* humans came on the scene thousands and not millions of years ago—that all humans are related—and that sin is universal. You do not need Genesis for that; as G. K. Chesterton said, "You only have to read the front page of any newspaper." Human sinfulness has been evident throughout the time before there was a Bible.

Connecting the age of the earth with our perceived need for atonement is unintelligible. Ken Ham himself wrote:

> Many great men of God who are now with the Lord have believed in an old earth... Scripture plainly teaches that salvation is conditioned upon faith in Christ, *with no requirement for what one believes about the age of the earth or universe.*[381]

We are dealing with cognitive dissonance. One immediate defeater of connecting the earth's age with the atonement is that believers who accept the science on the universe's age also see the need for atonement since the two ideas are unrelated.

YErs would object at this point, insisting that YEC is more than the belief in a young earth. But that is my point. YEC, its reform movement with presuppositions and claims (see chapter 1), and the extreme devotion to them are at issue on these pages, not the simple belief the earth is young based on literal interpretation. Christians have always been free to think that way no matter how wrong it is because it doesn't matter. The issue is extremism. YErs treating a clear nonessential as essential while admitting it is not really essential.

YEC would be correct or incorrect if it were just the simple belief that the universe is young, and we might debate it seriously. But claiming that YEC is the key to everything from biblical authority to preserving the "message of the cross," "the atonement," and whether God might be a liar makes it an ideology alien to Christianity.

The *faith* of non-young earth Christians is intact, no matter the claims of mainstream science about God or YE science about "flood geology." While science might *imply* that God exists or He doesn't, it cannot prove or disprove God because it is naturalistic, and God is not. On the contrary, *faith in God* may be compromised among YE reformists if:

- The earth is old.
- The universe is old.
- Animals (including marine life) were carnivorous before human sin.

---

381. Ken Ham, "Does the Gospel depend on a Young Earth?" November 10, 2013, AiG website.

- Animals die because they are mortal, not because humans sin.

- Evolutionary Creationism is true.

- Progressive creationism is true.

- The Big Bang is true.

- The Bible contains an error.

- Dinosaurs were absent on the Ark.

Under any of these circumstances, some YErs suggest they could never trust the rest of the Bible because any one of these "ifs" means God and Jesus are liars. What kind of Christians are these? They are on the slipperiest of slopes, and it is a fanciful one.

Nothing about the Creation could undermine the cross as Paul says:

For I am convinced that neither death, nor life, nor angels, nor rulers, nor things present, nor things to come, nor powers, nor height, nor depth, *nor anything else in all creation,* will be able to separate us from the love of God in Christ Jesus our Lord. (Romans 5:38–39 NRSV; emphasis mine)

Paul's words notwithstanding, for YErs zealots, an old earth is a most dangerous idea. Yet to suggest that anything can undermine the cross is to misunderstand the cross. The cross altered everything because of who its victim was—*the Creator—the Incarnate One.* Nothing can undermine the cross of Christ, let alone "destroy the message of atonement:"

For by [the Logos] all things were created that are in heaven and that are on earth, visible and invisible, whether thrones or dominions or principalities or powers...having forgiven you all trespasses...having nailed [them] to the cross. Having disarmed principalities and powers, he made a public spectacle of them, triumphing over them in it. (Colossians 1:16, 14–15 NKJV)

But according to YE rhetoric, an old earth can bring all that down.

YEC websites are devoted to establishing this age/cross "undermining." What do they mean by undermining? They mean if people believe the earth is old, they will eventually reject the Bible, Jesus, and who knows what else, as if there is a dependence on a young earth for *full acceptance of the Gospel,* which they desperately claim they don't believe. In a statement from YE scholars, we find this: "To be sure, we are not insisting that a person must be a young-earth creationist to be saved and in a right relationship with God. Faith in Christ alone is sufficient for that."[382]

Yet, at the same time, there is this:

---

382. From the "Prologue" in *Coming to Grips with Genesis,* a set of essays by YE scholars, August 2008, page 20.

As soon as you surrender the Bible's authority in one area [the age of the earth], you "unlock a door" to do the same thing in other areas. Once the door of compromise is open, *even if ajar just a little*, subsequent generations push the door open wider. Ultimately, this compromise has been a major contributing factor in the loss of biblical authority in our Western world.[383]

How does an incorrect estimate of the earth's age lead to such a slippery slope?

The phrases "surrender the Bible's authority" and "door of compromise" are YEC *"in speak."* They are prejudicial statements. The Bible's authority is not in whatever science existed at the time, any more than whatever was the existing engineering or plumbing. Taking the days of creation figuratively is not "surrendering the Bible's authority," especially when your motive is to respect the nature of God above all else. I could say, "Once you open a door that humanizes God, even if ajar just a little, subsequent generations will push the door wide open and worship an all too human God."

And isn't that what has happened?

With this, YErs commit the informal fallacy of *Appealing to the Consequences*.

Appealing to the Consequences

If you bring naturalism and its presuppositions to the early Chapters of Genesis, it is just a short step to denying all the miracles of Scripture —including the Resurrection of Christ.

—John MacArthur[384]

Here, MacArthur appears to confuse the philosophical worldview "naturalism" and its presuppositions with deep age ideas and science's naturalistic *methods*. Science is the study of nature, so its *methods* must be naturalistic. But *naturalism* is a different thing. Naturalism is not science or a method; it is philosophy.

Philosophical naturalism is the belief that nothing exists beyond the natural world. That is not a scientific statement; it is a statement within the branch of philosophy called *ontology*. Ontology is the theory of "being" or what has "existence." Philosophical naturalism (presupposes only physical things exist) and divine creation *are* at odds. However, naturalistic explanations of *how nature works* are not at odds with creation since God determined how nature works—naturally, that is. Nature is not the enemy. Neither how nature works

---

383. Ken Ham, "Does the Gospel Depend on a Young Earth?" January 1, 2010; last featured November 10, 2013, on the AiG website.

384. Terry Mortenson, Thane H. Ury, Foreword by John MacArthur, *Coming to Grips with Genesis* (2008), p. 14. MacArthur also claims that interpreting Genesis figuratively is a slippery slope of "epic proportions."

nor has worked in the past is not the enemy. We are free and encouraged to discover how nature functions (Psalm 139:14; Romans 1:20). The problem with some scientists is that they appear to take credit for how nature works by merely discovering its mechanisms.

Doing science is not much different from engineering, detective work, or mechanics. In those occupations are Christian believers and philosophical naturalists. They follow the natural law that governs their work that Christians believe God established. Atheistic scientists have a dominant platform to promote philosophical naturalism outside their discipline. Christianity vs. Philosophical Naturalism is what most people mean when they claim Christianity and science are at odds.

Let's look at MacArthur's quote again:

If you bring naturalism and its presuppositions [that nothing exists outside physical nature] to the early Chapters of Genesis, *it is just a short step* to denying all the miracles of Scripture—including the Resurrection of Christ.

MacArthur does not realize that naturalism and its presuppositions *already deny the resurrection and all miracles.* MacArthur appears to say that Progressive Creationism and Evolutionary Creationism build on *metaphysical naturalism,* yet neither is doing that because both are theistic. If God sustains nature's substances and processes that He created in the composition and development of living organisms, then that does not assert metaphysical naturalism, which requires "nature" (whatever that is) to be solely responsible for all life and existence itself. Evolutionary Creationism rejects this.

Science defines nature as "the physical force regarded as causing and regulating phenomena." Note the words "regarded as," which softens the definition. Read the same sentence without "regarded as," and it is more potent— "nature is the physical force causing and regulating phenomena." A physical force can be isolated and quantified, but that cannot be done with "nature" if it exists everywhere; since then, it would be omnipresent and immeasurable, which is more a description of the supernatural. If nature is not everywhere or all there is, then something that exists beyond nature, by definition, is unnatural or supernatural. In other words, "nature," aka "Mother Nature," is simply a substitute for God's operations upholding and sustaining the universe He created. Randomness in nature's movements is necessary to provide a context for rational beings possessing free will. Therefore, fundamentalists should use caution in attacking natural processes, which are nothing less than a visual of God's operations.

Ironically, even a literal interpretation of the creation of Adam and Eve can be construed as naturalistic, at least in part since it says God made Adam from the dust or earth, not a creation out of nothing. Adam means "earth" as Paul said, Adam was of the earth, earthly (1 Corinthians 40, 47–49), and God said to both Adam and Eve, "For dust you are, and to dust you shall return"

(Genesis 3:19). All creatures on this planet are composed of the elements of the earth. That is a fact, not a statement on metaphysical naturalism.

Metaphysical naturalism presupposes miracles such as the resurrection or supernatural beings like angels and God do not exist. So MacArthur's claim that if Christians apply naturalism to the creation (which denies God's existence), they might *reconsider* miracles, including the resurrection of Christ, shows confusion. Spirituality does not deny the evidence in nature for what has happened, whatever evidence may be in the cosmos or geological record. With that, MacArthur makes a fundamental mistake.[385]

Evolution is evidence of nature's causes and effects or processes in the development of life on earth—not to say evolution claims to have *caused* life or its existence but rather its development. Natural developments continue to this day. Naturalism does not explain *why* nature has causes or why and how cause and effect exist, nor can it explain existence as a phenomenon or the first appearance of life on this planet called *abiogenesis*.

Why are the laws of physics laws? Why do the laws of physics work? Why are the fundamentals fundamental and the constants constant? Identifying nature's processes hardly denies the One who created those processes. Metaphysical naturalism does deny Him. MacArthur is mistaken in his understanding of the terms.

There are different grounds for macroevolution in two broad categories: atheistic and theistic.

Neither atheism nor theism is science. In both categories, evolution is observable in nature. One is purposely put in motion and continually (not periodically) upheld and sustained; the other is neither. In Evolutionary Creationism, the process is intentional or purposeful by a Creator. In the atheistic version, evolution is incidental or may never have happened. Science can tell us about evolution's mechanisms or how physical states affect other physical states. But there is no accounting for how or why those mechanisms exist on atheistic grounds. The lack of accounting is not proof God exists; neither is it evidence against evolution. It suggests that a reasonable answer to how and why things exist may come from beyond nature.

There is much more potential for new evidence to emerge on evolution. That is not to say there is hidden evidence that evolution is false, but its processes understood today may be enhanced by related mechanisms that could add to our current explanations. We have likely unearthed only a fraction of that evidence. Why evolution exists—i.e., why life develops, or anything exists rather than nothing—is not explained by atheism. G. W. Leibniz (see his Contingency

---

385. It appears that either MacArthur misunderstands the difference between *naturalism* and *natural processes* or he expects his readers are oblivious to the nuances, which would be disingenuous. I think the former, not the latter.

Argument, 1646–1716) said, the most fundamental question is, 'Why is there something rather than nothing?'" The question goes to the heart of existence itself. Few of our finest minds in science, philosophy, and theology would disagree since many insist that those who don't take Leibnitz's question seriously don't understand it. Stephen Weinberg said even after we find a final theory of everything, why something rather than nothing "is just the kind of question we will still be stuck with." *Nothing* could have always been the alternative to something.

Evidence that physical states cause other physical states does not explain their existence. Evolution is a name given to an observable process; it does not *cause* that process; that is, evolution cannot cause itself. Something else causes it to exist, especially the deterministic quality in evolution. Everything that exists in this universe depends on something else for its existence. Where does the dependence end in the sequence of past events? It's a fundamental question since an infinite series of past events (an endless regress) is impossible.

Science does not explain *why* evolution exists because that is not a scientific question but a philosophical one. All life seems determined to survive. Why? Suppose cognitive faculties, in the case of humans, have been selected for survival value as in naturalism. Why is the vast majority of our faculties not about survival: mathematics, theoretical physics, chemistry, astronomy, literature, architecture far beyond shelter considerations, cars, ships, poetry, music, art, entertainment, landing on the moon, etc.?

Why should the first life forms strive to survive? From where did the "will" to survive come? Why instinct? Were the first creatures capable of exhibiting determination, or did something outside themselves determine survival? They had no consciousness. From where does determinism come? How does something never having existed insist upon it?—living things do insist on existing, but how or why they do is not so clear.[386]

YEC insists that evolution is, by definition, atheistic. Evolution is a natural process of causes. It is not the *first cause* from nothing. Nothingness cannot evolve into something, no matter how much time is available; time would not exist. Evolution is not a creator. Instead, evolution is how the creation *appears* to unfold; it just does. In Christianity, God created all the natural processes. In Evolutionary Creationism, the creator introduced those processes in the universe, especially on earth.

It is misguided to claim that YEC can reform the culture because it debunks evolution since YE science and theology are not peer-reviewed nor taken seriously by anyone but fundamentalists. They cannot compete with mainstream science or biblical scholarship, so they reject both. By doing so, they

---

386. There has been debate among evolutionary biologists on whether outcomes in speciation is deterministic or idiosyncratic or repeatable in the case of determinism, and unrepeatable with idiosyncratic outcomes.

alienate unbelievers. They sabotage young people who begin as Christians but fall away after buying into the false choice of science vs. six literal days, 6000 years ago. They also engage in the shallowest study of scripture, so they have no profound alternative explanations.

Consider the birth process. Sperm plus egg, plus gestation, and birth equals a newborn. Atheists credit natural processes only, while believers credit God for those processes. The developments are still the same, no matter the source credited for *causing* them. Both atheists and believers may even call the process "nature's miracle." But the phrase *nature's miracles* is an oxymoron. If nature is *fully* responsible, it is not a miracle.

The real miracle of nature is not how it works or its processes but its existence.

God is the continuous underlying reality upholding and sustaining everything that exists. Without God, nothing contingent could exist. Therefore, God did not create nature isolated from Himself only to intervene when things get complicated, aka the "God of the gaps." Divine intervention implies God comes on the scene where He had been absent, which is contradictory to omnipresent being. God is the soil for the garden of all existence.

A certain amount of randomness in the universe appears useful. Could God have grounded the universe in Himself from the instant of creation, so all things unfold within predetermined parameters while allowing freedom of motion in objects? In other words, the right balance of fine-tuning and randomness in the universe creates a platform for free will and determinism in lifeforms.

The singularity and Big Bang are analogous to how babies are born. YErs mistakenly believe that you are ipso facto a philosophical naturalist if you accept the Big Bang. That is no truer for someone who takes conception, gestation, and birth as a natural process. Christians that accept the Big Bang or the birthing process do not attribute purely naturalistic origins or *blind and undirected processes for their existence.* Unlike atheists, they don't need to. They believe in God. In Big Bang cosmology, the singularity is the universe in an "embryonic" stage, the initial swelling of expansion is "gestation," and the rapid inflation is the birth of a newborn universe. Science can speak of the birth of a baby and a universe without reference to any metaphysical cause, but Christians don't.

If the singularity came from nothing (as most atheists fear), it could not have a naturalistic explanation that merely pushes back the beginning to an original or ultimate singularity. The state of absolute nothing may or may not be natural, but *something from nothing* is decidedly unnatural. Origins have causes; ultimately, all causes are something or someone since the absence of anything cannot cause anything. The original or ultimate *someone* or *something* must transcend the universe's content (time, space, and matter/energy), or that content would not exist.[387]

All attempts to determine how God actually "did it" fail because the First Cause transcends the natural world that constrains us. Terry Mortenson and Thane H. Ury build on an easily recognizable mistake:

> Far more serious is the door to further compromise that this kind of thinking opens. Will those who think that homosexuality and adultery are condemned in Scripture be muzzled by the mere rhetorical device that such judgments reject the validity of the entire corpus of modern psychological research?[388]

Psychology, unlike physics, is not hard science. The often soft, even pseudoscientific research in psychology, especially on sexual norms, such as infinite genders, is not comparable to the overwhelming empirical data on the deep age of the universe in theoretical physics, theoretical chemistry, and the earth's age in geology. Equating the data-driven nature of physics with psychology's subjectivity on homosexuality and adultery are unwarranted comparisons.

Furthermore, celebrating the gay lifestyle and same-sex marriage is not the slippery slope but another slip on an existing slope, which began in psychology and sociology, not theology or the hard sciences.

Ironically, such births have increased significantly, especially considering over a million abortions performed annually since *Roe v. Wade* in 1973. The full impact of repealing this dubious constitutional right by deferring to the people of the states is unclear. The sexual revolution turned what society long considered healthy and necessary sexual behavior as nature's imperative into something recreational, a matter of personal taste or preference, like a balanced diet vs. fast food.

The continuing slide has brought us to partial-birth abortion on the verge of infanticide, an unlimited number of genders. Biological males identify as female, compete with biological females in high school sports, and shower together. Where psychology trumps biology, we are no longer talking about science. The cultural slide has reached the point of rejecting nature itself. That is well beyond concerns over biblical authority; it is insanity. It is also anti-science because science is about nature, not against it. On many things, science and Christianity are allies. But when one intrudes on the other, there is conflict. Yet, Christians participate in modern science because they love God's handiwork.

---

387. The two categories we know of that are without time, space, and matter/energy, are abstract objects and mind. Of the two, only mind is a causal agent. That means if the universe came from nothing (i.e., no time, space, or matter/energy) as it appears, then mind or consciousness is a possible explanation for it.

388. Terry Mortenson and Thane H. Ury, "Prologue," *Coming to Grips with Genesis* (2008), p. 17.

Using the Bible to support unchristian or unnatural behavior is nothing new, nor is homosexuality the worst. Appealing to the consequences that might lead to widespread acceptance of homosexuality or adultery among Christians is useful in fundamentalism for its bandwagon effect. Slavery, so many degrees worse, has been justified by the misuse of scripture, too; so has witch burning, abusive authority, and killing for God. Better interpreters of scripture must always defeat those who misrepresent the Bible. Misusing and abusing the Bible is not new. Still, the Bible continues to survive and thrive. Its pages are everywhere in the world. The difference is that the Bible is no longer the only (or nearly only) source of knowledge it once was. That can be good since all truth "belongs to our Master"—per Augustine. The Bible does not hold all truth.

Nonetheless, the Bible remains the primary source of the knowledge of Christ. That is why it has thrived. Knowledge of the Bible and tools for studying it have never been more available. People are free to accept or reject the Bible's tenants as always. It is up to Christianity to persuade people of the value of the scriptures without forcing dubious claims about them. Our first task as evangelists is not to convince people of the Bible's merits or win them to our cherished distinctives, whether they are essential or not. Our first task is to help people make contact with God so that they might come to Christ. As Jesus said in John 6:44, "No one can come to me unless the Father who sent me draws them, and I will raise them up at the last day."

None of this has anything to do with the age of the earth.

Ken Ham writes, "Even though it is not a salvation issue, the belief that earth history spans millions of years has very severe consequences."[389] Note, the consequences for believing the earth is old are not just severe; they are *very severe*. The fuel for YE excesses is *appealing to the consequences*. Of course, this is *fearmongering* over, of all things, the age of the earth.

It takes courage to change one's beliefs—especially the most cherished— the ones that give us an identity, even if it's a false one. There is nothing to fear since truth cannot *cause* falsehoods—instead, unwarranted connections or correlations with the truth mislead people. If truth leads a person into an error, that person is a poor steward of the truth or is unprepared to receive it.

Appealing to the consequences declares something is true or false not because it is true or false but whether the premise leads to desired or undesired outcomes. It is an if/then proposition: if "A" is true (the antecedent), then "B" will happen (the consequent). In other words, believing the earth is young is better because it leads to better consequences. However, to be a consequent, it must follow from the premises of the antecedent, or it cannot be an actual consequence. It is akin to the difference between causation and correlation. If

---

389. Ken Ham, "Does the Gospel Depend on a Young Earth?" January 1, 2010, last featured November 10, 2013, AiG website.

people conclude that God does not exist because the earth is old, they have drawn a conclusion that does not follow the premises. Instead, it appeals to emotion and is highly subjective.

Frankly, more people reject Christianity because of YEC (which is falsifiable) than because the earth is old (which the Bible allows). I do not mean the Bible teaches the earth is billions of years old. Rather, the Bible does not address the earth's age, which invites human discovery on the subject though it may be flawed.

A 2011 Barna Survey on American Christianity discovered six primary reasons young adults leave the Church. Reason number three is that "Churches come across as antagonistic to science." Twenty-three percent of young adults (formally Christian) polled by Barna say they have been "put off by the Creation and evolution debate."

We hear of young people devoted to YEC who lost their faith when studying science. At that point, the Bible they understood and science conflicted, and in the mind of the YEr, the two cannot coexist. Empirical evidence can be much more potent than a literary interpretation from the Late Bronze Age. A crisis of faith can occur with no recovery in sight when one's faith is in a misplaced view of the Bible. Real faith is not in a book but an authentic experience with a person—Jesus Christ. Nothing solidifies one's faith more than that experience.[390]

The Christian God has created a rational universe with surprises. He created an intelligible world for rational creatures to explore. God has left enough bread crumbs in our world for our critical thinking skills to follow. The universe is like a grand sandbox in our world's backyard. Modern science began in a Christian world, not a Muslim, Hindu, or Buddhist world. Many outstanding scientists have been believers. The competition is not between the Bible and scientific knowledge. Christians should be dedicated to science since it observes and delights in creation. Scientists unmistakably sense the wonders of our universe. With that wonder is the presence of God, whether those scientists know it or not. The real competition is between the interpreter's skillfulness and wisdom in unlocking nature and scripture and lacking such skills.

An August 2016 Pew poll with similar results to the Barna survey shows that an increasing number of Americans are abandoning belief in God. A prime reason is conflicts between fundamentalists and science. Science is more convincing on nature than is fundamentalism. The perception becomes that science should evaluate the Bible, which is absurd. We do not apply science to literary works because they are a different field of study requiring a different set of criteria or, as the physicist Stephen Jay Gould said, need a separate "magisterium."

---

390. By experience, I mean an unmistakable sense that God is present in the believer's life in both good times and bad that leads to a transforming faith.

The conflict between science and religion, in general, is a myth held by popular culture and fueled by fundamentalists who try to usurp the role of science and the mantle of Christianity in our culture. They are entitled to neither. The SDWC is a result of a misunderstanding of the Bible's role.

For example, in YEC, it is common to present macroevolution and the standard Big Bang model of the universe as false teachings and dangerous because they appear as "slippery slopes." YErs do not take the scientific evidence very seriously since they have particular words from the Bible. However, they acknowledge the need for some empirical science since words from a literary period cannot stand alone. The science they employ is their own brand for the sole purpose of securing their distinctives. YErs start with certainty and then search for evidence. That kind of inquiry does not go where the evidence leads; it leads where the inquirer wants to go.

And most YErs are duty-bound to "go there."

Many people, including many highly regarded scientists, have come to faith following their scientific work. They slipped the other way. Here is a small sampling of renowned scientists that converted:

Francis Collins of Biologos, already mentioned; Allister McGrath, Oxford biochemist and now Christian theologian, Founder of "Scientific theology;" Michael Reiss, a British bioethicist and now Anglican priest; Bernard N. Nathanson, an American medical doctor who helped found the National Association for the Repeal of Abortion Laws. He was the narrator for the controversial 1984 anti-abortion film *The Silent Scream*. George R. Rice, a geneticist who became an Evangelical Christian and wrote on the New Testament; Allan Sandage—a prolific astronomer—converted to Christianity later in his life, stated, "I could not live a life full of cynicism. I chose to believe, and peace of mind came over me." Gerald Schroeder, an MIT biologist responsible for converting Anthony Flew, the famed Oxford atheist, to theism by Schroeder's discoveries about God through his scientific research.

History records countless similar examples. The popular culture is not interested in them. Yet science confirms that "The heavens declare the wonders of God," and it further shows how wonderfully He made us.

If God does not exist, it does not matter how old the earth is. If God does exist, it still doesn't matter. His plan stands, no matter what, so the age of the earth does not matter. One would have to accept the false choice between God's integrity as a truth-teller or the universe's deep age. According to YEC, we can only pick one.

There is an inherent appeal to emotion by YErs since the *fear* of a consequence can prejudice one's judgment. And great monetary reward fuels the impression that God has blessed or validated an exclusive distinctive. Gain does not prove righteousness (1 Timothy 6:5).

The assumption that one's understanding of the Bible determines God's integrity is an ominous slippery slope. There can be no talking to people that think their opinion is infallible. *"Infallible opinion"* is an oxymoron. They treat their opinions on the Bible like a privately held "papacy." That would be profane if it were not preposterous. Do you honestly think YEC is capable of saving Western civilization? *The reformists do.* The idea is that if people believed the earth is young, they would believe in God and become Christians and the right kind of Christians—*"uncompromised."*

Many people believe that God exists but do not accept the Gospel. There are Jews and Muslims that believe the earth is young. As James wrote, "Even the demons believe that [God exists] and shudder" (James 2:19). Believing that God exists is not the Christian faith. Our faith accepts Jesus Christ, his identity, and what he said and did is centered in the Gospel, not literal days, flood geology, genealogies, or faith in a literal reading of Genesis 1–11.

Jesus said, "Here you are scouring through the Scriptures, hoping that you will find eternal life... What you don't seem to understand is that the Scriptures point to Me" (the Voice). Jesus is saying that we do not gain eternal life from the scriptures. Instead, the scriptures tell us *where or with whom* we may find it.

Believing in a literal Genesis is not coming to Christ. It is coming to YEC. It is not a given that one has come to Christ because one takes Genesis literally. After all, Genesis is a document in the Hebrew Bible under the old covenant. The Jews, more than any other people, lay claim to Genesis. We gain eternal life by coming to that person, not to a book called the Bible or a little book called Genesis or a single chapter in that little book.

Uncovering hidden references to Christ in the Old Testament can be a slippery slope, too, if misapplied. YErs see hints of Christ in the book of Genesis, such as sin and its consequences and the spiritual solution in Jesus. So do many Christians. But reading Jesus into Genesis requires an allegorical interpretation that can only occur after Christ appeared: "And I will put enmity between you and the woman, and between your offspring and hers; he will crush your head, and you will strike his heel" (Genesis 3:15).

It is hardly clear that Genesis 3:15 is about Christ, the Church, the Mother of Jesus, and Satan. It would then be an obscure allegory to be interpreted and cannot have a one-to-one correspondence to reality. Yet, YErs treat it and Genesis as equal to, or greater than, any New Testament scripture. They admit that a literal Genesis is key to all biblical teaching for them. But the fact is, there are allusions to Christ not only in Genesis but throughout the Hebrew Bible. Yet, the entire Old Testament is not the key to all biblical teaching. The life of Christ is that key.

As Keith Ward notes:

For a Christian, every part of the Bible must in some way, point to Christ, to the living person of Jesus who is the Christ, and to the unlimited, liberating love of God, which is revealed in Christ. To put it bluntly, it is not the words of the Bible that are 'the way, the truth, and the life.' It is the person of Christ, to whom the Bible witnesses.[391]

As I said in the "Preface," I was a pastor in a church with a Jewish Christian culture and a strong focus on the Old Testament. We believed Jewish Christianity was the best model for a Christian community, Jew and Gentile alike. Jewish Christianity was the culture of the earliest Church when we know the Holy Spirit filled the Church. We kept the seventh-day Sabbath because Jesus, Paul, and the early Church did, and most importantly, so did God (or so we thought) at creation. To be consistent, we observed the seven annual Sabbaths of Israel found in Leviticus 23. We kept those *biblical days* because God gave them and spoke them, but mostly because we saw Christian interpretations in them. The Word of God is not in the obligations in the law but their ultimate theological interpretation:

1. Christ is our Passover

2. Days of Unleavened Bread pictures coming out of sin.

3. Pentecost commemorated the giving of the Holy Spirit

4. Day of Atonement is really about Christ's atonement.

5. The Feast of Trumpets heralds the Second Coming.

6. Feast of Tabernacles pictured the millennial reign of Christ on the earth.

7. The seventh day of Creation was a type of Rest in Christ.

Since the Sabbath was one of the Ten Commandments and said to be perpetually binding, and Sunday never *explicitly* replaced the Sabbath in the New Testament, then the seventh day must still be binding—or so went our reasoning. Observing the weekly Sabbath in the Decalogue seemed inconsistent without keeping the annual Sabbaths God also commanded. We failed to make distinctions between New Testament *interpretations* and old covenant *prescriptions*. We carried the point too far.

What does this have to do with the SDWC?

YErs also have a zealous devotion to Old Testament days, but instead of the feast days in Leviticus, their dedication is to the six days in Genesis. It is one thing to interpret the days literally; it is quite another to be devoted to them or make their interpretation obligatory for an uncompromised faith.

The six days of YEC are unusual for days dedicated to one's faith. They are not observable. There are no ceremonial, liturgical, or traditional ways to celebrate them. They are just days of the week—every week—having no *theological*

---

391. Ward, *The Word of God*, p. 148.

significance to the days themselves. Frankly, There is far more theological significance for Christianity in Israel's holy days than in the six literal days of YEC.

It is common knowledge among scholars that Jesus's work seemed to follow the sacred calendar—from the Jubilee Year at the beginning of Jesus's ministry (Luke 4:18–20) to the Feast of Tabernacles (John 7:2–3) and Passover at the end of his ministry. The holy days of Israel understood in Christ outline the plan of salvation in more detail than anything found in Genesis. That fact, misused, can be misleading, too, by obligating people to Jewish Christianity or Old Testament prescriptions based on literal or symbolic interpretations.

Judging the quality of one's faith in Christ by such things is absurd.

The Old Testament generally points to Christ. He arrived. Misusing that general principle can become a slippery slope because it remains that the Old Testament books are not covenantal for Christians. The Old Testament does not command specific prescriptions for Church life not mentioned in the New Testament. The irony is that the seventh day of Creation week is the most important day of that "week."

A further irony is that the most momentous day in Creation week is, without a doubt, allegorical and eternal. That is why YEC would just as soon not talk about the seventh day of Creation. Note: they only speak of the six days of creation. That is because YErs do not observe the Sabbath, and rightly so. But to take the seventh day of creation literally and not keep it holy (as God did n the story) is a contradiction, especially if one takes the fourth commandment (keep the Sabbath) literally to justify six twenty-four-hour days of Creation week upon which YEC depends (see the section "The Fourth Commandment and Genesis" in chapter 24). In other words, YErs take the secondary words of the fourth commandment literally, *but not the command itself.* That is not just inconsistent; it is selective reading.

I am well-acquainted with exaggerating the importance of Old Testament teaching, which anticipates Christ as if those teachings reveal Christ. They do not. Only the Incarnation *reveals* Christ. Those Old Testament allusions are inspired, but they are not themselves the revelation to which they allude. They are hints that come into focus once the revelation appears. Theological interpretations of types uncover the reality in the typology. For example, the Law, with its temple services, pointed to Christ the reality. There is now the law of Christ: Galatians 6:2, "Carry each other's burdens, and in this way, you will fulfill the law of Christ." This use of "the law" is metaphoric. Christ fulfilled the scriptures concerning the Law and himself, who is the Law as he is the Word (Logos).

If the focus of YEC was on Christ, one could be more sympathetic. Instead, they focus on a misplaced concept of biblical authority. That can be a slippery slope to legalism and other theological blunders. YEC's remarkably inflated view of Genesis 1–11, making it the key to all biblical understanding, has led to a *low view of God*. Bibliolatry is a low view of God. Idolatry occurs when something is allowed to compete with God's rightful place in reality.

There can be no one-to-one correspondence to reality when the reality is God.

Christ reveals the types and analogies in the Hebrew Bible by transforming them into reality. Entering the Temple becomes joining God in our conscience. The mortal becomes immortal. "You shall surely die" becomes "You shall never die." Reality is in the Logos—Christ. Overemphasizing teachings found in the Old Testament as if they are the foundation of our covenant in Christ is getting the cart before the horse. The Old Testament came first, chronologically, but is not *foremost* in theological importance. Dietrich Bonhoeffer said of scripture, "In its entirety and in all its parts it is nothing but this witness of Christ, his life, his death, and his resurrection." Christians married to their tradition do not quite comprehend this.

The only consequences we should appeal to are the ones that end in Christ.

PART IV:
ORIGINS OF THE
YOUNG EARTH
REFORM MOVEMENT

THE EVOLUTION OF THE YOUNG EARTH REFORM MOVEMENT

When an intelligent [person] expresses a view which seems obviously absurd...
we should try to understand how it ever came to seem true.
—Bertrand Russell

We have seen that YEC is not the single view that the earth is a newborn in cosmic terms. It is a theological system with supportive presuppositions and claims. Young earth creationism is an *ism*. In the spirit of Bertrand Russell, how did the YE Reform Movement "ever come to seem true?"

Young Earthers are encouraged by many theologians from the pre-scientific age that thought the earth was several thousand years ago. But there was no sign of the *ism* we have seen in today's YEC. Theologians from the distant past did not all agree on a specific age, which is typical when using the Bible alone as a dating device. Nonetheless, most Christians believed the earth was young by today's estimates. We are reflexive to appeal to authorities that we hope bring credibility to our view. Yet, Thomas Aquinas said, "The argument from authority is the weakest of arguments." Why is that? While appealing to authority in *support of an argument* can be effective, asserting an authority *as an argument* is weak. The *reasoning* on the merits is what makes authorities authoritative.

Some ecclesiastical leaders of the distant past found a way to date the earth with scripture alone. But scripture was all they had. The cases they made were sparse and tentative. We forget that the most significant source of knowledge in Christendom, especially on origins, was the Bible. If one wanted to know how old the world was, one either searched the scriptures or believed the universe always existed, as in philosophy. *There were few other alternative sources of knowledge.*

We cannot rely on the pre-scientific world to tell us how old the universe is. For example, in the fourth century, Bishop Ambrose of Milan thought the earth was young or that Bishop Ussher, in the seventeenth century, fixed the date of creation on October 23, 4004 BC, do not answer the same questions of origins we have today.

Different questions confront us. Here are just a few:

1. Why did some of the best theologians *in the pre-scientific age* take the days of creation figuratively?

2. Why did most, if not all, theologians allow latitude on the nature of the days?

3. What would those theologians conclude today, given the advancements in knowledge of the Bible, the ANE, and science?

To suggest that these questions make no difference is wishful thinking.

There was no mathematical, scientific, archeological, or empirical data for an old earth/universe in the Middle Ages. There was the choice between an eternal universe and a created one—a beginning or no beginning. That world did not know what a solar system was; they thought the sun, moon, stars, and a few planets revolved around the earth. Nor did they know that stars are like our sun. They did not need to know such things since they used the stars for navigation and referencing the calendar, and for all they knew, those were their only purposes.

The ancients had no perspective on the visible stars for their size, purpose, and distance from earth, nor did they conceive that trillions existed. The Milky Way was the only galaxy known until the twentieth century. Dinosaur bones, paleontology, geology, and extreme distance between stars and other galaxies—not to mention DNA—did not yet present real alternatives to the universe's history or the history of life on earth. These recent sources of knowledge that developed long after the Bible cannot be special revelation. Instead, they reflect significant developments in our ability to measure our world through technology and mathematics. We no longer depend solely on the naked eye to discover what God has offered with general revelation.

Prehistory (before writing) was out of reach for humans until modern times.

Even theologians like Philo, Origen, Augustine, and others knew the days in Genesis were figurative. Still, they could not infer an accurate age of the earth, let alone the size of a universe that they could not possibly comprehend. Theologians of the past read their assumptions into the Bible too.

It is helpful that many of the best theologians were doubtful that the days of Genesis were literal because it shows there are reasons to take the days figuratively without modern science. But we have science today, which we cannot ignore, and we have a much better knowledge of ANE worldviews, languages, cultures, history, and prehistory. Because of our increase in knowledge in so many relevant areas, we know that Genesis is not the superficial document envisioned by fundamentalists. We see the nature of the cosmos much better.

Among all humans in history, we are more authoritative in these areas.[392]

---

392. Early theologians were much more versed in literary devices. They were not suspicious of allegory or significant use of figurative language, nor did they consider metaphor and allegory evil or somehow lying. Unlike YErs, earlier theologians, even during the inquisition, actually believed if science showed their opinion on scripture false, then their interpretation of scripture needed adjusting. They assumed the book of nature and scripture should be harmonious.

The Curious Seventh Day Adventist Connection

It is easier to fool people than to convince them they were fooled.

—Mark Twain

Historians like David Lindberg and Ronald L. Numbers have traced the modern Young Earth Reform Movement to its original roots in Seventh Day Adventism (SDA).[393] Ellen G. White, the "prophetess" of the SDA Church in the mid-1800s, claimed to have visions of Creation week. Before that, Christian geologists speculated that Noah's flood might have skewed the geological evidence with false appearances of deep age in the strata. After exhaustive attempts to verify their hypothesis with actual work in the field and at numerous sites, they were deeply disappointed to discover their speculations were wrong. The strata showed extreme age consistently throughout the world.[394]

These early Christian geologists fully expected their discoveries to confirm their theological assumptions because assumptions held fervently and long enough begin to look like facts. These geologists started with what they thought was special revelation and fully expected to find supportive evidence. Empirical

---

393. David C. Lindberg was the Hillsdale Professor Emeritus of History of Science and Past Director of the Institute for Research in the Humanities at the University of Wisconsin–Madison. He held a degree in physics from Northwestern University and a PhD in history and philosophy of science from Indiana University. Lindberg received numerous awards from prestigious organizations, including the John Simon Guggenheim Foundation, National Science Foundation, the National Endowment for the Humanities, the Institute for Advanced Study, History of Science Society, the Medieval Academy of America, and the University of Wisconsin–Madison. With Ronald Numbers, he co-edited two anthologies on the relationship between religion and science. Also with R. Numbers, Lindberg was general editor of the eight-volume Cambridge History of Science and, with Michael Shank, editor of its volume on medieval science. He served as president of the History of Science Society and received its highest award for lifetime scholarly achievement: the Sarton medal. ("David C. Lindberg," *Wikipedia*).

394. We know several things about the history of geology and the flood. Most of the early geologists were clergy (of the eighteenth and nineteenth centuries). Long before that, Tertullian and Augustine believed many animals went extinct during the flood. That indicates they did not take literally the reference "all the animals of the earth" were represented on the Ark, whether by twos for the unclean animals or seven pair of the clean animals. By the nineteenth century, the idea of flood geology was abandoned not by atheists but Christian geologists, *before Darwin*, such as the Reverend William Buckland and James Hutton who like many others believed God created the world with "active principles" that developed naturally. The idea that all geological strata were produced by a single flood was rejected by 1837 by Reverend Buckland who wrote: "Some have attempted to ascribe the formation of all the stratified rocks to the effects of the Mosaic Deluge; an opinion which is irreconcilable with the enormous thickness and almost infinite subdivisions of these strata, and with the numerous and regular successions which they contain of the remains of animals and vegetables, differing more and more widely from existing species, as the strata in which we find them are placed at greater depths. The fact that a large proportion of these remains belong to extinct genera, and almost all of them to extinct species, that lived and multiplied and died on or near the spots where they are now found, shows that the strata in which they occur were deposited slowly and gradually, during long periods of time, and at widely distant intervals." This was the assessment of the leading Christian geologists from actual evidence in the field, before Darwin, when evolution and deep age were not givens.

evidence—aka general revelation—does not care about our opinions regarding "special revelation." Special revelation cannot contradict general revelation (but we do not always understand either one). The former is metaphysical, while the latter is empirical. But our *opinions* on special revelation are not special revelation, nor does general revelation submit to our assumptions about special revelation. Science helps us understand general revelation.

The findings of early geologists were unexpected and disappointing, lending credibility to those findings. Some of them may have inspired Ellen G. White to an idea. Around the same time, she claimed to have visions of creation. Accordingly, Ronald Numbers, a former Seventh-Day Adventist and now Professor of the History of Science and Medicine at the University of Wisconsin-Madison, wrote:

> The Seventh-day Adventist Church was led by the prophetess Ellen G. White, whom Adventists regarded as divinely inspired. Following one of her trance-like "visions," *White claimed to have actually witnessed the Creation,* which [she said] occurred within a literal week. She also taught that Noah's flood had sculpted the surface of the earth, burying the plants and animals found in the fossil record, and that the Christian Sabbath should be celebrated on Saturday rather than Sunday, *as a memorial of a [literal] six-day creation.*[395]

YErs are quick to point out that no one witnessed the Creation except for God.

However, Seventh-day Adventists claim Ellen G. White witnessed the creation around 1860.[396]

Pressing the literal day theory gives credence to the primary Seventh-day Adventist distinctive—obligatory seventh-day Sabbath observance. It is no coincidence that SDAs promote vegetarianism, assumed obligatory in Eden. If the days of creation are twenty-four-hour days, the seventh day Sabbath

---

395. Ronald Numbers was a Seventh-day Adventist in his youth. He became a leading scholar in the *history of science and religion* and an authority on the history of creationism and creation science. Numbers received a PhD in the history of science from the University of California, Berkeley, in 1969. Currently, he is the Hillsdale and William Coleman Professor of the History of Science and Medicine at the University of Wisconsin–Madison. From 1989 to 1993, he was editor of *Isis*, an international journal of the history of science. With David Lindberg, he has co-edited two anthologies on the relationship between religion and science. Also with Lindberg, he is currently editing the eight-volume Cambridge History of Science.

396. The example of E. G. White is instructive because YErs treat Genesis 1 almost as a vision. They accept the authorship of Moses but that God showed Him, somehow, exactly what happened. How did God do that? Was it a vision? Genesis does not say anything like this and YErs do not say. The choices are dictation, rejected in Christianity, or some sort of miraculous infusion of precise words, which sounds a lot like dictation. That means either verbal dictation or dictation through a vision. The simple answer is that the author was moved to write a book on origins for the covenant people Israel, based on his experiences with God in the world he understood.

becomes an evangelistic tool to draw people to the SDA Church with a unique distinctive. The idea is if God kept the seventh-day Sabbath at the beginning of time, then it is not merely a Jewish institution. If God observes the Sabbath, who are we to refuse, especially since God Himself enshrined the Sabbath in the fourth commandment that scripture says He "wrote with His finger."[397]

But we should ask, did God observe the Israelite Sabbath or another rest?

Ronald Numbers writes that George McCready Price (1870–1963), a devotee of Ellen G. White and a self-taught geologist, determined to prove the earth was young by interpreting Noah's flood based on White's visions. Her visions declared that Noah's flood was the geological "smoking gun." Price's original work, *The New Geology*, published in the 1920s, enjoyed moderate but surprising success among Adventists and Lutherans, although Price never did fieldwork to test and verify his hypotheses.[398]

The geologist David R. Montgomery also writes:

[George McCready] Price sent copies of his book to eminent geologists seeking their reaction. Among the few who bothered to respond was David Starr Jordan, president of Stanford University and an expert on fossil fishes. In a letter to Price, Jordan warned him not to expect geologists to take him seriously because his argument was based on "mistakes, omissions, and exceptions"... Jordan tried for over two decades to convince [Price] to get some experience in field or laboratory work. Decades later, students on a fossil-hunting trip were astonished to discover that the world's leading creationist could hardly tell one fossil from another. The roots of modern [young earth] creationism run directly back to Price and honing arguments faithful to [Ellen White's] teaching.[399]

According to Ronald L. Numbers, Price provided the substance and inspiration for the book decades later entitled *The Genesis Flood*, co-written in 1961 by Henry Morris and John Whitcomb, neither a geologist. Price coined the *reform language* that today's YErs would eventually copy. But the reform language in Adventism had less to do with the earth's age than the obligation that a literal Genesis implied, namely obeying the fourth commandment to keep holy the seventh-day Sabbath.

---

397. To be fair to the SDA church, they would insist that Sabbath observance enhances the Gospel and their Christian life generally. That was true in my former fellowship. But that is what everyone does with his or her cherished distinctives—they glue them to the gospel to exaggerate their importance, often without realizing it. Yet, Sabbath observance cannot enhance the gospel. In fact, the gospel diminishes the importance of a weekly Sabbath by rendering it "a shadow of things that were to come, but the reality is found in Christ" (see Colossians 2:16–17)

398. The body of SDAs is large and their books often enjoy brisk sales if only to their own people.

399. David R. Montgomery *The Rocks Don't Lie: A Geologist Investigates Noah's Flood* (W. W. Norton & Company, New York, London, 2012), p. 187.

Today, some Adventists insist they interpret Genesis without relying on Ellen G. White. That may be, but that is today, after decades of effective criticism over the credibility of White's visions and writings. They can no longer speak officially on the centrality of her visions in SDA theology. Besides, the origin of the *"Reform Movement"* is the point here. The movement (not the nonessential belief that fostered it) is an extremist view of literalism in Genesis. But even Adventists are not as adamant on how the age of the earth affects animals having eternal life, or God being a liar, or that YEC is the key to everything, the vanguard of evangelism, the cross, and the atonement. Ironically, Adventists embrace a seven-day workweek for God because they are Sabbatarians, which White's visions also influenced.

As a result, Adventist theology is well-rooted in the Old Testament. Assuming that God works a six-day week and rests on the seventh day, as humans do, bolsters the case for obligatory Sabbath observance since an earthly work*week* continues to repeat and, therefore, has commemorative usefulness.[400] Unlike YErs, Adventists freely acknowledge seven days of creation week (not just six)—the Sabbath, when made holy, was created on that day.

It doesn't take a scholar to see the SDA's motivation for accepting the literal day theory with their primary distinctive—Sabbath-keeping—initially validated by White's visions. Millions of Adventists still believe in her visions. This SDA connection is lost on many YErs. Sunday keeping YErs reject it when informed. Perhaps Mark Twain was right: *"It is easier to fool people than to convince them they were fooled."*

Young Earth Reform Mutates

Before the 1960s, fundamentalists offered three primary explanations of Genesis 1.

1. The gap theory: Places an unknown gap of time between Genesis 1:1 and the first day of creation in verse three, allowing the creation of humans thousands of years ago while the universe may be eons older. Some ANE creation accounts state that the initial conditions of darkness and chaotic waters existed for eons, if not eternity.

2. The day-age theory: Defines the days of creation as long periods.

3. George McCready Price's seven literal days, several thousand years ago.

---

400. In contrast to an earthly workweek that repeats over and over again, the divine week does not end. This is analogous to the earthly sacrifices that had to be repeated daily whereas the sacrifice of the Son of God is once and for all times (Hebrews 7:27). So is the seventh day of creation; it never ceases, therefore, neither does creation week.

Before 1960, support for flood geology centered primarily in the Seventh Day Adventist church of George McCready Price and those influenced by that body, such as Lutherans, and some Calvinists. From the early 1960s through the 1990s, Henry M. Morris, a Baptist civil engineer, was the most influential voice in YE circles. He devoted the rest of his life to promoting flood geology, which he deemed "Creation Science." Morris's book, *The Genesis Flood*, co-written with John Whitcomb, was enormously influential. It brought Price's model of earth's history into non-Sabbatarian fundamentalism.

Meanwhile, in 1964, two radio astronomers, Arno Penzias and Robert Wilson, accidentally discovered the cosmic microwave background radiation (CMB). It was startling support for the redshift in the light spectrum that Edwin Hubble discovered in the 1920s. Edwin Hubble found a real game-changer with the most powerful telescope to date. The light from those galaxies shifted to the red portions of the light spectrum, meaning galaxies were receding—the universe was expanding.

Light waves are analogous to sound waves. Sound waves traveling toward us increase pitch along the sound spectrum until they pass. They decrease in pitch when moving away from us. This phenomenon is called the "Doppler Effect." Similarly, light waves emitted by objects moving toward us shift to the blue side of the color spectrum of light, while objects moving away shift to the red side. Color is to light what pitch is to sound. The *stretching* of the light wave frequency tells us that galaxies have traveled away from us for an extremely long period and at incredible speed (many times the speed of light) and increasing. A redshift in all directions means the entire universe is expanding. How that would affect the prevailing theory of the Steady State Model of the universe was not evident in the late 1920s. Nonetheless, it seemed to be a game-changer.

Game-changers invite questions.

Why was the universe expanding? What caused it, and what does it mean? The answers were surprisingly simple. The universe is moving farther and farther apart, which means it must have been closer and closer together, making its light and heat denser the further back in time we look. The math on rewinding the trajectory showed that the universe converges into a tiny, indescribably dense particle called the singularity. Rapid cosmic inflation would give birth to time, space, matter and energy, *and the laws of physics*.

David Berlinski describes this singularity:

> The retreat into the past ends in a state in which material particles are at no distance from one another and the temperature, density, and curvature of the universe are infinite. Such a state is known as a singularity. The cone tapering into the past must end. The lines of sight converge. The universe had a beginning.[401]

---

401. David Berlinski, *The Devil's Delusion: Atheism and its Scientific Pretensions*, p. 74.

This "cone tapering" reverses the present expanding universe back to its original pinpoint, creating a cone-shaped path backward (see figure 6 below). "The lines of sight converge." The CMB was empirical evidence of a universe-wide rapid expansion of radiation in all directions, sending immeasurable light and heat that birthed our universe.

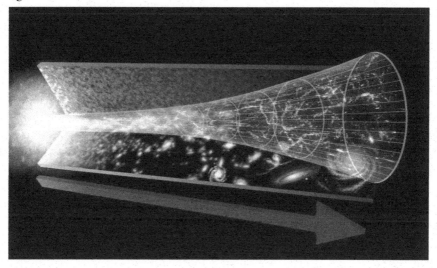

Figure 6. An artist's conception of the Big Bang shows the universe's expansion going forward and earlier stages of the universe when reversed.

There is more.

Galaxies in every direction still contain the thermal radiation left from the Big Bang. The CMB is the oldest radiated light in the universe and is still glowing, tucked away in the microwave background, the radio light spectrum's furthest region. Sensitive radio telescopes showed a faint background glow, stable in all directions and not associated with any star, galaxy, or other phenomena. *The glow is strongest in the microwave region of the radio spectrum, indicating extreme age.* That earned the Nobel Prize for both Arno Penzias and Robert Wilson.

The CMB was a snapshot of the oldest light in our universe when it was just 370,000 years old. It shows tiny temperature fluctuations corresponding to regions of slightly different densities, representing the seeds of all future structures: the stars and galaxies of today.[402]

The rate of expansion tempered by gravity required a magnitude of precision that appears too great for creating a life-permitting universe by accident. The singularity was like a "universe-seed"—a virtual cosmic "zygote." Seeds are a kind of divine signature. God does not seem to create many individual units

---

402. Eblin Dr. Torsten, "Planck Reveals an Almost Perfect Universe," *Max-Planck-Gesellschaft*. Retrieved June 3, 2013.

instantaneously. The *method* of creating Adam and Eve with dust and rib must be figurative since God does not breathe or hold his breath, and such creative acts are not *ex nihilo*. God seems to prefer things developing from within an environment prepared for it, like seed and soil.

Remember Augustine's prescient words, "In the beginning [God] created only the [seeds] or causes of life which were afterward developed in gradual course... *[At] least we know* that the [Genesis creation day] is different from the ordinary day with which we are familiar[403] (emphasis mine).

If the days in Genesis are no doubt literal, then Augustine continually missed the obvious. That was not something he was in the habit of doing. We know from his writings that Augustine struggled with Genesis throughout his life. He went to the grave, unsure of some of its meaning. One thing Augustine knew with certainty (his words) was that the days of creation were figurative. As we saw earlier, the earth's age is indeterminable in the Bible if any of the six days are figurative.

That is a fact.

The discovery of cosmic microwave background radiation left over from an early stage in the universe's development was a landmark test of the Big Bang model of origins. At the time, Roger Penrose and Stephen Hawking demonstrated that the singularity was inescapable. The universe had a beginning. Some atheistic physicists were/are baffled, even horrified by the CMB. For obvious reasons, Christians appreciated the beginning of the universe more than physicists did. The discovery of the CMB led Penzias to say these now-famous words:

> Astronomy leads us to a unique event, a universe that was created out of nothing, one with the very delicate balance needed to provide exactly the conditions required to permit life, and one which has an underlying, one might say, supernatural plan...

> The best data we have concerning the Big Bang are exactly what I would have predicted, had I nothing to go on but the five books of Moses, the Psalms, the Bible as a whole.

Knowing the deep age of the universe, Penzias embraces the Bible in praise.

According to the Standard Big Bang Model, this very tiny singularity contained what would become the entire universe. It was "infinitely" dense, "infinitely" hot, with no spatial or temporal relationships. "Infinite" has a special meaning here. It means no measurability in time/space, where mathematics itself breaks down. In other words, the singularity was without the laws of physics and was spaceless and timeless. Was the singularity a physical thing? That is not clear to some physicists.

---

403. *"The Literal Interpretation of Genesis,"* 5:2 (AD 408).

Time, space, and matter did not produce the Big Bang; it was the reverse. The Big Bang brought time, space, and matter into existence. In his book, *The Beginning of Time,* Stephen Hawking wrote, "The universe and time itself had a beginning in the Big Bang." Hawking gives Augustine credit for understanding time, many centuries before Einstein.

In the 1960s, scientists discovered that the universe began at a finite point in the past; that moment simply appeared, and nothing became everything in a cosmic burst of light and heat. The CMB is universe-wide that resulted from a cosmic-wide event—the universe's birth. CMB is the ultimate "smoking gun." It is official; the universe began from *nothing:* without time, space, or matter/ energy. If scientists were looking for a way to prove that Genesis is pure mythology, they had a strange way of doing it.

David Berlinski writes:

> If science has shown that God does not exist, it has not been by appealing to Big Bang cosmology. The hypothesis of God's existence and the facts of contemporary cosmology are consistent... "Perhaps the best argument in favor of the thesis that the Big Bang supports theism," the astrophysicist Christopher Isham has observed "is the obvious unease with which it is greeted by some atheist physicists."[404]

Let's face it, the resurgence of the YE Reform Movement in the 1960s through Morris and Whitcomb robbed Christianity of the high ground in the creation debate. Atheists tell the world there is proof that the universe came from an infinite burst of light and heat—*ex nihilo.* YErs said, "No. No. Look over here." Too many people looked over there. Too many listened.

Christianity's "See, I told you so" moment was shouted down by louder fundamentalist voices. Historical Christian teaching entitled us to that moment. Christianity virtually predicted the singularity/Big Bang, and there it was. We have no one to blame but our passive selves. I am not saying "Censor YEC." I'm saying Christianity should have driven the Big Bang bandwagon if only to say, "See, the universe had a beginning from nothing—the Bible tells *us* so. If there was a Big Bang, there must have been a Big Banger."

We let a "bull in a China shop" frame the debate, called YEC.

---

404. David Berlinski, *The Devil's Delusion,* p. 82.

29.
THE NEW TESTAMENT MASTERPIECE OF OLD TESTAMENT INTERPRETATION

> The Church has always claimed that the Hebrew Scriptures is the
> record of God's revelation to Israel, and the New Testament is the record
> of God's *final revelation* to the world, through His Son.
> Therefore, the Old Testament is *subordinate* to
> and interpreted in the light of the New Testament revelation.
> —Richard Swinburne[405]

The book of Hebrews is a masterpiece of Old Testament interpretation in the light of Christ. We do not know who wrote this book. There is no salutation identifying the author as in the epistles. Neither is there a clear tradition pointing to a particular author. Scholars believe the book of Hebrews was likely a sermon transcribed.

Hebrews is decidedly hermeneutical. However, there is no "*as written hermeneutic*" as the author interprets the Old Testament. The author uses an allegorical method of interpreting indicative of the Alexandrian School of the first century AD. Well-known luminaries of the school were Philo, Clement of Alexandria, and Origen.

The author introduces the concept of God's rest in Chapter 3. He begins by recasting the story (for Jewish Christians) of the Exodus from Egypt and the failure of that generation to enter the Promised Land. The original exodus wanderers did not enter "God's Rest" due to their unfaithfulness. God allowed only their descendants to enter the land. A new generation of Israelites would experience a new life with Yahweh in the Promised Land. It was supposed to be a national version of the Garden of Eden, where lavish blessings were waiting for them, "flowing with milk and honey" and an abundance of "vines and fig trees." The book of Hebrews describes this scene as a type of "God's Rest."

The author prepares the ground for equating the seventh-day rest at creation with Christ's rest. The Israelite Sabbath and entry into the Promised Land only symbolized that rest. The seventh day of creation finds fulfillment in Christ with the Messianic Age that has begun—the rest at creation and Christ's rest are, in fact, the same. In paganism, the "rest" in creation myths was for the gods and aristocrats. The Seventh-Day Rest of Genesis was an offer to join God.

Hebrews 3:7–11 quotes Psalm 95 about a *particular day*:

---

405. Richard Swinburne, *Was Jesus God?* (Oxford University Press, Oxford England, 2008), Kindle edition, location 1908.

The Holy Spirit says: *"Today,"* if you hear his voice, do not harden your hearts as you did in the rebellion, during the time of testing in the wilderness, where your ancestors tested and tried me, even though for forty years they saw what I did. That is why I was angry with that generation; I said...*"They shall never enter my rest."* (emphasis mine)

The author connects God's "rest" with the Promised Land, where Israel could find peace and fellowship with God, which they rarely experienced. He then makes the link explicit, showing that the offer of rest at creation is ongoing. Notice the next remarkable verses in Hebrews 4:4–7 from The Amplified Bible:

For in a certain place he has said this about the seventh day: *And God rested on the seventh day from all His works*... Seeing then that *the promise remains over* [from past times] for some [in David's day] *to enter that rest*, and that those who formerly were given *the good news*...did not enter because of disobedience. *Again he sets a definite day*... *Today*, [and gives another opportunity of securing that rest] saying through David [in Psalm 95] after so long a time [since they entered the land under Joshua]... *Today*, if you would hear His voice...do not harden your hearts." (emphasis added)

Note that the promise to enter the same rest in David's day shows that the seventh day of creation continues and that it was an invitation to communion with God.

The word *again* links the *seventh-day rest of creation* with entering the Promised Land under Joshua. The idea is that God invited all humanity to join in His rest at the beginning. Almost none accepted. God then began a carve-out plan with Abraham and his descendants, highlighting the ongoing offer of rest.

Notice that the weekly Sabbath in Israel is not the divine seventh-day rest in Genesis, which was the equivalent to entering the Promised Land, i.e., *"You shall not enter my rest."* That generation in the wilderness failed to enter God's rest under Joshua, yet they kept the Israelite Sabbath. But here is the more significant point: *those that eventually came into the land still did not enter God's rest because they continued to resist God in the land.*

God's rest is more than a literal garden or stretch of land. It turns out that eternal rest is in the soul joined to God by faith. That turned out to be a fragile joining for ancient Israel. According to the book of Hebrews, the old covenant did not lead the nation to God's rest because, ultimately, that rest is in Christ under a new covenant.

Real rest is made clear with David's offer of a *day* (*today*) *while he was in the promised land* indicates that the land was not the ultimate rest since the people were already there but were not all joined to God in *spiritual rest*, which is the true meaning of the seventh day of Creation. To join that rest means "you shall not surely die," i.e., spiritually. God offered the children of Israel rest or fellowship with Him, but like Adam and Eve in Eden, Israel failed in the Promised Land because of unbelief.

Furthermore, the Promised Land was not the rest but was symbolic because it was merely geographical, not spiritual. Israel was separate from the pagan world and could serve as a place for spiritual renewal. Hebrews points out that faith is necessary for entering God's rest (Hebrews 3:19). Jesus made it explicit to the Samaritan woman at the well that true worship is *not geographical* but in spirit, for God is Spirit (John 4:21–24).

The *divine rest* is not a specific place or length of *time*. The *rest* is peace with God, brought by an eternal transformation ultimately found in Jesus Christ. When we say farewell to those who have passed by saying "Rest in peace," we mean in heaven with God. It is not the rest in the ground of a dead body. God offered Adam and Eve eternal rest in fellowship with Him; instead, they struck out on their own.

The continuous offer of rest since Genesis shows that the seventh day of creation did not end. The mysterious author of Hebrews emphasizes the words *day* and *today* in keeping with the language of the seventh *"day"* of creation for *all times*. This "day" of rest cannot be temporal because it is *divine rest in the Lord*.

The absence of the recurring phrase "evening and morning" was needed to end the seventh day of Creation. That did not happen. It is pointless, not to mention inconsistent, to insist that the rest was twenty-four hours as if God was refreshed enough to start the next day's activity.

Our author continues:

For if Joshua had given them *rest* [in the Promised Land], he [David] would not speak afterward about another day." So then, *there is still awaiting a full and complete Sabbath-rest* reserved for the [true] people of God; For he who has once entered [God's] rest also has ceased from [the weariness and pain] of human labors, just as God rested from those labors peculiarly His own. (Hebrews 4:8–10, AMP)

Notice that God rests from the kind of labors *"peculiarly His own,"* according to His own nature. God's "labor" at creation was in saying things like "Let there be light," "Let this," and "Let that." It is doubtful that God literally said such things. To whom was He speaking? He certainly did not speak Hebrew. Genesis is in Hebrew, translating God's will. God's nature is without limits; therefore, "labor" and "rest" cannot be *literal* because they are human limitations.

The whole earth has yet to experience God's rest in the new creation. The eternal seventh-day rest connects the previous "six days" of creation to eternity.

The book of Hebrews indicates that creation *"week"* does not end until the seventh "day" ends, which cannot happen. God's creative works are like him: endless. God's nature tells us this. His creation continues forever (not in its current state), but as God currently upholds it. That is the continuous phase of creation as new things come into existence even now. Ultimately, He transforms His creation and continues it forever in the new heaven and earth.[406]

We think of the creation as being complete or that it ceased to continue. This conventional view is the misunderstanding of a literal reading since it is self-evident that the creation is still happening in new births, new stars, and galaxies forming daily. What ceased is the *story of creation* as told by the author of Genesis.

The creation appeared static to the ancients and moderns until Edwin Hubble discovered the red shift in the light spectrum in the late 1920s, and Wilson and Penzias found the CMB in 1964. The Steady State of the universe was the scientific model based solely on observation until the 1960s. We now know the universe is remarkably dynamic: increasing, expanding, and spreading its content. The ceasing of Genesis was in the apparent static nature of the world. It looked done, and for the author's purposes, it was. But Jesus said, "My Father *is always at his work* to *this very day*, and I too am working" (John 5:17). "To this very day" means from the beginning until now. Jesus referred to God's work in this universe, which is creative and redemptive.

Hebrews connects the unending divine week of Genesis with an analogous human week in Exodus. God did not really participate in daily labor, from sunup to sundown, or keeping the Hebrew Sabbath. Speaking a few words a day is not labor. It was a creation *story* in the Hebrew tradition with theological connections to the covenant people of Israel. The two types of weeks are not of the same nature any more than the participants are of the same kind. The rich typology in Hebrews provides a corrective for interpreting Exodus 20:8–11, literally:

> Remember the Sabbath day by keeping it holy. Six days you shall labor and do all your work, but the seventh day is a sabbath to the Lord your God. On it you shall not do any work, neither you, nor your son or daughter, nor your male or female servant, nor your animals, nor any foreigner residing in your towns. For in six days the Lord made the heavens and the earth, the sea, *and all that is in them*, but he rested on the seventh day. Therefore the Lord blessed the Sabbath day and made it holy.

As the author of Hebrews says, human labor is according to human nature, and divine labor is particular to God's attributes—i.e., temporal in the former, *eternal* in the later (Hebrews 4:4–8). "Eternal" means unending, implying no personal expenditure of energy; that is, without labor. God's rest and

---

406. The Commandment says, "In six days the Lord made the heavens and the earth, the sea, and *all that is in them*". Really? "All that is in them"? Well, not literally. It's a fact that creation never stopped. It continued with new species: stars, galaxies, and the expansion of the universe. The ceasing was literary and confirmed to the author by what appeared to him as a static universe. What ceased was *the story of creation as told by the author. We know creation* is dynamic in ways he could not know."

human rest can only be analogous since, according to the scriptures in both Testaments, God never "rests" and His Day of Rest is for us and continues into a perpetual age we call the New Heavens and New Earth.

The book of Revelation states that there will be no need for the sun in the new creation, which governs the beginning and end of the weekly Sabbath (Revelation 22:5). The divine Sabbath in Genesis and Revelation is not time-sensitive since it has nothing to do with solar days. Therefore, Christianity is not dependent on special days. We may celebrate them, but they do not define us. They are reminders of our core beliefs.

Many YErs believe God kept a twenty-four-hour Sabbath, blessed it, made it holy, obligated the Israelites to it, only to discard it when Christ arrived. They cite verses like Exodus 31:17, "It will be a sign between me and the Israelites *forever*, for in six days the Lord made the heavens and the earth, and on the seventh day he *rested and was refreshed.*" The *forever* is not the only term in this verse that is figurative. The words *rested* and *refreshed* are telltale signs that the passage is analogous, not literal.

Other translations have it:

- "He rested and relaxed."
- "He ceased and recovered."
- "He stopped and took a long deep breath."
- "He rested at His ease."[407]

These are possible translations, but none can be literal.

First, the *weekly* Sabbath obligation in the fourth commandment was not "forever," though written that way, but turned out temporary. Second, a literal reading does not work *here* for YEC because it violates the YE "literal historical narrative" and its supposed *one-to-one correspondence between words and reality.* The only Sabbath rest that is forever is God's rest in Genesis because it is not part of a physical week but a theological one. You can see that the nature of God is unaffected by any "literal historical narrative." It is not history to say God "relaxed," "recovered," or *"stopped and took a long deep breath,"* or that he *"relaxed"* or was at *"ease."*

The book of Hebrews (and the New Testament in general) interprets the Old Testament contrary to YEC's "as written" hermeneutic. The difference between these two interpretive methods cannot be starker. It is often difficult to see how New Testament writers arrive at their interpretation of Old Testament

---

407. See Biblegateway.com for references.

passages, i.e., their interpreting often has less correspondence to the passages they interpret.[408]

Notice this revealing observation from the YE scholar Steven W. Boyd, "But Genesis 1 states that the world developed in six days, not seven. The seventh day was *merely* for God to rest" (emphasis mine).[409] This remark is surprising; perhaps it shouldn't be.

How could Boyd and YErs generally ignore the profound meaning of the seventh day of Creation? They ignore its transcendent purpose by limiting it to a *weekly Sabbath* for "mere rest." Yet Paul says the weekly Sabbath is a *"mere"* shadow, so Boyd describes God's rest in the same *"mere"* terms. God does not *"merely"* do anything; His rest is the reality Paul refers to, not the shadow (see Colossians 2:17 NASB 1995). Therefore, the seventh day of creation cannot be the weekly Sabbath of the fourth commandment, as the book of Hebrews shows. The author is trying to wean his Jewish Christian readers from the chains of literalism.

Boyd considers the seventh day at creation as incidental or, in his words, "merely" for God to rest. Is he saying, "What value does the seventh day hold if it does not help establish the age of the earth? YErs have no interest in the seventh day (unless they are Seventh-day Adventists) since they have six literal days of labor." Notice the Creation *Science Encyclopedia* on Boyd:

> Dr. Boyd is most known for his linguistic studies. Dr. Boyd has done a detailed study of the words, mostly verbs, of poetic and narrative passages of Scripture. According to his analysis, the verb forms in Genesis 1 coincide with verb forms from other historical, narrative passages, not poetic passages. Therefore, the Creation story should be taken literally.

YErs repeatedly remind us that some of their evangelists have doctorate degrees. The *argument from authority* is a tactic used when one has a weak case,

---

408. This subject is too large for the space available here. The conclusion most scholars adopt is that New Testament writers are using interpretive methods familiar in the day. For instance, the Second Temple hermeneutic interprets Old Testament passages in the light of major events that occurred in and around the interpreter's day. The New Testament authors use a similar Second Temple hermeneutic by interpreting the OT in light of the Christ events. They radically reinterpret the biblical text because a new day had dawned. See G. K. Beale and D. A. Carson, eds., *Commentary on the Use of the Old Testament in the New Testament* (Baker, 2007). Craig Evans, "The Old Testament in the New," *The Face of New Testament Studies*, edited by Scot McKnight and Grant Osborne (Baker Academic, 2004). Craig Evans, "Jewish Exegesis," *Dictionary for Theological Interpretation of the Bible*, edited by Kevin Vanhoozer; Associate editors, Craig Bartholomew, Daniel Treier, and N. T. Wright (Baker Academic, 2005). G. K. Beale, ed., *The Right Doctrine from the Wrong Texts: Essays on the Use of the Old Testament in the New* (Baker, 1994). Richard Longenecker, *Biblical Exegesis in the Apostolic Period, 2nd Edition* (Eerdmans, 1999).

409. Terry Mortenson, Thane H. Ury, *Coming to Grips with Genesis*, p. 158.

and sophistry is likely to follow. Notice Dr. Boyd's false choice: Genesis is either a poem or literal history *based on verb forms.*

Are we to believe that those verb forms determine whether God *spoke* Hebrew at the beginning of time: *saw*, i.e., looked to evaluate, *labored* for six days, *retires* at night, *rests* on Saturdays, and *manages* His time by sunrise and sunset? Did He *breathe* oxygen from His lungs into Adam's nostrils? According to Dr. Boyd, since these verbs are in other contexts that he takes literally, the earth must be six-thousand years old. That was easy. So it takes a YEr with his Ph.D. to inform us that *verb forms* determine God's attributes and thereby date the universe.

Some verb forms!

The wholesale Christian change from Sabbath to Sunday suggests the cosmic impact of the Incarnation on *the new creation* by instituting this celebration of the resurrection for a new kind of covenant with all heaven and earth, not just Jews. This covenantal change shown in the Sabbath/Sunday transfer shows that literal days in Genesis are not essential to Christianity like John 1:1-14 is. We are back to the universal offer of rest at creation.

There is no explicit change or legal ruling in the New Testament declaring Sunday "observance" over Sabbath observance. Instead, Sunday celebrations (not observations) rose spontaneously within the new community to recognize the resurrection of Christ. The resurrection of God incarnate was a cosmic event—a new "In the beginning" for a new creation. The first day (analogous to an "8ᵗʰ day" of creation) was a sign of a new beginning and covenant with humanity no longer "in Adam" or obligated to Moses at Sinai but to Christ at Calvary. Not the Garden of Eden, but the Garden Tomb is key to all biblical doctrine.

There are many explicit commands to keep holy the Sabbath throughout the Hebrew Scriptures and several examples of Christ, Paul, and the early Church attending the synagogue on the Sabbath day. There is evidence that Christians routinely attended the synagogue in the first century to hear the scriptures read while celebrating Christ's resurrection on Sunday with communion.

The vast majority of people did not have a Bible, nor could many read it if they had one. It wasn't until the Gutenberg press of the sixteenth century that the Scriptures eventually became available to congregations. Yet, still, it took centuries before most households owned a Bible. Christians have always depended on teachers to disseminate the Bible's contents.

Judaism and Christianity officially split near the end of the first century when Jewish leaders pressured Jewish Christians still attending the synagogue incognito. Attendees were to recite a curse on Christ and his followers called the *Birkath-ha-minim*. Jewish leaders could identify the Christians in their midst when, in good conscience, those believers would not comply with the curse and thus purged from the synagogue for good.[410]

There is no command or teaching anywhere in scripture to assemble weekly on any day but the seventh day. Yet, regular and widespread Christian assemblies on Sunday are evident by the beginning of the second century. Sunday assembling emerged spontaneously to the person and work of Jesus, namely His resurrection, and not by reading Old Testament scriptures *as written* or paraphrasing the fourth commandment into "one day in seven." The spontaneous move toward resurrection Sunday indicates the work of the Spirit.

The divine seventh day at creation is a continuous offer of fellowship and communion with all humanity. Participating in divine rest is what God's plan has always been about, *not days of the week*. We can enter this rest today, tomorrow, and every day because of Jesus, *whose coming revealed the continuous nature of God's rest*. This rest revealed in Christ was determined before Sinai *and before the creation* (Ephesians 1:4).

Yet you will spend hours going through the Creation Museum in Northern Kentucky bombarded by six literal days, Old Covenant lessons, and a continuous diatribe on God's Word being true and man's word being false. It all ends on the sixth day, for some reason. When I went through the Creation Museum, there was no portion dedicated to the seventh day of Creation: hopefully that has changed. Seventh-day Adventists would have a good case for calling non-Sabbatarian YEC's compromisers. Of all the days of Creation week, the one "day" in which God personally participates, calls holy, and blessed is of little importance in YEC.

"The seventh day was *merely* for God to rest?" Thank you, Steven W. Boyd *Ph.D.*

---

410. For a comprehensive look at this development, see D. A. Carson, *From Sabbath to Lord's Day: A Biblical, Historical and Theological Investigation,* (Copyright 1999 by D.A. Carson).

30.
THE FOURTH COMMANDMENT AND GENESIS

Our hearts are restless until they find their rest in you.[411]
—Augustine

YErs use the fourth Commandment as Seventh-day Adventists do, i.e., to argue for their exclusive distinctives. Yet, both interpret the commandment very differently:

> "Remember the Sabbath day by keeping it holy. **9** Six days you shall labor and do all your work, **10** but the seventh day is a sabbath to the Lord your God. On it you shall not do any work, neither you, nor your son or daughter, nor your male or female servant, nor your animals, nor any foreigner residing in your towns. **11** For in six days the Lord made the heavens and the earth, the sea, and all that is in them, but he rested on the seventh day. Therefore the Lord blessed the Sabbath day and made it holy.

I'm especially familiar with the fourth commandment, having kept the weekly Sabbath for 32 years. The six days are not the subject of the command; the Sabbath is. Consequently, YErs virtually ignore the *command in the commandment* to keep the seventh day holy. Confusing the referent in any context always leads to misunderstanding. Besides, this verse is used to prove six literal days only if one is predisposed to seeing God in human terms.

But the fourth commandment is not about creation or even making holy "one day in seven," as many Christians and YErs believe (a compromise in SDA's eyes). The Decalogue *explicitly* commands the covenant community to keep holy *the seventh day*. Otherwise, the fourth commandment is meaningless. God didn't rest any day in seven. One rests from physical work after work, not on the first day before the workweek begins. The Sunday "rest" in Christianity is different from the Sabbath rest. The first day makes sense if it celebrates the spiritual rest Christ brought that starts a new life in an individual and the Christian community. The start of the week—Sunday— acknowledges Easter Sunday when Christ defeated the grave for us and fits the new covenant theology of a New Creation. The fourth commandment was a shadow of what has now appeared.

When Christians interpret this command as one day in seven, they still have one foot in the old covenant trying to satisfy the fourth commandment. No covenantal demand is made on New Testament Christians obligating them to "keep" any specific day. Sunday worship is not a commanded day of rest from weekly work. Rather, it celebrates Christ's atoning work that liberates us from the consequences of

---

411. Augustine's *Confessions* (1.1.1)

unfaithful works: "Those who enter into salvation's rest lay down their labors in the same way that God entered into a Sabbath rest from His" (Hebrews 4:10). Neither rest (Christianity's or God's) is literal rest from weekly work, but spiritual or eternal rest through fellowship with God.

But SDAs think God *labored* for six days and *rested* on the Sabbath; that's what it says. Therefore, we should observe the seventh day. That is an old covenant obligation and too literal since God does not actually labor or rest. SDAs have also believed God has a body, which skews their interpretations. God does not rest, nor does He labor governed by the sun, as humans do.

In Sabbatarianism, like the SDA church, the Sabbath is not just for those under the old covenant, the Jews. It was good enough for God, so it should be good enough for everyone. That train of thought appears justified since the fourth commandment links weekly Sabbath-keeping to the divine rest of Creation Week, so according to SDAs, obligating the new covenant Church to weekly Sabbath-keeping is justified. That is why they invented the YE Reform Movement in the first place: to compel Christians to observe the seventh-day Sabbath as their literal understanding of Genesis would demand (see chapter 28).

But in YEC, that takes this one-to-one correspondence to reality stuff too far.

YEC depends heavily on a false choice they continually project—there are six literal 24-hour days in Genesis, or each "day" must represent billions of years. The former is mistaken, while the latter is absurd. Only people who know little about the scriptures and the history of ancient Israel believe a Hebrew workweek intended to convey billions of years.

People use or misuse the Bible to figure out all kinds of dates: the birth of Jesus, the Second Coming of Christ, and the age of the earth/universe, to no avail. The Bible is not for that purpose. The seven days of Genesis and Exodus have nothing to do with how long God took to create. The common *and decidedly earthly* Hebrew workweek illustrates Yahweh, the God of their covenant, as Creator.

What the days mean in Genesis is how to understand them in Exodus. Augustine was right. They are figurative; they have always been figurative and always will be despite past assumptions or speculations on earth's age.[412] God is

---

412. Remember the *Manual of Catholic Theology of 1898* said *"The best Catholic authorities* [since Augustine tell us] that the whole act of creation was only *one instant of time, and that the division of it into six days is a way of presenting to the reader the order according to the connection of causes rather than the order according to the intervals of time (St. Aug., De Gen. ad Lit., 1. V.).* such is the opinion of St. Augustine, *and St. Thomas* thinks it highly probable (I., q. 66, a.i.) ...These and similar considerations, quite independently of natural science, have induced the *theologians of all times to allow a very free interpretation of the six days.* Obviously, modern science could not have influenced "theologians of all times."

not a Hebrew workman who labors and rests or follows the sun in any literal sense. That is an analogy. Exodus is saying, the rationale for the Sabbath command at the end of your workweek *is like* Yahweh's divine week. They cannot be identical because the correspondence between divine and human nature is too low. YEC does not appreciate God's nature, nor does it understand the purposes of the Bible, which have to do with God disclosing His nature and plans, not instruction on science.

Whether the YE misunderstanding of God's nature leads to confusing the Bible's purposes or vice versa, each confusion energizes the other and distorts the Christian Mission of preaching the Gospel and Discipleship grounded in the New Creation, not an exclusive or engineered version of the mission.

The special revelation" in John 1:1-14 is the point of scripture and gives us the Christian creation account. John 1 takes us from the first creation in verse 1 to the new creation in verse 14. Verse 14 reveals the staggering Incarnation, which was the purpose of creation in the first place. YEC dedicates itself to literalizing the Hebrew Genesis designed for old covenant Israel. They are like Geocentrists who dedicate themselves to literalizing phenomenological language in scripture when the purpose of the Bible is God's self-disclosure that culminates in the Incarnation and its implications for the world.

Interestingly, the Exodus version of the fourth commandment adds its own rationale for Sabbath-keeping: "For in six days the Lord made heaven and earth...but he rested on the seventh day; *therefore* the Lord blessed the seventh day and consecrated it." Note the contrasting phrase *"but he rested on the seventh day."* The contrasting "but" helps highlight the commandment's real focus—the seventh day. We saw that focus on seven in Genesis repeated painstakingly.

But why is God's rationale for the Sabbath in Exodus 20 completely different from His rationale in Deuteronomy 5? The two accounts were of the same event when it says God wrote the actual commandment with His "finger." Yet, the reason for the command in Exodus is not only missing in Deuteronomy, there *God wrote an entirely different rationale for the Sabbath command* that has puzzled scholars for centuries.

The same incident of the Ten Commandments repeated in Deuteronomy 5:22 was supposed to restate the historical event in God's exact words, including the fourth commandment that we just read in Exodus 20:11. But the command in Deuteronomy does not mention creation. The Sabbath rationale in Deuteronomy 5:15 reads: *Remember that you were slaves in Egypt and that the Lord your God brought you out of there with a mighty hand and an outstretched arm. Therefore the Lord your God has commanded you to observe the Sabbath day.* (emphasis mine)

Deuteronomy says nothing about the six days of creation week or even the seventh day of creation. If God wrote the Decalogue *by hand*, word for word, YErs would have a dilemma. Exodus and Deuteronomy contradict each other (or call it a conspicuous inconsistency) on the rationale for the fourth commandment. Yet, Deuteronomy 5:22 claims to be the same account as Exodus 20 when Moses says God wrote the 10 Commandments:

> These are the commandments the Lord proclaimed in a loud voice to your whole assembly there on the mountain from out of the fire, the cloud and the deep darkness; AND HE ADDED NOTHING MORE. *Then he wrote them on two stone tablets and gave them to me.* (emphasis mine)

So God "added nothing more" to the commands? Not according to Exodus 20:11. Deuteronomy DOES ADD something the Exodus account leaves out, and omits the other. That has to be a stunner for *the "literal historical narrative" and "one-to-one correspondence between words and reality"* crowd if they cared about reality. Do they decide what is real for themselves despite unsolvable hermeneutic problems? Don't get me wrong; this is not a big deal unless you are a YE reformist who believes God wrote the Bible, word for word. The author is more concerned about the theological point, not strict history.

In the fourth commandment, the labor/rest dynamic illustrated the Israelite's newfound liberty to live their lives moderately more than any other command. Their *freedom from slavery* obligated Israel to the Covenant. It was aptly sealed by the liberating Sabbath mandate. Jesus agreed with the liberating rationale for the Sabbath in Deuteronomy when he said: "Should not this woman, a daughter of Abraham, *whom Satan has kept bound* for eighteen long years, *be set free on the Sabbath day?*" in Luke 13:16 (emphasis mine).

In Deuteronomy, the Sabbath represented liberty from oppressive work like that of slavery in Egypt. Jesus elevates Deuteronomy's liberating purpose for the Sabbath: rest from oppressive work to rest from the oppression of Satan's world. According to Hebrews 3-4, the seventh day of creation is about eternal rest or liberty from sin and unbelief, showing the two rests mentioned in the fourth commandment are analogous, not identical.

Historians recognize the Pharisaic obsession with protecting the Sabbath command in Second Temple Judaism due to the catastrophic Babylonian captivity partly due to their constant lip service to the Sabbath. The glaring inconsistency between the Exodus and Deuteronic Sabbath command suggests the possibility that Exodus 20:11 is an editorial note that may have emerged after the exile to give more weight to the Sabbath command.

The Sabbath takes up significantly more space than the other nine in the Decalogue. It served as a seal or sign of the covenant. The two accounts of the all-important giving of the Ten Commandments establishing the covenant *"written with"* God's hand on stone tablets contain strikingly different fourth commandments. YErs claim that there is an exacting word-for-word accounting of this command set in a "literal historical narrative."[413] There weren't two sets of tablets with different wording preserved in the Ark of the Covenant, so which is historical? The more carefully one studies scripture, one sees that excessive literalizing fails.

The Sabbath command was of primary importance because it was a sign of the covenant: "It will be *a sign* between me and the Israelites forever, for in six days the Lord made the heavens and the earth, and on the seventh day he *rested and was refreshed*" (Exodus 31:17). The words *"rested and was refreshed"* cannot be literal. Though the word *"forever"* is not literal regarding the weekly Sabbath (its obligation ended with the old covenant), could it be a veiled reference to the unending seventh day of creation? All this suggests the verse is a theological statement, not a one-to-one correspondence between words and reality.

Some have suggested that Exodus 20:11 was an *editorial note* added after the exile by a copyist to relate the Sabbath command to Genesis?" If true, Exodus 20:11 came after Deuteronomy's original version of the fourth commandment and why Jesus seemed to agree with Deuteronomy. Is that reasonable or even possible?

Editorial notes in scripture are more common than most people realize. They could be commentary by the original author or may have been *marginal notes* alongside biblical texts for decades written by copyists or editors for clarity. Sometimes marginal notes became so familiar they eventually ended up in the biblical text. We know of several editorial notes in scripture, and there may be others not yet identified, and some will likely go undiscovered.

While Exodus 20:11 may be an editorial comment illustrating the pattern for Judah (not to mention avoiding the human tendency to be exiled as Adam and Eve from Eden), it is unnecessary to depend on that possibility for our discussion. Historical and linguistic criticisms suggest that Genesis 1 was written or edited around the time of the exile, centuries after giving the Ten Commandments at Sinai. On returning from exile, Judaism attempted reforms by building a "protective wall" around the Law, especially the Sabbath, to avoid further captivity and to expedite the Messianic kingdom. That may have led editors to strengthen the fourth commandment.

Even if this editorial comment originated as a marginal note, it does not mean it is false, or we should reject it. It still needs its meaning assessed as other

413. This is a critical point since the two accounts cannot both be definitive. That means that the biblical text has theological purposes that supersede strict reporting on the facts. That is not lying: it expresses truth idiomatically. Slavery in Egypt was a brute fact while comparing the creation week to the simple Hebrew workweek is theological since the divine week is metaphysical; the Israelite week is earthly. The two reasons given in the two accounts identify the Hebrew God as Creator (in Exodus) and *Deliverer from slavery* (in Deuteronomy). The latter justifies the covenantal obligations Yahweh places on Israel that He earned. The purpose of these verses is to teach the meaning of covenantal obligations theologically and not simply to reiterate them word for word.

editorial comments in scripture do. For example, consider the following verse regarding Abraham: "Abraham obeyed *my voice and kept my charge, my commandments, my statutes, and my laws.*" It is hard to imagine that in the first book of Moses, this verse could refer to anything else but the Law of Moses, who had not been born at the time of Abraham. The statement on Abraham's stellar obedience to all the Law is out of historical context.

What is happening?

This anachronism may be saying, "Abraham was one of us," a genuine Hebrew, though he was Chaldean by blood and worshipped pagan gods before Elohim called him. Since Abraham was circumcised (the future token for entering the covenant community) and obeyed God by faith, he was reborn as a spiritual Hebrew. It was common in the ancient world for authors to give heroic figures exceptional qualities that some may call legendary. A modern bias might label these qualities as "lies." Authors would describe extraordinary people with extraordinary attributes when ordinary language seemed inadequate. That was especially true of Semitic peoples of the ANE.

Another example is Numbers 12:3, "Now Moses was a very humble man, *more humble than anyone else on the face of the earth.*" If Moses wrote this, it is self-defeating since the most humble person in the world would not say, "I am the most humble person in the world." This evaluation of Moses is an editorial note, hyperbole, and opinion—no doubt a commonly held opinion. An editor must have recorded Moses's death in Deuteronomy 34:5–7. The description of his humility is a fitting epitaph.

Notice a well-known editorial comment in Mark 7:19 that says:

> Don't you see that nothing that enters a person from the outside can defile them? "For it does not go into their heart but into their stomach and then out of the body *(in saying this, Jesus declared all foods clean).*" (emphasis mine)

The words are in parentheses because translators recognize this as a later editorial comment by a copyist. Remember, Peter refused to eat the unclean animals in the vision of Acts 10. The vision would have been unnecessary, and Peter would have reacted to it differently if Jesus had openly declared all foods clean. Not until Acts 15, and with the help of Paul, did the disciples see a distinction between old and new covenant obligations.

Look. Maybe Abraham's obedience to the Law in every detail is a historical fact. Abraham could have miraculously kept the entire Mosaic Law; maybe Moses self-identified as the humblest person in the world, and maybe Jesus taught all meats were good to eat despite Peter's strange unfamiliarity with that change in scriptural teaching (Acts 10:13–14). These literal interpretations are possible, *but they are not reasonable.* Similarly, it is not reasonable for the unlimited God to work like a finite man, i.e., a Hebrew craftsman, during His most Almighty act—the Creation of the universe from nothing.

Editorial comments were necessary for the text to remain readable through dramatically changing times with intellectual advancement, war, invasions, captivity, exile, etc. Initially, in all its diverse genres, the Bible contained no punctuation, no space between words, paragraphs, chapters, and verses in either testament. All the letters of the Bible were in what we call "caps." We know editors added structural, grammatical, editorial changes, and parenthetical statements into the text for clarity. Names of cities, empires, landmarks, idioms, and who knows what can change over the centuries so that past references may not be recognizable. Editing is the primary reason the Bible is readable and remarkably coherent, considering its diverse genres, cultures, authors, subject matter, and evolving languages, compiled over a thousand years. This historical editorial process is only a problem for people that confuse inspiration with dictation.

The commentary within the fourth commandment in Exodus is striking. The comparative pattern of the human and divine workweeks is undeniable. But is the equivalence literal or analogous? *The nature of the principal actors decides this, not words only.*

Notice further that the fourth commandment is not in the first person. It does not say, "*I gave* you the Sabbath" or "For in six days, *I created* the heavens and the earth" or "*I rested*" the seventh day and "*I blessed it,*" etc. *The author says* "the Lord" did these things. But did the Lord speak and write down *the rationale* for the Sabbath on the tablets of stone?

Compare the first person references in the first commandment, "*I am* the Lord your God *who* brought you out of the land of Egypt, *etc.,*" (Exodus 20:2). Verse 1 says, "*God spoke all these words.*" This change of pronouns indicates the possibility that some editing for theological purposes occurred on the fourth commandment, especially since there are two diverse versions of this critical event at Mt. Sinai. Additionally, the fourth commandment is the longest of the commands in the Decalogue, suggesting its development and growing importance over time.[414]

The first commandment is next in length; the others are much shorter. The first and fourth commands were the most poorly kept by the Israelites and were the primary reasons for their captivity (Jeremiah 17:27; Hosea 2:11; Amos 8:5; Ezekiel 20). Both commands relate directly to worshiping Yahweh. Perhaps the length of the first and fourth commandments may be due to editors looking

---

414. There is linguistic evidence that a later copyist inserted this reference to creation in the fourth commandment around the time of the exile or early second temple period when most scholars believe Genesis 1 was written. In other words, Genesis 1 was written after Exodus 20 when an editorial note supporting the command is reasonable and not that the editorial comment appeared in the official stone tablets containing the Decalogue. There are linguistic and theological parallels that fit this hypothesis. This book is not the place to establish the certainty of this editorial note but only to state that it is a reasonable possibility and adds to a general uncertainty over some details that YEC relies on so heavily.

back from the exile to reinforce those commands so that future generations may avoid the tragic mistakes of their ancestors.

At any rate, the fourth commandment begins, "Remember the Sabbath," not "Keep holy the Sabbath," but *remember it*. God had given them the Sabbath earlier as they left Egypt (Exodus 16:23–29). They tended to neglect it. The Sabbath reference in Exodus 16 is the first mention of a Sabbath day kept by humans *and animals*. Animals underscore the earthly nature of the Israelite Sabbath and its fundamental difference from the seventh day of creation. The Sabbath was a reoccurring reminder that God freed Israel from bondage in Egypt and was at peace with God, provided they kept the covenant.

The exhortation to remember the Sabbath also suggests the tendency of the children of Judah to neglect it, which they did more seriously right before the time of Babylonian captivity in Jeremiah's day:

> But if you do not obey me to keep the Sabbath day holy by not carrying any load as you come through the gates of Jerusalem on the Sabbath day, then *I will kindle an unquenchable fire in the gates of Jerusalem that will consume her fortresses.* (Jeremiah 17:27)

Genesis does not say God *kept* the Israelite Sabbath, which Paul said was a shadow of Christ (Colossians 2:16–17). The word *Sabbath* does not appear in Genesis, suggesting a distinction between God's *rest* from the weekly Sabbath in Israel. It is incoherent to claim that the divine rest of creation is a shadow of the "true rest." The Israelite Sabbath, *as an institution,* arose during the Exodus and was not established until Sinai. God's rest at creation did not result in a human institution or an earthly Sabbath, and as we saw in Hebrews 3-4, God continued to offer the divine rest throughout Israel's history.

Israel was to use the Sabbath to commune with God in collective fellowship. Similarly, God offered *eternal fellowship* with all humanity by giving us the unending Rest of creation. The book of Hebrews leads us to the eternal rest in Christ anticipated by the Creation Rest meant for everyone, not the shallow notion of Stephen Boyd, that God *merely* rested.

The author of Hebrews describes the earthly nature of the old covenant worship system and its symbolism with the realities in the heavenly realm. The author mentions the seventh day of creation and its meaning—an abiding rest for the people of God. He mentions the priesthood and the role of the High Priest, the administration of the sacrificial law, ceremonies, rituals, and liturgy laid out by the calendar for the temple services: annually, monthly, and during the weekly Sabbath:

> It was necessary, then, for the copies of the heavenly things to be purified with these sacrifices, *but the heavenly things themselves with better sacrifices than these.* For Christ did not enter a sanctuary made with human hands *that was only a copy of the true one... Nor did he enter heaven to offer himself again and again,* the way the high priest enters the Most Holy

Place every year with blood that is not his own. Otherwise, Christ would have had to suffer many times since the creation of the world. But he has appeared *once for all* at the culmination of the ages to do away with sin by the sacrifice of himself...Christ was sacrificed once to take away the sins of many (Hebrews 9:23-27)

Note the words, "Nor did he enter heaven to offer himself again and again." Repetitious activity indicates the temporal efficacy of the activity, which is not a feature of the heavenly realm. The divine rest at creation is another case in point. God's rest is not like the weekly Sabbath in Israel for the same reason. The earthly Sabbath was repetitive and temporal. The divine rest introduced at creation and secured in Christ continues once and for all.

Everything in this fourth commandment is analogous to the relevant principles— "Six days you shall labor and do all your work, but the seventh day is a sabbath to the Lord your God," alongside "For in six days the Lord made... but he rested on the seventh day." The obvious analogies are between God's Personhood and human personhood, divine activity and daily labor, and God's eternal rest compared to repeated and temporal weekly rest in ancient Israel. These cannot be of the same nature.

What are the two natures of the workweeks, given the infinite gulf between the nature of God and human nature? Fundamentalists could not be more confident that Exodus 20:11 rests their case, that God is like a man (He hadn't created yet) and puts in a good day's work. Humans live seven days a week, and apparently, so does God (or so *did* God says YEC). He did His work every morning and retired every evening during a literal week, just as we do, and He rested. Therefore, YErs conclude the earth is 6000 years old.

Curiously, YErs avoid commenting on the seventh day of creation as much as possible, even though they rely on a literal reading of the Sabbath commandment in the Decalogue to make their case for six literal days. Upon visiting Ken Ham's Creation Museum, visitors find a large section devoted to the six days, vegetarianism, dinosaurs roaming in Eden, unicorns, real flying dragons that once existed, and many Old Testament themes, especially Genesis 1-11. I was especially interested in how they dealt with the seventh day of creation and was surprised that they dedicated no time or space to it when there. Might the reason be that the unending seventh day in Genesis is a real threat to six literal days?

YErs miss the fourth commandment's intent to *keep holy the sabbath* they deem is unnecessary to take literally. This inconsistency is glaring. The point of the commandment is set aside for what is not its point. The YE signature distinctive detracts from the divine intent in both creation "week" and the fourth commandment: rest in God. The difference is that the heavenly rest is eternal and spiritual, and the weekly rest is temporal and physical. God is not physical. Christians interpret Genesis in the light of Christ and the New Testament.

Revelation says the tree of life will be in the New Jerusalem. Of course, Revelation is an example of highly symbolic Jewish Apocalyptic literature. It means eternal rest and peace will finally come to the world, and the Lamb will rule. The Advent song in Luke 2:14 goes: "Glory to God in the highest heaven, and on earth *peace* to those on whom his favor *rests.*"

Therefore, since the seventh-day rest in Genesis extends beyond the scope of a single solar day, the correspondence between the "day" of God's rest and Israel's "Sabbath day" observance would be analogous, not identical. As such, there is every reason to believe that the eternal nature of the seventh day of creation must correspond to the nature of the previous six days because together, they make up one divine week. *In other words, since the seventh-day rest in Genesis is eternal, so must be the week. The week in Israel ends when the Sabbath ends, and a new week begins, which is all too temporal to characterize God's activity. The week does not end in Genesis with the consistent formula, "evening and morning were the seventh day." God's creative acts are endless since we know this creation continues unabated and will morph into its transfiguration—a new creation—the new heaven and earth.*

Of course, the old covenant Sabbath is not an obligation for New Testament Christians because it is a copy of the heavenly (Hebrews 9:23). It also falls short of God's self-disclosure in Christ, who offers eternal rest as God did in Genesis. The weekly Sabbath in Israel was a temporal bridge between the divine rest in Genesis and coming to Christ to find the rest he gives.

Our rest is in a person (the Logos made human), the reality that grounds the universe and ensures peace with God (Colossians 2:16–17). It is as if the resurrection on the first day of the week is a continuation of creation week that left us with an unended seventh day absent sundown, ready to rendezvous with Easter Sunday. Easter morning of 30 AD continued the creation plan, i.e., a baton had passed from the first creation to a new creation in Christ. That is a theological explanation, not a historical one.

If the two workweeks referred to in Exodus 20:11 are identical, and the Genesis creation account is the foundation upon which God's plan rests, then the weekly Sabbath could not be a mere shadow as Paul said (Colossians 2:16-17). And the SDAs would be correct to say there are no grounds for changing the fourth commandment. An unending seventh day sealed the creation account as told in Genesis, and the weekly Sabbath sealed the Israelite covenant at Sinai (compare Isaiah 56:6; Exodus 20:20). If they are the same, then they stand or fall together. But they are not the same because the weekly Sabbath has been set aside, and the seventh-day rest at creation continues forever (Hebrews 4:4, 9-11).

The New Testament does not explicitly change the seventh-day Sabbath to the first day of the week. One reason is that resting on the first day before any work is senseless. The new covenant is not about those things. The new covenant is about spiritual work with no covenantal obligation to material rest. *"My*

Father is always at his work to this very day, and I too am working" (John 5:17) *and we should be "about our Father's business"* (Luke 2:49). That alone shows we are dealing with a significant metaphor and that spiritual reality trumps shadows in the material world.

Why don't YErs take the *command* in the fourth commandment *as written*? After all, it was law. YErs also believe they are God's actual words spoken and written at Sinai. Is it God's eternal, perfect word as written, as YErs claim? Or is it a temporal word? Was not this command God-breathed written with His finger? Why is a literal workweek of greater importance to YErs than *the commandment's point*?

Because the YE point is not the same as the fourth commandment's point.

God says to remember the seventh day, not *one day in seven,* and certainly not to remember the age of the earth, which is never mentioned anywhere in scripture. Yet, Sabbath observance ceased to be obligatory with the new covenant on substantial theological grounds. That fact alone calls a literal day interpretation of the creation week into question. If God kept the weekly Sabbath, who are we to abandon it? The New Testament does not tell us to give it up for Sunday.

The connection may not be evident at first.

Nonetheless, an unintended consequence of literalism in Genesis 1 means that we could no longer apply the seventh-day Sabbath to Jews only; but to all humanity as far back as creation itself when there were no Jews nor an old covenant. This connection is why *the YEC Reform Movement was a Seventh-day Adventist invention and why today's "Sunday keeping" YErs virtually ignore the seventh day of creation.* SDAs and YErs believe God observed the literal seventh day, *blessed it, and made it holy, i.e., made it holy for us.* Would God do that for Jews only at the beginning of time? That does not make sense. Adam and Eve were not Jewish nor under the old covenant. God did not tell Adam and Eve to "remember the Sabbath;" they were enjoying it until disobedience disrupted the peace.

God keeping a weekly Sabbath is more *narrative license* than literal narrative. Why would an unlimited God *literally* observe a day of rest, bless it, and then personally sanctify it with His holiness if its usefulness was as temporal as the law of circumcision? The seventh-day rest in Genesis has theological importance, not material ones. We would not conceive of circumcising God. Then why is God resting from sunset Friday to sunset Saturday perfectly reasonable? An infinite God keeping a weekly Sabbath is contradictory.

Everyone knows actual rest for God is figurative. Fine. Both the Sabbath (seal of the covenant) and circumcision (the sign of admission into the covenant community) were central to the old covenant, but because of the overt and coarse nature of circumcision, no one uses it in any metaphorical sense with God. Yet, when it comes to the nature of God, literal Sabbath-keeping and circumcision are equivalent for one reason; they are both of the body, which God does not have.[415]

Circadian rhythms are a neurological response to daytime and night over a twenty-four-hour day and signal us to feel bright and awake in the morning and drowsy at night. Rhythmic exposure to light and dark affects our internal clock, conditioning us to function properly. Of course, this response is physiological. Therefore, day and night cannot govern God's activity and must be metaphorical. The Israelite Sabbath had liturgical and communal use, but theologically, it was a *shadow* of what was to come in Jesus. Thus *"what was to come"* had to do with our share in God's eternal rest introduced at creation and established by the covenant in Christ who said, "Come to me, all you who are weary and burdened, and I will give you rest" (Matthew 11:28).

Colossians 2:16–17 says:

Therefore do not let anyone condemn you in matters of food and drink or of observing festivals, new moons, *or sabbaths. These are only a shadow of what is to come, but the substance belongs to Christ.* (NRSV)

Or,

Such things are only *a shadow of what is to come and they have only symbolic value*; but the substance [the reality of what is foreshadowed] belongs to Christ. (Colossians 2:17 AMP; emphasis mine)

The "symbolic value" is in representing something more profound. Paul could not mean that the *seventh day of creation* lacked substance or was a shadow of things to come. The seventh day in Genesis is not the weekly Sabbath in Israel; it was the divine and unending offer of rest to humanity and union with God. God's rest remains offered *today* (Hebrews 4:4-5). We saw in the last chapter that the author of Hebrews equates the seventh day of creation (an unending "Today") with God's eternal rest for those who believe—*"those who formerly had the good news proclaimed to them did not go in [the Promised Land] because of their disobedience."* The Promised Land is analogous to Eden/rest.

The author calls this train of thought God's word when he says in verse 7, *"God again set a certain day, calling it Today. [God] did this when a long time later he spoke through David, as in the passage already quoted [Psalm 95:11]: "Today, if you hear his voice, do not harden your hearts."* The word "Today" cannot be a twenty-four-hour day because it continues to Christ through Joshua and David's day.

These verses help explain "God's rest" as something much more than a weekly rest. Israel did not find God's rest in Canaan because they did not fulfill the covenant faithfully (Hebrews 3:16–19). *God's rest is not the end of weekly work*

---

415. The Bible does use circumcision metaphorically as in "circumcision of the heart" (Romans 2:29). Nonetheless, Sabbatical rest lends itself much better as a metaphor for communion with God in peace and tranquility.

but anticipates the fulfillment of God's redemptive work, resulting in eternal blessings for all humanity.

The "Today" in Hebrews is a divine and eternal "Today" or a never-ending *now*—it is the continuous call to peace and fellowship with God from the beginning: call it the offer of eternal life, Heaven for the saints, union with God, or God's eternal rest; it all means the same thing. The author then says in verses 9-10, *"There remains then [continues to be], a Sabbath-rest for the people of God; for anyone who enters God's rest also rests from their works, just as God did from his,"* meaning there is an analogy. Humans *"Rest from their works of disobedience"* by faith, and God "rests" in His eternal way. That is spiritual rest according to the nature of each. We have an analogy, not literalism. The author concludes in verse 11, *"Let us, therefore, make every effort to enter that rest, so that no one will perish by following their example of disobedience."* The examples to avoid include Adam and Eve. Note that the author's choice of effort and rest in verse 11 is an interesting contrast, showing that physical labor is irrelevant to God's rest.

Entering God's rest today is not keeping a weekly, earthly Sabbath; it is spiritual rest that Christ offers, which solves the problem of spiritual death. That is the kind of rest God presented. If the earthly Sabbath and the Divine Sabbath were the same, then God needed time to rest, which would be the precise amount of time a human needs. His would be some kind of shadow, which is unacceptable. Was God's rest temporary and suitable for earthly work? Or was it a divine rest, ideal for heavenly work? It is odd to say that an omnipotent God rested for twenty-four hours, which means he returned to work on the eighth day. Knowing how absurd this sounds, YErs admit the seventh-day rest continues, but the seventh day ends. Why would the *rest* be eternal for a week's worth of *work*?

This YE reasoning is shooting from the hip into the foot.

YErs say the *rest* is figurative but continues. At the same time, the *day* is literal, but it ends. They say it ends, not because YErs are consistent or that they read the Bible as written or that whenever "evening and morning" accompanies a day, it is always twenty-four hours. Instead, YErs say the seventh day of Creation ends because— and only because— they are determined to remain YErs.

I, too, was determined to stay in a Jewish Christian tradition even when, at times, I thought maybe some of this wasn't correct. There seemed to be enough other "proof texts" reinforcing my overall beliefs.

There always is.

Cognitive dissonance among YErs, as with anyone else, is the product of maintaining one's opinion evidence to the contrary. The stronger that evidence is, the greater the dissonance. The confusion over an *eternal rest* on a twenty-four-hour day is a flat contradiction. Even this YE confusion illustrates how different the nature of a divine or eternal "day" is from a human or a solar day. There are no divine days, except in the figurative sense, e.g., "the Day of the Lord" or "In that Day, [God will...]" and "the Ancient of Days." The seventh day of creation is unbounded. It is not an actual day but a *continuous "Today,"* as the book of Hebrews repeatedly states (Hebrews 3:7, 13, 15, 4:7, 13:8). Moses illustrates that by abruptly ending the refrain "evening and morning" on day seven.

If the seventh day of creation ended, what happened on the eighth day? Circumcision? Circumcision, like the Sabbath, was a sign of the covenant (Genesis 17:10–14). The unending seventh day and no eighth day underscored the temporal nature of the first covenant. A priest circumcised the baby Jesus on the eighth day (Luke 2:21); the human Jesus also kept the *Jewish* Sabbath—the *infinite* Logos in heaven from the beginning did neither. The Logos did not turn into Jesus; The unlimited Logos remained in heaven. Instead, the Logos *assumed* or took on human nature in Jesus of Nazareth without changing His nature.

The nature of the Almighty is decidedly not human.

Hebrews 3–4 seizes on the seventh day, not ending in Genesis, so it must be allegorical according to God's word through Joshua and David. That was one of many brilliant observations from the author of this New Testament masterpiece. One conclusion is that the unending seventh day is a *corrective* to any thought by the reader that the previous six days of labor were literal. The days in Genesis are undoubtedly an anthropomorphic context and, therefore, figurative. Genesis is not about *physical* labor and rest, on *ordinary* days, during a *temporal* week, by an *infinite* God. That is what YEC is about.

There is no such thing as a six-day week in Judaism. In the Hebrew week, *the Sabbath brings the week to an end.* But if the seventh day of creation never ends, *creation week never ends. It is not just the seventh day that continues; the week continues, meaning we are not talking about a literal week.* While the word for "week" in Hebrew is שׁוּבָע (*shabua*: a period of seven days), by Paul's day, *Shabbat* or Sabbath could mean week depending on the context. For instance, 1 Corinthians 16:2 says, "On the first day of every week [σάββατον or "Sabbath" in Greek], each one of you is to put aside and save."

This reference cannot mean the seventh day of the week because there is no first day of every Sabbath day, but there is the first day of every week—Sunday. In other words, the term *Sabbath* often meant an entire week because, with it, the week completes.

The two Sabbaths (divine and human) are as diverse as the participants. The reality is the seventh day of creation meant the same thing when Jesus said, "Come, and I will give you rest." Jesus called himself "Lord of the Sabbath" (Matthew 12:8). Being the Logos at creation, the *Lord of the Sabbath* gives eternal rest, or he could not be its Lord.

God's rest shows His desire for fellowship that continued from the beginning through the Promised Land with Joshua, in the land with David, and punctuated in Christ's day, according to the author of Hebrews 4:8–11. N. T. Wright follows this biblical train of thought when he writes, "[Hebrews] 3–4 says the Old Testament speaks of a time of 'rest,' of entering the Promised Land, *even in writings which were written long after the entry into Canaan.* There must be a different, more permanent rest."[416]

Today, the seventh day of creation continues in Christ.

---

416. N. T. Wright, *Following Jesus: Biblical Reflections on Discipleship* (SPCK, Great Britain, Holy Trinity Church, London, 1994), p. 8.

31.
AND GOD SAW IT WAS ~~VERY GOOD~~ "PERFECT"

There was a perfect world to start with described by God as "very good."
—Ken Ham[417]

How revealing is it when someone misquotes God in front of all to see?

Ham corrects the biblical record; indeed, he corrects God. When Genesis describes the world as "very good," it quotes God in the story. According to Ham, Creation was not just *very good*. It was perfect. That amounts to editing the scripture by effectively scratching out "very good" and replacing it with *"perfect." So much for "as written."*

The *whole world* was not a paradise; instead, it was *"very good."* The Garden of Eden is distinct from the rest of the world since the author applies paradisal or idyllic imagery nowhere else in the story (Genesis 2–3). In fact, the opposite is true.

Michael S. Heiser writes:

Adam and Eve lived in the garden. The rest of the earth needed subduing... It was habitable. But it wasn't quite what Eden was, namely, it was not a garden. The whole world needs to be like God's home... [Adam and Eve] were supposed to make it happen. They were to do that by multiplying and following God's direction.[418]

There was still *unfinished* work to do in the world, and God wanted humans to participate in that work. Genesis says that wild animals inhabited the rest of the world, calling them "the wild beasts of the field [wilderness]." The Garden of Eden was marked by how different it was from the untamed outside world. That is obvious. Yet they are made homogeneous in YEC with the broad brush of perfection.

While YErs believe God created every living thing in a mature state, the text says that God personally planted seeds in the garden's soil, and they *sprouted*. Sprouts are new growth; that is, they are young shoots, not fully grown:

And the *Lord God planted a garden* in Eden to the east. And he *placed* there the human he had fashioned. And the Lord God *caused to sprout from the soil* every tree lovely to look at and good for food, and the tree of

---

417. From AiG website. YErs openly switch "very good" with perfect with no justification.

418. Michael S. Heiser, *The Unseen Realm: Recovering the Supernatural Worldview of the Bible* (Lexham Press, Bellingham, WA 98225, 2015) p. 51. Heiser is a biblical scholar and specializing in ancient Semitic languages.

life was in the midst of the garden and the tree of knowledge of good and evil. (Genesis 2:9–10, 15; emphasis mine)[419]

Every tree was *sprouting.*

Those trees began as young shoots, as all plants do. This verse describes the dawn of new life in the beauty and tranquility of a garden planted by God. If God created the garden mature at the outset, planting would make no sense. It is hard to deny the suggestion of an interval much longer than a day. Genesis 2–3 does not seem interested in singling out any day, such as day six, nor does it mark any time.

Robert Alter says the phrase "He placed there the human" could read, "God took the human and *set him down* in the garden."[420] This phrase is explicit in that God took Adam from the *outside* and placed him inside the protective garden. The way YErs apply the word *perfect* to the whole universe fails here because if indeed the whole is "perfect," as YErs claim, then no part can be more "perfect" than the whole. Therefore, if the garden was perfect, then the rest of the wilderness was neither the garden nor perfect. Still, *the author does not call the garden "perfect."*

After all, a tree associated with evil was at the garden's center, and a deceiver lurking around eventually pierced the garden's perimeter. A world where evil is there for the "picking" and a deceiver is present to serve it up is not a perfect world. Before Adam sinned, things were still *not good* for him until the arrival of Eve—"It is *not good* for man to be alone." It took the creation of a woman to declare the world "very good," not morally good, but well-ordered or *balanced* for human flourishing. A human world was now complete. The world was *ordered* for human habitation, and with gender completion, humanity could flourish, i.e., "be fruitful and multiply." Mortals cannot continue in a temporal world without gender completion. With Eve the world of humans was complete, not perfect.

The notion that whatever God makes must be perfect in the absolute because He is perfect is unjustified. It assumes the world possesses God's nature. YEC needs a perfect world to justify animal-eternal-life to reject deep age. A better word for Eden is *idyllic,* meaning ideal for humans as understood in the ancient world. Adam and Eve had the task of keeping the garden from falling into neglect, which indicates the second law of thermodynamics was operating in Eden. God made the world outside Eden, not perfect but as a diamond in the rough with the task of refining it on us. The Potter/clay metaphor illustrates this. Humans either possessed the ideal life for a time and then lost it, or we

---

419. Robert Alter, *Genesis: Translation and Commentary* (W. W. Norton and Company, New York and London, 1997), Kindle edition, location 878.

420. Ibid., location 883.

never really had it. The common belief in Christian thought is that we lost what we once had. Thus the fall.

God's active presence in the garden made it ideal. Undoubtedly, the created order was a *very good beginning* but not a *perfect* end. Perfection, an ultimate maturity, comes at the end in temporal reality, not the beginning, as plants and trees come from seeds in the ground that took nature's ordinary course to maturity.[421]

According to its design, a "very good" tree produces good fruit, not perfect produce in the absolute. The seeds that God planted sprouted into young shoots. They took time to mature, yet Adam and Eve needed an immediate food supply. If there was a time to create something mature, this was it. That does not happen. Therefore, mature plants were around before Adam. Coordinating all the details of events and accounting for every hour is not this author's concern. That is a YEC concern.

Adam's job, it appears, was to maintain the garden as it grew. That meant to harvest fruits and vegetables as they ripen, so they do not rot. The couple kept things neat by pruning, cultivating, and preventing grasses and unwanted plants from taking over. Otherwise, *dressing and keeping* are meaningless. Adam and Eve were supposed to spread idyllic conditions throughout the earth by their offspring (Genesis 2:15).

Conflating "very good" with "perfect" leads to one of the presuppositions of modern YEC, namely the belief that nothing *would* die in a "perfect" world before Adam sinned, that is, except plants. Poor plants; they were the only category of creatures in Eden that did not sin, yet the couple could eat them.[422]

Actually, the first sinner was a *wild animal*—a lying snake in the grass.

The story says God gave the serpent "special skills"—the "Liam Neeson of Eden."

Now the serpent was *more crafty than any of the wild animals* the Lord God had made. He said to the woman, "Did God really say, 'You must not eat from *any* tree in the garden?'" (Genesis 3:1)

One cannot help but notice that the first sentence, "Now the serpent was more crafty than any of the wild animals the Lord God had made," does not read

---

421. *Perfect* in King James English meant "mature."

422. This is a strange inconsistency in YEC. On the one hand, plants were subject to death in a so-called perfect world. On the other hand, YE literature describes the curses as effecting the plant kingdom with defense and attack mechanisms and even carnivorous abilities like the Venus flytrap. This is counterintuitive. How could the additional powers given to plants be curses? They were *more vulnerable* being eaten in a "perfect" world without those defenses. In other words, since plants were killed and eaten before the fall, it would be a blessing for them to acquire defenses and survival skills. Besides, those survival mechanisms promote the spreading of seeds and new growth assuring a flourishing ecosystem, which is no curse. We have to ask, "How well is YEC thought out?"

like a literal historical narrative. In fact, there is no example of literature any-where when animals, *by nature*, carry on a conversation, and trees are mystical that we consider in the genre of literal historical narrative or word-for-word lit-eralism. It sounds more like storytelling or fable, not unlike characters in *Aesop's Fables*. Interestingly, the Greeks said Aesop got his genre from Mesopotamia.[423]

Interestingly, YEC is just as much mythology as anything else. Consider YE notions of everlasting animals and bugs, eternal life, no carnivores, pet dino-saurs, trees that give eternal life or death should you pick the wrong one; literal supernatural curses for eating forbidden fruit, and creation from a rib similar to the much earlier Sumerian myth of Dilmun (see chapter 11). Like Jewish Apocalyptic, myths are not errors unless taken literally.

At any rate, if the sequence of the serpent is literal, then God made this animal "questionable," i.e., his shrewdness tainted his ethics. Yet real animals are not moral agents. Animals do not reason about God and His relationship with humans. A child might take these details literally, but the author is not writing for children. The story indicates that this wild "animal" started a chain reac-tion of sin from itself to Eve, Adam, and every person since. Some *wild* animal. Genesis explicitly places the serpent in the wild outside Eden, where things were much different. Yet this lying snake entered Eden.

What kind of world was on the outside?[424]

The specific words in Genesis 1:28 that refer to the role of humans over the creation are to *subdue* and *rule,* meaning they were to tame or domesticate and then dominate the world outside Eden. "Be fruitful and multiply, fill the land, and *conquer it. Rule* over the fish of the sea, the flying creatures of the sky, and over every animal that crawls on the land" (TLV).[425]

Does a perfect paradise need conquering?

---

423. Aesop was supposed to have been a slave in ancient Greece around 550 BCE. "When [Berossus] set down fables from the *Aesopica* in verse for a Hellenistic Prince 'Alexander,' he expressly stated at the head of Book II that this type of 'myth' that Aesop had introduced to the 'sons of the Hellenes' had been an invention of 'Syrians' from the time of 'Ninos' (personifying Nineveh to Greeks) and Belos ('ruler')." See *Wikipedia* article "Fable."

424. The serpent was a common symbol in the ANE for a spiritual being that had a place in the council of a pantheon. Scholars have suggested that this serpent may have been a member of Yahweh's council within the confines of the Garden which itself was symbolic of God's dwelling brought among humans. The Garden dwelling might include God's entourage. This may explain why the writer presents Eve as entirely comfortable in a conversation with a "serpent." It may also account for the words "Let *us* make man in *our* image." Some scholars also suggest that the serpent, later identified as Satan, originally played the role of a prosecutor as in the book of Job and that he may have played the same role in Genesis so that, technically, he was not lying but playing "the devil's advocate." That said, all this calls into question how literal we should take the details of the story.

425. The TLV (Tree of Life Version) is a new Bible translation produced by Messianic Jewish Christian and mainstream Christian scholars, which highlights the rich Hebrew roots of the Christian faith and language. It helps bridge gaps that often are lost in translation.

Notice God does not say "dress and keep" the wilderness. Other translations use terms such as *subdue*, *dominate*, and take *control*. God made Adam a son and steward of the garden but *lord* over the outside world. *Subdue* and *dominate* are not words used for a paradise where God was Lord. We also know those actions were relatively harsh in ANE cultures. The words in Hebrew are *ezer* and *kn*; which have warlike connotations. This is not about abusing the creation. Humans are God's stewards over the earth. The point is obvious. The world outside Eden was wild; it was not a paradise. It was not meant to be perfect since it is temporal.

Eden needed no such taming. It was ideal.

If you read the story literally, wild animals could not just talk; they could *deceive*. Who knows how many less-talented "wildlings" were roaming around? If they could lie, might stealing and murder be far behind? These are silly questions unless people insist that this is a literal historical narrative or a one-to-one correspondence with words to reality. We are not dealing with biblical scholars here.

Christians have long identified the serpent in the first book of the Bible as the same serpent in the last book—the devil of Revelation. Therefore, evil and sin were there before Adam and Eve. In keeping with the *as-written* hermeneutic, Satan appears to have corrupted the animals or at least one of them.

But let's be honest: the serpent sequence is imagery that casts a dark shadow over Eden.

The tree of the knowledge of good and evil assumes the existence of evil. God does not explain the concept to the couple who, you might think, didn't understand evil. Adam and Eve seem innocent in an immature way. God endowed human nature with the capacity to comprehend general revelation, natural law, or basic right and wrong. The innocence of ignorance that does not comprehend good and evil lacks wisdom.

It is counter-productive to keep adults or even older children from the knowledge of evil. Mature humans were brought up knowing the difference and learning to choose the good. Jesus knew of evil and good better than anyone, yet he always chose the good. How can we embrace good or avoid evil if we are not wise concerning them? To comprehend good and evil is good. It may be that eating from this tree of knowledge meant the first couple failed to choose good as defined by the Creator and not that they could now simply comprehend what evil and good are. The sin was not in understanding but in choosing the wrong path to enlightenment. Or perhaps the tree of knowledge is a story idolizing innocence in paradise, and not read more into it.

Whatever the case, notice that Moses does not explain the serpent or the two trees to his readers. The serpent and trees enter the story with the definite article "the"—*the* snake and *the* trees—with no attempt to identify them, implying an immediate familiarity among the intended readership. Textual scholars think there had been a previous Edenic story or oral tradition, likely an epic poem (alluded to in Ezekiel 28:11–19, 31:8–18) that the author of Genesis draws from to establish a new theology about the Creator and his relationship to heaven and earth.[426]

The Israelites understood things in the text about which we can only guess. The author does not have death explained to the first couple when he writes, *"On the day that you eat, you shall surely die."* The author is not interested in having death explained to Adam and Eve. Instead, he is showing that death is the result of disobedience. According to YEC, the couple had no experience whatsoever with death *of any kind*. Yet, Adam and Eve seem to know what death means, or the warning is pointless.[427] Still, even *we* are unsure what "death" means in this passage since Adam and Eve did not immediately die in the literal sense as God appears to have predicted. The original readers likely "breezed through" these passages without difficulty.

The serpent's entry into the story shows that evil already existed at the beginning of the created order, whenever that was, yet the author does not feel the need to explain. The idea is that evil existed outside paradise, where the lying snake appears to have roamed; then it entered Eden. We still have a hard time explaining how evil could start in a universe that was absent of it initially. Why does evil exist in all its manifestations, chiefly high levels of gratuitous evil? The author shows that all evils do not stem from eating a specific fruit. There is a significant layer of evil independent of human behavior. The serpent never ate from the tree of good and evil yet sinned in other ways. But that is overthinking.

This is a story.[428]

Plants could die by way of being eaten before human sin. Creatures had to eat something. But did their food have to be alive? Yes, it did. Food had to be a renewable resource in a temporal world. Do YErs believe that plants not eaten continued living forever in their understanding of the perfect world? Or could they die naturally by seasonal cycles like biennials? If they did die before

---

426. Umberto Cassuto and Israel Abrahams, "A Commentary on the Book of Genesis: from Adam to Noah," *Umberto Cassuto Biblical Commentaries 1* (1989), pp. 76–80. Cassuto is famous for rejecting the critical Documentary Hypothesis of Julius Welhousen. See also Nahum M. Sarna, *Understanding Genesis (The Heritage of Biblical Israel* (JTSA /Varda Books, 2014), Kindle edition, pp. 24–25. Sarna also rejected the DH.

427. If one assumes God took time to educate the first couple on the many concepts not explained in Genesis, then one admits to more elapsed time than we have in the text. That opens up the possibility of an unspecified amount of time-lapse unaccounted for in the story as we have it.

428. God placed the tree of knowledge in the center of the Garden in the full and constant view of the couple, tempting them with its tantalizing features like mice before a mousetrap. However, unlike mice, these humans could heed a warning, but they still bit. Our difficulty is that the story *reads* more like a morality tale than history. That is a reasonable consideration since morality tales are effective teaching tools, not lies.

sin entered the world, it would seem that God created them cursed, at least by one of the YE definitions of a curse on any living thing—death.

On the one hand, plants were not relevant to the fall if they could die before sin entered the world. But, on the other hand, according to YErs, plants received curses *after* the fall anyway. That is confusing. Maybe this is Elizabeth Mitchell's *cruel sense of irony.*

YErs believe that God cursed the entire universe, including the plant kingdom, with thorns and thistles that would reduce crop yield if left unchecked. I must admit to loving fresh artichokes, which happen to be in the thistle family. I suppose my taste buds could be cursed.

Some plants developed carnivorous ways like the Venus flytrap that captures insects and consumes them. See the YouTube clip, "World's Biggest Carnivorous Plant Catches Whole Sheep." That's right, some plants kill and eat mammals. Plants compete for living space aggressively. This behavior does not quite sit right. If plants could die before the fall, their newfound attack and defense mechanisms would be blessings, would they not? At least now, plants have a fighting chance.

Plants also have healing properties. Many of our most effective medications come from plants. They possess anti-inflammatory, anti-cancer, and heart health benefits. Are plants really cursed? Even poisonous plants and venomous creatures give us many critical medications.

The YE claim of the perfect world assumes too much. These are the traps, Venus or otherwise, that lie in wait for arguments that begin with dubious presuppositions and claims. Never mind that the Bible says nothing of many YE claims. Instead, the curses refer to human-related activities and snakes, not the entire universe.

Snakes were to get the worst of it among all animals: "The Lord God said to the snake, 'Because you did this, a curse will be put *on you.* You will be cursed, *as no other animal, tame or wild,* will ever be. You will crawl on your stomach, and you will eat dust all the days of your life'" (NCV). That puts a lot on one reptile.

The curses had a narrow application, whether literal or not.

We assume that future generations of snakes got the curse. But it does not say that. Genesis 3 tells us the curses last the lifetime of those cursed without reference to future generations, i.e., all the days of *your* life. The word *"your"* is plural and might refer to a whole class, but that is unclear, as will be seen.

If snakes got the severest curse, it would follow that the other animals that received no curse were either unaffected or far less so. But that would include the animals that went extinct. Animals go extinct because they cannot adapt. If that is not cursed, what is? Conversely, snakes are doing fine—too fine; they're everywhere. Absurdities abound with wooden literalism. Note that God does not tell the serpent it will die.

Why not? According to YEC, it had eternal life.

Death would seem worse than slithering around, which works well for this reptile. The serpent is anthropomorphized even in the curse. Slithering around with no legs would be a curse for humans, but not this reptile.

Why did God not include death in the serpent's curse if this animal had eternal life, as YEC presumes? Adam and Eve got the death curse, which cut off the tree of life. For them, eternal life was dependent upon eating the right fruit. If humans did not have eternal life, how would we take seriously the YE view on animals possessing eternal life, pre-fall?

There is not the dire sentencing to the serpent, "*You shall surely die,*" but instead, the snake gets the storybook phrase, "*All the days of your life.*" This curse does not shorten the life of the serpent. Let's be honest: humans did not have eternal life yet because they did not eat from the tree of life, so neither did animals. Remember, the cherubim prevented Adam and Eve from partaking of the tree of life and living forever. Adam and Eve had the potential of eternal life, not actual eternal life, but the presumed "ever-living" snake would live out the standard days—"all the days of its [own] life." If all this is literal, as YErs say, it is contradictory, so it is not literal, and why much of this is overthinking around a moral lesson.

Note Paul on this:

There is a physical body. So there is also a spiritual body. As the Scriptures say, "The first man, Adam, became a living person. But the last Adam is a life-giving spirit. The spiritual man did not come first. *It was the physical man that came first*; then came the spiritual. The first man came from the dust of the earth. The second man came from heaven. *All people belong to the earth. They are like that first man of earth*. But those who belong to heaven are like that man of heaven. *We were made like that man of earth,* so we will also be made like that man of heaven." (1 Corinthians 15:44–49)

The reason we all die is that our body comes from the earth. "Adam" means *earthling*. The earth in "*earth*ling" does not refer to the planet. In this case, it means *dirt*. Adam came from the ground. He was a "*dirtling.*" Being dirt, he did not have eternal life yet. Eternal life requires an ontological change or a new mode of existence. According to Paul, this body of dirt, dust, soil, or clay (take your pick) needs to transform into a spiritual body (1 Corinthians 15:44).

That Adam and Eve should *surely die* means the offer of eternal life was now off the table for them at that moment. YErs say the animals had eternal life, so death's curse should be particularly relevant for them. Or maybe death was not an applicable curse to the serpent since animal death was a given and future eternal life is not in the cards for animals. Or perhaps the serpent sequence is not dealing with a literal snake but a symbol. All things are not as they seem in this story, though the lessons are more apparent.

YErs claim that God cursed *all His creation* because of Adam's sin. However, the curses say nothing of the seas and the marine life in them or the day and night skies occupied by birds and celestial bodies. Moreover, most marine animals happen to be both predators *and* prey. If predation is inherently evil, the oceans are the evilest environment on earth. Yet, they are not recipients of any curse. The snake, Adam and Eve, and the ground, which Adam relied upon for food, are the center of the curses— those involved in the transgression. God would still provide food outside Eden, but it would be no Garden of Eden, no idyllic paradise.

Notice the specific curses:

So the Lord God said to the serpent, "Because you have done this, Cursed are you *above all livestock and all wild animals.* You will crawl on your belly and you will eat dust all the days of your life." *To the woman* he said, "I will make your pains in childbearing very severe; with painful labor you will give birth to children. Your desire will be for your husband, and he will rule over you." *To Adam* he said, "Because you listened to your wife *Cursed is the [soil]* because of you; through painful toil you will eat food from it all the days of *your life.* It will produce thorns and thistles *for you, and you will eat the plants of the field. You will have to work hard and sweat to make the soil produce anything,* until you go back to the soil from which you were formed. *You were made from soil,* and you will become soil again." (Genesis 3:14–8 GNT; emphasis mine)

The curse for Adam was on the soil's yield in food production. He was to consume plants in the open fields outside Eden and return to the ground from where he came. He would still eat plants, but not the ones God planted in Eden. The *field and wilderness* contrasted with the garden, where God's special grace operated. Did God alter the ground? Or did the absence of His special grace withhold blessings on crop yield?

How did the curse of reduced crop yield affect the next generation?

The field is where Cain killed his brother, Abel. After murdering him, Cain receives a curse for the first time. For it says the field's yield was strong for Cain. Hence, God says, "*Now you are cursed* from the ground, which has opened its mouth to receive your brother's blood from your hand. When you till the ground, it will no longer yield to you its strength" (Genesis 4:11–12 WEB).

"*It will no longer yield to you its strength*"? The ground produced for Cain bountifully. If you are following all this literally, something does not add up. Cain appears not to be the recipient of the same curse of the ground leveled against Adam in any practical sense. God richly blessed Abel too. Perhaps "*the sin of the father was not visited upon the children.*" Ezekiel addressed that idea. He said each person is accountable before God for his own sins, which is only just.

Further confusion comes in Genesis 8:20–21 when God says, "Never again will I curse the ground because of humans, even though every inclination of the human heart is evil from childhood." "Cursing the ground" may not refer to the whole earth but the ground used by specific individuals who received curses. This new divine declaration that cursing the ground used by persons like Adam would cease; God said to Adam, "the ground will no longer yield *to you* [Adam] its strength."

The concept of curses may simply mean that blessings are in short supply without God in our lives. Both Abel and Cain were prosperous in raising their sheep and crops. The point is there are idioms thrown down here, so we cannot be sure about the nature of the curses.

Some fundamentalists mistake the doctrine of the fall for the doctrine of *original sin*: Note these words, "As soon as Christians allow for [animal] death, suffering, and disease before sin, then the whole foundations of the message of the Cross and the Atonement *have been destroyed*. The doctrine of original sin, then, is totally undermined."[429]

Mark this well: this YE assertion means that the Gospel depends on animals having everlasting life and perfect health before Adam ate from a mystical tree. *YEC connects original sin to animals.* That concept, whatever you want to call it, is not good or even a Christian idea. My guess is not all YErs buy into this extreme view.

Not all branches of Christianity accept original or ancestral sin. The Orthodox Churches recognize the doctrine of the fall but do not accept original sin. I do not intend to resolve the question but simply point out that the more competing variables there are to a theory, the less sure it likely is. In other words, original sin is not a given in Christianity. That means we may not inherit the curses or that they might not be ongoing or even literal. The story of Noah is a kind of resetting of the relationship between God and all human beings. Genesis presents Noah's flood as something like a do-over. Gordon J. Wenham makes a similar point:

> The flood story may be read as a kind of commentary on the preceding chapters. They invite us to compare the account of the new creation with that of the first creation. The accounts share the same starting point: the Spirit or wind of God moving over the primeval ocean that covered the hidden landmass. The parallels continue with the ebbing of the waters, which discloses the dry land. Whereas Genesis 1 could be read as achieving this in a single day, it takes several months in Genesis 8. With the emergence of dry land vegetation appears: in the first account all sorts of

---

429. Ken Ham, "The Necessity of Believing in Six Literal Days," December 1, 1995, AiG website.

plants and fruit trees are seen, but only an olive leaf in the second. Finally, all the land-based creatures are "created" or come out of the ark.[430]

There are repeated themes throughout Genesis—and the entire Pentateuch, for that matter—that act as a commentary, further elaborating on previous themes. God makes several Noachian promises, including this often-overlooked promise highlighted by Wenham:

> All creatures that survived the flood are given this injunction in 8:17. An allusion to the fall and its consequences is found in 8:21, "I will never again curse the ground because of man" (cf. 3:17). Genesis 9:1–7 addresses the vegetarian diet prescribed for all creatures in 1:29–30.[431]

The curse over the ground appears to end with Noah, "I will never curse the ground again." My point is that building a dogmatic theological system based on uncertain concepts from antiquity does not further our understanding of what the language means. Therefore, no matter how well-meaning, a spiritual war against Christianity's main body by a small contingent over nonessential trivia is indefensible. YErs will insist that Christians choose man's word over God's word.

Technically, the pagan notion of a *literal* curse was a pronouncement of evil upon someone or something as an act of retribution. Are curses in the Bible an evil *spell* God casts on His handiwork, or does He inflict some other kind of ruination upon it? Today, people use the word *curse* routinely, such as when people say a good memory can be a "blessing and *a curse*"—i.e., it can create unavoidable problems.

The Red Sox "Curse of the Bambino" supposedly lasted for decades because they traded Babe Ruth to the Yankees. Many baseball fans and players are superstitious and devoted to rituals before and during a game. I grew up a Detroit Lions fan. Everybody "knows" the Lions are cursed. That's one I could take literally. Curses usually mean nothing goes right because of continuous mistakes and bad luck. I became more a Matthew Stafford fan (the Detroit quarterback) for the last ten years and was content when he won the Super Bowl his first year with the Rams. That "lifted the curse." All language is symbolic; it is not reality.

Estrangement from God creates instability. Call it a "curse." A curse may simply mean God was pulling away His active presence, leading to instability in an already changing world governed by the second law of thermodynamics. Things gradually break down that otherwise would remain stable under God's regulating presence. God created a world that is interdependent on Him and the stewardship

---

430. Gordon J. Wenham, *Rethinking Genesis 1–11: Gateway to the Bible* (DLS/Didsbury Lecture Series) (Cascade Books, Eugene, Oregon, 2015), p. 42.

431. Ibid.

of humans. The creation makes little sense without humanity, but humans cannot regulate the second law of thermodynamics. That requires cooperation with God.

A striking example of blessings and cursings is the covenant in Israel.

Read the *curses* from Mt. Ebal for Israel's disobedience found in Deuteronomy 28:15-68. They are horrifying compared to the mild curses in Genesis:

> The Lord will cause you to... become a thing of horror to all the kingdoms on earth. Your carcasses will be food for all the birds and the wild animals, and there will be no one to frighten them away. The Lord will afflict you with the boils of Egypt and with tumors, festering sores, from which you cannot be cured. The Lord will afflict you with madness, blindness and confusion of mind. At midday you will grope about like a blind person in the dark. You will be unsuccessful in everything you do; day after day you will be oppressed and robbed, with no one to rescue you. (Deuteronomy 28:25-29)

Suddenly, thorns and thistles, tough childbirth, and slithering snakes were kind.

Strangely enough, turning to God does the opposite:

> The *fruit of your womb* will be blessed, *and the crops* of your land [shall be blessed]... The Lord will send a blessing on your barns and *on everything you put your hand to do*. The Lord your God will bless you in the land he is giving you. (Deuteronomy 28:4)

The oldest Hebrew inscription was found on Mt. Ebal in Israel, dated around 1000 BC. It happens to be an ABBA Chiastic Parallelism on the subject of curses. It is also the oldest mention of God's name. It reads:

> "Cursed, Cursed, Cursed— cursed by God.
>
> You will die cursed.
>
> Cursed you will surely die.
>
> Cursed by YHW— cursed, cursed, cursed."[432]

Is there any doubt that curses are an ANE idea that has nothing to do with ruining the creation? Deuteronomy 28:4 describes not just life with curses but also with lavish blessings. Perhaps the curses in Genesis are conditional. Blessings and cursings are responses of God as people obey or disobey Him. "Blessings and cursings" are part of any covenant, not just those in Genesis.

Notice the words of Malachi as the Old Testament closes:

---

432. See The Jerusalem Post, "Researchers Decipher Oldest Known Hebrew Inscription On 'Cursed' Tablet: Mt. Ebal Discovery Aligns With Biblical Texts In Deuteronomy, Joshua." by Judith Sudilovsky, Published: March 24, 2022; Updated: March 26, 2022.

You are under a curse—your whole nation—because you are robbing me. Bring the whole tithe into the storehouse, that there may be food in my house. "Test me in this," says the Lord Almighty, *"and see if I will not throw open the floodgates of heaven and pour out so much blessing that there will not be room enough to store it. I will prevent pests from devouring your crops, and the vines in your fields will not drop their fruit before it is ripe,"* ... *"for yours will be a delightful land,"* says the Lord Almighty. Malachi 3:9–12 (emphasis mine)

That sounds Eden-like: I will "pour out so much blessing that there will not be room enough to store it," and "I will prevent pests from devouring your crops," and "yours will be a delightful land." This language describes God's active presence or special grace. *Curses do not mean God ruins His creation.* It can mean that estrangement from God makes blessings in short supply and that what we call the second law of thermodynamics will go unregulated. Nonetheless, if God ruined the ground, He stands ready to bless people with abundance—a hundredfold in this life:

"Truly I tell you," Jesus replied, "no one who has left home or brothers or sisters or mother or father or children or fields for me and the Gospel will fail to receive a hundred times as much in this present age: homes, brothers, sisters, mothers, children, and fields." (Mark 10:28–30)

Literal treatment of ancient writings with unrecognizable idiom is misinformed. This language in Mark sounds like the blessings of Eden might continue in the Church, explicitly regarding real estate, family, childbirth, and crop yield. Regrettably, fundamentalists have not thought this *curse thing* through. Could the ancients call some things curses that were nothing more than the effects of entropy built into the second law of thermodynamics made worse by God's absence from the scene? Matter decays, crops are overgrown; age, water, heat, bitter cold, violence, carelessness, and neglect can increase the speed of decay naturally built into the world. Physical things deteriorate. Mortals die. Everyone today dreams at some point that burdens inherent in nature and life might disappear with technologies that the ancients could not imagine.

It is quite a stretch to claim that the second law of thermodynamics *is* the curse since the Creation story in Genesis includes it, being that the garden needed upkeep, and reproduction (male and female) assumes the need to replace what is lost. Jesus clarified that immortality means no reproduction, "At the resurrection, people will neither marry nor be given in marriage; they will be like the angels in heaven" (Matthew 22:30).

Overall, *relying too heavily* on ancient ideas and idioms is suspect. That means theological systems built on obscure concepts are also dubious and do not justify an excessive orientation towards reform movements that amount to speculation. Christianity is the "reform movement" relevant to us.

We saw earlier that Ezekiel addresses the concept of sins carried down from one generation to the next and reinterprets the Law by declaring persons are responsible for their own sins.

"Why should not the son suffer for the iniquity of the father?" When the son has done what is lawful and right, and has been careful to observe all my statutes, he shall surely live. The person who sins shall die. A child shall not suffer for the iniquity of a parent, nor a parent suffers for the iniquity of a child; the righteousness of the righteous shall be his own, and the wickedness of the wicked shall be his own. (Ezekiel 18:19–20)

Notice it says, "The person who sins shall die." Ezekiel does not mean the person dies right away nor does it mean he goes on living forever if he does not sin. This language is similar to God's curse, *"You shall surely die."* Adam and Eve didn't die right away either. Scripture does not say the couple shall live forever, simply for not sinning. Eternal life does not come through a lifetime of omissions.

Adam and Eve were to eat of the tree of life, which likely symbolized union with God. Jesus did not sin and still died, but more importantly, he *could* die in a sinless state. Therefore, sinlessness for a mortal does not create immortality. A transfiguration is still necessary. Jesus did not have immortality of the body until his glorification. So what does all this mean? It means we are dealing with a world foreign to us, making inevitable mistakes, especially for laypersons without years of disciplined, systematic, and peer-reviewed studies. As Paul said, Adam and Eve were mortal, of the earth, earthly. They did not have eternal life; therefore, neither did the animals.

YErs say it was permissible to kill and eat plants. Plants were supposedly not subject to the sin/death symbiosis that YErs apply to everything else from humans to microbes, including the microbes attached to plants. Yet the curse involved individual plants, thorns and thistles, and the soil that impacts plants intended for food.

The *ism* in YEC is a web that entraps itself. YErs handle many objections to their views with *ad hoc* answers with seemingly little forethought. If plants are irrelevant to sin, why curse them? If plants were killed and eaten before Adam's sin, how worse off can they be with a "curse"? How can cursed things be the prime source of cures in medicine and vital for nutrition? Plants contain cancer-fighting compounds like flavonoids and antioxidants. Nutritionists continually tell us to *eat our fruits and vegetables;* it is a key to good health. Many plants of all kinds are beautiful. The only purpose for some flowers seems to be to please our senses. Genesis did not aim the curses at the plant kingdom or plants as a category. The curse on the ground is more likely on Adam's use of it—meaning God would not be obligated to bless his efforts.

Alienation from God simply increases the uncertainties in human activity and experience. Blessings and cursings are opposites. I suggest that blessings result from God's favorable involvement in our lives, and "cursings" mean increased instability resulting from His detachment.

YErs claim to take the curses literally, but to the contrary, they expand them beyond that mentioned in Genesis and apply them to all things everywhere, even galaxies far, far away, and heretofore immune plants. What if there is life on other planets? Would God have cursed them? What would possibly justify ruining everything?

Why ruin anything?

YEC says God cursed the entire universe by instigating some vague disordering of the creation that once was very good to its current "very bad" state. They apparently believe this mal-recreation was God-ordained. Would God change a "perfect" creation into a very bad one? Why would he do that? Why ruin everything when surgical removal of bad seed would do the trick? Fundamentalists say sin is the cause of the curses, not God. But do humans have the power to ruin the universe with simple behavior? What kind of fruit was that? Let's face it. Only God could alter the entire universe.

It is inconsistent to claim God could not have created a world with evil in it, then turn around and say He created universal ills from one end of the universe to the other because of an incident involving fruit. Why not let Adam and Eve die that very day, as God appears to predict, and start over with another pair (Genesis 2:17)? God does that on a much larger scale with Noah and his family, i.e., God starts over by judging the world and preserving Noah's family. God also rescinds the curse of the ground (Genesis 8:21).

The inconsistencies are too great for all this to be a word-for-word "literal historical narrative."

Noah was without blame in the Genesis context: "Noah was a righteous man, blameless among the people of his time, and he walked faithfully with God" (Genesis 6:9). So why didn't the reconstruction of creation with blameless Noah remove all curses as He did the "curse" of the ground (Genesis 8:20–21)? That would be consistent since all bad seeds, literal and metaphorical, perished in the flood. So we now have a clean slate. But maybe we are reading too much into this story.

God appears to kill the entire degenerate human family leaving a "blameless" one and his family alive. Why not kill the original couple, keep the world "perfect," and try again? Talk about "a cruel sense of irony." Our world is unstable not because God ruined it. "God is not the author of disorder" in any world (1 Corinthians 14:33). Whatever curses mean, it does not mean God brings chaos to his creation.

Here is the point: the story is not about changing conditions of the universe but about changing conditions between God and humans. When God distances Himself, or we distance ourselves from Him, things are not as they should be; things will be difficult or more likely to go wrong.

"We're not in Eden anymore."

32.
WELL ORDERED, IMPERFECTLY

The world is not endowed with the attributes of God.
—John Walton

YErs define *very good* as *perfect,* so what do they mean by "perfect?" They use the word *perfect* in both a moral and absolute sense as needed. The words "very good" appear on no other day but the sixth day when God creates humans. God does not call anything "very good" until He places humans in a well-suited environment.

Humans, the apex of God's physical creation, were not perfect in either the moral or absolute sense. If Adam and Eve were morally perfect, they would not steal. Because Adam went for a time without breaking the command given him, it does not mean he was perfect. Genuine perfection is not temporal. Otherwise, being perfect would be time-sensitive with a possible expiration date; we would be perfect while not sinning and imperfect while sinning, which is nonsense.

The notion that animals had eternal life is absurd, especially since humans did not have eternal life in their created state. They had the potential of eternal life in the tree of life. Living in a material world is, by definition, temporal. Notice again what Paul says:

> The body that is sown is *perishable*, it is raised imperishable; it is sown a natural body, it is raised a spiritual body. There is a natural body, there is also a spiritual body. So it is written: "The first man Adam became a living being"; the last Adam, a life-giving spirit. The spiritual did not come first, *but the natural*, and after that the spiritual. *The first man was of the dust of the earth;* the second man is of heaven. 1 (Corinthians 15:43-49)

Adam was always earthly; that is, mortal. He did not become a spiritual man as far as we know. His body needed a change. Like us, he was always subject to physical death. The story says Adam and Eve were to eat from the right tree to "graduate" from biological to spiritual life. That means mortal bodies are not a curse but a created state with the potential for glory. To gain eternal life, we need to eat from the tree of life, aka the True Vine, the Logos, Jesus Christ (John 15:5–8):

> I am the vine; you are the branches. If you remain in me and I in you, you will bear much fruit; apart from me you can do nothing. If you do not remain in me, you are like a branch that is thrown away and withers; such branches are picked up, thrown into the fire and burned... This is to my Father's glory, that you bear much fruit, showing yourselves to be my disciples.

Additionally, being *sin-free* is not perfection, as in *error-free* or accident-free. Since errors and accidents routinely occur in our experience, it makes sense that accidents might lead to serious harm without sin being the direct cause. For example, we find herds of animals in the fossil record killed by geographical and climate changes. The La Brea Tar Pits in Los Angeles buried thousands of animals with liquid asphalt seeped up from the ground for thousands of years. Leaves and debris often camouflaged the tar that appeared as solid ground to unsuspecting creatures.

God would have to prevent those things from happening in a world designed that allows them to happen. Our world is full of changing circumstances because it is temporal. Accidents can happen due to negligence, but they may also occur because of freedom of movement and simple gravity. Indeed, Adam and Eve were not free from error or accident; nonetheless, they were very good or well-ordered in their composition for God's purposes.

Notice that God calls his creative acts "good" on days one, three, four, and five. That is to say, so far, so *good*, but not *very good*, which He spoke only on day six. Surprisingly, God does not call anything on day two "good" in any sense, though He created the sky. Furthermore, His activity level appears abbreviated on day two (the sky is the only thing made and by a single spoken sentence) compared to the other days, especially the next day, day three, which is teeming with activity (Genesis 1:9–13).

What is going on?

Just one thing occurred on the second day: "Then God said, 'Let there be an expanse between the waters, separating water from water.'" That is all. God did not create the sky (expanse) directly. He made it by commanding the waters separate, perhaps by the wind or Spirit of God mentioned in Genesis 1:2 as in other ANE accounts, though that is not explicit. The second day appears finished in an instant:

> And God said, "Let there be a [expanse] between the waters to separate water from water."... And it was so. *God called the [expanse] "sky."* And there was evening, and there was morning—the second day. (Genesis 1:6-8)

Perhaps more is going on than the sum of the words.

Why does God *not* call the new and no doubt glorious sky "good" on day two? Did day two lack moral virtue? Well, no. John H. Sailhammer suggests, "The reason for the omission is that on day two, there was nothing created or made that was, as yet, 'good'—that is, beneficial to humanity."[433]

---

433. John H. Sailhammer, *Genesis (The Expositor's Bible Commentary), Revised Edition:* ISBN 978-0-310-53172-2 (Zondervan, 3900 Sparks Dr. SE, Grand Rapids, Michigan 49546, 2008), EPUB Edition, location 2453.

Sailhammer's observation is unsatisfactory since essential resources for human flourishing would be first: air to breathe, then water, food, and shelter. Thus, air or "sky" (created on day two) is not only beneficial to human life but also critical and worthy of being called good. Is nothing good about day two, or is there something else behind the omission?

The waters appeared to be the main subject and were still problematic until day three when God finished "dealing" with them. If day two is a veiled treatment of chaotic waters, it reinforces *that the waters in Genesis 1:2 are not part of day one.* Day one is like day two in that one simple thing is spoken into existence (light), *but in sharp contrast, God calls the light "good."* The waters existed before day one and, therefore, were not mentioned on that day. If the sky is not called good on day two, how is the initial light that fills the sky called good? *More puzzling is that light was created on the first day before there was a sky, which was created on day two.* That adds credence to the idea we saw earlier: the light on day one is not an object that throws light like the sun, but light itself. The waters are not the subject on day one; instead, they become the subject on day two, finishing on day three."

In contrast, the waters are not good or "useful" until day three, after God gives them their function. God appears to call only the new things He creates "good," not something that existed before day one. Perhaps God creates things in a raw state only to fine-tune or polish them later. However, that argues against the YEC's view that God created everything instantly and matured during the six days.

Furthermore, this questions whether the author thinks God created those waters in the first place or they were the primordial waters before creation understood throughout the ANE. The focus on day two does not seem to be the critical sky equally important as the light on day one *but the divided waters themselves.* This focus is odd since the only new thing on day two is the sky that divided the waters. God merely rearranged the waters that still needed further attention on day three.

Undoubtedly, the waterworks were not complete on day two. The author chooses to deal with the waters directly over days two and three so that the word *good* shows up twice on the much "*longer*" day three. However, day three is not supposed to be "longer" if both days are ordinary. After the shortest work on day two—a simple command—notice all that happens on day three:

> Then God said, "Let the water under the sky be gathered into one place, and let the dry land appear." And it was so. God called the dry land "earth," and the gathering of the water he called "seas." *And God saw that it was good.* Then God said, "Let the earth produce vegetation: seed-bearing plants and fruit trees on the earth bearing fruit with seed in it according to their kinds." And it was so. The earth produced vegetation: seed-bearing plants according to their kinds and trees bearing fruit with seed in it

according to their kinds. *And God saw that it was good*. Evening came and then morning: the third day. (Genesis 1:9–13, CSB) (emphasis mine)

(Note that the land officially receives a name—earth. This naming gives the newly created earth a function—now it can produce vegetation.)

God utters two statements *on the third day* and creates two broad sections: oceans separated from land and God letting the land produce vegetation. The phrase "and it was so" *appears twice*, and God evaluates each of the two completed sections with the refrain, *"And God saw that it was good,"* as if day three could be two separate days. One must wonder why God took the entire second day for a single command to split the waters without an evaluation while day three loads up on creative activities enough for two days. This question is unavoidable because of the *twice-mentioned* phrase on day three— *"And God saw that it was good."* It is as if the first part of day three belongs to day two. Take a moment to compare day two with day three again.

The difference between days two and three is striking.

Is this a mistake by the author not getting God's daily activities down consistently? Or was God not into it on day two? Or maybe God does not always manage His time efficiently? All God did on day two was utter a statement that took seconds. If Genesis means to show the strict duration of daily activities, there is a strange and inexplicable imbalance between days two and three that questions a clock. God could create the universe in no time at all. Days two and three do not seem literal because the *time expenditures,* which workdays are all about, are sharply inconsistent.

This is not accidental.

With short work on days one and two, it is as though God eases into creative activity. The Jewish Talmud says God begins with light like a king that builds a palace when the site is in darkness. "He first kindled lamps and torches to see where to lay the foundations."[434]

On day two, God's sole activity divides the waters, opening up a sky as though God is still getting started. Not until day three does God's level of activity increase substantially as He finishes dealing directly with the waters. God's activity continues at a high level until day seven.

We saw earlier that day five parallels day two by filling the waters and the sky with suitable life. However, the author does not abbreviate the work level on day five as on day two. So God does a significant amount of work on day five comparatively.

Day six parallels day three. Similarly, there are two work evaluations on day six with the words "good" and "very good," as on day three. On day six, God

---

434. Umberto Cassuto, *A Commentary on the Book of Genesis* (Varna Books, 2005), p. 25. The king analogy is quoted from the Talmud Bereshith Rabba III, 1.

makes animals and humans fill the land created on day three. *Day three and six are the most productive, but day six's activity exceeds all the others. Like day three, the author might split the sixth day into two without missing a beat. However, this author is committed to a Hebrew workweek that must finish with the seventh-day rest.*[435]

Widely inconsistent activity levels each day, including the seventh day, suggest that the Hebrew workweek is simply a vehicle to communicate the theological point that the Creator of heaven and earth is *the work* of the Hebrew God. In other words, the Hebrew workweek, complete with a Sabbath rest, conveys two ideas simultaneously: that Israel's tribal God is also the God of the universe. Moreover, absent the seventh-day rest and monotheism, the six-day outline could naturally fit into other ANE cosmogonies. God is the revelation, not physics, geology, or the age of the earth.

In EE, order out of disorder begins after the war among the gods ended with Marduk splitting Tiamat (ocean waters) in half by a north wind creating a sky in between. Marduk uses Tiamat's ribcage to hold up the waters above the sky (in some ANE creation accounts, the primordial waters exist simultaneously with the wind). This crucial act of Marduk in EE is the equivalent of the second day in Genesis but with mythic imagery. In both accounts, God/god divides the waters to create the sky, but for Marduk, it took an arduous battle.

Genesis is about Yahweh; the waters have no name; they are just waters. Like EE, a wind (Spirit) of God is active. What suspends the waters above is the mysterious firmament (also translated as a vault, dome, expanse, and sky)? We also saw other stories from the ANE with a similar theme as in the Baal Cycle at Ugarit, where Baal defeats a sea monster (waters) with a wind. This battle against the sea/sea monster was what most ANE accounts exalted because *it is the key event that brings basic structure to the universe.* In addition to monotheism, the relevant difference between these accounts and day two of Genesis is that the mythological language and imagery are absent in Genesis though that language shows up elsewhere in scripture, as we have seen. There is no titanic battle in Genesis.

Now notice that the flow of the days is abruptly changed.

On day two, God spends the whole day uttering a single sentence to separate the waters. There is no "And God saw it was good" statement, which is unusual because it is the only day of creation with nothing God could see that was good. It is as if that line of communication on day two is interrupted.

---

435. The striking variations in workload from day to day with the accompanying commentary suggests that Genesis 1 was based on an earlier account of creation. Our Hebrew author recasts the account to fit the covenantal workweek ending in a Sabbath rest. This is speculative, and an analysis of the possibility is too much here.

Day three continues God's work on the waters that He did not finish on day two. Day three has much more activity with God giving His work a "good appraisal" twice. The first appraisal on day three could easily belong to day two. That may suggest either a *veiled* struggle with the waters that took more time, which the original readers would immediately recognize, or dividing the waters was not a simple task. It took all day. The original readers must have understood this because the author does not explain the inconsistencies to our loss. Yahweh does fight primordial waters elsewhere in scripture in mythological terms:

> It was you who split open the sea by your power; *you broke the heads of the monster in the waters. It was you who crushed the heads of Leviathan...* you established the sun and moon. It was you who set all the boundaries of the earth; you made both summer and winter. (Psalm 74:13–17; emphasis mine)

And there is this from Psalm 89 in the Expanded Version:

> You rule the ·mighty [raging; surging] sea and calm the stormy [rising] waves. *You crushed the Rahab* [a sea monster, representing chaos (Job 26:12; Is. 51:9)...] *The skies [heavens] and the earth belong to you.* You made the world and ·everything in it [its fullness]. (Psalm 89:8–11 EXB; all comments are the EXB)

Psalm 89 mentions the "skies" after crushing Rahab (representing the waters), as does day two. These mythical versions of creation (also in Job) are older than Genesis 1, suggesting to some scholars that an epic on creation may have existed in Israel's early history.

All this commentary on inconsistencies between day two and the other days may be interesting, but some speculation puts it together. My use of the words *perhaps*, "seems to," *suggests*, and "it is as though," indicating uncertainty. There is so much we do not know. That is why any dogmatic declaration on Genesis 1 is likely to overreach.

Regardless, the waters above the sky did not originate as thick cloud cover as some have suggested. The ancients imagined the waters were above the expanse, *beyond the skies that included the stars, and stored for intermittent use.* The waters above did not fall down into the sky until released as rain clouds and other types of precipitation. Less clear are *all* the waters below the expanse. They would include oceans, lakes, and river systems, to be sure. But there were also waters said to be *below* the earth. It appears that people thought there were waters below the whole *earth*, not merely below its surface. In some illustrations, the waters below the earth contained pillars that supported the earth. That is the way people thought. It cannot be the way God thinks.

Notice Genesis 1:6–8:

> Then God said, "Let there be a space to separate the water into two parts." So God made the space and separated the water. Some of the water was

above it, and some of the water was below it. God named that space "sky." There was evening, and then there was morning. This was the second day. (ERV)

Here is the Expanded Version:

Then God said, "Let there be ·something to divide the water in two [L a firmament/dome/expanse in the midst of the waters to separate/divide the waters from the waters]." So God made the ·air [L firmament; dome; expanse; C rain clouds] and placed some of the water above the ·air [L firmament; dome; expanse] and some below it [C referring to the rain and the oceans, lakes, and rivers]. God ·named [called] the air [L firmament/dome/expanse] "·sky [heaven]." Evening passed, and morning came [1:5]. This was the second day. (EXB)

Notice verse six says the expanse separated "waters from waters," implying a significant division, e.g., an even split as we see elsewhere in the ANE. The splitting of the Red Sea echos a divine signature in the ANE, i.e., the dividing of waters. What started as one body of water became two when separated.

Additionally, Genesis 2:5 says God had not sent rain to the earth, meaning no rain clouds. "Rain" and "clouds" were not obscure terms; the author could easily use them if he meant them. The author could have said, "God created the clouds" on day two. But clouds are not permanent fixtures; they come and go (far less in arid climates) and would not stand out to itemize them among created things, especially with obscure language— i.e., *"waters above the expanse."* Aren't clouds *in* the expanse as opposed to *above* them?

There were both evening and morning skies. The night sky revealed the stars. Beyond the stars were the waters above. Throughout the ANE, this universal view of a World Ocean is what we saw from Cassuto—a primordial cosmic ocean that dominated the universe perceived in the ANE.

We have already seen on day four that giving names like "sun" and "moon" (Canaanite deities) to the luminaries could imply personhood that might deify them in the minds of the Israelites. The same principle might apply to these waters that had mythical status throughout the ANE world.

Day 2 is too vague and abbreviated to draw any hard conclusions.

The author's suggestion that it took two whole days for God to rearrange the darkened waters is significant, not because God needed the time or that these waters necessarily existed as described but that the darkened deep is consistent with the prevailing assumptions of the day. It also fits the storyline in Genesis that moves from uninhabitable conditions to a well-ordered world. Though veiled, the intention might be that God tames and subdues the waters as man is to tame and subdue the earth. However, man can tame the land significantly; he cannot tame the sea.

Genesis declares God's rule over all things literal and mythical.

At any rate, God evaluates the *completed* creation as "very good." God evaluated His work like a man, step-by-step until He was satisfied with the whole. God declared the final product *very good* not because of some moral superiority the sixth day exercised over the other days or that it would be immoral for animals to act out their design as YErs believe. It was what God intended for His purposes. Days 1–5 created the conditions for day six to succeed, which is a very human way to describe God's "*workmanship.*"

The *holiness* given to the seventh day comes closer to moral content than the first six days since it alone has a spiritual and eternal function—peace with God. "Very good" clearly refers to the orderly development of a completed work that could support human flourishing but not "perfect" as *moral perfection or flawlessness.*

Therefore, the instinct of animals does not undermine a well-ordered world; it contributes to it. That is not to say that the world outside the garden needed no attention. On the contrary, human responsibility was to tame and rule the earth as God's imagers (Genesis 1:28).

God formed the entire universe to accommodate the arrival of humans on this planet. Atheistic scientists like the infamous Richard Dawkins corroborate this shaping of the universe for rational beings like ourselves. This part of the universe gives us ideal lines of observation for the Hubble Deep Field images in a virtual table set for discovery, though atheists do not credit God for this. Fred Hoyle initially ridiculed the notion of the Big Bang because it sounded like "Let there be light." Yet, he also conceded that the laws of physics and the fine-tuning of the constants and quantities that permit all life, particularly human life on this planet, are conspicuously noticeable in the universe's design.[436]

"For forty years, physicists and cosmologists have been quietly collecting examples of all too many 'coincidences' and unique features in the underlying laws of the universe that are necessary for life. If any one of them were different, even minutely, the consequences would be lethal." Hoyle said it was as if "a super-intellect has monkeyed with physics."

Brandon Carter coined the term "the *Anthropic Principle*," suggesting that the fine-tuned constants in the universe anticipate observers like human beings. In other words, scientific observation of the universe by carbon-based life as humans would not be possible if the constants were different. Proponents

---

436. Earth is in a unique position in the universe with fine-tuned conditions that must exist to produce and sustain human life. Surprisingly, our position in the solar system is such that we can view, for the first time, the farthest reaches of the universe with our Hubble telescope. The level of darkness in the night sky in this part of the Milky Way galaxy, together with portions in our night sky that provide a lane into deep space for our view, makes this place in the universe most advantageous for observing it. If the Copernican revolution displaced the earth at the center of the universe, fine-tuning restores humanities central place in a universe that is fine-tuned for observers like us. Ironically, physicists resisted the Anthropic Principle because of its theological implications with no natural explanation; that is, until they invented the multiverse.

of the anthropic principle argue that it explains why this universe has [deep] age and the fundamental physical constants, both necessary to accommodate conscious life since if either had been different, we would not have been around to make observations—thus, the *anthropos* (man) in Anthropic.

The Anthropic Principle deals with the notion that the universe seems to be purposely fine-tuned. Moreover, a version of the anthropic principle proposed by John D. Barrow and Frank Tipler states that the universe, in some sense, *had* to have conscious and sapient life emerge within it.[437]

Paul C. W. Davies observes, "Scientists are slowly waking up to an inconvenient truth—the universe looks suspiciously like a fix."[438]

Genesis describes an obvious progression toward orderliness from the darkened formlessness at the opening of day one through the sixth day of creation week. Yet, there were things "not good" at various points. For example:

1. Darkness persists (to this day), unlike in Revelation 22:5, where God removes it.

2. The loneliness of man is explicitly *not good*. It reads as if God may have initially intended the man to be alone and that the creation of Eve was to solve the emerging problem of loneliness. Of course, that can only be an anthropomorphic thought process for God.[439]

3. The Tree of the Knowledge of Good *and Evil* amid the Garden.

4. Since the Garden was idyllic, the outside world called the "field" or "wilderness" was not so tranquil. The entire earth could not be idyllic, or how should readers distinguish it from Eden, which refers to a limited area near the Tigris and Euphrates rivers? In the wild kingdom outside, conditions were not as "good."

5. A cunning serpent enters Eden from the wild—not good.

6. Finally, Adam and Eve, the apex of God's creation, sinned while living in the Garden. That is not good. God is responsible for making beings who can sin. Though God is not responsible for evil deeds, he cannot delegate the responsibility for creating persons capable of such deeds.

---

437. See *Wikipedia* article, "The Anthropic Principle."

438. Paul C. D. Davies is Professor of Physics at Arizona State University and author of *The Goldilocks Enigma: "Why is the Universe Just Right for Life".* (Penguin Press, Great Britain, 2006).

439. Certainly, God intended all along to make us male and female, but that is not how the story *is written*. Adam is given a choice of a helper among the creatures God made. Then God sees he must create a "special" creature like Adam—a female. Could it be the author's way of creating some drama or suspense to heighten the arrival of Eve? Of course, God is Creator, yet there are theological reasons in the author's mind for God's behavior that are not necessarily meant to be historical ones.

Remember, this is a story. We should read it in that spirit.

The word *good* is relative and has various connotations. Good might mean moral goodness or orderliness, as in the condition of a car. It could also refer to the value of something like a piece of art. God was not likely to declare Adam and Eve "morally good" on day six since that is a verdict requiring time and testing. Furthermore, animal predation has no moral component, as YEC claims.

It is senseless to call dirt, air, water, fish, animals, plants, and stars *morally* good. Those evaluations are category errors. However, they may be well ordered. With the progress in the creation account directed at improving conditions, we can safely conclude that "very good" in Genesis means "well-ordered" for life, mainly human flourishing. With God's active presence, a well-ordered world is what God made.

Nonetheless, since created beings, visible and invisible, can disturb the order, that alone is imperfection. God intended the potential for both good and evil. Those potentials are inherent in contingent beings possessing free will. The freedom given to imperfect persons is how evil emerges. God allowed this. He intends to eradicate evil and *finish* the work of perfection He started, but not by force. It follows naturally that perfection with free will requires our *willing* cooperation.

So far, as a race, we have been unwilling.

33.
ANIMAL SUFFERING AND DEATH

The lions roar for their prey and seek their food from God.
—Psalm 104:21

The YE line of reasoning connects animal death directly to human sin and indirectly to the Gospel, the cross, and the Atonement, yet leaves no room for redeeming those same animals. Cursing and condemning animals for human sin, when animals are incapable of sinning but offer no hope of restoration, is an inexplicable disconnect, not to mention *unjust* next to the natural and straightforward concept of animal mortality before and after the fall. That is the nature of animals without an immortal soul. In other words, that is how God made them. How we think he should have made the animal kingdom is irrelevant.

Recall Elizabeth Mitchell's idea again that *there can be no argument*; the fossil record is a graveyard full of carnivory, suffering, and death, and that "if God had called that world *very good,* then he either had a cruel sense of irony or didn't know what he was talking about, or worse, he is a liar."

The fossil record is not a graveyard of carnivory, suffering, and death. Dead bodies go back to the soil from where they came. That is how this works. Everything on earth remains on the planet. Where else are things going to go? The rare bones that occasionally surface are fossilized either by sediment or in hermetically sealed environments inaccessible to air and scavengers, which preserve them much longer. Some 99.99 percent of all animals, including their bones, become part of the soil. The tiniest fraction becomes preserved.

Furthermore, without this recycling feature that breaks down corpses into dust, multiple billions of skeletal remains would overwhelm the globe, creating a literal graveyard. That is not what we find. Instead, we find several mass extinctions caused by acts of God: asteroids, climate change, and geological changes. You can walk through the woods that have sustained millions of animals over the centuries and will not find a graveyard. Dead animals go back to the soil to produce the vegetation that feeds the world, including animals. Without them, there would be fewer plants and fewer seeds for the vegetarians, thus less food for the animal kingdom. It is called the *cycle of life,* not the hyperbolic "graveyard of suffering and death."

God ordered the world with its cleanup and sanitation systems with countless scavengers, including insects, to do the work. Why would God create a planetary sanitation system for a perfect world where nothing is supposed to die? Why would he create a remarkable reordering system as a necessary response to His *disordering* curses? YEC assumes that God made a perfect world, then cursed it with evils, and then brought an elaborate *"Crime Scene Clean Up"* system in nature to remove the "evidence."

None of this makes sense.

Of course, there are remains in the soil, no matter how deaths occur—carnivorous or otherwise. The geological strata hold trace evidence for several vast and global extinctions and innumerable smaller ones by "acts of God" that rival the number of deaths due to predation or disease. Asteroids, meteors, floods, climate changes, and earthquakes have snuffed out billions of creatures very quickly, not to mention a worldwide flood that YErs insist destroyed nearly all the creatures God created on the earth. God appears to be the apex predator. That would be a cruel sense of irony.

God does not seem squeamish regarding animal death, even if they did nothing to "deserve" it. "Deserve" is anthropomorphic. Also, simple predation and disease occur to weaker animals, and scavenging is part of an ingenious clean-up system. These are indeed functions in a well-ordered world.

Interestingly, most animals on land are not carnivores, unlike the oceans, where nearly all are carnivores and prey. Think about it. There is universal predation with marine life, yet God is curiously silent about cursing them. They were unaffected by the flood. How did they get a pass? Water is not the only way God can kill. He could have filled the oceans with dirt the refilled them with water. Marine life does not seem to be touched by curses or God's judgment, though the vast majority are predators, and the sea was a source of chaos and evil in the ANE.

In the Messianic kingdom, the behavioral changes to land animals like the lion and the lamb lying down together do not have a marine life equivalent. Why not something like the killer whale swimming with the seal? Perhaps the ANE fear (some say superstition) regarding the menacing oceans prevented using such language on marine life for the Messianic Age. John in Revelation says *there will be no sea* in the new earth as if God will finally evaporate the evil menace. We love the beach. Since the book of Revelation is Jewish apocalyptic, the symbolism is extensive. The language concerning the sea mirrors the ANE's fears about the primal waters. In Revelation, the sea becomes a symbol of evil and chaos when the multiheaded serpent arises from its depths: "And I saw a beast *coming out of the sea*. It had ten horns and seven heads, with ten crowns on its horns, and on each head a blasphemous name" (Revelation 13:1).

Is that the way it will be in the new earth? Or is that merely the ANE impression about the way it will be? The prophets attempted to describe an ideal world with concepts familiar to them. Their impressions are more the point than the details. The prophets do not explain the nature of the glorified state. The glorified state is beyond everyone, including New Testament authors: "Dear friends, now we are children of God, and what we will be has not yet been made known. But we know that when Christ appears, *we shall be like him,* for we shall see him as he is" (1 John 3:2).

Ironically, the fossil record demonstrates the enormous success animal flourishing achieved at various periods despite numerous catastrophic events, including those mass extinctions due to acts of God. We think of humans as the most successful creatures on the planet. In most ways, we are. In terms of longevity as a species, it is not even close.

The fossil record also shows that apex carnivores from the distant past, such as dinosaurs, mega-oceanic predators, and gigantic mammalian and avian predators, appear *cleared away* to create a new world for us. When modern humans appeared, the world was significantly and "coincidently" tamer, more easily manageable, and ideal for human flourishing. By that time, grasses flourished across the globe, opening the way for large-scale agriculture.

Timing is everything.

Over billions of years, the vast numbers of extinct creatures buried with layer upon layer of flora and fauna left enough energy in the ground to launch the rapid advance of civilization that, in short order, led to man landing on the moon and the capability for the Gospel to blanket the world. The prehistoric worlds have provided an endless supply of goods God saw in the beginning.

Now a human cemetery is a graveyard complete with funerals. But we would not say that *human life* is only suffering and death simply because we are mortal. Life is a beautiful thing; it beats the alternative. Life is an opportunity even in a fallen world. Life is how we look at it for the most part. To be sure, there is too much suffering. We can be perplexed, but suffering and tears will end (Revelation 21:4). Christians ought to have a *glass-half-full* perspective on life because all will be well. Living in this world is a mix of triumphs and tragedies but ultimate victory. It is what Louie Armstrong said it is—a wonderful world.

Christians especially should be joyous.

According to scripture, suffering can include joy. "You *suffered* along with those in prison and *joyfully* accepted the confiscation of your property because you knew that you yourselves had better and lasting possessions" (Hebrews 10:34). Besides that, Hebrews 12:2 reads, "Fixing our eyes on Jesus, the pioneer, and *perfecter* of faith. For the *joy* set before him, he endured the cross, scorning its shame, and sat down at the right hand of the throne of God."

These are not poems.

Every mortal thing dies. Shouldn't that go without saying?

Look, suffering is not good ultimately. It makes sense only in a temporal material world. That is the nature of our universe. Sure, a cemetery is full of people "dying to get in," but not all of us would say life, in general, is nothing but suffering and death. In the YE "scholarly" work, *Coming to Grips with Genesis,* page 94, is this admission:

We must note that [Martin] *Luther did in fact allow for animal death before the Fall*, not because God is angry at them. On the contrary, "for them death is...a sort of temporal casualty, ordained indeed by God but not...as punishment. Animals die because for some other reason it seemed good to God that they should die." (emphasis mine)

So Martin Luther accepted animal death before human sin entered the picture. Did Martin Luther "destroy the message of the cross and the Atonement?" Today, no compelling voice insists that animal death is *punishment* for human sin. YErs seem to believe some version of this, so they cannot agree with Martin Luther. Christianity has always said that animals are not morally culpable. They are nonrational and, therefore, without moral intelligence capable of making ethical decisions.

Furthermore, humans have a soft spot in our hearts for animals. God made animals to serve us. They belong to us. We named them; we own them. We love them. Animals do not serve God per se except by serving us and the environment. We serve God directly. He named us; he called us. He loves us. We are in the soft spot of God's heart.

We want God to have the same deference toward animals as we do, but they do not relate to Him as they do to us. It is not that God is indifferent to animals. Animals exist to serve a lesser purpose than humans do. Therefore, it is reasonable that justice for humans is of a higher order than animal justice.

Jesus, Animal Suffering, and Death

Remarkable verses in the New Testament tell us that Satan is:

1. Prince of the power of the air.

2. The "god" of this world.

3. Capable of influencing the behavior of humans and animals.

1 and 2 are typologies.

On 3, remember that Jesus cast demons out of a man into a drove of two thousand pigs (Mark 5:13). As a result, they scrambled down a bank into the sea in unison like locusts. Battered and bruised, they all drowned. That demonstrated Jesus' authority over the spiritual and material realms in one miracle. His authority was now indisputable since no one could suggest that swine could be part of fraud perpetrated by Jesus. Swine cannot conspire. This incident convincingly illustrated that Jesus was who he said he was. That made the loss of two thousand pigs worth it. All mortal creatures die whether we like it or not; some are good for food, and some are not.

Why would Christ initiate the bloodshed, suffering, and mass killing of thousands of pigs just to make a point? How long did those animals take to die from their wounds? Was this a heartless act? Call it what you want; there it is for everyone to see. Why not make the same point compatible with the scruples of the more sensitive? The killing of an animal is not necessarily evil, or Jesus would not have involved himself in killing two thousand of them. This incident shows that slaughtering animals is not an innate evil when serving humans and their higher needs, *even if not used for food*. God created them to serve higher purposes.

Animals do not misuse other animals in predation. Carnivores are designed for and so entitled to prey for food. Predators appear evil when we anthropomorphize them; we want them to empathize with prey animals when they cannot. We judge them by human moral standards, which is another category error. Predation is suitable for a balanced ecosystem, and sometimes it is neither good nor evil but merely the way things are in a temporal world. Surprisingly or not surprisingly, God ensures that carnivores get their meat: *"The lions roar for their prey and seek their food from God."* (Psalm 104:21) and *"Who provides food for the raven when its young cry out to God and wander about for lack of food"* (Job 38:41). If God feeds predators like this and Jesus' swine massacre was evil, Elizabeth Mitchell might have something in her charge against God having a *"cruel sense of irony."*

Animals do not have immortal souls; therefore, they cannot lose what they did not have. Beasts and critters do not sin, so they cannot suffer the fate of sinners; that is why they do not enjoy redemption as sinners can. Taking from the tree of life is not for lower creatures because it is a conscious choice. Such YE ideas are foreign to historical Christianity.

Furthermore, sin was in the universe before Adam. The serpent in the Garden implies that. Elizabeth Mitchell's charge that God lied if he called the creation "very good" if creatures died is reckless. It is like the farmer scanning his crop after the harvest that calls his work "very good" while someone insists he is lying because of the thousands of insects he crushed by plowing and reaping. Feeding thousands of human beings is very good despite the passive sensitivity of some over large-scale "insect massacres."

PART V:
THE CHRISTIAN MISSION
VS.
THE YE REFORM MOVEMENT

34.
THE GOOD NEWS OF WARNING PEOPLE

We warn people that compromising God's Word in Genesis is an authority
issue, a gospel issue, and indirectly, a salvation issue.[440]
—Ken Ham

Go into all the world and preach the gospel to all creation.
—Mark 16:15

The above phrase, *"indirectly, a salvation issue,"* attempts to sound serious
but is supercilious. YErs will admit that one does not need YEC to receive *salvation* or accept the Gospel, acknowledging that YEC is not essential for those
things. Though not about "direct salvation," Ham says, YEC is essential for
"indirect salvation." What "indirect salvation" means, he does not say. You will
not find its definition in any theological dictionary.

Note the presumption of personal authority—"*We* warn people." YErs
warn other Christians about an ominous threat to the faith that scripture is
silent about and is not essential for salvation: at least not the direct sort. We
have seen many claims and comments like this among YErs. Yet, there are no
warnings in scripture about mistaking the age of the earth, nor is there any history in Christian thought about the *central importance* of six literal days or how
long ago creation took place.

All Christians believe that God is Creator and that Genesis has its place
in the Old Testament canon and Judeo-Christian theology. That is quite different from the YE Reform Movement and its overarching message of proclaiming
when the creation occurred and basing all biblical authority and doctrine on
how long ago they insist it happened. So they *warn people.*

About what exactly?

Norman Geisler (1932–2019) was a respected scholar and apologist among conservative Evangelicals and one of the framers of the *Chicago
Statement on Biblical Inerrancy*. He did not accept YEC though he was sympathetic to those who did. After being publically maligned by YErs over his
expertise, and biblical inerrancy, he wrote:

The founders and framers of the contemporary inerrancy movement
(ICBI)... explicitly rejected the Young Earth view as being essential to
belief in [biblical] inerrancy. They discussed it and voted against making it a part of what they believed inerrancy entailed...even though they
believed in the "literal" historical-grammatical view of interpreting the

---

440. Ken Ham, "Should I Have Dinner With Biologos?" October 14, 2014, AiG website.

Bible... One is surprised at the *zeal by which some Young Earthers* are making their position a virtual test for evangelical orthodoxy.[441]

Geisler says some framers of inerrancy were sympathetic to a more literal view of Genesis among this Evangelical brain trust yet rejected the notion that biblical authority is at issue. Instead, it is a difference of opinion on the text, which may or may not be correct. They notably rejected the movement that connects YEC to biblical inerrancy and, therefore, biblical authority because YEC is a mere set of opinions. YEC is not "the Word of the Lord to the prophet [fill in the blank]."

YErs have no authority to warn people about their private test of orthodoxy since their *reform movement* is unorthodox in the ways we have seen. The *activists* among them are a significant minority group in Christianity, increasingly on the fringe as scientific and theological advancements march forward. They make a lot of noise. Even if they grow in numbers, their theology is taken less and less seriously by Christianity and especially unbelievers, making evangelism much more difficult. You can find countless debates on Facebook, where unbelievers love to exploit YErs on their unfamiliarity with science and the Bible, with believers and the occasional unbeliever who knows the scriptures better. Geisler was concerned about the YE movement's excesses where YErs "warn people" with the zeal of Old Testament prophets. Ham says, "I must admit: there are times when I believe I have gotten an inkling of what the prophet Jeremiah felt after he warned people about their departure from God's Word."

There is nothing wrong with admiring the Old Testament prophets. But we shouldn't aspire to be one. The biblical periods of the Law and the prophets are over. John the Baptist was the last of *the prophets* whose commission was to warn:

"Cry aloud, spare not, and show God's [covenant] *people* their sins." Jesus ends that prophetic period because he cleanses all sin for all time. Therefore, we are not in the time of the Prophets when a word from God came exclusively to an individual such as Ezekiel's "watchman," to warn Israel of war drums:

"But if *the watchman* sees the sword coming and does not blow the trumpet to warn the people and the sword comes and takes someone's life, that person's life will be taken because of their sin, but I will hold the watchman accountable for their blood." (Ezekiel 33:6)[442]

---

441. Norman Geisler, "A Response to Ken Ham and Answers in Genesis," online.

442. This is not to say that no remnant of the prophetic spirit is left in Christianity but only that it is no longer the occupation and certainly not the preoccupation of the Christian Mission. God's Son supersedes the prophets and is now the heart and soul of Christian messaging.

The New Testament relegates this kind of evangelism to history: "*In the past, God spoke...through the prophets...but in these last days he has spoken to us by his Son*" (Hebrews 1:1–3). Faith in the Good News of Jesus is now the message. The Christian warning is not to reject Christ.

While the New Testament declares that the *methods* of the prophets reside in the past, YErs like Ken Ham disagree: "AiG [is] bold and unashamed in contending for the faith, like the *watchman* in Ezekiel, *to warn people* about those who undermine the authority of God's Word [in Genesis]."[443] That would be news to Ezekiel and not the good kind. Ham prides himself on his boldness, but he tends more toward rudeness.

The old Worldwide Church of God (and its spinoffs) had an "Ezekiel's Watchman Mission," too. "Being bold" was a phrase we used often. We thought the Watchman role was our calling and duty, but that mentality came from an excessive and covenantal orientation to the Old Testament.

To Ham, this is "war," and he is the "Watchman" standing over the towers glassing for the enemy and its belief in "millions of years." One wonders what Ezekiel might think, knowing YErs coopted his mission as Israel's Wartime Watchman in the service of six literal days. Ham wrote:

> I believe AiG is a leading supplier of the most advanced "weaponry" designed to counter the enemy's attacks in this era...I praise God for the advances that many believers are making on various battlefronts as a result of the Lord using AiG to be a part of equipping them for this war.[444]

Believing the earth is young is one thing; making it the warning message to the Church is bizarre.

YErs say that we can deny YEC and still be Christian while warning us of dire consequences. If YEC is central to *all bible teaching*: if it is the foundation of God's plan, and denying it is calling God a liar, if an old earth destroys the Atonement and the Cross's message, then rejecting YEC is not compromise; *it is apostasy*.[445] But of course, we all know it is not apostasy, nor is it the other dire things YErs asserts, which are nothing more than YE obsessions.

For YE evangelists, it is essential to preach the nonessential, YEC.

---

443. Ken Ham, "Watchmen for the Church," June 3, 2014, AiG website. A cursory survey of AIG and other YE websites will uncover similar statements.

444. Quoted from the AiG website.

445. It is tempting to distrust YErs comments on the saving force of YEC. Remember Ham's quote above: "Compromising God's Word in Genesis is a gospel issue, and, *indirectly, a salvation issue.*" Ham gives the impression that he wants to get as close as possible in making YEC necessary for both the Gospel and salvation without committing Himself, which is hedging. YEC is for him and many others the calling of their lives. That should be a warning to them. "Prophet, warn thyself" or at least reassess your opinions.

How do you know if a Christian or a pastor is an obsessive YEr? Just ask the following questions:

1. "If the earth is old, is God a liar?" If the answer is "yes," there is no need for the next two questions. If they endlessly avoid the question, that means yes.

2. "If the earth is old, is the Bible untrustworthy?"

3. "Is proclaiming YEC the key to reforming the Church and culture?

How objective could they be to answer "yes" to these inquiries? What is the likelihood of reasoning together if they accuse you of calling God a liar? Or if a YEr calls God a liar if they are wrong. They don't know the difference between biblical authority and biblical opinion. They confuse Christian evangelism with their private YE evangelism, something unthinkable in Church history. How well could they understand God's attributes, the Bible's purposes, or the Church's Mission?

When engaging most YErs, you'll eventually find their underlying motivations—suspicion and conspiracy theories so that they see any reasoning contrary to YE opinions as a deception. Those can be cult-like motivations that we also had in the WCG and some of its offshoots.

When YErs engage other Christians, many come off defensive and accusatory. YEC is their primary identity, and *effective* disagreement feels threatening. It doesn't matter how compelling the case may be, YE reformists are certain their detractors are deceivers, and the worst "deceptions" are the most convincing.

We wed our life's mission to what we identify with most and may not be aware of it. Can there be any doubt that winning the SDWC is YEC's first mission? When that becomes apparent, YErs claim they are not *Young Earth* Creationists but "biblical creationists." Who isn't? A persistent, overly judgmental posture toward a *nonessential* can only be a by-product of misunderstanding the Mission, particularly when the subject is objectively marginal. Paul addresses a similar fervor, "I can testify that they have a zeal for God, but it is not enlightened" (Romans 10:1–3). The truth is *overzealousness* is never enlightened.

My main point should be clear by now.

The *excesses* of "warriors" in the YE Reform Movement can discredit the mission of the Church in the minds of unbelievers. Unbelievers have piled more ridicule onto Christianity for the mistaken assumption that Christianity accepts Late Bronze Age "science" over modern science. I've debated atheists that insist Genesis is literal because of YEC assumptions. They reject any attempt to explain Genesis as literature in its context. Many atheists want to debate YErs because they are so easy, and some get a kick out of it. Tragically, these atheists believe they are defeating Christianity to the point that they deny any other view of Christianity.

That is a problem.

In March 2011, the Great Homeschool Conventions, Inc. board voted to disinvite Ham and AiG from future conventions. Conference organizer Brennan Dean stated *Ham had made "unnecessary, ungodly, and mean-spirited statements that are divisive at best and defamatory at worst."* Dean said further, *"We believe Christian scholars should be heard without the fear of ostracism or ad hominem attacks."* The disinvitation occurred after Ham criticized Peter Enns of the BioLogos Foundation, who advocated a symbolic, rather than literal, interpretation of the fall of Adam and Eve. Ham accused Enns of espousing *"outright liberal theology that totally undermines the authority of the Word of God."* [446]

It was not YEC teachings that led the Great Homeschool Conventions, Inc., to disinvite Ken Ham and AiG. In fact, the invitation was initially to hear their perspective, which is appropriate. It was Ken Ham's over-the-top judgmental behavior. He again confused rudeness for boldness toward Peter Enns, a moderate (fundamentalists say liberal) scholar. Ham has done similar things toward decidedly conservative scholars like Norman Geisler, Bruce Waltke, and Apologists like William Lane Craig and Hugh Ross. [447]

Christians should not engage in *cancel culture* or warring against other Christians to silence them over honestly held opinions or threaten careers over a nonessential. Unchristian behavior is a separate issue. Ham's recent personal attack was against William Lane Craig, who has written on the historical Adam and identified the genre of Genesis 1–11 as mytho-history.

There can be no doubt that Genesis 1–11 has similar stories considered myths of the ANE. However, Genesis does not present those stories as myths but gives them a historical backdrop that is neither strictly myth nor history. Instead, it is a way of saying that origins, as they commonly understood them in the ANE, are the work of Israel's God and not the result of other gods written as epic myths.

As I wrote earlier: It would be like God revealing Himself for the first time today if the whole world had no knowledge of God but maintained our commonly understood science in the public domain. With today's physics and

---

446. Jennifer Riley, "Ken Ham Disinvited from Homeschooling Event over 'Ungodly' Remarks," *Christian Post*, March 27, 2011.

447. William Lane Craig's work at Reasonable Faith is unsurpassed in Christian Apologetics, especially his debates with some of the best scientists and philosophers in the world (see *reasonablefaith.org*). I do not recommend Ross's work in biblical studies. He is a concordist who attempts to read modern science into the scripture. His value as a Christian Apologist is his main field of study—astronomy (see *ReasonstoBelieve.com*). One point about the Discovery Institute is an ambivalence on evolution. They appear to reject Neo Darwinian evolution yet, some among them accept it and even Stephen Myer does not rule out common descent in an interview with Jim Stump. For an explanation and defense of Evolutionary Creationism see *BioLogos.org*.

biology, a modern Moses writing a contemporary Genesis might incidentally credit God for the Big Bang and *guided* evolution while rejecting philosophical naturalism.

The Big Bang and evolution would not be the point of a modern Genesis. Today's standard theories would not be the revelation since the world would already know some version of them. Therefore, as with Genesis, God is the revelation, not the naked eye cosmology of the ANE or theories in physics and biology in our modern era.

Craig is not the first to suggest the mytho-history genre of Genesis 1–11, but since Craig is influential among Evangelicals, Ham got personal:

> [Craig's] pseudo-intellectual arrogance that mocks God and his Word and instead exalts the word of fallible man above God's holy, infallible Word. He's destructive to the Church and will have to give account to God for his blatant compromise of God's Word and for leading many astray.[448]

Craig responds:

> [Ken Ham] accused me of pseudo-intellectual arrogance and mocking God's Word. I think those are very, very serious charges to level against another person... I differentiated between criticizing a person's view and criticizing a person's character. I certainly think that my views are open game for anyone to criticize, but when it comes to personal attacks on character I think that's a really serious matter.[449]

Many YErs believe they have God's mandate to reform the Church. They believe YErs are the only Christians who have not compromised the faith—a posture bound to sink into a warning message about judgment. But it is fanciful that YE zealots or reformers think of themselves as the best Christianity offers. They are like Old Testament prophets, steeped in Old Testament scriptures with an Old Covenant-inspired mission. They have dedicated museums and built a life-size Ark like an altar to the flood.

YE reformists are mainly about Genesis 1–11.

If a literal reading of Genesis is isolated from YEC's excesses, the worst case is that it's mistaken. But aiming YE reform at Christianity or attaching it to the Gospel with dire consequences if rejected, we have an *off-brand* of Christianity. Such mistakes are like that of Terry Mortensen: "[OEC] has severely damaged the Bible's teaching...assaulted the character of God, thereby

---

448. Ken Ham, "Are We Wrong to Call Out Compromise?" January 4, 2021, featured in Ken Ham's blog. Note the assumption of compromise. The title should be "Are We Wrong to Charge People of Compromise?" Maybe not. But charging people with compromise over a nonessential is incoherent. It suggests that YErs really think *six literal days* are essential after all.

449. See "William Lane Craig: What Is His Response to Ken Ham?" YouTube.

undermining the authority and reliability of the Word of God and subverting the Gospel." [450]

Note the intemperate words: "severely damaged the Bible," "assaulted God," and "subverting the Gospel." These are militant terms. Yet, by Mortensen's admission, YEC is unessential for both salvation and the Gospel.

Mortensen's confusion is about our three overarching concepts established in this book:

1. *The nature of God:* Deep age of the universe is "assaulting the character of God," meaning deep age is calling God a liar.

2. *The Bible's purposes:* An old earth is "severely damaging the Bible's teaching," as if the Bible is about things like the earth's age and flood geology.

3. *The Church's Mission:* An old earth is "subverting the Gospel," meaning YEC establishes the Gospel or the Gospel depends on YEC.

The marshal terms: assaulting, severely damaging, and subverting, are a confused call to arms by a militant reform movement and its misguided view of Christianity.

The "Disease of Millions of Years"

According to Ken Ham, "The idea of millions of years is like a disease, and biological evolution is like the symptom. Many Christians are willing to deal with the 'symptom' [evolution] but not the 'disease' [millions of years]." [451]

Many YErs reduce all contrary views against YEC to "the belief in millions of years." "Belief in millions of years" is YE inspeak describing Christians who think the earth is old. The irony is that the only Christians that put their faith in years are YErs. They are obsessed with the earth's age while other Christians are not. Never mind that science measures the age of the earth in billions of years, not millions. One could reduce all YE views to "the belief in thousands of years" if so inclined. Christians generally do not speak this way.

Then why these strange phrases?

Most Christians accept the Big Bang as the initial creation set in motion. Since God is the source of all truth (per Augustine), these Christians do not ignore evidence pointing to truths, including scientific truths or facts discovered

---

450. Dr. Terry Mortenson, "Old-Earth Creationism—Is It A Sin?" July 1, 2012; last featured July 12, 2020, on AiG website. By "assaulting the character of God," Mortenson means that OErs call God a liar by believing the earth is old. Yet, YEC is an anthropomorphic and, therefore, a low view of God.

451. Ken Ham, "The 'Disease' of Millions of Years," May 21, 2012, AiG website.

by scientists.[452] Science has helped biblical interpretation by confirming some ideas in scripture that should be understood figuratively or as incidental, like geocentric passages where the sun goes around a stationary earth.

Additionally, most Christians believe God directed changes after the Big Bang at strategic points, especially in the development of life. That is possibly anthropomorphic if it suggests that God has to respond to challenges in cosmic or terrestrial changes He didn't anticipate. The idea of continuously upholding and sustaining a universe is about being the ground for things to exist or the underlying reality that gives existence to everything that is not self-existing. We do not know how God operates; we can only see the effects (John 3:8). But we know God is the God of all "gaps" and non-gaps.

Others, like Augustine and Aquinas, believe God endowed all the development the universe has seen with little or no need to intervene along the way since He upholds the creation and sustains it continually. Such divine operation following the Big Bang is reasonable for a believer but is suppositional. Creationism of a specific kind, from YEC to Evolutionary Creationism, is not finally a brute fact but a mix of empirical data and sound or unsound philosophical and theological reasoning. It may be impossible to distinguish between changes God built into the universe from an instant beginning and the possibility of interacting with His creation as He pleases, though the evidence for the former is stronger than the latter for created things. But the Incarnation is the ultimate divine invasion into this universe. We simply do not know the details in nature, only that Christians believe God continuously impacts every particle in the universe by maintaining their existence.

All Progressive creationists and Intelligent Design advocates recognize the deep age of the cosmos, i.e., they accept the Big Bang. Still, most do not accept Neo-Darwinism[453] or the massive biological changes in species by *blind*

---

452. If we apply Thomas Aquinas's 4 types of Law to truth, there are 4 types: (1) Eternal truth— that only God knows; (2) divine truth—revealed by God, e.g., in scripture; (3) natural truth—a subset of divine truth discoverable in nature through reason; (4) and human truth—made by humans reflecting God's image.

453. Not all Intelligent Design advocates reject macroevolution and common descent.

and undirected processes.[454] Many Christians fall somewhere in this category. In other words, there is wide acceptance of an old earth/universe in Christianity but no widespread conviction on *evolutionary processes that are unguided or wholly unintentional.* That presents a tactical problem for YE evangelists because their initial grievance was over Darwin's common descent of all species from a single ancestor where God is not responsible for the process, which almost no Christian believes.

It is easier for YErs to accuse Christians that are Evolutionary Creationists of unbelief because they assume God wrote the Bible and would never use a natural process like macroevolution. Yet, this universe is all about natural processes, so much so that "naturalism"— that everything arises from natural properties and causes *only*— is a popular worldview among atheists and agnostics. But if evolution is purely naturalistic, then our cognitive faculties have been selected for survival value, not truth. Then it's ultimately irrelevant whether some of our beliefs happen to be true if they do not have survival value. What would matter, then, is whether natural selection responding to environmental pressures and mutations is beneficial for passing along genes.[455] In other words, if naturalism is true, we must be unsure about the reliability of our faculties for knowledge. Hence, we can have no confidence in the truth of naturalism formed by the same unreliable faculties.

Furthermore, as I said earlier, natural selection for survival value does not explain why so much of our faculties do not seem dedicated to mere survival. Evolutionary Creationism upheld by God can account for faculties far exceeding survival, producing mathematics, theoretical physics and chemistry, astronomy, literature, architecture way beyond shelter, cars, ships, poetry, music, art, landing on the moon, etc.

All nature and evolution may just be substitute words for God's operations; maybe "Mother nature" is another term for God. Not that nature is God. The title "Creator" is operational (His acts), not ontological (His nature). The same is true of all processes God has made. "But the creation is not perfect;

---

454. Evolutionary biologists define *random* mutations as specific changes from a wide pool of possibilities that might be beneficial, neutral, or detrimental and not necessarily the result of blind chance since beneficial changes are more likely to continue. Similarly, a random sperm cell (healthy or not) might fertilize an egg, but it comes from a complex that is not haphazard. If the vast majority of fertilized eggs were from unhealthy spermazoa the species may be threatened with extinction. Beneficial mutations endure and pass on. In other words, there does seem to be a general progress in evolution even with randomness, but science as a discipline rules out divine direction because the methods of science cannot establish divine presence of a transcendent God. The role of science is to detect physical evidence, not comment on an undetectable presence. On the other hand, theism and atheism are philosophical concepts, not science. The atheist and theist that depend on science alone to establish their philosophy of God are imposing on science something it cannot do—speak for any realm beyond this one.

455. Bill Nye the Science Guy candidly stated, "The meaning of life is pretty clear: Living things strive to pass their genes into the future." So past the age of reproduction, is one's life meaningless?

there is too much chaos or randomness," some say. No changing world is perfect. Randomness allows free movement and an authentic context for freewill agents.

Christians who accept the science of common descent present a much smaller pool of proselytes for YEC. They are harder to convince because they likely know the science better than YErs. YErs blur the lines between unguided evolution and anything associated with deep age, namely the Big Bang, the redshift in the light spectrum, the cosmic microwave background radiation, and the overwhelming geological and DNA evidence for deep age. A Big Bang believer is automatically labeled an "evolutionist" by reform movement YErs.[456]

Many YErs like Ham and Mortenson focus directly on *deep-time* so that the vast majority of Christians might provide an immense pool of prospects for YE evangelism. Therefore, Ham isolates *age* (millions of years) and pigeon-holes it as "a disease." Ham is saying, "It is not enough to reject unguided or even guided macro-evolution; you still compromise biblical authority which depends on a young earth." Or something like that.

The YE objective is to make the real enemy (macroevolution) impossible in the minds of Christians by severely reducing the age of the earth. YErs believe a world thousands of years old would eliminate all doubt. A young earth certainty means one can dismiss evolution without serious thought.

However, it is conceivable that God could condense the process of evolution into thousands of years as when YErs claim that God concentrated all the considerable geological evidence for deep age during Noah's flood—neither one is a reasonable solution, of course, but theoretically possible for an omnipotent God. According to YEC, the flood compressed what appears like deep age in the fossil record into a single year. So was evolution also compressed into a single year? Well, no. The problem with condensed age by a flood doesn't answer why everything else in our solar system: moon rocks, rocks from Mars, asteroids, and meteors also date to 4.5 billion years unless YErs are ready to insist that Noah's flood was a solar-system event.

Similarly, a hundred *real* rings in a tree cannot hide its actual age, whether it arrived instantly or by natural processes—its actual age is the same. In other words, if genuine rings are how God created trees, they must be authentic in every respect, including age. Otherwise, YErs are talking about a fake tree or magic, which God does not do.

Ham's symptom/disease metaphor positions "unguided evolution" as secondary, i.e., "the symptom," and *deep time* as primary—the disease itself. Since

---

456. There is an orgy of labels levied at non-YErs. I have been called: a humanist, atheist, Bible hater, God hater, destroyer of the Church, destined for hell, worker with the devil, Satanic and other epithets— all that over a nonessential!

many Christians accept deep time in the Big Bang model and reject Darwin, that larger pool of prospects governs YE evangelism.[457]

YEC's primary focus is not to convert unbelievers to Christianity but to convert Christians to YEC. For most Christians, the Big Bang does not require macroevolution as a necessary finish; they separate the two because they believe God intervened and orchestrated life's development at specific times. Others believe that God planted all the designs in the universe, including life, in the singularity in a similar way that the zygote carries a complete human. Is the spectacular growth from a zygote to an adult human with 65 trillion cells nature's doing or God's? Most evolutionary creationists believe God continuously upholds and sustains nature and its laws as He created them. The same may be true of the singularity's spectacular growth into a mature universe.

Since YErs object to deep-time, their "in-speak" includes the rather lame mantra, "*the belief in millions of years*," which has morphed into the amateurish "*disease of millions of years.*" So "millions of years" is the disease, and "thousands of years" is the cure. Old Earthers are the patient, and YEC is the physician. Imagine the Pharisees asking the disciples, "Why does your master eat with tax-collectors and *Old Earthers*?" And Jesus said, "YErs don't need a physician, "but those infected by millions of years do" (Matthew 9:12).

All Christians credit God for the Creation of the universe, including life. In Christianity, macroevolution, *Theistic* Evolution, and "Evolutionary *Creationism*" show God's authorship with the words "Theistic" and "Creationism." The Evangelical think tank, Biologos, founded by Francis Collins, coined the phrase "Evolutionary Creationism." Biologos also accepts the Bible's authority, recognizing that biblical authority is hardly the sole jurisdiction of fundamentalists and that a six-thousand-year-old universe has nothing to do with that authority.

Many Christians question evolution with all the misinformation surrounding it because of its common association with atheism. The practical difficulty with evolution is that species development by countless minute changes through deep time is hard to grasp. You can't watch it, and seeing is believing for most people. But deep time is analogous to deep space; you can't get your mind around either. It is easier to accept deep space because we can see it with extremely high-powered telescopes. We cannot watch deep time in real-time, but we can see its effects in the universe and speciation.[458] Yet both deep time and deep space are one in this universe.

---

457. This is not suggesting that Christian evangelists targeting a specific audience for evangelism is improper; but "evangelizing" other Christians with warnings over nonessentials and with what amounts to sophistry is senseless if not unethical.

458. Deep time can be seen in the redshift in galaxies throughout the universe. Galaxies said to be 13 billion years old, means that the light emanating from them is 13 billion years old. The galaxy may no longer exist.

Most unbelievers look upon YEC with contempt not because it evokes God but the kind of God it suggests—one that wrote the Bible and created an inconceivably vast universe in six literal days. A universe that is six-thousand years old is not reasonable. If unbelievers think that belief in God includes YEC, they will have contempt for the God of Christianity. Augustine warned of this. A literal Genesis is not enough to convince unbelievers; YEC is unconvincing to the vast majority of Christians for theological and scientific reasons.

Generally speaking, the Bible, especially literalism, is not the tool to evangelize atheists or non-Christians. Paul did not refer to scripture when evangelizing the Athenian philosophers in Acts 17, and they were highly religious people (verse 22). He was all things to all people. He did not allow petty differences to undermine the Gospel. If the Gospel is relevant and effective in today's world, evangelists must allow for deep age, if only as a side issue.

Many Christians outside the YE ranks are their main field to proselytize. They feign a "reform movement" within the Church because nobody outside will take them seriously. At least some in the Church will listen. Ham's solution is to recast his anti-evolution stance with the disease/symptoms metaphor over "millions of years." Ironically, Ham, who sometimes insists that figurative language is lying, does not seem to grasp his own metaphor.

According to Ham, if you believe in millions of years (the Big Bang), you have the plague. But if you believe in biological evolution, you only have the symptom —"sores" and such. It does not dawn on Ham that by his reasoning if a Christian rejects Neo-Darwinian evolution (the symptom), she is symptom-free. Ham concludes his train of thought: "The idea of millions of years is like a disease in the Church; *biological evolution is just a symptom.* Your support of AiG, with God's blessing, will help prevent the disease [millions of years] from spreading further."[459]

One wonders what the impact this YE messaging has on the *real work* of the Church. A scan of the AiG website and others like it will uncover many intemperate statements like the following excerpt:

> We often deal with the *"enemy"* from within. The *attack* from within is *more dangerous and destructive* than from without—you see, *it's an attack on biblical authority from those who claim to be biblical. I must warn you of the deadly compromise* teachings of an organization promoting what is called "progressive creationism.[460]

Note the militant terms: *enemy, attack, destructive,* and *deadly.* But all that over the earth's age? I thought we did not need to be YErs and that salvation is in Christ alone. Ham warned his readership about Hugh Ross's ministry, Reasons to Believe. Ross is a respected astronomer from the University of

---

459. Ken Ham, "The "Disease" of Millions of Years," May 21, 2012, AiG website.

460. Ken Ham, "The Enemy Within," August 9, 2003, AiG website.

Toronto and a fellow at Caltech. Since Ross accepts the Big Bang, he must be dangerous, even though he rejects Neo-Darwinism. Because of this, Ham calls Ross an *"enemy of biblical authority,"* meaning Ross disagrees with YEC. *Ross has the "disease."*

Ham claims, in no uncertain terms, that the earth's age is unrelated to the Gospel and salvation. He wrote, "Scripture plainly teaches that salvation is conditioned upon faith in Christ, with no requirement for what one believes about the age of the earth or universe."[461] Yet Ham still warns Christians that believing the earth is old is *lethal—"a deadly compromise"* of the Christian faith.

YErs seem to think people won't take YEC seriously or pay attention to it without outrageous threats. Since salvation and the Gospel are independent of the geological record, as YErs profess, geology should be in secular hands, like engineering and medicine as in other sciences.

All biblical traditions: Jewish, Catholic, Orthodox, Protestant, Evangelicals, and even fundamentalists, have interpreted the Bible, including Genesis, both literally and figuratively. Whether the scripture is literal or figurative is not a matter of biblical authority since that authority can be in either interpretation.

In other words, *the Bible does not lose authority when it speaks figuratively.*

What is more, if an interpreter takes scripture figuratively when it should be literal or literal when it should be figurative, the interpreter has made a mistake. *The interpreter loses authority.* Therefore, the issue is not biblical authority but knowledge, skill, and wisdom in interpreting scripture. Yet, mistakes can still happen with those skills and many years of serious study. We may never discover some errors. That is why only essentials should unite us.

Ham continues his warning:

The Lord has raised up *creation ministries* around the world to call the Church back to the authority of God's Word in Genesis—but Satan will do whatever he can to undermine *this vital work* from outside the Church, *and from within.* I really wish I *didn't* have to share *the battles with you.* But you need to know. Indeed, *there's an urgent need to help restore the Bible's authority worldwide...* Your gift during the summer... will help proclaim biblical truths, including the precious gospel message.

---

461. Ken Ham "Does the Gospel Depend on a Young Earth?" January 1, 2010, AiG website. Contrast this article where YEC is not necessary for the Gospel or salvation with an article by the same author entitled, "The Necessity for Believing in Six Literal Days," December 1, 1995, AiG website. In this article, Ham insists, "*It is vital to believe in Six Literal Days for many reasons. The foremost reason is that allowing these days to be long periods of time undermines the foundations of the message of the cross.*" These two lines of reasoning create cognitive dissonance. The truth is, unless YEC is seen as vital to the faith, no one would care about it.

Please continue to stand with us, *in this fierce battle*, with your practical support and prayers.[462] (emphasis mine)

Attacking a person's opinion is not an attack on the individual's virtue or piety. But it is easy to feel attacked when one ties their central identity to a cherished distinctive when scrutinized. In a world of "identity politics," Christians should not lose sight of their primary identity—God's image restored in Jesus and not another "identity theology," which can be an idol. Identity politics is non-Christian: "There is [now no distinction] [between] Jew nor Greek, slave nor free. There is no male and female; for you are all one in Christ Jesus" (Galatians 3:28 AMP). Even the American founders chose individualism over tribalism.[463]

Many YErs are devout. Henry Morris was, and Ham certainly seems to be. But Ham thinks simple disagreement attacks the sincerity and devotion of YErs like himself. Yet he viciously attacks people like the mild-mannered Hugh Ross, Norman Geisler, Bruce Waltke, Peter Inns, and recently, William Lane Craig. Continuing Ham's attack, he wrote: "[Craig's] main thrust is to compromise the pagan religion of evolution/millions of years with God's Word. He is helping atheists undermine the Word of God and capture the minds of genera tions of people."

Note the silly epithet, "the pagan religion of *evolution/millions of years.*" So "millions of years" is both a disease and religion. That is odd since Ham's devotion to thousands of years is religious while "millions of years" is secular.[464] Ham then ends with an Old Testament prophet's warning in his day: "'Woe to the shepherds who destroy and scatter the sheep of my pasture.' declares the Lord" (Jeremiah 23:1).

There is nothing wrong with quoting an Old Testament prophet unless doing so is a fixation that crowds out the gospel. How can a disagreement over a nonessential make an enemy of biblical authority? Notice the significant space Ham gives to *war rhetoric* (most of the above article is this way).[465]

At the same time, a single phrase regarding the Gospel is an afterthought at the end of the article, where he writes, "Your [donation]...will help proclaim biblical truths, *including the precious gospel message.*" The governing word is

---

462. Ken Ham, "The Enemy Within," August 9, 2003, AiG website.

463. American progressivism with its intersectionality, tribalism, and moral relativism is decidedly anti-Christian. Christians that try to hold both views misunderstand one or both worldviews. That is why movements from the far Left often push back against only one religion: Christianity. It is the last line of defense against any Neo-Marxist tendency of the radical left or any State control over the conscience.

464 I realize that some revere science like a religion. But fanaticism is a human failing found in many secular pursuits. We are using an analogy; extreme devotion to anything is like religious fervor even with no connection to spirituality. In YEC, "thousands of years" is religion.

465. Ken Ham, "The Enemy Within," August 9, 2003, AiG website.

precious. However, the Gospel's preciousness to a Christian organization should not be in the rarity of its proclamation.

In Ham's "*warning mission*," there is no real attempt to warn the reader of any threats to the gospel of Jesus itself. Instead, Ham justifies his warnings about "millions of years" with an unrelated warning from Paul. He writes:

> Paul gave *a warning* in Acts 20, *which we need to apply even today*: "Keep watch over yourselves and all the flock of which the Holy Spirit has made you overseers... Even from your own number men will arise and *distort the truth* in order to draw away disciples" (emphasis mine).

Ham implies that Christianity is trying to siphon off YErs to the mainstream, i.e., "*to draw away disciples*" when YErs are evangelizing Christians. So Ham interprets Paul's warning about *distorting the truth* when he writes:

> Here are just a few things...that "distort the truth:"

1. Noah's Flood was just a local event.

2. Secular geology, with its *millions of years* for the age of fossils/earth and the entire evolutionary "sequence of events," *must be accepted*.

3. Secular/evolutionary cosmology and the big bang are true.[466]

The first thing that stands out is the artificial use of the word *secular* attached to *geology* and *evolutionary cosmology*. It implies that the "right" geology has a priestly class or religious authority when it is necessarily a secular pursuit, not a religious one, except in YEC.

Obviously, Paul could not have had those three points in mind since they have nothing to do with "the truth" (or its distortions) that Paul declared. Ham is exploiting a tender moment in the life of the apostle. Paul was saying farewell to the Ephesian elders, knowing his life would end soon. Paul makes clear the truth he refers to with this:

> I have declared to both Jews and Greeks that they must *turn to God in repentance and have faith in our Lord Jesus*... My only aim is to finish the race and complete the task of *testifying to the good news of God's grace*... They all wept as they embraced him and kissed him. What grieved them most was his statement that they would never see his face again. (Acts 20:21–38)

Somehow Ham misses this.

Christians see the gospel as the central truth of the Bible, not unessential distinctives.

Note Ham's words again, "The Lord has raised up *creation ministries* around the world to call the Church back to the authority of God's Word in

---

466. Ibid.

THE SIX DAY WAR IN CREATIONISM

Genesis—*but Satan will do whatever he can to undermine this vital work from outside the Church, and from within.*" So YEC is a vital nonessential?

Forget the paranoia for a moment and ask, What is a "creation ministry?" Ham can only mean a "YE ministry." It is harder to see "creation ministry" as a ministry rather than another YE Reform Movement misnomer. No Christian rejects the Creator or creation. There is no such thing as a "creation ministry." The words *"Call the Church back to the authority of God's Word in Genesis"* are inexplicable since there never was an "authority of God's word in Genesis" period in Church history. This phrasing echoes Jude's words to contend for the faith once delivered (Jude 3). The "faith once delivered" was not YEC; it was the person of Jesus and his ministry. The YEC idea of authority in Genesis means a contrived authority invested in six literal days, which means the authority of YEC is only in the minds of radicalized YE reformists.

In reality, the nature of God, the divinity of Christ, the giving of the Holy Spirit, inspiration (not dictation) of the Bible, the Gospel of Jesus, Salvation by grace through faith, the community of saints, a core number of sacraments, and the Judgment have historically been the essential distinctives throughout Christianity. Never in Church history has the earth's age been at the vanguard of Christian thought, though God as Creator has, but not *when* he created or how long He took. The Apostle's Creed is a Catholic and Orthodox confession that all the branches of Christianity confess. Its opening phrase is, *"I believe in God, the Father Almighty, creator of heaven and earth."* The vast majority of Catholics, Orthodox, and more than two-thirds of Protestants are not YErs.

So, why use the phrase *"vital creation ministry"* in evangelism?

It appears that a YE belief on its own is not enough to gain a following. What do you do when your most important identifying distinctive is inconsequential to people? You connect it to something vital like the theology of creation or biblical authority and, if not salvation, then "indirect salvation" and the "beginning of the gospel" (see next chapter). You tell the unsuspecting that they call God a liar if they disagree. For YErs, biblical authority is less about God's self-disclosure in Christ than six literal days and flood geology. Christendom's main concern with what I call the SCWC is that unbelievers assume YE ministries speak for Christianity *when they only speak for themselves.*

Determining the age of the earth is a scientific and secular question. Make no mistake; a "gospel" about the earth's age is secular, having nothing to do with Christ, the Bible, or the Church's Mission. YErs attempt to force their ideology to the top of the theological food chain with indiscriminate warnings. Christians believe in Jesus—big deal. YE reformists position YEC as daring, exciting, and *bold*; now you have something. If true, YEC would give YErs special status over scientists. But is YEC the vital ministry that will *reform* Christianity and the culture?

Not in a million years.

35.
THE "CREATION GOSPEL" AND JESUS

The whole message of the Gospel falls apart if one allows millions of years for the Creation of the world.
—Ken Ham[467]

And never forget, the Gospel begins in Genesis.
—Mike Riddle [468]

[This is] the *beginning of the Gospel* about Jesus the Messiah, the Son of God.
—Mark 1:1

YE evangelists proselytize Christians—not unbelievers so much, but Christians—with their self-styled "creation gospel" and "creation evangelism." The primary YE mission is to proclaim a literalization of Genesis 1-11, not the Great Commission to preach the Good News of Jesus Christ to unbelievers without mixture and make followers of Jesus, though some may do that secondarily. Genuine Christian evangelism proclaims the Gospel of Jesus to the world found in the New Testament, preferably in a way the culture might find credible (Matthew 28:18–20; Luke 24:44–49). YEC does not do that, and frankly, neither do OEC zealots. Both are intrusions into the text.

Since he didn't return as expected, Jesus' followers documented his life and teachings so future generations may know *what* the gospel is, *preach it,* and instruct new disciples on the life and teachings of Jesus. YEC was not in their vocabulary. Nothing in the Old Testament could address the advent of the Messiah in two separate stages, and after announcing a New Creation, a literal interpretation of Genesis could only offer less.

Note, however, the following collective statement by YE Reform scholars about their mission:

> May this [book] help to convince many to believe, proclaim, and defend the truth of Genesis 1–11. This is no arcane debate over trivial matters. Instead, it is all about glorifying the Creator's name... and strengthening His Church for the purpose of bringing to salvation many sinners from every tribe and tongue and people and nation.[469]

---

467. Ken Ham, "The Necessity for Believing in Six Literal Days," December 1, 1995, AiG website.

468. Mike Riddle, "The Gospel," April 1, 2010, AiG website. This article starts out minimizing the importance of YEC for the Gospel. Yet, Riddle ends with the statement that "the Gospel begins with Genesis." He means the Gospel begins with a literal six days in Genesis.

469. *Coming to Grips with Genesis*, p. 21.

The abrupt insistence that "this is no arcane debate over trivial matters" makes one think this may be an *arcane debate over trivial matters.* Otherwise, it might go without saying. So what do these YE scholars say Christians should "*believe, proclaim, and defend?*" The gospel? Nothing so orthodox. They say we should "believe, proclaim, and defend Genesis 1–11." And why? "For the purpose of bringing to salvation many sinners." Really? That's how we bring many people to salvation?—preaching a literal Genesis 1-11. This "mission reassignment surgery" in YEC is not the Great Commission but the "*great omission.*"

The Genesis 1–11 mission is the sole property of YEC; it is unique in the annals of Christendom.

Ask any Christian about the one thing they should believe, proclaim, and defend. They would not hesitate to answer, "The Gospel." Paul said, "The word is near you; it is in your mouth and in your heart," that is, the word of faith that we proclaim" (Romans 10:8). Christ is that Word of saving faith that we should proclaim. Mixing anything else with him is the definition of compromise.

As participants in a new creation, we are to be "fruitful and multiply and fill the earth," not by spreading genes (as in Genesis) nor by spreading the good news of a literal Genesis but by spreading the Gospel of Jesus Christ for a *new kind of creation.* He is the Word, the "seed" sown for eternal life.

Note the parable of the sower and the seed from the NKJV:

Therefore hear the parable of the sower: When anyone hears the word of the kingdom, and *does not understand it,* then the wicked one comes and snatches away what was sown in his heart. This is he who received seed *by the wayside.*

The devil is not the primary problem; misunderstanding is. Those who don't have understanding end up on "the wayside." They lose their way with the word, which is the Gospel with all its implications. "But he who received seed on the good ground is he who hears the word *and understands it,* who indeed bears fruit and produces: some a hundredfold, some sixty, some thirty."

The seed is *the word,* and the word is the Gospel. The word that historical Christianity preaches is not Genesis 1–11, flood geology, or even biblical authority. Jesus did not say, "Preach the very first verse," but "*Preach the Gospel to all nations...even to the ends of the earth*" (Matthew 8:18; Acts 1:8). This call to action in the world is the new creation equivalent to "Be fruitful and multiply and fill the earth" because it multiplies reborn children of God. Nothing is here about proclaiming Genesis 1–11 to the whole world. Proclaiming Jesus's Gospel is the point of the Bible.

The Gospel is, in fact, the eternal, inerrant, and Holy Word of God in the world.

The Bible is critically important because it contains the Gospel and provides a meaningful context for understanding its implications and the mandate to proclaim it. What value might the Bible have if it did not include the Gospel with Jesus's life and teachings? That would be the Hebrew Bible without the life and teachings of Jesus; its value may still be considerable, but considerably less, and a small portion of the Hebrew Bible, Genesis 1, is comparatively less than that, since many places throughout the Scripture speak more significantly of Creation (see Psalm 104:5-30; John 1:1-14). Additionally, *the seventh day of creation is the only day explicitly referred to again in scripture and revealed as an eternal seventh day (Hebrews 3-4:9).*

Genesis 1–11 is like an introductory montage of primeval events, understood throughout the ANE but reinterpreted in ancient Israel. Genesis is a beginning, *not an end.* Genesis did not reveal nor declare the realities we know in Jesus. It was not time for that. Promising a Messiah would be confusing at the time of Israel's covenant at Sinai since they had just experienced a deliverer in Moses, not to mention Yahweh Himself saved and ruled them.

The Hebrew tribes descended from Abraham were recently set free from centuries of slavery. They needed food, shelter, clothing, and a home. They needed a clear identity and to feel safe. The Israelites needed a tradition that united them to Yahweh and a cultural narrative tying them to each other that made sense in the Late Bronze Age. Thus the covenant at Sinai.

Six literal days have never been a *feature* of the Gospel, evangelism, or theology in any Christian community before the YE Reform Movement began in the 1920s. The Seventh-day Adventism of George McCready Price and Ellen G. White laid the foundation for today's YEC (see chapter 27). But the SDAs divided their affections between YEC and the two distinctives most important to them—seventh-day Sabbath-keeping and prophecies about the Second Coming (Adventism).

But there is a more critical distinction to be made.

Contrary to YE notions, the *beginning* of YEC *did not* originate with the first theologians that believed the earth was young. There was no "Young Earth Creationism." Early theologians did not have the same YEC presuppositions, claims, and assertions we have seen, nor did suspicion and conspiracy theories weigh them down. Likewise, they did not know modern science and ANE literature, which would have made a difference in determining the literal versus figurative understanding of the six days in Genesis.

YErs confuse their *theological system* with the simple idea that the earth is thousands of years old. No theologian of the past thought that taking the six days in Genesis figuratively compromised the faith, called God a liar, or any other excessive claims in YEC. They were not obsessive or part of a *movement* for the "belief in thousands of years." And that was when most people believed the universe was eternally old.

According to YE evangelist Mark Riddle, the Gospel of Jesus of Nazareth *begins* with the six literal days in Genesis. However, Genesis 1 is theology and *cosmology* in the *old covenant* tradition, while John 1 is theology and cosmology in the *new covenant* tradition; Jesus is *explicitly* the point in John. There was no Jesus of Nazareth until the Incarnation. The sin problem presents itself in Genesis, but the solution (the Incarnation) was to come later. New covenant theology has its roots in the Old Testament when it says things like this: "'The days are coming,' declares the Lord, 'when I will make a *new covenant* with the people of Israel'" (Jeremiah 31:31–34). Nevertheless, Jesus of Nazareth gets credited for articulating and proclaiming *his Gospel*, not from "the very first verse" but *for the very first time.*

Therefore, giving Moses credit for introducing the Gospel of Jesus is absurd.[470]

The Gospel is about Jesus, not solar days, animals with eternal life, curses, vegetarianism, genealogies, or flood geology. YErs know this in theory but are ambiguous in practice. New Testament theology emerges from Old Testament theology like a butterfly from the chrysalis. Both the butterfly and the New Testament transcend their predecessors.

At no time does the butterfly long to be the caterpillar.

The Good News about a new creation *began* with the union of divinity and humanity in Christ. As "Let there be light" was the first creative act in the first creation; *"Let there be the Light"* in the Incarnation was the first creative act for a New Creation (John 1:4–5). John 1 trumps Genesis 1 as the new creation trumps the old. Therefore, according to Mark 1:1, the *beginning* of the Gospel that Christians preach is the ministry of Jesus. This distinction has never been disputed or even unclear in the history of Christianity until the YEC Reform Movement.

Imagine if Jesus *began* his Gospel with six literal days.

The AiG website links articles to Mike Riddle's assertion. It does so with ten *essential* things Christian creationists *must know* that caught my eye. So what are the ten necessary things every creationist *"must know?"* Note that they *begin* with six literal days:

Ten Basics *Every* Creationist *Must Know*:

1. Six Literal Days.

2. Radiometric Dating.

3. Variety Within Created Kinds.

4. The uniqueness of Man.

5. Distant Starlight.

6. Global Flood.

---

470. My experience as a Gentile Christian proclaiming Jewish Christianity to other Gentiles makes this point more striking (see Preface).

7. Dinosaurs on the Ark.

8. One Race.

9. Suffering and Death.

10. The Gospel.

You have seen test questions asking which item does not belong on a list. Here is a perfect example. The first nine "must-knows" belong to YEC only, while the tenth (the odd one out) belongs to something else—Christianity. Once again, the Gospel appears as an afterthought in YE literature. The author seems to slip the Gospel into his list so people won't wonder about YEC's affections.

Here are 10 things *Christians* "must-know:"

1. In the beginning, was the Word (Logos).

2. The Word was with God and was God.

3. All things were made *by* Him and *for* Him.

4. Humans are in His image.

5. Jesus Christ is the Word made human: a union of divinity and humanity.

6. Ultimately, the Gospel is the union of *all* humanity and divinity made possible by the personification of that union, Jesus Christ.

7. The Word that the Church must proclaim is the Gospel.

8. The Church (Christ's body) enjoys union with God now but is waiting for a comprehensive union at the consummation.

9. Christ will transform all universes into one New Universe (dimension).

10. There will be a Judgment.

Other variations of this list are possible and valid. But none contain anything about YEC.

Young Earth *"Missionary Trips"*

[Genesis 1-11] is the foundation of the Gospel.
—Terry Mortensen[471]

And this gospel of the kingdom will be preached in the whole world as a testimony to all nations, and then the end will come.
—Matthew 24:14

An absurd example of "mission reassignment" among YErs is when YE evangelists like Terry Mortensen embark on a *"missionary journey."* The

---

471. Dr. Terry Mortenson, "William Lane Craig's Mytho-History vs. Historical Genesis," December 19, 2020, AiG website.

question is not whether his trip was a missionary journey, but on what mission was it? It turns out that Terry Mortensen's mission is preaching the "truth" of a literal Genesis. His purpose is to evangelize Christians to YEC and "reform the Church."

The attempt happened recently.

In a telling article about Mortensen's "missionary trip" to Russia, we have this heading: "For eleven days [we] had the privilege of presenting the *truths of [YEC]* in Russia, a huge country of 11 time zones and 140 million people."

Mortensen writes:

There were a few key Christian leaders who were influenced by the [YE] messages. Several American missionaries who believe Genesis in *a straight-forward way were* strengthened to see its foundational importance—and their need to influence others to see this. A couple of missionaries who are *compromised on the idea of millions of years* were challenged to rethink their position, and it appeared that some lights were going on in their heads as I spoke. The manager of a large Christian bookstore began to see the importance of this subject as a result of my visit; he will now carry some creationist books in his store.

Also, the pastor who leads all the Baptist churches in a million-people region of Siberia (three time zones east of Moscow) heard me speak on the *foundational importance of Genesis,* and he would now like to have me come and speak in their area in the future. He said there is a great need for this message in Siberia.[472]

Mortensen found a gold mine for converting Christians to YEC as "lights were going off in their heads as he spoke."

In language that mimics the book of Acts, Mortensen parts with Acts by altering the apostle's *mission* during his unorthodox *"missionary trip."* Here is how the book of Acts describes a missionary journey of a Christian evangelist:

They *preached the gospel* in that city and won a large number of disciples...and when they had *preached the word* in Perga, they went down to Attalia. From Attalia they sailed back to Antioch, where they had been *committed to the grace of God* for the work they had now completed. (Acts 14:21–27)

Mortensen continues:

God has used [our] persistent faithfulness to teach many others and to open several doors for me to minister... Pray that they will be able to

---

472. Dr. Terry Mortensen, "Proclaiming the Truth in Russia... From the Very First Verse," May 20, 2006, AiG website.

spread the message of the truth and importance of Genesis to impact the Church and to lead many to the Savior.[473]

But repentance and faith move people to the Savior, not the YE *"importance of Genesis."*

Like early Christian evangelists in Acts, Mortensen believes God opened "doors," not for proclaiming the Gospel but for proclaiming the good news of YEC. That is not Christian evangelism; it is *marketing* a nonessential distinctive by speeches and selling books.

Many Christians know the word *evangelism* comes from the Greek *euangelion*—a noun meaning a *good news announcement*. To *evangelize* is a verb meaning to proclaim the Good News. An evangelist spreads the Gospel. A Christian missionary trip is like a concert tour for preaching the Gospel throughout a region from one city to another; it is not about opening doors for understanding the "importance of Genesis" in Mortensen's supposed *"straightforward way."*

Compare Paul on his missionary journeys: "And pray for us, too, that God may open a door...so that we may *proclaim the mystery of Christ*, for which I am in chains" (Colossians 4:3). One can hardly imagine Terry Mortensen carried off in chains over the "dangerous" idea of an earth six-thousand-years-old. The sobering reality is that real Christian missionaries are being murdered every day in several countries for preaching the Gospel, which is a genuine threat to tyrants.[474]

"The mystery of Christ," as Paul put it, is not preaching a creative angle on flood geology. The mission is to proclaim the Gospel of the Incarnate Christ and the new creation he brings, clearly, without additives. Mixing the Gospel with nonessentials dilutes it.

We've seen YErs practically say that a young earth interpretation of Genesis is the key to the Gospel. Of course, they deny this, which you would expect and hope is true, but they do so ambiguously. They make the statements that we have seen: "the Gospel falls apart" or "the message of the cross is destroyed" if the earth is old, and that we should *"believe, proclaim, and defend* the truth of Genesis 1–11...*to bring to salvation many sinners."* They go on missionary trips explicitly to push YEC. They are on record, and the record is long.

Notice again how "unnecessarily necessary" YEC is to salvation, the Gospel, and Christianity by revisiting this:

[An old earth] creates an insurmountable problem regarding the Gospel... As soon as Christians allow for death, suffering, and disease [of animals]

---

473. Ibid.

474. Jayson Casper, "The Top 50 Countries Where It's Hardest to Be a Christian," *Christianity Today*, January 15, 2020.

before sin, then the whole foundations of the message of the Cross and the Atonement *have been destroyed*. The doctrine of original sin, then, is totally undermined.[475]

Does that statement sound like YEC is irrelevant to the Gospel? According to this statement, "Christ and the Atonement" are *not* the foundation for YEC (of course, it isn't)—YEC is the foundation of the Cross and the Atonement. Notice carefully, without YEC, "*the whole foundations of the message of the Cross and the Atonement have been destroyed.*" Here, AiG's lesser accusations of "compromising" and "undermining" the faith are not strong enough. An old earth does not simply compromise the Gospel for these YErs; it "*destroys*" it. This theology has no precedence in Church history. It is, in fact, nonsensical.

The YE Reform Movement has undermined the Christian Mission since Christianity is the reform movement, and the Gospel is its vanguard. It needs no other. Diluting is compromising. When the world thinks defeating YEC is the same as defeating Christianity, it brings shame to the Church, and its Mission is damaged. On the contrary, it is a privilege to be persecuted for the Gospel's sake.

YErs insist their nonessential is *the key* to bringing the culture into Christianity. How can *the key* be nonessential? Are not keys essential to locks? Without a doubt, YEC is central to the brand of Christianity for YErs and is the key to only one thing: the existence of YErs. What would happen if organizations like AiG, CRI, and IRC stopped emphasizing YEC? Would the purity of the Gospel keep them afloat? Would people look to them for spiritual understanding or guidance? The tie that binds them is the "Gospel of YEC." YEC theology is why these organizations exist, so they are, by definition, "YE Evangelists" for their creation gospel.

Notice what follows the above list of ten "must-knows" in the article:

Creation evangelism...is not just for pastors and evangelists; it's for everyone, old and young alike. Perhaps you might want to try one of these [must knows] to reach people with the truth of God's Word from the *very first verse.*[476]

This confusion is an example of mixing the Gospel with personal opinions to the point where it bears no resemblance to the Apostles' preaching in the New Testament. The earth's age does not help spread the Gospel, and the Church's Mission is not about "the very first verse." Of course, teaching the theology of the book of Genesis has its place in discipleship training, the classroom,

---

475. Dr. Terry Mortensen, "Proclaiming the Truth in Russia... From the Very First Verse," May 20, 2006, AiG website.

476. "Creation Evangelism—from A to Z," September 19, 2006, AiG website. The article implies that the Gospel is "the truth of God's word from the very first verse." The Bible is not the Gospel. The Bible contains the Gospel, explicitly in the New Testament. The Gospel is not literalizing whatever portions of the Bible preoccupy us.

biblical studies, sermons, etc. However, YEC has no place as a competitor or the vanguard of the Gospel.

The truth is that accepting a young earth or even believing there is a God is not the same as following Him or experiencing a genuine faith in Christ. Adam and Eve were acutely aware of God, who cared for them in an ideal setting. They had every advantage, and according to YEC, the first humans believed the earth was only *six days old*. The only God they knew was the Creator. They experienced His presence. Despite this, humans went astray right away.

Humans go astray under the best circumstances. That is not the "good news" in Genesis; it is bad news *from* Genesis, especially its early chapters when the spread of evil was unstoppable until the flood. Moreover, the Old Testament holds no clear *promise* of eternal life. The Good News we know today, hinted at by the prophets, was first introduced by Jesus (Mark 1:1).

Christians would agree; real faith in Christ defines a Christian. Think of it; you can be a YEr and not Christian; there are Jewish and Muslim YErs. But you are a Christian if you believe the Gospel of Jesus without being a YEr, which is the case for many believers. That alone illustrates YEC's nonessential character. Therefore, a literal Genesis cannot be *"the beginning of* the Gospel of Jesus." Instead, Mark states the obvious—the Gospel of Jesus began with Jesus.

On his journey to Corinth, Paul "knew nothing but Christ and him crucified" (1 Corinthians 2:2) while missionaries for a young earth like Terry Mortensen *focused* on YEC and flood geology. Trusting God in Christ is how conversion *begins*. Accepting opinions regarding the universe's age is not *the Way,* nor is it *on the way.*

The Logos that created everything became incarnate as a man with many signs and wonders. He rose from the dead and ascended to the right hand of God (Ephesians 1:19). Yet only about 120 committed followers assembled after Christ's death (Acts 1:15). If divine wisdom with signs and wonders did not reform that culture, a six-thousand-year-old universe has no hope. YEC repels more unbelievers than it can attract. That does not prove YEC is wrong; it does show it is not the key to reforming the world. What eventually changed the culture of the Roman Empire? It was the spread of the Gospel, in the Spirit, proclaiming the resurrected Christ with authentic missionary trips, and only secondarily, speaking out against *real* evils, not *pseudo* evils.

Christ is Creator. Pinning a YE or OE label on him is an indignity. Jesus was not a Republican or Democrat, Catholic, Orthodox, Protestant, Evangelical, or Fundamentalist—all humanly designed. Christianity has never led its evangelistic efforts with six literal days. YErs do. I have noted that YErs will admit YEC's relative insignificance *vis-à-vis* the Gospel, salvation, or when others challenge them or when their zeal reaches embarrassing levels.

Ham assured his followers about the unessential nature of his distinctive with this emphatic statement:

Numerous [scriptures] could be cited but *not one of them* states in any way that a person has to believe in a young earth or universe to be saved... Many great men of God who are now with the Lord have believed in an old earth... *Scripture plainly teaches that salvation is conditioned upon faith in Christ, with no requirement* for what one believes about the age of the earth or universe.[477]

So in trying to clarify the YEr position on the Gospel, Ham says, *"Many great men of God"* did not accept YEC, that there is *"no requirement"* on the earth's age for salvation or the Gospel.[478] However, later in the same article, we read: *"All biblical doctrines, including the gospel itself, are ultimately rooted"* in Genesis or *"from the very first verse."* The word *ultimately* intends to muddle the thought by softening the word *rooted* but fails to soften it since *all biblical doctrines* are not rooted in a *literalized* Genesis (YEC).

Ham asks, "Does the Gospel *Depend* on a Young Earth?" and gives his first answer: "Scripture plainly teaches that salvation is conditioned upon faith in Christ, *with no requirement for what one believes about the age of the earth or universe."* So the reader assumes the answer is an unambiguous "no." But Ham's final answer states that the Gospel is "ultimately *rooted in,"* meaning eventually "controlled by" or *"ultimately depends on"* a literal six days.

YErs think that human sin in Genesis leads to the need for a Savior is the same as a literal six days leading to the need for a savior. In reality, the lessons in Genesis and YEC have nothing to do with each other.

So Ham's answer to the question "Does the Gospel Depend on a Young Earth?" is *no* but "ultimately" *yes*. This equivocation is on the thinnest thread from "Genesis," as he understands it, to the Gospel. Ham muddies the water when he connects the earth's age with the theological importance of Genesis (and the Gospel) as if they are synonymous. What connects Genesis to the rest of the Bible is not the earth's age or animal-eternal life; it is not even that God created the universe. Many places throughout scripture tell us God is Creator, especially John 1, which is independent of Genesis and arguably the ultimate revelation on creation.

The real connection between Genesis and the rest of the Bible is God's self-disclosure begins there and runs through the life of Abraham and his descendants. It is (to use Ham's phrase) *"ultimately rooted"* in the son of Jesse. Paul quoted Isaiah saying: "There shall be *a root* of Jesse; And He who shall rise to reign over the [Nations], In Him the [Nations] shall hope" (Romans 15:12). Isaiah and Paul connect Jesus with the "root of Jesse" not because of Genesis but

477. Ken Ham, "Does the Gospel Depend on a Young Earth?" November 10, 2013, AiG website.

478. In reality, very few Christians have been Young Earth Creationists because the modern system of YEC is much more than the belief in a young earth. It is also the things we have been citing that depart from historical Christianity, especially regarding the nature of God, the purposes of the Bible and the Mission of the Church.

from the Incarnation demonstrated by the resurrection and ascension of Jesus into heaven.

YErs assume that it always means six literal days whenever the Bible refers to Genesis or creation. For example, note how AiG tries to make the connection:

> Who delivered us out of the authority *of* darkness and transferred *us* into the kingdom *of* the Son...in Whom we have the redemption, the forgiveness *of* sins—The Son Is The Preeminent Head of All Creation, *Because* He Created All Things ... Who is *the* image *of* the invisible God, *the* firstborn *of* all creation, *because* all *things* were created by Him in the heavens and on the earth, the visible *things* and the invisible *things*— whether thrones or lordships or rulers or authorities. All *things* have been created through Him and for Him. And He Himself is before all *things,* and all *things* have existence in Him. (Colossians 1:13–17, DLNT)

Ham then writes, "Thus, the doctrine of creation [by that he means YEC] is vital to an understanding of the Gospel." [479]

However, this verse is not about YEC, OEC, or even Genesis. Instead, Paul *identifies* Christ in two ways: Creator and "the image of the invisible God," to justify him as the one able to save the world "*by him and for him.*" These verses are about *who,* not *how* or *what.* Note that the tense of the passage is current, not the past, as Paul concludes that right now, "*all things have existence in Him.*" Nothing can exist, on its own, apart from God. That is Logos. It does not refer to, let alone establish, YEC. The personhood of Christ again takes a backseat to the YE Reform Movement in YEC.

Furthermore, Colossians 1:13-17 reflects the Bible's purposes—God's self-disclosure in Christ, *who was before the creation*—all things exist by him and for him. The age of the earth is irrelevant, and so is animal-eternal-life, genealogies, and flood geology. Whenever YErs see the word "creation" in scripture, they try to smuggle in YEC into the mainstream "doctrine of creation," as if YEC is that doctrine.

Very few people of faith have been Young Earth Creationists because YEC is not only about the earth's age. It includes the presuppositions and claims, such as God lied if the earth is old, that animals had eternal life, that dinosaurs were on the Ark, or that it is the key to all biblical doctrine, and now YErs say the Gospel is "ultimately rooted in YEC." The theological system of YEC, with its presuppositions and claims, is foreign to historical Christianity (see chapter 1, subtitle, "Presuppositions and Claims").

Ham recently uttered some fire and brimstone at William Lane Craig regarding Craig's book *"In Quest of the Historical Adam,"* saying that Craig "will have to give an account to God [in the Judgement] for his blatant compromise

---

479. Ken Ham, "What Is the Gospel?" July 1, 2002, Last Featured January 2, 2016 at AiG website, and *Why Won't They Listen?*

of God's word and for leading many astray." Craig acknowledged that his work is his opinion but an educated one.

As an academic, Craig expects critique, preferably in peer-reviewed studies, to point out any error in his work and not simply attack him personally. Peer-reviewed studies are not what Ham does. He made no effort to engage in analysis. He only harangued. Craig did not lash back but appeared to take the condemnation soberly, then welcomed critiques of his work, hopefully without *ad hominem*. That is what genuine scholars do; they welcome peer reviews because the pursuit of truth is the point. Qualified reviews can help everyone involved develop a clearer understanding.

YE leaders must sometimes qualify their position on the Gospel because of their judgmental posture, often with the *"Repent or face the Judgment"* routine. But one cannot be a "great man of faith" while compromising it, nor would a great woman of faith be an *"enemy of biblical authority."* Neither does the "God is a liar" mantra circulate among great persons of faith, yet it does among YErs.

Here is the thing: If we can't specify what difference a belief makes to a Christian's relationship with God, then that belief is insignificant. As William James said, it has no *"pragmatic criterion of truth."*[480]

YErs appear ambivalent on the relevance of YEC to our personal relationship with God because it is more legalistic than devotional.

And isn't our relationship with God what Christianity is all about? Yet, nothing changes in the Young Earth Reform Movement; its primary mission remains YEC. "Creation Gospel" and "creation evangelism" mix theological fabrics. "Creation Gospel" is not the Gospel. It is sloganeering.

Preaching the Gospel does not require avoiding every subject that is not essential to salvation. That's impossible. The Gospel is often presented juxtaposed against real evils in the world that need confronting such as totalitarianism in the culture like 1930's Germany, and moral issues: slavery, decadence, moral relativism, genuine bigotry, child molestation of all types, persecution of the Church, etc., etc., not differences of opinion on the age of the earth. This means not confusing essentials for salvation and human flourishing, with any distinctive that captivates a group.

The Apostles' preaching identifies Jesus as the Incarnate Son and things about his life: his death for all evils, his resurrection, and the inauguration of a new kind of world. Ultimately, the Gospel is about how God fulfills His plan, the union of all things to Himself through Christ.

---

480. Peter Kreeft, *Socrates' Children: The 100 Greatest Philosophers, Volume II: Medieval Philosophers* (St. Augustine Press, South Bend Indiana, 2019), Kindle edition, location 274.

36.
COMING TO CHRIST AND
A LITERAL GENESIS

On the AiG website, we read, "Understanding the foundational aspects of *the gospel in Genesis* is a vital *key* to unlock a powerful method of evangelism to reach the world for Christ." Consider the words "foundational aspects of the Gospel in Genesis."

"Foundational aspects" blurs the rest of the phrase *"the Gospel in Genesis."* Since sin entered in Genesis, the world needs forgiveness, and since the Gospel is about forgiveness, Genesis is fundamentally about the Gospel according to YEC.

But identifying a need does not supply the solution.

Is there any doubt this YE phrase: "The foundational aspects of the Gospel in Genesis" means preaching YEC evidenced by their YE missionary trips? YEC is all about six literal days, six thousand years ago, based on their presuppositions and claims. For YErs, it is not Genesis but the YE literalized version of Genesis (including animal-eternal-life, literal magic trees, talking serpents, and casting curses) that are the "foundational aspects" of the Gospel.

What would it say about a new believer's faith if they needed to accept six literal days, six thousand years ago, before turning to Christ? That would be backward. To believe in a literal Genesis, one already assumes belief in the God of Genesis—*Not the God who wrote Genesis, but the one it reveals.* Only after believing in God could they also accept the New Testament that gives us the actual Gospel of Jesus. These two steps are necessary for the *third step* in converting to YEC—embracing a literalization of Genesis. But if one's faith in the first two steps is authentic, namely genuine belief in God and the Gospel, what need is there for the third? So why evangelize that way at all? Why fasten a millstone around the neck of proselytes with a dubious nonessential, presuming it would be easier to convince them of Christ?

Christ-centered evangelism would not be very different in a young earth world.

The many centuries of evangelism before the modern era attests to that. For two millennia, the Church preached Christ in a world that believed the universe was not just old but that *it always existed*—that it had no beginning—a greater challenge to defeat since it was the dominant view until the 1960s. The relevant point for our issues came from Judaism and Christianity that said "the universe had a beginning because someone created it," which is what Genesis

1:1 states explicitly: "God created the Heavens and the Earth," but Moses does not add the "when."[481]

Today, most people agree with Christianity on the critical point in cosmology, the once-radical view that the universe had a beginning. Ironically, now atheist physicists routinely refer to the beginning as *"creation."* That was not true before discovering the Big Bang. Creation implies a beginning. Stephen Hawking himself said as long as the universe had a beginning, there remains the possibility of a creator. Of course, it doesn't take a Stephen Hawking to figure that out. Yet YErs assert that the Big Bang denies the Creator, which is backward since *the one thing the Big Bang does deny is YEC.*

I realize YErs are not open to mainstream scientific discoveries and empirical data associated with the universe's beginning. Even so, the standard Big Bang model has more in common with Genesis than the previous science that assumed a universe eternal in the past. It is odd for the Big Bang to be part of a conspiracy against Genesis. It was a Catholic priest, mathematician, astronomer, and cosmologist named Georges Lemaître who first formulated the modern Big-Bang theory when, *in the 1920s,* he wrote that the universe began in a rapid expansion of a small primeval "super-atom."[482]

The fact is many atheists would prefer that the Big Bang never happened. The universe is infinitely younger than they ever thought, not to mention that a beginning for everything from nothing is problematic for an atheist. That is why they scramble to find something they can *call nothing,* such as the multiverse. At least things are going in the right direction if you are a YEr. It is misguided to think people will believe in God and become Christians if they first accept the earth is young. The reverse is true. They would have to first believe in God, then the Bible, then Jesus, and after that become Christians who accept six literal

---

481. It may come as a surprise that some theologians believe the creation of the universe does not necessitate a beginning, that it could have been eternal in the past yet still created, i.e., "eternally created." The Cappadocian Fathers to Aquinas said creation is about *existence*, not the succession of physical states. In other words, even if the universe has always existed, the miracle is in its existence or the state of existing that must be given. Whether the universe had a beginning or not, its existence must be upheld by necessary existence since the universe is a bundle of contingent things and all contingencies are, by definition, necessarily dependent on something for their existence. Therefore, the first contingent thing to exist depended on necessary being. Even so, theologians generally accept the beginning of the universe.

482. Lemaître was a "Belgian priest...and professor of physics at the Catholic University of Louvain. He was the first to identify that the recession of nearby galaxies can be explained by a theory of an expanding universe which was observationally confirmed soon afterwards by Edwin Hubble. He was the first to develop what is commonly known as Hubble's law, but since 2018 was officially renamed the Hubble–Lemaître law, and made the first estimation of what is now called the Hubble constant, *which he published in 1927*, two years before Hubble's article. Lemaître also proposed what later became known as the 'Big Bang theory' of the origin of the universe, initially calling it the *'hypothesis of the primeval atom.'"* See article "Georges Lemaître," *Wikipedia*.

days, six thousand years ago (or similar sequence)—the weak link in this chain is obvious.

One may wonder if the Gospel is compelling enough for YErs. The focus of evangelism should be Jesus' words:

> This is what is written: The Messiah will suffer and rise from the dead on the third day, and repentance for the forgiveness of sins will be preached in his name to all nations, beginning at Jerusalem. You are witnesses of these things" (Luke 24:46–48).

That is not the focus of YEC, which crowds Jesus' Gospel.

Evangelizing people into YEC before or when they accept Christ adds a burden never practiced in Church history. For critical thinkers, accepting YEC is an impossible barrier to the Gospel. It is not just that there is no empirical evidence for a young earth; its that all existing evidence is to the contrary. That indicates that we are dealing with absurdity. Under those conditions, a critical thinker would conclude that it is meaningless to "examine evidence" that doesn't exist. Realistically, YE evangelism can turn atheists, agnostics, and other unbelievers away from the Gospel because *a six-thousand-year-old universe is harder to believe than the existence of God!*

YEC is an unnecessary obstacle to faith for countless people. It is also a potential path to a crisis of faith if a YEr eventually sees the universe's deep age. Diehard YErs might believe that God lied to them. They already admit the possibility. That results from misunderstanding the Bible's purposes, which warps a group's central mission.

The Gospel can withstand scientific theories irrelevant to the Gospel, and accepting Christ is not merely a cognitive exercise in replacing dating methods with Bible verses or "creation science." Rebirth is an *internal* spiritual union with God; it is a mystery. It is not about accepting information on flood geology or animal death; dinosaurs on the Ark will not help. It is the internal presence of Christ that unbelievers must receive after hearing the Gospel, and not YE opinions about a nonessential distinctive.

On the Answers in Genesis website, Ken Ham recounts an extraordinary dialogue with a newly baptized woman who did not understand that the Gospel indeed depends on YEC. In a piece entitled "What Is the Gospel?" Ham writes:

> She didn't want to admit that without Genesis, she could not answer the question [what is sin?]. *Because the meaning of anything is dependent on its origin, you could not define sin without referring to the literal event of the Fall in Genesis. The literal rebellion of Adam,* as recorded in Genesis, is the foundation necessary to understand *the meaning of sin.*[483] (emphasis mine)

---

483. Ken Ham, "What Is the Gospel?" Last featured on January 2, 2016, on AiG website.

Note the word *dependent*. Here, repentance is dependent on a literal Genesis. This incident with a new convert reveals Ham's answer to the previous question: "Does the Gospel *Depend* on a Young Earth?" According to Ham, if a proselyte is not a YEr, they will not know the meaning of sin. How then could they turn to God in repentance?

This woman was a new Christian, and this is how Ham witnesses to her?

Ham's priorities inform her that to "truly" repent of sin, she would have to accept his literal interpretation of Genesis. But the literal transgression of Adam and Eve was eating a piece of fruit that imparted knowledge. Is that the ultimate definition of sin? Is it any definition at all? A specific sin is not a definition. It is an act. You can see how literalism can lead to legalism.

Was simply eating the literal fruit equal to *literal rebellion,* as Ham indicates, or is there symbolism in the story? The trees themselves were symbolic (literal trees are not morally good or evil, nor do they impart knowledge or eternal life), and so was the fruit. Even consuming the fruit was symbolic of sin since Jesus said eating something cannot defile a person (Mark 7:18–20). Eating unclean foods symbolized ritual defilement in the temple under the old covenant. Eating pork cannot spiritually defile a human being. Neither can eating the wrong thing be the defining example of sin. Applying defilement to food is old covenant and ANE thinking. The story illustrates that humanity did not embrace God but went separate ways.

All sins, then and now, illustrate separation from God; therefore, Ham's innovative theology on "genuine repentance" breaks down. The Holy Spirit convicts one of sin unto repentance; YEC has nothing to do with it. To declare otherwise is heresy.

Ham says we must know the two trees as a literal incident to understand what Jesus did. But unfortunately, Ham trips on a fallacy unknowingly, namely, "the meaning of anything is dependent on its origin." That commits *the Genetic Fallacy,* which assumes that how something originated dictates its present meaning or relevance:

> The genetic fallacy (also known as the fallacy of origins) is based solely on...a thing's history, origin, or source rather than its current meaning or context. This overlooks any difference to be found in the present situation... The fallacy, therefore, fails to assess [a] claim on its [current] merit.[484]

This fundamental fallacy Ken Ham makes shows people everywhere, including some in YE circles, that Ham is incompetent as an exegete. Ham's fallacy does not consider how the meaning of sin developed over time and how context and changes in covenants with different obligations cast new light on

---

484. *"Genetic Fallacy," Wikipedia. See also Ted Honderich, ed., The Oxford Companion to Philosophy (Oxford University Press, 1995),* ISBN 978-0-19-866132-0.

the meaning of sin and righteousness. Christians mainly consider the New Testament refinements on the meaning of right and wrong that Jesus brought— "If you lust after a woman you commit adultery in your heart."

Jesus is our standard, not the writings of Moses.

Ham's blunder is a strange one. He means that one cannot know what sin is without embracing YEC. That is a grave departure from historical Christianity. Unfortunately, Ham tells a woman who put her faith in Christ that she could not do so knowingly unless she accepted things like literal fruit, six literal days, 6000 years, and animal, eternal life.

For YErs, it is not the lesson of Adam and Eve that gives us truth: but whether the details are brute facts. Ham conflates truth in a story with whether the story happened as a set of literal facts when the lessons and factual data are quite capable of being independent of each other. Ham insists that moral and theological truths are dependent on scientific facts too.

The fact is: that while all facts are true, *not all truths are facts.* As stated earlier, Jesus is indeed the "Lamb of God," but that is not a fact since Jesus was human and not, in fact, a lamb. That statement is true in one way (theologically) but false when misunderstood (i.e., literally). *Truth may trump the literary medium that transports it.* Metaphor is more typical of ancient Semitic literature than strictly factual data. The literal definition of words is not the final arbiter of truth:

> The Holy Spirit does not provide an unambiguous interpretation of every given text... we have to interpret what we read. *Interpreting just means making sense of a text*—it is not a special skill reserved for difficult passages. The ways we go about making sense of the Bible will be influenced by our frames of reference and cultural expectations... Keeping in mind the origin of the Bible and overall purpose of Scripture can help orient our expectations as we read.[485]

A nonessential distinctive promoted obsessively will overshadow the Gospel. That is already happening in many Christian communities where their exclusive distinctives and traditions are paramount. Unbelievers get the wrong ideas about Christianity because of this tendency. In his anecdotal example above, Ken Ham imposes his nonessential distinctive upon a new Christian. Lamentably, Ham plants doubt in a new Christian's faith in Christ for the sake of his pet distinctive.

It is a serious thing for a Christian leader to undermine a new Christian's faith by imposing a legalistic nonessential on them. For Christians, accepting creation means accepting the Christian God as Creator. That is all it means

---

485. Biologos.org, Common Questions, *How Should We Interpret the Bible?* Online.

since it is impossible to know how God created everything, especially from nothing.[486]

To accept the so-called "creation *gospel*," one must confess that creation took six literal days several thousand years ago, which is not really about the Creator who transcends time and space; it is about a tradition that has erupted into a strange "reform movement." Worse, the novel "creation gospel" has nothing to do with the actual Gospel of Jesus.

"Creation Gospel" is a meaningless phrase.

Does the Garden story give us the literal "meaning of sin?" If so, sin would be eating real fruit from a natural tree that was off-limits yet curiously planted right in front of Adam and Eve's noses. If it was a "unique tree" that doesn't exist anymore, we could never commit the same sin. Therefore, we are all guiltless of Adam's sin! Here literalism leads to absurdity.

Besides, why create a tree that bears fruit not meant for food? If the tree was off-limits and not intended for food, why plant it? To test the first couple, perhaps? God could test them in any number of ways. This drama of sin in paradise is not science or strict history; it is storytelling with a moral, recognizable in the author's day with its gardens, magical trees, talking serpents, forbidden fruit, and curses—*welcome to the ANE!* The tree was symbolic, and symbolism does not supply Ham's literal meaning.[487]

According to Jesus, nothing that enters a person from the outside defiles him: "Are you so dull?" he asked. "Don't you see that nothing that enters a person from the outside can defile them? [Spiritually, that is]. For it doesn't go into their heart *but into their stomach,* and then out of the body"—the biological truth (Mark 7:18–20). Jesus did not need lessons from Moses on the meaning of sin. If a Christian wants to know what sin is, look to Jesus first, not Moses.

More is going on in Genesis than the *literal words* would indicate. There is no concept of "unclean fruit" in the Bible. It is unlikely the first couple ate from a real *tree* that grows out of seed and soil. Otherwise, we would have to concede that its chemical composition contributed to the fall and, at the same time, increased the cognitive skills of the first humans since *"their eyes were opened."* If the tree was symbolic, we do not know the specific sin they committed. Perhaps the story represents general sinfulness the first humans entered into, such as wanting autonomy from God, or perhaps plain disobedience is the point, which is not a special revelation.

486. For example, many fundamentalists believe God created Adam from literal dust and Eve from the literal rib of Adam and literally breathed into Adam's nostrils. One might reasonably believe all that or creation of humans *from nothing* but cannot believe both.

487. Fruit trees and edible plants were an integral part of everyday life in the ANE. They often served as symbols of good and evil as in the paradisiac story of Dilmun (see chapter 11).

What makes more sense is that Eden warns of sin's *attractiveness* and the *resulting* alienation from God, not the *meaning* of sin. Later biblical authors define sin in much clearer and fuller terms than in Genesis. In ancient Israel, the Sinai covenant was the basis for sin and righteousness, blessings and cursings, with substantial detail (Roman 5:13–14). Throughout the Old Testament, writers define sin as idolatry, disobedience, adultery, abomination, murder, coveting, envy, lust, lying, disrespecting parents and elders, acts contrary to nature, injustice, and on it goes. The sin in Eden was symbolic of one or more of these and other evils.

There are seven deadly sins in Proverbs 6:16–19.

Satan's sin is pride or an extreme sense of self-importance, especially the attempt at actual rebellion to overthrow God (Revelation 12:3–5). When you read the life of Adam and Eve, they do not come across this way as rebels fighting against some "divine patriarchy." Perhaps we might call them rebels. The idyllic setting makes the act seem more senseless. But the general tendency to interpret the first couple's sin shows its metaphorical power to explain man's current relationship with God and creation.

Eve goes on to praise God for her first pregnancy. That is not what you would expect from an insurrectionist. For example, there is no place in scripture where the devil (a real insurrectionist) is thankful or praises God. Adam and Eve raised Abel and Seth, two righteous figures in the Bible. Noah, David, and Jesus were direct descendants, going back to many great patriarchs in Adam. Speaking of fruit, Jesus said an evil tree cannot bear good fruit (Matthew 7:18). Adam and Eve bore some good fruit. They represent humanity, whose *family tree* is both good and evil.

Humanity follows good and evil lines throughout Genesis, as suggested by the tree of good and evil. Unlike Satan, who is never good, Adam and Eve are not presented as rebel agents anywhere in scripture. Instead, Genesis tells us the couple gave birth to two lines of descendants, one righteous, the other wicked. The author illustrates our good and evil character with Abel's descendants, who continued more or less in righteousness while Cain's descendants grew progressively worse.

Instead of being insurrectionists, Adam and Eve were like most of us: a combination of good and evil. Paul said the serpent deceived Eve, but Adam knew better. According to the story, Adam's act could be cowardice or resignation. The author records that sin increased to an alarming rate beyond the first couple's example and primarily along a single line of descendants.

I am not saying that Adam and Eve's disobedience appears minor or what Catholics might call a venial sin. It resulted in a separation from God. *I am saying it is absurd to claim that a literal Genesis gives a new convert the ultimate definition of sin necessary for them to repent and become a Christian.*

According to the literal interpretation of the story, Adam and Eve ate natural fruit from a literal tree that imparts divine knowledge. In what way do YErs expect every Christian to *define* sin accordingly? Beyond simply disobeying a direct command (Romans 5:14). Adam and Eve's sin might suggest the desire for autonomy. Perhaps they wanted more distance from God. They certainly got it. Maybe they were naive, easily fooled. Many have assumed their sin was sexual. However, all this is speculation on a quite vague and dreamlike text, including any *definition of sin*, outside of doing something prohibited. A five-year-old knows this. The wide range of interpretations of the couple's sin shows no clear definition or meaning. The point is that Adam and Eve do not seem interested in leading a rebellion. There wasn't anyone to lead.

Rebellion or insurrection is the language of militants.

According to Jesus, sin is anything contrary to love toward God and neighbor. Jesus defines it:

> "Teacher, which is the greatest commandment in the Law?" Jesus replied: "Love the Lord your God with all your heart and with all your soul and with all your mind. This is the first and greatest commandment. And the second is like it: Love your neighbor as yourself. *All the Law and the Prophets hang on these two commandments.*" (Matthew 22:36–40)

The greatest commands in this central teaching of Jesus do not come from a systematic law code. He does not say anything about eating, and Genesis is not on the table. The love that Jesus refers to finds its best definition in Jesus's life and teachings, not in Mosaic writings. John wrote, "And this is his command: to *believe* in the name of his Son, Jesus Christ, and to love one another as he commanded us" (1 John 3:23). Faith and love are ultimate commands.

The Light of Christ illuminates the meaning of sin most profoundly, especially in the crucifixion, where all the sins of the world are on display by the Romans (a corrupt government), the Jewish Sanhedrin (a corrupt clergy), and the crowd (a corrupt populous) that condemned Jesus. The disciples also lost their faith due to cowardice. Those perpetrators do not represent ethnic groups; they are stand-ins for all of us. The blame is all around. We are participants in the world's sinfulness.

Contrary to the popular myth, Christianity is unlike any other religion that offers various ways to reach God. In Christianity, God reaches down to us. Jesus shows that *systemic* immorality makes God's condescension into this world necessary. *Episodic* sin—or simple behavioral issues such as eating a piece of forbidden fruit or cookies from a cookie jar—can be modified, but a systemic condition of degradation needs an intervention.

The notion that without Genesis 2-3, we cannot define sin is not a Christian idea. It is not even a Jewish idea. The early chapters of Genesis show that the *problem* of evil is acute, but it is not where sin and redemption find their clearest explanation. Above all others, Christians understand sin and its ramifications from the contrasting beauty of the life, teachings, and death of Jesus, not from YEC.

I am spending significant time on this YE idea since it has bruised a new Christian.

The new Adam appears insufficient for comprehending sin among some radical YErs to the point that they will discourage a woman newly converted to Christ. You can see that the YE Reform Movement is not one idea about the age of the earth. Instead, this "reform" babble is a theological perspective that distorts the Christian understanding of the Bible, and the Gospel. It is clear that the woman to whom Ham "witnessed" was doing the witnessing, but he was not open to it, nor did he seem to comprehend it. Can you see how mixing the Gospel with nonessential distinctives corrupts it to the point of abusing a new Christian's faith?

Blessed are Your Eyes

Notice Jesus's words concerning himself in Matthew 13:16–17, "Blessed are your eyes, for they see, and your ears, for they hear. Truly I tell you, many prophets and righteous people longed to see what you see, but did not see it and to hear what you hear, but did not hear it" (NRSV).[488]

Again, this:

In the past, God spoke to our ancestors through the prophets at many times and in various ways, *but in these last days he has spoken to us by his Son*, whom he appointed heir of all things, and through whom also he made the universe. *The Son is the radiance of God's glory and the exact representation of his being, sustaining all things by his powerful word.* (Hebrews 1:1–3; emphasis mine)

These passages show where God's self-disclosure has come, where it is now and is to come. The Incarnation brings into focus all previous revelations in scripture. You can see that God's self-disclosure is the purpose of scripture, not dating the universe. The Logos made human is God's ultimate disclosure that God is capable of union with us; Jesus demonstrates this in his dual nature. As Hebrews says above, the human Christ *"is the radiance of God's glory, the exact representation of his being"* (Hebrews 1:3). *Jesus unites us in his being that is in union with God.* Jesus was not a theophany, and no theophany in the Old Testament was an Incarnation. Jesus Christ was a new creation. The unlimited Logos, the second of the Trinity, is uncreated and continued unchanged after the Incarnation when He took on human nature.

God's purposes are not in the YE six-day, or a six-thousand-year-old adaptation of creation, with the Babylonian numerological twist on the numeral

---

488. Notice the sensory terms Jesus uses: eyes that see and ears that hear; 1 John 1:1 adds, "And our hands have touched." The divine is now thoroughly immanent in Christ.

six. Instead, Genesis is a Hebrew account with the number seven elevated to an overwhelming extent, complete with an eternal seventh-day rest that YErs would just as soon ignore. As we have seen, the seventh day of Creation-week points to God's intention—"a Sabbath rest for the people of God" (see Hebrews 4:9).

YErs curiously avoid a thoughtful analysis of the seventh day. In YEC, a literal Genesis is the foundation of God's plan centered on six days, not seven, though only the seventh day foresees God's plan from what we learned in Hebrews 3-4. The YE creation idea is more Babylonian than Hebrew, though it is probably neither. Creation does not give God's plan purpose. God's plan provides the purpose for creation. The New Testament shows us that the seventh day of Genesis pointed to that purpose. Frankly, YErs overlook the seventh day of Creation because it defeats the literal day theory single-handedly. If the Sabbath does not end, every Hebrew knew neither does the week, meaning the week in Genesis 1 is not literal, despite other words that may give that impression."

The plan of God was still a mystery during the relatively enlightened period of the prophets. That is one reason most Jews missed the Messiah when he came. Paul writes about the mystery:

> The mystery of Christ was not disclosed to people in former generations as it has now been revealed to his holy apostles and prophets by the Spirit... I became a servant of this gospel according to the gift of God's grace...given, to proclaim to the [World] the unfathomable riches of Christ and to enlighten everyone about God's *secret plan—the mystery that has been hidden for ages in God* who has created all things. The purpose of this enlightenment is that through the church the multifaceted wisdom of God *should now be disclosed to the rulers and the authorities in the heavenly realms.* (Ephesians 3:4–11 NEB; emphasis mine)

Therefore, God's plan was:

1. Unknown before Christ.

2. Purposely hidden by God.

3. Planned before creation: i.e., *"before the world began."* (1 Corinthians 2:7 ERV)

In a strange opening to his article, Dr. William Varner asserts, "The Gospel is not something God hid until Jesus came in the flesh." Why does Varner assert this? Because he writes, "After Adam's fall, God shared the seeds of a plan he had already worked out before time began" (Genesis 3:15).[489] Varner's statement is convoluted because "the seeds of a plan" are not the plan; any more

---

489. Dr. William Varna, "Seed of Promise in Genesis 3:15," April 1, 2015; last featured August 14, 2016, Answers in Genesis website.

than seeds are plants; they *anticipate* plants. Varner uses "seed" as a metaphor but interprets it as if "seed" is God's plan.

Literary seeds are hints that anticipate an uncovering. In this case, what Varner calls "the seeds of God's plan" were not recognizable as hints *until Jesus came in the flesh.*" Looking back, we can say that Genesis 3:15 may be an illusion of Christ's coming: "And I will put enmity between you and the woman, and between your offspring and hers; he will crush your head, and you will strike his heel." However, even now, this connection is obscure at best, so scholars are divided on its meaning.

Catholicism interprets Genesis 3:15 as an allegorical reference to Mary, Satan, and Jesus. This obscurity is Varner's so-called "revealing" of God's plan to ancient Israel. Yet, no one claimed this passage referred to the Incarnation until *after* Christ came. Thus, Varner's comments here are inarticulate since all the generations before the Incarnation missed his so-called "reveal."

Varner's naked assertion, that his seed theory "reveals" the plan to incarnate the Son "is not something God hid until Jesus came in the flesh", defies reason. It is also contrary to Paul's explicit statement about "God's secret plan—the mystery that has been hidden for ages in God...that he accomplished in Christ Jesus our Lord" (Ephesians 3:7–11). This Pauline passage is not obscure as Genesis 3:15. It is explicit: a God incarnate Messiah was hidden. Varner uses obscurities to negate explicit statements of scripture like Ephesians 3:7–11, the meaning of which is not controversial.

Peter wrote, "[Christ] was chosen before the creation of the world, but was revealed in these last times for your sake" (1 Peter 1:20). Note that Christ was *revealed in these last days,*" not the first days, or the YE mantra—"from the very first verse." Varner makes the mistake of interpreting an obscure and mysterious passage and then declaring that his thought on it is an obvious fact.

Genesis and the Creation have a crucial place in Christian theology. However, Genesis accounts for the Creation in paleo Hebrew for theological and religious purposes in context with the ANE and covenant Israel. YEC does not add to the essential theology of creation. Of course *Genesis* is important and owns its place, not as science but in the Old Testament canon and theology. YEC does not have such a place. The *system* of YEC is a foreign intrusion into the theology. Therefore, a YEC Reform Movement is unjustified.

The Creation happened; it is fading away, only to become transfigured:

> In the beginning, Lord, you laid the foundations of the earth, and the heavens are the work of your hands. *They will perish,* but you remain; they will all wear out like a garment. You will roll them up like a robe; like a garment they will be changed. But you remain the same, and your years will never end. (Hebrews 1:10–12)

New Testament revelation says the new has come, is coming, and is yet to come, meaning the New Creation is in progress (Revelation 1:8). The first

THE SIX DAY WAR IN CREATIONISM

creation is one step in an infinite number of "steps" toward fulfilling God's ultimate purposes that will unfold throughout eternity.[490]

I have made it plain that a simple belief in a young earth is not the central issue in the SDWC. Let people read their Bibles, hopefully with an open mind, and listen to teachers who have earned the right to teach. The YE "movement," i.e., the "war," is the problem. Some YErs are passionate about reforming the world and Christendom with six literal days and flood geology. But I learned long ago that such ambitions are more fantasy than reality.

---

490. It may not be that the New Testament reveals the ultimate ends of God's plan. The New Testament takes us to a new heavens and new earth in the presence of God who is described as "all in all." How can we possibly know what that means or what God has in store for us beyond that? It is simply not possible to connect a "literal Genesis" to any of this or force an artificial significance of six temporal days onto God's eternal plan and then condemn others for not recognizing a pseudoscience. After all, we are talking about a nonessential.

37.
WHY GOD CREATED THIS WORLD

[God's] intent was that now, through the Church,
the manifold wisdom of God should be made known to
the rulers and authorities *in the heavenly realms.*
—Ephesians 3:10

The short answer to why God created this world is because it holds value to Him. As He said in the beginning—"this is very good." It is extraordinary that the transcendent should value the lowly to this extent: "God so loved the world that he gave His one and only Son" (John 3:16). The Incarnation illustrates the inestimable value of the world and the human race in particular. It was a very good world initially, and it still is, or God would not give His only Son for it.

There is the assumption among the main branches of Christianity of an *ultimate end* to God's plan beyond getting us saved. Our salvation is not an end but a beginning. The final or ultimate reason for our existence suggests our real value and why this world is worth preserving.

In this chapter, I do not claim that the following thoughts are definitive, nor are they the only way to understand God's ultimate purposes that are largely beyond us. Rather, I rely mainly on the NT's language with help from theologians. I do so to show how meaningless the SDWC is.[491]

So why create *this* kind of world?

A material creation like ours holds unique forms of good and beauty (value) that may not present themselves in an immaterial world. It follows that this realm offers outcomes that the Creator desires *in the context of all the other domains He has created or may create.* For example, we identify the beautiful through our senses: sight, sound, smell, touch, and taste. Ideas and mathematical formulas can be beautiful or elegant, reflecting a nonsensory or immaterial side to our nature that would exist in an incorporeal world. However, *sensory* beauty would not exist in a nonsensory world, at least not in the way it exists in a material world. Our world could finally fit into the fuller context of all realms with its capacity to be transformed. All other worlds are in God's view but are mainly opaque to us.

---

491. The language of scripture does not answer all our questions and often creates new ones. Biblical authors record various ways of looking at profound concepts because no single set of words capture everything given our limited capacity to understand. Nonetheless, seeing in part, seems to be sufficient for us as far as God is concerned (1 Corinthians 13:12). It is all we can expect.

Existence in a material world means we cannot experience nonsensory worlds. They are in dimensions that are "offline," we might say. That is why we cannot see or hear those who have passed. Christians believe our bodies decay back into the soil while our immaterial nature *passes* from the material world of sights and sounds to an incorporeal realm.

Since we do not experience the fuller context of all created realms, we are often lost when bad things happen. When we lose someone, people will say, "Heaven needs so and so more than we do," or "It's all part of God's plan." Is everything or every event God's plan? Possibly. God's plan is likely broader than every detail of existence. God built some randomness into this universe that allows some freedom of motion, which provides a context for free will to emerge in rational creatures.

Free will is essential to God's purposes. Yet, while God does not plan or *will* all events, tragedies, and sufferings, no amount of those things can alter God's ultimate plan; in fact, God may use all things in service to His plans: "We know that in all things God works for the good of those who love him, who have been called according to his purpose" (Romans 8:28).

Christians trust there are good reasons why God allows inexplicable things. What appears unexplainable, impossible, or even horrifying, God can resolve easily—that idea is behind the ancient symbolism of God's victory over the "mythical chaos monster" in Psalm 74. This monster is a symbol of the evils in the world that humans cannot control. No matter how invincible evil seems, God will crush it. Consequently, our kind of world necessitates faith or confidence in God in addition to our faculty of reason that provides a platform for faith.

Faith is evidence of things not *seen* (Hebrews 11:1). This verse is a highly philosophical and theological statement. God is the great *unseen*. Augustine said, "Faith is believing what you do not see; its reward is to see what you've believed." In other words, faith is a kind of vision for "seeing" the invisible God sustaining our sensory universe (Hebrews 11:27). God is not perceptible without faith. The atheist looks at the universe and concludes God is not possible, while faith enables us to reason that without God the universe is not possible.[492]

"Faith involves placing trust in what you have reason to believe is true"— J.P, Moreland. The importance placed on faith was a unique and visionary hallmark in Christian thought from the start, based on reason and evidence (Hebrews 11:1).

Trust is not much to ask of the creature by an all-knowing Creator. The Incarnation justifies our trust in Him, though the world seems to betray us or

---

492. The irony is the multiverse that atheists depend on to counter creation from nothing is not only without evidence; there can be no evidence forthcoming. The leading physicists, Roger Penrose and Stephen Weinberg, have made that clear.

we betray ourselves. Our kind also betrayed him. Nonetheless, because this world remains valuable to God, things will work out in the end. After experiencing the risen Christ, Paul could confidently say, "All things work for good" (Romans 8:28).

God created a world where bad things, even the unspeakable, *can* happen when humans separate themselves from Him. An idyllic world depends on the Creator's *active presence*. He does not force Himself on us. Humanity can choose between good and evil, to live outside the Garden or inside. God, in effect, asked humans, "What would you like, a paradise with Me, or the outside world to yourself?" According to Genesis, we took the outside world, so here we are. Like spoiled children that run away from home and need rescuing, God had a plan for that eventuality.

Most Christians believe God did not intend our world to function well without His full participation.[493] Therefore, as the Garden story illustrates, there will be instability when we separate ourselves from God. I believe the ancient Hebrews expressed instability as "curses" resulting from God withholding His active presence and blessings. In other words, the "curses" are nothing more than the result of God's inaction, not direct action by ruining His creation.[494]

Things have a greater potential to go wrong in a world alienated from God. "Curses" do not mean that God damaged anything. God is not a warlock, or like Endora in *Bewitched*, who often cursed Darrin for being human, or like a spoiled child who breaks things when he does not get his way. God does not behave this way. A well-ordered world requires God's full engagement; as Genesis 1 indicates, *"it was very good."* Yet, God does not allow anything that thwarts His plan. He did not create a universe with that possibility. The human race apparently wanted distance from God, and we got it.

Again, Paul said, "God's *intent* was to *reveal* His wisdom to the heavenly realm *through the Church*" (Ephesians 3:10). Stop for a moment. What reveal? What *wisdom of God* did the heavenly realm receive that involved the Church? Christ and His Church are the spiritual or internal rebirth of a new creation. The Incarnation began a chain of events that will lead to a metamorphosis of all created realms. In our beginning, God created a temporal universe as a "seed" that will give birth to a new universe like Paul's concept of the resurrected body, where our physical bodies are like "seeds" that will birth glorified bodies (1 Corinthians 15:35–44).

Ephesians 3:10 means Christ incarnate highlights God's wisdom in creating this kind of world capable of being redeemed (shown in the Church) despite its fall. The spiritual realm appears to have experienced a limited fall in

---

493. Christianity has rejected Deism and determinism, historically, despite the tendencies toward Deism in the Newtonian world of the American founders.

494. See Deuteronomy chapters 11, 27, and 28 for the blessings and curses in Israel.

that a minority turned away from God. Nonetheless, a divine/human redeemer can reach down and bring back a fallen world like ours. That reveals God's wisdom to the spiritual realm in creating this realm as He did—free to choose but redeemable should we make wrong choices. This wisdom is how the Jewish Christian Rabbi named Paul interpreted the Christ events.

After the fall, the human condition may have left spiritual beings wondering about this world's fate. It fell entirely. Was it worth creating?[495] Spiritual beings are not omniscient. So Paul indicates that the Incarnation and the new creation (begun in the Church) revealed God's wisdom to spiritual beings. See Paul's words again: "God intended that now, *through the Church*, the manifold wisdom of God should be made known to the rulers and authorities *in the heavenly realms.*"

The Church is the result of the Incarnation. This "manifold wisdom" is not a simple thing. The angelic realm may have been unprepared for the capacity God gave humans for repentance, faith, renewal, redemption, and the surprising way He provides it. The solution found in the Incarnation revealed the *full extent of God's love*, which was a revelation to spiritual beings, too, as Francis W. Beare, and Theodore O. Wegel wrote:

> Can it have been a marvel, as [Ephesians 3:10] suggests, *to the principalities and powers in the heavenly realm?* [RSV] It may strike us as mythological speculation, yet it expresses a deep insight. Man the sinner, the prodigal son forgiven and returned to a father's arms, *knows a love of God which even angels may not know.* (emphasis mine)[496]

This world's value is in the extent of God's love that can operate in it, which has been a revelation to all realms. No doubt, an endless array of surprises awaits us.

Humans seem to be born fallen though some Christians disagree with that idea. I think Paul is saying that the Grace of God in the Incarnation and its results "reveal [God's] manifold wisdom to the heavenly realm."

No created being, human or otherwise, can know all God's intentions. The Incarnation brings all realms "up to speed." The Incarnation reveals the nature of God: (triune), the purposes of the Bible: God's self-disclosure culminating in Christ, and the Church's mission: to preach Christ, no matter the earth's age.

But why create worlds with the potential for unrestrained evil?[497]

---

495. One Jewish tradition states that it would be better if God never created this world. Of course, they did not know Jesus.

496. Francis W. Beare, Theodore O. Wegel, *The Epistle to Ephesians: Introduction, Exegesis and Exposition, The Interpreter's Bible in Twelve Volumes, Volume 10* (Abington Press, Nashville, 1984), p. 672.

497. It's worth considering that God has restrained evil more that it appears.

YErs insist that God created a *perfect* world.[498] The claim that the universe was perfect until we ruined it is in serious doubt. Do perfect things come with *latent* imperfections? Were Adam and Eve perfect until they sinned as if perfection could expire? Indeed, Adam and Eve were not perfect the way the glorified saints shall be. In the New Testament, being made perfect is permanent: "For by one sacrifice he has *made perfect forever* those who are being made holy" (Hebrews 10:14; emphasis mine).

It is likely that God created us *for* perfection, not *in* perfection, because we are not sculptures. We need an *internal formation* that can only occur after our initial creation. If God created a perfect race, He would have accomplished His plan already, we could not have fallen, and we would not be where we are. If we understand it correctly, the created spiritual realm was imperfect, too, in that one-third of the angels may have revolted before the rest received their finished perfection (Revelation 12:4).[499] Nevertheless, the righteous angels now seem to possess angelic perfection obtained at some point. However, we cannot be sure about this with limited and obscure information.

Instead of allowing chaos in the heavenly realm, God "cast" the devil and his demons to the earth (Revelation 12:9; 2 Peter 2:4; 1 John 3:8). This idea is apocalyptic and likely symbolic. We fell from grace; they fell from heaven like heaven was a cosmic Garden of Eden. God banished the fallen angels to earth and exiled Adam and Eve to the wilderness.

What do we make of this?

We can deduce that a perfect world with perfect creatures created by fiat is not what we see in either realm. We know what happened in ours. We did not fall from perfection; we fell from grace; that is, we fell from an original position of favor with God that would have *led to perfection* without so much evil and suffering. Genesis indicates that human sin complicated matters, so our behavior required a needed discipline before God would continue perfecting us. The world now needed redemption that eventually came with Jesus. Perhaps Adam and Eve may not have sinned if they had let God perfect them, or it may be that sin is the imperfection of an incomplete creature or an unfinished creative work of God. We can't be sure of all our explanations:

An unfinished creative work has not been brought to a completed state. Its creator may have chosen not to finish it, [due to] circumstances... Such

---

498. The KJV uses the word *perfect* as in "be perfect as your father in heaven is perfect" but at the time of King James English, *perfect* meant "mature." Humans should be all a human ought to be that God intended, not all that God is. How to define perfection in glory is unknown, except that we cannot fall from it.

499. Revelation 12:4 is highly symbolic. The fraction one-third is used throughout the book of Revelation, indicating it may not be literal or that a significant minority of angels rebelled.

[works] are often the subject of speculation as to what the finished piece would have been like had the original creator completed the work.[500]

Unlike human artisans whose lifeless subjects have no say in their refining, choosing from the tree of life symbolized embracing God's finishing work in humanity. Michelangelo's rough outline of David on the unfinished marble slab could say nothing. God gives his rational subjects a choice for the finished product because perfection in a rational being necessitates free will, and free will needs choices. God's purpose is to finish all creation by drawing all realms to Himself.

What does "draw all realms to Himself" mean? Unfortunately, we cannot be sure.

The Bible's words for it are *glorification, transfiguration*, and "union with God." Glorification is oneness or union with God set in motion by the divine-human Jesus. Glory means reflecting the gift of divine nature, in which humans will more fully participate. So Peter wrote, "He gave us the very great and precious promises. [So that] With these gifts you can share in [partake of] the divine nature, which enables us to live forever" (2 Peter 1:4 EXB). The result is an ontological transformation or a kind of metamorphosis.[501]

God shares His glory by infusing value into us with Himself. Beyond that, we cannot say very much about union with God. It is incomprehensible in the current state of our being and may always be so. According to Paul, "No human mind has conceived the things God has prepared for those who love him" (1 Corinthians 2:9).

J. I. Packer described God's purposes when he wrote:

"Heaven and earth will, *in some unimaginable way,* be re-made. His servants shall serve him: and they shall see his face...and they shall reign forever and ever" (Rev. 22:3–5). This is the plan of God, says the Bible. *It cannot be thwarted by human sin, because human sin itself is taken up into it, and defiance of God's revealed will is used by God for the furtherance of His will for events.* [502] (emphasis mine)

Packer is simply repeating New Testament language in Hebrew idiom ("servants," seeing "his face," "reign," etc.) in recapping God's plan without really comprehending it, for Packer says this change comes "*in some unimaginable way.*" It is essential to face the purposes of God with humility. Instead, *some* fundamentalists know everything from the age of the earth to who is going

---

500. See "Unfinished Creative Work," *Wikipedia.*

501. In Matthew 17:2, it says Jesus was "transfigured." The Greek word is *metamorphoo.* It simply means "change in form."

502. J. I. Packer, *The Plan of God (Annotated),* permissions@fig-books.com, Kindle Edition, location 79.

to hell. They have scripture and verse, and that is all they want. We all are in for surprises.

God does not seem to want a "perfect" world *by fiat*. Such a world would merely parrot its creator's wishes. It would be Deism's mechanical world: determined, without free will, but with robotic causes and effects, and worse—artificial intelligence. Our current age is the first to appreciate AI. There is a creepiness in robots, especially the more sophisticated ones that appear alive until some odd behavior in their eyes or voice betrays them.

We were made incomplete without union with God. It is a given that rational creatures possessing free agency will fall unless they fully embrace God, like a five-year-old attempting a two-wheeler without parental support. A union between God and humans would have led to the whole creation, both heaven and earth, becoming one—the best possible world—which God intended from the beginning.

Adam and Eve did not choose union with God offered with the seventh-day imagery and symbolized by the tree of life. It is reasonable to assume that rational creatures must *consent* to the Creator's intentions before enjoying peace with God through a union. Consent or acceptance of God's offer must be on His terms, or perfecting is "halted."

Creatures do not set conditions for their Creator. The Cherubim that blocked the tree of life illustrates this. We cannot take eternal life for ourselves. It must be by contract or agreement, aka a covenant. A contract between Creator and created is gracious since creators have dictatorial rights over their creations.

That many angels did not fall is an example of this consent to perfecting grace (see 1 Timothy 5:21). For creation to possess a perfection corresponding to its nature, God has made a creation capable of receiving God's infusion. God's "pouring out" is an analogy that theologians have used for centuries.[503]

What does "*pour Himself into creation*" mean? The question is problematic because it is about a mystery described by an analogy, and answering it is necessary with another analogy like a "dance." What does any of this mean? Today, God upholds the creation by *sustaining* its existence. That is His *minimal* participation. If God could be bored, minimal participation would cause it. God intends to participate in a complete living union with all things in the warm *embrace* like a free-flowing "dance" might suggest.

God places such importance on free will that He allows horrific evil and risks rejection for its sake. The most persuasive argument against God is the argument from evil. Rejection of God in a world like this is a real possibility. Nonetheless, the *Argument from Evil* is weak logically but potent psychologically. If people love us, we expect them to stop our suffering if they can. God is

---

503. One example is St. Francis De Sales who said, "Therefore, God willed it for His sake, *to pour Himself out into creation.*"

rarely interested in immediate relief, though the availability of pain medications and anesthesia is not coincidental. God is in it for the infinitely long haul. Love risks rejection. It does not impose itself but wants the other to be free to love or not to love. That is necessary for love to be genuine (1 Corinthians 13:4–7).

Everything in this world is derivative, with the *possible* exception of free will. Free will is, by definition, self-generating. It must be *of the person*, uniquely expressed by each. Free will makes us personal and worth relating to. When relations are free and rich, dynamic and harmonious, there is delight that some compare to a free-flowing dance. *Flow* in dance means *"continuity of move-ment."* Motion is said to be free-flowing when energy is released freely and ably between two persons in dance. In that sense, union with God is like a free-flow-ing dance between souls.

The human *freedom* that God intends ultimately requires a state we have not yet received.

Our *will* needs harmony with the Creator's will to be ultimately free. Our free will is for turning toward God. God designed us that way, so there is no getting around it; it would be insane to try. In Jesus, the divine will became one with human will, with no loss of human freedom or alteration of the divine will. How can this be? We believe that the Logos *became* everything that makes us human: mind, body, soul, and spirit, including the will. We might say the Logos existed in two dimensions— infinite, timeless, without the universe as the Logos in heaven; and finite, in time, and within the universe as the human Jesus. Jesus still had divine nature and will, but he submitted them to his human nature.[504] Jesus endured testing and temptation in all things like any of us: He was *tempted in every way, just as we are—yet he did not sin"* (Hebrews 4:15). Jesus was free to choose. Therefore, Jesus's humanity was not a contrivance.

Jesus demonstrated all that a human should be. Of course, a human can-not possess perfection as Jesus does. We could never be equal to Jesus, the "first-born" who is both divine and human by nature. *Our nature*, our soul, will always be completely human. Though we *reflect* the divine, we can participate in the divine, but we cannot *generate* divinity as Jesus does. Any divine nature radiat-ing in us is the glorified Christ sharing our consciousness. That is infusion—the divine pouring out—the free-flowing dance, etc.

This ultimate relationship with the divine awaiting us is why we and our world exist and why it is very good. Jesus will "transform our *lowly* bodies so that they will be like his glorious body" (Philippians 3:21). Our bodies are mortal by nature; they die. Other translations describe our current body as lower, humble,

---

504. Some believe Jesus of Nazareth was omniscient because he was God. However, Jesus was God made human. It may not be accurate to say Jesus was omniscient any more than he was omnipresent. He was human and so the Logos voluntarily submitted to human limitation as Jesus on earth. The infinite Logos continued to be transcendent, omniscient, omnipotent, and omnipresent, etc., in heaven.

weak, vulnerable, vile, dying, earthy, a humiliation, i.e., compared to our destiny. All those bodily references can be summed up by the word *mortal*; bodies decay. Contrary to YEC, animals were never any different in this respect.

Atheists criticizing God because they discovered weakness and flaws in the human body are shortsighted. We are unfinished. That would be like nit-picking on an embryo for not being a fully functioning human. God is refining the human person through rebirth and will transform our bodies and all universes into a New Universe. That is the Christian hope. Mortal things degenerate; *they are temporary.* Perfection is coming. *It is permanent.*

We shall receive a body like Christ's glorified body with an incorruptible nature.

Paul wrote, "We are transfigured by the Spirit of the Lord in ever-increasing splendor (glory) into his own image" (2 Corinthians 3:18 PHI). God's self-disclosure is inexhaustible. His infinite beauty and attributes guarantee His *continuous* self-disclosure throughout eternity. The more transformed we become, the more Christ radiates in us, and our union with God is more intimate. The complement is also true; the more intimate our union with God, the more transformed we become. Where all of this is going, we cannot know.

Our ultimate end is unending ultimately.

38.
A WORLD WHERE GOOD CAN RESPOND TO EVIL

We live in a world of good *and* evil. Perhaps that is what the author of Genesis assumed by the tree of good and evil. Maybe he meant to say the world is more evil than good. Whatever the case, we experience both. Jesus said, "Though you are evil, [you] know how to give good gifts to your children" (Luke 11:13). This verse may be hyperbole or an overstatement like we saw earlier. Perhaps Jesus meant, "Though you are evil *by comparison* to God, you also give good gifts to your children as He does. How much more then will God give you good gifts?"

While evil does not produce good ("an evil tree cannot bear good fruit"), good can be a response to it. The freedom to choose good and evil can create higher moral value than forced or contrived good. If one manufactures a robot that always follows its programming, it is a "good" robot, mechanically speaking. But there are no *moral* robots. Robots are contrived, artificial "persons," meaning they are not persons at all but machines. Good forced upon or programmed into us would be of little value to an all-wise, absolute, or all-loving one.[505]

There are also unique and intricate goods that could only emerge as a response to evil. Contrast is illuminating; sharp contrast is most illuminating. It follows that some of the highest goods might be a response to the worst atrocities. There are countless stories of profound good and virtue found in concentration camps during WWII or the gulags of the Soviet Union.

The Greeks taught that courage is a primary virtue upon which other virtues depend. A coward is less likely to be virtuous in other ways when tested. Yet, the primary virtue of courage does not exercise itself without danger or risk of facing various types of evil. "Patience" is also a virtue. How much patience will we need in glory? What about "perseverance?" These are virtues for a world of good and evil. The best example of good responding to evil is the life, death, and resurrection of Jesus, who met all evil in the world with a demonstration of the highest good—the full extent of God's love. Ultimate good overcomes all evil (Romans 12:21).

When tragedy makes its way into the news, no matter how horrible, there are often heroes of extraordinary selflessness. Most are ordinary people that renew our hope for humanity. The Charleston, South Carolina Church massacre of nine African Americans in 2015 saw a remarkable response by the surviving members of Emanuel African Methodist Episcopal Church when without hesitation were ready to forgive the murderer collectively. While many

---

505. That is why the debate between free will and determinism in Christian thought is important.

people could not comprehend the gesture, those Christians were clearly on the side of good.

The point is that unique goods often emerge from tragedy, so our fund of knowledge about good and evil increases. Could it be that the more we understand good and evil, the better we know God: God said, *"The man has now become like one of us, knowing good and evil"* (Genesis 3:22). That tree is still with us.

At times evil appears to "want" good to exercise itself. An extreme example is when serial killers want law enforcement to catch them or are relieved when caught. Their conscience wears them out. Confession really is good for the soul.

The cross was God's direct response to all the unchecked evil in creation. The judgment will settle matters. The cross was an act of God's judgment on sin and a monumental act of grace for the sinner (Colossians 2:13–15). Sin, death, suffering, and injustice cannot overcome the good because the source of all good is infinite. A redeemable creation capable of union with God is suitable for fulfilling God's purposes. He made it that way. We cannot, nor do we need to comprehend everything about this. The cross gives us enough to justify trusting God for all outcomes.

The passion of Jesus at the cross reveals the seriousness of evil, but more importantly, it discloses the full extent of God's love, which is the point of redemptive history. Divine love is the answer to everything. "All you need *is* love" if it is divine love. It covers a multitude of sins (1 Peter 4:8).

Divine Love in this universe is sacrificial. The Greek word for this kind of love is *agape*. Many practicing Christians know this Greek word. Agape is giving the self for the sake of others. The Passion disclosed the full extent of divine love, and a universe like ours was necessary for the Passion of Christ to be valuable. There could be no value in a Passion where evil and sin do not exist. And if the cross was *not* the only possible way to save the world, as many theologians have speculated, choosing the Passion becomes more revealing about *divine agape*.

A material world like this inevitably deteriorates, not because it is cursed but because it is temporal. Conditions in this world are changing toward some end. Even in biological evolution, there is a drive toward a developed outcome and randomness that appears intentional. Beginnings imply ends. *There is a telos to world history and an eschaton to salvation history*:

> If anyone builds on this foundation using gold, silver, costly stones, wood, hay or straw, their work will be shown for what it is, because the Day [of judgment] will bring it to light. It will be revealed with fire, and the fire will test the quality of each person's work. If what has been built survives, the builder will receive a reward. If it is burned up, the builder will suffer loss yet will be saved—even though only as one escaping through the flames. (1 Corinthians 3:12–15)

Of course, we sometimes experience evil and suffering for no apparent good, though there may be some imperceptible good. In Christianity, the permanent value of free will outweighs any temporal suffering in this life because the rewards lead to a superior life in eternity. Paul wrote, "I consider that our present sufferings are not worth comparing with the glory that will be revealed in us" (Romans 8:18). God selects evil and suffering for elimination once any usefulness expires (Romans 8:18; Revelation 21:4).

We might ask, "Why create a world with the potential of evil and suffering only to eliminate evil and suffering?" Besides the importance of free will, another reason to allow evil is that *experiencing* what is contrary to God is also contrary to our own self-interest and not merely taking God's advice to avoid it, which we appear unwilling to do anyway. Knowledge plus experience is most convincing. In any case, Adam and Eve did not take God's advice. They chose the hard way by experiencing evil. Their story tells us that our wills should be compatible with God's. He should know; He designed us. But a person's will needs to be free, or it is not that person's will; therefore, allowing evil is worth the risk.

The universe seems governed by laws and cyclical processes, from the orbit of planets to particles and probability waves in atoms. There are spiral galaxies, seasons of the year, and the cycle of life and death in a temporal world. Destructive forces like volcanos can form landscapes and islands of spectacular beauty with ecosystems suitable for countless life forms. Entropy guarantees that the universe's general trajectory will lead to destruction if God does nothing about it. Then the universe will "give itself up" to an integrated new heavens and earth, and our bodies shall give way to imperishable ones.[506] And the death of this universe will give way to a new realm permeated by God.

We believe the end will be a new beginning. Actually, every end is a beginning. Every sunset is a sunrise. Things come and go, giving rise to new things. Stars implode, and new ones form. Supernovas form a myriad of new stars, and galaxies collide, creating greater ones. Living things die and then nourish new life. We understand and accept this kind of (call it) *"sacrificial"* process for plants, animals, and inanimate objects because nature imposes it upon them.

But we are different.

When a human sacrifices the self, it is a matter of conscience—a moral choice that may reflect divine love, which is surprisingly suitable, even integral for life in our world. Sacrificial love is not the only form of love that God generates, but according to Jesus, it is the highest love *we can generate* (John 15:13). Our art and music often reflect a love that is *all in* "forever and a day." In popular

---

506. In 1 Corinthians 15:36–44, Paul likens our bodies to seeds that must first die to give rise to an imperishable body.

music, a song like *Bridge over Troubled Waters* is a powerful lyric with the line *"I will lay me down."* The rest of nature lacks this kind of choice.

Nature participates instinctively in a sacrificial world according to its design.

Since an essential expression of God's nature is sacrificial love (1 John 4:8), His creation would reflect a similar love that corresponds in kind. The highest demonstration of this love in this world is the cross of Jesus. As God's imagers, humans can reflect sacrificial love to a higher degree than the rest of nature because reason enables moral choices, and faith calls it to action.[507]

Most things in nature spend themselves to serve other purposes. Not consciously but by design. Destroyed matter changes in form, creating new things out of the destruction. Like it or not, predation is a natural part of the universe. That is self-evident. The sacrifices exhibited in nature, say a prey animal's life spent for the life of the predator and its offspring, help regulate the balance in a temporal ecosystem.

A bizarre example is the male counterpart to the black widow that voluntarily roles over (almost eagerly) after mating, only to be consumed by his soon-to-be "widow." That kind of "sacrifice" is not conscious and, therefore, not of the same value as agape reflected in humans. If the black widow is evidence of a curse, it is an unnecessary and extraordinary one that says much more about its Creator than the loss of *"spider, eternal life,"* asserted by YEC.

We tend to anthropomorphize animals as we do God. We project the horror of a person eaten alive onto the deer taken down by wolves or a falcon plucking and eating a dove while alive. It "feels" wrong because we intuitively project ourselves into the scene with the human capacity for empathy. It is a mistake to conflate the nature of humans with the nature of God or animals. These are three distinct natures with attributes unique to each.

Yet, a grizzly bear feasting on salmon about to spawn does not evoke the same horror. Perhaps the overwhelming number of salmon swimming at once or the lack of blood and their watery existence sufficiently detach us from the drama. They do not appear to suffer much. These salmon were already on a path to die anyway, so what is the big deal? Yet spawning has not always occurred when the grizzly feasts on them. The eggs end up as dessert. The salmon's entire life's purpose is overtly sacrificial for both a new generation of salmon and grizzly. How better for the grizzly to store sufficient energy to survive hibernation?

What is happening?

---

507. There is more to say on why evil exists. An afterlife goes a long way to resolve the problem of evil. But my intention is not to resolve the question of evil but to say, contrary to YEC, that a "very good" universe can allow evil and suffering for morally sufficient reasons, some of which may be unknowable.

We have humanized the deer but less so the salmon without justification. The deer is a mammal, and so are we. But more than that, the deer is Bambi—a humanized innocent. Salmon that sacrifice themselves to birth new life while sustaining bears and other creatures are remarkable examples of "imitation agape" by a lower animal. We respect salmon for their sacrifice and endurance. They are amazing. But to suggest that the life cycle of salmon is proof of a curse suggests something less inspiring than the salmon.

The more a creature has corresponding similarities to ourselves, the stronger the feeling of kinship and horror upon perceived suffering. The Asian delicacy of eating monkey brains "on the half skull" is especially nauseating to most westerners even when the chef dispatches the monkey "humanely" in advance, though not always done. It feels like cannibalism. Association and suggestion, not reality, condition us that way.

Knowing that does not help much.

The wild has its own set of "mores" (the law of the jungle) quite apart from ours. Animals lack the depth of conscience we have—we are more intentional. We intend. Intentionality is necessary for moral decisions. Animals do not choose between good and evil; they choose between eating or starving, living or dying, raising offspring, or dying out. Therefore, we do not *properly* refer to wildlife in terms meant for humans, such as having eternal life or losing eternal life due to human sin or expressing empathy. Many experiences in the animal kingdom are, more appropriately, analogous but not the same as ours.

It is mistaken when YErs refer to creation as perfect in a moral or absolute sense. Perfection cannot exist in an ever-changing world since any change would spoil perfection. We need a different term if we are not talking about absolute perfection in creation. Why not use *the biblical phrase* "very good" or "excellent," "beautiful," or "well-ordered?" These are relative terms appropriate for a changing world—this world.

The YE presupposition that the world was perfect is fatal to the YE case, particularly when it insists that perfection requires that all living creatures be total vegetarians. Who knows how many microbial creatures inhabit every vegetable and how many larvae are in shelled nuts humans and animals consume daily? There happens to be a whole world of living beings in a single drop of water resting on a rose petal. Is water cursed too? There is nothing moral about vegetables. Even vegetation can be carnivorous, and not only the Venus flytrap.[508]

There are good reasons why a human might choose self-sacrifice—even sacrifices that are responses to evil—to save a life or multiple lives of family, friends, strangers, or even enemies. One may sacrifice the self for an *ideal* greater than the self. Unlike instinct, this is a moral or ethical decision of a rational mind informed by a standard, though that standard might be unidentifiable or subconscious.

We are the only moral beings of this kind we know in our world. Animals are extraordinary but not in the same category as God's imagers. They can mimic the good. When animals prey on other animals for food, it is not murder, as in *homicide*. Murder and homicide are unique to humans. Terms like that applied to animals are anthropomorphic.

Furthermore, killing is distinct from murder in Christian and Jewish theology and most secular law codes. Murder is unjustified homicide or knowingly killing an innocent. Murder is a sin. Animals kill; they cannot murder because they do not judge innocence or guilt. They do not choose to murder; they need to eat. They do not comprehend death as we do. They understand hunger only goes away by eating. We do too, but we can also choose to fast.

Even the scripture says God provides meat for predators. We saw earlier that *"The lions roar for their prey and seek their food from God"* (Psalm 104:19–21). Job 38:41 says, *"Who provides for the raven his prey when his young ones cry to God and wander about for lack of food."* Of course, God provides for these creatures. He made them and designed them brilliantly as carnivores.[509]

Animals partake of God's provisions.

Animal instinct is not evil; it is *drama*—the natural drama of life and death in a temporal world. Animals can show tenderness to each other and toward their young as much as their nature allows, which is behavioral, not moral. The predator's primary role in an ecosystem is to cull the old or weak, which will soon perish. Their functions are not conscious but instinctive and, therefore, neither moral nor immoral. When animals are hungry, you can see

---

508. The tropical pitcher plant, the genus *Nepenthes*, is different from other carnivorous vegetables in its choice of prey. They prey on lizards, amphibians, and even mammals. The doomed animals are attracted by the plant's sweet-scented nectar, and once they fall into the pitcher shaped "veg-a-beast" digestive tract, digestion can take as long as two months. About 150 *Nepenthes* species are scattered around the world. There are carnivorous plants in the fossil record dating to some 40 million years ago. See the article, "Meet 12 Carnivorous Plants That Eat Everything from Insects to Mammals" by Bob Strauss, the ThoughtCo., part of the Dotdash Publishing Family, June 30, 2019, found online.

509. I reject the notion that Satan altered the physiology of creatures converting them to carnivores or that he may have created prehistoric beasts like dinosaurs and the sabretooth tiger. Satan is nowhere credited as a creator and God is said to have created *all things visible and invisible.*

their programming in the hunt; predators do not think about the ecosystem; they are looking for the easiest meal their God-given physiology will provide. Instinct helps ensure prey and predator consistently do their part in the environment. The lack of moral content in animals underscores the profound differences between them and us.

Ever notice that we see very few of the millions of animals that die worldwide yearly? *Nature has accounted for the cleanup.* It is not *"Crime Scene Cleanup"* (CSC). It is the recycling of life in a material world.

Humans marvel at creation, especially animals. But our affections do not change reality. We also have strong attachments to inanimate objects: art, cars, homes, antiques, clothes, etc. We often say we love those things. It is painful if they are damaged. Our affection is magnified with living things because we can relate to them.

Our empathies should be relative to their objects. We apply empathy in descending order according to the worthiness of the subject. For example, we usually empathize less with inanimate objects than with plants, less for plants than animals, and less for animals than humans. The moral value of animals is not how *they* treat each other, which is instinctive and largely contrived by their defining structure. God has made it clear that we are different from animals. The arbitrary YE assertion that animals had eternal life gives them a level of equality with us that is unreasonable, especially considering we never had eternal life. They are less purposeful creatures whose primary role is to serve us and the environment. We serve God. We are more like God than any creature we know.

The *moral value* in animals for persons like ourselves is how we should interact with them. It is *indirect* and *twofold,* as I see it:

First, an animal's moral value to us is in how we, as God's imagers, manage them to uncover their total value. We can exploit or empower them to serve the greater good, including their own. A prime example of both exploitation and empowerment of the wild is the expansion into the American West. Advancing technology played an important role in taming the wilderness to the extent that humans threatened much wildlife. Animals that were abundant such as the buffalo, grizzly bears, wolves, elk, beavers, and turkeys, were disappearing at an alarming rate due to excessive hunting and trapping. By the early twentieth century, a new approach to the wild became the focus—conservation.

We now see that wildlife is not as formidable as it was to the ancients. The wild is no match for humans. Just a hundred years before conservation, people hunted whales to near extinction with primitive technology by today's standards—a point in time caught by Herman Melville in *Moby Dick.*

The animal kingdom is relatively harmless compared to the human family. Today, a single person could send a few armed drones into the woods and wipe out the population in no time. It is silly now to suggest wild animals threaten human or animal flourishing, their design is evil, or they once possessed eternal life (a most preposterous notion). Contrary to Elizabeth Mitchell's harangue, God did know what he was talking about when He evaluated this creation as *very good*.

We now understand all too well that we must find a balance in managing the risks and rewards of integrating the wild. We must manage energy sources as basic as fire and technologies with enormous rewards and acceptable risks. It so happens that God said the same thing in the beginning; we are to subdue the wild, manage it, and not just keep it, but keep it *safe* so it may flourish in a well-ordered world.[510]

Under the right circumstances, you can see how an ideal analogous to Eden might become global if humanity, in cooperation with God, would "dress and keep," i.e., *manage* the entire earth:

> And God blessed them and said to them, "Be fruitful, multiply, and fill the earth, and subdue it [using all its vast resources in the service of God and man]; and have dominion over the fish— of the sea, the birds of the air, and over every living creature that moves upon the earth..." And God saw everything that he had made, and behold, it was very good (suitable, pleasant) *and* he approved it completely. (Genesis 1:28, 31 AMPC)

The prehistoric world is not relevant to God's evaluation of the world of modern humans as "very good" on day six. How could it be? Technically, we did not exist during the first five days, as the story goes. Creation had not reached the point described on day six as "very good." We would not evaluate God's creative skills by the darkened primordial deep. You cannot judge the final product before finished.

The creation is still not finished since it has yet to be perfected. The unfolding nature of a developing creation illustrates why the earth's age is inconsequential to the New Testament's stated Commission of the Church to preach the Gospel of Jesus Christ to the world. The mission is the same no matter the times. Odd presuppositions and bizarre claims on God's nature, the Bible's purposes, and the Gospel have led the YE Reform Movement into *excesses* that all except zealous YErs can see.

Secondly, the animal kingdom's moral worth reveals something about its creator: from the lion's regality to the awesome power of a blue whale (all 180 metric tons of it), from the spirited stallion to the athleticism of a cheetah. Even in the silverback gorilla, there is beauty in the beast. Consider the blessed utility

---

510. Some Christians are so devoted to our duty to the environment they attach it to the Gospel almost like YErs do with the age of the earth. Our passions too easily get in the way of the primary Mission given to us. Teaching stewardship of the earth is about discipleship training (a secondary mission). Listing the duties of a Christian (which are many) is not the point of evangeling unbelievers. Preaching the Gospel is about making believers out of unbelievers by sharing the meaning of the life, death, and mainly the resurrection of Jesus Christ, which inaugurated *a new creation that is superceding the old*.

of animals like cattle, sheep, poultry, and the horse that happens to fit a human perfectly on its back.

Think of the ascetic beauty and delicacy of butterflies, hummingbirds, and the spectacular fireworks of deep-sea creatures that light up the deep like a floating neon garden. In all these can be found hints of the values of God. Humans can create and discover genuine good and beauty in nature that may work toward some end or simply provide an aesthetic reprieve in a world that can be ugly. Flowers are themselves works of art. Besides aesthetic beauty, the cycle of life and life spent for new life plays itself out continually.

Life is a canvas for divine and human compositions in moral and aesthetic beauty in the face of ugliness. God made the world capable of producing the highest good, dazzling beauty, and disturbing evils. That is how the awesome beauty of Yellowstone National Park came from a caldera and the Hawaiian Islands from volcanos. Art's beauty is about contrasts. Darkness displays the light: "In him was the light of all mankind. The light shines in the darkness, and the darkness has not [apprehended] it" (John 1:4–5). In this world, good is clearest and brightest when juxtaposed against the shadows.

The central question is why this kind of creation exists in the first place—not how old the universe is, why destruction can happen to material things, or whether nature should sacrifice goods for the greater good in a temporal world. The nature of God is perfect and therefore, unchangeable. The nature of this universe is changeability. *Therefore the flaws in this universe are not due to the nature of God, but rather the nature of the universe He chose to create. This world is in constant change and, therefore, imperfect, or unfinished; and so it can be perfected.*

God is the ultimate unchangeable.

God's plan rests in Christ for whom, by whom, and through whom all heaven and earth exists. Through him, perfection *is coming*. Genesis, indeed the Old Testament, did not reveal the mystery revealed to us—the hypostatic union of divinity and humanity that leads to a cosmic union of universes when all darkened shades of evil fade away. The age of the earth is *immaterial* and *inconsequential* to that revelation.[511]

Therefore, YEC is what we said it is: nonessential.

That is a fact.

---

511. The Hypostatic Union is the doctrine of the two natures of Christ in one person—divinity and humanity in one person and what it means to all creation. *This is the mystery, the revelation, and the Word.*

39.
WHY GOD BECAME HUMAN

> The primary reason for the Incarnation is that God might
> communicate Himself outside Himself... The Incarnation is the ultimate
> self-communication of God to man. Therefore, God willed it for
> His sake, to pour Himself out into creation.
> —St. Francis De Sales

> No greater wonder could be accomplished than God should become man.
> —Thomas Aquinas

The Incarnation's *full* implications for God's end purposes have been a subject of intense interest for theologians through the centuries. There are traditions in all branches of Christianity of an ultimate end for humanity.[512] According to St. Francis De Sales, the Incarnation's primary purpose is God's self-communication by pouring Himself into humanity, i.e., a comprehensive union with God.

For Catholics, God's ultimate end is the beatific vision; for the Orthodox, it is theosis or apotheosis; for Reformed Protestants, it's to glorify God and enjoy Him forever. Other traditions suggest various versions of heaven. "Divination" or "deification" are synonyms the Orthodox use for the ultimate destiny of humanity but can be misleading. We share in God's nature through Jesus Christ by an act of grace, not by making our essence the same or equal to God's, which is not possible.[513] Admittedly, all these are rather vague. Can anything more be said about where all this is leading? Enter the Incarnation.

Why did God become human?

Most Christians would say that the Son *had to die* to save the world from sin. One must be mortal to die. Therefore, the Logos, the eternal Son, became Adam's son to save us. "In Adam, all have sinned, and in Adam, all die." The phrase "in Adam" is another way of saying we are of the same nature—earthly and mortal. But Jesus is a new Adam through whom all shall be made alive. He was of heaven and earth, sinless, yet he died. A dying sinless man is contradictory

---

512. It is impossible to know what our final change or the realm we will inhabit shall be like. Most of my language in "Part V" comes from the New Testament, but I do not profess that all that the language implies is knowable.

513. It is impossible for God to do the intricately impossible such as making a finite being infinite or a contingent being a necessary being. Once contingent, always contingent and if necessary, always necessary, in being, that is. The creature cannot be equal to the Creator.

if his death is due to his sin. Therefore, since a perfect man can die, the body's death is natural (see 1 Corinthians 15:42-49).[514]

Jesus is the "Lamb of God," and the empty cross is the iconic symbol of Christianity for good reasons. Jesus's life, death, resurrection, and ascension together have atoning power because God accepted it as such, which is His right. But dying was not the only reason Jesus became human. Suffering and dying proved Jesus's humanity and that his humanity was not a contrivance but an integral part of God's plan.

Becoming human was necessary for the divine plan of uniting heaven and earth to God. God's plan is not only about saving people from their sins. Atonement and a comprehensive union with God is a two-sided coin. Atonement means what the compound word suggests—at-oneness. Jesus became human to "atone" for our sins *in order to "bring together all things both in heaven and on earth:"*

> He has enlightened us to the great mystery *at the center of His will*. With immense pleasure, He laid out His intentions through Jesus, a plan that *will climax* when the time is right *as He returns to create order and unity— both in heaven and on earth*—when all things are brought together under the Anointed's *royal rule*." (Ephesians 1:9–10, The Voice).

Note that God's plan for creation is incomplete until "[Christ] returns to create unity in heaven and earth...when *all things are brought together* under him." The comprehensive union with God merges all realms, including a multi-verse, should it exist. The birth of Christ was a new creative act that conceived a new creation. Various Christian traditions land on one perspective or another on any mystery as we attempt to understand them.

The choice of Incarnation in a *fallen world* meant that death for Jesus was inevitable.

Given the corrupt human heart, it is no extraordinary feat for omni-science to predict what would happen to Jesus. Even humans know blood will flow when a righteous and resolute man confronts debased men who wield power. But death would not prevent the Incarnation; it would aid it because the God/Man is the *only possible means to accomplish a comprehensive union of all things with God.*

It was essential for the Incarnation to proceed unrestricted and without contrivance because it was more about the infusion of life into the world and not simply about dying. Jesus said, *"I have come that you may have life and that you may have it more abundantly"* (John 10:10 KJV). Christ's death is not enough

---

514. It may not be enough to say that the world's sins placed on Jesus is what made it possible for him to die physically. The sins of the world placed on Jesus is a theological truth not a biological cause of death. It is more likely that Jesus could die because his body was mortal like all genuine humans.

for this. Paul said the cross without the resurrection was useless (1 Corinthians 15:17). Useless? Yes, *futile* because then Jesus would have proven to be *only* another dead prophet without divine nature, which does us no good. Christ's dual nature—*the Incarnation itself*—was the point because it was the seed for God's plan for the union of all things to Himself. That is why participating in the new creation must be through Jesus.

God proceeded with the Incarnation despite *all* the dangers that were in waiting. God used those dangers. He was unwilling to prevent the free will actions of corrupt men despite the resulting bloodshed. This was real. No manipulation of events on God's part was necessary. God did not kill Jesus or have him murdered to fulfill biblical prophecy. Humans freely chose to murder Jesus—a perfectly predictable event. What is impressive about the Old Testament prophecies is the manner of death Jesus would endure (see Psalm 22:1, 14–1; Zechariah 12:10) and how long he would be in the grave, i.e., his body would not see corruption: "For Thou dost not leave my soul to Sheol [grave], Nor allowest thy saintly one to see corruption" (Psalm 19:10 YLT).[515]

Through the centuries, some theologians like Aquinas thought that God has the power to declare us saved or forgiven upon repentance alone, as he did with David when he committed adultery with Bathsheba and had her husband, Uriah the Hittite, murdered by an act of treachery. "Then David said to Nathan, 'I have sinned against the Lord.' Nathan replied, *'The Lord has taken away your sin.'* You are not going to die" (2 Samuel 12:13).

God simply removed David's sin and death upon confessing and repenting of heinous sin. God can do this. Later, the Psalmist saw that God was not interested in sacrifice or he would offer it. "You do not delight in sacrifice, or I would bring it; you do not take pleasure in burnt offerings. My sacrifice, O God, is a broken spirit; a broken and contrite heart you, God, will not despise."

Our sins are against God; therefore, He is entitled to forgive as He pleases. He chose a way that demonstrates mercy and justice, and the concept of sacrifice was understandable in the first century, especially in Israel. Genesis tells us that when God wills something, *it is so*. Since that is true of the creation, perhaps it is true of the new creation. In other words, if God said, "Let there be forgiveness," would it be so? With an anthropomorphic vision of God, one might think God *has to* do things a certain way, work things out one step at a time, or form strategies to respond to challenges or execute justice as a legal requirement upon Him. His nature is not like that. No conditions imposed upon God outside

---

515. In ancient Judaism, physical corruption or decay in a dead body was thought to begin after three days, which was also proof of death. In biology, we know organs begin to decompose after the first twenty-four hours, the rest of the body in three to five days. It was by observing outer bodily changes after three to five days that led the ANE to conclude decomposition began after three days. Natural sight (and smell) was what they had. Even so, it appears Jesus was dead for only one day and two nights according to all four gospels.

Himself are possible. So could God have chosen an alternative way to save us other than the death of His Son?

The synoptic Gospels *imply* the answer.

The manner of Jesus's request for another way in the Garden of Gethsemane *suggests* the possibility. In Matthews's account, Jesus says, "*If it were possible*, let this cup pass from me." *It is inconceivable that Jesus wanted to abandon saving the world by passing up the cup.* Jesus likely meant one of two things. If there was another way *possible* to save the world according to:

1. God's *abilities;* or

2. God's *willingness.*

The answer may be in Jesus's next words: "Not as I will, but as *you will.*" Matthew seems to mean, "If it were possible that God might *will another way,*" not that there was no other way. But Matthew is not explicit.

Luke's account does not say, "If it were possible," but "Father, *if you are willing,* take this cup from me; yet not my will, but yours be done" (Luke 22:42). This statement allows for God to choose another way *if He were willing.*

Now notice what Mark says: "Father...*everything is possible for you.* Take this cup from me. Yet not what I will, *but what you will*" (Mark 14:36). The question in all three gospels centers on *God's will,* not His abilities. Mark suggests another way was possible. *"Everything is possible"* with God, but not all choices best communicate God's will or intentions. God *chose* the way; He was not stuck with it. God wanted to convey justice and mercy in the atonement. Sin must be a grave matter to God, and justice can illustrate that gravity to creatures like us since it stresses forgiving a debt or righting a wrong.

Despite Jesus's request, the way chosen *would not change* because it was according to God's will and not because God's abilities were limited. Paul wrote: "the Messiah had to suffer and rise from the dead" (Acts 17:3). God's *decision* was a decisive display of self-disclosure.

Beyond conveying divine mercy and justice, *the cross demonstrates the full extent of God's love.*

Let's face it; saving the world would not be difficult for God to pull off. Nonetheless, to express the fullest extent of His love to unreceptive humans would take something extraordinary—something beyond humanlike justice or mercy. It would take what we are most receptive to—extraordinary love.

The Passion is the maximal revelation of God's love possible in this reality.

The cross expressed God's love with the richest pathos that might move the hearts of fallen humanity. While simply declaring us forgiven upon repentance was God's prerogative, it does not have the same impact on captivating the world. God was willing to put up with the ultimate atrocity—the cross—perpetrated by inferior creatures for the eternal benefit of those same creatures. We have every reason to believe God's choice has been compelling throughout the history of humankind. And since another way could have saved the world, the cross is a divine "extra mile" that further demonstrates the love of God *freely given* to us.

Christ closes the distance between all relationships separated by estrangement and provides the basis for union with God. All this implies purposes for the Incarnation beyond the ability of the Son to die. The main point is his *glorified life*. Romans 5:10 says, "For if when we were enemies we were reconciled to God through the death of His Son, *much more, having been reconciled, we shall be saved by His life.*" In other words, the cross without the resurrection does not save; the resurrected Jesus is necessary to validate who he claimed to be, i.e., not a prophet, but *the Son*. "And if Christ has not been raised, your faith is futile; you are still in your sins" (1 Corinthians 15:7).

The sacrifice of Jesus was a *freewill offering*. Jesus *volunteered* to submit to evil's tyranny: *"No one takes [my life] from me, but I lay it down of my own accord." I have authority to lay it down and authority to take it up again"* (John 10:18). The Logos knew his coming as a man would lead to death without having to force anything. God did not kill Jesus nor have him killed.

Jesus was murdered.

Peter said, "God, following his prearranged plan, *let you use the Roman government to nail him to the cross and murder him"* (Acts 2:23 TLB). This verse may surprise some Christians because they may believe Jesus had to die or God had to make sure it happened. But that would be an unnecessary conspiracy to murder. The cross occurred because humans made the free choice to murder Jesus. God and Jesus were willing to let it happen. *"Letting it happen," not making it happen, is the sacrificial nature of the cross.*[516]

Jesus offered Himself to illustrate that God clears humanity of all charges and clears the way to unite all humanity to divinity. Jesus's death was *self-sacrifice* based on his will and that of the Father. God let it be and accepted it according to a "prearranged plan," as Peter said (Acts 2:23). The idea of a sacrifice applied to the cross is a theological way of saying Jesus fulfilled all mediating efforts of a human priesthood and sacrificial system.

Make no mistake; the sacrifices of Jesus were numerous and real from the moment he became human and freely limited his divine prerogatives. The Incarnation was *primarily* about an infusion into this world of a new kind of life that only a genuine union of God and man could create. Christ's entire life is effectual for salvation. Jesus's sacrifice *began* not at the cross where it was "finished" but at conception. The influential evangelical scholar F. F. Bruce

---

516. Humans were free not to murder Jesus and could have avoided doing so or else the cross would have been a contrivance.

observed, "*His Incarnation itself is viewed as an act of submission to God's will, as such, an anticipation of his submission to that will in death.*"[517]

The Creator became the servant of the created.

That was unthinkable in Judaism, especially in an age when traditions about class distinction, idolatry, and blasphemy were sharp. The Incarnation is a spectacular way to show how valuable we are in God's eyes and why the creation is "very good" even now. God not only became one of us, but He also became our servant to assist us.

> Who, being in the form of God, thought it not robbery to be equal with God: But made himself of no reputation, and took upon himself the form of a servant, and was made in the likeness of men: And being found in fashion as a man, he humbled himself and became obedient unto death, even the death of the cross. (Philippians 2:6–8)

No other theology thinks this way. Other religions give strategies for reaching up to God. In Christianity, God gives up His reputation, power, and status, becoming obedient to his creatures and serving the servant. The Incarnation alone might have been sufficient to save humanity if God was so willing. *But without the cross, the fullest extent of God's love and commitment would not be on display.*

Jesus's whole life, from conception to Ascension, was sacrificial. Jesus shows His love for his bride in startling and unforgettable ways. There is no "until death do us part" because death does not part with Christ. It reconciles and works for good (Romans 8:28). This love is sacrificial because it covers a multitude of sins (1 Peter 4:8).

Christ was always going to free the world from sin, which was His plan before the beginning. Sin has no hope; it never did.[518] God will give us the grace to remain sinless in the glorified state, which completes creation and redemption. However, that is not the ultimate end of God's plan either. God's plan is more than rewarding good people and punishing bad ones. Once transfigured into the glorified state, then what?

No doubt something.

Thomas Aquinas gave five motivations for the Incarnation:

---

517. F. F. Bruce, *The New International Commentary on the New Testament: The Epistle to the Hebrews: With Introduction, Exposition, and Notes* (WM. B. Eerdmans' Publishing Co. Grand Rapids, Michigan, 1990), p. 234.

518. Sin is a theological term that resonates with believers but is lost on many unbelievers today. It has come to mean bad acts. Sin is more than that; it is the condition of sinfulness that only God can "cure." A non-theological term that unbelievers might relate is that of an *unfinished* human being. We are neither finished in mind or body. There is a change coming. It seems we must live out our lives in this world. Genesis shows choosing sinfulness alienates God and stands between God and our perfection. Therefore, God requires that we turn to Him for the finishing. We have failed to do that as a race from the beginning, but now there is great hope in Christ.

1. It illuminates our faith.

2. It strengthens our hope.

3. It inspires our love.

4. It provides us with a model.

5. *It affects union with God.*[519]

Number 5 is the most significant. The Incarnation reveals God's prime motivation in expressing His love—the union of heaven and earth through that personal union, the divine-human Jesus—but it does not explain what such a union would look like except by analogy. To understand a world outside and unlike our own, we must enter it. As John wrote, "Dear friends, now we are children of God, and what we will be *has not yet been made known.* But we know that when Christ appears, *we shall be like him,* for we shall see him as he is" (1 John 3:2). To know a reality is to participate in it.

The essential passages on God's purposes are in the New Testament. Does that mean God did not inspire the Old Testament? No. If the Old Testament were a celestial body, it would be the moon, while the New Testament is the sun. Once the noon sun is at full strength, the moon's light is much less functional but is still there.

Obsessing over the early chapters of the Bible is howling at the moon.

Logos Flesh

May they also be in us...so that they may be one, as we are one, I in them and
you in me, that they may become *completely one.*
—John 17:20–23 (NRSV; emphasis mine)

The Apostle John is known to students of the Bible for his unique theological concepts and phrasing. He gave us "born from above" or "born again," "eat my flesh and drink my blood," the "I am" statements, the Vine and branches, the Bread of Life, and other sayings unique in scripture.

A Greek professor of mine once shared an overlooked subtlety in John 1:14a where its literal translation is "The Logos flesh became." "Flesh" here means human. The word "Logos" and the choice of "flesh" are set side-by-side, for a reason. The phrase even helps visualize the *union* of divinity (Logos) and humanity (flesh) in Jesus. The irony is that in the same Gospel, John states emphatically that *"no one has ever seen God"* (John 1:18).

John was under no illusions. He knew God was incorporeal, but in some way, He became human, and so John says, "That which was *from the beginning, which we have heard,* which *we have seen with our eyes,* which we have looked at and *our hands have touched*—this we proclaim concerning the Word [Logos]

---

519. St. Thomas Aquinas, *Summa Theologiae III*, Q. 1, a. 2, 5.

of life" (1 John 1:1). Note the sensory language—heard, seen, and touched. It would not be necessary to use sensory terms if Jesus was only a man, which would state the obvious. But this Person was "from the beginning." He was the Word, the "Logos of life."

"The Word became flesh" may *imply* the Virgin Birth:

The Virgin birth naturally did not form part of the first cycle of Apostolic teaching. The Apostles bore witness to their own experience and to the growth of their own faith, and they knew Jesus Christ first as a man. Apart from the evidence for the fact, *it has seemed to most Christians in all ages that the idea of a new creative act is naturally associated with the occurrence of the Incarnation.*[520]

The miraculous nature of Jesus's birth in Matthew and Luke and John's statement that the Logos became human are synonymous.

God's self-disclosure reveals Himself in this world as triune:

1. The Father is God transcendent, the planner beyond the universe.

2. The Son, Logos/Word, communicates the divine will and built the universe.

3. The Holy Spirit is God's active presence in the world.

Jesus of Nazareth is the *corporeal presence* of God in the world—"*For in Christ all the fullness of the Deity lives in bodily form*" (Colossians 2:9). In other words, Jesus is God entering time, space, and matter in Galilei. God purposefully created human nature able to accommodate the Incarnation. The Father and the Spirit are not incarnate and do not exist in, nor is their essence of, time, space, or matter. Neither does the second person of the Trinity—the limitless Logos—have His existence in the universe. The Logos entered this space through the hypostatic union with human nature in the New Man Jesus—human within this world while remaining infinite without it. We do not know how the preexistent Logos became the Man Jesus and cannot explain it, but we can verbalize what happened and present it plausibly for reasonable people to consider and seekers to believe. Christianity has done this for centuries.

The Logos humbled Himself, not by altering His nature or changing it in any way but by submitting it to human nature. We accept this for one important reason: we think Jesus revealed it; that is to say, since Christ makes this claim and others like it (John 8:23, 42, 58–59, 15:26 RSV), God validated those claims by raising Jesus from the dead and accepting him into heaven. God would not validate a blasphemer if the Incarnation were not true. (The scholarly literature

---

520. "Incarnation:" *Hastings' Dictionary of the Bible: A Dictionary of the Bible (4 Volumes in One)*, Kindle Edition, Locations 55608, www.DelmarvaPublications.com.

on the resurrection of Jesus, shows the resurrection's credibility is arguable with objective standards of historiography.)[521]

In John's day, extreme dualism was the philosophical position throughout the Greco/Roman world. Pagan dualism framed a view of the cosmos controlled by deities that fated the world toward good or evil. In short, the spiritual world of the "light" was good, and the material world of "darkness," most characterized by the flesh, was evil. In Hellenism, it was unacceptable for the Logos, the Light of the world, to become flesh; darkness (flesh) cannot exist in the light (Logos). Hellenism dismissed the resurrected body as a contradiction (see Acts 17:32). However, in Christianity, the material universe is very good by nature and redeemable if fallen.[522] The universe remains very good. The extreme YE view that God ruined the entire universe with a blanket curse is an erroneous presupposition that leads to many mistakes we have seen.

John leaves no doubt about the Incarnation by injecting the in-your-face, side-by-side juxtaposition of *"Logos flesh."* The Greek looks like this: *Ο' Λόγος σάρξ έγινετο*—with the consecutive terms *Logos (Word)* and *sark (flesh)*—*"the Logos flesh became."*

This phrase indicates that the divine Logos entered this universe by becoming human—an incarnation. "Incarnation," as used about Jesus, is not a reincarnation from a previous state, an embodiment, or a theophany. The "appearances" of God recorded in the Old Testament are material *representations*, not incarnations. Such appearances are not a hypostatic union of two natures. The theological term for them is "theophany."

Theophanies are temporal. They are a single occurrence for a specific audience or a particular time and place. A theophany is not an actual or permanent becoming. The divine may manifest a theophany in another time and place that looks nothing like the previous manifestation because God does not look like any theophany. God has no look known to us. Jesus, on the other hand, will *always* be God who became human.

The Incarnation produced a new kind of person—the New Adam or the God/Man. In other words, the Logos flesh *became*. The *Hastings Dictionary of the Bible* gives three results of the Incarnation:

---

521. For a defense on the credibility of the resurrection see *The Son Rises: The Historical Evidence for the Resurrection of Jesus,* by William Lane Craig, Wipf and Stock Publishers, Eugene Oregon, 2000; Gary R. Habermas and Michael L. Licona *The Case for the Resurrection* (Kregel Publications, Grand Rapids Michigan, 2004), and N. T. Wright's *The Resurrection of the Son of God* (London, Great Britain, 2003). The plausibility of the resurrection takes into account conditional probability based on all lines of verification including oral, documentary and physical evidence.

522. Docetism was the gnostic heresy that rejected any union of the divine Logos with flesh that Christianity claimed of Christ.

1. Consummation of the universe and of humanity—St. Paul (Eph. 1:
   10) speaks of the purpose of God 'to sum up all things in Christ, the
   things in the heavens and the things upon the earth' (cf. Heb. 2: 10)...
   The idea here is that the universe is progressing toward a focal point—
   the union of heaven and earth. The Logos is the beginning and the end
   of this progress.

2. The Supreme revelation of God—The Old Testament is the history
   of a progressive revelation which is always looking forward to more
   perfect illumination, and the whole history of man is, according to
   the NT, the history of gradual enlightenment culminating in the
   Incarnation (Heb. 1: 2, Joh. 14: 9, Col. 1: 14).

3. Restoration of man— It has been a common subject of speculation in
   the Church whether the Incarnation would have taken place if man
   had not sinned.[523]

The New Testament takes us back "before" the foundation of the world, declaring that God's purposes in the Incarnation were preordained. God hid his ultimate intentions *until* Christ arrived. Therefore, according to the Apostle Paul, God hid His purposes for the Incarnation from Moses and was, at best, undeveloped in Old Testament written works, Genesis being one of them. Only after the resurrection and ascension could hints in the Old Testament be interpreted as incarnation.

While YErs come to the New Testament from the vantage point of the Old Testament (*"from the very first verse"*), Christians come to the Old Testament from the New Testament, beginning with Jesus, who brought a new beginning—a new creation—*a New Genesis.* Putting so much stock in a literal *or figurative* interpretation of details in Genesis can be misleading because only the New Testament is a collection of covenantal documents for Christianity. In John's version of the new creation, Logos flesh is unique to Christianity. The main point of Genesis is that Israel's God is Creator, and He has a plan for creation that He revealed gradually.

We may understand Old Testament writings in their covenantal context, but the Church interprets and applies them in the light of the new covenant that Jesus established. John 1 is preeminent on creation, and Christian discipleship replaces the Mosaic Law. Logos enlightens and transforms our understanding. Our covenant is new because we received a revelation unknown to the prophets.

The real purpose of the Bible, God's ultimate self-disclosure, is realized in Jesus. He said, "If you have seen me, you have seen the Father" (John 14:9). It is not that the Old Testament fails or that something is missing in Genesis, but its revelation is simply in covenant with ancient Israel. Genesis 1–2 is what it

523. "Incarnation," *Hastings' Dictionary of the Bible: A Dictionary of the Bible* (4 Volumes in One), Kindle Edition, locations 55630–55647, www.DelmarvaPublications.com.

intended to be—Hebrew cosmogony in the ANE revealing who the Creator is. The *fullness of time* had not yet come (Galatians 4:4).

The Trinity doctrine was born in a quest to understand God's self-disclosure in Jesus, beginning with the early Apologists of the second century. Unresolved hints in the Bible and early Christian writings indicated oneness and threeness in the Godhead. The charge of polytheism against the Church led theologians to resolve the tensions created by their inconsistencies. Progress continued through the Councils of Nicaea and consolidated in Thomas Aquinas.

Development of the Trinity was necessary to be consistent with the divinity of Christ and the giving of the Holy Spirit. For example, Aquinas's idea of divine simplicity means (among other things) that what proceeds from God cannot be less than God. Otherwise, if something comes forth said to be "part" of God, God would be divisible, which is impossible for the Infinite.

Jesus said, *"I proceeded and came forth from God"* (John 8:42 RSV). That is an important theological concept. If Jesus proceeded or "came forth" from God and all that proceeds from God is God, then Jesus must be divine. When we say Jesus is the *only begotten* Son of God, we mean that Jesus is the only one "generated" (Greek) from divinity. Christian thought says the infinite Logos is eternally begotten, i.e., He always generates or proceeds from the Godhead in eternity as the infinite Logos before the advent of the human Jesus.

The classical illustration of this is the Logos or "Word" in John 1—"the Word was with God and was God" (John 1:1). As a person's word and thoughts generate from his being, the Logos (like thought) proceeds from the Godhead. That is the meaning of the *"Only Begotten."* "Beget" and "begotten" are dated words in English but in Greek (*gennao*), meant *to generate* or *produce*. *Gennao* referred to a physical father generating his son from his "loins" (i.e., siring).

Aquinas' argument looks like this:

1. Whatever proceeds from God is divine.

2. The Logos eternally proceeds from God.

3. The Logos proceeded from God into this universe becoming Jesus.

4. Therefore, Jesus is divine.

This is fundamental to classical Christology.

40.
THE MARRIAGE OF THE LAMB

Fruit begins by the union of one thing and the other.
—Thomas Howard[524]

Recall God's own words in Ezekiel 16:8: "I came by again and saw that you were ready for love and a lover. I took care of you, dressed you, and protected you. I promised you my love and entered the covenant of marriage with you. I God, the Master, gave my [vows]. *You became mine.*" (MSG)

The comprehensive union between husband and wife inspires the most intimate language for love we have. God "bears his heart" with a passionate declaration of His intentions for His people as a young Jewish man might declare his undying love to his betrothed. But God is not a young Jewish man ready for romance. He condescended by relating to His people in the most intense love they knew. Of course, Israel knew the language was anthropomorphic since they did not plan a honeymoon. The Hebraic idea underneath this union originates in the Eden story: "That is why a man leaves his father and mother and is *united to his wife, and they become one flesh.*" Other translations say:

1. "Two people become one" (ERV); and

2. "The two become like *one person*" (CRV).[525]

This all-inclusive union between husband and wife is a metaphor for the ultimate union between God and all creation. The Marriage of the Lamb is the way the New Testament puts it. God made Eve from Adam's side means more than the couple should walk side by side together. Adam and Eve are two persons of one substance with opposite but compatible designs that form a comprehensive unity. Such opposites attract, not repel. So the human family is one substance and one race of people; DNA confirms this.

The Incarnate Son is two substances in one person—divinity "poured" into humanity (per St. Francis De Sales). In Jesus, we have the Hebraic *firstfruits* or the start of a New Creation. "But Christ has indeed been raised from the

---

524. Thomas Howard, *Chance or the Dance: A Critique of Modern Secularism, Second Edition* (Ignatius Press, San Francisco, 2018), Kindle Edition, location 162–162.

525. I am not aware of similar language like Ezekiel 16:8 used for any of the supreme deities in ANE literature. This is actually romantic and obviously meant as a translation of God's love and commitment into "earth-speak." While this is one of the most beautiful expressions of God's love for humanity, at the same time it illustrates the inadequacy of words in any human language and the shallow breadth of our experience to comprehend God's love. Only the life, death, resurrection, and ascension of Jesus could reveal the fullest extent, the fullest height, and the fullest depths of God's love expressible in this universe.

dead, the *firstfruits* of those who have fallen asleep" (1 Corinthians 15:20). As Howard states above, "[This] is how *fruit* begins, by the union of one thing and the other." In this case, divinity and humanity.

The ancients called the offspring of a union— "fruit." In this case, the Incarnation (the *hypostatic union* in Jesus) bore fruit—the born children of God, the Church (John 1:13). The hypostatic union illustrates how Jesus is the foundation of God's plan for uniting heaven and earth. Jesus is the beginning of the union of both realms. He is the "seed" for more fruit. The marriage of the Lamb is another way of illustrating it. You can see that YEC cannot possibly be "the foundation upon which God's plan rests."

According to Genesis 2, God created humanity from matter, i.e., dirt and rib, and so the process was: soil (or dust) to Adam, Adam's side to Eve, and Eve to all humanity (Genesis 2). Genesis 2 implies that every human comes from existing matter: ourselves, our parents, and their parents before them, all the way back to dust. But the tradition in Christianity is that the First Cause created the initial universe out of nothing, including Adam and Eve.

Whether God actually formed Eve from Adam's side or Adam from the soil is not the point.

The theology or the intended meaning is that Adam and Eve were one substance; they were of the earth, and so are we. That makes us unequivocally mortal— *"you shall surely die."* Some Christians may object, saying humans are immortal because we have souls. However, humans are a unity of body and soul. If any part of that unity is mortal, in this case, the body, then the *person* is properly mortal; therefore, *"This mortal must put on immortality"* (1 Corinthians 15:53). The only way to enter eternity is with God's presence radiating in our conscience.

The New Testament declares Jesus the first *fruit* of a new creation. The resurrection of the saints is like a harvest of glorified children of God. As spawning salmon return home and give up their life for countless new lives—this universe and our existing bodies are to be given up for a harvest of transformed souls. Paul presents this concept:

> But someone will ask, "How are the dead raised? With what kind of body will they come?" How foolish. *What you sow does not come to life unless it dies.* When you sow, you do not plant the body that will be, but just a seed... So will it be with the resurrection of the dead. The body that is sown is perishable, it is raised imperishable; it is sown in dishonor, it is raised in glory; it is sown in weakness, it is raised in power; it is sown a natural body, it is raised a spiritual body. (1 Corinthians 15:35–44)

The caterpillar illustrates this concept when it appears to die buried in a "coffin," the chrysalis while being reborn. Our old person begins to die, and a new person begins to form or regenerate. Our old person's corrupting nature is being discarded like the caterpillar while a new incorruptible person joined in

Christ is born in us. The new creature in our conscience rises incorruptible; it is always incorruptible; otherwise, "incorruptible" is meaningless since the word means *not corruptible*. Our corruptible side will not go on; it is dying. Only the new person continues. The butterfly and the glorified human rise a new creature—no longer the simple caterpillar, no longer the "old or corruptible person."

The interlocking union of one and *the other* in a new heavenly family seeded by the divine/human Jesus and, by extension, his Church reveals God's chief end. The resurrection of Jesus is *the beginning* of God's outpouring into His creation ending in a bountiful family.

The rest of us follow Jesus:

> He who raised Christ from the dead will also give life to your *mortal bodies* through [union with] His Spirit who dwells in you... For as many as are led by the Spirit of God, these are children of God...and heirs of God and joint heirs with Christ, that we may also be glorified together. (Romans 8:11–14)

Christians also have the first fruits of the Spirit as Romans 8:23 declares, "We ourselves, who have the first fruits of the Spirit, groan inwardly as we wait eagerly for our adoption to sonship, the redemption of our bodies." In this case, the outpouring of the Holy Spirit in us begins a union with God that glory will consummate as the imagery of the marriage between Christ and His Church symbolizes.

Some theologians describe union with God as a cosmic "dance" between God and all realms—each made new to accommodate the union. "Marriage," "metamorphosis," or a "dance"—analogies abound because we cannot spell out what a comprehensive union with God is or what it will be like. How God will transform our reality so it can merge with a reality currently outside ours is unknowable. We know that humans must say "yes" to God to participate. There is no consummation, no marriage to the Lamb, without the equivalent of an "I do."

Jesus makes God's plan explicit; to prepare each realm to receive the other with God at the center. In John 17, we have this remarkable prayer of Jesus:

> My prayer is not for [the twelve] alone. I pray also for those who will believe in me through their message, that all of them may be one, Father, *just as you are in me and I am in you. May they also be in us* so that the world may believe that you have sent me...that they may be *one as we are one—I in them and you in me—so that they may be brought to completely one*... Father, I want those you have given me to be with me where I am, and to see my glory, the glory you have given me because you loved me *before the Creation of the world*. (John 17:20–24; emphasis mine)

This prayer's deepest meaning is mysterious since the phrase "*completely one*" may be impossible to define. Nonetheless, Paul did say, "What God has planned for people who love him is more than eyes have seen or ears have heard. It has never entered our minds!" (1 Corinthians 2:9 CEV).

Paul also said that some "things cannot be put into words," literal or figurative (2 Corinthians 12:4). Asserting that God's plan and all biblical doctrine hinge on something as prosaic as six solar days or that the deep age of the universe compromises the faith *trivializes* the inexpressible gift of God revealed in Jesus. The blunder of the YE Reform Movement is disproportionality; it is not the foundation of God's plan but instead trivializes it. It is not enough to say YEC strains at gnats and swallows camels, but to say *'what a man considers distasteful must be measured by what he eagerly swallows.'*[526]

Jesus spreads the new creation through His Church, the community of saints. Paul uses the analogy of a temple expertly framed on a foundation with Jesus as the cornerstone. "In [Christ] the whole building is joined together and rises to become a holy *temple* in the Lord" (Ephesians 2:21).

The Church is something like a temple or a new Garden of Eden. Gardens and temples often occupied the same grounds where people believed heaven and earth met. The Church is a temple in that sense. Jesus said he is in the midst of us when "two or more gather in [his] name" (Matthew 18:20). That is "temple language."

Union with God is the divine seventh-day rest symbolized by a universal "garden temple." That has been God's intention, but an ANE way of putting it. The glorified Church is the realization of the seventh day of creation—the point of creation week—without which the six days have no purpose:

> His *purpose* was that all the rulers and powers in the heavenly places will now know the many different ways God shows his wisdom. They will know this *because of the Church*. This agrees with the plan God had *since the beginning of time*. He did what he planned, and he did it through Christ Jesus our Lord. (Ephesians 3:10–13, ERV)

Sure, YErs admit that the age of the earth has nothing to do with any of this. But, at the same time, they claim it is the key to the Gospel, the cross, the atonement, and reforming the Church and culture. The YE Reform Movement is the first time in Church history that a nonessential opinion on six literal days competes with Christ as the key to spiritual and cultural reform in a group's evangelistic efforts.

The Church is where we enter God's Rest *Today* as we saw in Hebrews 4:4-11, not through a literal building on a day called Sunday, but having come to Christ, we then experience rest as the people of God in a spiritual temple (Matthew 11:28; Hebrews 4:7–9). Having left "spiritual Egypt," we are "tabernacling" with God on the way to the "promised universe."

---

526. David Berlinski, *The Devil's Delusion: Atheism and its Scientific Pretensions*, p. 152.

Genesis is most relevant for Christians as the New Testament reinter-prets it, especially in the first chapter of John's Gospel—"*In the beginning* was the Word" who created all things. Genesis 1 and John 1 are theological: one under the first covenant, the second under the new. John 1 takes precedent in Christianity, but that is not clear in YEC, where Genesis 1 overshadows John 1. YEC claims Genesis 1 is the key to everything, but the real key is John 1.

When the "fullness of time" came, the Logos entered time-space as Jesus healed and taught the people, made the journey to the cross, rose from the dead, ascended into heaven, and began a community of renewed humans with the birth of the Church. Jesus is the new Adam—the *origin* of a new humanity—a new creation. None of this would fit anywhere in YEC's Reform Movement, with animal-eternal life, vegetarianism, six literal days, 6000 years, genealogies, or flood geology. A new creation is a new beginning—a *new Genesis* (John 1:1-14).

It is hard to know where YEC fits in the Church's Mission and where YErs fit in preaching the Gospel. Only Jesus *reveals the plan* of union between *heaven and earth* by personifying that union—his human nature being from this universe and his divine nature from heaven (John 3:13). As Jesus said to Pilate, "My kingdom is not of this world" (John 18:36 KJV). The YEC's world is this one. They put too many eggs in an unraveling basket.

Jesus is the King of a heavenly kingdom, not an earthly one. He joins his kingdom to our world by a "royal wedding" to the spiritual "daughter" of earth, the Church. *Church* is a word we use for redeemed humanity, which eventually will include people of all nations, ethnic groups, and walks of life, not just what we think of as Christendom. In the Judgment, our membership in a denomina-tion will not be relevant, and YEC will be absent from the discussion.

Humans enter union with God through Jesus, who alone makes it possi-ble because *only he is the living body of this union.* He is the channel on behalf of all destined for unity with divinity. Like no other can, Christ— with his body, the community of saints— generates union with God. That is why eternal life is in Christ alone. Eternal life is more than being kept alive by God.

Eternal life *is* union with God through the Incarnate Christ.

When we say eternal life is through Christ alone, we do not mean people must join a church or pick the right religion for salvation. A Christian should be in a Church because it's a place for growth, service, discipleship, community worship, and hearing the word. But the power of salvation is God's grace. God has determined that eternal life *is* union with God through Christ.

The only way for a human to unite to God is through the one that leads the way— who already unites both in himself, the God/Man who said, "No one comes to the Father except *through me*" (John 14:6). "*Through me*" has real meaning. Jesus became the "conduit," the "vine," the "river" between God and Man when both natures manifested in him. This is real. That is why salvation can only be in Christ. He is the only means a comprehensive union of humanity and divinity can happen. In Christ, we'll enter a new universe transfigured. This is not religious exclusivism. Jesus is the only way union is possible.

Jesus is the tree of life. He offers God's rest by telling all to come.

If we are not in Christ, we block ourselves from the tree of life; God doesn't do that anymore because of Jesus. If we are one in Christ, and Christ is one with God, then we are one with God— the purpose of creation, the age of which is irrelevant. We are also one with all who are one with God; as Jesus said, "Father, *just as you are in me and I am in you. May they also be in us* so *that the world may believe* that you have sent me. I have given them the glory that you gave me, *that they may be one as we are one*" (John 17:21–22).

It is only through Christ that we find the *means* for eternal life. Our traditions are not the means. The person of Christ is the way God does it. Eternal life does not consist of God simply keeping us alive forever or remaking us so we can't die. It does not mean we must act right to go to heaven; that is impossible.

There is a specific *way* that God provides eternal life— "This is the word He spoke: God gave us life that lasts forever, *and this life is in His Son*" (1 John 5:11, NLV). Union with God, in Christ, by the Spirit empowers that life. We enter union with the Triune God through Christ, who said, "*that they may be one as we are one*" (John 17:22). The joining of the divine Spirit with the human spirit to the Father established by Christ accomplishes this— "*The Spirit Himself joins our spirit in testifying that we are God's children*" (Romans 8:16 EHV).

This union in Spirit *is* eternal life:

Metamorphosis requires an ontological change in us that only God's active presence in our consciousness can make. That is the purpose of creation and why only the Creator can accomplish this. It is not about being good ourselves; it is about the final stage in human creation achieved by the Creator, the Logos who became Jesus Christ.

Our willingness to accept this "final stage" of our creation is essential. We have to be willing, that's all. God reaches down in the Incarnation to create a new person in every willing human. He works in us. That is how God forms or "reforms" a new human, not by YE reform. Freedom of choice is necessary, or our transformation is forced or contrived.

Jesus is not just the way; *he is the only way it is done*. Like a bridegroom, Christ chooses those with whom he unites; those who say, in effect, "I do." It is not up to us or our tradition to say whom Christ has received. There is no injustice in this; it is supremely just since all can participate; all are invited to the wedding—Catholic, Orthodox, Protestant, Fundamentalist, Jew, Muslim, Hindu, and anyone else willing to come.

God's grace has opened eternal life to anyone willing to receive it.

We have seen that the focus of YE evangelism is to *"believe, proclaim, and defend"* the literal interpretation of Genesis 1–11. Unfortunately, one unintended consequence of the YE Reform Movement is it distracts from the Church's Mission. But worse, an extremely high view of scripture that distorts its purposes can lead to a low view of God. *The God that puts in a good day's work is a caricature of the true God.*

Unbelievers can see the absurdity of such a God. Augustine saw this over 1,500 years ago. He feared that our scriptures and the God they portray would look silly to unbelievers after hearing self-styled scientists and theologians among Christians explaining nature with a wooden understanding of scripture.

The heart and soul of scripture is the Incarnation—the Bridegroom's coming. The Bridegroom's arrival is in two stages, just as a first-century Jewish marriage was in two stages—first the betrothal, then the consummation. At his first coming, Jesus "proposes marriage" to humanity and "consummates" or completes *union* with God at the second coming. Wedding plans are now underway (Revelation 19:7–8). In the Marriage of the Lamb, we will not be one flesh as in earthly marriage but one glorified humanity in God and Christ. A literal marriage or wedding ceremony is not the point.

Instead, a comprehensive union analogous to marriage is what the New Testament has in mind.

This marriage scene is one of the high points of the book of Revelation written in Jewish apocalyptic. We are dealing with symbolism, specifically Jewish customs regarding betrothal and marriage applied to the union of Heaven and Earth. Nonetheless, that which the metaphor symbolizes is true. It is the most crucial truth of all—God will be "all in all" or "fill everything in every way" with Himself (see Ephesians 1:23).

This is the "Marriage of the Lamb."

41.
GOD'S AIM IS *TO FINISH IT*

> God's goal was to finish his plan...that *all things in heaven and on earth* be
> joined together with Christ as the head.
> —Ephesians 1:10 (ERV)

The heavenly or spiritual realm is a topic of interest today because of the ANE worldview of a "divine council" shared to some extent by ancient Israel. Recent writings by Michael Heiser (now deceased) concentrated on the ANE *concept* of a divine council of spiritual beings identified as lesser "gods" (*elohim*). They have various ranks led by a supreme tribal or cultural deity called the "Most High God."[527]

The Bible also speaks of "elohim" or "divine" beings and the realm they occupy that sound similar to other ANE Semitic writings that have survived, notably the tablets found at the seaport city of Ugarit in northwestern Syria. Archeologists discovered cuneiform tablets from the fourteenth to twelfth centuries BC and spoke of "the Council of El [God]" that met in an *idyllic garden*. Semitic expressions like "sons of El" and "the Most High El" appear in these tablets. Praises to Baal, such as "King above all gods" (elohim) are similar to biblical references to the God of Israel as Psalm 95:3 says, "For the Lord is the great God, the great *King above all gods*." These phrases are idiomatic for this region and time in the ANE.

A similar idiom between peoples does not necessarily mean their theology is the same. For example, Jews, Muslims, and Christians declare "God is one." However, only Christians believe God is one Being in three distinct Persons—not *separate* Persons—but *distinct*, such that God remains one. Hence, Christian monotheism is different from the monotheism of Judaism and Islam.

This heavenly realm worldview may account for enigmatic verses in the Bible, especially Psalm 82:1, "God [Elohim] has taken his place in the divine council; in the midst of the gods [elohim] he holds judgment." Again, Psalm 95:3 says, "For the Lord [Yahweh] is a great God [Elohim], and a great King above all gods [elohim]." There was no lower-case lettering at the time. All letters were uppercase, so the two terms *ELOHIM* and *elohim* were identical, but the referents were different. Scholarship's role is to interpret those passages

---

527. In their early history, the Israelites believed there were other gods that were inferior to Yahweh. Of course, every tribe believed their god was superior to others. Around the time of the prophets, most worshippers of Yahweh believed all other gods were false. Yahweh was the `living God' or the God that is alive because they actually experienced him, unlike the statuary based only on myths about pagan deities.

carefully and in context, not bound by an exclusive distinctive that can corrupt interpretation.

The two uses of Elohim/elohim may also account for obscure references like, "Let *us* make man in *our* image and *our* likeness." The key to understanding the Hebrew word *elohim* is that it can be a generic term for a powerful *being*. Nonetheless, among all elohim, only the God of Israel is *Yahweh* (the self-existing and covenant deity. Exodus 3:14; 20:1-3).

The ancients perceived this divine council as an administrative center in the heavenly realm connected to secondary centers that corresponded to earthly realms. The earthly kingdoms mentioned in scripture are Israel and the seventy Gentile nations in Genesis 10. The phrase *"whole earth"* generally applied to Israel's land and the lands of these seventy nations, ranging from modern-day Iran in the east to the Iberian Peninsula in the west. Beyond Spain, Portugal, and Northwestern Africa was the Atlantic, a foreboding sea beyond "the world" (the Romans called the northern coast of Spain the "end of the earth"). People were afraid to navigate the straights of Gibraltar for fear of falling off the edge of the world.[528]

The spiritual realm and its divisions appear connected to the Israelite understanding of these nations and their traditional boundaries. The tablets at Ugarit demonstrate further that the narrative in Genesis on the Garden of Eden is a product of the ANE from a Hebraic point of view. That shows Genesis 1-3 is authentic to the period (Late Bronze/Early Iron Ages) and that a garden concept similar to Eden was not unique.

Many Old and New Testament verses refer to an organized heavenly or spiritual realm. For instance, Paul writes, "For in [Christ] all things were created: things in heaven and on earth, visible and invisible, whether thrones or powers or rulers or authorities; all things have been created through him and for him" (Colossians 1:16).

Why are the references to *thrones and powers in both realms* relevant? Because in Judaism, their purposes and functions appeared to be in concert. It implies that the Garden of Eden is the *Hebraic vision* that converges the heavenly realm (God and His Hosts) with a human and earthly domain to which Israel and her neighbors might relate. A temple compound, for instance, with royal palaces was a temporal location believed to reflect a similar layout in a corresponding heavenly place. Jesus makes the fulfillment of a "New Garden of Eden" possible since heaven and earth converge in him and his Church.

The pagans housed carved *images* of their tribal deities in temples. No image or likeness representing God was allowed in Israel because, unlike pagan deities, nothing corresponds to Yahweh in nature, including the human

---

528. See "Kings and Things: 5 Incredibly Well-Preserved Romans Buildings," YouTube clip.

image.[529] That was a leap forward on the nature of God. Israelites believed God's *invisible presence* was in the Holy of Holies, the temple sanctuary's inner chamber. Prohibiting images of any kind led Israel to realize that Yahweh was the *living* God. The pagans were preoccupied with statuary.

But even this advance of a living God in the Holy of Holies was inadequate. Jesus said:

> "Believe me, a time is coming when you will worship the Father neither on this mountain nor in Jerusalem... the true worshipers will worship the Father in Spirit and in truth, for they are the kind of worshipers the Father seeks. God is spirit, and his worshipers must worship in the Spirit and in truth" (John 4:22-24).

The temple that God dwells in is the human spirit.

Paul said to the Athenian philosophers, "The God who made the world and everything in it is the Lord of heaven and earth and does not live in temples built by human hands" (Acts 17:24). Temple grounds such as the Parthenon in Athens often graced mountains or hills with lush trees planted throughout, presenting a vision of beauty and tranquility. Temple landscapes, especially in Mesopotamia, and Egypt, flourished on mountains or hills, alongside river systems and waterworks, all financed and decorated with silver, gold, and precious gems (see the Eden of Ezekiel 28:13-14; 31:1-18).

In ANE symbolism, serpents were divine-like beings like cherubim, the guardians of sanctuaries that generally faced the east. *Divine-like* does not mean equal to God, nor does it refer to any of God's infinite attributes. In Israel, the uncreated God created these beings called *"elohim"* (lowercase), and some went bad. The language can confuse moderns because the ANE and its idioms are alien. The Bible is part of that world and is also foreign to us in ways that do not register without extensive familiarity with the ANE, including aspects of the region's theology, history, philosophy, and archeology. The ANE is the context for the Old Testament.

This secondary use of the word "elohim" describes beings that reflect God's image beyond the likeness humans currently reflect; namely, spiritual beings are invisible, without body, and more powerful than humans (Psalm 8:5). They wield more influence than humans do. Spiritual beings also live in a realm beyond ours and can affect our domain to some extent. It is not clear how we might affect their realm.

---

529. The image and likeness of God in humans does not mean God is like us or looks like us. Humans are in the position to rule the earth and manage it on behalf of God. Humans reflect God; God does not reflect humans.

Some ancients believed Satan could come and go in both realms (see Job 1:6-7).[530] Genesis depicts Eve as unsurprised to find a talking serpent (representing a spiritual being) in the Garden who might have talked about resembling God (Elohim) or possibly becoming one of the lesser gods (elohim). People ask, 'Isn't it possible that the serpent, the two trees, and the Garden narrative are literal?' And couldn't God make Adam and Eve from dust and rib? Theoretically, we assume it is possible because all things are possible with God. *But it is not reasonable or more faithful to apply literalism to God's nature, especially since God has no literal hands to mold things or lungs with breath.* Just because a thing is possible for God to perform doesn't mean we must take it literally or risk being unfaithful to God and scripture. This concern is a misguided devotion to a literal, interpretive method. It fails to see that the scriptures do not make such demands.

Whether the explanations of these references to "elohim" are literal regarding the spiritual realm, they illustrate how far removed we are from the ANE world. At a *minimum,* it makes sense to assume that a spiritual world exists. God is Spirit and Creator, so an immaterial or spiritual world is a likely choice of worlds He might create. Our world is puzzling since we assume spiritual beings are more like God than we are. God seems to have made the spiritual world first (Job 38:4–7). If an *infinite* number of universes in a multiverse exists, then a spiritual realm must be one of them.

It is reasonable to assume that such spiritual beings are intelligent, powerful, and free to make choices and that some abused their freedom. So we likely have two fallen realms that God is responsible for creating and seems intent on salvaging. So the only conclusion is that both worlds must be worth salvaging.

How would God preserve them together?

The Primacy of Christ

This Son, radiance of the glory of God, flawless expression of
the nature of God, Himself the upholding principle of all that is,
effected in person the reconciliation between God and man and then
took his seat at the right hand of the majesty on high.
—Hebrews 1:3[531]

The phrase "effected *in person* the reconciliation between God and man" may be a veiled reference to the two natures in Christ, i.e., the reconciliation between God and man effected in an "incarnational atonement." A *genuine* reconciliation between two distinct realms might be "effected *in one person* if he

---

530. The reference here in Job is "the Satan," meaning "the adversary" or something like a prosecuter. The devil and Satan had not been equated together at the time of Job, but was a much later development.

531. Phillips Translation.

inhabits both realms." Ancient kingdoms facilitated peace by marriage— mixing royal bloodlines—a son from one domain and a daughter from another.

Christ has the prerequisite for reconciliation between God and humanity by a genuine union of the two when he became human—the "marrying" of two natures creating a new realm. Peace through "marriage" is a simple *analogy* that expresses what God is doing. "Therefore, since we have been justified through faith, we [the Church] have peace with God through our Lord Jesus Christ" (Romans 5:1).

Note the words, "The Son *is Himself the upholding principle of all that is*" (Hebrews 1:3). That is the meaning of Logos, the grounds upon which *all creation* rests. Jesus of Nazareth is the glorified man who will sit on the throne "at the right hand of the majesty on high." We somehow share in that glory. Jesus is entitled to sit on the throne as the Logos made Man, and we are in him. Of course, "throne," "right hand," and "sitting" are metaphors. But they are metaphors that apply to Christ in a way unlike any other person. Jesus is the Firstborn, the First, and the Last; we are not (Colossians 1:15, 18).

Ephesians 1:19–23, Paul writes:

What is the incomparable greatness of *his power toward us who believe*... This power he exercised in Christ when he raised him from the dead *and seated him at his right hand in the heavenly realms, far above every rule and authority and power...not only in this age but also in the one to come.* And God put all things under Christ's feet, and gave him to the Church as head over all things.

Perfected humanity as God intended had not occurred in Eden. Therefore, consider the possibility that God made Adam and Eve incomplete or unfinished and banished them from Eden in that state. By *unfinished,* I mean something is missing in us that God intended to supply if we were willing to cooperate (we are, after all, the creature, and He is the Creator). Those cooperative conditions were not satisfied in Eden since the first humans did not eat from the tree of life, symbolizing all the *necessities* for eternal life otherwise absent.

Consequently, Adam and Eve were not in union with God and, therefore, not glorified. An unglorified human is incomplete, not yet a butterfly, and more like a living temple without a deity. Adam and Eve, like all humans, were potential "temples" of the Holy Spirit. But God never set up residence in them as eating from the tree of life indicated, as eating from the true vine also shows (John 15:1).

Blaise Pascal said humans have a God-shaped hole in their hearts that God would fill with Himself *if we were willing.* Our free will must be fully engaged, suggested by two lovers who wholeheartedly commit to each other. Should God accept anything less?

Pascal's metaphor may have implied that God once filled that hole, but because of sin, it is now emptied. But we are working with metaphor. What if

God never filled the void in humanity's heart? But left it open for each person willing or ready to accept Him, as He does now. Whether one believes that Adam and Eve were historical or literary figures, the lesson is the same—humans resist God.

We know Adam and Eve never ate from the tree of life. Jesus said in his day, "You refuse to come to me and receive life" (John 5:40). Jesus was talking to Jews. But Jews are just people who can become legalistic, exclusivists, and stubborn; any of us can, even over "ordinary" days. With few exceptions, we play *hard to get* with our Creator.

The new Adam inaugurated a new beginning by the creative power of the Incarnation. He came to clarify God as Father and reveal His will for all people. That means something was always missing in the human heart necessary to be fully human—to be the finished product, complete and reborn with the divine presence fully taking up residence in us as *His* living temple.

Rebirth is but a *down payment* for glorification in the coming new universe. Every Christian has a new person in them that is a fledgling of what they will become. "The Spirit," Paul wrote, "is the *first payment that guarantees* we will get all that God has for us. *Then we will enjoy complete freedom*" (Ephesians 1:14 ERV). That new inner person has eternal life, not our current bodies that are temporal:

> If anyone builds on this foundation [Christ] using gold, silver, costly stones, wood, hay or straw, their work will be shown for what it is because the Day [of Judgement] will bring it to light... If what has been built survives, the builder will receive a reward. If it is burned up, the builder will suffer loss but yet will be saved. (1 Corinthians 3:12–15)

The mistake many unbelievers make is assuming eternal life is about being a good person and that many unbelievers are no worse than most Christians, so where is the behavioral advantage in being a Christian? Eternal life is not primarily about the earthbound you, as the butterfly is not mainly about the caterpillar. It is about a new birth of an invisible you that will discard the old you and enter eternity in a new state of being. It is you transformed. That gestation is now forming in the Christian consciousness by divine design. Our old person will "burn up...yet we [a new we] will be saved." We are in transition like the caterpillar that is an unfinished butterfly. The resurrection and ascension of Jesus solidify this Christian teaching.

Paul concludes the point by saying, "Don't you know that you yourselves are God's temple and that God's Spirit dwells in your midst?" United to God's Spirit, our soul is a new person, and collectively, we are the new humanity waiting for glorification of the body. That is life eternal that Christians possess now in earnest—"Whoever believes in the Son *has eternal life*" and "This is the bread that comes down from heaven, so that one may eat of it and *not die*" (John 3:36, 6:50). Our earth-bound self dies, but a new person emerges.

The tree of life is "open" again.

Paul confirms 'the mystery of His will' this way: "God's goal was to *finish his plan* when the right time came. *He planned that all things in heaven and on earth be joined together* with Christ as the head" (Ephesians 1:9–10, ERV; emphasis mine). That is the point of all created things. Union of His creations is His ultimate plan, and Christ is the foundation, the grounds for that union.

In what sense is the age of the earth the foundation for any of this?

Uniting divinity to humanity is the ultimate atonement (oneness of personhoods). Jesus becomes the seed, the "singularity" that plants one new universe. Paul said, "The promises were spoken to Abraham and to his seed..." [not seeds, but seed] "meaning one person, who is Christ" (Galatians 3:16). Christ is the genesis of all personhood.

The YEC claim that an old earth "destroys the atonement'" is a mistaken view of Christianity. We are dealing with Christians who do not really understand the most fundamental Christian doctrines though they may be able to verbalize them. Trying to glue a literal six-day Genesis to the foundations of God's plan confuses *logistics* in a simple creation account (a schedule of activity) with God's *purposes* for all Creation. God's plan will outlast the natural world and its initial created order. Peter wrote, "On that Day the heavens will *disappear* with a shrill noise, the heavenly bodies will burn up and be destroyed, and the earth with *everything in it will vanish*" (2 Peter 3:10 GNT). *That is why the age of the earth is irrelevant and so is the YE Reform Movement.*

Peter says the physical heavens (stars) and earth will dissolve, and a new universe combined with any realms beyond the stars will replace it. Peter's statement on the demise of the universe is similar to theories in modern physics, except God's plan is Peter's point. That is how first-century Christianity illustrated the transformation of all existence. Likewise, our bodies will change in form to participate in such a universe. God planted the seed of the New Universe with the Incarnation and resurrection of Jesus. That is what Christianity means by the Incarnation changed everything.

The Incarnation exposed the material universe as a lesser reality and not our permanent state since ultimate reality grounds our world; it *reached down* to draw our realm into ultimate reality. God always intended to do that. Furthermore, the oneness of two natures in the Incarnate Christ was in the plan before sin entered the picture. *Salvation* is not the union of two realms per se, but a necessary step toward it. Like the children of Israel were *delivered* ("saved" Exodus 14:13, 15:2 RSV) from Egypt, yet, that generation did not enter the land that was a type of paradise with its "milk and honey" and "vines and fig trees." The generations that were in the Promised Land never found God's ultimate rest. Today we declare that the new has come and is still coming because it is renewed creation in transition. Therefore, creation did not find the finish line in Genesis, and God finishes what He starts.

From the Bible, we gather that sin is disorder or anarchy (1 John 3:4) developed first in the spiritual realm and entered our world. Hence, both fallen and upright spiritual beings have some access to this world and can influence it. To what extent their influence reaches us, we do not know; their control is likely quite limited.

Spiritual beings were supposed to influence our world for good; it appears that some have (Daniel 12:1). Others left their first responsibility and left it a mess (see Jude 6). Sin and the disorder it brings are evidence of an incomplete state, not of God's finished work. Chaos happens for one reason— estrangement from God. Resisting God is absurd since it fights one's destiny. Christ came to restore our finish line.

The point is that *unfinished* created beings with *free will* are always capable of evil. We can assume two-thirds of the angels that did not fall were willing to let God "complete" them. The rest resisted. While some angels fell, the spiritual realm seems more stable and less susceptible to falling than our material world. When sin came to humanity, something about our nature made its impact easily spreadable. God cleanses, rehabilitates, restores, and will perfect humans. The redeeming quality of our world is that it is by nature redeemable.

Evil has touched this universe from the fallen spiritual realm. According to the story, the forked-tongue serpent was already in the world when humans arrived. Why else would there be a tree of good *and* evil before humans sinned? Why would there be any concept of evil if it did not exist? God gave the first humans a choice between two existing trajectories—good and evil, symbolized by a tree. A choice between two things assumes both are in view to make an informed decision. The point is evil existed before humans.

These are theological and moral stories, sometimes called mytho-historical literature. This genre used known myths that were imaginative to account for the world's condition without the epical form. They provided a context to explain a troubled world with reissued stories from a cultural lexicon. Perhaps those stories are factual, but *they do not need to be factually correct to be theologically true* about the current state of affairs. Therefore, a reform movement over literalizing them is meaningless.

Adam sinned by attempting to govern—not just the world, which was his right—but the knowledge of good and evil, to which he had no right. Like the Sophists in ancient Greece and their modern relativist reincarnations; the lesson in Adam and Eve may be about humans wanting to be *"the measure of all things."* That was the effect of their actions. The final say on good and evil is a divine right ("you shall be like God") and not a human right since all humans shall remain human. Because God always intended to unite both heavenly and earthly realms, both rise or fall together.

What does all this have to do with the SDWC?

By contrasting God's actual plan for creation with the YE claims that a literal Genesis is the foundation of the plan, it puts the nonessential nature of the SDWC into perspective. YEC claims it is the foundation for God's plan. We looked at God's plan. There is no connection. The YE Reform Movement cannot be the key to all biblical teaching, the key to reforming the Church and culture or preserving biblical authority.

Rejecting YEC's ideas is not calling God a liar.

We are dealing with Christians in the YE movement that have a mistaken view of historical Christian thought. They do not fully comprehend some Christian doctrines, so they mishandle them. That is cause to be patient with YE *laypeople.* They are vulnerable to sophistry in that they don't detect uncritical lines of thought that begin with mistaken presuppositions and claims. The average YErs in church honestly believe everything they say despite the cognitive dissonance, which is not enough to overcome their conditioning. They don't have the tools to reassess their beliefs, nor are they taught them.

The deep cognitive dissonance YErs routinely display leads detractors to think they are liars. How else do you account for the most noticeable mistakes when shown to them, yet they remain steadfast? That's easy. Reading scripture over and over again in a certain way is powerful. "God" always trumps critical thinking for many fundamentalists. I experienced the same thing in the Worldwide Church of God, and worse, believing Jewish Christianity is the only uncompromised tradition focused mainly on the Old Testament.

The bottom line is that God has *not given* Christians the right to war with each other over nonessentials for salvation or compromising the Gospel's primary place in evangelism. Christians are free to accept various views on Genesis because it is literature foreign to modern western thinking. We cannot make it fit without compromising it. Genesis was under the old covenant and with different purposes. John 1 is decidedly Christian.

Warring over such nonessentials is a rupture in Christianity.

John Duns Scotus and the Absolute Primacy of Christ

Theologians have long speculated that had Adam and Eve not sinned, the divine Logos would still come Incarnate to glorify humanity in Himself. Glorification works the same whether it occurs to sinless humanity or a redeemed one. The Incarnation is necessary for this transformation under any circumstances. The Incarnation was not only to save us *from sin* but to finish creating us for *a comprehensive union with God.* The new creation leaves Genesis 1-11 where it belongs—in old covenant theology.

The scholastic John Duns Scotus (AD 1266–1308), among others, championed the love of God in Christ as the *primary* motivation for the Incarnation because it leads to a warm embrace of that "cosmic dance" with

God; as Paul wrote, "May [you]...grasp how...deep is the love of Christ, and to know this love that surpasses knowledge—that you may be filled to the measure of all the fullness of God" (Ephesians 3:18–19). God is the measure of all things, and He fills all things. The hypostatic union of God Incarnate was the reason for creating this universe (Romans 1:20; Ephesians 1:4). Creation has no eternal purpose without it. The Incarnation is the means of bringing all creation into eternity.

And so God's ultimate purposes that began with the Incarnation are not *reliant* on anything earthly, including any emergent need of fallen humans or a historical Adam, or an inerrant Bible. God set his plan in advance, no matter what happened. Nothing in the creation and nothing *about creation* can alter the aim of comprehensive union with God revealed in the Incarnate Christ. Paul wrote:

> For I am convinced that neither death nor life, neither angels nor demons, neither the present nor the future, nor any powers, neither height nor depth, nor anything else in all creation, will be able to separate us from the love of God that is in Christ Jesus our Lord. (Romans 8:38–39)

For Scotus, Paul's concept of predestination is crucial to the Incarnation. Paul says, "For he chose us in him *before the creation of the world... In love, he predestined us* for adoption to sonship *through Jesus Christ in accordance with his pleasure* and will" (Ephesians 1:4–7). Predestination shows God's plan cannot be stopped, period. Notice that the *emphasis* is on God's *love* and *pleasure* to adopt us regardless of how a Christian interprets Genesis 1–11 because that love was "*before the creation of the world.*" Paul adds in verse 8 that God's plan to adopt us through Jesus Christ is based on His "*lavish grace,*" not a literal Genesis.

God's ultimate aim surfaces in verses 9–10, "He made known to us the *mystery* of his will... *to bring unity to all things in heaven and on earth under Christ.*" "Heaven and earth" is an ANE merism for all things, i.e., the universe. The completed plan is an ultimate universe with God at the center. It is beyond belief that *everlasting animals, 6000 years, dinosaurs on the Ark, genealogies, and feigned "biblical authority"* are relevant.

For Scotus, the Incarnation is absolute, meaning it was not dependent on any need or circumstance that arose at or after creation. God set His aim "before" the beginning, before the appearance of the singularity and Big Bang. His plan was the reason for the singularity, and all that followed.

A new creation in the Incarnation/Virgin birth conceived by the Holy Spirit such that the notion of *any* theory on the age of the earth undermines God's purposes is bizarre, especially for a Christian. God bases His plan on His intrinsic goodness and shall "pour out" that goodness into creation as an ultimate act of grace. What do six literal days have to do with this?

Not a thing.

The coming of Christ was also for His own sake, meaning it was something He cherished before the world. God receives divine pleasure in His creation. God would not predestine Jesus *because* of sin only. The Incarnation is the supreme work of God *ad extra* (outside of Himself) for the expressed purpose of bringing all things into Himself.

The Incarnation is too spectacular and extravagant to be caused solely by the flaws of contingent creatures.

Undoubtedly, the love of God, and not human actions, is what brought us the Incarnation. Jesus simply mowed sin down like so many insects at harvest. The predestination of Christ and the creation of all things were one simultaneous decision.

There are five observations about the Incarnation derived from Scotus:

1. The first thing God wills, relevant to the creation, is Christ.

2. God predestines Christ, the saints, and angels to glory before any occurrence of sin by angels or humans.

3. It is backward to predestinate the height of created glory (the Incarnate Son) and God's infusion into His creation based solely on an inferior creature's fall.

4. Creation is incomplete without the Incarnation.

5. Nothing in creation, including the creation itself, gives meaning to the Incarnation. Instead, the Incarnation gives meaning to creation.[532]

Why is this important? It exposes the claims and presuppositions of YEC for what they are. The book of Hebrews says we persevere to the end by *"fixing our eyes on Jesus, the pioneer and perfecter of [our] faith"* (Hebrews 12:2). Only taking our eyes off Jesus Christ compromises our faith.

Six *figurative* days do not.

In the light of God's infinite plan and His real aim for His finished work, it is clear that the resources and energy dedicated to the Six-Day War in Christianity for a nonessential reform movement such as YEC is a misguided chapter in the history of Christian thought. Through the Incarnate Christ, the astonishing plan of God "insists" that the earth's age cannot possibly be essential to it.

The SDWC detracts us from the mission of making known the Gospel's objective—the invitation to the new creation in Christ—to complete His

---

532. Fr. Maximilian M. Dean FI, *Bl. John Duns Scotus on the Incarnation: Overview, The Absolute Primacy of Christ,* July 2012.

work in all creation. Our mission is to announce the Good News globally to convict the world's conscience to participate in Christ's work.

That work will inaugurate all universes into a *single, unbounded, perfectly functioning, glorified universe.*

God will finally put everything under Christ's feet (a Hebraic idiom) so that God will be *all in all* (1 Corinthians 15:28). God flows through Jesus and embraces us. We are in Jesus to embrace God, which the seventh day of creation anticipated and that YEC seems to avoid; as YE evangelist Stephen W. Boyd said, the seventh day was "merely" for God to rest.

The "divine pouring out" permeates our being with His active presence without compromising our personhood, identity, or free will. Though marriage is analogous, two people remain individuals, a spiritual union of beings in a spiritual dimension is more intimate in that two or more persons may share thoughts. Perhaps that goes too far; who knows? Language is all we have to describe the indescribable.

Remember, here in Part V, we have synthesized explicit, implicit, and idiomatic ideas in scripture and how theologians may have understood them in the past. The resurrection of Jesus underwrites all of it. Beyond that, it does not fully appear to us what God has in store for the world—"Eye hath not seen, nor ear heard, neither have entered into the heart of man, the things which *God hath prepared for them that love him"* (1 Corinthians 2:9).

We can never reach God's realm because He is infinite, and the Trinity is a divine singularity, indivisible. But God can reach down into ours and has—"For in Christ all the fullness of the Deity lives in bodily form" (Colossians 2:9). That *fullness in bodily form* will live with us through the living Christ. His name is Immanuel, meaning "God with us." He will always remain so.

The creation account in John 1 reveals the Word who created all things and identifies him as God and as Jesus. Genesis does not do that. Nothing against Genesis: the early chapters are about origins, not ends, and more about problems than solutions. Even with the coming of Christ, Genesis has its share of obscurities. Christ, without the text of Genesis 1–11, is undiminished. Also, John 1 apart from Genesis 1 can stand alone undiminished.

Six literal days are not in the game.

42.
HOW PERFECTION COMES

These [heroes of old] were all commended for their faith...
since God had planned something better for us so that only
together with us would they be made perfect.
—Hebrews 11:39–40

Notice it, only together with us would [the faithful of old] be made perfect. So God perfects all people *at the same time*. That is because all created realms or universes will be perfected at once, of which we are only a part. This perfection of God's people calls to mind Jeremiah, where God instructs him:

> "Go down to the potter's house, where I will give you my message." So I went there and saw the potter working at his wheel. Whenever a piece of pottery turned out imperfect, he would take the clay and make it into something else. *Then the Lord said to me, "Don't I have the right to do with you people of Israel what the potter did with the clay? You are in my hands just like clay in the potter's hands"* (Jeremiah 18:1–6).

God is like a Master Potter whose plan is to take an unfinished human race made of clay and polish body and soul in a spiritual realm.

In Genesis, our world was "very good" for its intended purpose—biological life. Everything in this world combines particles and probability waves in motion. All is in a state of flux (except the constants), constructing and destructing, making this an imperfect world.

"Perfection" in created beings occurs when they become all that God intended. To be "perfect" as in "holy" means "wholeness" or "completeness" not absolute perfection, but rather a fully finished creation. Jesus is the model for this life and the next. Though we will be a lesser version of the glorified Jesus, who is the *unique* Son of God, our bodies will be like his (see Philippians 3:21). Compare these verses:

Matthew 13:43, "Then shall the righteous shine forth *as the sun* in the kingdom of their Father."

Matthew 17:2, "[Jesus] was transfigured before them: his face did shine *as the sun*."

Philippians 3:21, "[Christ] will transform our lowly bodies so that they will be *like his glorious body*.

Matthew uses similar language for both the glorified saints and the transfigured Jesus. However, "shining like the sun" is a simile. Intense sunshine, the symbol of glory in ancient times, still does not define or demonstrate the glorified state. Nonetheless, we can assume that some of the abilities Jesus displayed after his resurrection will be true for us. Jesus's appearances were not an exhaustive demonstration of his transfigured state but were for the moment's sake. His appearances in the book of Revelation are in Jewish Apocalyptic and, thus, highly symbolic.

Paul states that the new nature makes us incorruptible in eternity (1 Corinthians 15:42–44, 54–58). No compromise to our free will occurs in this change because we have chosen it and participated by cooperating with God, which is necessary as the ultimate exercise of our free will. Continuous eating from the tree of life symbolizes an eternal bond with God. *Incorruptibility and immortality have never been characteristic of this world. This world must "put on incorruption and immortality" (1 Corinthians 15:53).*

Christians believe there is an ultimate self in each of us destined to blossom. Forming the final person is the concept behind metaphors for the Spirit's work: the *tree of life,* the *bread of life,* and the *true vine* are nurturing concepts. These relational metaphors describe a comprehensive and *continuous* connectedness to the source of life, power, and goodness (1 Corinthians 15:28).

Adam and Eve were not perfect. How do we know? They sinned. A perfect person, the glorified person, is not able to sin. Incorruptibility for the whole person is in the future when we shed the caterpillar and burst into glory—"It will happen suddenly, quicker than the blink of an eye. At the sound of the last trumpet, the dead will be raised. We will all be changed, so that we will never die" (1 Corinthians 15:52 CEV). That is our hope in 1st-century idiom.

The New Testament says that perfection is given simultaneously to all people of faith: past, present, and future (Hebrews 11:39–40). Evil will be a thing of the past. Paul said, "The body is 'sown' in corruption; it is raised beyond the reach of corruption... It is sown in weakness; it is raised in power" (1 Corinthians 15:42 PHI).

Another fall from grace will be impossible.

God does not force perfection on us since it comes through a divine, human union—a mutual embrace. It takes two to embrace each other honestly; we must want it and agree. "Union" and "embrace" are terms for intimacy. There is always some loss of intimacy unless both are one. A forced union is a violation like a shotgun marriage or worse. Therefore, God finishes perfecting those willing to receive it. A six-thousand-year-old earth and its YE trappings will never come to mind in glory.

"Willingness" means turning to God in humility—a simple concept that, for some reason, is very difficult for us to do. However, that stubbornness may be a good thing in one sense; if a genuine willingness and cooperation with God emerge out of the obstinacy, the resulting turnaround would be that much more *authentic.* New Testament examples are Paul and James (Jesus's brother), who rejected Christ in no uncertain terms: Paul accused Christianity of blasphemy, and James believed he was dealing with a delusional brother who thought he was the Messiah the Son of God. No brother would buy into Jesus's claims under pain of death outside something extraordinary, and Paul was not open to discussion. Their immediate turnaround occurred when *the resurrected Jesus appeared to them.* Consequently, their credibility as converts became unassailable. God calls the weak to do the extraordinary, so His hand is more noticeable (John 9:1–3; 1 Corinthians 1:27).

From the beginning, all humanity has had the same choice. How each person chooses may manifest itself in the number of ways there are people. The choices expected of Adam and Eve were in symbol—the two trees. The new Adam did not sin; he showed human nature as God intended, so he replaced the first Adam and began humanity reborn as a heavenly race. "Just as we have borne the image of the earthly man, so shall we bear the image of the heavenly man" (1 Corinthians 15:49). "Our citizenship is in heaven" (Philippians 3:20). This language is a theological way of looking at the authentic things Jesus accomplished. His kingdom is a heavenly one. The new will subsume the old, so God's creative works continue.

Some literalists believe Adam and Eve had to keep eating the fruit to keep immortality. First, it's a story. If they had immortality, they would not need to eat *anything.* In reality, repeated eating of this tree was symbolic of the continuous stream of life that union with God brings, like the true vine, which is not a literal vine. A miraculous tree that sustains life means God sustains life, not a literal tree. The soul or spirit in humans unites with God's Spirit and "plugs" into life. The symbolism of the tree of life was the continuous nature of this union.

Union with God becomes more comprehensive in glory. Christians walk in the Spirit now, which means God is "streaming" in them. But the stream will become rivers like the Euphrates, Tigris, Pishon, and the Gihon (Genesis 2:10–14). In glory, it will be a "deluge"—the only flood that matters in the end.

God waited patiently in the days of Noah while the ark was being built. In it, only a few people, eight in all, were saved through water, and this water symbolizes baptism that now saves you also—not the removal of dirt from the body but the pledge of a clear conscience toward God. It saves you by the resurrection of Jesus Christ. (*1 Peter 3:19–22*)

Since Christ, we now know that the *significance* of Noah's flood for Christians is not its geology or whether it was a global flood but its theological implications for the saved. Technically, Noah and his family were not saved by or through water but *from* the water. But that is typical of New Testament interpretation of Old Testament themes, i.e., highly theological.

Noah's flood symbolized baptism in water and the Holy Spirit (John 3:5). In the end-time outpouring of the Holy Spirit, Isaiah writes, "For I will pour *water* on the thirsty land, and streams on the dry ground; I will pour out my *Spirit* on your offspring and my blessing on your descendants" (Isaiah 44:3). This verse is a compound *parallelism* where the first two parts say the same thing as the following two parts but with different words. It means water for a thirsty land is the equivalent of the Spirit that fills the emptiness in the human heart, which Pascal referred to poetically.

Isaiah anticipates the New Testament concept of baptism in the Spirit, the "essential deluge." Noah's flood is to baptism what the tower of Babel is to Pentecost—Genesis 1 is to the creation what John 1 is to the New Creation.

YEC is left out.

Our ultimate destination will unfold to ever-new vistas of God's self-disclosure and the most lavish grace allowing us to partake in His nature (2 Peter 1:4). In the *"dance"* between God and all creation, God will lead us into an ever-increasing intimacy with Him, disclosing His infinite beauty and attributes without end (2 Corinthians 3:18). Thus, there will be eternal beauty and splendor in the new creation unknowable in this one.

There is a peculiar explanation of this eternal "dance" between God and Creation at Answers in Genesis: "*In regard* to God's plan for the new heavens and new earth... *Have you ever wondered what the garden of Eden looked like? Well, the new heavens and new earth will give us a "taste" in the future.*"[533]

This muse is surprising, even after all the YE commentary we have seen. Perhaps I misunderstand it. A "taste" is a hint of fullness. Apparently, to some YErs, the Garden of Eden was the ultimate state for humanity, more delightful than the new heavens and earth. In this case, transfiguration in the new heaven and earth is a "taste" of the Garden of Eden. How much thought went into this? The usual amount, it seems.

Sometimes we speak of experiences giving us a "taste of heaven." You understand that. It is not heaven but a hint of it, like a blazing sunset or the taste in the tiny pink spoon at Baskin-Robbins. You want more. But to say our ultimate destination is a *"taste"* of the Garden of Eden is, again, a spectacular blunder of disproportionality on the plan of God. But then, what would you expect from people who think the foundation of God's salvation plan is six literal days? One can only imagine YE evangelists like Ham in heaven, longing for the "real thing." If Ham misspoke in his article (I'd like to think he did), you still have to wonder how he *could* misspeak like this and how his editors would let it go. Do they all feel the same way?

Such cognitive dissonance on a nonessential leads to *babble.*

Uniting all things in Christ is a higher reality than a literal Garden spot on earth since God will fill all existence with Himself. I am not insisting that Eden was a literal garden. Literalists do. Assuming it was a literal garden, such gardens in the ANE were also temple grounds where the tribal deity and its image resided. However, if Eden is symbolic of a temple site and a temple is

533. Jeremy Ham, "What Is God's Plan for Heaven and Earth?" Biblical Authority Devotional: Consistency of Scripture's Message, Part 11, August 11, 2010, AIG website.

symbolic of the heavenly realm, then Eden was two steps removed from the reality it symbolized—the real kingdom we are all longing to receive: "Then the King will say to those on his right, 'Come, you who are blessed by my Father; take your inheritance, the kingdom prepared for you *since the creation of the world*" (Matthew 25:34); and it's not the garden of Eden!

A comprehensive union of heaven and earth has never existed. Lange comments on this:

> Heaven and earth have become places of sin (2:2; 6:12); indeed heaven was the first theatre of sin when a part of the angels fell (1 Tim. 3:6; 1 John 3:8; Jas. 2:19; 2 Pet. 2:4; Jude 6); thence it came to earth in ever greater dimensions (1 Cor. 10:20, 21).[534]

The Incarnation is the means of uniting all realms.

The future new heavens and earth are just that—new. It is a change or a changing into something, not a reverting to a previous garden spot near the Tigris and Euphrates Rivers any more than our glorified bodies will revert to some previous bodily state. To be sure, the New Testament speaks of *restoration,* but it refers to God's active presence before our fall from grace that restores us, that is, the restoration of humanity's intended place in union with God. Jesus has restored the grace we fell from, *which is the key to transforming all things in our world.*

What also needs restoring is God's active involvement in world affairs that the prophets described in Messianic terms by restoring Israel, illustrated in the New Testament when the disciples asked—"Lord, are you at this time going to *restore* the kingdom to Israel?" (Acts 1:6). The only theocracy that works is with God openly governing, not by humans pretending to lead one.

Restoring the Jews to their promised land in 1948 indicates there may be something to Israel's place in all this. A restored Israelite kingdom on earth may or may not be literal. It is not the purpose of this book to determine that. Nonetheless, the Jews were justified in fighting their Six-Day War in 1967 to maintain the land, not to mention their existence. The *Six-Day War in Creationism* is not justified for anything meaningful.

For fundamentalists, "restoration" is like an episode of reality TV where the featured stars restore an old beat-up car to "like-new" condition. If the restoration of all things means going back to pre-fall conditions, we must assume those conditions would allow the possibility of another fall from grace that leads to death. That is out of the question. Therefore, we are not discussing a simple restoration back to the garden.

Christianity teaches there will be some continuity between the old and new creations as our new selves will still be identifiable; otherwise, the new

---

534. *Lange's Critical, Doctrinal, and Homiletical. Commentary on the Holy Scriptures* (Volume 7—Acts to 2 Corinthians), Kindle Edition.

creation would be a total otherworldly reality and not *our world* transformed. There will still be something of the caterpillar in the butterfly. The glorified body will not revert to one like Adam's before sin. This is absurd. Adam was of the earth, mortal and corruptible—"The first man was of the *dust of the earth*; the second man is of heaven. *As was the earthly man, so are those who are of the earth*; and as is the heavenly Man, so also are those who are of heaven" (1 Corinthians 15:47–48).

"Not that I have already obtained all this," Paul said, "or have already [been *perfected*]... But our citizenship is in heaven. And we eagerly await a Savior from there, the Lord Jesus Christ, who... *will transform our lowly bodies so that they will be like his glorious body*" (Philippians 3:12, 20–21). The new heaven and earth is not mere restoration but transformation. Otherwise, it would not be new, and we must assume that evil could emerge in the new creation just like the initial creation. Instead, God eradicates evil in the new heaven and earth, something never done.

The tree of life and its symbolism will be there (Revelation 22:2, 14), but the tree of good and evil will not. Therefore, the original creation was not the ultimate ideal or a final product. That is another YE mistaken assumption. To be fair, this over-idealized view of a *perfect creation* is relatively common among Christians. The story of Eden is idyllic to contrast the damage a fall from grace or moral degradation inflicts. Eden was an ideal look at what this world might be like before it is transfigured. It was not the glorified state for which we hope. This world could have been ideal but has never been perfect. YEC has built an elaborate and contrived theology around this overreach.

Furthermore, the Gospel of John says the Word gives believers "the power to become the sons [children] of God" (John 1:3–4, 1:12). There is an essential qualifier in all this. We will not be "sons" or "daughters" in the same way Jesus is *the Son*. While our bodies will be the same kind that the glorified Jesus bears, we will not be equal to the glorified Christ. Jesus has two natures—God made human.[535]

Furthermore, we will not be humans made God in any literal sense. By an extraordinary act of God's grace, we will be humans that only "partake" of or "participate" in the divine nature (see 2 Peter 1:4). By contrast, Christ does not "partake" of the divine nature, nor does God give it to him by grace. Christ's divinity

---

535. Pope Leo the Great said of the Incarnation, "This is a marvelous exchange. He humbled himself to share in our humanity so that we might be raised up to share in his divinity." The word "share" can be an equivocation if understood incorrectly. The Logos shares our humanity by becoming human; we do not "share" in Christ's divinity by becoming God. The Logos took humanity; we cannot *take* divinity. Only a "share" can be given to us by grace, which shows we cannot be God.

belongs to him by nature. Jesus is not merely a glorified man as humans will be; he is the only glorified God/Man. The glorified Christ is the Incarnate Son transfigured: [536]

> *After six days* Jesus took with him Peter, James and John the brother of James, and led them up a high mountain by themselves. There he was *transfigured* before them. *His face shone like the sun, and his clothes became as white as the light.* Just then there appeared before them Moses and Elijah, talking with Jesus. (Matthew 17:1–3; emphasis mine)

Interestingly, this transfiguration occurs on the seventh day (i.e., *"after six days"*) when Jesus's face shone like the sun. It points to God's real rest. The incident confirms Jesus as the Messiah, his Messianic kingdom (Moses, Elijah with the Church), and the seventh day of creation that shall never end (Isaiah 9:7). What comes next helps make these connections: "Then Peter answered and said to Jesus, 'Lord, if You wish, let us make here *three tabernacles*: one for You, one for Moses, and one for Elijah'" (NKJV; emphasis mine). The Feast of Tabernacles or booths (sukkot in Hebrew) pictures the thousand-year reign of Christ on earth. The Jewish Apocalyptic of Revelation implies that world history is a week of seven one-thousand-year days: six-thousand years of human rule and corruption followed by a thousand-year sabbatical reign of Christ, which is a theological and eschatological concept of history and not a precise chronology.

The transfiguration event of Jesus included Moses, Elijah, and his disciples, showing that Christ and his Church represent God's Kingdom by fulfilling the Law (Moses) and the prophets (Elijah). Judaism referred to the scriptures not as "the Bible" but as "The Law and the Prophets," sometimes adding a third division, "The Writings" (see esp. Matthew 7:12, 11:13, 22:40; Acts 13:15, 24:14, 28:23; Romans 3:21). Luke 24:44 says "the Psalms" when Jesus makes clear that he fulfills the promises.

No documentary boundary was called "the Bible" at the time. Canonization occurred decades (for the Old Testament) and centuries later (for the New Testament). The transfiguration illustrates that the Bible is subservient to Christ, who is the Word. He had the power to change biblical injunctions and inaugurate a new covenant that superseded the old. Jesus and the Bible are not equals any more than Moses and Elijah are equals to Christ. These two prophets symbolize all that has gone before in the old covenant, only here transfigured in Christ.

---

536. Pope Leo the Great said of the Incarnation, "This is a marvelous exchange. He humbled himself to share in our humanity so that we might be raised up to share in his divinity." The word "share" can be an equivocation if understood incorrectly. The Logos shares our humanity by becoming human; we do not "share" in Christ's divinity by becoming God. The Logos took humanity; we cannot take divinity. Only a "share" can be given to us by grace, which shows we cannot be God.

A week of a thousand years is likely symbolic since it appears only in Jewish Apocalyptic literature and comes full circle to creation week with the unending seventh-day rest of God. There will be no end to Christ's rule: "All things have been delivered to Me by My Father... Come to Me, all *you* who labor and are heavy laden, and I will give you *rest*" (Matthew 11:27–28).

The unity of all things is what all the realms of creation contribute to the puzzle. Humanity itself is one organism, though we do not always look at it that way in the Protestant world. On Romans 5:12–17, Lange's Critical Commentary offers this insight that *"Christ has gained far more for us than Adam lost"*:

> Paul evidently views the human race as an organic unit. Adam and Christ sustain to a central and universal relation, similar to that which the root has to the tree and its branches. *Adam was not merely an individual...* and his transgression was not an isolated act... So it is with Christ. He calls Himself emphatically *the* (not a) Son of Man, the universal, normal, absolute Man, the representative head of regenerate humanity, which is from heaven, heavenly, as Adam's fallen humanity is "of the earth, earthy" (1Co. 15: 47-48)...*Christ has gained far more for us than Adam lost— namely, eternal unity with God, in the place of the temporary union of untried innocence* [in Eden]. The resurrection of humanity in Christ is the glorious solution of the dark tragedy of the disastrous fall of humanity in Adam. In view of the greater merit of Christ and the *paradise in heaven...* It is God's infinite wisdom and mercy alone, which overrules the fall of man for [God's] own glory.[537]

Notice the phrase, "eternal union with God, in the place of the temporary union of untried innocence [in Eden]." Adam was not perfect. Eden is a story with lessons. Catholic and Jewish thought view humans as a single organism ontologically speaking. However, before God and the Law, inalienable rights mean we are judged individually, rejecting tribalism. The U.S. Constitution, when understood, is the most progressive Law. We are one organism of individuals ("out of many, one"). Our bodies are of the same substance but separated by time-space. Our souls/consciences make us unique.

This distinction is in the prayer of Jesus but in sharper terms:

> I ask not only on behalf of these, but also on behalf of those who will believe in me through their word, that they may all be one. *As you, Father, are in me and I am in you, may they also be in us...* The glory that you have given me I have given them, so that they may be one, *as we are one, I in them and you in me, that they may become completely one.* (John 17:20–23 NRSV; emphasis mine)

537. *Lange's Critical, Doctrinal, and Homiletical. Commentary on the Holy Scriptures (Volume 7— Acts to 2 Corinthians)*, Kindle Edition, Location 55723.

The phrase *"as we are one, I in them and you in me"* cannot be of the body.

It is hard to believe a fisherman named John from first-century Galilei could make this up. Because of that, many people do not think John wrote it. Three centuries later, the doctrine of the Trinity found a voice—God is one Being in three distinct but inseparable "Persons" (Gk. *hypostases*). Put in a modern sense, God is a singularity of three divine "consciences."

Before the discovery of the Big Bang, a cosmic singularity of time, space, and matter was unknown. By analogy, God reveals Himself in our universe as an undifferentiated singularity of Father, Son, and Holy Spirit. He is like a singularity, a realm, or "dimension,"[538] so Jesus asks the Father for the Church to be one in the Father and Son as the Father and Son are One in each other. This union is a spiritual reality.

We will be one in Christ yet distinct persons, each with our own identity in a similar but incomprehensible sense. So there will be some continuity from this world to the next. Jesus said to the Sadducees, who did not believe in the resurrection, that the God of Abraham, Isaac, and Jacob is *"not the God of the dead but of the living."* This and resurrection would make no sense if people were unrecognizable to themselves and others. After his resurrection, the wounds in Jesus's hands and feet suggest some enduring continuity and personal identity within the profound oneness the transfigured state brings.

Peter writes, "He has given us his very great and precious promises, so that through them *you may participate in the divine nature*, having escaped the corruption in the world" (2 Peter 1:4). We will still be human but glorified; that is, humans that partake of the divine nature by the special grace of God. That has always been our destiny. God does not intend to live apart from us. Paul wrote, "Our citizenship is in heaven. And *we eagerly await a Savior from there*, the Lord Jesus Christ, who...will *transform our lowly bodies so that they will be like his glorious body*" (Philippians 3:20–21). God made us for this.

Notice John's words again, "Dear friends, now we are children of God, and *what we will be* has not yet been made known. But we know that *when Christ appears, we shall be like him,* for we shall see him *as he is*" (1 John 3:2; emphasis mine). We cannot know *what* we will be like because it is beyond our

---

538. The Greek word for "person" in the doctrine of the Trinity is the philosophical term *hypostases*, which meant something like "the ground of being" or "subsistence being." There is no clear translation in English. Each member of the Trinity is His own ground of being or perhaps conscience. The three hypostases are distinct but not separate; i.e., they are one essence (God). Nonetheless, the numbers *one* and *three* are not meaningful; they are unavoidable for finite persons with limited language. Our language and limitations betray us. The Trinity is about "one" *infinite* God in "three" *infinite consciences*. "Being" and "person/hypostasis" are not synonyms and the numbers used of limitless nature are forced upon us. God is a singularity of Father, Son, and Spirit where there are no separations, like the singularity before the Big Bang was undifferentiated time, space, and matter/energy.

comprehension and remains so until we are in the glorified state. Humanity will share in the life of the transfigured Christ.

"*The belief in thousands of years*" is receding further into our rear-view mirrors.

In the beginning, the Word was in continual existence. He entered our space so that now all things would continue forever. The Incarnate Son's resurrection is the first of the first fruits in one fully functioning unbounded new universe.

The New Testament's view of God's plan for a New Creation is beyond earthly things, beyond history, and beyond comprehension.

How much more is this *New Genesis* beyond six literal days?

"Behold, I make all things new."

—Revelation 21:5

CLOSING REMARKS:
THE CHRISTIAN SOLDIER

Christians have always been free to interpret Creation Week literally or figuratively. However, the *Young Earth Reform Movement* is a new phenomenon, claiming that YEC is essential and warning Christians of severe consequences for rejecting it—consequences they never clarify since they admit many great Christians have interpreted the six days figuratively. So why the confusion?

We've seen three historical teachings in Christianity overshadow The Six-Day War in Creationism that holds all soldiers accountable:

1. The *nature* of God;
2. The *purpose* of the Bible; and
3. The *Mission* of the Church.

God's infinite attributes provide a corrective for interpreting Genesis too literally. The sun's rising and setting does not govern God's activity, nor does He expend energy that needs replenishing. Those earthly attributes are not possible because God is not of the earth. The Hebrew workweek is a triumphal way of saying the creation is *the work* of the God who saved Israel from bondage and secured for them an abundant life with livable work. He gave them Sabbath rest weekly, annually, and continuously by living free in their own land. Creation week was a cosmogony expressed in covenantal language.

The *purpose* of the Bible has been to leave a record of God's increasing self-disclosure and His plan for creation. God's self-disclosure was a progressive revelation unfolding throughout the history of ancient Israel that culminated in the Incarnation, and we find it preserved in the Bible for future generations.

God did not write the Bible, nor did he micromanage each word. The Spirit moved biblical authors to compose genuine works in real-time. The prophets transmitted messages from God orally to the people, then reproduced them in written form for posterity. Authors like Luke did the research, prepared their material, and did the work; they wrote the books. God now speaks through His Son, who is *"the radiance of God's glory, the flawless expression of the nature of God, and is Himself the upholding principle of all that exists"* (Hebrews 1:1–3).

God withheld the central piece of His plan until the right time, *"When the fulfillment of the time came, God sent his Son, born through a woman"* (Galatians 4:4). In other words, God finally unveiled the mystery of His plan by *generating* the Logos Incarnate in this universe.

The *Church's mission* is twofold: to proclaim the Gospel *explicitly* for unbelievers and make disciples. One follows the other. Unessential distinctives and specialized ministries characteristic of a group should not be prerequisites for preaching or accepting the Gospel. Discipleship training continues for life.

God determines when we have accomplished our primary mission. And if we understand that correctly, the end comes: Jesus said, "This gospel of the kingdom will be preached in the whole world as a testimony to all nations, *and then the end will come*" (Matthew 24:14). The mission also includes building the Church with disciples of Jesus to help spread the Gospel exponentially. It is not about making disciples of any competing nonessential teaching hiding behind biblical authority. Knowing the mission helps recognize who is doing the real work of the Church and who is not.

The Gospel promises a new creation "seeded" by the divine-human Jesus. Galileo was right, "The Bible tells how to go to heaven, *not how the heavens go*." These and other teachings of Protestantism, such as "unity in essentials, and charity in nonessentials" are markers of the Christian Soldier that do not reflect well on reformist ideology.

We saw that YEC is more than the belief in a young earth. A simple YE has an innocence—some say naiveté. But there is no innocence in the excesses of YEC's inarticulate "reform movement." The YE Reform Movement is an extreme theological ideology on shaky ground that is unique in Church history. The reason Christians are free to accept a young or old earth without compromising their faith is that age is unessential and irrelevant. Everyone knows this, including many YErs, who, as a result, suffer from a most reverberating cognitive dissonance.

The dissonance is knowing on an intellectual level that the earth's age is nonessential but at the same time not accepting that fact in practice. Cognitive dissonance occurs when anyone cannot defeat facts or arguments yet cannot admit to the possibility of being wrong or even reassess one's presuppositions and claims. It is surprising to hear so many YErs claim they cannot possibly be wrong no matter how much they are shown to be and when their errors are obvious.

Honesty demands we do a fundamental analysis to find reasonable responses to our case's weaknesses and be open (not without caution) to refinements. If we do neither, sophistry and activism replace integrity and analysis.

Let's ask Bertrand Russell's question: "Why do Young Earth Reformers believe things that are obviously false, even absurd?" Because they have a naïve view of God's nature and take narratives dependent on anthropomorphisms and metaphor, literally; they also misunderstand the purposes of the Bible, which often leads to legalism, and they compromise the Christian Mission for their own Young Earth mission.

YEC is inconsistent with God's attributes, irrelevant to the Bible's purposes, and of no consequence to the Church's mission. What is consequential is if one answers *yes* to any of the following questions:

1. If the earth is old, is God a liar? (on the nature of God)

2. If the earth is old, is the Bible unreliable? (on the purposes of the Bible)

3. Is proclaiming Genesis 1-11 the key to reforming the Church and culture? (on the Mission of the Church)

Those who answer yes to any of these questions are indeed *soldiers* in the SDWC. They are fighting the wrong battle. These three fundamental excesses have led to many others we have seen. Is there any greater symbol of excess than the Ark Encounter in Northern Kentucky? The life-size replica of Noah's Ark appears to tempt God to send a flood and launch it. The wood could have been carved into a billion crosses and sent to China!

We cannot serve two masters (Matthew 6:24). By a bold embrace of one, we may squeeze the life out of the other. One master will push out the other like a dominant chick that removes a weak sibling from the nest. Our allocation of time, treasure, and the focus of our message will indicate the kind of soldiers we are.

If we die on the wrong hill, no life is left to give. "No soldier of God is entangled with secular business" (1 Timothy 2:4). Measuring the age of the earth is a scientific matter, not a biblical one, and, therefore, serves secular purposes.

Christian soldiers serve their Captain, who is about his *Father's business*.

INDEX

ACKNOWLEDGMENTS

I must thank several people whose impute proved valuable to this project. My brother Chuck, without realizing it, inspired me to write a book like this one. Stephen Evilsizor helped early on with style, which set the pace. Elizabeth Nouhan was helpful in clarifying some of my language and argumentation. Ted Johnson was insightful on some content editing and affirmed many of my conclusions. Jason and Mauro Mautone provided a positive sounding board from two very different perspectives. Gary Jones, a high school friend, gave me insight into how some people might respond to my scholarship, especially on the nature of God, which never occurred to me. I especially want to thank Dr. Brian Law who gave me a platform to teach my apologetics class to a well-informed group. I was able to use some of my lectures as a basis for several chapters of this book. Finally, I thank my wife Susan, who is a natural writer and gave constructive criticism and encouragement. She also put up with me ignoring domestic duties I conveniently overlooked with endless research, writing, and editing, mostly from my personal library, during Covid lockdowns.